MARTIN VAN BUREN
AND THE
AMERICAN POLITICAL
SYSTEM

MARTIN
VAN BUREN
AND THE
AMERICAN POLITICAL
SYSTEM

DONALD B. COLE

PRINCETON UNIVERSITY PRESS
PRINCETON, NEW JERSEY

FOR DOUG AND CAROLYN,
BOB, DAN AND MARYELLEN,
SUE AND JEFF

CONTENTS

LIST OF ILLUSTRATIONS

PREFACE

I first became interested in Martin Van Buren in the 1960s while doing research for a book on Jacksonian Democracy in New Hampshire. As Isaac Hill and Levi Woodbury prepared for the election of 1828 in the Granite State, they corresponded with Van Buren and learned, as so many did, what a sociable man he was. Van Buren dined at the Woodbury mess in Washington and invited both Hill and Woodbury to visit him in New York. Intrigued by these letters, I resolved to learn more about Van Buren, who was so different from the irascible Hill and the pompous Woodbury.

In the years since then, many kind people have helped me find that Van Buren was more than just a sociable man. Henry F. Bedford, Henry W. Bragdon, James C. Curtis, Aida D. Donald, Edward Pessen, and Robert V. Remini read all or part of various drafts of the manuscript and helped me immeasurably in describing and evaluating Van Buren. Margaret Cohen did a skillful job of copyediting the manuscript.

My many conversations with Professor Curtis while we were both studying at the Library of Congress sharpened my thinking about Van Buren. Richard E. Ellis strengthened my understanding of Van Buren's response to the political scene after the War of 1812 and shared with me a paper he had written on New York and the nullification crisis. Paul E. Johnson generously shared the results of his study of local activists in New York in 1828.

I am grateful to the following for permission to quote from manuscript collections: the Astor, Lenox and Tilden Foundations of the New York Public Library, the New-York Historical Society, the New York State Library, the Columbia University Library, the Manuscripts Department, University of Virginia Library, and the Historical Society of Pennsylvania. Librarians at these libraries and societies were generous with their time and advice. The Avery Architectural Library of Columbia University and Richard V. Upjohn granted permission to publish the rendering of Lindenwald by Richard Upjohn. The staff at the Martin Van Buren National Historical Site took time to review chapter 1 and furnished photographs of Lindenwald. George W. Franz, Director of the Van Buren Papers project, helped me with information from the files of the project. Peter V. Denman provided me with a

xi

copy of a letter from the John P. Van Ness Papers. I am particularly indebted to Jacqueline Thomas and the staff of the library of Phillips Exeter Academy for assistance at every stage of the work. After spending a year at the Library of Congress, I owe more than I can say to the staff of that great institution. Like so many scholars in the early national period I have benefited from the advice and friendship of John McDonough, manuscript historian of the Library of Congress.

Much of the research for this study was accomplished during a sabbatical leave granted by the Trustees of Phillips Exeter Academy. The research was also supported by a grant-in-aid from the American Council of Learned Societies. Helen G. Hardardt, Betty M. Kukesh, Irene E. Little and Kathleen A. Pottle cheerfully and efficiently typed the drafts and final copy.

My friends, colleagues and family have steadily encouraged me, and have listened patiently to stories about Van Buren. They are pleased that the job is completed. Without Tootie it could not have been completed.

Donald B. Cole
Exeter, New Hampshire
August, 1983

ABBREVIATIONS IN FOOTNOTES

Argus	*Albany Argus*
Autobiography	John C. Fitzpatrick, ed., "The Autobiography of Martin Van Buren," *Annual Report of the American Historical Association for the Year 1918*, II (Washington, D.C., 1920)
CUL	Columbia University Library
Flagg Papers	Azariah Flagg Papers, New York Public Library
HSP	Historical Society of Pennsylvania
King Papers	Rufus King Papers, New-York Historical Society
LC	Library of Congress
MVB	Martin Van Buren
NYHS	New-York Historical Society
NYPL	New York Public Library
NYSL	New York State Library
UVL	University of Virginia Library
VBP	Martin Van Buren Papers, Library of Congress

MARTIN VAN BUREN
AND THE
AMERICAN POLITICAL
SYSTEM

INTRODUCTION

On December 5, 1782, as George Washington waited at Newburgh, New York, for news of the peace treaty with Great Britain, Martin Van Buren was born in the town of Kinderhook farther up the Hudson River. Almost eighty years later on July 24, 1862, as Abraham Lincoln continued his search for a general to oppose the Confederate army, which was soon to invade Maryland, Van Buren died in his old home town. Born at the end of the Revolution and dying during the Civil War, Van Buren represented the second generation of American political leaders—those who lived between the generation of Washington and that of Lincoln. The year 1782 is a convenient date to mark the beginning of this generation because Daniel Webster, Lewis Cass, Thomas Hart Benton and John C. Calhoun, as well as Van Buren, were all born that year.[1]

The leaders of Van Buren's generation were born too late to fight for independence and died too soon to fight over the Union, but they made important contributions in other ways. They fought off the British challenge to American independence in the War of 1812, held the nation together during the sectional crises that began with the debate over slavery in Missouri, pushed the frontier westward from the valley of the Ohio to the big bend of the Missouri, and extended the nation's borders to the Pacific. At the same time they responded to the economic and social changes that were transforming America in the first half of the nineteenth century. Between 1820 and 1850, while the second generation was controlling the nation, the infusion of capital and labor from Europe and the impact of inventions such as the railroad and the reaper so strengthened the American economy that the annual value of manufactures rose to a billion dollars. The new economy helped breed a new society less rural and less homogeneous, more mobile and more modern than before. The leaders of the second generation responded anxiously to these changes and yearned for the security they imagined existed in the Revolutionary era; yet

---

[1] Birth dates for other members of the second generation include the following: Andrew Jackson 1767, John Quincy Adams 1767, William Henry Harrison 1773, Roger B. Taney 1777, James K. Polk 1795. So many leaders of the generation died close to 1850 that that date can be used to mark the end of the era. Death dates are as follows: Harrison 1841, Biddle 1844, Jackson 1845, Adams 1848, Polk 1849, Calhoun 1850, Clay and Webster 1852, Benton 1858, Van Buren 1862, Taney 1864, Cass 1866.

3

they carried the Republic forward until it was the second most powerful manufacturing nation in the world.[2]

And the most democratic. Even though the new economy created new inequalities, it also contributed to the rise of a political system far more democratic than before. In 1812, for example, in half of the states the presidential electors were chosen by the state legislatures, but by 1832, all but two of the states had turned this process over to the people, and in almost every state, property qualifications had been dropped in favor of universal adult white male suffrage. As a result, the number of those voting for President rose from less than 400,000 in 1824 to 2,400,000 in 1840. Although the second generation looked back on the aristocratic Washington and Jefferson as their heroes and gave their hearts to the aristocratic Lafayette, they also built a democracy. When Alexis de Tocqueville visited America in 1831, he found this new society so modern and so democratic that he became convinced—even fearful—that democracy would succeed everywhere, and he made Van Buren's generation immortal in *Democracy in America.*

The key to Van Buren's career is the way in which he adapted to the new society and the part he played in building the new political system. A Northerner of yeoman stock who grew up in the country and then moved to the city, he was in many ways a typical American of his era. For Van Buren the adjustment was never easy. He too yearned for the security of the past, but he accepted change and let his career be shaped by it. He spent half a century building, perfecting, and defending a new system of political parties at first the state and then the national level. In New York he reorganized the Republican party and set up the Albany Regency to keep the party in power. Then he moved on to Washington where he did more than anyone to construct the Democratic party, which dominated American politics down to the Civil War. Caught between the old and the new, he was never ideologically secure and not always consistent. Like others of his generation he too had aristocratic heroes and he too sought aristocrats for his models and sometimes his associates. In making hundreds of political decisions and moral choices during his career, Van Buren sought to maintain a balance between what he considered the repub-

---

[2] The tension between yearning for the past and striving for change has been a central theme throughout American history, but the enormous economic, technological and social change between 1815 and 1840 meant that this generation experienced the tension more than most. For a perceptive study of the changes in America in the 1820s and 1830s, see Douglas T. Miller, *The Birth of Modern America, 1820-1850* (New York, 1970).

lican principles of his youth and the demands of the democratic system that he was building. When balance was impossible and something had to give way, politics took precedence over ideology. He was never as republican as he might have liked and never as democratic as he might have been. But he cared about ideology and he was more than just a self-seeking politician. In the end he became the quintessential party man who represented the best and worst in the new politics.

· I ·

NEW YORK POLITICIAN
1782-1821

1. Martin Van Buren's Birthplace in Kinderhook

·1·

A REPUBLICAN IN A
FEDERALIST WORLD

Like Webster, Clay, and others of his generation, Martin Van Buren
had roots deep in American colonial history. In 1631, Cornelis Maessen (Cornelis, son of Maes) of the village of Buren in Holland, sailed
to America, where he leased a plot of land from Kiliaen Van Rensselaer
near Fort Orange, now Albany, on the Hudson River. After a trip
back to Holland, he returned with a wife and two children to a farm
at Papsknee, on the east bank of the Hudson south of Albany. He
was soon producing a thousand bushels of wheat, oats, rye, and peas
a year, employing two hired men, and was rich enough to buy a
valuable plot of land on Manhattan Island. When he and his wife died
suddenly in 1648, they left five children and a large amount of property.[1]

Cornelis' eldest son called himself Marten Cornelisen Van Buren
(Marten, son of Cornelis from Buren) and thereby established the Van
Buren family name in America. Twice married, a member of the Dutch
Church of Albany and a captain in the regiment of Colonel Pieter
Schuyler, he was a man of substance; he leased half an island south
of Albany and bought outright a plot of land in Kinderhook Village.
His son Pieter, grandson Marten, and great-grandson Abraham were
freeholding farmers during the eighteenth century. When Martin Van
Buren, son of Abraham, was born in 1782, he was one of the sixth
generation of Van Burens in America.[2] Though successive generations
of Van Burens had progressed from leaseholder to freeholder, they
had displayed little of the fabled American mobility. Abraham Van
Buren tilled the soil in Kinderhook, only a few miles from where his
ancestors had first settled, and he was less prosperous than Cornelis
Maessen. Abraham did, to be sure, own six slaves, but the value of

[1] A.J.F. Van Laer, trans., ed., *Van Rensselaer Bowier Manuscripts, Being the Letters
of Kiliaen Van Rensselaer, 1630-1643, and Other Documents Relating to the Colony
of Rensselaerswyck* (Albany, 1908), pp. 176-181, 306-312, 412, 492, 814, 818; Harriet
C. Peckham, *History of Cornelis Maessen Van Buren . . . and His Descendants* (New
York, 1913), pp. 27-28; Frank J. Conkling, "Martin Van Buren, with a Sketch of the
Van Buren Family in America," *The New York Genealogical and Biographical Record*,
28 (1897), 122-124; *Autobiography*, p. 10.
[2] Peckham, *History of Cornelis Maessen Van Buren*, pp. 51-56, 68, 88; Conkling,
"Van Buren," pp. 207-210.

his real estate was only about average for the town, and he had been forced to turn his farmhouse into a tavern in order to support his family.[3] Martin Van Buren rose from a "small freeholder" family, like many others in Kinderhook and the rest of the United States, a family not unlike those of Clay, Benton and Webster.[4]

The isolated farming community in which he grew up was similar to those of his famous contemporaries. Like Webster's Salisbury in New Hampshire, Clay's Hanover County in Virginia, and Benton's Hillsboro in North Carolina, Kinderhook was a placid backwater that had changed little with the passage of time. Washington Irving drew the scenes and characters for "The Legend of Sleepy Hollow" from the life he observed on a visit to Kinderhook. According to the story, a "drowsy, dreamy influence" hung over the town, making it "one of the quietest places in the whole world," a town in which "population, manners, and customs remain[ed] fixed." Located on the east bank of the Hudson River in Columbia County twenty miles south of Albany, Kinderhook in the 1790s was isolated. Roads were rudimentary, and steamboat travel to New York City was two decades away. Most residents of Kinderhook lived as their ancestors had on farms surrounded by pines and decorated by lilacs, cherry and plum trees. The boyhood world of Martin Van Buren had the same "drowsy tranquillity" that Irving described in another of his famous tales, "Rip Van Winkle."[5]

In Martin Van Buren's boyhood, Kinderhook was still a Dutch town. The names of the heads of families in 1790 were mostly Dutch with Van Shaacks, Van Valkenburghs, Van Nesses, and Vosburghs rivalling Van Burens in frequency. The steep-gabled houses that the early Dutch settlers had built with oak sills, pine frames, and tiles imported from Holland still adorned the town. Dutch farmers still worshiped at the Dutch Reformed Church erected in 1727. Dutch was spoken in many

---

[3] For property statistics for Kinderhook, see Edward A. Collier, *A History of Kinderhook* (New York, 1914), pp. 121-123; for New York, see Franklin B. Hough, *Census of the State of New-York for 1855* (Albany, 1857), p. ix. Of 730 heads of family in Kinderhook, 174 owned slaves. Abraham Van Buren's real estate was worth £300. United States Bureau of the Census, *Heads of Families at the First Census of the United States Taken in the Year 1790. New York* (Washington, D.C., 1908), pp. 67-70.

[4] The "small freeholder" quotation is from George Bancroft, *Martin Van Buren to the End of His Public Career* (New York, 1889), pp. 1-2.

[5] Washington Irving, "The Legend of Sleepy Hollow," *The Sketch-Book of Geoffrey Crayon, Gent.* (Chicago, 1886), pp. 337-339; *Kinderhook, N.Y., the Village Beautiful. The Story of To-day* (Kinderhook, 1910); Collier, *Kinderhook*, p. 552; Henry C. Van Schaack, *An Old Kinderhook Mansion* (reprinted from *Magazine of American History*, Sept. 1878), p. 2. The "drowsy tranquillity" quotation is from Irving, "Rip Van Winkle," *Sketch-Book*, p. 48. Silas W. Burt, "Personal Reminiscences," MS, NYHS, I, 76.

homes. Washington Irving caught the Dutch flavor of old Kinderhook. Ichabod Crane, wrote Irving, enjoyed the "ample charms of a genuine Dutch country tea-table" with "sweet cakes and short cakes, ginger cakes and honeycakes," and spent evenings with "old Dutch wives, as they sat spinning by the fire, with a row of apples roasting and sputtering along the hearth." Crane listened apprehensively to "their marvellous tales of ghosts and goblins, and haunted fields and haunted brooks."[6]

The early Van Burens were as Dutch as Kinderhook. They spoke Dutch at home, they were members of the Dutch Reformed Church, and they married into other Dutch families. From the moment that Cornelis Maessen married in Holland until the American Revolution, Martin Van Buren's ancestors married only Dutch men and women. Surnames such as Hoes, Van Alen, Van Dusen, and Van Schaick were common in the family tree. Intermarriage was not unusual: Martin's father and grandfather each married women with Van Buren blood.[7]

There was a pattern in the family history that the men waited a while before they married, and when they finally took the step, married women considerably younger than themselves. Martin's paternal grandfather, for example, who married at thirty-three, was thirteen years older than his bride. Once married the Van Burens had large families; Martin's father, grandfather and great-grandfather were all members of families with at least eight children. By 1780, there were seven Van Buren families in Kinderhook.[8]

Martin Van Buren's immediate family followed the Van Buren tradition. After remaining single until he was thirty-nine, in 1776 Abraham Van Buren married the widow Maria Hoes Van Alen, a woman ten years his junior, who already had two sons and a daughter. Before a year had passed Maria gave birth to a daughter, Dirckie, and then in short order produced another girl, Janetje, and three boys, Martin, Lawrence, and Abraham. By the time he was ten in 1792, Martin's siblings including all these children, numbered seven, ranging in age from four to twenty-four.[9]

Martin's family and community helped to shape his emerging per-

[6] United States Bureau of the Census, *Heads of Families 1790. New York*, pp. 67-70; *Kinderhook, the Village Beautiful*; Lila James Roney, "Inscriptions of the Historic Stones, Kinderhook, New York," typescript (1925), p. i; Joel Munsell's Notes to Gorham A. Worth, *Random Recollections of Albany from 1800 to 1808* (Albany, 1866), p. 27; Burt, "Reminiscences," I, 74; Irving, "Legend of Sleepy Hollow," *Sketch-Book*, pp. 344, 357; *Argus*, Aug. 3, 1827.

[7] Conkling, "Van Buren," pp. 122-124, 207-210.

[8] *Ibid.*

[9] *Ibid.*

sonality. His father was both a political and a gentle man. A captain in the militia and a tavern keeper whose tavern served as a polling place, Abraham was a leading figure in the politics of Kinderhook. The epitaph on his gravestone describes him as "tender and indulgent . . . benevolent and charitable, a good man [of] mild temper and conciliatory manners." It is easy to surmise that this "amiable" man, as Van Buren described him, taught his son how to get along with people and introduced him to politics.[10] As for his mother, tradition holds that she recognized Martin's potential and saw to it that he got as much education as possible. On her death Van Buren recalled her "domestic virtues [and] undeviating fidelity." Van Buren received help and cooperation in varying degrees from other family members. One of his sisters helped bring up his children after his wife died. His brother Lawrence, although described as a "weak purposeless man," took over the family farm with Martin's blessing. In the 1840s, while former President Van Buren lived on his estate Lindenwald in Kinderhook, Lawrence ran a variety store, where he sold toys, candy and ice cream. Martin exchanged friendly letters with his other brother Abraham, who served in the War of 1812 and had a modest law practice. His two half brothers helped him when they could, one by lending money, the other by taking him in as a law partner. From the scanty evidence available it appears that Martin received love and support from his family, having no heavy-handed father, overbearing mother or challenging siblings to shake his security.[11]

He was also influenced by years spent in the convivial, busy atmosphere of a village tavern. Abraham Van Buren's crowded one-and-a-half-story farmhouse sheltered two adults, eight children, six

---

[10] Roney, "Inscriptions," p. 19; *Autobiography*, p. 10; Franklin Ellis, *History of Columbia County, New York with Illustrations and Biographical Sketches of Some of Its Prominent Men and Pioneers* (Philadelphia, 1878), p. 221; Conkling, "Van Buren," p. 210; Election advertisement, Sept. 26, 1801, VBP. James Parton called Abraham Van Buren illiterate, but it is difficult to understand how an illiterate could have been town clerk, as Abraham was. James Parton, *Life of Andrew Jackson* (New York, 1860), III, 121.

[11] For Van Buren's mother, see Denis Tilden Lynch, *An Epoch and a Man: Martin Van Buren and His Times* (New York, 1929), pp. 28, 165. The description of Lawrence is drawn from Burt, "Reminiscences," I, 89, 118-119. For Abraham, see MVB to Abraham Van Buren, Oct. 2, 1819, VBP; for the transfer of the farm, see Thomas M'Elhiney, *Life of Martin Van Buren* (Pittsburgh, 1853), p. 117. Abraham was surrogate of Columbia County, 1822-1836. Franklin B. Hough, *The New York Civil List from 1777 to 1863* (Albany, 1863), p. 458. For the loan, see *Autobiography*, p. 15; John J. Van Alen to MVB, May 26, 1803, VBP. See also Peckham, *History of Cornelis Maessen Van Buren*, pp. 88-89, 113-114; Conkling, "Van Buren," p. 122; "Statement of Van Alen and Van Buren's Business from Commencement of Firm until March 19th, 1805," VBP.

slaves, and paying customers; a favorite stopping-off point on the road from New York City to Albany, it introduced Martin to a wide variety of people. Years of living at close quarters not only with his family but also with strangers conditioned Van Buren to seek ways of adjusting to others, sometimes accommodating himself to them, at other times manipulating them to gain his wishes. In short he learned the art of compromising for which he later became famous. As amiable and political as his father, Martin developed into a pleasant, outgoing person who got on well with people.[12]

But beneath the cheerful, sociable exterior lay insecurities that followed him throughout his life, and it is this combination of outward sociability and inner insecurity that helps explain Van Buren's behavior both as a boy and as a man. Part of the insecurity came from Kinderhook, where slavery and the patroon system had created a class society in which people knew their places. Although slavery was outlawed in New York soon after the Revolution, it was not completely eradicated until 1827. In 1790, slaves made up fourteen percent of the population of Kinderhook, and a quarter of the heads of families owned slaves; but although he owned six slaves Abraham Van Buren stood well down in the social hierarchy of the town.[13] Conscious of this position, Martin learned as a boy to defer to those above him and continued to do so throughout his life. In his autobiography he recalled the upper-class Silvesters as "persons of much reputation and distinction" and as "men of no common mark." A half-century later he still recalled painfully an incident in which Peter Van Ness refused to speak to him, and Van Buren described with much satisfaction how he bought the Van Ness mansion and made it his own country estate.[14] At times Van Buren exaggerated his lowly beginning, as, for example, when he boasted that he had risen from rags to riches, but there is little doubt that his inferior status bothered him. It is striking that never once in his correspondence or other writings did he admit that his father had been a common tavern keeper.[15]

[12] Holmes Alexander, *American Talleyrand: the Career and Contemporaries of Martin Van Buren, Eighth President* (1935; reprint, New York, 1968), p. 16.

[13] The number of slaves in Kinderhook exceeded that in every other town in Columbia County. United States Bureau of the Census, *Heads of Families 1790. New York*, pp. 67-70; Collier, *Kinderhook*, pp. 552-559. See also Edgar J. McManus, *A History of Negro Slavery in New York* (Syracuse, 1966), pp. 197-200. New York ranked sixth in the United States in number of slaves. J.D.B. DeBow, *Statistical View of the United States, a Compendium of the Seventh Census* (Washington, D.C., 1854), pp. 45, 63-66, 82-86.

[14] *Autobiography*, pp. 13-20; Alexander, *American Talleyrand*, p. 29.

[15] Van Buren bragged in his *Autobiography*, p. 21, that he was not "worth a shilling" at the start of his career. William Hunt, an early biographer, called Van Buren a "self-

Van Buren was also ill-at-ease about his lack of education. His only schooling was at the village academy, where he learned to read and write, and received enough instruction in Latin to help him in his career in the law. With his lack of academic training Van Buren differed from Webster, who attended Phillips Exeter Academy and Dartmouth, Benton, who studied briefly at the University of North Carolina, and from John C. Calhoun, who graduated from Yale. Van Buren envied such men. "How often," he confessed, "have I felt the necessity of a regular course of reading . . . to sustain me in my conflicts with able and better-educated men." He cautioned his young readers against letting the prospects of fame tempt them into entering a profession too early in life, pointing out that he would have been more successful if he had had a better education.[16]

Van Buren's rivals and colleagues were well aware of his deficiencies. His New York political crony, James A. Hamilton, later wrote that Van Buren had not been adequately prepared for the State Department by his education, "which was very limited." When Andrew Jackson appointed Van Buren minister to England, John Randolph of Virginia warned the President that Van Buren could not "speak, or write the English language correctly," and would substitute "will" for "shall." Randolph was being unfair. Van Buren found writing so difficult that he rewrote his letters over and over and often relied on his sons and others to write for him. But even so he managed to turn out a prodigious quantity of letters and public papers. His writing was tangled, wordy, ornate, and confusing, but often by design and with the intent to obscure rather than from lack of skill. The important point is that Van Buren was painfully conscious of his lack of training. In recalling Randolph's criticism years later, Van Buren claimed that he and Jackson merely laughed at the assessment, but the fact that he told the story suggests that for Van Buren it was not a laughing matter.[17]

Van Buren's insecurity continued to dog him when he left home in 1796 to be apprenticed to the lawyer Francis Silvester. Working for the aristocratic Silvesters Van Buren was constantly reminded of his

---

made man." William Hunt, *The American Biographical Sketch Book* (New York, 1848), p. 49. Although Van Buren did not rise from rags to riches, his was a success story. He, Abraham Lincoln and Grover Cleveland were the only Presidents to have been elected with no college education, no military career, and without prosperous parents.

[16] *Autobiography*, pp. 11-13.

[17] James A. Hamilton, *Reminiscences of James A. Hamilton; or Men and Events, at Home and Abroad, During Three Quarters of a Century* (New York, 1869), p. 97; John Randolph to Andrew Jackson, Mar. 18, 1832, John S. Basset, ed., *Correspondence of Andrew Jackson* (Washington, D.C., 1926-1935), IV, 420; *Autobiography*, p. 12.

inferior social position, while at the same time receiving his baptism in New York state politics. Supported by the Livingstons and the Clintons, the Jeffersonian Republicans had won the elections of 1789 and 1792 in New York, but in 1795 the Federalists under Alexander Hamilton succeeded in electing John Jay governor. The bitter battles between Republicans and Federalists showed an embryonic two-party system at its best, and provided Van Buren with an ideal that he never forgot. Van Buren found himself among Federalists, for his employer was the son of Peter Silvester, Federalist state senator from Kinderhook, and was related to two other prominent Federalist families, the wealthy Van Schaacks and Van Rensselaers. Peter Van Schaack and Jacob R. Van Rensselaer led the famous Columbia County Junto, which kept the county staunchly Federalist. It was obvious to Van Buren that on all counts Federalists outranked Republicans in his community.[18]

The Silvesters did all they could to force Van Buren into the Federalist mold, particularly in 1798, when Peter Silvester was running for reelection. When Silvester was declared victorious, Federalists in Kinderhook staged a jubilant celebration; they fired cannon and caroused late into the night. Instead of joining in the festivities, the fifteen-year-old Van Buren retreated to his bed in the back of the Silvester store, where Francis Silvester's brother, Cornelius spent over an hour trying to convince the boy to become a Federalist. In the days that followed Van Buren found that the constant Federalist pressure of the Silvesters made his situation extremely unpleasant.[19]

The way in which he responded to this situation suggests a good deal about the sort of person he had become and foreshadows the way in which he would deal with similar situations and similar threats to his security throughout his life. The easy course would have been for him to join the Federalists, but he resisted and moved rapidly into Republican politics. One reason he was able to make this difficult decision was the strong support he got from his family. Even though Kinderhook had been the home of Tories during the Revolution and Federalists thereafter, his father had been an ardent patriot and a convinced Jeffersonian who made his tavern a gathering place for

---

[18] William M. Holland, *The Life and Political Opinions of Martin Van Buren Vice President of the United States* (Hartford, 1835), p. 34; Adrian Joline, "Martin Van Buren, the Lawyer," *The Autograph Hunter and Other Papers* (Chicago, 1907), p. 63; *Autobiography*, pp. 18-19. Dixon Ryan Fox called the members of the Junto and other Federalists "The Few, the Rich, and the Well Born." Dixon Ryan Fox, *The Decline of Aristocracy in the Politics of New York 1801-1840* (New York, 1919), ch. 1.

[19] Lynch, *Epoch and a Man*, pp. 36, 41; *Autobiography*, pp. 13-14.

Republicans in the 1790s. Legend has it that the famous Republican Aaron Burr often frequented the tavern on his way from New York to Albany. Ideology also played a part. For Martin Van Buren, who grew up on tales of the Revolution and learned from the political battles of the 1790s, the ideas of the Revolution seemed better articulated by Thomas Jefferson than by Alexander Hamilton.

Van Buren took advantage of his ability to adapt to new situations. His experiences in the family, in the tavern and in Kinderhook had taught him to compromise, accommodate, and even to defer in order to succeed. They had also taught him that appearances counted. When he first started to work for the Silvesters, he was so poorly dressed that his employers suggested that he get a new wardrobe. Instead of reacting angrily, he decided to acquiesce, and with the help of his family was soon able to deck himself out in clothes similar to those worn by his master. From that point on Van Buren was able to use his fine clothes and his attractive physical appearance to his political advantage. Though short and slight (he was only five feet six inches tall), he carried himself erectly, and his sharp, well-formed nose, blue eyes, and curly blond hair attracted attention. His reputation as a dandy followed him wherever he went. Not only was his attractive appearance a political asset, but it also helped him to compensate for his social insecurities.[20]

To his further advantage Van Buren found that he could use aristocrats even when he felt inferior to them. For example, to help him escape the Silvesters and succeed both in politics and in the law, Van Buren turned to the aristocratic Van Nesses, who led the Republicans in Kinderhook. The Van Nesses helped him become a delegate to the Republican party caucus in Troy in 1801, and he in turn helped John P. Van Ness win a seat in the United States House of Representatives the same year. Van Ness repaid Van Buren by lending him enough money to move out of Kinderhook, and Van Ness's brother William made a place for Van Buren in his new law office in New York City.[21]

Van Buren's five years with the Silvesters gave him the opportunity to develop the political style that he used throughout his career. Handsome, attractively dressed, pleasant, deferential, and accommodating, Van Buren made an impression that was hard to resist. But this agreeable exterior hid not only the old insecurity but also a strong resolute

[20] Lynch, *Epoch and a Man*, pp. 34-35. For a description of Van Buren dressed as a dandy, see John S. Jenkins, *Lives of the Governors of the State of New York* (Auburn, 1851), p. 374.
[21] *Autobiography*, p. 14.

character. Although he had learned to accommodate and defer, he had not learned to give in.

The next two years—1802-1803—his first away from Kinderhook, were difficult and uncertain. When he wrote to Congressman Van Ness requesting money and asking advice on such matters as attending the theater, Van Ness could spare only forty dollars, but was more liberal with his advice. On the one hand, he pointed out the advantages of the city and recommended that his young friend mix with "good society." On the other hand, Van Ness warned of the "temptations to vice," especially the vice of "idleness." Van Buren might properly attend the theater, but he should not make it a habit. The congressman was urging the young lawyer to work hard and move up in society, advice that the ambitious Van Buren followed without much prompting.[22]

The years in New York with William P. Van Ness drew Van Buren into Republican state politics at the right time. When George Clinton defeated Stephen Van Rensselaer for governor in 1801, Republicans took control of the state, which would never again go Federalist. Since Van Ness had studied with Mayor Edward Livingston and was close enough to Aaron Burr to serve as his second in the duel with Alexander Hamilton, Van Buren had an entrée into the New York City Republican organization. Burr accorded him so much attention that Van Buren felt his sympathies aroused by the notorious politician.[23] Still not twenty, Van Buren had widened his experience to include politics and politicians at the state level.

In the early nineteenth century until the constitutional convention in 1821, state politics in New York began every year with an election in April. Members of the legislature were elected annually and the governor was elected for a three-year term, commencing the following January. Even though he was working in New York City, Van Buren kept his ties with Kinderhook and returned there regularly in April. His experiences in the 1802 election show how deeply he remained involved in the politics of Kinderhook. In order to trick the local

[22] *Autobiography*, pp. 14-15; John P. Van Ness to MVB, Jan. 6, Nov. 3, Nov. 11, 1803, VBP.

[23] *Autobiography*, p. 15. The superficial similarities between Burr and Van Buren (both were small, scheming, successful New York machine politicians) led some to hint that Burr, not Abraham Van Buren, was the father of Martin Van Buren. There was even some circumstantial evidence because Burr frequented the Van Buren tavern the year before Martin's birth, but there is no direct evidence to support the allegation. Edward M. Shepard, *Martin Van Buren*, rev. ed. (Boston, 1899), pp. 17-18; Alexander, *American Talleyrand*, pp. 19-20. See also Gore Vidal, *Burr* (New York, 1973).

Republicans, the Federalists announced that they planned to run only a few candidates. They also tried to divide their opponents by including several Republicans among these candidates. Then, three days before the election, the Federalists suddenly offered a completely Federalist ticket and predicted that they would win with a majority of one hundred votes. On the first of the two election days Van Buren reported that "it went vote for vote" (there was no secret ballot), and by nightfall the Republicans were one or two votes ahead. But overnight the Federalists rallied and the next day "their waggons were continually going fetching the Lame the blind & the aged to the poll." For their part the Republicans "were not wanting in activity," and at three in the afternoon the Federalist momentum failed and the Republicans went ahead. "Not even the Machiavellian arts of Federalism [could] withstand the Irresistible ardor of Freedom of Republicans," wrote Van Buren, who had already learned the techniques and rhetoric that spelled victory.[24]

In November 1803, Van Buren was admitted to the bar and soon thereafter moved back to Kinderhook, where his half brother, James J. Van Alen, took him in as a partner. Van Alen had been practicing in Kinderhook since 1794 and had been elected town clerk. The partnership was such a success that by the end of the two years they had $821.17 in cash, $2,501.33 in accounts receivable, and debts of only $253. The fees were small, ranging from $3 to $60, but there were enough of them to make Van Buren sanguine about the future. In a revealing note he confided to himself that at this rate he would have $120,000 by 1849, having made $2,500 a year over expenses for forty-three years. The ambitious Dutchman had already learned how to get along with people, how to get out of difficult situations, and how to beat Federalists. Now he had learned how to make money and was ready to plan his future.[25]

In 1804, Van Buren felt independent enough to desert the Van Nesses when Aaron Burr ran for governor against Morgan Lewis. While regular Republicans led by George Clinton and Edward Liv-

[24] Van Buren to John P. Van Ness, April 6, 1802, Papers of General John P. Van Ness, 1769-1846, in the possession of Mrs. John Van Ness Philip, Talavera, Claverack, N.Y. I was given a copy of this letter by Peter V. Denman, who has completed a doctoral dissertation on the Van Ness Family. Denman, "From Deference to Democracy: the Van Ness Family and Their Times, 1759-1844" (University of Michigan, 1977).

[25] "Statement of Van Alen and Van Buren's Business from the Commencement of Firm until March 19th, 1805," VBP; Ellis, Columbia County, p. 112; Peyton F. Miller, A Group of Great Lawyers of Columbia County, New York (Hudson, 1904), p. 4; Autobiography, p. 15. In 1805, Van Buren helped found the Kinderhook Law Society, which held weekly debates. Kinderhook Law Society, "Minute Book," MS, NYSL.

ingston backed Lewis in this election, dissident Republicans including the Van Nesses, along with many Federalists, supported Burr. When John P. Van Ness made a special trip back to Kinderhook in April for the election, he tried in vain to talk Van Buren over to the Burr side. Van Buren recalled painfully in his autobiography that Van Ness became so angry that their friendship was in abeyance for some time. Van Ness's powerful father and Peter Van Schaack—both for Burr— even tried to embarrass Van Buren by using a technicality to challenge his right to vote on election day. But like the Silvesters the Van Nesses discovered that Van Buren put Republican party regularity over personal friendship and could not be bullied, and when Lewis won the election, they realized that Van Buren had learned how to end up on the winning side.[26]

Events in the summer of 1804 restored Van Buren's ties with the Van Nesses and rearranged the shape of New York politics. On the morning of July 11, William P. Van Ness acted as second for Aaron Burr when he killed Alexander Hamilton in a duel, and was soon indicted as accessory to murder. Called upon to help, Van Buren successfully defended Van Ness in court and intervened on his behalf with the governor. Burr fled from New York to start his notorious conspiracy in the Southwest, and his political organization collapsed.

The election of 1807 pitted Lewis, whose backers included some of the Livingstons and some Federalists, against Daniel D. Tompkins, who was supported by George Clinton (now Vice President) and his nephew DeWitt, mayor of New York City. Tompkins descended from a Yankee family that traced its roots to Concord, Massachusetts, in 1640. After graduating from Columbia in 1795, he took up law in New York City and joined the Republican party. A gracious, warm-hearted, good-natured man, Tompkins had a wide following in the state, where he was popularly called the "farmer's boy." Still seeking party regularity and party success, Van Buren joined the Clintons and helped Tompkins carry the state. Van Buren would maintain a close political relationship with Tompkins for the next decade and a half. (It was with Governor Tompkins that Van Buren intervened on behalf of William P. Van Ness.) In backing Tompkins Van Buren again courted hard feelings in Columbia County, which voted for Lewis as it had for Burr in 1804. Van Buren's bitter political experiences between

---

[26] Van Buren complained to William P. Van Ness that he was being attacked by the friends of Van Ness in 1804, but insisted that he could not be "scolded out" of his position. MVB to William P. Van Ness, Mar. 13, 1804, VBP. See also William P. Van Ness to Van Buren, Feb. 22, 1804, VBP. Van Buren recalled the events in the *Autobiography*, pp. 15-16.

1798 and 1807 provided stern schooling for the years ahead. They soured him on the factional politics represented by Burr and Lewis and sent him in search of a better political system based on party regularity.[27]

With money coming in at the law office and with his political candidates winning, Van Buren at twenty-four was ready to think of marriage. Like the other Van Burens before him, Martin turned to a Dutch woman whom he knew well and whose family was related to his. Hannah Hoes was descended from a Dutch family named Goes (they had changed the spelling of the family name after frequent mispronunciations), who had lived for several generations in Kinderhook, where Hannah was born in March 1783, three months after Van Buren. The Hoeses and the Van Burens were interrelated in several ways. Hannah's father had married a Quackenboss, just as the original Marten Van Buren had done in the seventeenth century. Hannah Hoes was Martin Van Buren's first cousin once removed—her grandfather was the brother of Martin's mother Maria Hoes—and Hannah's brother Barent later married one of Van Buren's sisters. Martin and Hannah grew up in the same town, went to school together, and gradually became sweethearts. In February 1807, they slipped off to Catskill, New York, where on the twenty-first they were married at the country estate of Hannah's brother-in-law, Judge Moses I. Cantine.

Although little is known about Hannah, at her death Van Buren wrote that she was a "modest and unassuming" woman with a "mild" disposition. If she was, she was remarkably like her husband's parents and siblings, who were also mild and far from aggressive. Accustomed to sweet, loving people in his home, Martin chose the same sort of person for his wife. As a lawyer and politician, Van Buren had accepted a contentious way of life. He sought and found peace, love and support in his family. Hannah was pretty and tiny enough to be smaller than Van Buren. Unlike several of his ancestors, Martin did not marry a woman who was already pregnant, but he and his wife produced a child exactly nine months after the wedding.[28]

[27] *The Leading Citizens of Columbia County New York* (Boston, 1894), p. 591; Lynch, *Epoch and a Man*, pp. 67-73; Fox, *Decline of Aristocracy*, pp. 61-83; Elisha Jenkins to MVB, April 22, 1807, Reminiscences of Van Buren's Contemporaries, 1853, VBP; Ellis, *Columbia County*, p. 51; *Autobiography*, p. 16; Ray W. Irwin, *Daniel D. Tompkins: Governor of New York and Vice President of the United States* (New York, 1968).

[28] Robert V. Remini, "Hannah Hoes Van Buren," *Notable American Women 1607-1950: a Biographical Dictionary*, ed. Edward T. James (Cambridge, Mass., 1971), III, 505-506; *Argus*, Feb. 9, 1819; Lynch, *Epoch and a Man*, p. 73.

With his marriage in 1807, Van Buren had come of age as a politician, lawyer and family man in Kinderhook. Despite bitter hostility he had maintained his Republicanism in a county that was Federalist and in a party that was split into factions. Though he had not yet developed a philosophy, he was already being congratulated on his (yet undefined) "truly republican principles." By February 1807, he had been admitted as a counselor before the supreme court of New York; crowds were beginning to attend his court appearances. A month later he was made surrogate of Columbia County. Twenty-four years old, with a growing income and a growing family, he had come a long way from the uncertain thirteen-year-old lawyer's apprentice. He was now ready to move out of the narrow world of Kinderhook.[29]

ON August 17, 1807, a few months after Van Buren's marriage, Robert Fulton's steamboat *Clermont* started north from New York City, and after several stops for firewood, pulled into Albany thirty-two hours later. The voyage of the *Clermont* symbolized a transportation revolution that shook the stability of old Kinderhook. The isolation of Kinderhook disappeared as Yankee pioneers traveled the new roads from Boston to Albany. Some settled in the upper Hudson Valley; others continued west along the Mohawk toward the rich Genesee land and the Great Lakes. The invasion was so large that New York grew more rapidly than any of the seacoast states in the first decade of the nineteenth century.[30]

As the population grew, the society of the Hudson Valley changed. Immigration from New England meant that Yankees began to challenge the Dutch in numbers and influence. As early as 1787, Troy had been founded as the Yankee rival to Dutch Albany, and by 1803 Yankees outnumbered the original inhabitants in Albany as well. The newcomers rose rapidly in New York politics. Since the cocksure Yankees often scorned the Dutch, accusing them of ignorance and lack of enterprise, tensions mounted. In the "Legend of Sleepy Hollow," Irving ridiculed the Yankee schoolmaster Ichabod Crane, and

---

[29] Van Buren was appointed surrogate on March 20, 1808, replacing his half brother and partner, James J. Van Alen. Jabez D. Hammond, *The History of Political Parties in the State of New-York from the Ratification of the Federal Constitution to December 1840* (Cooperstown, 1840), I, 262-263; John C. Hogeboom to MVB, Mar. 14, 1803, VBP.

[30] David M. Ellis, "The Yankee Invasion of New York, 1783-1850," *New York History*, 32 (Jan. 1951), 1-17; Ellis, *Columbia County*, p. 127. The population of New York in 1790 was 340,120; in 1810, 959,049. George Tucker, *Progress of the United States in Population & Wealth in Fifty Years* (1855; reprint, New York, 1964), p. 57.

James Fenimore Cooper attacked the sly Yankee Aaron Thousandacres in *The Chainbearer*. Irving and Cooper, who grew up at the same time as Van Buren, picked up this hostility in their boyhoods.[31]

Progress from agriculture to commerce, industry and finance accompanied the social changes. New York State, which ranked fifth in exports in 1790, had climbed to first by 1807. Three years later the state had 33,069 looms, 12,293 spindles, 427 fulling mills, 124 hatteries, 11 blast furnaces, 48 forges, 867 tanneries, and 591 distilleries. The change was particularly noticeable in Van Buren's own Columbia County, which ranked among the leading manufacturing counties. The number of banks in the state grew from three in 1799 to twenty in 1812.[32]

Van Buren was able to take advantage of the opportunities offered lawyers by the economic advances. In 1808, soon after his first son Abraham was born, he moved his family to nearby Hudson, a commercial town founded by Yankee Federalists on the Hudson River.[33] Here he formed a partnership with Cornelius Miller and began to compete with the members of the Columbia County bar, one of the strongest legal rosters in the United States; William W. Van Ness, Jacob R. Van Rensselaer, Thomas P. Grosvenor, and Elisha Williams were all lawyers of great renown. The same energy and determination that marked Van Buren's apprenticeship enabled him to prosper in Hudson. Thanks to the changing economy the new partnership was soon enjoying so much business that Van Buren was making $10,000 a year.[34]

Backed by careful research and armed with a superb memory, he

[31] Ellis, "Yankee Invasion," pp. 11-16; Dixon Ryan Fox, *Yankees and Yorkers* (New York, 1940). At the same time, the density of black population in New York dropped and slavery was gradually abolished. McManus, *Slavery in New York*, pp. 122-143, 172-200.

[32] Timothy Pitkin, *A Statistical View of the Commerce of the United States of America: Its Connection with Agriculture and Manufactures: and an Account of the Public Debt, Revenues, and Expenditures of the United States* (Hartford, 1816), pp. 51-54; Hough, *Census of New York 1855*, p. lvi; Treasury Department, *A Series of Tables of the Several Branches of American Manufactures, 1810*, Part II, *Tabular Statement* (Philadelphia, 1813), pp. 32-38; *Argus*, Jan. 1818. For a list of banks founded 1781-1812, see William M. Gouge, *A Short History of Paper Money and Banking in the United States* (Philadelphia, 1833), Part II, pp. 42-44.

[33] Holland, *Van Buren*, p. 57; Fox, *Decline of Aristocracy*, pp. 39-40.

[34] Miller, *Great Lawyers of Columbia County*, pp. 6-7; Joline, *Autograph Hunter*, p. 63; Holland, *Van Buren*, p. 34; two letters to Benjamin Butler, 1819, Charles Butler Papers, LC; William Emmons, *Biography of Martin Van Buren, Vice President of the United States* (Washington, D.C., 1835), p. 7; statement of sums due Van Buren, 1810, VBP; M'Elhiney, *Van Buren*, p. 42.

overwhelmed his opponents with elaborate briefs, careful arguments, and rapid rhetoric. Spectators enjoyed seeing the suave little lawyer stand up to his more impressive rivals. Outside of court his tact, cleverness and tenacity enabled him to win settlements. If necessary, Van Buren could insist on the letter of the law. Once he demanded that Peter I. Hoes, one of his relatives, fulfill the obligations of a note. His reputation even led Edmond (Citizen) Genêt, who had been minister to the United States during the French Revolution and was now living in New York, to ask Van Buren for legal help.[35]

The great Federalist lawyer Elisha Williams also respected Van Buren. From 1809 to 1819, Williams was Van Buren's professional opponent in many cases at the bar of Columbia County. With his speaking skill, his wit and his invective, Williams was a superb defense lawyer, winning verdicts from juries. Van Buren, on the other hand, with his skill in research and his ability to analyze, was the master at winning appeals to judges. Van Buren openly admitted that it was hardly "possible to excel [Williams'] skill in the examination of witnesses or his addresses to the Jury," but he criticized his opponent for being "seldom well prepared."[36]

Men enjoyed comparing the tall, "God-like" Williams with the short, capable, but not brilliant Van Buren. No one compared them better than the future United States Attorney General Benjamin Butler, who as a young law student had witnessed many clashes between the two:

> Both were eloquent; but the eloquence of Williams was declamatory and exciting, that of Van Buren insinuating and delightful. Williams had the livelier imagination, Van Buren the sounder judgment. The former presented the strong points of his case in bolder relief, ... indulged in more unlicensed and magnificent invective, and gave more life and variety to his arguments. ... But Van Buren was his superior in analyzing, arranging, and

[35] Joline, *Autograph Hunter*, p. 68; William A. Butler, *Martin Van Buren: Lawyer, Statesman and Man* (New York, 1862), p. 37; Holland, *Van Buren*, pp. 60-61; MVB to Peter I. Hoes, May 31, 1817, Aug. 5, 1820, Hoes to MVB, July 29, 1820, VBP; Genêt to———, Sept. 1817, Edmond C. Genêt Miscellaneous Papers, NYSL.

[36] Oliver Wendell Holmes was once told that Williams was the most remarkable man in America. Olvier Wendell Holmes, *The Poet at the Breakfast-Table* (Boston, 1891), pp. 330-331; Fox, *Decline of Aristocracy*, p. 41. Van Buren called Williams his "professional antagonist" in *Autobiography*, pp. 21-22. There is a good sketch of Williams in William Raymond, *Biographical Sketches of the Distinguished Men of Columbia County* (Albany, 1851), pp. 1-3.

combining the insulated materials . . . in unraveling the web of intricate affairs.[37]

It was Van Buren's lot in 1810 and throughout his career to be compared with lawyers and politicians more dramatic, more exciting than himself. He would never attract people as easily as did Williams, DeWitt Clinton, Henry Clay, Andrew Jackson, or Daniel Webster. No one knew it better than Van Buren, whose autobiography reveals the awe he felt for his rivals even when he was besting them. He wrote that he approached Williams with "apprehension"; that he regarded Jackson as a man of "perfect purity and unconquerable firmness"; that Clinton was a man of "stateliness [and] hauteur." From the first chapter—in which John Randolph is described—to the last, which is devoted largely to Daniel Webster, the *Autobiography* is the work of a man who was self-conscious about his rivals.[38]

Van Buren's legal career contributed immeasurably to his success in politics. Lacking schooling, he secured his training in his legal studies and in his day-by-day preparation for his cases. From 1796 to 1821, when he entered the United States Senate, Van Buren's life was spent for the most part in the law. Through 1840, all Presidents except Washington were lawyers, but being a lawyer meant more to Van Buren than to the others. All of the others had experiences that diluted the impact of the law. All but Jackson went to college and traveled abroad; Monroe and Jackson had military careers; plantation responsibilities distracted Jackson and the Virginians; the Adamses taught school. Until he went to England in 1831, Van Buren did none of these. Most of the others had outside incomes, but for many years Van Buren depended on the law alone. Even when he entered public life, it was often in a legal capacity as surrogate and later as attorney general. In *Democracy in America*, Alexis de Tocqueville commented that "lawyers belong to the people by birth and interest, and to the aristocracy by habit and taste; they may be looked upon as the connecting link between the two great classes of society." The upward-looking, class-conscious Van Buren, who traveled the long road from a humble tavern to a country estate, epitomized this assessment.[39]

---

[37] Shepard, *Van Buren*, pp. 20-21. For a summary of descriptions of Williams, see Fox, *Decline of Aristocracy*, pp. 41-43.

[38] *Autobiography*, pp. 12 (Randolph), 21 (Williams), 167 (Clinton), 229 (Jackson). Marvin Meyers has commented on Van Buren's admiration for powerful decisive leaders in *The Jacksonian Persuasion: Politics and Beliefs* (Stanford, 1957), pp. 146-147.

[39] Edward M. Shepard best summarized the impact of legal training on Van Buren. See Shepard, *Van Buren*, ch. 2. Alexis de Tocqueville, *Democracy in America* (1835; Bradley edition, New York, 1945), I, 282-290, quotation, p. 286; Donald M. Roper,

Measured by his professional career, Van Buren was one of the most competent lawyers to reach the White House. Benjamin Harrison matched him in scope of practice; Chief Justice William Howard Taft outstripped him in scholarship and national renown; but no other President surpassed Van Buren as a lawyer. The caution, care, and respect for detail that mark successful lawyers characterized Van Buren in politics as well. Only brilliance and excitement were lacking.[40]

From 1807 to 1828, Van Buren appeared frequently before the state supreme court, the state court of errors, and the state court of chancery. After 1812, he was a member of the court of errors, where he delivered in 1813 a significant opinion in a case involving John W. Barry, who had been imprisoned for debt. According to a modification of the law, debtors who posted a bond were allowed outside jail, providing they stayed within certain boundaries. When Barry pursued his cow a few feet across the line, his creditor sued for the amount of the bond and won before the supreme court. In his opinion, which resulted in a reversal of the decision, Van Buren not only attacked the opinion of the famous chief justice James Kent, but also lashed out against imprisonment for debt. Debtors were put in jail, Van Buren argued, "for the misfortune of being poor; of being unable to satisfy the all-digesting stomach of some ravenous creditor." In addition to sympathy for debtors, his lengthy opinion demonstrated a comprehensive understanding of procedures.[41]

Beause of the continued in-fighting among Republican factions and Federalists, Van Buren's political and legal career generated much bitterness. In the election for governor in 1810 President James Madison's unpopular trading restrictions against the British helped the Federalists, who were supporting General Jonas Platt against Republican governor Daniel D. Tompkins. During the campaign Van Buren

---

"Martin Van Buren as Tocqueville's Lawyer: the Jurisprudence of Politics," *Journal of the Early Republic*, 2 (Summer 1982), 169-189.

[40] Three students of Van Buren and the law who rank him with Harrison as one of the leading lawyer-Presidents of the nineteenth century are Edward M. Shepard in *Van Buren*, p. 31; Adrian H. Joline in *Autograph Hunter*, pp. 55-56; and Claude G. Bowers in *The Party Battles of the Jackson Period* (Boston, 1922), pp. 53-54.

[41] In 1855, Smith Van Buren prepared a list of his father's appearances before three upper New York courts, VBP. For interesting cases see William Johnson, *Reports of Cases Argued and Determined in the Supreme Court of Judicature, and in the Court for the Trial of Impeachments and the Correction of Errors in the State of New-York*, 3 (1808), 3rd ed. (Philadelphia, 1832), pp. 175-178, 422-423, 499-505. The debtor case (Barry *v.* Mandell), 10 Johnson, 563-587. Several cases are discussed in Joline, *Autograph Hunter*, pp. 70-82; in Holland, *Van Buren*, pp. 66-73; and in Shepard, *Van Buren*, pp. 25-27.

complained to party chief DeWitt Clinton, who was the Republican candidate for lieutenant governor, about the way in which Federalist landlords manufactured votes by giving land to landless Federalists for a few days, thus making them eligible to vote. Van Buren, who learned from the opposition, did not accuse the Federalists of fraud, but reported ironically that his opponents had "made" more votes than he had been able to. He informed Clinton "with shame," that the county had given a majority of 527 votes to Platt, even though Tompkins carried the state.[42]

Conflict over the incorporation of banks intensified political conflict, for in the state's expanding economy, control of credit became a widely sought political prize. During the 1790s, when Federalists controlled the state, New York had only four banks, all of them in Federalist hands. After Republicans gained political power at the turn of the century, they set up two banks of their own, Aaron Burr's Manhattan Bank in New York City and the State Bank in Albany. Capitalized at $2,000,000, the Manhattan Bank became the largest bank in the state. It was also the most controversial because, in drawing up the charter in 1799, Burr had slyly asked the state to incorporate a waterworks with banking as a subsidiary feature. When the corporation turned out to be a Republican bank, Federalists were outraged.[43]

Concern over banking increased in 1810 and 1811 as the charter of the Bank of the United States was about to expire and plans for new banks came before the legislature. Within two years the New York legislature had chartered ten new banks, increasing the number in the state from ten to twenty and the projected capitalization from $5,680,000 to $22,280,000. Most of the new banks and capitalization were for New York City, where the branch of the Bank of the United States closed in 1811, but charters were also granted for establishments in the upstate towns of Utica, Albany and Troy. At the start of the War of 1812, New York had overtaken Massachusetts as the leading banker in the nation.[44]

---

[42] Francis P. Blair used the word "acrimonious" to describe Van Buren's career. Fox, *Decline of Aristocracy*, pp. 112-116, 142-146; MVB to James J. Van Alen, June 28, 1810, Blair to MVB, Jan. 25, 1856, VBP; MVB to DeWitt Clinton, April 19, April 28, 1810, DeWitt Clinton Papers, CUL. See also De Alva S. Alexander, *A Political History of the State of New York* (New York, 1906), I, 255.

[43] Republicans Ambrose Spencer, John W. Taylor, Elisha Jenkins, and Thomas Tillotson organized the State Bank at Albany. Ellis, *Columbia County*, pp. 49-51. For lists of early American banks, see Gouge, *Short History*, Part II, 42-44, and Bray Hammond, *Banks and Politics in America from the Revolution to the Civil War* (Princeton, 1957), pp. 144-145. Hammond used and corrected Gouge; he discusses the Manhattan Bank episode, pp. 149-158.

[44] Exactly when New York overtook Massachusetts is uncertain but on January 1,

The chartering of the Bank of America in 1812 produced an economic and political crisis. With a proposed capital of $6,000,000, the Bank of America would be the largest bank in the nation and would make New York City the nation's financial center. The struggle over the bank transcended party lines, for Republicans, including former state treasurer David Thomas and state printer Solomon Southwick of Albany, joined Federalists in support of the bank. Opponents of the new bank charged that Thomas and Southwick had resorted to bribery. They also accused Van Buren's Federalist rivals Elisha Williams, Jacob R. Van Rensselaer and William W. Van Ness, of the Columbia Bank in Hudson, of supporting the Bank of America in return for promises of a low-interest loan. Republican governor Tompkins attacked the Bank of America in his address to the legislature in January of 1812. When that failed to stop the bank, he prorogued the legislature in April and May, but the charter sailed through when the legislature reconvened.[45]

Van Buren's position on the Bank of America was more political than ideological. Since he was a Republican, he found it politically expedient to oppose a bank organized by Federalists in New York City and supported by Federalists in Columbia County. He did, to be sure, insist later that he had tried "to arrest the bank mania of the times" for philosophical reasons. When in 1811, Vice President George Clinton cast the deciding ballot in the United States Senate to defeat the recharter of the Bank of the United States, Van Buren referred to Clinton's "glorious casting vote." Van Buren also spoke strongly against the Bank of the United States at a Republican convention held in Albany in 1811. In his book on the origin of American political parties published after his death, he attacked Alexander Hamilton, the Bank of the United States, and the "money power."[46] But Van Buren was

---

1811, Massachusettes had 15 banks capitalized at $6,292,144, and New York had 8 banks capitalized at $7,522,760. On January 1, 1815, Massachusetts had 21 banks capitalized at $11,050,000, New York 26 banks capitalized at $18,946,318. These figures are for actual capitalization and are smaller than those cited in the text, which are for projected capitalization. The figures in the text are taken from Gouge, *Short History*, Part II, pp. 42-44; those in this note for 1811 and 1815 are from Albert Gallatin, *Considerations on the Currency and Banking System of the United States* (New York, 1831), pp. 101, 103. In 1815, there were 208 banks capitalized at $82,300,000 in the entire United States, of which 47 banks capitalized at $29,996,318 were in the Empire and Bay states. *The Statistical History of the United States from Colonial Times to the Present* (Stamford, 1965), p. 623.

[45] Hammond, *Political Parties*, I, 299-314; Hammond, *Banks and Politics*, pp. 161-164; Ellis, *Columbia County*, p. 178.

[46] For references to Van Buren's opposition to the Bank of America, see *Autobiography*, pp. 28-29. For Clinton's casting vote, see Bancroft, *Van Buren*, p. 16; and *Autobiography*, p. 411. The anti-Bank of the United States convention is mentioned in

no doctrinaire opponent of banks. He was director of the Hudson
Bank, and two of his closest friends, John C. Hogeboom and Gorham
Worth, were president and cashier. He also had close ties with the
Mechanics' and Farmers' Bank in Albany, and held back from at-
tacking Southwick and Thomas for bribery because Southwick was a
Republican and president of that bank.[47]

A longstanding debate over the large estates in the Hudson Valley
also involved Van Buren in controversies that were both political and
ideological. In Columbia and Rensselaer counties the Livingston and
Van Rensselaer families held a large share of the land, with patents
dating back as far as the original Dutch land grants of the seventeenth
century. Ever since the Revolution, tenants had contested the legality
of these patents. In 1811 Van Buren advised a committee of tenants
that the Livingston patent was void and that the land belonged to the
state because the patroons had used "fraudulent misrepresentation."
Letters, quite likely written by Van Buren, also appeared in the Hudson
Advocate claiming that both the Van Rensselaers and the Livingstons
had acquired their land corruptly. The legislature promptly directed
Attorney General Thomas A. Emmet to start a suit for the state against
the landlords.[48]

After the proceedings began, the rumor circulated that Jacob R. Van
Rensselaer had said on the floor of the assembly that the tenants were
not capable of governing themselves, and needed a master. Van Rensselaer, worried about the effect of the rumor on his bid for reelection
the next spring, asked Van Buren to repudiate the story. He replied
that he would do so only if the assemblyman denounced malicious
tales about Van Buren circulating in the Federalist press. Van Rensselaer refused and called a public meeting to accuse Van Buren of
recommending delay on the suit until the time of the election. After

---

Bancroft, *Van Buren*, p. 17. Apprehension about Hamilton and the "money power" is
evident throughout the first 200 pages of Van Buren's *Inquiry into the Origin and
Course of Political Parties in the United States* (New York, 1867). Note especially p.
166.

[47] Ellis, *Columbia County*, p. 178; Hogeboom to MVB, Mar. 14, 1803, MVB to
Worth, Dec. 16, 1817, April 27, 1818, Nov. 1, 1851, VBP; *Argus*, Jan. 6, 1818; Robert
V. Remini, "The Albany Regency," *New York History*, 39 (Oct. 1958), 342, 347; Frank
Otto Gatell, "Sober Second Thoughts on Van Buren, the Albany Regency, and the Wall
Street Conspiracy," *Journal of American History*, 53 (June 1966), 25-26; "Biography
of Martin Van Buren," *Argus Extra*, 1832; Smith Van Buren, "Notes on Martin Van
Buren's Early Political Career, 1812-1815," 185-?, VBP.

[48] *Autobiography*, pp. 22-24; David M. Ellis, *Landlords and Farmers in the Hudson-
Mohawk Region* (Ithaca, 1946), pp. 152-153; MVB to Benjamin A. and Others, Committee, July 28, 1811 (copy), VBP.

sending out handbills and publishing a denial in the newspapers, Van Buren called his own rally at which he accused Van Rensselaer to his face of distorting the truth. The latter angrily offered to forfeit a $500 deposit if Van Buren had the nerve to sue him in court. Although Van Buren brought no suit, he continued the debate in the press.[49] The legislature failed to take land away from the patroons, but the issue was revived years later, in the Anti-Rent War.[50]

When Van Buren attacked the credibility of one of the landlords' surveyors in court, John Suydam, who was an attorney for the Van Rensselaers, denounced him. At a banquet at the Van Rensselaer mansion the next day, Suydam drank too much and challenged Van Buren to a duel. To save face Van Buren accepted, but the duel was never fought because Suydam's second refused to participate. Van Buren came out of the episode with honor when he challenged Suydam and the latter refused.[51]

Loyal Democrats later used the battle over the manor lands to present Van Buren as a democrat in his defense of the common man against the landlords. Van Buren, said one account, had to fight "an opposition at once powerful, personal, and peculiar." A few old families, who were generally Federalists, owned most of the land and, backed by the merchants and professional men, held "uninterrupted ascendancy" in Columbia County. Van Buren was attacked because he "would neither worship at the shrine of wealth nor court the favour of the powerful." A decade later the historian George Bancroft praised Van Buren for defending the small freeholders against the landlords. On Van Buren's death the New York *Evening Post* recalled that he had been "the object of bitter animosity from the federal leaders of the time."[52] Not everyone saw Van Buren so favorably. One opponent portrayed him as a "pettifogger," who took the side of the farmers because he had been ignored by the Livingstons. Another maintained

---

[49] MVB to Francis Stebbins, Aug. 19, 1811, MVB to Jacob R. Van Rensselaer, Aug. 19, 1811, Van Rensselaer to MVB, Aug. 24, 1811, VBP; Ellis, *Landlords and Farmers*, pp. 153-154; *Autobiography*, pp. 24-26.

[50] *Autobiography*, p. 24. For the aftermath, see Ellis, *Landlords and Farmers*, pp. 154-155; and Henry Christman, *Tin Horns and Calico: a Decisive Episode in the Emergence of Democracy* (New York, 1945). James Fenimore Cooper described the Anti-Rent War in his *Satanstoe, The Chainbearer,* and *The Redskins.*

[51] *Autobiography*, pp. 26-28; MVB to John Suydam, Nov. 25, 1811, Richard Riker to MVB, Feb. 17, 1812, VBP; Lynch, *Epoch and a Man*, pp. 81-84.

[52] "Corrector," *Letters Addressed to Martin Van Buren, Esq. Secretary of State: Correcting Many Important Errors in a Late Biography of That Gentleman* (New York, 1830), p. 3. See also Bancroft, *Van Buren*, p. 9; and the obituary of Van Buren in the New York *Evening Post*, July 24, 1862.

that Van Buren got involved in the manor lands affair simply because he needed the money. But neither attack challenged the importance of the cases, the height of the passions, or the role of Van Buren.[53]

And neither view was wholly correct; Van Buren was neither a heroic tribune of the people nor a cheap pettifogger. The small farmers on the manor lands had a grievance, but for decades they had done little about it. By openly attacking the Van Rensselaers and Livingstons, Van Buren turned discontent into a crisis. But it is going too far to say that the landlords were out to get Van Buren. During these years Van Buren occasionally took cases for the Livingstons, and even helped eject farmers from manor land. The most sensible assessment of Van Buren's role in the manor affair appears in his own autobiography, in which he tells the story in a straightforward way. In this version Van Buren emerges as a careful, correct lawyer helping those in need, and as a clever politician looking for popular support, but not as a hero endangering his career in a battle against the landlords.[54]

Van Buren benefited politically from the episode when he ran for the state senate in 1812. He used his reputation as a defender of the people to outmaneuver his two opponents for the Republican nomination, both of whom had better family backing than he did. In the April election, he opposed Edward P. Livingston, grandson of Philip Livingston, signer of the Declaration of Independence. Since Livingston was backed by the Federalists, the Livingstons, the Van Nesses, and the supporters of the Bank of America, he seemed to stand for the high and mighty. Van Buren, in contrast, could be said to represent the main body of Republicans. As the results began to drift in, it appeared that Livingston had won. The first week in May, amid the smirks of his opponents, a discouraged Van Buren boarded the steamboat at Hudson for New York City, but a few miles downstream, at Catskill, a rowboat pulled alongside with the news that Van Buren was the winner. His margin was less than 200 votes.[55]

[53] "Corrector," *Letters Addressed to Van Buren*, pp. 4-5; Alexander, *American Talleyrand*, p. 77.

[54] *Autobiography*, pp. 21-28. Other balanced accounts appear in Ellis, *Landlords and Farmers*, pp. 152-155, and to a lesser extent, in Lynch, *Epoch and a Man*, pp. 79-84. A number of Van Buren's biographers simply omitted references to the episode or made little out of it. See, for example, Holland, *Van Buren*; Emmons, *Van Buren*; M'Elhiney, *Van Buren*. Alfred Young suggests that New York Republicans used anti-manor sentiment against the landlords to get votes, but were unwilling to join the tenants in challenging the landlords. Van Buren went further than the Republicans Young describes. Alfred E. Young, *The Democratic Republicans of New York: the Origins, 1763-1797* (Chapel Hill, 1967), pp. 568, 580.

[55] *Autobiography*, pp. 28-33; Holland, *Van Buren*, pp. 86-87; Ellis, *Columbia County*, p. 89.

It was fitting that Van Buren should have been aboard a steamboat when the good news came. The steamboat and other changes had helped expand his simple world, providing the economic opportunities that shaped his career and led him to the state senate. It was fitting also that the manorial and banking interests were lined up against him in the election, for Van Buren had built a somewhat inflated reputation for republicanism by opposing them. And it was especially fitting that the episode should have taken place in Federalist Columbia County, for with his election Van Buren had completed over a decade of political training as a young Republican in a Federalist world.

· 2 ·

PRINCIPLES AND PARTY

The years that followed Van Buren's election to the senate offered him the opportunity to continue his political education—to articulate a philosophy and to perfect techniques. Before long he was expressing the "truly republican principles" on which he had been congratulated before, and he was building the sort of political party that would become the basis for a new political system. During these years he continued to be in the center of the same sort of legal and political controversy that had marked his career down to 1812, only now the struggles were at the state rather than the town or county level. These were the years in which he matured from an inexperienced twenty-nine-year-old state senator in 1812, to an experienced thirty-eight-year-old party leader in 1821.

These were also the years of the War of 1812 and its aftermath. The War of 1812, which began a few weeks after Van Buren was elected to the senate, was crucial for both the new senator and his state. Like other politicians of his generation, Van Buren launched his state and national career during the era of the war. From 1807, when the Embargo Act effectively closed the port of New York, to 1820, when Van Buren successfully defended Governor Daniel D. Tompkins' handling of wartime funds, issues associated with the War of 1812 were central to New York politics. Many parts of the United States were indifferent or hostile to the war, but New York was vitally concerned because so much of the fighting took place within or near its borders. From the Niagara campaign of 1812 to the Battle of Lake Champlain late in 1814, New York was under siege. To a degree the War of 1812 was the New York War.

Soon after moving to Hudson, Van Buren had begun to support Republican maritime measures against the British. In the waning months of the Jefferson administration when Federalist landlords called meetings of their tenants to denounce the embargo, Van Buren held a counter-meeting in Hudson. Urging his followers to support their President, he said that "war, submission to European despots, or prohibition of commerce" were the only alternatives.[1] At the county meeting that followed, Republicans adopted Van Buren's resolutions, pledging

---

[1] [Albany] *Balance and New-York State Journal*, Feb. 4, 1809; Bancroft, *Van Buren*, p. 12.

to fight in defense of their country. In 1810 and again in April 1811, Van Buren drafted resolutions in Hudson supporting the administration, and he based his campaign in 1812 partly on a platform backing President James Madison. He was as much a war hawk as Henry Clay or John C. Calhoun.[2]

But even so, in 1812 he turned against James Madison to support DeWitt Clinton's campaign for the presidency. Until the death of Vice President George Clinton of New York in February, Republicans in the Empire State seemed likely to support renomination of the Madison-Clinton ticket. Then, after Clinton's death, hostility toward Virginia began to surface as many New Yorkers were no longer content with second place on the ticket. A resolution in Schoharie County at this time reminded New Yorkers that they were not inferior to Virginians. During the spring Lieutenant Governor DeWitt Clinton, who was also mayor of New York City, received growing support for President. The state Republican caucus nominated him on May 29, less than two weeks after the caucus in Washington had nominated Madison and only three weeks before war was declared on England.[3] Van Buren, who had been a Clinton man for several years, had to support him. The mayor had helped Van Buren with his senatorial race, and was the nominee of the regular party caucus.[4] In addition, Van Buren thought he had Clinton's backing for state attorney general; in August when someone else was named to the post Van Buren wavered, but in the end he swallowed his pride, paid a call on Clinton, and promised to support his campaign.[5]

It was embarrassing for Van Buren that Federalists had begun to flirt with Clinton during the summer. By 1812, the Federalist party had lost so much strength that the old two-party system had largely collapsed. Certain that no member of their party could defeat Madison, the Federalists counted on Clinton to do the job; the mayor was willing

[2] Bancroft, *Van Buren*, pp. 12-15; Lynch, *Epoch and a Man*, pp. 88-89.

[3] In notes written c. 1853, Van Buren stated that the New York Republicans had endorsed Madison in March, but this is not corroborated elsewhere. "Notes of Martin Van Buren on the Republican Presidential Nominations in 1812," [1853], VBP; *Albany Register*, April 21, May 1, June 26, 1812.

[4] MVB to Clinton, April 19, April 28, 1810, DeWitt Clinton Papers, CUL; *Autobiography*, p. 29.

[5] Van Buren lost the job partly because he was too young and partly because Tompkins did not think Van Buren would prosecute Solomon Southwick and David Thomas for bribery involving the Bank of America. *Autobiography*, pp. 38-43; Smith Van Buren, "Notes on Martin Van Buren's Early Political Career, 1812-1815," 185-?, Martin Van Buren, Jr., "Reminiscences about Van Buren's Appointment to the Office of Attorney General," 1853?, Richard Riker to MVB, July 21, 1812, VBP.

to cooperate. To those who favored war, he promised more efficient prosecution; to those who wanted peace, he talked peace. On September 15, seventy Federalists from eleven states met in New York City, passed ambiguous resolutions opposing Madison, and departed, having tacitly agreed to support Clinton for President.[6]

When the legislature met in November to select presidential electors, the situation was difficult for the New York Republicans, who were still split into factions. Although the Republican caucus had nominated Clinton, many Republicans opposed the mayor. Angry at Clinton for consorting with Federalists, these factions wanted a Madison slate. In addition, the war was going so badly in New York that it seemed disloyal to oppose the President. General Stephen Van Rensselaer had failed in his attempt to invade Canada at Niagara in October, when most of the New York militiamen refused to leave the state. General Henry Dearborn had a similar experience at the Canadian border near Lake Champlain in November. If Clinton were elected, it would appear that New Yorkers had repudiated the war.[7]

Into this situation stepped Van Buren, his age, reputation, appearance, and personality all commanding attention. At twenty-nine, the youngest person save one who had ever been elected to the senate, he brought with him a reputation enhanced by his political and legal successes in Columbia County. His appearance defied but invited description. According to one writer he arrived "dressed in a green coat, buff breeches, and white topped boots, and withal, bearing himself somewhat jauntily." Van Buren, who had dressed well in order to advance as a lawyer, did the same in politics. Small, poorly educated, from an undistinguished family, Van Buren was always the outsider, eager to please and eager to make an impression. Observers enjoyed comparing the sociable, pleasant Van Buren with the haughty DeWitt Clinton. One writer said that Van Buren

> had less genius, but more practical tact. Mr. Clinton had more self-reliance, Mr. Van Buren greater self-command. The one was wilful, headstrong and impatient; the other calm, cautious and prudent. Mr. Clinton was reserved in manner, but gave free utterance to his thoughts,—Mr. Van Buren was frank in manner, but concealed his thoughts. Mr. Clinton was always bold and decided,—Mr. Van Buren only so at the proper time. The former

[6] Fox, *Decline of Aristocracy*, pp. 165-171; Robert V. Remini, "The Early Political Career of Martin Van Buren, 1782-1828" (Doctoral dissertation, Columbia University, 1951), pp. 68-76; Alexander, *Political History*, I, 199-206.

[7] *Autobiography*, pp. 41-43; Fox, *Decline of Aristocracy*, pp. 171-173.

studied books,—the latter men. The one could scarcely control himself, much less govern others; the other was complete master of himself, and therefore, easily obtained the mastery over others.

With these perceptive remarks the observer summarized the differences between the two men, one the greatest of the old-style, aristocratic factional leaders, the other a man who was to become the standard for a new style of party politicians.[8]

The exciting, imaginative Clinton had the dramatic personality that made men follow him, but having no practical plan for winning the New York electoral votes, he wisely turned that task over to Van Buren.[9] The young senator had to cope with a legislature in which the assembly was controlled by Federalists, the senate by Clintonian Republicans. In addition, there were a few Madisonian Republicans in each House. According to the New York constitution, each House was to select a slate of presidential electors. Those whose names appeared on both slates would be declared elected; the rest were to be selected by joint ballot. Van Buren's problem was to have Clintonian electors chosen without giving any hint of a deal with the Federalists.[10]

To solve the problem, Van Buren turned to the party caucus—a device he would use many times. Calling Republicans of both Houses together, he lulled the suspicions of the Madisonians by nominating one of them for chairman. Van Buren then proposed a Republican electoral slate in which the Madisonians would have only token representation. When they balked, he nominated a slate made up entirely of Clintonians. The caucus voted it in. Madisonians were furious, but Van Buren was able to say that they had had their chance. In the election the Federalist assembly submitted an entirely Federalist ticket, while the senate backed the Clintonian slate drawn up at the caucus. In the joint election that followed, most Madisonian Republicans refused to vote, and enough Federalists voted the Clintonian Republican slate (by prearrangement) to ensure that the Republicans got credit for giving New York's electoral votes to Clinton.[11]

Van Buren had bailed out Clinton and the New York Republicans, but at great cost to himself. When despite New York's vote, Clinton failed to win the presidential election, his political standing in the state

[8] Alexander, *Political History*, I, 207; Jenkins, *Lives of the Governors*, pp. 374, 436-437.

[9] *Autobiography*, p. 42; Hammond, *Political Parties*, I, 321.

[10] Alexander, *Political History*, p. 208.

[11] *Autobiography*, pp. 39-41; Hammond *Political Parties*, I, 320-322; Remini, "Early Political Career of Van Buren," pp. 82-87; Smith Van Buren, "Notes," VBP; Alexander, *Political History*, I, 209-210.

withered, leaving Van Buren in a precarious position. Having antagonized the Madisonians and lacking support from the political club at Tammany Hall in New York City, Van Buren found his political career in jeopardy. Since Republican power in New York lay with Justice Ambrose Spencer of the supreme court, and Governor Daniel D. Tompkins, Van Buren had to reestablish himself with them.

The first opportunity arose in February 1813, when the legislature took up the election of a United States senator. After the senate nominated Federalist Rufus King and the assembly countered with Republican James W. Wilkin, Van Buren and others heard the rumor that enough Clintonian Republicans would desert Wilkin to elect King. The Clintonians would be repaying Federalists for voting for Clinton for President. When Van Buren confronted Clinton with the rumor, he denied it, but the vote in joint session—64-61 for King—convinced Van Buren that the stories had substance. Back in the senate chamber Clinton said he hoped that Van Buren no longer had any "suspicion." "No," replied the ironic Van Buren, playing with Clinton, "My suspicions have become convictions." While voting for Wilkin, Van Buren let the word pass that he really preferred Ambrose Spencer. King was elected senator. By quarreling with Clinton, by voting for the regular party candidate, and by speaking out for Spencer, Van Buren had taken steps toward reestablishing himself with the main body of the party.[12]

Van Buren took the next step when the Republican caucus met to nominate candidates for governor and lieutenant governor. Although the renomination of Daniel D. Tompkins for governor was guaranteed, few expected DeWitt Clinton to be renominated for lieutenant governor, especially since Tompkins was opposed to Clinton. When Clinton, still hopeful, asked Van Buren to nominate him, he agreed to do so, but made it clear that he expected to fail and would go along with the nomination of Judge John Tayler instead. In his nominating speech, Van Buren succeeded both in nominating Clinton and at the same time defeating him. Van Buren first reviewed the events leading to King's election to the Senate, hinting that Clinton had engineered the deal; then after weakly nominating Clinton, he agreed to "support cheerfully" a Tompkins-Tayler ticket. Clinton was defeated. From then on, according to Van Buren, he and Clinton were never again political

---

[12] *Journal of the Senate of the State of New-York*, 36th session (1812-1813), 82-83; *Autobiography*, pp. 45-46; Smith Van Buren, "Notes," Charles Holt to MVB, Jan. 20, 1813, VBP; Remini, "Early Political Career of Van Buren," pp. 79-82; Alexander, *Political History*, I, 211-212; Hammond, *Political Parties*, I, 344; Fox, *Decline of Aristocracy*, p. 173.

friends, and from that day it was apparent that Van Buren was on the Tompkins bandwagon.[13]

For his twists and turns at the start of the war Van Buren paid dearly in terms of his future political reputation. His support for Clinton led critics to say that he had helped the enemy in wartime. Others condemned the tricky way in which he won New York's votes for Clinton. Van Buren was also criticized for abandoning Clinton so rapidly after he failed to win the election. To defend Van Buren in 1832, the *Albany Argus* published an extra entitled "Mr. Van Buren and the War," trying to prove that Van Buren was always "on the side of his country." A good deal of political ammunition was fired on both sides.[14]

But Van Buren had to do what he did. As a young politician who had worked for Clinton and had received his help, Van Buren could hardly have opposed him. Nor could he have gone against the party caucus. After Clinton lost, all bets were off. To dispel charges of disloyalty, Van Buren went through the motions of nominating Clinton, but it was only sensible at the same time to indicate support for Tompkins and Tayler. There was little else he could do. The episode shows that Van Buren put party regularity ahead of principle and personal loyalty. It also helped harden his growing conviction that a new two-party system was needed to replace the factional system that had led to Clinton's presidential nomination.[15]

Van Buren emerged from the affair a state rather than a local politician. From then on no one was more in command in the senate than Van Buren, who chaired committees, drew up resolutions, brought in bills, and called for votes. The party needed his leadership because the most prominent Republicans were busy in other parts of the gov-

[13] *Autobiography*, pp. 46-47; Lynch, *Epoch and a Man*, p. 118; Alexander, *Political History*, I, 212; Hammond, *Political Parties*, I, 354; Smith Van Buren, "Notes," VBP.

[14] For critics, see Hammond, *Political Parties*, I, 322; Hammond to MVB, Oct. 17, 1843, VBP; Henry Adams, *History of the United States of America during the Administrations of Thomas Jefferson and James Madison* (1889; reprint, 9 vols. in 4, New York, 1930), VI, 409-410; Alexander, *American Talleyrand*, pp. 103-104. For the defense, see "Mr. Van Buren and the War," *Argus Extra*, 1832; Holland, *Van Buren*, pp. 90-94; Bancroft, *Van Buren*, pp. 24-46.

[15] Van Buren insisted that he behaved as he did because he felt obliged to follow the dictates of the party caucus. *Autobiography*, p. 37. His son Smith agreed. "Notes," VBP. Jabez Hammond denied that Van Buren was inconsistent. Hammond, *Political Parties*, I, 355. Edward M. Shepard said that Van Buren "had a stronger sense of allegiance to his party in the Senate than to his party at Washington." Shepard, *Van Buren*, p. 59.

ernment, and he had his hands full because the Federalist assembly was bent on blocking important war legislation.[16]

Military setbacks during the winter of 1812-1813 encouraged the Federalists. In the west William Henry Harrison sustained such heavy losses at Frenchtown in January that he postponed further campaigns. Along the coast the British were tightening their blockade. Hopeful that they could turn public dissatisfaction with the war into political victory, the Federalists nominated Stephen Van Rensselaer to run against Governor Tompkins. Patroon of his vast family estate and one-time lieutenant governor, Van Rensselaer was a strong, well-known candidate. Unfortunately, however, he had been in command at Niagara the previous October when most of the New York militia had been so unwilling to fight. The Patroon's dismal military record and Tompkins' popularity enabled the Republicans to win the governor's chair as well as the state senate. But the Federalists held the assembly.[17]

When Van Buren was selected to write the Republicans' annual "address" for the campaign, it gave him a chance to define his republicanism. In the document the new senator took up some of the topics and developed some of the themes that Thomas Jefferson had addressed in his first inaugural a dozen years earlier. But the circumstances surrounding Van Buren's effort were different from those surrounding Jefferson's. Written by a young New Yorker rather than an old Virginian, the address represented the views of the new, not the old generation, and a rising, not a declining state. It was a wartime message, delivered with the republic in greater peril than it had been in 1801. It was delivered to a state rather than to a national audience. As a result, Van Buren's republican principles in the address differed considerably from those expressed by Jefferson.[18]

More openly democratic than Jefferson, Van Buren began by telling his "fellow citizens" that they did not have to submit to "the arbitrary mandates of despotic power," nor to the "seductive wiles and blandishments of the corrupt minions of aristocracy," but should rather listen to the representatives of the people. In a government, he said, where ultimate power rested with the people, voting was extremely important. The state officials about to be selected were the people's "most important functionaries." Van Buren expressed a democratic version of Jefferson's state-rights republican ideal.

Like Jefferson and other early Americans, Van Buren considered the republic a unique experiment on display. The "only free people on

---

[16] "Van Buren and the War," *Argus Extra.*

[17] Fox, *Decline of Aristocracy*, pp. 175-176; *Autobiography*, p. 49; Hammond, *Political Parties*, I, 358; "Van Buren and the War," *Argus Extra.*

[18] "Van Buren and the War," *Argus Extra.*

earth," he wrote, blessed by a "munificent Providence," Americans were to be envied; they were free from "the tempest of passion and lawless violence [that] raged in the countries of the old world." Like John Winthrop, who spoke of a "city upon a hill," Van Buren reminded his readers that Europe was watching them. But he was more concerned about the future of the republic than Jefferson had been. As New Yorkers went to the polls, Van Buren warned that the "efficacy [of their] mild and wholesome form of government" was being tested. The United States, he said, was "the last republic," and the rulers of Europe had predicted that republics could "never stand the rude shock of war." The voters must decide "whether man is capable of self-government, whether our republic must go the way of its predecessors." Van Buren believed that Americans must show the world that their republican experiment could succeed.

As a result Van Buren's republicanism was more nationalistic than Jefferson's. In 1812, he said, "WAR, AND WAR ALONE, *was our only refuge from national degradation.*" Americans could not have surrendered to the orders-in-council, or to the "detestable practise" of impressment. Americans could not have bowed before the nation that "sought to strangle us in our infancy." Those who refused to rally to the defense of their native land were "parricidal." Americans should perform the duty they owed their country so that future generations would know that the "spirit" of those who fought at Saratoga had not been vanquished.

Van Buren was more partisan than Jefferson. "No falsehood is considered too glaring [by the Federalists]" claimed the New Yorker, "to seduce your affections from your native land." Federalists lied when they said that Republicans were enemies of commerce and under French influence. On the contrary, the administration was waging war to defend the rights of commerce, and Republicans would hardly succumb to French influence when Frenchmen were so unpopular in the United States. Federalists were simply exploiting the fears of New Yorkers. Unlike the founding fathers, Van Buren willingly accepted the idea of political parties, arguing that it was "not in the power of circumstances to destroy the virulence of party spirit." Rather than destroy the opposition, he preferred to defeat it.[19]

[19] Roger H. Brown has developed the thesis that fears for the republic led Americans into the War of 1812. Brown, *The Republic in Peril: 1812* (New York, 1964). Richard Hofstadter has argued that Van Buren "arrived at a coherent view of party politics" after the War of 1812, and that his "ideas on party were fully expressed as early as February 1828." Richard Hofstadter, *The Idea of a Party System: the Rise of Legitimate Opposition in the United States, 1780-1840* (Berkeley, 1969), pp. 223-224. Max M. Mintz claims that Van Buren was the first political leader to accept the idea of parties.

As a spokesman for the Republican party in New York, Van Buren returned to several of these themes later in the war. He was consistently bellicose, in one statement asking Americans to fight on until their "multiplied wrongs" were avenged, and denouncing the British for their "cold blooded murder of peaceful and unarmed individuals." He was always anti-Federalist: the Federalists had opposed a just war, had supported sectional policies against the nation's interests, and had sowed "the seeds of Jealousy and disunion" between the North and the South. But Van Buren accepted political opposition and political parties, arguing that differences of views were often "productive of much national good."[20]

Van Buren's rhetoric marked the shift from the republicanism of the 1790s to the more national version of the War of 1812, and it gave hints also of a new philosophy of government and new political ideas that later became the core of Jacksonian Democracy. Van Buren was more democratic, more nationalistic, and more comfortable with trade and commerce than Jefferson. There was little of the traditional Jeffersonian strict interpretation of the Constitution and defense of state rights. Brought up on tales of the Revolution but not a member of the revolutionary generation, Van Buren found it easier than Jefferson to appeal romantically to the "spirit which actuated the heroes of Breedshill." Neither a planter nor an aristocrat, Van Buren could adjust to the commerce and business that had recently arrived in the Hudson Valley. But Van Buren had not yet adopted the rhetoric that identified the Jacksonians in the 1830s. He made no appeal to the people, no reference to "plain farmers," or to the working class, no attack on the "money power." He was a nationalistic New York Republican.

Despite Van Buren's rhetoric, his opponents after 1815 often suggested that he had not contributed much to the war effort. He had, they said, supported Clinton in 1812 and had stayed in Albany in "snug quarters" while heroes such as William Henry Harrison, Andrew Jackson, and even Van Buren's brother Abraham, were risking

---

Mintz, "The Political Ideas of Martin Van Buren," *New York History*, 30 (Oct. 1949), 430. See also MVB, *Letter of Ex-President Van Buren* (Philadelphia, 1856), p. 4; Hammond, *Political Parties*, passim. The evidence suggests that Van Buren had accepted political parties earlier than the date given by Hofstadter, as early as the March 1813 address. Lynch, *Epoch and a Man*, p. 120.

[20] *Journal of New York Senate*, 37th session (1814), 38-40; *Autobiography*, pp. 50-52; "Reply to the governor Sept. 27, 1814," in Emmons, *Van Buren*, pp. 68-73. *Journal of the Assembly of the State of New York at Their Thirty-Eighth Session* (1814-1815), 189, 211.

their lives in battle. Moreover, he had turned down a commission when Secretary of War James Monroe and Major General Winfield Scott, who was a friend of Van Buren, offered him one. Years later, Davy Crockett made fun of Van Buren's reluctance to go to war.[21]

The critics were unfair, for Van Buren performed valuable services, especially in the final year of the war. The situation looked ominous for New York as the year began. A two-pronged assault on Montreal the previous fall had collapsed along the St. Lawrence and Lake Champlain. The British had just burned Buffalo, captured Fort Niagara, and set the Indians loose on settlers near Niagara Falls. In the legislature in January, Federalists in control of the assembly blocked the senate's attempt to have New York pay its quota of the federal direct tax. In the early months of 1814, Van Buren was deeply involved in working for war legislation and in campaigning against the Federalists.[22]

He also played a part in the court-martial of General William Hull. The unfortunate Hull, who served valiantly in the American Revolution, was almost sixty when called back into action at the start of the War of 1812. Entrusted with the western theater, he surrendered Detroit in August 1812 without firing a shot. Lack of naval power on Lake Erie and the failure of General Henry Dearborn to divert the British by an assault on Montreal contributed to Hull's defeat. At worst, he was guilty of incompetence, but an outcry rose against him, and he was brought to court-martial on the charge of cowardice. General Dearborn, whose reputation was also at stake, was—incredibly—selected to preside over the trial. Van Buren was appointed special judge advocate to help prosecute the government's case.[23]

Van Buren handled himself well during the trial. At the start, he had the task of examining Colonel Lewis Cass, who had served honorably under Hull and was subsequently appointed governor of the Michigan Territory before being called to Albany to testify at Hull's trial. Cass and Van Buren had similar careers that intersected at a number of points, particularly in 1848, when both were candidates for President. Van Buren began to question the colonel flippantly, but

[21] Richard Hildreth, *The Contrast: or William Henry Harrison versus Martin Van Buren* (Boston, 1840), p. 20; David Crockett, *The Life of Martin Van Buren, Heir-Apparent to the "Government," and the Appointed Successor of General Jackson* (Philadelphia, 1835), pp. 35-36; Alexander, *American Talleyrand*, p. 88; Winfield Scott to MVB, Oct. 22, 1814, VBP.

[22] *Journal of New York Senate*, 37th session (1814), 11-12, 51.

[23] *Report of the Trial of Brig. General William Hull* (New York, 1814), p. 3; Samuel C. Clarke, *Memoir of General William Hull* (Boston, 1893), p. 19; MVB to A. J. Dallas, Jan. 5, 1814, Winfield Scott to MVB, Oct. 22, 1814, VBP.

as soon as he realized that he could not get away with that, he became more respectful. It was typical of him that he altered his tactics when he found that his first approach was not working. The energy, adaptability, verbosity, and skill that he displayed in the court-martial were consistent with his earlier court appearances in Columbia County. Hull was sentenced to be shot for cowardice, but his sentence was remitted by the Secretary of War.[24]

In the senate Van Buren worked to promote war legislation. When the Federalist assembly blocked several bills proposed by the senate, conferences were held at which committees of both Houses debated before joint sessions of the legislature. According to reports, the debates were conducted eloquently before large crowds. Van Buren, who was often principal speaker for the senate, spoke with such "dexterity [and] powerful reasoning," according to the *Argus Extra*, that he won great applause.[25]

The debates were aimed at the voters as well as the legislators. Van Buren started the political campaign with a speech in which he pleaded with New Yorkers to support a "righteous war." In his address to the Republicans in April, he accused the opposition of depriving the government of "the two great sinews of war—men and money." Van Buren later declared that the election was "the most important of any ever held in the State." The result was a Republican victory in both assembly and senate, "the complete humiliation," said Van Buren, of the Federalists, and he later recalled that the triumph "gladdened the heart of every patriot." According to one account, the news was received in Washington "with an exultation only inferior to that with which was received the news of the victory of New Orleans." The Washington *National Intelligencer* called the New York results a great victory for the administration.[26]

Confident of support at last from a Republican legislature, Governor Tompkins called a special session to meet September 26, 1814. When the legislators gathered, the United States seemed to be losing the war. A month earlier the British had burned Washington, D.C. Only a brilliant naval victory by Captain Thomas MacDonough on Lake

[24] *Hull Trial*, pp. 2-14, 156; William T. Young, *Sketch of the Life and Public Services of General Lewis Cass* (Philadelphia, 1851), p. 77; Adams, *History*, VII, 417.

[25] "Van Buren and the War," *Argus Extra*; Holland, *Van Buren*, pp. 105-106; Benton to Davis, Dec. 16, 1834, in Emmons, *Van Buren*, pp. 162-163.

[26] *Journal of New York Senate*, 37th session (1814), 38-40; *Autobiography*, pp. 51-53; Holland, *Van Buren*, p. 108; "Notes and resolutions of a Republican general meeting held at the Capitol at Albany, April 14, 1814," VBP; Alexander, *Political History*, I, 226; *National Intelligencer*, May 5, 1814, quoted in Bancroft, *Van Buren*, p. 42.

Champlain two weeks before the special session, prevented British forces from threatening Albany. In Massachusetts the legislature was preparing to call for the convention that met at Hartford. With only a little exaggeration, Van Buren wrote later that the attention of "friends of the Country in all directions" was turned to New York when the legislature convened.[27]

In a burst of energy the legislature responded by "turning out war measures,"—as one historian put it—"like cloth from a loom." The legislators paid New York's share of the federal direct tax; they raised the pay of the state militia above that of the United States Army; they encouraged privateering by New York sea captains, and they reimbursed Governor Tompkins for war expenses that he had taken from his own pocket. They also established a joint committee to devise ways of raising troops.[28]

Two proposals for troops were brought to the floor of the senate from the committee. A plan for volunteer soldiers came from Erastus Root, who had migrated to New York from Connecticut in time to lead the fight against the Bank of America and in favor of the War of 1812. The very next day Van Buren proposed a special classification bill that would enable the state to draft soldiers rather than rely on a voluntary system. Van Buren recalled that in two days of heated debate he fought "the violent opposition of the Federalists aided by General Root, who denounced [the classification bill] with great bitterness." Van Buren, however, had the aid of his friend Major General Winfield Scott, who was one of the heroes in the War of 1812 because of his brigade's heroism at Lundy's Lane. Scott helped defeat the volunteer plan, which lost by a vote of 20 to 8. In rapid order Van Buren's bill passed the senate on October 14, was amended a few days later, had passed both Houses by October 21, and was accepted by the council of revision on October 24—only five days after Massachusetts elected delegates to the Hartford Convention.[29]

Van Buren's classification bill, which Senator Thomas Hart Benton later called "the most energetic war measure ever adopted in our America," authorized the state of New York to enlist twelve thousand free white males, eighteen to forty-five, for a period of two years. Militia company commanders were ordered to make lists of all such men living within the towns. If no one from a given group within a

[27] Emmons, *Van Buren*, pp. 68-73; *Journal of New York Senate*, 38th session (1814-1815), 4-6; *Autobiography*, pp. 53-55.

[28] Alexander, *Political History*, I, 226.

[29] *Journal of New York Senate*, 38th session (1814-1815), 7-72; *Autobiography*, p. 56; Holland, *Van Buren*, pp. 108-109; Bancroft, *Van Buren*, p. 46.

town volunteered, then the group was required to "procure" a soldier or pay a fine of $200. The bill never went into effect because the war was ending, but Secretary of War James Monroe was sufficiently impressed to use it as a model for a similar national draft bill proposed in December 1814 but never passed.[30]

In the council of revision that endorsed the war measures, the only opposition came from Chancellor James Kent, the famous Federalist who had been appointed to the court of chancery in 1814. Kent, who became a symbol for early nineteenth-century conservatism, was born in New York in 1763 and graduated from Yale in 1781, the year before Van Buren was born. He practiced law in Poughkeepsie and New York City before reaching the supreme court in 1798. Kent was a more learned scholar than Van Buren but a less skillful lawyer and politician. Failing to block the war measures in the council of revision, Kent carried the dispute to the press, calling the privateering act immoral and unconstitutional. The classification act, he said, asked a state to contribute too much to the defense of the nation, put insufficient restrictions on the use of the troops, and did not properly exempt those who had already served.[31]

Kent's outburst first brought Speaker Samuel Young into the fray. Young, who used the pen name of "Juris Consultus," pointed out that the war bills had passed the legislature by margins of at least two to one, and that Kent had no support on the council of revision. Young denied that the privateering act was unconstitutional, reminded Kent that British soldiers were hardly moral when they burned the Capitol, and refuted Kent's constitutional interpretation of the classification act.[32]

When Kent attacked Young, Van Buren came to the speaker's rescue with two articles signed "Amicus Juris Consultus." In the first article Van Buren cited such authorities as Hugo Grotius, Samuel Von Pufendorf, Matthew Hale, and Domenico Azuni to prove the privateering act constitutional. In the second Van Buren called on more scholars and a half-dozen treaties to show that nations at war had always

[30] MVB, "Notes on the Classification Bill," Oct. 24, 1814, included with Martin V.B. Wilcoxon to MVB, Dec. 17, 1855, Scott to MVB, Oct. 22, 1814, MVB, "Copy of the endorsement of the original draft of the Classification Bill, filed in the office of the Sec. of the Senate," Feb. 20, 1815, VBP; "An Act to Authorize the Raising of Troops for the Defense of this State," taken from *Laws of New-York*, and published in *Argus*, Nov. 4, 1814; Holland, *Van Buren*, p. 108; Shepard, *Van Buren*, pp. 61-62; *Autobiography*, pp. 55-57.

[31] "Juris Consultus to James Kent," *Argus*, Nov. 11, Nov. 25, 1814; "Answer to Amicus Juris Consultus," Dec. 1, 1814, VBP; *Autobiography*, pp. 57-58.

[32] "Juris Consultus to Kent," *Argus*, Nov. 11, Nov. 25, 1814.

engaged in privateering. Since Kent had published a card in the *Albany Gazette* accusing Van Buren of "tear[ing] asunder the bonds of friendship," the senator published his own card declaring that the chancellor had started the fight and should get out of politics if he did not like his statements questioned. Van Buren may have bored his readers with his tedious list of authorities and quotations, but he had the last word.[33]

With his victory over Chancellor Kent, Van Buren emerged at the end of the War of 1812 as one of the leading Republicans in New York. Like other members of his generation—Andrew Jackson, William Henry Harrison, Henry Clay, and John C. Calhoun, to name a few—he used the war to establish a reputation. The war revealed Van Buren as a new kind of adaptable pragmatic politician. In three hectic years, he was flexible enough to win a seat in the senate, to run Clinton's presidential campaign, to detach himself from Clinton, to promote the war, and to help defeat the Federalists. Different from charismatic figures such as Washington, Jefferson and Clinton, Van Buren was typical of the new kind of broker-politician who came to dominate American politics in the 1830s. Political rather than ideological, conciliatory rather than implacable, he always seemed to win when pitted against aristocrats such as Williams, Clinton and Kent. Even though Van Buren opposed the ideas of the Federalists, he was willing to use their votes. He was never personal. When charged with "cruelty" in the dispute with Kent, Van Buren insisted that he remained "a true friend of the Chancellor." Van Buren, in the War of 1812, gave Americans a glimpse of what their new leaders were to become.[34]

He also helped Americans redefine their concept of republicanism at a time when that concept was undergoing a profound change. During the war Van Buren showed that he was more willing than Jefferson had been to accept nationalism, political democracy, party structure, and a commercial economy. Unburdened by the traditions and demands of southern landholding, Van Buren could far more easily represent the new plain citizens of the North, who were beginning to dominate America. Van Buren, above all, had the advantage of being from New York. In a report to the state senate on February 24, 1815, calling for a loan to the federal government to pay off the militia, Van

---

[33] "Amicus Juris Consultus to Amicus Curiae [Kent]," *Argus*, Nov. 29, Dec. 9, 1814; MVB, "A Card," *Argus*, Dec. 9, 1814; *Autobiography*, pp. 57-58.

[34] In addition to those cited, Lewis Cass, Richard Mentor Johnson, Zachary Taylor, Winfield Scott, and Daniel Webster also began their careers during the war. The War of 1812 brought a new generation of political figures into prominence. *Autobiography*, p. 62. Richard Hofstadter calls attention to this change in politicians in his *Idea of a Party System*, pp. 223-224.

Buren remarked that the loan would show not only New York's devotion to the Union, but also the high rank that the state had achieved because of its efforts during the war. No state had changed as much as New York during the era of the war, and no man was better equipped to adapt to and guide the changes in the years to come than Martin Van Buren.[35]

As the war ended Van Buren set out to create a new political system that would be better suited than the old factional politics to the new techniques and doctrines he had developed. Starting in 1815 he and other young Republicans turned their attention to stripping Ambrose Spencer of his control of the party. Spencer, who inspired admiration, respect and often fear, had dominated state politics ever since he shifted from the Federalist to the Republican party and was elected to the council of appointment in 1800. Prepared for the law at Harvard and in various law offices, he was admitted to the bar in Hudson, New York, in 1788 and served on the state supreme court from 1804 to 1823. Despite his position on the bench Spencer remained head of the Republican party after the War of 1812.

The rebels scored immediate victories when Ruggles Hubbard was elected to the council of appointment and Nathan Sanford to the United States Senate. Spencer tried to retaliate by backing a candidate against Van Buren for attorney general, but Van Buren was elected. Van Buren did not hesitate to use a shrewd political maneuver to obtain one more Republican vote in the assembly when that body was electing the council of appointment. He secured the vote by seeing to it that Henry Fellows, a Federalist, was unseated for a few days because some of his ballots had been improperly marked "Hen. Fellows." With a Republican temporarily replacing Fellows, the assembly elected a speaker and a council of appointment favorable to the rebels.[36]

Van Buren's struggle for power was soon transferred to the presidential election of 1816. Ever since DeWitt Clinton's defeat in 1812, New Yorkers had been eager for another chance to dislodge the Virginia Dynasty. This time they hoped that wartime governor Daniel D.

[35] "Mr. Van Buren and the War," *Argus Extra*, 1832.

[36] Sanford to MVB, Dec. 28, 1814, Hubbard to MVB, Jan. 3, 1815, VBP; J. M. Gitterman, "The Council of Appointment in New York," *Political Science Quarterly*, 7 (1892), 113. Gitterman estimates that the council of appointment controlled 14,950 positions in New York. See also *Autobiography*, pp. 66-69, 73; Harriet Weed, ed., *Autobiography of Thurlow Weed* (Boston, 1883), pp. 45-48; Hammond, *Political Parties*, I, 392-393, 412; Smith Van Buren, "Notes," VBP; Fox, *Decline of Aristocracy*, pp. 186-187.

Tompkins would win the Republican nomination over James Monroe of Virginia, and Secretary of War William Harris Crawford of Georgia.[37] In the fall of 1815 Tompkins' chances began to fade when President Madison appointed Solomon Southwick postmaster of Albany, and Southwick began to use his *Albany Register* to back Monroe for President. At the same time Van Buren received a letter from his friend Justice Smith Thompson of the New York supreme court supporting Southwick's appointment. Since the justice was for Monroe and later became his Secretary of the Navy, it appears that both Thompson and Madison were trying to help Monroe win votes in New York.

Van Buren and his followers were faced with a dilemma. If they climbed on the Monroe bandwagon, they risked alienating their supporters in New York and being saddled with a President who favored DeWitt Clinton. If they backed Crawford, they risked installing a President who favored Ambrose Spencer. And if they backed Tompkins, they might split the anti-Virginia vote and let Monroe win anyway. To check the political climate Van Buren visited Washington during the Christmas season. While there he learned from Senator William Bibb of Georgia, that Crawford was not eager to fight for the nomination. When members of the New York congressional delegation asked Van Buren how they should vote in the congressional nominating caucus, he answered without much enthusiasm, "We say Tompkins, of course," and then was unavailable for the rest of his stay.[38]

Historians have read into Van Buren's behavior that he was plotting to desert Tompkins and back Monroe, but it is more likely that he was uncertain about what course to take. On returning home he received a letter from his friend Samuel R. Betts in Washington saying that Tompkins had little chance for the nomination and that the only way to unseat the Virginians was to push Crawford into running. But when the New York Republican caucus met in Albany on February 14, 1816, with Van Buren present, the majority failed to take a strong position. They ignored Crawford and recommended that the delegation in Washington present Tompkins as a candidate and oppose any

[37] *Albany Advertiser*, Dec. 16, Dec. 20, 1815, Jan. 27, 1816; Samuel R. Betts to MVB, Feb. 5, 1816, VBP; Alexander, *Political History*, I, 237-240; *Autobiography*, p. 122; Hammond, *Political Parties*, I, 411. In analyzing Van Buren's role in the election of 1816, I have profited from Robert V. Remini, "New York and the Presidential Election of 1816," *New York History*, 31 (1950), 308-324, but I have followed more closely Joseph G. Rayback, "A Myth Reexamined: Martin Van Buren's Role in the Presidential Election of 1816," *Proceedings of the American Philosophical Society*, 124 (1980), 106-118.

[38] Smith Thompson to MVB, Nov. 24, 1815, Hammond to MVB, Jan. 23, 1816, VBP; Hammond, *Political Parties*, I, 411-412.

Virginian. During the next month, however, the collapse of the Tompkins campaign and increased support for Crawford encouraged a number of the New York congressmen to vote for the latter. As a result, at the congressional caucus on March 16, 1816, fifteen New Yorkers voted for Crawford, four voted for Monroe, and two were absent. Monroe narrowly defeated Crawford for the nomination, 65-54, and went on to defeat the Federalist Rufus King in the election.[39]

Since Crawford would have come within one vote of winning if all twenty-one New Yorkers had voted for him (making the vote Monroe 61, Crawford 60), some historians have held Van Buren and New York responsible for Monroe's victory. But as Joseph G. Rayback has demonstrated, the evidence proves otherwise. Crawford supporters from other states who failed to vote for him were more at fault than those from New York, and Van Buren took no steps to undermine Tompkins or Crawford. Van Buren preferred Tompkins, but realizing that the time was not right to break the Virginia monopoly, he decided to let events take their course. He maintained his position in New York by going on record for Tompkins. National politics could wait.[40]

By the time the caucus met in March Van Buren was more interested in the state election than in national politics. Anxious for a strong Republican effort in the election because he was running for reelection to the state senate, he had made certain that Tompkins was renominated for governor even while he was being considered for President. During the campaign that spring Federalists criticized Tompkins for running up a million-dollar debt in the war, and Spencer did his best to organize a faction against Van Buren within the Republican party; but despite the opposition both Tompkins and Van Buren were reelected.[41]

[39] Samuel R. Betts to MVB, Jan. 19, Feb. 5, Feb. 24, Mar. 17, 1816, Nathan Sanford to MVB, Mar. 14, 1816, Jabez Hammond to MVB, Jan. 23, 1816, VBP; V. Birdseye to John W. Taylor, Taylor Papers; Charles Francis Adams, ed., *Memoirs of John Quincy Adams, Comprising Portions of His Diary from 1795 to 1848* (Philadelphia, 1875-1877), V, 439-440; *Albany Advertiser*, April 3, 1816; Adams, *History*, IX, 123; *Niles' Register*, 10 (1816), 59-60; Hammond, *Political Parties*, I, 411-412; Alexander, *Political History*, I, 240; Remini, "Early Political Career of Van Buren," pp. 160-184; Remini, "Election of 1816," pp. 317-321.

[40] Hammond, *Political Parties*, I, 409-412; Alexander, *Political History*, I, 239-240; Remini, "Early Political Career of Van Buren," pp. 160-184; Remini, "Election of 1816," pp. 308-324; William G. Morgan, "The Origin and Development of the Congressional Nominating Caucus," *Proceedings of the American Philosophical Society*, 113 (1969), 193. See also Parton, *Jackson*, III, 127-128; Alexander, *American Talleyrand*, pp. 141-147; John S. Jenkins, *History of Political Parties, in the State of New York* (Auburn, 1849), pp. 195-198; Irwin, *Tompkins*, p. 209; *Autobiography*, p. 122.

[41] Hammond, *Political Parties*, I, 428; Fox, *Decline of Aristocracy*, pp. 186-192; *Albany Advertiser*, June 15, 1816; *Autobiography*, p. 73; *Argus*, Mar. 5, April 23,

Just before the election Van Buren moved with his wife Hannah and their three sons to Albany, where reports soon spread about the "splendor" of their new home, especially the sideboard, which supposedly cost a thousand dollars. With money coming in steadily from his law practice and with an income of $5.50 a day plus expenses, from his position as attorney general, he was able to invest in western lands. He purchased several lots in the new town of Oswego on Lake Ontario and considered speculating in land at Niagara Falls. With his growing affluence and his great influence in the senate, Van Buren had achieved success and had apparently wrested political power away from Spencer.[42]

Looking for help, Spencer turned to his old rival DeWitt Clinton in the spring of 1817. When Tompkins was elected Vice President in the previous fall, Spencer set out to check Van Buren by backing Clinton for governor. Van Buren tried to avoid holding an election, first by arguing that Tompkins could be Vice President and governor at the same time, and then by suggesting that Lieutenant Governor John Tayler take over as governor. When these ploys failed, Van Buren backed two different candidates against Clinton in the Republican caucus, but Clinton won both the nomination and the election that followed. Just a year after moving to Albany in triumph, Van Buren had been badly beaten.[43]

One reason for Clinton's comeback was the popularity of his canal policy. Ever since colonial days New Yorkers had talked of linking the Hudson River with the Great Lakes. As a member of the canal commission, which was appointed in 1810, Clinton had explored a possible route and had become known as the leading exponent of the canal plan. Retired from office in 1815, he had the leisure to promote his plans, which were already being discussed in the legislature.[44]

The enthusiasm for the canal embarrassed Tompkins, Van Buren

1816; *Albany Register*, April 23, 1816; Robert Tillotson to MVB, May 4, 1816, Smith Thompson to MVB, May 5, 1816, VBP.

[42] For Van Buren's western investments, see Enos T. Throop to MVB, Aug. 24, 1811, and Peter Porter to MVB, June 14, 1815, VBP. Jabez Hammond's assessment of Van Buren's "influence" in the legislature is taken from Hammond, *Political Parties*, I, 422; from Hammond to MVB, Jan. 23, 1816, VBP. See also Benjamin Butler to MVB, July 31, 1816, Benjamin F. Butler Papers, NYSL; Joel Munsell, *The Annals of Albany* (Albany, 1853-1859), VI, 123.

[43] *Autobiography*, pp. 73-79; Hammond, *Political Parties*, I, 431-439; Porter to Smith Thompson, MVB and Moses I. Cantine, Feb. 13, 1817, Robert Swartwout to MVB, Feb. 26, 1817, Enos T. Throop to MVB, Mar. 15, 1817, John Swartwout to MVB, Mar. 17, 1817, VBP; Alexander, *Political History*, I, 249-252.

[44] Ronald E. Shaw, *Erie Water West: a History of the Erie Canal 1772-1864* (Lexington, 1966); Alexander, *Political History*, I, 241-245.

and other Republicans, who philosophically opposed government projects. Tompkins, whose backers in New York City hated both Clinton and his canal, ignored the project in his messages in November 1816 and January 1817. Aware that the majority of his political party were against a canal, Van Buren also knew that most Federalists, including his particular enemies Jacob R. Van Rensselaer and Elisha Williams, were in favor of the idea.[45]

When the canal issue came to the senate, Van Buren was lukewarm at best. In 1816, he voted for more surveys, but succeeded in striking out clauses permitting construction to begin. Though Van Buren later denied that he had been influenced by the bill's "political bearing," his opponents at the time thought differently. In a broadside entitled *The Grand Canal Defeated by a Democratic Senate*, they blamed Van Buren and his followers for defeating the bill. The Federalist *Albany Advertiser* pointed out that Van Buren, "the leading and most influential democratic member" of the senate, had made the fatal motion. In the winter of 1816-1817, as Clinton and Spencer drew together, Van Buren opposed both them and the canal.[46]

As the gubernatorial campaign of 1817 approached its climax, Van Buren began to have second thoughts about opposing the canal. His friend Enos T. Throop advised him that Clinton had strong support in northern New York because he was promising a canal, and Van Buren's brother-in-law Moses I. Cantine, a "very ardent" opponent of Clinton, now "earnestly" supported the project. After a speech by Elisha Williams, the assembly passed—on April 10, 1817—a bill to start construction. Since Van Buren controlled a number of anti-Clintonian votes in the senate, where bills for a canal had failed before, pressure mounted on the attorney general.[47]

On April 14, two days before the election, he decided to support the bill. After explaining lamely that he had voted against construction the year before because the senate lacked sufficient information, he declared that the situation had changed. Dramatic increases in the

[45] Alexander, *Political History*, I, 246; Fox, *Decline of Aristocracy*, pp. 148-159; *Autobiography*, p. 84; Crockett, *Van Buren*, p. 65; William O. Stoddard, *The Lives of the Presidents: Andrew Jackson and Martin Van Buren* (New York, 1887), p. 274.

[46] Shaw, *Erie Water West*, p. 54; *Autobiography*, p. 84; *The Grand Canal Defeated by a Democratic Senate* (n.p. 1816); Fox, *Decline of Aristocracy*, p. 155; *Albany Advertiser*, April 27, 1816.

[47] Enos T. Throop to MVB, Mar. 15, 1817, VBP; *Autobiography*, pp. 84-85 (including the references to Cantine); Fox, *Decline of Aristocracy*, p. 154n; David Hosack, *Memoir of DeWitt Clinton* (New York, 1829), pp. 444-451.

value of New York real estate now made it possible to finance the canal with an additional tax of only one mill per dollar. The benefits from the canal would be well worth the added tax; goods from the "wilderness" around the Great Lakes and produce from the farms of western New York would find their way to the sea by way of Albany and New York City rather than through Montreal. The farmers and manufacturers of the state would begin to supply Pittsburgh and Louisville to the west. The port of New York would outstrip Baltimore and Philadelphia. Letting his imagination soar for once, the usually cautious Van Buren concluded that the project would "raise the state to the highest possible pitch of fame and grandeur." Since the "People" were for the canal, the legislature should base construction on the broad credit of the state rather than on the limited credit of the canal fund. With this open appeal to economic interests and to the people, Van Buren had found a way to come out strongly for the canal.[48]

When the speech was over, the hall crackled with excitement, and DeWitt Clinton forgot his customary haughtiness to rush forward and shake Van Buren's hand. One reporter admitted later that he became so excited as the speech unfolded that he failed to keep pace with Van Buren's rapid delivery. The reporter was particularly struck by Van Buren's "graceful" style, which he said, could be "animated" and even "impassioned." The speech swung five anti-Clintonian votes including Van Buren's, to support of the canal, enabling the bill to pass, 18-9. By abandoning his Jeffersonian opposition, Van Buren showed once again his ability to adapt to new economic conditions and his willingness to bend his policies for political gain. Even though he lost the election, he strengthened his position for future campaigns. Van Buren's ideological flexibility was a mark of the new-style politician he had become.[49]

But with his forced change of heart on the canal question and his defeat in the election in 1817, Van Buren had suffered a severe setback. The three years that followed were filled with anxiety as one heavy

[48] MVB, "Notes on the Erie Canal, preparatory to his speech (April 15, 1817) in favor of the bill for its construction," VBP; William L. Stone to Hosack, Feb. 20, 1819, in Hosack, *Memoir of Clinton*, pp. 451-454; *Autobiography*, p. 85; Shaw, *Erie Water West*, p. 75.

[49] William L. Stone to Hosack, Feb. 20, 1819, Hosack, *Memoir of Clinton*, pp. 451-454; *Autobiography*, p. 85; Hammond, *Political Parties*, I, 441; Bancroft, *Van Buren*, pp. 56-58. Nathan Miller contends that Van Buren simply got on the canal bandwagon and late at that. Miller, *The Enterprise of a Free People: Aspects of Economic Development in New York State during the Canal Period, 1792-1838* (Ithaca, 1962), p. 45.

blow followed another. Facing serious adversity for the first time, he responded with uncharacteristic bitterness, insecurity, and indecision. When the Clintonians widened their margin in the election of 1818, he wrote Gorham Worth an extremely despondent letter saying that the people had turned their backs on him and calling Clinton's brand of government "Jacobinism." By using this epithet, which had had such nasty connotations in the 1790s when Van Buren was a boy, he revealed how bitter he had become.[50]

His uncertainty increased when Smith Thompson stepped down as chief justice of the state supreme court. Thompson urged Van Buren to seek the seat, warning at the same time that he must not make a deal with the Federalists because "plots and intrigues [were] on foot." Van Buren then learned that the inner Clintonian circle was plotting to appoint him chief justice just to get him out of the way. Van Buren was tempted; he knew that the council of appointment might remove him as attorney general and he was not certain that he could be reelected to the senate in 1820, but he settled the matter by turning down the proposal and facing continued uncertainty.[51]

Family heartaches also contributed to Van Buren's despondency. During the campaign of 1817 his father died and his mother Maria's death followed in February 1818. Around this time, he became increasingly alarmed about the condition of his wife Hannah, who had contracted tuberculosis in 1816. The birth of her fourth son in January 1817 left her weaker than before, and from then on she became progressively more nervous, timid and weak. On February 5, 1819, she too died.[52]

Van Buren's feelings for Hannah remain an enigma. He almost never referred to her in his correspondence and never once mentioned her in his autobiography. There is no indication, however, that the silence reflected a lack of affection. The inscription on the gravestone, written by Van Buren, and the obituary in the *Albany Argus*, presumably written by him, reflect his love. He remembered her as a "tender mother and a most affectionate wife," who, after a "lingering illness," calmly awaited death. Now with his father, mother and wife dead, and with his brothers less close than before, Van Buren was bereft of the gentle,

---

[50] MVB to Gorham Worth, April 27, 1818, VBP.

[51] Thompson to MVB, Nov. 3, Dec. 8, Dec. 25, 1818, Jan. 23, 1819, Nathan Sanford to MVB, Nov. 4, 1818, MVB to Gorham Worth, Nov. 26, 1818, VBP; *Autobiography*, p. 90; Hammond, *Political Parties*, I, 499.

[52] Lynch, *Epoch and a Man*, pp. 165, 169-170; MVB to Worth, Nov. 26, 1818, VBP; Laura C. Holloway, *The Ladies of the White House; or, in the Home of the Presidents* (Philadelphia, 1881), pp. 335-336; *Argus*, Feb. 8, 1819.

loving people who had given him so much security. At the age of thirty-six he was on his own with sons aged eleven, eight, six, and two, to care for. Van Buren rarely complained, but he did tell his friend Benjamin Butler that the "anxiety" aroused by Hannah's death had left his health in a "delicate" condition. Since the tragedy occurred at a time of pressing political decisions, the events of the winter precipitated a psychological crisis that had political as well as domestic consequences.[53]

The death of his wife drastically altered Van Buren's life. First there was the anxiety of providing for the boys. Although one of his sisters and his wife's sister, Christina (Mrs. Moses I. Cantine), shared the responsibility for the next few years, Van Buren bore a heavy burden for a long time to come. Since he liked female company, he escorted many women to parties and exchanged witty letters with many others, but he never became intimate enough with any of them for marriage— or even scandal—to result.[54]

In this period of mourning and frustrating political setbacks, Van Buren turned viciously against DeWitt Clinton. Van Buren's letter to Gorham Worth in the spring after Hannah's death was filled with anger at Clinton. The Magnus Apollo, sneered Van Buren, had never had to run a business, support himself, or carry through on any project, and yet Clinton was the object of Worth's "idolatry." That this unusual letter gives vent to such jealousy, scorn and bitterness, is partly attributable no doubt, to Van Buren's despondent state.[55]

Clinton responded in kind, showing his low regard for Van Buren in a series of salty letters. "Whom shall we appoint," Clinton asked one correspondent, "to defeat the arch-scoundrel V.B., [whose] treachery and duplicity [make him a] confirmed knave?" After winning the assembly in the election of 1819, Clinton felt strong enough in July to remove Van Buren as attorney general. It was one more in a series of setbacks that had dogged Van Buren since 1817.[56]

By the summer of 1819, Van Buren's career had reached a dangerously low point. He began at last to take steps to restore his political and personal momentum. His anger at Clinton made him all the more

[53] The gravestone inscription is quoted in Lynch, *Epoch and a Man*, p. 170. The obituary is from *Argus*, Feb. 9, 1819. The letter is MVB to Butler, Feb. 11, 1819 (copy), VBP.

[54] Roger Skinner to MVB, Feb. 15, 1823, VBP.

[55] MVB to Worth, April 22, 1819, VBP.

[56] John Bigelow, "Dewitt Clinton as a Politician," *Harper's New Monthly Magazine*, 50 (1874-1875), 409-417, 568-571; *Argus*, Mar. 23, June 4, July 13, July 16, 1819; MVB to David E. Evans, May 10, 1819, Samuel R. Betts to MVB, July 23, 1819, Mordecai Noah to MVB, July 13, 1819, VBP.

determined to destroy the factional system that had enabled Clinton to regain power. In its place he dreamed of returning to the old days, which he remembered so nostalgically, when parties rather than leaders dominated New York politics. Having failed to gain control of the old Republican party, he decided to organize a new party called the Bucktails, a term that had first appeared in the 1790s when Tammany Hall made the tail of the buck its official badge. Surrounding him were a number of young Republicans, many of whom would move later into the Albany Regency and the Democratic party: veterans of the battles over the War of 1812, Samuel Young and Roger Skinner; old opponents of Spencer, Jonathan Dayton and Erastus Root; former critics of the canal, Lucas Elmendorff and Peter R. Livingston; Walter Bowne and Michael Ulshoeffer represented New York City, Moses I. Cantine had family ties with Van Buren, Henry Seymour brought strength from western New York, and Senator Nathan Sanford and Vice President Daniel D. Tompkins reported to Van Buren from Washington.[57]

The strength of the new organization was revealed as early as the Republican caucus on January 4, 1819. Though preoccupied with his dying wife, Van Buren saw to it that all Bucktails were present, while the casual Clinton was caught with a number of his legislators absent. In the balloting for speaker of the assembly the caucus chose Bucktail William Thompson over Clinton's nominee, Obadiah German. But when the election was held in the assembly, Clinton ignored the caucus and backed German, who won with the help of Federalist votes. Even though his man was elected, Clinton's treatment of the caucus and use of Federalist votes antagonized many Republicans.[58]

Clinton continued to lose ground later in the winter. At the Republican caucus to select a candidate for the United States Senate for the term beginning in December 1819, Clintonians had a majority, but let the meeting break up without a vote. In the legislative balloting that followed, they supported Ambrose Spencer's son John, while Bucktails stuck by Samuel Young, and Federalists backed the incumbent, Rufus King. At this point, Clinton angered a number of Federalists by refusing to back King, and the election was put off until the next winter. At the same time, however, Clinton widened the gap

---

[57] Hammond, *Political Parties*, I, 451-457; Remini, "Early Political Career of Van Buren," p. 208; Fox, *Decline of Aristocracy*, p. 215n.

[58] *Argus*, Jan. 8, 1819; *Autobiography*, pp. 89-90; Hammond, *Political Parties*, I, 478-481; Alexander, *Political History*, I, 257-260; John King to Rufus King, Jan. 8, 1819, Charles R. King, ed., *The Life and Correspondence of Rufus King* (New York, 1894-1900; reprint, 1971), VI, 102. Alexander wrongly assigns these events to January 1818, and the letter is incorrectly dated Jan. 8, 1818.

with the Bucktails by joining with the Federalists to gain control of the council of appointment.[59]

To counteract Clinton's influence over the council Van Buren sought to dominate the canal commission, which controlled a vast number of jobs. When a position on the commission opened up in 1819, Van Buren cooperated with the Federalists to have Henry Seymour elected. As Van Buren smugly commented in his autobiography, the Bucktails "derived more advantage from the patronage and influence attached to [the canal commission than] the Governor obtained from the Council of Appointment." Van Buren gained this advantage because he was able to exploit two new developments—the digging of the canals and the splintering of the Federalists.[60]

Van Buren also used traditional means of strengthening his party. During the 1819 campaign the Bucktails began to hold their own caucuses. They also established a committee of correspondence made up of Van Buren, Rufus King's eldest son, John, and ten others. Most important, they employed a partisan press. When Clinton tried to shift the state printing contract away from the *Albany Argus*, the Bucktails won the support of the *Argus* by blocking the move. Editor Jesse Buel of the *Argus* joined the Bucktail committee of correspondence and opened the columns of his newspaper to his new colleagues.[61]

Another Bucktail convert was William L. Marcy of Troy, who had annoyed Clinton by writing an article in the *Argus* calling on Republicans who had backed the War of 1812 to oppose the governor. Clinton had retaliated by removing Marcy and his followers from state jobs. When Marcy's group refused to support Clintonians in the election of 1819, Federalists carried Troy. Like Van Buren and Buel, Marcy was anxious to destroy Clinton.[62]

[59] *Argus*, Feb. 5, 1819. John King to Rufus King, Jan. 8, Jan. 14, Jan. 28, Feb. 2, 1819, King, *Correspondence*, VI, 102, 192-193, 199-204; Hammond, *Political Parties*, I, 482-487; Alexander, *Political History*, I, 267.

[60] *Autobiography*, p. 91; Alexander, *Political History*, I, 261.

[61] In New Hampshire another Republican, Isaac Hill, was setting up a similar committee of correspondence. Donald B. Cole, *Jacksonian Democracy in New Hampshire, 1800-1851* (Cambridge, Mass., 1970), p. 18. For the Albany committee, see *Argus*, Mar. 23, 1819. For an analysis of Albany newspapers, see *Argus*, Dec. 26, 1815. References in this paragraph are from the *Argus*, Feb. 17, 1818, Jan. 8, Jan. 15, Feb. 23, Mar. 9, Mar. 23, Mar. 26, May 23, June 4, 1819, and passim. In February 1819, a month before the attempt to shift the printing to the *Albany Register*, the *Argus* was still independent enough to support John C. Spencer, the Clintonian candidate for United States senator, instead of Samuel Young, the Bucktail candidate. *Argus*, Feb. 26, 1819. In New Hampshire the *New-Hampshire Patriot*, ed. Isaac Hill, was a Republican journal comparable to the *Argus*.

[62] Ivor D. Spencer, *The Victor and the Spoils: a Life of William L. Marcy* (Providence, 1959), pp. 28-29.

In the struggle between Bucktails and Clintonians both sides sought help from the dwindling number of Federalists. Although a majority of the Federalists had gone over to Clinton, one faction, which included Rudolph Bunner, Michael Hoffman, Gulian Verplanck, the sons of Alexander Hamilton, and members of the King family, inclined toward Van Buren. This was the group the governor had antagonized by refusing to back Rufus King for senator. King, who at sixty-four was a generation older than most of the others, had built an awesome reputation as one of the founding fathers. Dignified and statesmanlike in his bearing, he was considered by many the finest orator at the Constitutional Convention. After moving from Massachusetts to New York City, he married into a wealthy merchant family, and was one of the first two United States senators from the state. He next served as minister to England and ran unsuccessfully for Vice President in 1804 and 1808, before returning to the Senate in 1813. There he remained (his bid for the presidency in 1816 failed), and if there was a "Mr. Federalist" after the death of Federalism, it was Rufus King.

Perhaps the most intellectual and satirical of this faction was "Gilley" (Gulian) Verplanck, who had begun writing pamphlets during the press war that followed the Columbia College commencement riot of 1811. Verplanck turned against Clinton at that time because the latter had presided at the trial in which Verplanck was fined $200 for defending a student involved in the riot. James A. Hamilton, the third son of Alexander Hamilton, practiced law in Hudson while Van Buren was living there and later served as a brigade major in the War of 1812. Clever and smooth, Hamilton was a confidant of Van Buren during the 1820s even though some of Van Buren's party distrusted the major because of his Federalist background. In 1819, Verplanck, Hamilton and others founded the New York *American*, which was little more than a political sheet aimed at freeing the state from control of DeWitt Clinton.

During the second attempt to choose a senator in December, Van Buren and Marcy tried to attract these Federalists by publishing a pamphlet supporting King. Republicans, they said, should be willing to support the Federalist King because he had fought in the Revolution and had backed the War of 1812. Van Buren then inserted an article in the *Argus* endorsing the pamphlet and told Mordecai Noah, editor of the *National Advocate* in New York City, that there should be no "fluttering" on the subject of King. Van Buren also ordered Benjamin Butler to write "a short elegant piece" in favor of King for the newspapers. The night before the election Van Buren and Erastus Root reminded Republican legislators how to vote. Dazzled by Van Buren's clever handiwork, Bucktails joined Federalists in supporting King, who was easily elected.[63]

The campaign for Rufus King shows Van Buren so intent on building a new party that if he had to back someone with Federalist principles, he would do so. The episode is also typical of his attitude toward aristocrats. Throughout his career, especially in the early years, Van Buren felt ill-at-ease with men he considered superior in birth, breeding, education, and reputation. Some of these men—Elisha Williams, James Kent, Ambrose Spencer—he defeated. Others—DeWitt Clinton, Spencer for a while, and King—he joined. The senatorial election gave him the opportunity to win the favor of a respected old statesman who had fought in the Revolution and helped write the Constitution. From 1819 on, Van Buren deferred to his colleague, and the *Autobiography* is full of warm references to the old man. King in turn wrote that he was "particularly obliged" to Van Buren, and their good relationship was influential in helping Van Buren to overcome his depression.[64]

King's reelection coincided with the debate over slavery in Missouri. On February 13, 1819, Republican congressman James Tallmadge of New York, proposed an amendment to the Missouri enabling act, to prohibit the further introduction of slaves into the state. After passing the House, the amendment foundered in the Senate despite two speeches by King in favor of restricting the spread of slavery. Before Congress resumed in December, King published his speeches expressing his fear that the spread of slavery west of the Mississippi would threaten "the repose, if not the security of the Union." After his reelection in December, King delivered two more speeches against slavery in Missouri. According to John Quincy Adams, King "spoke with great power, and the great slaveholders in the House, gnawed their lips and clutched their fists as they heard him." In spite of King's efforts, the Jesse Thomas amendment prohibiting slavery north of 36°30' in the Lou-

[63] John King to Rufus King, Jan. 8, 1819, King, *Correspondence*, VI, 102; Robert Ernst, *Rufus King: an American Federalist* (Chapel Hill, 1968); Robert W. July, *The Essential New Yorker: Gulian Crommelin Verplanck* (Durham, 1951); Fox, *Decline of Aristocracy*, pp. 207-228; MVB, *Considerations in Favour of the Appointment of Rufus King, to the Senate of the United States. Submitted to the Republican Members of the Legislature of the State of New-York* (Albany, 1819); Shepard, *Van Buren*, pp. 68-71; *Argus*, Dec. 14, 1819; MVB to David E. Evans, Nov. 17, 1819, MVB to Noah, Dec. 17, 1819, Noah to MVB, Dec. 19, 1819, MVB to Butler (copy), Dec. 29, 1819, VBP; John King to Rufus King, Jan. 8, 1820, King Papers; *Autobiography*, pp. 100-101, 138-139.

[64] Shepard, *Van Buren*, pp. 71-72; *Autobiography*, pp. 100-101, 108, 130-132, 139-141, 147, 154-155; Rufus King to John King, Mar. 18, 1820, King Papers.

isiana Purchase, but admitting Missouri as a slave state, passed the Senate. King wrote sadly that he had been "conquered" and the South had "triumphed."[65]

The Missouri question stirred the North—especially New York, where it became a political issue. Federalists there had often used the antislavery movement as a weapon, accusing Republicans of being the tools of slaveowners. New York Federalists had also led the fight for the abolition of slavery and had controlled the black vote. As Federalism fell apart, many Republicans—particularly Southerners—worried that in the North, Republicans and Federalists would amalgamate into an antislavery party led by DeWitt Clinton. He had split with southern Republicans in 1812, and had united with Federalists to control the legislature in 1819. Many of Clinton's friends including the Spencers, Solomon Van Rensselaer, William W. Van Ness, and Charles G. Haines, were well-known opponents of slavery. There were also rumors that Rufus King hoped to use the issue in a last effort to get himself elected President. Smith Thompson bluntly warned Van Buren that the Clintonians and Federalists who advocated slavery restriction looked to Rufus King for leadership.[66]

Van Buren refused to swallow the notion that King was plotting to set up a northern party. King's views, said Van Buren, were "honorable and correct." Aware that King had shown his contempt for Clinton in 1812, and that King's sons had already started a Federalist movement away from the governor, Van Buren considered the alliance of King and Clinton unlikely. Correctly assuming that King had no selfish political goals, Van Buren tried to turn the Missouri question in the

[65] Robert Ernst, *Rufus King*, p. 365. "The substance of Two Speeches on the Missouri Bill Delivered by Mr. King in the Senate of the United States," Rufus King to Messrs. John B. Coles and John T. Irving, Nov. 22, 1819, Rufus King to R. Peters, Jr., Nov. 30, 1819, J. Adams to Rufus King, Dec. 7, 1819, Rufus King to John King, Feb. 11, Mar. 4, 1820, Rufus King to C. Gore, Feb. 17, 1820, Rufus King to John King and Charles King, Mar. 5, 1820, King, *Correspondence*, VI, 216-217, 233-237, 240, 269-270, 276-278, 288-292, 690-703; Adams, *Memoirs*, IV, 523-524. John A. Dix, a future member of the Albany Regency, was also impressed. John A. Dix, *Memoirs of John Adams Dix compiled by His Son Morgan Dix* (New York, 1883), I, 60.

[66] MVB, "Notes on meetings in Albany and New York on the Missouri question, 1819-1820," 185-?, Smith Thompson to MVB, Jan. 23, 1820, VBP; Richard W. Smith, "The Public Career of Martin Van Buren in Connection with the Slavery Controversy through the Election of 1840" (Doctoral dissertation, Ohio State University, 1959), pp. 34-35; *National Intelligencer*, Nov. 20, Nov. 23, 1819; Glover Moore, *The Missouri Controversy 1819-1821* (Lexington, 1953), pp. 175-189; Salma Hale to John W. Taylor, Dec. 27, 1819, Taylor Papers; Haines to Van Rensselaer, Nov. 20, 1820, Mrs. Catharina V. R. Bonney, *A Legacy of Historical Gleanings*, 2 vols. (Albany, 1875), I, 354-355; Thomas Hart Benton, *Thirty Years' View, or a History of the Working of the American Government for Thirty Years, from 1820 to 1850* (New York, 1854-1856), I, 10.

right direction. By wooing the Kings, he would keep DeWitt Clinton and Rufus King apart, and thus prevent a plot.[67]

But Van Buren did suspect Clinton of making political capital out of the Missouri question. In his autobiography Van Buren claimed that those opposing slavery in Missouri sought to "bring the politics of the slave states and the standing of their supporters in the free states into disrepute through inflammatory assaults upon the institution of slavery." As a Republican Van Buren could not join a Clintonian-Federalist attack on slavery, but at the same time he did not dare lose support by openly defending slavery. He therefore moved cautiously when Clintonians and others called a meeting on Missouri in Albany. He added his name to the list of those calling the meeting, but on the day it took place he arranged to be out of town. On his return he used his absence as an excuse not to sign the antislavery memorial that came from the meeting. Van Buren's suspicions were aroused on January 4, 1820, when Clinton in his governor's address, referred to his "deep anxiety" about the Missouri debate. Calling slavery "an evil of the first magnitude," he asked the legislature to pass a resolution opposing the "progress" of the southern institution. Van Buren later admitted candidly that he did not favor the proposal, but was ready to vote for it so as not to be accused of defending slavery. Van Buren avoided declaring himself when a resolution against the spread of slavery passed the senate without a recorded vote.[68]

Even after the compromise, the Missouri question refused to die in New York. The following summer the Bucktail *National Advocate* called the affair a Federalist plot; the *Albany Argus* accused Clinton of trying to use the "unhappy controversy" to organize "a northern confederacy." In retaliation the Clintonian *New-York Statesman* in Albany published a "History of a Bucktail," saying that Van Buren's side was supporting slavery. Then, in November, Clintonians attacked the constitution of Missouri for backing slavery, and Bucktail Erastus Root responded, criticizing the "political knight errantry [of] declaring war upon Missouri."[69]

[67] MVB to Noah, Dec. 17, 1819, VBP; Tallmadge to Taylor, Jan. 11, Mar. 2, 1820, Clinton to Taylor, 1819-1820, Taylor Papers.

[68] *Autobiography*, p. 137; MVB, "Notes on the Missouri question," MVB to Mordecai Noah, Dec. 17, 1819, Henry F. Jones to MVB, Jan. 19, 1820, MVB to Henry F. Jones, Jan. 21, 1820, VBP; MVB, *Opinions . . . in Reference to the Abolition of Slavery* (Washington, D.C., 1836), p. 11; "New York Joint Resolution," Jan. 17, Jan. 20, 1820, King Papers; *Autobiography*, pp. 99-100; Charles Z. Lincoln, ed., *Messages from the Governors* (Albany, 1909), II, 1022-1023.

[69] *National Advocate*, Aug. 24, 1820; *Argus*, Jan. 28, 1820, Mar. 23, 1821; Moore, *Missouri Controversy*, pp. 190-192; MVB, "Notes on the Missouri question," VBP; [Albany] *New-York Statesman*, Aug. 8, Nov. 14, 1820.

Nor did Van Buren and King forget Missouri. In March, after the compromise, Van Buren assured King that the public was not so excited over Missouri as King supposed. King did not continue his fight over the issue, but a year and a half later it was still on his mind. As he and Van Buren traveled to Washington for the opening of Congress in 1821, King spoke with feeling about the "influence" that slavery had had on the government. He blamed the long string of Republican victories since 1800 on the "unanimity of the slave states caused by the slave interest." Van Buren replied that the Republicans had won not because of slavery but because Republican principles were superior to Federalist.[70]

Contemporary observers and subsequent historians have differed in interpreting Van Buren's reaction to the Missouri question. In the 1830s, when Van Buren was running for Vice President and President, his southern detractors tried to show that he had been antislavery in 1820. Historians since then have occasionally suggested that he was secretly antislavery, but the evidence is lacking. Van Buren grew up in slaveholding Kinderhook, his father owned slaves, and so briefly did Van Buren himself. Van Buren admitted that he played along with the antislavery movement only to prevent Clinton from getting an advantage. In 1835, a campaign biography and an essay by his friend Benjamin Butler both went out of their way to show that he was not hostile to slavery. The burden of proof is on those who would make Van Buren into an opponent of the peculiar institution.[71]

A more convincing interpretation argues that Van Buren took advantage of the Missouri controversy to revive the old New York-Virginia alliance. According to Richard H. Brown, the Bucktails were "anxious for peace" in the Missouri debate and "supported the corporal's guard of Northern Republicans [who] made peace possible." Brown is referring to the eighteen compromisers who either voted for the Missouri Compromise or else absented themselves from the vote. The New Yorkers were Henry Meigs, Henry R. Storrs, Walter Case, Caleb Tompkins, and Harmanus Peek. Meigs was, indeed, a Bucktail close to Van Buren, but Storrs was a Federalist-Clintonian, and the

[70] MVB to King, Mar. 23, 1820, King Papers; *Autobiography*, pp. 131-140.

[71] For the effort to show that Van Buren was antislavery and the Van Buren defense, see *Inconsistency and Hypocrisy of Martin Van Buren on the Question of Slavery* (n.p., n.d.); MVB, *Abolition of Slavery*; Holland, *Van Buren*, pp. 143-147. Several historians have tried in vain to suggest that Van Buren was sympathetic to the antislavery point of view. Remini, "Early Political Career of Van Buren," pp. 250-251; Smith, "Public Career of Van Buren in Connection with Slavery," pp. 40-59; Jenkins, *Lives of the Governors*, p. 383.

others were obscure politicians. It is hard to prove from this group that New York Bucktails were responsible for the compromise. Brown goes on to say that twenty months later, Van Buren took off for Washington where he set about restoring the alliance of New York and Virginia. But that was two years later. Little that Van Buren did during the Missouri debates bore immediately on the crucial North-South alliance.[72]

It makes more sense to explain Van Buren's reaction to Missouri in terms of politics in New York. The Missouri controversy hit New York in the midst of the bitter struggle between Clinton and Van Buren. Van Buren backed King for senator partly to gain Federalist support and partly to prevent an alliance between King and Clinton over slavery in Missouri. To keep Clinton from making political gains from the Missouri question, Van Buren straddled the slavery issue. In 1819 and 1820, Van Buren was more interested in helping his state party by checking Clinton than in reestablishing a New York-Virginia party at the national level.

The gubernatorial election of 1820 gave Van Buren an immediate opportunity to defeat Clinton. When the Bucktails nominated Tompkins to run against Clinton, Van Buren was worried because Tompkins was drinking heavily and was under attack for misusing funds in the War of 1812. On January 19, Van Buren wrote Rufus King asking if he and President Monroe could prevail on Smith Thompson to replace Tompkins as a means of checking "Mr. Clinton's career." He enclosed a letter for Thompson assuring him that the Bucktails really preferred him to Tompkins. Thompson was tempted, but after writing Van Buren three letters within a few days, decided not to run. King had no success convincing Tompkins to drop out. Van Buren finally gave in and decided to support Tompkins when the Vice President traveled up the Hudson and entered Albany amid "cheers from the surrounding multitude."[73]

In attempting to undermine Tompkins, Van Buren showed once again that his first priority lay in defeating Clinton. In his letters to

[72] Richard H. Brown, "The Missouri Crisis, Slavery and the Politics of Jacksonianism," *South Atlantic Quarterly*, 65 (1966), 55-72.

[73] *Autobiography*, pp. 95-99; Lynch, *Epoch and a Man*, pp. 180-181, 195-196; MVB to Daniel D. Tompkins, Jan. 17, 1820, MVB to King, Jan. 19, 1820, VBP; MVB to Thompson, Jan. 19, 1820, John King to Rufus King, Feb. 24, 1820, King, *Correspondence*, VI, 252-255, 281-282; MVB to King, Feb. 2, Feb. 23, 1820, King Papers; Thompson to MVB, Jan. 23, Jan. 28, Jan. 30, 1820, King to MVB, Jan. 31 (two letters), Feb. 6, 1820, "Address to the public in favor of their nominees, Daniel D. Tompkins for governor and General Mooers," Feb. 22, 1820, VBP.

King and Thompson he had asked a Federalist (King), a Bucktail (Thompson), and a southern Republican (Monroe) to cooperate in putting down Clinton. As in the Missouri affair, Van Buren sought to use King against Clinton. His interest in an alliance with the Virginian Monroe was as a means of saving the Bucktails in New York. King's reelection to the Senate, the Missouri Compromise, and Tompkins' renomination for governor all came within a span of four months. In each case Van Buren behaved in a manner best calculated to defeat Clinton.

The outcome of the election hinged partly on charges of corruption against Tompkins. As wartime governor, Tompkins had been so careless in mixing personal with state money that auditors had turned up a shortage of $120,000 in his accounts. To clear his record the legislature voted to consider this amount as money advanced by Tompkins during the war; therefore he owed the state nothing. Tompkins then precipitated a debate by demanding another $130,000. To save the day Van Buren proposed a compromise in which Tompkins would receive $12,000, and the entire matter ended in the courts. The election in April was not quite as decisive as Van Buren had hoped, for although the Bucktails gained control of the legislature and the council of appointment, Clinton was reelected governor. Smith Thompson was exaggerating somewhat when he wrote that Clinton's "sting" had been "plucked."[74]

Van Buren's behavior during and after the campaign suggested that he had not yet conquered the tension, uncertainty and bitterness that had gripped him ever since Clinton's victory in 1817. Just before the election an exhausted Van Buren confided that for ten days he had "scarcely had time to take [his] regular meals" and that he was "pressed by at least a half dozen unfinished concerns growing out of this intolerable political struggle." He had decided not to run for reelection to the senate in 1820, partly because he was not certain he could win. He had considered moving his law office to New York City, then gave up the idea when Clinton was reelected. Soon after the election Van Buren wrote to Gorham Worth: "I had intended to have left here for New York this fall, in the event of the War [against Clinton] being ended," but he concluded, "my desire to serve your friend *the Great*

[74] Fox, *Decline of Aristocracy*, pp. 226-228; Alexander, *Political History*, I, 275-282; Hammond, *Political Parties*, I, 521-525; MVB, *Speech of the Hon. M. Van Buren of the Senate, on the Act ... of the 13th April, 1819, for the Settlement of the Late Governor's Accounts* (Albany, 1820); Smith Thompson to MVB, May 9, 1820, VBP.

Clinton will keep me here a few years longer." The sarcasm exposed the insecurity that lay beneath Van Buren's calm, pleasant exterior.[75]

The events of the next twelve months did much to restore the old Van Buren. Even before the election he had been fighting to increase his share of federal patronage in New York. He complained to Bucktail congressman Henry Meigs that the "rascality" of some Clintonian postmasters made it impossible for Bucktail newspapers to circulate freely in New York. He asked Meigs to intervene with his relative, Postmaster General Return Meigs, to "alarm" the opposition by removing postmasters at Bath, Little Falls, Oxford, and elsewhere. The congressman replied promptly that the Postmaster General would remove anyone who tampered with the mails. On June 1, Bucktails in Herkimer wrote to the Postmaster General demanding the removal of the postmaster in that village. When six deputy postmasters lost their jobs, the opposition cried "proscription" and the *New-York Statesman* suggested that Van Buren should be made Postmaster General to save him the trouble of "*dictating*" to Meigs. After digging up a copy of Van Buren's letter to Meigs, Clinton complained that it was "equally offensive to grammar and truth." He was even more annoyed when the administration appointed a Bucktail, Jonathan Thompson, as customs collector in New York City.[76]

Van Buren also ended the uncertainty about his future by announcing that he would like to replace United States Senator Nathan Sanford, whose term expired in 1821. Election to the Senate was not easy because Sanford, a loyal Tammany Hall Republican, wanted to keep his seat. When both Van Buren and Sanford were nominated at the Bucktail caucus on February 1, 1821, the caucus voted 58-24 for Van Buren, but Sanford still had a chance because he had Clinton's support. As Clinton tried to defeat Van Buren in the legislature, two different concepts of party government were seen to be opposed. Van Buren stood for caucuses, party regularity, and the two-party system, while Clinton hoped to continue the amalgamation of parties that had char-

[75] MVB to King, April 13, 1820, King, *Correspondence*, VI, 331-332; Lynch, *Epoch and a Man*, pp. 195-199; *Argus*, Sept. 22, Oct. 3, Oct. 17, 1820; MVB to Worth, June 1, 1820, VBP.

[76] MVB to Henry Meigs, April 4, 1820, Henry Meigs to MVB, April 10, 1820, John R. Drake to Henry Meigs, April 15, 1820, Herkimer County Inhabitants to Return Meigs, June 1, 1820, VBP; *Argus*, May 30, 1820, Jan. 23, 1821; *Statesman*, June 2, June 9, June 16, 1820; Alexander, *Political History*, I, 283-286; Clinton to Solomon Van Rensselaer, Mar. 17, Nov. 27, Nov. 29, 1820, Bonney, *Historical Gleanings*, I, 349, 352, 358; Clinton to Henry Post, Nov. 27, 1820, Henry Post Papers, UVL; Hammond, *Political Parties*, I, 557; Rufus King to Charles King, Nov. 22, 1820, King, *Correspondence*, VI, 357-358.

acterized the Era of Good Feelings after the War of 1812. The former prevailed when almost every Bucktail, even those favoring Sanford, voted for Van Buren. Soon after the election the Clintonians revealed their misunderstanding of the new politics when the *Statesman* complained that Sanford would have won had not the Bucktails agreed in caucus to back Van Buren unanimously. The *Statesman* had missed the point because caucus rule was at the heart of Van Buren's system.[77]

Another weapon in Van Buren's system that winter was the council of appointment, which consisted of the lonely governor and four Bucktails—Roger Skinner, Walter Bowne, John T. Moore, and David E. Evans. After the election the *Albany Argus* had predicted that the Bucktail council would "cleanse the Augean stable," and the *Statesman* sadly agreed. They were correct. In early 1821, the new council struck, replacing Clintonians right and left with Bucktails. Gone were Comptroller Archibald McIntyre, who had served since 1806, Attorney General Thomas J. Oakley, who had replaced Van Buren in 1819, Adjutant General Solomon Van Rensselaer, the hero of Fallen Timbers, and Recorder Peter A. Jay, the son of John Jay. Gone also were Mayor Cadwallader Colden of New York City, and Gideon Hawley, the first superintendent of common schools in the state. As they fell, so did sheriffs, surrogates and district attorneys "in windrows." According to the *Statesman*, it was a "bloody inquisition."[78]

Replacing the fallen Clintonians and Federalists were hundreds of Bucktails—often younger men than those they replaced—who formed the nucleus for the New York Republican/Democratic party in the 1820s and 1830s. Many of the new officeholders were close friends of Van Buren: Attorney General Samuel A. Talcott, whom Van Buren had personally enlisted; Adjutant General William L. Marcy, who had helped write the pamphlet to reelect King; District Attorney of Albany Benjamin Butler, who was Van Buren's law partner; Treasurer Benjamin Knower, later Marcy's father-in-law; and Van Buren's brother Abraham, the new surrogate of Columbia County. At the same time Van Buren's brother-in-law, Moses I. Cantine, was elected state printer.[79]

[77] MVB to Rufus King, Jan. 14, 1821, John King to Rufus King, Feb. 2, 1821, MVB to Smith Thompson, Feb. 2, 1821, King Papers; Judge Van Ness to Gen. Van Rensselaer, Feb. 7, 1821, Bonney, *Historical Gleanings*, I, 363; *Statesman*, Feb. 6, Feb. 9, 1821; Lynch, *Epoch and a Man*, pp. 206-207; Alexander, *Political History*, I, 286-287. Jabez Hammond, though a Clintonian, voted for Van Buren because he felt Van Buren had more talent than Sanford. Hammond, *Political Parties*, I, 561-562. Rufus King congratulated Van Buren after his election. Rufus King to John King, Feb. 11, 1821, King, *Correspondence*, VI, 384-385; Rufus King to MVB, Feb. 18, 1821, VBP.

[78] *Autobiography*, p. 105; *Argus*, Aug. 29, 1820; *Statesman*, Sept. 12, 1820, Feb. 20, 1821; Alexander, *Political History*, I, 287-289.

[79] Alexander, *Political History*, I, 289-294; *Statesman*, Feb. 20, Feb. 27, 1821; *Argus*,

By the spring of 1821, the Bucktails had established themselves in New York and Van Buren had emerged from his depression. In the nine years since 1812, he had overcome many setbacks including political defeats, the death of his wife, and a siege of anxiety. During those years politics in New York had shifted from a complicated struggle among a number of Republican and Federalist factions to a two-party battle between Bucktails and Clintonians. Political power had passed from one Republican to another—from Tompkins in 1815 to Spencer in 1817 to Clinton in 1819 to Van Buren in 1821. To win control of New York Van Buren had formed useful political alliances and had adjusted rapidly to economic and political changes. First Tompkins and then King served Van Buren well. He reacted shrewdly to the advent of canals, to the concern over slavery, and to the decline of the Federalists. He started out working within the New York system but had changed the system by 1821. Van Buren used the years to define his republicanism and to hone the skills and techniques that would make his political organization the envy of the nation.

Sept. 17, 1822; Kalman Goldstein, "The Albany Regency: the Failure of Practical Politics" (Doctoral dissertation, Columbia University, 1969), p. 8; Stephen C. Hutchins, *Civil List and Constitutional History of the Colony and State of New York* (Albany, 1880), pp. 154, 159, 161, 357, 364.

·3·

THE ALBANY REGENCY

Even after his many triumphs in 1820 and early 1821, Van Buren knew that his control of New York was not yet assured. Despite laboring to rid the state of Clinton, the Bucktails had only partly succeeded. They had won the legislature and had appointed hundreds to office, but Clinton was still governor and many of the counties and towns were still controlled by Clintonians. The provisions of the state constitution, which gave the council of appointment great power over patronage, made a Clintonian comeback entirely possible. If the Clintonians won back the assembly, which was usually theirs, Clinton would regain control of the council, which would then throw the Bucktails out of office. And since the constitution gave the governor a three-year term, Clinton had almost three years left. To maintain themselves in power Bucktails needed to replace Clinton as governor and strengthen their party organization. To do that they needed a new constitution. Only nine months away from the start of a new career as United States senator, Van Buren had still not finished building his party in New York. His organization in Albany was still not fully developed.

The opportunity to do something about the state constitution came in the spring of 1821, when the question of calling a convention to revise the constitution was put before the voters. The outmoded constitution of New York dated from 1777, when the founders of the new state had checked the governor with a clumsy system dividing power among the council of appointment, the council of revision, and the supreme court. Ever since the War of 1812 demand for change had mounted, but most political leaders, including Van Buren, had at first resisted. After the election of 1820, the prospects of a convention brightened because Bucktails saw it as an opportunity to strengthen their grasp on the state.[1]

On the other hand the prospect of a convention alarmed the Clintonians. As early as the fall of 1820 the *Statesman* predicted that the Bucktails would first use the council of appointment to put their men in power and would then call a convention to rearrange the govern-

---

[1] Rufus King claimed that 300 of the 356 towns in the state were "federal." King to John King, Oct. 6, 1821, King, *Correspondence*, VI, 409. MVB to Gorham Worth, June 1, 1820, VBP.

ment in their own favor. The Clintonians particularly feared a convention that would change the judiciary, most of whom were Federalists and followers of Clinton. If a convention had to be called, Clintonians wanted one with strictly limited powers that would not be able to alter the court system. When the Bucktails passed a bill calling for an unlimited convention, Governor Clinton used his vote in the council of revision to veto the plan. But the Bucktails pressed on, submitting the question to the people, and in the spring election of 1821, the voters overwhelmingly endorsed a constitutional convention with no limit to its powers.[2]

Van Buren was silent while a convention was being discussed and did his best to reassure conservatives that the Bucktails offered no threat to property owners. In a letter to Rufus King Van Buren insisted that he had not led in proposing a convention because he was "timid in all matters of innovation." He was, furthermore, "thoroughly convinced that temperate reform" was the sole motive of the Bucktails who were urging a convention. The rights of property, he said, stood in no danger from Bucktail Republicans at a convention; if there was "safety for property and protection for principle to be expected from any quarter," it was from the Bucktails. They represented the "yeomanry of the State, who though they [had] not individually the largest, [had] collectively the greatest interests at stake." The Clintonians were the ones to fear. They were the "bankrupt," the "political blacklegs [who had] betrayed all parties"; they were the "nefarious band of speculators [who had] preyed upon the very vitals of the government" during the War of 1812.[3]

With its cautious words such as "timid" and "safety," the letter indicates that Van Buren and the Bucktails were far from radical reformers in 1821. The contents can also be read as evidence that Van Buren formed a link between Jefferson and Jackson. Like Jefferson he feared the "bankrupt" and the "speculators," but there are hints of Jacksonian Democracy in Van Buren's dependence on the "yeomanry" and in his easy use of the term "party." Van Buren did not propose the idea of a constitutional convention any more than he invented the canal system. At first, in fact, he opposed both, but when he saw that a majority wanted change, he went to work to deliver it. Van Buren did not initiate change, but he adapted to it quickly.

The composition of the constitutional convention, which met in

---

[2] *Statesman*, Sept. 12, 1820; Alexander, *Political History*, I, 295-298; *Autobiography*, p. 102; Hammond, *Political Parties*, I, 545.

[3] MVB to King, Jan. 14, 1821, King Papers.

Albany on August 28, reflected the state of American society early in the nineteenth century. With large-scale immigration still a quarter of a century away, only one of the one hundred twenty-six delegates was foreign-born. But the substantial internal migration in America was shown by the fact that fifty-nine delegates were born outside New York. Over half of the delegates were of Yankee stock, with ancestors originally from the British Isles. In preindustrial America it was natural that a majority of the delegates should be farmers, but there were also thirty-seven lawyers and nine merchants.[4]

With over three-fourths of the delegates, the Bucktails controlled the convention. They elected Daniel D. Tompkins presiding officer; Tompkins in turn chose Bucktails to chair the standing committees. Prominent Bucktails Samuel Young, Erastus Root and Peter R. Livingston stood out in the debates. So did Van Buren, even though he had had a hard time getting elected to the convention. Aware that he could not be elected by Albany or Columbia counties, he had arranged to be sent by the safe Bucktail county of Otsego. Despite their minority status, the handful of old Federalists at the convention carried considerable weight because of their personal prestige. These influential conservatives included the celebrated chancellor James Kent, the former attorney general Abraham Van Vechten, the Great Patroon Stephen Van Rensselaer, and the Federalists from Columbia County—William W. Van Ness, Elisha Williams and Jacob R. Van Rensselaer. In changing the constitution the Bucktails had to contend with these Federalists.[5]

The debates started on September 3 with a committee report on the council of revision, and ended on November 10 when a new constitution was passed by a vote of 98 to 9. In between, the delegates'

---

[4] *Argus*, Nov. 16, 1821; Ellis, "Yankee Invasion," p. 13; Fox, *Decline of Aristocracy*, pp. 229-231; Nathaniel H. Carter and William L. Stone, reporters, and Marcus T. C. Gould, stenographer, *Reports of the Proceedings and Debates of the Convention of 1821, Assembled for the Purpose of Amending the Constitution of the State of New-York* (Albany, 1821), p. 690 (hereinafter cited as *Debates*).

[5] One of the committee chairmen was Rufus King, a Federalist who had gone over to the Bucktails. Ninety-eight of 126 delegates were Bucktails. For lists of delegates and committees, see *Debates*, pp. 27-28, 38. For biographical data, see *Debates*, pp. 687-689. For a list of those who took the most part in the debates, see *Debates*, p. 690. Other biographical material may be found in Fox, *Decline of Aristocracy*, pp. 237-244; Alexander, *Political History*, I, 298-299; John A. Casais, "The New York State Constitutional Convention of 1821 and Its Aftermath" (Doctoral dissertation, Columbia University, 1967). For Van Buren's election, see *Argus*, June 19, June 22, 1821; *Autobiography*, pp. 105-106. Jabez Hammond emphasized the point about Bucktail dominance at the convention. Hammond, *Political Parties*, II, 6n-7n.

agenda moved, with digressions, from the executive branch, to the bill of rights, to the voting franchise, to the appointing power, and ended with the judiciary. The powers and organization of the legislature came up repeatedly.[6]

Reform of the executive branch began with the council of revision. The constitution of 1777 had kept the governor in check by forcing him to share the power of veto. By 1821, the majority of New Yorkers agreed that the council was unpopular, undemocratic and unwise. In the convention James Tallmadge attacked it for violating the theory of separation of powers. According to Daniel D. Tompkins, it had all too often based its decisions on political expediency. Van Buren objected because it consisted of members of the judiciary, who were not "directly responsible to the people." Opposition to the council, he said, arose during the War of 1812 when the council had found constitutional arguments against laws designed to raise troops. By a unanimous vote the convention decided to amend the constitution and abolish the council of revision.[7]

With the council abolished, the convention turned to the power of veto. Radical Bucktails Root and Livingston, who wanted to enlarge the powers of the legislature, suggested—quoting Jefferson—that a simple majority of both Houses rather than two-thirds be sufficient to pass a law over the governor's veto. The more moderate Van Buren, who feared that the public would refuse to ratify radical changes in the constitution, argued that the legislature was not infallible. "A bare majority," he said, "did not necessarily prove that a favorable measure [was] correct," for "great weight of character and powerful talents" were often in the minority. It should take a two-thirds vote to override a veto. Turning Jefferson on the radicals, Van Buren pointed out that the great Virginian had once criticized the Old Dominion for concentrating too much power in the legislative branch. Unfettered majority legislative rule, concluded Van Buren, "would agitate and excite the fears of the community." Van Buren had his way; the convention voted 100-17 to give the governor the veto and to require a two-thirds vote to overrule it.[8]

In the debate over the governor, Van Buren was once again in the middle between conservatives such as Elisha Williams, who wanted to retain the three-year term of office, and radicals such as Erastus Root, who wanted the governor "subjected to the ordeal of public

[6] *Debates*, pp. 42-43, 657.
[7] *Ibid.*, pp. 47, 68-76, 79.
[8] *Ibid.*, pp. 70-76, 120.

opinion once a year." Though Van Buren agreed that the public wanted a reduction in the three-year term, he felt that one year was not long enough. He wanted the people to test the governor, "not by the feelings of temporary excitement, but by that sober second thought, which is never wrong." In one year, he declared, no governor could "make himself acquainted with the interests, the wants, and condition of this great state." The best solution was to give him a two-year term. The convention voted with Van Buren.[9] When Daniel D. Tompkins tried to weaken the governor's power of pardon by requiring him to disclose his reasons to the legislature, Van Buren successfully opposed the motion, but tried in vain to give the governor the power to commute punishments.[10]

Van Buren was also unsuccessful in a curious effort to oppose attaching a bill of rights to the constitution. According to his argument, a bill of rights was "a privilege," a "concession extorted from the king in favor of popular liberty," which did not apply in a free republic. After reviewing the history of the bill of rights in England, but ignoring the American bill of rights, he concluded that it was inappropriate to add such a list of rights to the constitution of a free people. In a similar vein he opposed giving absolute freedom of speech to members of the legislature. Despite his efforts, however, the legislators were guaranteed freedom of speech, and a bill of rights was drawn up and passed.[11]

Van Buren displayed characteristic moderation in the debate over the elective franchise. After a committee chaired by Nathan Sanford brought in a report calling for something close to white manhood suffrage, discussion arose over the word "white." In 1821, the six thousand free adult male blacks in New York enjoyed the same voting rights as whites. Sanford's proposal denied all blacks the vote. When an amendment was proposed giving blacks the same rights as whites, the convention divided in an unusual way. Many of the more radical Bucktails, who favored expanding the franchise, voted against the blacks, while conservative Federalists, who hated to extend the franchise, voted for blacks. One reason for the anomaly was political: Federalists had traditionally received black support in New York while Republicans had few ties with blacks. In addition, the Bucktails who spoke revealed a fundamental belief in black inferiority. Samuel Young insisted that Negroes had long been social outcasts in New York and

[9] *Ibid.*, pp. 137-140, 147-148, 177, 551-552.
[10] *Ibid.*, pp. 124, 133-136, 147, 177-178.
[11] *Ibid.*, pp. 170, 172, 665-666.

therefore did not deserve the vote; moreover in his view, "the minds of blacks [were] not competent to vote."[12]

Van Buren would not go that far. He argued in favor of giving blacks the franchise because he did not want to deprive those who had been allowed to vote in the past. Many blacks, furthermore, paid taxes, and Van Buren did not want to take their money and then keep them from voting. After moderate Bucktails including Van Buren joined the Federalists, the blacks were granted the right to vote. Later, however, when it was proposed that blacks be excluded from voting unless they possessed a freehold worth $250, Van Buren went along, saying legalistically, that "the right [to vote] was not denied." If blacks worked hard, he said, they could vote, for the provision "held out inducements to industry." Van Buren was too democratic to exclude blacks from the vote, and too antiblack to grant them equality. His pragmatic views represented those of the majority both at the convention and throughout the North.[13]

For white voters the committee on the franchise made two proposals: one ended the distinction between those voting for governor and senators, and those voting for members of the assembly; the other removed the property qualification, giving the right to vote to any adult white male who paid taxes, or served in the militia, or worked on the roads. As a result, the number of those eligible to vote for assemblyman would increase from about 200,000 to about 260,000 and those voting for governor and senator from about 100,000 to 260,000.[14]

The debate opened with an amendment requiring those voting for senator to have a freehold worth $250. Chancellor Kent supported this proposal with his famous speech on the suffrage. The history of Europe, said Kent, proved that universal suffrage had been "productive of corruption, injustice, violence, and tyranny." To prevent this disaster Kent counted on "the stability and security of a senate, bottomed upon the freehold property of the state," and based on agriculture, "the foundation of national wealth and power." Kent was fearful of change. New York, he said, was no longer a simple farming republic, but had become "a great nation, with great commerce, manufactures,

---

[12] *Ibid.*, pp. 178-192.

[13] *Ibid.*, pp. 202, 377. Van Buren's quotation is in Holland, *Van Buren*, p. 187. See also Alexander, *Political History*, I, 299-300; Fox, *Decline of Aristocracy*, pp. 269n-270n; Casais, "New York Convention," pp. 181-184.

[14] Hough, *Census of New York 1855*, pp. ix-x; Richard P. McCormick, "Suffrage Classes and Party Alignments: a Study in Voter Behavior," *Mississippi Valley Historical Review*, 46 (1959), 405.

population, wealth, luxuries, and with the vices and miseries they engender." The growth of New York City with its "unwieldy population" and its "burdensome pauperism" frightened Kent. He was afraid that universal suffrage would enable the city to "govern this state." To prevent such a disaster he wanted to leave the senate in the hands of the prosperous farmers of New York.[15]

Van Buren's speech on the amendment was less famous and less eloquent than Kent's, but it was far more representative of the views of the delegates. A stranger hearing Kent, said Van Buren, would have assumed that "we were on the point of prostrating with lawless violence, one of the fairest and firmest pillars of the government, and of introducing into the sanctuary of the constitution, a mob or a rabble, violent and disorganizing, as were the Jacobins of France. . . . Those fears and apprehensions were wholly without foundation." The amendment was unfair, for it would exclude renters, "mechanics, professional men, and small landholders, . . . constituting the bone, pith, and muscle of the state." By excluding personal property from representation, the amendment failed to keep faith with the spirit of the Revolution, which had held that "taxation and representation were . . . indissoluble." The amendment lost, 100-19.[16]

After rejecting the conservative arguments of Clintonian Federalist James Kent, Van Buren fell in line with the conservative amendment of Bucktail Federalist John Duer, who proposed that the vote be restricted to those who paid taxes on real or personal property. This would have eliminated those who owned no property but who worked on the roads or served in the militia. Van Buren liked Duer's plan because he felt that the committee had taken the delegates closer to universal suffrage than their constituents desired. Pointing out that they had "already reached the verge of universal suffrage," Van Buren warned that "there was but one step beyond," and he did not wish to take it. He was willing, he said, to go as far as any man to extend liberty; but he would not "undervalue this precious privilege, so far as to confer it with undiscriminating hand upon every one, black or white, who would be kind enough to condescend to accept it." After Duer's amendment was rejected, the suffrage question was sent back to committee.[17]

Van Buren's slide toward the conservative side on the suffrage question continued when the issue returned from committee. First the convention decided to grant the vote to all who paid taxes or served

[15] *Debates*, pp. 215, 219-222.
[16] *Ibid.*, pp. 255-265, 270.
[17] *Ibid.*, pp. 271-277.

in the militia. Then discussion turned to those who worked on the roads. Van Buren first opposed giving road workers the vote, but then agreed in order to forestall a more radical plan to give complete manhood suffrage. Sounding more and more like Kent, he referred to "the many evils which would flow" from the plan, one being that it would give New York City about twenty-five thousand votes. Such an increase would, he said, render the elections in the city "a curse rather than a blessing [and] would drive from the polls all sober minded people." Universal suffrage would take representation away from the "hardy sons of the west" and give it instead to "the worst population" of the cities. The highway provision passed, but universal suffrage lost.[18]

The most important political issue at the convention was the question of how to appoint some fifteen thousand officeholders. Since the Bucktails had used the council of appointment so effectively in the spring, most observers assumed that Van Buren would devise some scheme to retain the council but keep it under Bucktail control. As Tompkins started to appoint committee chairmen, he smiled knowingly when Van Buren announced that he would like to chair the committee on the appointing power. Van Buren took advantage of these assumptions to outwit his opponents on the committee. "I rather mischievously," he wrote, "delayed calling the committee together until the suspicions . . . had time to mature." When the members finally did meet, Van Buren refused to give his views first, saying suavely that it "would be contrary to parliamentary usage, according to which the Chairman is regarded as a mediator."

Since Van Buren's opponents assumed that he would propose a continuation of the council of appointment, they wasted a lot of time preparing speeches to oppose such a plan. When Van Buren proposed abolishing the council and dividing the appointing power among the governor, the legislature and the people, the committee was surprised and some accused him of "radicalism." Van Buren was no radical. In the debates that followed, he prevented the committee from making surrogates, sheriffs and county judges elective; instead they would be chosen by the governor with the consent of the senate. His opponents were so outtalked and outmaneuvered that the committee adopted almost all of Van Buren's proposals. One exception involved the justices of the peace, whom Van Buren wanted chosen by the governor. The committee insisted that they be elected by the people instead.[19]

[18] *Ibid.*, pp. 356-368.

[19] *Autobiography*, pp. 106-107; Alexander, *Political History*, I, 307-308; Casais, "New York Convention," pp. 209-210; *Debates*, pp. 159-162, 296-300; Remini, "Early Political Career of Van Buren," pp. 294, 307-308.

In presenting the committee report and defending it in the debates that ensued, Van Buren denied that he was trying to centralize the appointing power. He pointed out that the committee had left only 531 of 14,943 officers at the disposal of the governor. These included the chancellor, the adjutant general and the justices of the supreme court, as well as the surrogates, sheriffs and county judges. The secretary of state, comptroller, attorney general, and treasurer would be chosen by the legislature; local officials such as district attorneys, clerks of courts, and mayors would be chosen on a local basis; lower militia officials would be elected by the rank and file; the choice of other officials was left to the discretion of the legislature.[20]

But Van Buren insisted that he wanted the justices of the peace chosen by the governor instead of by the people. The 2,556 justices were important to Bucktail control because they were the most influential figures in most towns, where they heard cases at the lowest level and settled neighborhood disputes. The justices handled five times as much business as the rest of the courts in the state. According to Rufus King, control over their appointment brought more political power than all the remaining patronage in New York. Van Buren argued that these officials if elected, would be so concerned about reelection that they would be poor judges. He outlined a plan whereby the justices of the peace would be appointed by the county supervisors and the county judges. If the supervisors and judges did not agree, which was likely to happen, then the governor would make the decision. With an eye toward compromise Van Buren hinted that he would be willing to have sheriffs and surrogates elected by the people in return for letting the governor have a hand in selecting the justices of the peace.[21]

Bucktail response to Van Buren's proposal varied. Samuel Beardsley of upstate New York, agreed that to protect the party, the justices should be chosen in Albany. But Michael Ulshoeffer of New York City, opposed having officials chosen in Albany while the legislature was sitting. Rufus King, who always worried about partisanship, suspected a plot to center patronage in Bucktail hands. Although the people, he wrote, were considered wise enough to elect the highest officers, Van Buren considered them "unworthy and not safe" to elect justices of the peace. Any plan, King complained, by which "local chiefs can obtain these offices at Albany, suits officeholders and demagogues better than election by the people." The differences of opinion

[20] *Debates*, pp. 159-162, 296-300, 315, 322; Alexander, *Political History*, I, 307-308.

[21] *Debates*, pp. 159-162; Alexander, *Political History*, I, 308; Holland, *Van Buren*, pp. 188-190.

within the party left the convention, said King, "in great conflict and disorder," with meetings going on "from house to house."[22]

Responding to his critics Van Buren denied that his plan was undemocratic. The committee report, he said, "had given to the people, the right of choosing more than eight thousand militia officers: Was this nothing?" In addition the report left three thousand six hundred civil officers to be appointed as the legislature saw fit: "Was this nothing?" Those choosing the justices in the counties would surely consult the people before making their lists. "And is this," asked Van Buren, "giving chaff to the people?" "We do not," he declared, "deny the competency of the people to make a proper choice." But if the justices were to be elected, they would know who voted for and against them, and thus be biased in their judicial decisions.[23]

Then he went on to a remarkably open defense of party politics. "We all know," he began, "the partiality and attachment, which men of the same political sentiments have for each other." His plan for selecting justices of the peace, he conceded, would sometimes favor one party, and sometimes another. When the governor made the final choice, he would select those whose politics were the same as his. Van Buren did not agree that the plan would add too much to the governor's power. "That power," he argued, "would be put in the hands of the executive, not for himself, but to secure to the majority of the people that control and influence . . . to which they are justly entitled." The governor would be the agent of the party and the party would be the agent of the people. Van Buren was expressing a fundamental belief in the new party politics. He was not trying to strengthen the governor; he was trying to develop a powerful party. His speech anticipated basic doctrines of Jacksonian Democracy.[24]

When Van Buren's amendment to give the governor a role in choosing the justices of the peace came to a vote, it failed, 58-56, largely because of Tammany Hall, the political organization in New York City, which ordinarily supported the Bucktails against the Clintonians. According to King, the jealousy of Tammany Hall destroyed any "confidence or cordiality" between the sachems and Van Buren. Some of the Tammany leaders even went so far as to say that an open council of appointment would be better than hidden control of appointments at Albany. With Bucktail control of the convention in jeopardy, Van

[22] Samuel Beardsley to Ela Collins, Sept. 20, 1821, Michael Ulshoeffer to MVB, Sept. 21, 1821, VBP; Rufus King to John King, Oct. 2, 1821, King, *Correspondence*, VI, 407.
[23] *Debates*, pp. 339-340.
[24] *Ibid.*, pp. 341-342; Casais, "New York Convention," p. 219.

Buren resorted to his favorite political device—the party caucus—and called a meeting of all Bucktails, especially those from Albany and New York City. After the caucus a modified version of Van Buren's compromise plan passed. The governor was allowed to help select the justices of the peace, but he lost the right to select sheriffs, who were to be elected by the people. The Bucktail organization had won at least part of the patronage power it wanted.[25]

With the councils of revision and appointment gone, the last target was the supreme court. Many Bucktails wanted to destroy the old judicial system just to get rid of the unpopular justices of the supreme court William W. Van Ness, Jonas Platt and Ambrose Spencer. There were also legitimate grievances against the system. Local courts were often incompetent, and the supreme court and the court of chancery were overworked. Erastus Root offered a plan to abolish the existing courts, to set up a new supreme court with district judges, and to transfer powers of equity from the court of chancery to the courts of common pleas. Even after this plan was defeated, Root continued his efforts to remove his enemies. Van Buren, who did not wish to support such openly vindictive proposals, delivered two speeches opposing Root's plans. Van Buren said primly that he did not wish "to commit to the winds a system which had justly been considered the proudest pillar in our political fabric." He refused "to descend to pulling down obnoxious officers [instead of] amending . . . principles." In the end, both Root and Van Buren could claim victory. The convention retained the old court of chancery and its distinguished chancellor James Kent, but all members of the supreme court were dismissed and a new high court established. In addition, a new system of circuit courts was set up with four to eight circuit judges.[26]

Van Buren was more ruthless in revamping the legislature. The committee on reapportionment chaired by Rufus King, proposed on October 17 that the convention replace the four senatorial districts with seventeen. Since the number of senators would remain thirty-two, King's proposal meant that ordinarily two senators would represent each district instead of the six to nine who represented the four

[25] *Debates*, pp. 356, 384, 389; Rufus King to Charles King, Oct. 15, 1821, MVB to John King, Oct. 28, 1821, King, *Correspondence*, VI, 416-417, 422; Casais, "New York Convention," pp. 220-223; Remini, "Early Political Career of Van Buren," pp. 310-313; Peter A. Jay to John Jay, Oct. 10, 1821, Henry P. Johnston, ed., *The Correspondence and Public Papers of John Jay* (1890-1893; reprint, 4 vols. in 1, New York, 1971), IV, 452.
[26] *Debates*, pp. 517, 520, 527, 535, 596, 624; Holland, *Van Buren*, pp. 201-205; Alexander, *Political History*, I, 302-306.

large districts in 1821. Federalists and Clintonians preferred having so many districts because their strength was concentrated in enclaves such as Albany, Columbia and Oneida counties. One Clintonian proposed single-member districts, which would have given his party the best hope in the senate. But as the old system had enabled Republican Bucktails to hold the senate over Federalists and Clintonians, even while losing the assembly, Bucktails would consent to no more than eight districts. When the outcome was in doubt, Van Buren slyly suggested passing the problem along to the legislature, where Bucktail control was assured. Such a diversion proved unnecessary; the convention set up eight senatorial districts, of which the Bucktails were likely to win six, the Clintonians two (one of them district three, which included both Columbia and Albany counties). Van Buren then tried to win control of this district by suggesting that Columbia County be moved out of it and two Bucktail counties moved in. Recognizing the stratagem, Elisha Williams sarcastically remarked, "in the third district you have a Gerrymander. The monster will curl its tail on the mountains of Jersey—coil along the borders of Pennsylvania, wind its scaly and hideous carcass between the crooked lines of counties, and finally thrust its head into Bennington. Disguise it as you will, the object will be visible, and the people will understand it is to exclude federalism from every senatorial district." Williams won this particular joust as Van Buren's greedy plan was defeated, 68-36.[27]

The work of the convention, which was promptly ratified by the people, brought about important changes in New York. Responding to the growth of democracy, the delegates removed the freehold qualification for voting, thereby almost trebling the number of eligible voters. But the change was still not complete, and free white manhood suffrage did not become a reality until 1826. Since New Yorkers in 1821 no longer feared the power of the executive as they had in 1777, the convention granted the governor the additional powers of appointment and veto. No longer convinced that the lower house should dominate the government, the delegates added to the powers of the senate. The abolition of the councils of appointment and revision made the government more efficient. Jacksonian and Progressive historians have exaggerated these reforms. They did not add up to "a momentous revolution," as George Bancroft maintained, nor did they bring about "the decline of aristocracy in the politics of New York," as Dixon Ryan Fox concluded. Revisionist historians have erred in the opposite direction. Any convention that increased the number of eligible voters

[27] *Debates*, pp. 413-416, 560.

from 100,000 to 260,000 was hardly a victory for "the conservative opposition to universal suffrage," as Lee Benson described it. The new constitution was neither a victory for democracy nor a rear guard reform by reactionaries, but was instead a practical revision that was long overdue.[28]

As contemporary New Yorkers realized, the political implications of the convention outweighed the constitutional. None saw this distinction more clearly than Jabez Hammond, who wrote his history from personal observation. Hammond painted the convention in sharp colors, dividing the delegates into political categories—Bucktail, Clintonian and Federalist; he preferred these terms to the words "radical," "moderate" and "conservative" that some later writers employed. Recognizing the political importance of the convention, Hammond stressed the political struggle over the appointing power more than the ideological debate over the suffrage. "The Bucktails," he said, "were desirous to give the control of these appointments . . . to the central appointing power of the seat of government . . . while the Clintonian part of the convention . . . strenuously opposed the system." The two parties felt as they did, said Hammond, because the Bucktails had control of the legislature and the Clintonians did not.[29]

[28] For the Jacksonian interpretation, see Bancroft, *Van Buren*, especially p. 107. The best Progressive interpretation is Fox, *Decline of Aristocracy*, ch. 9. For Benson's quotation, see Lee Benson, *The Concept of Jacksonian Democracy: New York as a Test Case* (New York, 1961), p. 8. For the vote on the new constitution, see Hutchins, *Civil List*, p. 128. I agree with Marvin Meyers that the differences among radicals such as Erastus Root, moderates such as Van Buren, and conservatives such as Chancellor Kent were not very great. All wanted the people to rule, all shared an uneasy fear of the city mob, and all believed in republican principles. I do not, however, believe that the convention supports Meyers' thesis that the "Jacksonian Persuasion" was an attempt to "recall agrarian republican innocence." It was more forward-looking than that. Meyers himself concedes at the end of his section on the convention, that important changes had taken place. "Henceforth," he writes, "the issues of political debate were to be formed entirely within a framework of democratic institutions and democratic language." Well-aware of the changes that had taken place, the embryo Jacksonians did occasionally look back at a republican dream, but they also looked ahead to democratic reality. At the convention of 1821 they reconciled the two. See Meyers, *Jacksonian Persuasion*, pp. 15, 237-253. Richard P. McCormick calls attention to the importance of the convention in *The Second American Party System: Party Formation in the Jacksonian Era* (Chapel Hill, 1966), pp. 104-115. In "Suffrage Classes and Party Alignments: a Study in Voter Behavior," McCormick argues that the liberalizing of voting qualifications had little effect on voting in New York. See also Richard P. McCormick, "New Perspectives on Jacksonian Politics," *American Historical Review*, 65 (Jan. 1960), 288-301.

[29] Hammond, *Political Parties*, pp. 76-77. Compare Hammond's interpretation with that of John A. Casais, who used the terms "radical," "moderate" and "conservative,"

Hammond was correct; the convention was a political landmark, called for partisan reasons. Clintonians would never have called it because they had done well under the old system; Bucktails, on the other hand, sought to alter a system that had made it difficult for them to gain power. Once the decision to introduce changes was made, the elections for delegates were held on a partisan basis (Van Buren even had to go to a county more reliable than his own in order to be elected), and when the convention met, it was organized on a similarly partisan basis, with Bucktails in command. Dominating the convention was the most partisan politician in New York—Martin Van Buren.

Van Buren and the Bucktails knew that the convention gave them the chance to solidify their political position. Ever since 1817, when Clinton had been elected governor, the chief executive had used Clintonian control of the assembly and the powers of the governor's office to maintain his strength. Control of the assembly gave him control over the council of appointment because the assembly elected most members of the council. As governor, he appointed all the justices of the council of revision. If the Bucktails could weaken the assembly and abolish the councils, they would gain ground.

By the time the convention was over, the Bucktails had done all that and more. Since they had the best organized party in the state, they insisted on changes that strengthened the role of political parties in New York. By reducing the term of governor from three years to two, they made the office of governor more responsive to the people and more closely affiliated to a political party. Moreover, the new plan meant that Clinton would have to run again in 1822 rather than in 1823. By doing away with the council of appointment, they ended a system in which patronage depended on factions and maneuvering in an assembly that was often Clintonian. Under the new constitution most positions were elective and thus responsive to party control; the rest were appointive, generally by order of the governor and the senate. These new arrangements reduced the role of the assembly, which the Bucktails had not often controlled, and increased the power of the senate, which they were sure of controlling. But the Bucktails did not want to depend wholly on popular elections once they were in power. Within their organization control of villages and towns depended on the more than 2,500 justices of the peace, and to influence as many of these as possible Van Buren made certain that the governor was given a share of the power to appoint them. When the convention

and Dixon Ryan Fox, who emphasized the debate over the suffrage. Casais, "New York Convention," pp. 73-103; Fox, *Decline of Aristocracy*, pp. 248-264.

completed its work in December 1821, it left New York with a form of government that Van Buren's political organization was able to control for most of the next two decades.

Interpretations of Van Buren's role at the convention have shifted along with changing views of Jacksonian Democracy. The immediate reactions were partisan. In his 1835 campaign biography of Van Buren, William M. Holland argued that Van Buren fought for democracy at the convention. Van Buren was always guided, said Holland, by "the *opinion of the people*; to the people he always referred as the just arbiters of all political measures and the only source of legitimate authority." Another Jacksonian, George Bancroft, also portrayed Van Buren as the hero of the people, establishing manhood suffrage despite the opposition of the Federalists. Like Holland, Bancroft found it necessary to explain why his hero opposed complete manhood suffrage. He did so, said Bancroft, because " 'The sober sense of the community' . . . had not demanded 'deep and dangerous innovations.' "[30]

In the presidential campaigns of 1836 and 1840, writers interpreted Van Buren's role differently. One pamphlet, entitled *The Claims of Martin Van Buren*, pointed out that Van Buren had opposed the popular election of justices of the peace and had stood against popular manhood suffrage. *The Contrast*, by the Whig historian Richard Hildreth, accused Van Buren of having been undemocratic in supporting the veto power for the governor. Even Jabez Hammond, who was a supporter of Van Buren, conceded in 1842 that Van Buren had held back democratic reform by keeping the appointment of justices of the peace in the hands of the governor.[31]

In the twentieth century, writers have been equally divided. The Progressive view held that Van Buren led future Jacksonian Democrats in a successful battle for manhood suffrage against the reactionary stand of Chancellor Kent and the Federalists. Van Buren's speech, according to De Alva Alexander writing in 1909, "made the deepest impression." Arthur M. Schlesinger, Jr., went much further. He held that Van Buren "marshaled the liberal forces in the New York constitutional convention and delivered the most crushing reply to the neo-Federalist arguments of Chancellor Kent on the question of the suffrage." Consensus historians, however, considered Van Buren almost as conservative as Kent; Lee Benson, for example, said that Van

[30] Holland, *Van Buren*, pp. 149-205; Bancroft, *Van Buren*, pp. 74-107.
[31] *The Claims of Martin Van Buren to the Presidency* (n.p., n.d.), p. 4; Hildreth, *The Contrast*, pp. 22-25; Hammond, *Political Parties*, II, 80.

Buren led the "conservative majority." Even historians sympathetic to Van Buren portrayed him as bent on building his own political machine rather than facilitating democracy in America.[32]

Van Buren was neither an ardent advocate of democracy nor a reactionary opportunist. His behavior at the convention was consistent with his behavior before and after. He did not originate ideas; he did not lead the demand for reform. At the same time he did not stand in the way of change. He was not simply carried along by events, nor did he merely try to make the best deal for himself. Instead Van Buren was a master at determining the direction in which events were moving and then directing those events along the route that was best, as he saw it, for himself, his party and his state. He understood the demand for manhood suffrage, but realized that it would be best for his organization at Albany if he kept the vote away from the lowest elements in New York City. He realized that the people wanted to elect public officials, but he saw that he could help the Bucktails if he gave the governor a role in selecting the justices of the peace. By strengthening the governor's office and the senate, and by altering the method of nominating officials, Van Buren took large strides toward establishing his organization.

He knew that he was in a difficult position at the convention, where he had to deal with a variety of opponents including the Federalists and Clintonians. He was also at odds with the delegation from New York City and many Bucktail Federalists; in addition he had to hold back "a small number of Mad-caps among the old democrats," who considered "nothing wise [that was not] violent," and who thought that they "merit[ed] Knighthood by assailing everything that [was] memorable in old institutions." He was "exposed to the detraction of some dozen hair brained [sic] politicians," and was accused of "radicalism" by one side for giving the choice of so many offices to the people, while the other "much censured" him for not insisting on complete adult manhood suffrage. According to John King, Van Buren lost ground with the radicals because he had "flinched upon the ques-

---

[32] Alexander, *Political History*, I, 301; Arthur M. Schlesinger, Jr., *The Age of Jackson* (Boston, 1945), p. 48; Benson, *Concept of Jacksonian Democracy*, p. 8; Alvin Kass, *Politics in New York State 1800-1830* (Syracuse, 1965), p. 90. Robert V. Remini is one of the historians sympathetic to Van Buren who argues that he sought to build the Albany Regency at the convention. Remini, "Early Political Career of Van Buren," pp. 308-312; Remini, "Albany Regency," p. 341. See also Casais, "New York Convention," pp. 204-233, 297. I cannot accept Casais' argument that the new constitution strengthened the Regency by weakening the governor. The convention actually strengthened the governor by giving him the power of veto and additional appointment power, and this increased power of the governor helped strengthen the Regency.

tion of suffrage" and had fought too hard to keep control of the appointment of officers who were "supposed to have influence in the counties." Peter A. Jay reported that "the more violent members of the convention [were] enraged" when Van Buren opposed the election of justices of the peace. None of this seemed to bother the optimistic Van Buren. He wrote in the midst of the convention that he was "very well pleased with the actual state of things & happy in . . . having been a member of the convention." By the end Van Buren had made his way safely past all obstacles.[33]

The New York constitutional convention was part of the process by which Van Buren began his transition from state to national politician. It also marked the culmination of events that enabled him to rid himself of his anxiety and indecision. The convention came at exactly the right time—in the fall of 1821—just before he took his seat in the Senate in December. After playing such an important role in the proceedings he was not likely to be awed by politics in Washington, where Thomas Hart Benton, Nathaniel Macon and Richard Mentor Johnson would be no harder to deal with than James Kent, Ambrose Spencer and Erastus Root.

In the year and a half that followed the constitutional convention Van Buren and his Bucktails moved swiftly to tighten their hold on the state. Since Van Buren anticipated spending much of his time in Washington, he began to seek ways to improve the connection between Capitol Hill and Albany, and in New York the Bucktails turned their attention toward winning the governor's seat in the November election of 1822. As a result of their efforts the Bucktail organization grew so strong that it became known as the "Albany Regency," and so successful that it became a model for political organizations for years to come.[34]

A patronage squabble involving Congressman Solomon Van Rensselaer gave Senator Van Buren his first opportunity to manipulate the Regency from Washington. In January 1822, the story circulated that

[33] Van Buren to Rufus King, Oct. 28, 1821, King, *Correspondence*, VI, 422; *Autobiography*, pp. 107, 112; John King to Rufus King, Oct. 26, 1821, King Papers; Peter A. Jay to John Jay, Oct. 10, Oct. 28, 1821, Jay, *Correspondence*, IV, 452-455.

[34] The term "Albany Regency" was common by 1824. John C. Calhoun, for example, referred to the "Regency at Albany" in November 1823. Calhoun to Samuel L. Gouverneur, Nov. 9, 1823. Samuel L. Gouverneur Papers, NYPL. See also John Cramer to John W. Taylor, Jan. 6, 1824, Taylor Papers; DeWitt Clinton to Francis Granger, Jan. 25, 1824, Gideon and Francis Granger Papers, LC; Remini, "Albany Regency," pp. 341-342.

Solomon Southwick had defaulted on his accounts and would be removed as postmaster in Albany. Since the postmastership was a political plum, the Regency was disturbed when word spread that the Clintonian Van Rensselaer was about to be appointed. In Washington Van Rensselaer stole a march on the Regency lining up twenty-two members of the New York delegation, including some Bucktails, to back him. Furthermore, he asked his cousin, the Great Patroon Stephen Van Rensselaer, to intercede with Van Buren and Senator Rufus King. For a Clintonian, Solomon Van Rensselaer, to seek support from Bucktail members of Congress, showed how far from clearly defined parties in New York still were.[35]

Van Buren took steps that drew party lines more sharply and gave a good indication of how the Albany Regency would work during the next two decades. After assuring himself of the support of Rufus King and Vice President Tompkins, Van Buren asked Postmaster General Return Meigs and President Monroe to delay two weeks before making the appointment. He then instructed Republicans in Albany to call a caucus to draw up a petition opposing Van Rensselaer. Van Buren reminded the party members that Van Rensselaer was too "partisan," but cautiously warned them to be neither "offensive [nor] threatening or scolding." He insisted that they use the "utmost delicacy" in their letters and that they argue positively for a Republican instead of negatively against a Federalist. Van Buren also called a caucus of Bucktail congressmen, hoping to get them to support the delay of two weeks. Finally, he met with Secretary of the Navy Smith Thompson, who had already come out against Van Rensselaer. In three days Van Buren had involved dozens of Bucktails in both Albany and Washington. He had been quick, thorough, partisan, but always cautious. His caution did not, however, prevent tempers from flaring. Monroe reported that Thompson had "objected in the strongest manner" to the appointment.[36]

Van Buren got a prompt response. His pressure apparently disturbed Monroe because the President called a special cabinet meeting on

[35] Southwick had been appointed postmaster in 1817. *Statesman*, July 14, 1820; Solomon Van Rensselaer to the Patroon, Dec. 26, 1821, Thomas R. Ross to Return Meigs, Dec. 31, 1821, Bonney, *Historical Gleanings*, I, 369-372; King, *Correspondence*, VI, 438-439; Adams, *Memoirs*, V, 479-480.

[36] MVB to Meigs, Jan. 3, 1822, Meigs to King and MVB, Jan. 4, 1822, Tompkins, King, and MVB to Meigs, Jan. 4, 1822, Meigs to Tompkins, King, and MVB, Jan. 4, 1822, MVB to Monroe, Jan. 5, 1822, VBP; Tompkins to Jonathan Thompson, Jan. 4, 1822, MVB to Benjamin Knower and Others, Jan. 5, Jan. 6, 1822, Bonney, *Historical Gleanings*, I, 373-377; Adams, *Memoirs*, V, 479-480.

January 5, just two days after Van Buren had started his campaign. The members of the cabinet including John Quincy Adams, William Harris Crawford and John C. Calhoun, were much interested in the struggle over patronage, but only Thompson opposed the immediate appointment of Van Rensselaer. A long debate took place over whether the President had the right to interfere or whether the power of appointing postmasters rested exclusively with the Postmaster General. The next day Van Buren held his caucus with the eleven Bucktail congressmen who were supporting Van Rensselaer, and got seven of them to ask for a two-week delay. Van Buren sent another letter to Meigs, saying that Van Rensselaer was unacceptable, and recommending former chancellor John Lansing. It was all in vain, for on the following day the President announced that he would not interfere in the Albany appointment, and the Postmaster General named Van Rensselaer.[37]

Van Buren had lost, but the affair strengthened the Regency by helping to establish lines of communication between Albany and Washington. As early as January 6, Van Buren's brother-in-law Moses I. Cantine was reporting to Van Buren on politics in the state capital. Clintonians, he said, were divided between those who supported Van Rensselaer and those who wanted to retain Southwick, while many Bucktails favored Cantine himself. Partisanship became so nasty that Cantine felt obliged to send a second copy of his letter from Catskill because he feared that Southwick might intercept the original copy mailed from Albany. Another report, from Michael Ulshoeffer, described the "indignation" that had arisen in Albany over the appointment. In a letter to Rufus King, William A. Duer also reported great "disgust amongst the Republicans" over the affair. Charles Dudley of Albany, asked Van Buren to remind Monroe of "the great importance" that the Republican party of New York had been to his administration. The organ of the Regency, the *Albany Argus*, summed up the sentiment of the party. Disgust, said the *Argus*, had swept the city when the appointment of Van Rensselaer was announced, because he was "as bigoted a federalist as ever existed in this state."[38]

[37] Adams, *Memoirs*, V, 480-482; William B. Rochester to Solomon Van Rensselaer, Jan. 7, 1822, Solomon Van Rensselaer to Dr. William Bay, Jan. 7, 1822, *Evening Post* correspondent, Washington, D.C., Jan. 7, 1822, Bonney, *Historical Gleanings*, I, 377-380; Tompkins and MVB to Meigs, Jan. 7, 1822, Meigs to Tompkins, Jan. 7, 1822, VBP; Monroe to MVB, Jan. 7, 1822, James Monroe Papers, NYPL; Rufus King to Charles King, Jan. 14, 1822, King Papers.

[38] Daniel D. Tompkins also believed that mail was being opened in Albany. Tompkins to Jonathan Thompson, Jan. 4, 1822, Bonney, *Historical Gleanings*, I, 373. Moses I.

A meeting of Bucktail legislators took place on January 21, with Charles Dudley in the chair and Benjamin Knower secretary. Letters were published, resolutions attacking the appointment were passed, and a committee drew up a partisan memorial for President Monroe that declared: "we can neither repress nor disguise our strong conviction, that in filling important vacancies, political consideration ought not to be overlooked; but on the contrary, that devotion to Republican principles, should be required, appreciated, and rewarded." In response a Clintonian meeting supported the nomination and attacked the Bucktails for getting the federal government involved in "petty party feuds."[39]

The episode put Van Buren in the limelight. A member of the Van Rensselaer clan, Catharina Van Rensselaer Bonney, later concluded that "the wires of this political puppet show were all pulled at Washington by the invisible but skillful hand of the crafty [Van Buren]." Newspaper articles up and down the Atlantic coast reported on the Van Rensselaer appointment. Some of the attention was hostile as party lines became more sharply drawn. At the Clintonian meeting in Albany, the presiding officer John W. Taylor attacked Van Buren personally for supporting one Federalist, Rufus King, but opposing another, Solomon Van Rensselaer. Michael Ulshoeffer reported, with evident understatement, that a "few" in Albany were "unfriendly" to Van Buren, and warned of possible unpleasantness for Van Buren in Washington because the House delegation would be criticized and might take it out on the new senator. But on the whole Van Buren believed that the post office affair had helped his party.[40]

Another opportunity to help the party and get rid of Clinton came in the state election in the fall of 1822. The provisions of the new constitution reduced the governor's term of office from three to two years and shifted the election from April to November. When the party tried to nominate Van Buren for governor, he refused on the grounds that he had "seen enough of state politics for many years." But Van

---

Cantine to MVB, Jan. 6, 1822, Michael Ulshoeffer to MVB, Jan. 13, 1822, VBP; William A. Duer to Rufus King, Jan. 13, 1822, King, *Correspondence*, VI, 447-448; Charles Dudley to MVB, Jan. 14, 1822, Bonney, *Historical Gleanings*, I, 385; *Argus*, Jan. 15, 1822; Rufus King to John King, Jan. 19, 1822, King Papers.

[39] Bonney, *Historical Gleanings*, I, 387; *Argus*, Jan. 22, Jan. 29, Feb. 1, 1822; Charles Dudley and Others to Tompkins and MVB, Jan. 22, 1822, VBP.

[40] According to the *Argus*, Federalist newspapers along the coast were supporting Van Rensselaer, while the Baltimore *Patriot* applauded Van Buren's part in the affair. *Argus*, Feb. 1, Feb. 5, Feb. 15, 1822; Bonney, *Historical Gleanings*, I, 385, 395; Samuel A. Talcott to MVB, Feb. 7, 1822, Ulshoeffer to MVB, Jan. 27, Jan. 31, 1822, VBP; MVB to John King, Feb. 18, 1822, King Papers.

Buren had no intention of abandoning state politics. In the summer of 1822 he returned to Albany to run the campaign. For a time the Bucktails debated running Erastus Root or Nathan Sanford for governor, but finally agreed on Joseph C. Yates, a member of the state supreme court. When Clinton decided not to run, Van Buren had finally accomplished what he had set out to do in 1815. Yates was easily elected in November.[41]

Although the election of Yates gave the Bucktails control of the state, they still faced the task of reconciling groups within the party. The Regency, which stood in the middle, had to balance off the conflicting demands of radicals led by Root and Samuel Young, and conservatives under Yates. Before Van Buren left Albany, rumors spread that he had held a party caucus to lay down instructions for the new governor. Van Buren denied the charge, but as soon as he reached Washington, he wrote to Yates recommending a number of Bucktails for jobs. After resisting for a short time, Yates gave in and named two Bucktails, including one who had been suggested by Van Buren, to the new supreme court.[42]

With the governor as well as the legislature on their side, the Bucktails were able to round out their political organization. In addition to the two justices of the supreme court, the Regency named five Bucktails to the new state circuit courts. Many Bucktails who were already in office were reappointed, including Benjamin Knower as treasurer and Samuel A. Talcott as attorney general. William L. Marcy was named comptroller. Even more important, thousands of Bucktails took over local offices. The Bucktail sweep that had begun in the spring of 1821 was now complete.[43]

By 1823, the Regency had already become a well-organized, smoothly running machine, the pride of its supporters, the envy of its rivals, and the prototype of political machines for the next century. Policy was made at the top by a directorate, or "Regency," in Albany. Many of these leaders, but not all, held high political positions such as governor, United States senator or Secretary of State. If a problem or crisis arose,

---

[41] Van Buren had been rumored as a candidate immediately after Clinton's victory in 1820. *Statesman*, Aug. 11, 1820; MVB to Root, Jan. 16, 1822, MVB to Gorham Worth, Feb. 18, 1822, Ulshoeffer to MVB, Mar. 11, Mar. 19, 1822, Knower to MVB, Mar. 4, 1822, VBP.

[42] Cantine to MVB, Dec. 2, 1822, MVB to Yates, Dec. 10, 1822, VBP; R. M. Livingston to John W. Taylor, Jan. 1, 1823, Taylor Papers.

[43] Jacob Sutherland and John Savage were named to the supreme court, Samuel R. Betts, William A. Duer, Nathan Williams, Samuel Nelson, and Enos T. Throop to the circuit courts. Silas Wright became surrogate in St. Lawrence County. Hutchins, *Civil List*, passim; *Argus*, Feb. 18, Mar. 28, April 1, April 11, April 22, April 25, 1823.

the leaders would meet or letters would flow back and forth until a consensus had been reached on how to act. Once the decision was made, orders would come down to the party caucus in the legislature and would then be transmitted across the state by the party press or by roving emissaries. The new circuit judges, appointed by the governor, played an important role as they traveled about their circuits spreading the party line from Albany. At the grassroots the Regency controlled the choice of thousands of justices of the peace, county judges, surrogates, and masters and examiners of chancery, all of whom exercised great power at the local level.[44]

At the heart of the organization was the party press, headed by the *Albany Argus*. When the Bucktails in the legislature named the editor of the *Argus*, Moses I. Cantine, state printer, they gave the newspaper the sole right to print the state laws at public expense. In addition the *Argus* received the profitable right to publish notices of insolvency and mortgage sales. With these lucrative privileges the *Argus* enjoyed a wide circulation throughout the state. Van Buren knew how important the *Argus* was as mouthpiece of the Regency. "Without a paper thus edited at Albany," he wrote, "we may hang our harps on the willows. With it the party can survive a thousand . . . convulsions." The opposition also recognized the role of the *Argus*. There was "no office to fill," protested one disgruntled writer, that was not "first arranged in the office of the *Albany Argus*." Other Regency newspapers included the *Plattsburgh Republican*, the *Elmira Gazette*, and the *Patriot* in Orange County. When an opposition editor was particularly difficult, the Regency sometimes bought the newspaper out from under him. In 1828, for example, the *Buffalo Emporium* complained that the Regency had bought out the *Buffalo and Black Rock Gazette*, which henceforth would echo "the will of Pope Martin the First."[45]

Patronage held the organization together. The New York journalist Beman Brockway recalled that "if a man wanted an office at the hands of the governor, it was necessary that he should be on good terms with the county judges, be a straightout democrat." Once a member

---

[44] MVB to Benjamin Butler, Dec. 12, 1826, Silas Wright to MVB, Jan. 13, 1833, VBP. For the best description of the Albany Regency, see Remini, "Albany Regency." See also Goldstein, "Albany Regency," pp. 1-10.

[45] Milton W. Hamilton, *The Country Printer: New York State 1785-1830*, 2nd ed. (New York, 1964), pp. 115-135; MVB to Jesse Hoyt, Jan. 31, 1823, William L. Mackenzie, *The Life and Times of Martin Van Buren* (Boston, 1846), pp. 190-192; New York *Courier and Enquirer*, April 25, 1832, quoted in Goldstein, "Albany Regency," p. 9.

of the Regency reached the office of governor, treasurer, comptroller, attorney general, or secretary of state, he could be counted on to appoint party men to subordinate jobs. Before long the Regency controlled the canal commission with its vast potential for patronage. And not all the jobs were state and local; with the right administration in Washington the Regency could name federal judges and marshals, postmasters, and, most important of all, the collector of customs for the Port of New York. The latter, who controlled the greatest source of patronage in the United States, was so crucial to the Regency that one of Van Buren's first acts as a United States senator was to oppose a bill that threatened to reduce the collector's commissions.[46]

The Regency was well-disciplined. It was not easy, first of all, to get into the upper levels of the organization. When one opponent tried to set terms for changing sides, Van Buren replied sternly that no such "stipulations" were possible. Once enrolled, according to Beman Brockway, members of the Regency had to "swear allegiance to the powers that be," and there was no mercy for the disloyal. "The first man we see *step to the rear*," said Silas Wright of the Regency, "we *cut down* . . . they *must* not falter or they perish."[47]

AT the head of the Regency, commanding the admiration and respect of his colleagues, stood Van Buren. Benjamin Butler found Van Buren one of the most agreeable men in conversation that he had ever met. "So much ease, politeness, vivacity and good nature at the social board," he said, "[were] rarely to be met with." William L. Marcy, who felt the same way, recalled that he had always deferred to Van Buren's "better judgment." Even members of the opposition recognized Van Buren's supremacy. One called Van Buren the most popular Bucktail in New York, while another remarked that he was "a host in himself, the *idol and pride* of his party." Van Buren's political reputation had grown so great by now that he became known as the "Magician," a term used by both friend and foe throughout the rest of his career.[48]

[46] Beman Brockway, *Fifty Years in Journalism Embracing Recollections and Personal Experiences* (Watertown, 1891), pp. 27-28; *Annals of Congress*, 17th Congress, 1st session (1821-1822), 26, 131-136, 184-204; William Hartman, "The New York Custom House: Seat of Spoils Politics," *New York History*, 34 (1953), 149-163.

[47] Wright to Azariah Flagg, Jan. 28, 1833, Flagg Papers; MVB to George Tibbitts, Oct. 1820, VBP; Brockway, *Fifty Years of Journalism*, pp. 27-28.

[48] Benjamin Butler to Harriet Allen, Nov. 25, 1816, Butler Papers, NYSL; Marcy to Albert Gallup, Sept. 23, 1837, William L. Marcy Papers, LC; William B. Rochester to Henry Clay, June 23, 1823, James F. Hopkins, ed., *The Papers of Henry Clay* (Lexington, 1959—), III, 445; P. L. Tracy to John W. Taylor, July 10, 1828, Taylor Papers.

In 1823, four years after the death of his wife, Van Buren had adjusted to being a widower. Winters were spent in Washington, early spring often included a trip to the South, summers and falls found him in Albany practicing law and tending to the Regency; every August he spent a few weeks at Saratoga or some other watering place. In Georgetown he lived comfortably in a pleasant boardinghouse with Rufus King and other senators. Whenever Van Buren visited New York City, he was fussy about his housing, once demanding a sitting room in addition to a bedroom, and on another occasion insisting that his rooms not be on an upper floor.[49]

He had many friends. Political allies, among them Senator Mahlon Dickerson of New Jersey, accompanied Van Buren on trips to Saratoga and the South. He explored the law with Benjamin Butler, drank with Jesse Hoyt, talked philosophy and politics with Rufus King. Van Buren was especially at ease with women, particularly those with whom he corresponded. To Lucy Evans, the wife of Bucktail David E. Evans, Van Buren sent a copy of Sir Walter Scott's *Kenilworth*, warning her that the ending was "distressing." On another occasion he sent her a twig from a cedar next to the tomb of Washington at Mount Vernon. One of the reasons Van Buren enjoyed moving to Washington was the opportunity to carry on polite flirtations with a variety of women; he had the ability to suit his mood and tastes to many different kinds of men and women.[50]

At this point Van Buren was free to devote his attention to politics because his children were cared for by others. In the summer of 1820 only the oldest of his sons—twelve-year-old Abraham—was living with his father. When Van Buren departed for Washington in 1821, he left Abraham with the boy's aunt, Christina Cantine. In 1823, Abraham, now fifteen, journeyed to West Point to enroll in the United States Military Academy; since Martin was off on a political trip at the time,

---

For the use of the term "Magician," see Bonney, *Historical Gleanings*, I, 385; *Richmond Enquirer*, Mar. 20, April 13, April 24, May 15, 1827, July 31, 1829; Silas Wright to Azariah Flagg, Aug. 8, 1833, Azariah Flagg–Silas Wright Correspondence, NYPL; John Forsyth to MVB, Aug. 5, 1835, William A. Butler, *A Retrospect of Forty Years 1825-1865* (New York, 1911), pp. 78-79; Francis P. Blair to Andrew Jackson, Mar. 17, 1840, Jackson, *Correspondence*, VI, 54; John Dix to Azariah Flagg, Aug. 16, 1832, Flagg Papers.

[49] MVB to Hoyt, Nov. 17, 1819, Mackenzie, *Van Buren*, pp. 183-184; MVB to Hoyt, Nov. 14, 1822, William L. Mackenzie, *The Lives and Opinions of Benjamin Franklin Butler . . . and Jesse Hoyt* (Boston, 1845), p. 36.

[50] MVB to Dickerson, June 20, 1821, Hugh Hughes Papers, LC; MVB to Lucy Evans, Mar. 23, 1821, Mar. 10, 1822, VBP; Charles Butler to Benjamin Butler, 1819, copy by William A. Butler, Charles Butler Papers, LC.

he could not accompany his son and had to content himself with giving advice. Abraham's "future character and usefulness" depended, said the father, on "industry and fidelity." That same year, his second son John, aged thirteen, went to live with Rufus King on Long Island while attending school nearby. The two youngest sons, Martin and Smith, stayed behind with Christina Cantine and Van Buren's sister.[51]

Van Buren depended on his law practice to help support his family. In June 1820, Benjamin Butler gave up an unsuccessful venture in banking to renew his partnership with Van Buren. Their office was at 111 State Street, Albany, down the hill from the capitol building, where they occupied the entire first floor, Van Buren in front with a library and Butler in back. It was, boasted Butler, the most attractive office in Albany. Van Buren worked as hard as ever, often rising at four thirty in the morning and pushing himself harder than was wise. Once when he was ill and insisted on speaking for three hours before the court of chancery, he had to spend the next three weeks in bed. Despite such industry, he was often hard-pressed for cash. In 1820, he kept after his brother Abraham to repay a loan of $150, and two years later Van Buren was furious with Peter I. Hoes for losing several thousand dollars of their money in a bad investment. Fortunately for Van Buren his law practice kept money flowing in.[52]

Second in command of the Regency after Van Buren was William L. Marcy. With his large head, black hair and tall, commanding presence, Marcy looked surprisingly like Daniel Webster, though Marcy's features were "coarser" (according to one source) and his oratory not in a class with Webster's. Marcy, whose father fought at Saratoga, grew up on a farm in Sturbridge, Massachusetts, graduated from Brown, and in 1808, moved westward to Troy, New York, where he became clerk in a law office. Aligning himself with the Republican party, Marcy gave his first political speech at the age of twenty-three on Columbus Day, 1809. Three years later Ensign Marcy of the Troy Invincibles led five men into a building on the Canadian border where they captured forty-five Voyageurs and brought back a British flag. That encounter and Marcy's four "Vindex" articles defending the War of

[51] Fourth Census of the United States, 1820, Population Schedules, II, Albany County, New York; MVB to Rufus King, May 31, 1822, May 9, 1823, King Papers; MVB to Colonel Sylvanus Thayer, May 30, 1823, Cindy Adams, ed., *The West Point Thayer Papers 1808-1872* (West Point, 1965), IV.

[52] *Argus*, Sept. 5, 1820; Munsell, *Annals*, VI, 123; Charles Butler to Benjamin Butler, July 27, 1819, Charles Butler Papers, LC; Martin Van Buren, Jr., "Reminiscences of [Van Buren's] contemporaries," 185-?, MVB to Abraham Van Buren, May 31, 1820, MVB to Peter I. Hoes, Oct. 17, 1822, VBP. Butler wrote the description of the law office in a letter to Jesse Hoyt, June 24, 1820, Mackenzie, *Van Buren*, p. 165.

1812 established his reputation. In 1818, when Marcy was removed from office for publishing a strong anti-Clintonian article, he moved rapidly into the Bucktail inner circle. When Clinton threatened to sue the *Albany Argus* that year for a particularly sharp attack, Marcy attended the Bucktail meeting that discussed how to respond. In December 1820, Marcy secretly helped Van Buren with his pamphlet supporting Rufus King for senator, and he was the obvious choice for adjutant general of the militia in 1821 and comptroller in 1823. Marcy's sense of humor, his ability to write clear prose, and his attention to detail all made him an invaluable stand-in when Van Buren was in Washington.[53]

In the early years of the Regency Van Buren leaned heavily on several others. Samuel A. Talcott first came to his attention by making political surveys of Oneida and Oswego counties. By 1821, the brilliant but erratic Talcott had become attorney general. Another lawyer, Roger Skinner, joined the Regency because he felt such personal hostility toward DeWitt Clinton. Benjamin Knower, an Albany hat maker, brought his talents in business to the service of the Regency, and the marriage of Knower's daughter Cornelia and Marcy in 1824 united two of the leading families in the organization.[54]

Later in the 1820s, younger men moved to the fore. Like Van Buren, Benjamin Butler had been born the son of a tavern keeper in Kinderhook. Butler, who was attorney general of Albany County, was content to remain in Albany while his partner advanced his political career in Washington. When Van Buren needed something done in Albany, he often called on Butler. In 1824, for example, when he wanted the legislature to nominate William Harris Crawford for President, Van Buren told Butler to "get some of the most prudent and confidential men together at your house and read them this letter." In a few days

[53] Brockway, *Fifty Years in Journalism*, p. 43; Spencer, *Victor and the Spoils*, pp. 1-33, 111, 221; Weed, *Autobiography*, p. 67; Goldstein, "Albany Regency," pp. viii, 6; Remini, "Early Political Career of Van Buren," p. 328; Remini, "Albany Regency," p. 342.

[54] For Talcott, see *Autobiography*, pp. 173-176; Talcott to MVB, Mar. 31, 1819, April 15, 1820, VBP; Weed, *Autobiography*, p. 103. For Skinner, see *Autobiography*, pp. 103, 144; Skinner to MVB, Feb. 15, Dec. 30, 1823, Dec. 1, Dec. 24, 1824, VBP. For Knower, see Spencer, *Victor and the Spoils*, pp. 28, 38-39, 42-44, 50, 57-58. In nine of the major political crises faced by the Regency, 1817-1824, Van Buren was involved in all nine, Marcy in at least five, Talcott, Skinner and Knower in at least four. In their descriptions of the Regency, Thurlow Weed, De Alva Alexander, Dixon Ryan Fox, Robert V. Remini, and Kalman Goldstein all agree that Marcy was in the inner circle in the early years. Four of the writers list Talcott, three Knower, but only two mention Skinner. Weed, *Autobiography*, p. 103; Alexander, *Political History*, I, 294; Fox, *Decline of Aristocracy*, pp. 281-284; Remini, "Albany Regency," p. 342; Goldstein, "Albany Regency," pp. 5-8.

Butler assembled Marcy, Knower, Talcott, Skinner, and a few others to see what could be done. At Butler's funeral in 1859, Van Buren declared that he could never forget the "pale, refined and intellectual cast" of his friend's face.[55]

The self-effacing Butler found a kindred soul in Silas Wright, who was born in 1795—the same year as Butler—in Amherst, Massachusetts. Like many of his contemporaries, Wright taught school to pay his way through Middlebury College, from which he graduated in 1815. Four years later he was admitted to the bar in New York State, and began to practice in Canton, near the St. Lawrence River. Rapidly accepted by the Regency, Wright was soon appointed surrogate for St. Lawrence County by Skinner's council of appointment. Wright served in the state senate from 1824 to 1827, then moved on to the United States House of Representatives. After an unbroken career as comptroller, United States senator, and governor, he retired in 1846 and died in Canton in 1847. Like Butler, Wright was honest and unselfish, ever willing to subordinate personal interests to those of the Regency, but like the unfortunate Skinner, he drank too heavily for his own good. In a tribute Van Buren wrote that the "close relations" between himself and Wright were never thoroughly appreciated. Not one single occasion, he said, ever "disturbed . . . the calm confidence of my feelings towards him"; nor did Wright's "respect and esteem" for Van Buren ever waver. Van Buren deferred to Wright's judgment and was never "tempted to regard [himself] as superior" to Wright. According to Van Buren, Wright "had no superior in the sincerity, simplicity, and strength of his public and private virtues, and in that important attribute of a truly admirable statesman, perfect disinterestedness—he stood above any man I ever knew."[56]

Another young figure in the Regency was Edwin Croswell, the editor of the *Albany Argus*. In 1820, Van Buren had arranged to have the *Argus* sold to Moses I. Cantine and Isaac Leake. When Cantine died in 1823, the Regency brought in Croswell, who was editing a newspaper in Catskill, New York. The quiet and studious Croswell was an immediate success and within a year had bought out Leake, taken over the *Argus*, and assumed the role of state printer. According to the Whig politician Thurlow Weed, the Regency "found in Mr. Cros-

---

[55] William D. Driscoll, "Benjamin F. Butler: Lawyer and Regency Politician" (Doctoral dissertation, Fordham University, 1965); MVB to Butler, Feb. 17, 1824, Butler to MVB, Mar. 27, 1824, VBP; *Proceedings and Addresses on the Occasion of the Death of Benjamin F. Butler of New York* (New York, 1859), p. 1.

[56] The best treatment of Wright is in John A. Garraty, *Silas Wright* (New York, 1949). For Van Buren's tribute, see *Autobiography*, p. 728.

well . . . sound judgment, untiring energy, great devotion, and rare ability."[57]

Two other men—one in Albany, the other in New York City—rounded out the Regency. The tiny, dark-complected Azariah Flagg was born in Vermont, worked his way through college, and moved to New York, where he made a name for himself in the War of 1812. After editing the *Plattsburgh Republican*, Flagg was elected to the state assembly in 1823, and named secretary of state in 1826. In the 1830s, Flagg and Marcy ran the Regency in Albany while Wright and Van Buren were busy in Washington. In New York City the Regency was ably represented by Churchill C. Cambreleng, who had moved to the city from North Carolina. Arriving in 1802, a year after Van Buren, he soon established himself as a successful merchant and worked for a while with John Jacob Astor. A congressman from 1821 to 1839, Cambreleng became well-known as an advocate of low tariffs and as spokesman for the Regency. Short, stocky, earthy, and cynical, he expected the worst of human beings and loved to report the latest gossip to eager listeners such as Van Buren.[58]

Although collectively the Albany Regency enjoyed enormous success, there were no extraordinary figures, no one with the commanding presence of an Alexander Hamilton or a DeWitt Clinton. Physically they were a rather drab lot, ranging from the small Van Buren, Flagg and Croswell to the stout, middle-sized Marcy and Wright. The men were not particularly young or precocious. Butler, Croswell and Wright were, to be sure, in their twenties when the Regency began, but they themselves did not take command until 1830, when the average age of the seven top members of the Regency was thirty-eight years. There were no wealthy aristocrats, no Van Rensselaers or Livingstons. Nor could they boast that they had risen from rags to riches. Descended from simple yeoman stock, they grew up as Van Buren did, not in poverty, but in moderate circumstances. Some were sons of tavern keepers, some had taught to pay their way through college, some had lived on farms. Like many Americans, the members of the Regency

---

[57] For the sale of the *Argus* to Cantine and Leake, see Leake to MVB, May 28, 1820, Peter I. Hoes to Van Buren, July 29, 1820, MVB to Hoes, Aug. 5, 1820, Mordecai Noah to MVB, Dec. 29, 1820, Feb. 15, 1821, VBP; *Argus*, Aug. 18, 1820. For the death of Cantine and the hiring of Croswell, see MVB to Jesse Hoyt, Jan. 31, 1823, Mordecai Noah to Hoyt, Feb. 23, 1823, Mackenzie, *Van Buren*, pp. 190-192; Roger Skinner to MVB, Feb. 15, 1823, VBP; Weed, *Autobiography*, p. 8.

[58] For Flagg, see Brockway, *Fifty Years of Journalism*, p. 44; Spencer, *Victor and the Spoils*, pp. 39-40; Flagg to Wright, Nov. 28, 1823, Flagg-Wright Correspondence; Mordecai Noah to Flagg, Jan. 18, 1824, Flagg Papers; Flagg to Jesse Hoyt, Jan. 11, 1824, Mackenzie, *Van Buren*, p. 173. For Cambreleng, see Cambreleng to MVB, Jan. 1, 1829, VBP.

took advantage of the new opportunities to move up in society, becoming as James Gordon Bennett observed, "capitalists—land agents, speculators, bankers, caterers, brokers." And as they moved up, they moved from place to place. Like many other New Yorkers, Marcy, Knower, Wright, and Flagg started in New England. They were representative middle-class Americans; they were the "plain Republicans of the north" that Andrew Jackson would later claim as his own.[59]

These were practical, cautious, moderate men, who made a virtue of planning ahead. Whether it was Van Buren estimating his future worth, or Wright calling a meeting to get advice on how to act in the Senate, or Marcy sending an advance copy of a speech to Van Buren for approval, they left little to chance. They were not bound by rigid doctrines, but were willing to compromise to reach carefully selected goals. At the convention in 1821 Van Buren compromised time and again in order to gain his political victories. And in winning, the Regency men were willing to hold back and not destroy the opposition. Van Buren, for example, had no intention of taking the jobs of Federalist judges at the convention, and many members of the Regency were on intimate terms with their political rival Thurlow Weed. They sought office, but not complete domination; they were ambitious, but not controlled by ambition. Van Buren, the most intent on success, did raise himself from fence-viewer to President, but Butler and Flagg chose to spend most of their lives in Albany, and Wright turned down the vice presidency when it was offered to him. The Regency were men under control.

Above all they were profoundly loyal to each other, sociable and "true to their friends," said Bennett. "Their females kiss each other when they meet—their men shake each other heartily by the hand—they dine, or drink, or pray, or take snuff . . . in each other's company." In a letter to Andrew Jackson a few years later, Van Buren demonstrated how the Regency operated. He wrote in haste, he said, because he had been so "very busy with [his] friends." He had sounded out Butler on a post in Washington, and had had talks with Marcy and his friend Enos T. Throop. In a postscript he added that he had discussed all matters "*in confidence*, with my friends Marcy, Wright, Flagg, Croswell, and Butler and they concur[red] fully."[60]

Although the Regency was based on the spoils system, its leaders were not corrupt. As men in tune with a modernizing political system, they realized that political parties needed machinery and that money

[59] James Gordon Bennett, Diary of a Journey through New York [June 12-Aug. 18, 1831], July 28, 1831, NYPL.

[60] Bennett, Diary, July 28, 1831; MVB to Andrew Jackson, Nov. 29, 1832, *Autobiography*, p. 598.

and jobs fueled such machinery. Their motives in distributing jobs to their friends were political not personal. Privately the members of the Regency were old-fashioned men with simple tastes, who did not succumb to the temptations that accompanied success. Van Buren liked good wines, comfortable rooms, stylish clothes, but he did not seek luxurious living and he did not become wealthy on party money. His idea of a good time was a quiet tour of the Hudson Valley with his good friend Washington Irving. Marcy entertained well and liked fine furniture, but he was happiest when reading in solitude. Croswell and Flagg had scholarly interests and enjoyed good books. Butler and Wright had a puritanical strain that made them suspicious of great wealth. The day before Wright died he was busy on his farm digging a ditch. Thurlow Weed, who fought the Regency but sympathized with its methods, summed it up best when he wrote that he had never known a body of men who "possessed so much power and used it so well"; "they were men of great ability, great industry, indomitable courage, and strict personal integrity."[61]

The Regency revolutionized American politics, not only by creating a new type of political machine, but also by popularizing a new theory of political parties. In the eighteenth century Americans had disapproved of political parties because they believed that parties, or factions as they were called, were led by selfish men interested only in their own personal welfare. According to the founding fathers the ideal society was one in which unity and harmony prevailed. If parties existed, there must be something wrong with society. James Madison in Federalist Number 10 and George Washington in his Farewell Address agreed on what Washington called "the baneful effects of the Spirit of Party." Little wonder that Americans in the 1790s were alarmed when Federalists and Republicans demonstrated that the spirit of party was flourishing. One reason for the collapse of the two-party system during the Era of Good Feelings was the belief that these early parties had been harmful to the new republic.[62]

The Regency changed all that by developing a new political theory,

[61] Spencer, *Victor and the Spoils*, pp. 108-111, 145-146, 184, 283; Weed, *Autobiography*, pp. 8, 103; Shepard, *Van Buren*, p. 112. Lee Benson exaggerates the degree to which members of the Regency made money. Benson, *Concept of Jacksonian Democracy*, pp. 65-70.

[62] There has been a good deal written about the evolution of the American concept of political parties. I have drawn heavily on Bernard Bailyn, *The Origins of American Politics* (New York, 1967), especially pp. 36-37, 125-130; Gordon S. Wood, *The Creation of the American Republic 1776-1787* (Chapel Hill, 1969), especially pp. 53-65; Hofstadter, *Idea of a Party System*, ch. 1, ch. 2; Michael Wallace, "Changing Concepts of Party in the United States: New York 1815-1828," *American Historical Review*, 74 (1968), 453-491.

a theory that considered parties a positive good rather than a menace to society. According to the doctrine, political parties were democratic organizations that enabled the people to take part in government. More than that, political parties protected the state against selfish individuals by subordinating the individual to the will of the party. Van Buren summed up the theory in his autobiography: "All men of sense know," he said, "that political parties are inseparable from free governments," that the "disposition to abuse power . . . can by no other means be more effectually checked." Silas Wright best expressed the ideal of the loyal party man; he intended, he said, to "live up to what [he understood] to be the course of a political party man." He wanted nothing that would not serve "the best interests of the great republican party [of New York]."[63]

The Regency's new theory of party was premised on a new concept of society—one based not on consensus but on unavoidable conflict. In such a society, said the *Argus*, with so many different "interests," parties provided the essential "bond of national union." Without them "there would arise local jealousies and geographical distinctions, which would array the north against the south," and destroy "the integrity of the republic." Moreover, said the *Argus*, parties checked "the passions, the ambition, and the usurpations of individuals."[64]

Inspired by this new vision of party the members of the Regency talked openly about their political aspirations. When Van Buren left New York in 1821, his ambition was to restore "the old democratic party." Some years later William L. Marcy made the classic statement on partisan politics by boasting that the Regency saw "nothing wrong in the rule, that to the victor belong the spoils of the enemy." Van Buren devoted several of his waning years to writing his own *Inquiry into the Origin and Course of Political Parties in the United States*. And when Nathaniel Beverley Tucker wrote his anti-Van Buren novel in 1836, Tucker called it *The Partisan Leader*. Van Buren and the Regency had become synonymous with partisanship and political parties.[65]

While Van Buren was building the Regency, similar organizations were being formed in Virginia, Tennessee, and New Hampshire. Members of the Roane family and Thomas Ritchie, the editor of the *Richmond Enquirer*, led the way in Virginia with the Richmond Junto,

[63] Wallace, "Changing Concepts of Party"; *Autobiography*, p. 125; Wright to MVB, Dec. 17, 1828, VBP.

[64] *Argus*, Jan. 29, 1822, Oct. 8, 1824.

[65] MVB to Charles Dudley, Jan. 10, 1822, Bonney, *Historical Gleanings*, I, 382; *Register of Debates in Congress*, 21st Congress, 1st session (1831-1832), 1325-1327; Nathaniel Beverley Tucker, *The Partisan Leader* (1836; reprint, Chapel Hill, 1971).

which was fully in place by 1816. In Tennessee a political faction controlled by the wealthy banker and landowner John Overton of Nashville, outmaneuvered a rival faction by exploiting the popularity of Andrew Jackson after his triumphs over the British and the Indians. Overton's Nashville Junto became even stronger when it arranged to have the Tennessee legislature nominate Jackson for President in 1822. Isaac Hill began to build his own party in New Hampshire during the war of 1812, but his Concord Regency was not effective until he merged forces with former governor Levi Woodbury in 1825.

The four organizations had much in common. Each was controlled by a small elite and dominated by a single leader. Martin Van Buren, Thomas Ritchie, John Overton, and Isaac Hill all became prominent by the end of the War of 1812, and by 1828 were the leaders of four of the strongest state Democratic parties in the land. They differed greatly in personality and physical appearance. Tall, slender and elegant, "Father" Ritchie, as he was called, was the opposite of Van Buren. Born and married into a socially superior family, and better educated, Ritchie was never an outsider like Van Buren. He moved easily in society and became famous for his editorials, his after-dinner toasts and his performance on the dance floor. Overton was no outsider either. He had been a partner of Andrew Jackson in a number of land deals and was considered the wealthiest man in Tennessee. Even more important, he had the ability and the presence to be considered Jackson's equal—a status few men achieved. Hill, at the other extreme, was even more of an outsider than Van Buren. Hill was tiny, his family was poor, his father was insane, and he himself suffered an injury in his childhood that left him lame for life. A harsh, bitter man with a vindictive pen, Hill made a mark with his savage editorials in the *New-Hampshire Patriot*. The single quality that united these men was their consummate political skill.

The four political machines had other similarities. Each depended on a partisan newspaper. Each called itself Republican and professed loyalty to the Jeffersonian ideals of state rights and limited government, but none of them hesitated to enlist Federalists. Lawyers, bankers, editors, and men of yeoman stock were prominent in all four; planters and men of wealth only in the two southern groups. Each quickly adopted techniques that were still employed by political parties a century later. All four joined together to help elect Andrew Jackson President in 1828. John C. Calhoun observed enviously as early as 1823, that there was a "vital connection" between the Albany Regency and the Richmond Junto. By 1828, the connection had expanded to include all four organizations and Calhoun's in South Carolina as well.

But the surface similarities hid substantial differences. Of the four only the Albany and Concord regencies were able to control patronage sufficiently to build up local organizations throughout their states. As a result only those two were able to dominate state politics for a sustained period of time. Hill's regency was more successful in this regard than Van Buren's. Between 1828 and 1846, the Concord Regency controlled the governor and one of the United States senators every year, and controlled the second senator in all but five of those years. The Albany Regency did well, but it surrendered the governorship four years out of seventeen and could control only one of the two senators. The southern juntos did less well. Ritchie and his men rarely approved of the governor of Virginia and never named more than one senator. The Nashville Junto named both senators during most of Andrew Jackson's administrations but rarely the governor. By the end of Jackson's term of office the issues of banking and the tariff had split the Nashville Junto into two groups.

Of the four leaders only Hill and Van Buren headed organizations that served as the forerunners of modern political machines. Theirs were the only regimes that fully developed the modern techniques of caucuses, patronage and party press. The Nashville Junto soon fell prey to old-fashioned factionalism. The Richmond Junto used the modern techniques but also depended on such old-fashioned tactics as family alliances, intermarriage, and control of the state courts. In some ways Concord outstripped Albany, but not in all. Through their speeches and writing, only Van Buren and his friends were able to express their new faith in party politics in a coherent body of work. Only Albany had Van Buren, who came to symbolize the new system of politics. For a while at least his name was a household word; the names of Ritchie, Overton and Hill were not. And, finally, only the Albany Regency was able to exercise great power in national politics over a long period of time.[66]

[66] For the Richmond Junto, see Harry Ammon, "The Richmond Junto, 1800-1824," Joseph H. Harrison, Jr., "Oligarchs and Democrats: the Richmond Junto," *Virginia Magazine of History and Biography*, 63 (1955), 395-419; 78 (April 1970), 184-198; Charles H. Ambler, *Thomas Ritchie: a Study in Virginia Politics* (Richmond, 1913). For the Concord Regency, see Cole, *Jacksonian Democracy in New Hampshire*. For the Nashville Junto, see Charles Sellers, "Banking and Politics in Jackson's Tennessee, 1817-1827," *Mississippi Valley Historical Review*, 41 (June 1954), 61-84; Sellers, "Jackson Men with Feet of Clay," *American Historical Review*, 42 (April 1957), 537-551; Sellers, *James K. Polk Jacksonian 1795-1843* (Princeton, 1957), pp. 68-70, 135-137; Robert V. Remini, *Andrew Jackson and the Course of American Freedom 1822-1832* (New York, 1981), pp. 42-50. See also Calhoun to Samuel L. Gouverneur, Nov. 9, 1823, Samuel L. Gouverneur Papers, NYPL.

· II ·
NATIONAL POLITICIAN
1821-1829

2. Martin Van Buren c. 1828, after an engraving by H. W. Smith

· 4 ·

REVIVING THE OLD CONTEST

While the Regency was taking command in New York, Martin Van Buren was embarking on a new career as United States senator. His shift of interest from state to national politics paralleled a similar change across the land, where problems took on a national character and national affairs took precedence over local. It was a time when debate over the first great set of national problems dominated politics: the tariff, internal improvements, banking, and slavery. In the wake of the War of 1812 and the modernizing trend within the country, the United States Congress became a forum where large federal issues were discussed. With the rise of these national issues, national elections and national political parties began to surpass state elections and state parties in importance. As a senator during the 1820s Van Buren had to adjust to these developments: he had to take a stand on the issues and to play a role in national as well as state politics. In doing so he was able to build a national party as skillfully as he had built the Regency in New York.

America was changing dramatically as Van Buren began his senatorial career. A transportation revolution stimulated American commerce as the steamboat, which had taken command on the Hudson, now commanded the Ohio, the Mississippi and the Atlantic as well. New technology revolutionized the nation's economy. The cotton gin and steel plow enabled farmers to specialize and produce greater crops than before, while textile mills springing up on the streams of New England and New York allowed manufacturing to start competing with agriculture and commerce for economic leadership. The rise of banks and the growth of cities furthered the transformation of the economy.

And the society was undergoing transformation also. By 1820, New York City had passed one hundred thousand in population and was on its way to a million. Indian defeats before and during the War of 1812 opened the Old Northwest and the Southwest, initiating a westward movement that was approaching the Mississippi. Americans by the thousands moved westward or to the city to seek the new opportunities of an expanding economy. New extremes of wealth and poverty unheard of in 1800 reflected a new class structure with wealthy bankers and manufacturers at one end of the scale and poor workers at the other. America was still basically an agrarian society, but no longer the simple society into which Van Buren's generation had been born.

Van Buren and his peers were well aware that they were a new generation facing a new world. The visit of Lafayette and the laying of the cornerstone of the Bunker Hill monument in 1825 reminded Americans that half a century had passed since the Revolution. The passing of the founding fathers caught the attention of the nation. The remarkable coincidence of the deaths of Jefferson and Adams on the Fourth of July 1826, brought home the fact that most of the old heroes were gone. In Albany the Regency's *Argus* was wreathed in black; a few weeks later it carried a table of the deaths of the signers of the Declaration of Independence.

The new generation greeted its new world with a mixture of anxiety and anticipation. Fires, steamboat explosions and urban disasters confirmed the fears of many that the new industrial order was inferior to the old agrarianism. Some feared that political leaders in the new democratic society would not be able to cope with the new problems. In 1828, a newspaper in Albany pointed out that the nation could no longer count on the services of the "Revolutionary worthies," and would have to elect its next President "from a later and less worthy generation." In Richmond, the *Enquirer*, which devoted many issues to the death of Jefferson, warned that the passing of the Revolutionary generation would open an era of fierce political warfare, but elsewhere, the new generation greeted the opportunities and challenges of the new world enthusiastically without looking back. The great majority of Americans—Van Buren and his Regency associates among them— retained their reverence for the past while building the new political and economic institutions that the new society demanded.[1]

For the states of Virginia and New York the decade of the 1820s was particularly decisive because during those years the Old Dominion was declining both economically and politically, while the Empire State's power was increasing at a rapid rate. Between 1817 and 1829 land values in Virginia fell from $206,000,000 to $90,000,000, and exports dropped from $9,000,000 to $3,000,000. "Virginia is rapidly sinking in the scale of the Union," wailed a correspondent in the *Richmond Enquirer*. Another commented sadly on the "poverty" of

---

[1] Fred Somkin, *Unquiet Eagle: Memory and Desire in the Idea of American Freedom, 1815-1860* (Ithaca, 1967); Miller, *Birth of Modern America*; Alfred D. Chandler, *Visible Hand; the Managerial Revolution in American Business* (Cambridge, Mass., 1977); *Argus*, July 10, Aug. 14, 1826; *Richmond Enquirer*, July 7, July 11, July 14, July 18, 1826, June 12, 1827; *Albany Morning Chronicle*, Jan. 19, 1828.

the once rich state. When the Virginia constitutional convention gathered in 1829, fear of a slave revolt increased the anxiety that gripped the delegates.[2]

Both Virginians and New Yorkers agreed that the Empire State was another story. Advocates of change in Virginia used New York as an example of a state that had solved its transportation problem. The *Albany Argus* spoke for many New Yorkers when it boasted in 1823 that the prosperity of New York was an "envied spectacle." Demographic and economic statistics confirmed these impressionistic views. In 1790, Virginia was the largest state in the Union with over twice as many people as New York; by 1820, New York had surged ahead and ranked first. By 1825, customs receipts in New York were almost $16,000,000 out of total United States treasury receipts of less than $27,000,000; and on October 26 that year, cannon roared all across New York as the first barge on the Erie Canal prepared to depart from Buffalo. When the boat finally reached New York City, speakers pointed out to the nation that New Yorkers had "subdued the wilderness of the west."[3]

But New Yorkers were not satisfied that they had received the political rewards their economic gains deserved. One convention in New York complained that for thirty-six out of forty years Virginia had supplied the United States with Presidents, even though New York contributed more than one-third of the revenues of the United States. John A. Dix, who would later join the Regency, held similar views while he was serving in the army in Washington, D.C., in the early 1820s. Dix, who was "astonished at the decay" in Virginia, reported that the land was "exhausted," the farming "miserable," and the state "on the wane." He considered it "humiliating" that the North, even though superior in resources, still wielded less political influence. In describing a match race between two horses, one owned by New Yorkers and the other by Virginians, Dix expressed the hostility that existed between the two states. "My only solicitude," Dix wrote, "is

[2] Robert P. Sutton, "Nostalgia, Pessimism and Malaise: the Doomed Aristocrat in Late-Jeffersonian Virginia," *Virginia Magazine of History and Biography*, 76 (Jan. 1968), 41-55; *Richmond Enquirer*, Mar. 25, Oct. 11, 1825, Mar. 1, April 29, 1828; John Floyd to Claiborne W. Gooch, Feb. 16, 1825, Gooch Family Papers, UVL.

[3] For population figures, see Tucker, *Progress of the United States*, p. 57. In 1790, the population of Virginia was 748,308; New York 340,120. In 1820, Virginia had 1,065,379 people, New York 1,372,812. Statistics on treasury receipts are to be found in John H. French, *Gazetteer of the State of New York* (Syracuse, 1860; reprint, 1969), p. 111. See also *Argus*, April 15, 1823. For a description of the opening of the Erie Canal, see *ibid.*, Oct. 4, Oct. 18, Oct. 24, Oct. 28, Nov. 1, Nov. 5, Nov. 7, Nov. 8, 1825.

that these consummate braggadocios from Virginia may be put down." Dix was rewarded when the Virginia horse came up lame and then again when a substitute was beaten by the New York horse. "Never," he gloated "was boasting more effectually humbled." Virginia, he added, had "received a useful lesson from the North." Dix could only hope that the Old Dominion would receive a similar lesson in the field of politics.[4]

Van Buren the senator was influenced by the new issues, the new society and his role in the new generation; and like Dix he sought to increase the political role of New York. But unlike Dix Van Buren felt no hostility toward Virginians and other Southerners. As the son of a slaveowner he had demonstrated his sympathy for the South in the Missouri controversy; and as a dedicated Jeffersonian he shared many of the republican beliefs of Virginians and Carolinians. The key to his career as senator is the interaction of his adjustment to the new America and his empathy for the republican traditions of the South.

VAN BUREN left for Washington with two goals. Having restored the two-party system in New York, he now sought to do the same at the national level. With his nostalgic memories of the party battles of the 1790s and his deep faith in political parties, Van Buren thought it was time to end the blurring of party lines that had characterized the Era of Good Feelings. He agreed with the *Albany Argus*, which denounced what it called "the Utopian notion of . . . the amalgamation of all parties." On leaving New York, according to Charlemagne Tower, Van Buren pointedly remarked that he planned to "revive the old contest between the federals and the anti-federals and build up a party for himself." He yearned to restore the old Jeffersonian alliance of New York and Virginia. Soon after reaching Washington, in the midst of the fight over the Albany postmastership, he wrote that this was "the proper moment" to begin a "resuscitation of the old democratic party."[5]

[4] "Address to the Electors of Montgomery County on Behalf of the People's Ticket," NYPL, quoted in Kass, *Politics in New York State*, p. 70. John A. Dix to Dr. George Cheyne Shattuck, April 20, 1820, Nov. 20, 1822, "Letters from John Adams Dix to Dr. George Cheyne Shattuck, 1816-1848," Massachusetts Historical Society, *Proceedings*, 50 (1916-1917), 139-142, New Yorkers were correct in their perception that they had not received their just political rewards. Between 1789 and 1809, Virginians had held the most important United States political positions for 72 man-years; New Yorkers, only 24 man-years. In the 20 years that followed (1809-1829), Virginians held the same posts for 66 man-years; New Yorkers, only 28 man-years.

[5] Charlemagne Tower MS diary, April 1831, CUL; MVB to Charles Dudley, Jan. 10, 1822, Bonney, *Historical Gleanings*, I, 382-384; MVB to John King, Feb. 18, 1822, King Papers; *Argus*, Jan. 29, 1822, Oct. 8, 1824.

In order to lead such a party Van Buren knew that he would have to establish his position on the national issues. His second goal was to find answers that would satisfy enough sections and enough interests to pull a new party together. In particular, he would have to appeal to the republican traditions of the old South. Although he had gained a reputation as a leading northern Republican, his state career had given him little opportunity to demonstrate how he stood on the rights of the states and the role of the central government. He was willing to respond to change, but he knew that he must also maintain some of the traditions of the earlier generation. As he groped for just the right formula, Van Buren found it difficult to be consistent because political often outweighed ideological considerations.

Because of his goals and his political reputation, Van Buren attracted attention at the opening of the Seventeenth Congress in December 1821. The observant William Plumer, Jr., of New Hampshire, commented shortly after Van Buren's arrival that the New York senator was "perhaps the greatest manager" in the city. Congressman Henry Warfield of Maryland, who was less generous, called Van Buren "a pleasant good tempered facetious little fellow," who "look[ed] quite through the Deeds of men." Warfield was afraid to trust Van Buren because he was so "subtle and intriguing." But such voices were in the minority. Partly because of his reputation and partly because the Senate lacked strong leadership at the time Van Buren became a prominent senator from the very start. In a senate that boasted no one more famous than the aging Nathaniel Macon or the untried Thomas Hart Benton of Missouri, the new senator from New York was hard to ignore.[6]

Surrounded by a host of new and old friends Van Buren enjoyed himself immensely in Washington society. On several occasions he joined festive theater parties, on another he traveled to Philadelphia to drink wine with Nicholas Biddle, president of the Bank of the United States. Since Van Buren was a dashing widower in a new environment, rumors frequently linked him with eligible young women. Congressman Louis McLane of Delaware, filled his letters home with stories of Van Buren's flirtations. Tongues began to wag when Thomas Jefferson's granddaughter, Ellen Wayles Randolph, who was seen often with the blond Van Buren, asked the Marine Band at a dress ball to play "The Yellow-haired Laddie." Van Buren had only to set foot in Virginia and word spread that he was about to marry Miss Randolph

<hr>

[6] William Plumer, Jr., to William Plumer, Jan. 3, 1822, Everett S. Brown, ed., *The Missouri Compromises and Presidential Politics 1820-1825 from the Letters of William Plumer, Junior* (St. Louis, 1926), p. 74; Henry R. Warfield to Henry Clay, May 30, 1822, Clay, *Papers*, III, 210-211.

or one of her sisters. Benjamin Butler's wife Harriet chided Van Buren for flirting in Washington while sending messages to two women in Albany and not discouraging a third woman from wearing the "emblematic color" for him. The nosy Harriet asked Van Buren whether she should warn a certain "Elvira the fair" that there was no chance for her. When Churchill C. Cambreleng spread the tale that Van Buren was about to marry "Mrs. O. L.," Van Buren called him a "rogue" for putting him in a "peck of trouble."[7]

Van Buren did much of his flirting by mail. "Nothing serves so well," he wrote Harriet Butler, "to season the . . . perpetual dissipation of this Sodom as an occasional letter from a kind hearted & sensible female friend." He told one woman that he hoped he deserved "half of the compliments" that she had given him. "Your letter," he wrote, "has been to me a green shoot in the midst of a desert of political cares." Van Buren liked "to hear the gossip of the female world . . . for those small concerns [are] among the real comforts of life." Sometimes a testy husband interfered. Louis McLane got so tired of the steady flow of letters between his wife Catherine and Van Buren, that he jealously accused Van Buren of being "morally licentious." After his correspondence with a certain Mrs. Taylor broke down, Van Buren was afraid that "her *little* husband [had] interdicted it." Van Buren made up with the husbands, and went right on exchanging letters.[8] Family cares occasionally distracted Van Buren from his social life, as for example when son John spent too much money while attending Yale, but friends or relatives were usually quick to help.[9]

In choosing his political messmates, Van Buren was drawn toward the upper class. After spending the first few weeks in Washington at Strother's Hotel on Pennsylvania Avenue with several New York congressmen, he soon moved out to Peck's Hotel in Georgetown, where he lived with such wealthy and elegant members of Congress as senior

[7] Mrs. Samuel Harrison Smith, *The First Forty Years of Washington Society*, ed. Gaillard Hunt (1906; reprint, New York, 1965), p. 170; MVB to Biddle, Dec. 15, 1826, Biddle to MVB, Dec. 19, 1826, Nicholas Biddle Papers, LC; John A. Munroe, *Louis McLane: Federalist and Jacksonian* (New Brunswick, 1973), pp. 161, 172; Rufus King to John King, Jan. 19, 1822, King Papers; Ambrose Spencer to MVB, Mar. 28, 1822, Ulshoeffer to MVB, April 2, 1822, MVB to Cambreleng, Dec. 9, 1828, VBP; Mrs. Benjamin Butler to MVB, Jan. 25, 1826, Benjamin F. Butler Papers, NYSL.

[8] MVB to Mrs. Benjamin Butler, April 12, 1826, Butler Papers, NYSL; MVB to Mrs. William C. Rives, Jan. 9, Feb. 21, 1829, William C. Rives Papers, LC; Munroe, *Louis McLane*, pp. 171-172.

[9] Hunt, *Biographical Sketch Book*, p. 51; MVB to John Van Buren, Jan. 19, 1826, Sept. 3, 1830, VBP; John Van Buren to Jesse Hoyt, Nov. 28, 1827, Nov. 13, 1828, Mackenzie, *Van Buren*, pp. 202, 205.

senator Rufus King and Congressman Stephen Van Rensselaer of New York, Harrison Gray Otis and Benjamin Gorham of Massachusetts, Fenton Mercer and Andrew Stevenson of Virginia, Henry Warfield and Louis McLane. Half of his new messmates had Federalist backgrounds; all but one were college educated. Although Van Buren later insisted that he made the shift because he found "the mess at Washington too gay," the reason was more likely that he welcomed the opportunity to live with King and his prominent friends. Michael Ulshoeffer of the Regency warned Van Buren that he was being criticized for living with "aristocratic republicans," and for being "wedded to Mr. King." Van Buren did defer to King, who assigned rooms to the members of the mess. After leaning on the aristocratic Clinton and Spencer in rising to power in New York, Van Buren used another set of aristocrats to climb the ladder in the Capital.[10]

It was also significant both then and later that many of Van Buren's friends, including six of his messmates, were Southerners. Within a few hours of his arrival in Washington in 1821, the new senator received a call from Secretary of War John C. Calhoun. Van Buren considered Calhoun a "fascinating man," and spent many evenings with him, talking and playing cards. Congressman John Randolph also impressed Van Buren as "a most extraordinary man [who] could launch imputations by a look, a shake of his long finger, or a shrug of his shoulders." Randolph, who had expected to dislike Van Buren, found himself enjoying the new senator's company. The two spent much time together, often riding horseback on the roads about Washington.[11]

Among Van Buren's southern friends were two young men who would be important in the next generation. From the moment he arrived in Washington, Van Buren became an intimate companion of Louis McLane, who was about his own age. The two congressmen were accustomed to bantering with each other and when separated exchanged amusing letters. In the spring of 1823, for example, McLane

---

[10] Robert V. Remini suggests that Van Buren probably moved to Georgetown because it was less expensive, but the list of messmates convinces me that Van Buren had other motives. Robert V. Remini, *Martin Van Buren and the Making of the Democratic Party* (New York, 1951), p. 18. Judah Delano, *The Washington Directory* (Washington, D.C., 1822), pp. viii-xiv; Ulshoeffer to MVB, Feb. 17, 1822, VBP; MVB to King, Nov. 4, 1823, King Papers; *Autobiography*, pp. 574-576. Van Rensselaer, King, Otis, Gorham, McLane, and Warfield had been Federalists.

[11] Letters to and from Southerners are rare in the VBP at the LC until December 1821. From then until December 1828, there are at least fifty such letters. Elizabeth H. West, *Calendar of the Papers of Martin Van Buren* (Washington, D.C., 1910); *Autobiography*, pp. 205, 233, 429, 513.

scolded Van Buren for failing to visit the McLanes on his way home. In a letter to McLane's wife Catherine, Van Buren complained that her husband took unfair advantage of his seniority and popularity in the Congress, and contrasted McLane's boldness with Daniel Webster's caution. The other Southerner, William C. Rives of Virginia, came to the Congress two years after Van Buren. The two men shared similar views on state rights and presidential candidates, and were soon on close terms. Van Buren, who used his bachelorhood wisely and well, exchanged letters with Rives's wife Judith as often as he did with Catherine McLane.[12]

Another southern acquaintance of Van Buren was Andrew Jackson of Tennessee, who had been elected to the Senate in 1823 by the Tennessee legislature, a year after it had nominated him for President. Since Jackson was in Washington for only two of the seven years that Van Buren was senator and since the two men lived in different boardinghouses, they did not become close friends at that time; but they did at least have the opportunity to take the measure of each other. Jackson was able to judge the character of the notorious political manager from New York, while Van Buren was able to judge the political philosophy of the frontier hero. According to Van Buren, his "personal intercourse" with the general was "uniformly kind and courteous."[13]

ALTHOUGH Van Buren adjusted readily to Washington society, he showed signs of his old insecurity when he delivered his first speech in the Senate—on a land claim in Louisiana. After stumbling nervously for a few minutes, he "retreat[ed] with as good grace as possible [and] resumed [his] seat." But he soon regained his composure, got back on his feet and spoke for two hours. His initial embarrassment and the realization that he spoke too rapidly and too softly to be an effective orator convinced Van Buren to forgo speechmaking and resort to his old New York technique of working behind the scenes. Thanks to his skill, his reputation and the lack of competition, he rose rapidly and was soon chairman of the Judiciary Committee.[14]

---

[12] *Autobiography*, pp. 574-576, including McLane to MVB, April 30, 1823; MVB to Mrs. McLane, Feb. 6, 1825, Alexander Hamilton Papers, Hamilton-McLane Series, LC; MVB to Rufus King, Nov. 4, 1823, King Papers; Munroe, *Louis McLane*, pp. 128-129; MVB to Mrs. William C. Rives, Feb. 21, 1829, MVB to William C. Rives, May 5, 1829, Rives Papers, LC; Raymond C. Dingledine, "The Political Career of William Cabell Rives" (Doctoral dissertation, University of Virginia, 1947), pp. 88-91, 118.

[13] *Autobiography*, p. 233.

[14] Shepard, *Van Buren*, pp. 150-151; "Biography of Van Buren," *Argus Extra*, p.

Van Buren used his position in the Senate to defend the interests of New York and thereby strengthen his political base of power. As William Plumer, Jr., observed, Van Buren and the Bucktails had arrived in Washington "determined to make their great state felt" in national politics. Van Buren's unsuccessful effort to keep Solomon Van Rensselaer from becoming postmaster at Albany—and thus controlling a central patronage post—was aimed at helping the Regency. So was Van Buren's successful move to oust political rival, well-known Clintonian John W. Taylor, as speaker of the House of Representatives. Under instructions from Van Buren and the party caucus in Albany, the New York delegation in the House led the movement to unseat Taylor. When Southerners, who disliked Taylor for opposing slavery in Missouri, joined in, Taylor was replaced by Philip P. Barbour of Virginia.[15]

The new senator also sought to protect the Regency. A key clause in the customs bill of 1822 threatened the power of the port collector of New York, the kingpin of the Regency patronage system, by reducing his income from commissions by $4,000. Van Buren introduced an amendment that succeeded in restoring $2,000 of the proposed reduction. He also tried in vain to secure a federal grant of $1,500,000 for the Erie Canal.[16]

But in forming a new political party, Van Buren had to consider more than the interests of New York. He had to build a political reputation, not an easy task because during the Era of Good Feelings the old political and ideological terms had become badly confused. Supporters and opponents of President James Monroe both called themselves Republicans, and many Republicans supported nationalist policies that Republicans in 1800 would have opposed. After the War of 1812 the leading opponents of the nationalism of Monroe were the so-called "Radicals" of the North, including Van Buren and James Buchanan of Pennsylvania, and the "Old Republicans" of the South, led by Nathaniel Macon, John Randolph and John Taylor of Caroline County, Virginia. The Radicals did not share a consistent political

---

10; *Register of Debates*, 19th Congress, 1st session (1825-1826), 785; 20th Congress, 1st session (1827-1828), 203, 477. For Van Buren's first speech, see Van Buren to Benjamin Butler, Feb. 12, 1822, VBP; *Autobiography*, pp. 128-129.

[15] William Plumer, Jr., to William Plumer, Jan. 3, 1822, Brown, *Missouri Compromises*, p. 89. For the ouster of John W. Taylor as speaker, see MVB to John Van Ness Yates, Nov. 6, 1821, Martin Van Buren Papers, NYSL; Edward K. Spann, "The Souring of Good Feelings: John W. Taylor and the Speakership Election of 1821," *New York History*, 41 (1960), 379-399; Taylor to D. Ford, Jan. 18, 1822, Taylor Papers.

[16] *Annals of Congress*, 17th Congress, 1st Session (1821-1822), 26, 131-136, 184-204; Charles Dudley to Van Buren, Dec. 23, 1821, VBP.

ideology, but the Old Republicans were united in their opposition to national tariffs, national internal improvements and a national bank. Since Van Buren hoped to restore the Jeffersonian Republican party based on an alliance of North and South, he was anxious to develop close rapport with these Old Republicans. To do so he would have to oppose economic nationalism and support the concepts of state rights and strict construction of the Constitution.[17]

One of the first national issues facing Van Buren was slavery. The bill of 1822 organizing the territory of Florida, had one clause that imposed severe restrictions on the importation of slaves into the new territory. Although he joined his antislavery colleague Rufus King in supporting the clause, Van Buren was not a committed opponent of slavery. At the time of his vote he was still technically a slaveowner even though his slave Tom had run away eight years earlier. When Tom's whereabouts were finally discovered, Van Buren tried to sell the slave for $50. Van Buren pleased some Northerners by opposing the spread of slavery, while at the same time pleasing Southerners by defending slavery in the states where it existed.[18]

On the question of internal improvements Van Buren had difficulty establishing a reputation for strict construction of the Constitution. His first chances to vote on internal improvements came in 1822 and 1823, on bills to raise funds to repair the Cumberland Road. Old Republicans including Nathaniel Macon voted against the bills, but Van Buren voted yea with the majority. Although he justified his position on the grounds that the road needed repairing, Van Buren regretted his votes because they put him at odds with the South and undermined his claim that he was a strict-construction Republican.[19]

By 1824, Van Buren had staked out a position closer to that of the Old Republicans. On January 22 that year, he proposed a constitutional amendment preventing federal internal improvements unless the state involved gave permission and directed the work. A year later he sided with Macon twice, in voting against extending the Cumberland Road and against building the Chesapeake and Delaware Canal. In

[17] Norman Risjord, *The Old Republicans: Southern Conservatives in the Age of Jefferson* (New York, 1965), pp. 1-10, 162-177, 228-237, and passim.

[18] *Annals of Congress*, 17th Congress, 1st session (1821-1822), 275-277; A. G. Hammond to MVB, Dec. 23, 1824, VBP. I cannot agree with Richard W. Smith, who feels that Van Buren's vote against slavery in Florida proves that Van Buren was opposed to slavery. Smith, "Public Career of Van Buren in Connection with Slavery," pp. 97-98.

[19] *Annals of Congress*, 17th Congress, 1st session (1821-1822), 444; 2nd session (1822-1823), 84, 92; *Autobiography*, pp. 302-303; MVB, *Abolition of Slavery*, p. 15.

1826, he voted against two appropriations for the Cumberland Road, against bills for a Louisville and Portland Canal, a Baltimore-Philadelphia road, and a canal through the Dismal Swamp in Virginia. By this time a number of future Jacksonians, including Hugh L. White of Tennessee, and Levi Woodbury of New Hampshire, had joined Macon and Van Buren in opposing these projects. But proto-Jacksonians were not unanimous because Jackson himself, who was a staunch nationalist, voted for several of the bills on the grounds of military necessity.[20]

In 1826 and 1827, Van Buren went to great lengths to prove that the founding fathers had opposed internal improvements at federal expense. In a letter to James Madison, for example, Van Buren criticized one writer's "lame attempt to make out" that George Washington had favored internal improvements. A correspondent told Van Buren that Washington had insisted that the states construct all internal improvements themselves. Van Buren also received a letter from Alexander Hamilton's son John, who had found a statement by his father opposing canals without an amendment to the Constitution. Van Buren was not alone in his interpretation of the issue. In the winter of 1826-1827, representatives of both the northern Albany Regency and the southern Richmond Junto agreed with him that the federal government should not get involved in internal improvements.[21]

It was difficult for Van Buren to join Old Republicans in opposing the tariff because many interests in New York favored protection. Although New York City shippers supported a low tariff, farmers in the interior wanted stiff protection for raw wool and flax, and manufacturers backed protection for textiles. In his first session of Congress Van Buren presented a memorial from the American Society for the Encouragement of Domestic Manufactures asking for tariff protection. During the long debate over the tariff of 1824, Van Buren pleased many New Yorkers and other Northerners by voting to protect articles manufactured from flax or hemp. But he also sought to please low-

[20] *Annals of Congress*, 18th Congress, 1st session (1823-1824), 134-135; *Register of Debates*, 18th Congress, 2nd session (1824-1825), 666, 681; 19th Congress, 1st session (1825-1826), 20, 364, 619, 643, 718, 765; *Niles' Register*, 25 (1824), 336; 29 (1825), 269; Holland, *Van Buren*, pp. 269-270. Jackson supported internal improvements in 1822. Jackson to James Monroe, July 26, 1822, Monroe Papers, NYPL.

[21] MVB to Madison, Sept. 28, 1826, John C. Hamilton to MVB, Dec. 26, 1826, J. A. Alexander to MVB, Dec. 27, 1826, VBP; *Richmond Enquirer*, Dec. 7, 1826, Michael Hoffman to Azariah Flagg, Jan. 8, 1827, Azariah Flagg–Michael Hoffman Letters, Flagg Papers, NYPL.

tariff Southerners by voting in favor of some of the amendments to lower other parts of the tariff, including Nathaniel Macon's proposal to eliminate the tariff on cotton bagging. Just before the tariff bill passed, Van Buren wrote an ambiguous letter in which he straddled the issue.

On tariff policy Van Buren often differed with Andrew Jackson—just as the two had disagreed at times over internal improvements. In 1824, the nationalistic Jackson was far more committed to tariff protection and to internal improvements than was the southern-leaning New Yorker. In response to questions that year about his views on the tariff, Jackson had replied that he favored a "judicious tariff" as a means of protecting the American market. When Macon's amendment against protection for cotton bagging came before the Senate sitting as a committee of the whole, Van Buren voted yea, but Jackson's nay vote defeated the amendment, 24-23. Dismayed to find that his vote in favor of protection had irritated Southerners, Jackson tried to get Van Buren to change his vote so that the margin of victory would be wider (25-22), but to no avail. On the final vote on the amendment Jackson changed his own vote and so joined Van Buren in helping defeat the tariff on cotton bagging.[22]

On the issue of the Supreme Court Van Buren had no trouble at all in taking the state-rights position favored by the Old Republicans. His arrival in the Senate coincided with the start of a decade-long attack on the Court by these politicians. Southerners in particular were angry at decisions such as Fletcher *v.* Peck (1810), Martin *v.* Hunter's Lessee (1816), and McCulloch *v.* Maryland (1819), in which the Court had used both the contract and elastic clauses of the Constitution and Section 25 of the Judiciary Act to reverse decisions of southern state legislatures and courts. On December 12, 1821, Richard Mentor Johnson of Kentucky, proposed an amendment to the Constitution giving the states the right of appeal to the Senate in all Supreme Court cases in which a state was a party. Van Buren, who was anxious to back the South, supported this amendment. When Senator John Holmes of Maine, tried to strike the appeal clause from the amendment bill, Van Buren argued that Holmes was out of order. Despite Van Buren's efforts, Johnson's amendment made no headway.[23]

[22] *Annals of Congress*, 17th Congress, 1st session (1821-1822), 130, 154; 18th Congress, 1st session (1823-1824), 583, 708, 743-744, 3221-3226; *Autobiography*, pp. 239-243; MVB to Stephen Van Rensselaer, May 6, 1824, Lee Kohns Memorial Collection, NYPL. Van Rensselaer in reply told Van Buren that there were many in New York who opposed tariff protection. Van Rensselaer to MVB, May 14, 1824, VBP.

[23] For efforts to reform the judiciary, see Charles Warren, *The Supreme Court in*

In 1824, New Yorkers joined the South in opposing the power of the Supreme Court after Marshall's court ruled against New York in the case of Gibbons *v.* Ogden (1824). In early March, a few days after the decision, Van Buren reported a bill providing that no state law could be declared unconstitutional except by a vote of five of the seven members of the high court. The bill failed. Two years later he again showed his hostility to the Court in the debate over a bill to increase the Court by three members. Van Buren insisted that all justices of the Supreme Court serve on the circuit courts of appeals. Unless the justices appeared in the circuit courts, said Van Buren, they would hide in Washington and incompetence would go undetected. He went on to say that if he could reorganize the courts completely, he would strip the Supreme Court of most of its authority and give it to the state courts. He complained that the all-powerful Court sat "in final judgment" upon the acts of the states and had become the "highest legislative body" in the country. The contract clause alone, he said, had given "the jurisdiction of the Supreme Court a tremendous sweep." He particularly resented the spirit of "idolatry" that had grown up around the Court, and he was certain that it was not "the safest depository of *political power.*" With these arguments Van Buren both demonstrated that he held strong republican convictions and anticipated the Jacksonian attack on the Court that would follow.[24]

Van Buren also defended state rights, especially the rights of large states such as New York and Virginia, on the issue of the popular choice of presidential electors. When Thomas Hart Benton proposed that the people vote directly for President without using electors, Van Buren opposed the plan because it took too much power away from the states. He proposed instead that the people in each state choose the presidential electors, instead of giving state legislatures the option of choosing. If no one received a majority of the electoral votes, then the electors would choose between the top two, instead of deciding the matter in the House of Representatives. Van Buren argued that a decision in the House was unfair to the large states because all states

---

United States History, rev. ed. (Boston, 1926), I, ch. 17. See also *Annals of Congress,* 17th Congress, 1st session (1821-1822), 23, 68-94, 96-114.

[24] *Annals of Congress,* 18th Congress, 1st session (1823-1824), 336, 575; *Register of Debates,* 19th Congress, 1st session (1825-1826), 30, 409-423, 460, 566-569, 571, 668-671; *Niles' Register,* 26 (1824), 45; Warren, *Supreme Court,* I, 670; Shepard, *Van Buren,* pp. 134-137. For Van Buren's 1826 speech attacking the Court, see *Register of Debates,* 19th Congress, 1st session (1825-1826), 409-423; Holland, *Van Buren,* pp. 223-232. In 1828, Richard Riker told Van Buren that all cases involving a state should be "reviewable by the Senate," Riker to MVB, April 14, 1828, VBP.

had an equal vote. After his plans foundered, Van Buren warned that the power of the central government was reducing the "influence . . . and . . . respectability of the State governments."[25]

In his final major address in the Senate, Van Buren returned to the strict-construction, state-rights stance favored by the Old Republicans. The issue was a motion to give the Vice President the power to call members of the Senate to order during debate. Those supporting the motion relied upon loose construction of the Constitution, saying that the power to call to order was implied in the power of the Vice President to preside over the Senate. Opponents insisted that a senator should be allowed to appeal to the Senate every time he was called to order; Van Buren, who agreed, used the opportunity to attack those who wished to expand the central government. Ever since the Revolution, he pointed out, those who sought to "condense . . . all power [in] a single head" have opposed those who preferred to "limit the extent of executive authority." Like the latter, Van Buren believed that the states "richly deserve[d] the confidence" of the people. "Under the broad shield of state laws," he argued, "private rights [have] been protected, while public prosperity [has been] promoted." Van Buren warned that men with antirepublican views such as John Quincy Adams had "gone far beyond the utmost latitude of construction" of the early Federalists. "We have scotched the snake," Van Buren concluded, "not killed it."[26]

These Jeffersonian ideals, which Van Buren had sought to establish during his years in the Senate, remained with him throughout the rest of his career. In the campaign of 1828, for example, he warned that the states needed to exercise "perpetual watchfulness." Four years later he maintained that the federal government could not spend money on internal improvements without an amendment. In both 1836 and 1840, he insisted that the federal government could not establish a bank. Van Buren summed up his republican views in his *Origin and Course of Political Parties*. Ever since his boyhood days, he wrote, politics had been a battle between the enlightened views of Thomas Jefferson and the dangerous position of Alexander Hamilton. After losing in 1800, the Federalists had used the power of the federal courts to undermine the rights of the states. Congress should long ago have repealed the clause in the Judiciary Act giving the Supreme Court the right to review the decisions of state courts. "Ours was a confederacy

[25] *Annals of Congress*, 18th Congress, 1st session (1823-1824), 65-73, 170-204, 327, 355-362, 366-374, 381-399, 417-418; MVB, "Notes for a Speech in the Senate," Dec. 29, 1823, VBP; *Niles' Register*, 25 (1824), 285.
[26] Holland, *Van Buren*, pp. 285-297.

of sovereign states," said Van Buren, in which the federal government had only those powers the states "deemed necessary."[27]

Van Buren had begun to find the formula for which he had been groping. Arriving in the Senate with a reputation as a clever New York party manager, he had been anxious to take state-rights positions on national issues that would enable him to attract the Old Republicans of the South and restore the old Jeffersonian Republican party. At first he paid more attention to state issues than national, but increasingly as the years went by he began to establish a national reputation. Although he sometimes disappointed Southerners on the tariff, his positions on internal improvements, on the Supreme Court, and later, on the power of the President of the Senate brought him close to those of the Old Republicans. He was much closer to these Southerners than was Andrew Jackson, who was an avowed nationalist before anything else.

If Jackson and Van Buren were to unite politically in the years to come, they would have to reconcile the general's nationalism with the New Yorker's sympathy for republicanism. Inconsistent as Van Buren was, there was a strong theme of Old Republicanism recurring throughout his career in the Senate. Its origins were partly ideological, stemming from Van Buren's early career as a Jeffersonian in New York, but its thrust was strongly political, given his desire to please the Old Republicans. In short Van Buren took positions with which he was ideologically in sympathy, but which also promised to bring political rewards. Whenever he had to choose, politics took precedence over ideology. The leader of the New York Regency was thus making it possible for himself to unite northern and southern Republicans to form a new national coalition.[28]

[27] MVB to William Coleman, April 4, 1828, VBP; *Niles' Register*, 43 (1832), 124-125; 51 (1836), 25-30; 58 (1840), 393-396; MVB, *Political Parties*, pp. 227, 258, 265, 281, 297, 299, 307, and passim.

[28] Before dismissing Van Buren as simply a pragmatic politician, historians should consider his fight to abolish imprisonment for debt. After several attempts, Van Buren and Richard Mentor Johnson succeeded in 1828, in having the Senate pass a bill to abolish imprisonment for debt. *Annals of Congress*, 17th Congress, 2nd session (1822-1823), 98, 105, 129-139, 148; 18th Congress, 1st session (1823-1824), 346-353; *Register of Debates*, 18th Congress, 2nd session (1824-1825), 230; 20th Congress, 1st session (1827-1828), 68-69; Holland, *Van Buren*, pp. 211-212; Shepard, *Van Buren*, pp. 98, 116, 142.

Historical interpretation of Van Buren in the 1820s ranges from Robert V. Remini, who argues that Van Buren was a true "Jeffersonian," to Alvin Kass, who maintains that Van Buren's "ideological concern [was] always subordinate" to politics. Remini, *Van Buren and the Democratic Party*, p. 15; Kass, *Politics in New York State*, p. 132. Remini's view is also held by Richard H. Brown, " 'Southern Planters and Plain Re-

WITH his growing reputation as a state-rights Republican Van Buren was able to start building his coalition in the presidential campaign of 1824. At first, however, he refused to commit himself to any one candidate. In January 1822, William Plumer, Jr., observed that the Bucktails had "come on, in a body, to make their fortunes by joining the strongest party." They had "declared for no one in particular," he added, "but were waiting, and watching the progress of events." According to Henry Warfield, the "searching, ambitious, indefatigable" Van Buren had "no particular attachment" to anyone, but was "trying to find out whose chance" was best. Some said that Van Buren favored John C. Calhoun, but others believed that he had shifted to Henry Clay, or to William Harris Crawford. No one connected Van Buren with Andrew Jackson.[29]

In order to rebuild the Republican party, Van Buren was looking for a Jeffersonian Southerner. In February, he warned John King to "stand aloof" from John Quincy Adams of the North, and later in the year Van Buren scoffed at the "pretensions" of Henry Clay, who represented a border state. Van Buren's interest in the South surfaced in March when he took the steamboat down Chesapeake Bay and up the James River to Richmond, to pay a call on Old Republican Spencer Roane. Although Roane was ill, he sat up in bed and talked with his northern visitor for several hours. Van Buren pleased Roane by agreeing with the Virginian's opposition to John Marshall's nationalism, and Roane reciprocated by criticizing President Monroe for appointing Van Rensselaer as the Albany postmaster. Van Buren later described

---

publicans of the North': Martin Van Buren's Formula for National Politics" (Doctoral dissertation, Yale University, 1955). Kass' progenitors include Benson, *Concept of Jacksonian Democracy*, pp. 40-41. I am more sympathetic to the interpretation of Marvin Meyers, in his *Jacksonian Persuasion*, pp. 142-162, 252-253, 280-282; he portrays Van Buren as "one of the new young career men in American politics," self-consciously seeking a political philosophy appropriate to a changing world. Richard Hofstadter also portrays Van Buren as a new-style professional politician with a well-developed political philosophy. Norman Risjord argues that Van Buren was not an Old Republican, but was the leader of the radical new Republicans, who cared more about party than doctrine. Risjord is correct that Van Buren was not doctrinaire on banks and the tariff, but I believe that Van Buren did hold an Old Republican position on internal improvements. See Risjord, *Old Republicans*, pp. 230-231.

[29] *Autobiography*, p. 131; Rudolph Bunner to Gulian Verplanck, Jan. 18, 1822, Gulian Verplanck Papers, NYHS; William Plumer, Jr., to William Plumer, Jan. 3, 1822, Brown, *Missouri Compromises*, p. 74; Warfield to Henry Clay, May 30, 1822, Clay, *Papers*, III, 211; Peter Porter to Henry Clay, Jan. 29, 1822, Calvin Colton, ed., *The Private Correspondence of Henry Clay* (New York, 1855), pp. 62-63; Stephen Van Rensselaer to Solomon Van Rensselaer, April 9, 1822, Bonney, *Historical Gleanings*, I, 402; Jesse Hoyt to MVB, Dec. 5, 1822, VBP.

Roane as "a hearty and bold Republican of the old school." The visit did not go unnoticed; one newspaper that supported the Monroe administration referred to "a great plot to revive the Republican party." When Congressman William S. Archer of Virginia, who was also an Old Republican, came north the next summer to accompany the Radical Van Buren on a political tour of New York and New England, the New York-Virginia alliance was clearly being renewed. Neither the Albany Regency nor the Richmond Junto admitted that there was such an alliance in 1822, but Van Buren had laid the foundation for future political cooperation.[30]

By the fall of 1822 New Yorkers had begun to take sides in the presidential campaign. Many farmers and manufacturers were for John Quincy Adams or Henry Clay, because both favored internal improvements and protective tariffs. Adams enjoyed the backing of Rufus King, Clay that of Peter Porter of Buffalo. Calhoun was popular in New York City, where he was supported by the city postmaster, Samuel L. Gouverneur, and Secretary of the Navy Smith Thompson. Other New Yorkers, including Mordecai Noah of the New York *National Advocate*, were in sympathy with the aspirations of William Harris Crawford.[31]

Van Buren turned to Crawford for both ideological and political reasons. Although Crawford was too much of a nationalist to be a convincing Old Republican, his belief in economy and simplicity of government gained him the support of many former Jeffersonians including Nathaniel Macon, Mordecai Noah and Van Buren. Of all the candidates Crawford came the closest to being the Old Republican for whom Southerners and Van Buren were looking; or as Van Buren put it later, Crawford best deserved the title of "democrat." More important, Crawford already had a political following and offered the

[30] MVB to John King, Feb. 4, 1822, Rufus King to John King, Mar. 11, Mar. 17, 1822, King Papers; Gorham Worth to MVB, Mar. 16, 1822, Michael Ulshoeffer to MVB, April 2, 1822, MVB to Johnston Verplanck, Dec. 22, 1822, VBP; *Autobiography*, p. 126. Archer and the northern tour are mentioned in MVB to John King, Mar. 29, 1822, King Papers. See also *Argus*, Jan. 29, Aug. 23, 1822. The first reference to Van Buren in the *Richmond Enquirer* was July 4, 1823. *Richmond Enquirer*, 1822-1823, passim. Richard H. Brown and Robert V. Remini both conclude that the New York-Virginia alliance was underway in 1822, but concrete evidence is scant. Brown, "Southern Planters and Plain Republicans," pp. 22-23, 32-33; Remini, *Van Buren and the Democratic Party*, pp. 28-29.

[31] For an economic analysis of the candidates, see Rufus King to John King, Jan. 1823, and Rufus King to C. Gore, Feb. 9, 1823, King, *Correspondence*, VI, 495-496, 499-501. For Noah's position, see Rufus King to MVB, Sept. 24, 1822, VBP; and Rufus King to Charles King, Feb. 26, 1823, King, *Correspondence*, VI, 504.

best opportunity to "preserve the unity of the Republican Party" by uniting the North and the South. He was already considered the logical successor to the Virginia Dynasty. On the way back to Washington in November, Van Buren claimed that he was still "evaluating" the candidate, but by February he had made up his mind: "au fond," according to Rufus King, Van Buren was for Crawford.[32]

But before announcing for Crawford, he had to deal with Smith Thompson. Fearful that Crawford would carry New York, supporters of Adams and Calhoun began to consider Thompson for President. On February 1, 1823, Thompson met with King and Van Buren to suggest that the New York legislature submit a presidential nomination. When Thompson sounded out Van Buren by asking him what he thought of Crawford, the senator "parried" the question. King recalled that after the meeting, he urged Van Buren to discuss the presidency with Thompson, but Van Buren hesitated because "he had not thought much on the subject, and did not see his way clear." When the two finally met on March 4, they sparred with each other. Thompson warned that Adams had a good chance in New York because Calhoun was about to drop out and back the Secretary of State. Van Buren replied that Calhoun was in the race to stay, but that Clay and Adams would falter and their supporters would go over to Crawford. Thompson would be wise, said Van Buren, to settle for Vice President. Thompson refused to bite, and with feelings inflamed by too much wine, the confrontation ended on a bitter note. Convinced that it was now time to act, Van Buren huddled with Crawford a few days later, promised to back him for President, and then left for New York.[33]

As soon as Van Buren reached New York, he received a letter from Thompson that changed the situation. Supreme Court Justice Brockholst Livingston had died and President Monroe had offered to appoint Thompson to the vacant seat. With the presidency on his mind, Thompson was uncertain about accepting and wondered if he should recommend Van Buren. The latter's response revealed another facet of his rather complex character. He was shrewd enough to suspect that Thompson wanted him out of the way, but ambitious enough to be tempted and conceited enough to think that he might be appointed. With his usual caution he went out to Long Island to get the advice

---

[32] *Autobiography*, p. 131; Rufus King to MVB, Nov. 3, 1822, Root to MVB, Jan. 3, 1823, VBP; Rufus King to Charles King, Feb. 26, 1823, King, *Correspondence*, VI, 504; Risjord, *Old Republicans*, p. 249.

[33] Rufus King, memoranda, n.d., Mar. 4, April 7, 1823, King, *Correspondence*, VI, 507-511, 520-521. Just before his second meeting with Thompson, Van Buren took another southern trip. Roger Skinner to MVB, Feb. 15, 1823, VBP.

of Rufus King and Regency man Michael Ulshoeffer. The two told Van Buren bluntly that if he joined the Court, he would have to make an "absolute" decision—like "taking the vow and veil" of the church—to give up politics "wholly and forever." After several days of thinking it over, Van Buren decided that if the appointment were offered, he would accept it, invite his friends to an enormous dinner, and announce his retirement from politics. If at the age of forty Van Buren was willing to abandon politics for the Supreme Court, his goals were not as firmly tied to politics as many of his contemporaries believed.[34]

For the next few weeks there was a flurry of letters on Van Buren's behalf. Rufus King wrote that Van Buren was a man of "superior talents," whose appointment would be *better than any other* from New York. John Quincy Adams told Monroe that Van Buren would be a good justice because he would "follow in the track of Marshall [as a] sound interpreter of national principle." It was preposterous for Adams to say that the Jeffersonian Van Buren would follow Marshall and "national principle," but Adams and King were eager to have him on the Court. Van Buren correctly suspected that these "distinguished individuals" were plotting to get him out of the way in order to help Adams in New York.[35]

But the plot, if there was one, made no headway. Monroe delayed, waiting for Thompson or someone other than Van Buren to accept the seat on the bench. As time passed, Van Buren complained that he was "disappointed" at Monroe's "habitual indecision," and King accused the President of "imbecillity [sic] and . . . a hesitating mind." Van Buren became suspicious when Thompson admitted that he had not definitely turned down the appointment, and suspicion turned to anger when Van Buren learned that Thompson had been whispering that the "insincere" senator would not be named to the Court. Van Buren asked for explanations, but Thompson's response was evasive. Finally, four months after being offered it, Thompson wrote to Van Buren asking permission to accept the nomination. King advised Van Buren that he had every right to be angry, but Van Buren merely told

[34] Thompson to MVB, Mar. 17, Mar. 21, Mar. 25, 1823, MVB to Thompson, Mar. 30, 1823, VBP; Rufus King, memoranda, April 7, 1823, King, *Correspondence*, VI, 521-522; George Bancroft to Mrs. S. D. Bancroft, Dec. 27, 1831, Mark A. DeWolfe Howe, *The Life and Letters of George Bancroft* (New York, 1908), I, 194-195.

[35] At the time Van Buren believed that King "sincerely thought the appointment a desirable one," but later began to suspect that King had other motives. King to Adams, April 1, 1823, King to Monroe, April 2, 1823, Adams to King, April 7, 1823, King, *Correspondence*, VI, 512-515; *Autobiography*, p. 141; George Bancroft to Mrs. S. D. Bancroft, Dec. 27, 1831, Howe, *Bancroft*, I, 195.

Thompson to take the seat. Throughout that spring and early summer Van Buren's usual astuteness and common sense deserted him, but his caution protected him. He should have known that Monroe would not appoint him, yet when the affair was over, he may have been disappointed, but he had not lost the friendship of Thompson or King, and the Crawford movement in New York was not compromised.[36]

In the spring and summer of 1823, the Crawford campaign in New York came alive. In May, the state Republican caucus adopted resolutions drafted by Van Buren instructing the delegation in Washington to support the traditional system of nominating presidential candidates by a congressional caucus. The *Albany Argus*, which spoke for the Regency, announced for Crawford, who was described as a man of the old "Jeffersonian school." As summer turned into fall, the *Argus* developed the case that Crawford represented a revival of the original Republican party based on a North-South alliance.[37]

Van Buren continued to promote this alliance. On April 27, he wrote Crawford inquiring about political conditions in the South. On May 1, Samuel Smith of Maryland, asked Van Buren how many New York congressmen could be counted on to back Crawford. Nine days later Crawford wrote to Van Buren in support of his possible appointment to the Supreme Court and to boast that sixty-eight "friendly" congressmen had been elected in the South. At the same time the Albany Regency and the Richmond Junto began to cooperate. The *Richmond Enquirer* quoted from an editorial in the *Argus* praising Crawford and began to publish flattering references to Van Buren. In addition a warm personal relationship grew between Van Buren and Thomas Ritchie, editor of the *Enquirer* and head of the Junto. Before long the opposition was complaining that the *Argus* was uniting with the *Enquirer* and that the Regency and the Junto were planning to run the country.[38]

---

[36] Monroe to———, Mar. 31, April 6, April 14, June 9, July 20, 1823, John Wills to Monroe, April 29, 1823, William Wirt to Monroe, April 29, 1823, Monroe Papers, NYPL; MVB to Thompson, April 4, April 15, June 4, July 25, 1823, Thompson to MVB, April 6, June 26, July 11, 1823, King to MVB, April 18, July 15, 1823, VBP; MVB to King April 14, 1823, Rufus King to John King, April 17, 1823, King to J. Q. Adams, April 18, 1823, Thompson to MVB, April 25, 1823, King, *Correspondence*, VI, 516-517, 524; MVB to King, July 10, July 18, July 25, 1823, King to MVB, May, July 22, 1823, King Papers.

[37] Rufus King, memoranda, April 28, 1823, MVB to King, May 2, 1823, King, *Correspondence*, VI, 527-528; *Argus*, Dec. 17, 1822, Mar. 25, May 13, June 17, July 11, July 27, Aug. 1, Sept. 7, Sept. 12, 1824.

[38] Smith to MVB, May 1, 1823, Crawford to MVB, May 9, 1823, VBP; *Richmond Enquirer*, 1823, especially April 4, July 4, Aug. 8, 1823; *Argus*, July 29, 1823; Ritchie to MVB, July 2, 1838, Charles H. Ambler, ed., "Ritchie Letters," *The John P. Branch*

The Crawford campaign that summer kept Van Buren on the go. In mid-May, he asked Rufus King to join him on a trip to Boston, hoping that King's presence would allay suspicions that it was a political jaunt. The ruse was not entirely successful; Henry Clay received at least two letters reporting on the visit and the rumor spread that Governor William Eustis of Massachusetts would run for Vice President on the Crawford slate. From Boston Van Buren traveled to Philadelphia and then invited Smith Thompson to accompany him to Virginia. Thompson did not go, but it was typical of Van Buren that he could hope to get political support from a man with whom he had personal differences. Even when he was on vacation at Saratoga Springs, Van Buren managed to combine politics with pleasure.[39]

Next to Crawford, John C. Calhoun had the most active campaign in New York that summer. Recognizing the importance of the Empire State, Calhoun told his supporters that the fight must take place in New York. "Let New York do her duty," he added, and "all will go right." In addition to Samuel L. Gouverneur and Thompson, Calhoun enjoyed the backing of such prominent figures as Winfield Scott, United States Supreme Court reporter Henry Wheaton, and Port Surveyor Joseph G. Swift. In an effort to straddle, Calhoun conceded that "the rights of the State [were] essential to liberty," but he branded the state-rights philosophy of Van Buren and Crawford as "Radicalism . . . the most dangerous enemy of Republicanism." Although Calhoun believed in political parties, he attacked Van Buren's party, saying that it was made up of "unprincipled" politicians who relied upon "political dexterity." In New York City a new journal called *The Patriot* was started to present the Calhoun side.[40]

Instead of attacking the Regency, Henry Clay and his New York

Historical Papers of Randolph-Macon College, 3 (1911), 229; Ambler, *Thomas Ritchie*, pp. 89-90; John C. Calhoun to Samuel L. Gouverneur, Nov. 9, 1823, Gouverneur Papers, NYPL.

[39] MVB to King, May 9, 1823, King, *Correspondence*, VI, 529-530; MVB to King, July 10, 1823, King Papers; Charles Miner to Clay, June 29, 1823, David Woods to Clay, Aug. 1823, Clay, *Papers*, III, 436, 475-476; *Richmond Enquirer*, Aug. 8, 1823; MVB to Thompson, June 4, 1823, Thompson to MVB, June 26, 1823, VBP.

[40] Scott to Gouverneur, April 8, 1823, Calhoun to Gouverneur, April 28, May 25, June 6, 1823, Gouverneur Papers, NYPL; *Richmond Enquirer*, April 4, 1823; Calhoun to Swift, April 29, Aug. 24, Oct. 14, 1823, Thomas R. Hay, ed., "John C. Calhoun and the Presidential Campaign of 1824: Some Unpublished Calhoun Letters," *American Historical Review*, 40 (Oct. 1934), 84-94; Calhoun to Charles Fisher, June 11, Aug. 1, 1823, A. R. Newsome, ed., "Correspondence of John C. Calhoun, George McDuffie and Charles Fisher, Relating to the Presidential Campaign of 1824," *North Carolina Historical Review*, 7 (Oct. 1930), 480-482; Martin Lichterman, "John Adams Dix: 1798-1879" (Doctoral dissertation, Columbia University, 1952), pp. 23-30.

lieutenant Peter Porter hoped to carry the Empire State by winning the support of Van Buren, perhaps by offering him the vice presidency. Clay's backers reported favorably on Van Buren and his followers. According to Henry Shaw, who practiced law in western Massachusetts, the members of the Regency were "really able men"; Congressman Albert H. Tracy of New York remarked on Van Buren's "astuteness and his known reluctance to be on the losing side." To retain the support of his backers, Clay played on the rivalry between New York and Virginia. He argued that if Crawford, a Southerner, were elected, it would mean, in effect, a continuation of the Virginia Dynasty. To prevent that, New Yorkers should make certain that he, Henry Clay, won the presidency.[41]

Andrew Jackson and John Quincy Adams attracted less attention in New York than the other candidates. At the conclusion of his campaign against the Seminoles in Florida, Jackson had visited New York City in February 1819, at the height of the struggle between the Clintonians and the Bucktails. At a dinner given in his honor by the Tammany Society, which was opposed to DeWitt Clinton, Jackson dismayed almost everyone present by offering a toast to Clinton. Van Buren, who was there, recalled that those present were "very much stirred up at being thus snubbed" by the general. New York Republicans suspected that Jackson advocated the amalgamation of parties because he had urged Monroe, when President-elect, to lay party feeling aside and appoint moderate Federalists to office. Even so, the editor of the *Albany Argus* was attracted to Jackson because the general was "of the revolutionary school," but feared that he might set up a "military despotism."[42]

John Quincy Adams' nationalist views attracted the support of a number of Clintonians and former Federalists such as Rufus King and his sons, but they alienated those in New York who believed in the Old Republican tradition. Adams was the second choice of many, especially the Calhoun men, and would pick up valuable support if Calhoun's drive collapsed. In the summer of 1823, Adams had the

[41] Clay mentioned the possibility of offering the vice presidential nomination to Van Buren in Clay to Peter Porter, Mar. 18, 1823, Clay, *Papers*, III, 401. Not all Clay men respected Van Buren. David Woods, for example, called him "slippery as an eel." Clay also argued that if Crawford carried New York, it might enable Adams to win the election. Peter Porter to Clay, Jan. 29, Feb. 12, 1823, Clay to Porter, Feb. 2, Feb. 3, June 15, 1823, Henry Shaw to Clay, Feb. 11, 1823, Albert H. Tracy to Clay, April 27, 1823, David Woods to Clay, May 22, 1823, Clay, *Papers*, III, 356, 363-366, 373, 379, 412, 420, 432-433.

[42] John S. Bassett, *The Life of Andrew Jackson* (Garden City, 1911; reprint, 2 vols. in 1, 1967), pp. 287, 339-343; *Autobiography*, pp. 232-233; *Argus*, May 13, 1823.

enthusiastic backing of Thurlow Weed, who was a Clintonian even though he had a social and environmental background similar to that of many members of the Regency. Weed, whose grandfather had fought in the Revolution, was born in New York State in 1797, his parents having moved there from Connecticut. Since his father barely supported the family by unloading ships along the Hudson River, young Thurlow grew up "always poor" and had to seek work at the age of eight. He pumped a blacksmith's bellows, did odd jobs in a tavern, served as a cabin boy, and was apprenticed to a printer. After brief service in the War of 1812, he became a Clintonian and went to work for the *Albany Register* and later for the *Rochester Telegraph*, the first newspaper to come out for Adams. He was soon helping manage the Adams campaign in New York.[43]

In late summer 1823, Van Buren was forced to reconsider his decision to back Crawford when the Secretary of the Treasury suffered a paralytic stroke that left him speechless and nearly blind. Although his speech and sight improved enough to let him stay in the race, he never fully recovered. Crawford's illness gave Van Buren a good excuse to change candidates if he wanted to do so. He was on good terms with Calhoun, was close enough to Clay to joke about the presidency, and would soon become acquainted with Jackson in the Senate. John Quincy Adams felt that Van Buren owed him "some personal obligation" because he had supported Van Buren for the Supreme Court. Politicians on all sides were shifting about: John A. Dix, for example, who had left the army for a law career, changed his allegiance from Calhoun to Jackson to Adams during the campaign. But Van Buren stuck with Crawford because he still believed that Crawford could win—especially if the election went to the House of Representatives—and because only Crawford gave Van Buren the chance to create the type of party that he wanted.[44]

To keep the Crawford campaign going, Van Buren had to exert party discipline because many members of the Regency who had never been enthusiastic about Crawford became restive when they learned he had had a stroke. In September, Judge Roger Skinner suggested that he might shift from Crawford to Clay, and in October, Assemblyman Azariah Flagg and Surrogate Silas Wright agreed that they preferred Calhoun or Clay to Crawford. Even Crawford's strongest backer, Lieutenant Governor Erastus Root, reported from Albany that

[43] Weed, *Autobiography*, pp. 1-121.

[44] Parton, *Jackson*, III, 24; Clay to Porter, June 15, 1823, Clay, *Papers*, III, 432; Adams, *Memoirs*, VI, 365; "Letters from Dix to Shattuck," pp. 139-147.

his man was "*in trouble.*" Many other Republicans were said to be "disgusted," but nonetheless Van Buren, who had a powerful hold on the Regency, kept his organization in line. Flagg agreed to continue support for Crawford on the grounds that "unity among Republicans must be preserved," and the *Argus* continued to defend Crawford. As Van Buren prepared to return to Washington at the end of the fall, reports spread that he was forcing Republicans in New York to stick with Crawford. The reports cited "the necessity of *party discipline,*" but that was only partly correct. Van Buren was using party discipline at home to build a national party.[45]

Back in Washington during the winter of 1823-1824, Van Buren used the vice presidency to shore up the Crawford campaign. According to Rufus King, Crawford's friends "approached those of Adams in hopes of prevailing on him to accept the V. Pr." When they were refused, they went to work on Clay. Van Buren made "unwearied efforts" to get Clay to run for Vice President alongside of Crawford as a means of "preserving the republican party, then threatened with destruction." The approach was made through Thomas Hart Benton, who "pressed the matter upon Mr. Clay with his usual earnestness." Even though Clay declined, Van Buren was still optimistic in February 1824 that the Kentuckian would eventually withdraw from the presidential race.[46]

At the same time Van Buren resorted to the Republican technique of calling a congressional nominating caucus. Opposition to the caucus had mounted because many considered it simply a means of perpetuating the Virginia Dynasty, but Van Buren and others insisted on holding the caucus, which met February 14, 1824. When only sixty-six Republican congressmen and senators came out of over two hundred, there was a motion to postpone, but Van Buren succeeded in defeating it. The caucus promptly nominated Crawford for President and Albert Gallatin, who had just retired from public life, for Vice President.[47]

---

[45] Flagg to Wright, Oct. 28, 1823, Wright to Flagg, Nov. 12, Dec. 10, 1823, Flagg-Wright Correspondence; Flagg to Van Buren, Nov. 12, 1823, VBP; Porter to Clay, Sept. 6, Oct. 4, Nov. 17, 1823, Clay, *Papers*, III, 487, 494, 523; Rufus King to Charles King, Feb. 13, 1824, King, *Correspondence*, VI, 551; Goldstein, "Albany Regency," pp. 70-74; C. H. Rammelkamp, "The Campaign of 1824 in New York," American Historical Association, *Annual Report for the Year 1904* (Washington, D.C., 1905), p. 180.

[46] Rufus King to Christopher Gore, Feb. 1, 1824, King, *Correspondence*, VI, 551; *Autobiography*, pp. 665-666; MVB to Butler, Feb. 17, 1824, VBP. In March, Adams denied persistent rumors of a Crawford-Adams coalition. Adams, *Memoirs*, VI, 256.

[47] *Argus*, Feb. 24, 1824; *National Intelligencer*, Feb. 7, Feb. 16, 1824; Parton, *Jackson*, III, 26-30; William Plumer, Jr., to William Plumer, Feb. 16, 1824, Brown, *Missouri Compromises*, pp. 99-101; MVB to Benjamin Butler, Feb. 15, 1824, VBP. For a pro-

Immediately after the nomination Van Buren wrote to members of the Regency explaining how the caucus fitted into his scheme of party politics. He brushed off the meager attendance, saying that if Republicans disregarded the caucus on those grounds then the "whole power of the party" could be undermined by "a few members." What was at stake was no less than "the continuance of the old party division." Van Buren could not believe that any Republican could refuse to support the nomination, knowing that the "existence of the party" depended on it. He said that the caucus had nominated Gallatin instead of Richard Rush for Vice President although the former was foreign-born, because the latter was something even worse—a former Federalist. The choice of Gallatin, concluded Van Buren, would "revive old feelings" of solidarity.

The names of those taking part in the caucus suggest that Van Buren was well on his way toward creating a Republican alliance of Northerners and Southerners. The list includes a number of northern Republicans, many of them Radicals, such men as John Holmes of Maine, Churchill C. Cambreleng of New York, and Samuel D. Ingham of Pennsylvania, who opposed Adams' nationalism and who, like Van Buren, were seeking southern allies. The Southerners were a mixture of Old Republicans and new state-rights politicians interested in forming a new party: from Virginia, the Barbours, Andrew Stevenson, William C. Rives, and William S. Archer; from farther south and west, Joel Poinsett and Robert Y. Hayne of South Carolina, John H. Eaton and Sam Houston of Tennessee, and Richard Mentor Johnson of Kentucky. Leading them from his seat in the Senate was Van Buren and from his desk in Richmond, Thomas Ritchie. The new alliance formed the nucleus of the Crawford campaign of 1824, and more importantly, it formed the basis of the Jackson campaign of 1828.[48]

As the session of Congress drew to a close in the spring, the contours of the presidential election slowly took shape. Jackson's stock began to rise early in March when a Republican state convention in Harrisburg, Pennsylvania, nominated him for President, thereby forcing Cal-

vocative discussion of the relationship between foreign and domestic policies in the election of 1824, see Ernest R. May, *The Making of the Monroe Doctrine* (Cambridge, Mass., 1975).

[48] MVB to Benjamin Butler, Feb. 15, 1824, Van Buren to Charles Dudley, Feb. 1824, VBP; Parton, *Jackson*, III, 26-27; *National Intelligencer*, Feb. 7, Feb. 16, 1824; Francis F. Wayland, *Andrew Stevenson: Democrat and Diplomat 1785-1857* (Philadelphia, 1949), p. 66; Brown, "Southern Planters and Plain Republicans," pp. 32-39; Saunders to Bartlett Yancey, Dec. 31, 1823, A. R. Newsome, "Letters of Romulus M. Saunders to Bartlett Yancey, 1821-1828," *North Carolina Historical Review*, 8 (1931), 439-441; Adams, *Memoirs*, VI, 273.

houn to withdraw from the race. Since Jackson believed that New York, Pennsylvania and Virginia would go in a bloc, his success in Pennsylvania convinced him that he would win all three states. Jackson did not consider Van Buren powerful enough to "*manage* New York" for Crawford. The supporters of Adams were still confident that their man was in the lead, especially Rufus King; in March he was convinced that when Crawford's situation became "desperate," Virginia would swing behind Adams and make him President, but King along with many others believed that it was "in the power of New York to decide the election."[49]

Van Buren agreed. In the month and a half following the congressional caucus the Magician did all he could to get the New York legislature to nominate Crawford. If only they would pass a resolution in favor of Crawford, he wrote, it would "settle the result of the Presidential election." When his efforts failed, Van Buren resumed his lecture to the Regency on how the new party system should work. Firmness, consistency and cooperation between the state party and the national party formed the "sheet anchor" for the system. "Every honest democrat" must be made to see that every point in the system depended on every other and that it was necessary to defend "the whole to save a part." State support for the caucus nomination was, therefore, essential. If they left the "door open," he argued, they would encourage further debate over the presidency; but if they nominated Crawford, they would "close the door upon all the differences of opinion." He also insisted that decisiveness at this point would rid New York of outside pressure in the state election. Since many New Yorkers, he pointed out, were originally from other states, they were often influenced by friends back home. Once convinced that there was "no doubt" about New York, outsiders would leave the state alone.

According to Van Buren's optimistic scenario, the "Jackson fever" had not spread beyond Kentucky, Missouri, Indiana, and Illinois, and "Pennsylvania would be left to repent of her frenzy at her leisure." Virginia had ratified Crawford's nomination "with unprecedented unanimity," the Carolinas and New Jersey were safe, and once New York spoke, Ohio and most of New England would fall in line. Van Buren warned that if New York hesitated the election was likely to go to the House of Representatives, but if she acted, then the election

[49] Parton, *Jackson*, III, 18, 29; Jackson to Major General George W. Martin, Jan. 2, 1824, Jackson, *Correspondence*, III, 221; MVB to Benjamin Butler, Feb. 17, 1824, VBP; MVB to Jesse Hoyt, Mar. 3, 1824, Mackenzie, *Butler*, p. 39; Rufus King to Charles King, Mar. 10, 1824, King, *Correspondence*, VI, 554-555.

would "be made by the people," and New York would get "the credit [for] the good work."[50]

These letters to the Regency show the extent to which Van Buren's ideas on party politics were bound up with the Crawford campaign. They emphasized first of all his conviction that the party should come before the individual, that once the party had made a decision all its members should rally behind it. There could be no quibbling over individual issues or candidates, for that could lead to the breakup of the party. Rejecting Monroe's amalgamation of parties, Van Buren held to his ideal of the Republican party based on a North-South alliance. The last letter in particular revealed his emerging concept of how state parties should work in concert with the national organization. Above all Van Buren sought to prevent the election from going to the House of Representatives, where his new party system might not be able to operate effectively. After bringing order to New York politics, he sought to do the same in national politics.

Even though he was sure of Virginia, Van Buren continued to bring pressure to bear on the Old Dominion. In October 1823, he had written to James Barbour to say that they would be on the same side in the coming "contest," and after Congress adjourned in May 1824, Van Buren made another trip to Virginia, this time to visit Thomas Jefferson at Monticello. Here Van Buren spent several memorable days driving about the estate and listening to Jefferson's conversation. On the way back he spent some time in Richmond tightening the bonds between the Regency and the Junto. The trip so worried Henry Clay that he warned Justice Francis T. Brooke of Virginia, that Van Buren was off to the Old Dominion to discuss the Crawford illness, while John Quincy Adams thought that Van Buren was about to shift from Crawford to Clay. Sam Houston agreed, but Andrew Jackson heard that Van Buren went south to see if "Virginia could be induced to vote for Mr. Adams." According to Jackson's informant, Van Buren was "not content [to use] his talents for intrigue in his own state, [but] must try his powers with [the] *ancient Dominion*."[51]

In one of his letters to the Regency Van Buren warned that indecision in Albany would only increase the debate there over the manner in which the state's presidential electors were to be chosen. Since he felt

[50] MVB to Charles Dudley, Feb., Mar. 26, 1824, VBP.

[51] MVB to James Barbour, Oct. 9, 1823, James Barbour Papers, NYPL; *Autobiography*, pp. 182-183; Clay to Brooke, May 23, 1824, Clay, *Private Correspondence*, p. 93; Brooke to Clay, May 28, 1824, Clay, *Papers*, III, 733; Adams, *Memoirs*, VI, 365, 372-373; Col. Charles P. Tutt to Andrew Jackson, June 12, 1824, Jackson, *Correspondence*, III, 255.

that the Regency could control the legislature, Van Buren wanted the electors chosen by that body as in the past. Others, especially the supporters of Calhoun and of Adams, demanded that the people be given the right to vote for electors. When the legislature adjourned in 1823 without taking any action, the People's party was formed to carry on the fight in the fall election. Led by former congressman James Tallmadge and by Henry Wheaton, who was now in the state assembly, the People's party was made up of Clintonians, former Federalists, and other opponents of the Regency and Crawford. Van Buren was determined to defeat the plan for popular choice of electors because he believed it would cost Crawford New York. He also realized that it was "a matter of great delicacy," and that it was "awkward" for a party that "prided itself on being" in favor of the rights of "the People" to oppose such a democratic reform. One member of the Regency cynically reported that the "magic words, '*the people*,' '*the people*,' '*the people*,' were rung through a thousand changes." In the end a number of Regency men came out in favor of the new plan in order to make certain that they would be elected. Enough Bucktails managed to win in November 1823 to give the Regency firm control of the senate and a slim margin in the assembly. Since this would be the legislature that would choose the presidential electors in 1824, Crawford might be able to carry New York—unless the choice of electors was given to the people.[52]

After the election, the Regency continued to oppose the popular choice of electors. Edwin Croswell, the new editor of the *Albany Argus*, claimed that if the electoral laws were repealed, the People's party would run DeWitt Clinton for President, Republicans would be divided, and the Regency would lose the governor's seat, the electoral ticket and the assembly. Such a result would be intolerable, said Croswell, because those behind the People's party were simply "the old & implacable enemy under a new name." Croswell admitted that it was a matter of "expediency," but he rationalized that the "real people" did not favor electoral reform. State Comptroller William L. Marcy also believed that Clinton would be elected if the people chose the electors. Several Bucktails found that they were "hampered [by] their indiscreet pledges" before the election and had to act like "conspir-

---

[52] MVB to Dudley, Jan. 14, Mar. 26, 1824, MVB to David E. Evans, Feb. 25, 1824, VBP. Rufus King supported the popular choice of electors in a letter to John King, April 20, 1823, King, *Correspondence*, VI, 518-520. The *Argus* called the plan a "pretended reform." *Argus*, June 27, 1823. *Autobiography*, p. 142; Jacob Barker to Benjamin Butler, Oct. 2, 1823, Miscellaneous Papers, LC; Rammelkamp, "Campaign of 1824," p. 185.

ators." Benjamin Butler summed up the stand of the Regency when he recommended that they "stick to principles," which he defined as "adhering to the old forms and established doctrines of the party." For the Regency democracy meant saving the party.[53]

The electoral issue put Governor Joseph C. Yates in an awkward position: to be renominated by the Regency he had to oppose the reform; to be reelected by the people he had to support it. When Van Buren and the Regency dangled the vice presidency in front of Yates, he stopped short of backing the reform but instead recommended an amendment to the federal Constitution requiring the popular choice of electors. Since there was no chance that the amendment could be ratified before the presidential election, the proposal would not damage Crawford's chances in New York. Later that winter Van Buren, who was working in tandem with Yates, proposed a similar plan in the United States Senate.

Yates's proposal caused a rift between Van Buren and Rufus King. When the text of Yates's address arrived one evening, Van Buren, King, Andrew Stevenson, Stephen Van Rensselaer, Louis McLane, and others were having dinner at their boardinghouse in Georgetown. Expecting to hear that Yates had come out in favor of popular elections, King proposed that the message be read out loud. When Stevenson, who was reading, came to the proposal for an amendment, Van Buren noticed that "a lowering frown chased the smiles from Mr. King's face." "Mr. Crawford's friends," the old senator blurted out, "ought to send the Governor a drawing of the Vice President's Chair." When Van Buren "with some feeling" denied the charge that they had bribed Yates, King left the room in anger. He became even angrier when he received a letter from New York documenting his charge that Yates had been promised the vice presidency. King wrote back to his correspondent that as long as the legislature chose the electors, "unworthy Juntas" would control the elections and the people would not be "the keepers of their own liberties."[54]

During the rest of the winter the Regency was hard-pressed to keep the legislature from passing a new electoral law. Henry Wheaton reported gleefully that "the V.B. men [were] all in dismay." "We *whack* them on the floor," boasted Wheaton, and the Bucktails were "obliged

[53] Croswell to Flagg, Dec. 9, 1823, Flagg Papers; Marcy to MVB, Jan. 11, 1824, Jacob Sutherland to MVB, Jan. 24, 1824, VBP; Benjamin Butler to Jesse Hoyt, Jan. 29, 1824, Mackenzie, *Butler*, pp. 168-169.

[54] Hammond, *Political Parties*, II, 142; Rufus King to Charles King, Dec. 12, Dec. 19, Dec. 20, 1823, John King to Rufus King, Jan. 9, 1824, Rufus King to C. Gore, Jan. 20, 1824, King, *Correspondence*, VI, 538-541, 545-547; *Autobiography*, pp. 146-147.

to Caucus *all night* to make up for what they lose in the day time."
It was, he concluded, "truly a contest with 'the powers of Darkness.'"
Despite the efforts of "Little Flagg," as Wheaton called Azariah Flagg,
the Regency leader in the assembly, a bill was passed giving the choice
of electors to the people. After learning the bad news, Van Buren sent
a letter north, asking the Regency to arrange for a resolution in the
legislature nominating Crawford. The Regency failed to deliver, but
in the senate, Regency man Silas Wright managed to secure a postponement of the electoral bill until after the election.[55]

With the choice of electors safely in the hands of the legislature, the
Regency tried to improve its democratic image by nominating Samuel
Young, a consistent supporter of electoral reform, for governor. In so
doing they summarily abandoned Joseph C. Yates, who had lost popularity by straddling the issue at their bidding. In addition the Regency
hoped to break up a growing Adams-Clay alliance that was already
planning to run Young as its candidate. When Young "complacently
turned his back on his Clay friends" and accepted the nomination,
Thurlow Weed conceded that Van Buren had pulled a "bold flank
movement"; and DeWitt Clinton, who feared cooperation between
the Crawford and Clay camps, declared that Van Buren had arranged
"the purchase of Young, of Peter B. Porter, and with them of Clay's
party."[56]

Having enlisted Young, the Regency next moved to destroy Clinton.
Behind all the intricate Regency maneuvers lay the fear that DeWitt
Clinton would carry New York for Adams or Clay or Jackson, or
even for himself, all at the expense of Crawford. The Regency was
particularly afraid that the People's party would nominate Clinton for
governor. To hurt Clinton Roger Skinner engineered an elaborate plot
on the last day of the legislature to remove Clinton from his post as
canal commissioner. Thurlow Weed recalled graphically how a messenger carried the resolution for removal from the assembly to Silas

---

[55] Thurlow Weed reported that there was so much popular sentiment against the
seventeen who voted against the bill that they were soon "consigned to retirement."
According to Weed, Van Buren rewarded a number of them with political jobs. Weed,
Autobiography, pp. 107-108. Wheaton to Samuel L. Gouverneur, Feb. 3, 1824, Gouverneur Papers, NYPL; Rufus King to Charles King, Feb. 13, Mar. 25, 1824, King,
Correspondence, VI, 551, 558; Marcy to MVB, Feb. 15, 1824, MVB to Butler, Feb.
17, 1824, Butler to MVB, Mar. 27, 1824, VBP.

[56] John Quincy Adams was indulging in wishful thinking when he wrote in his diary
that the Young nomination revealed the weakness of the Regency and the "decay" of
Van Buren's influence. Adams, *Memoirs*, VI, 284, 340. See also Weed, *Autobiography*,
pp. 108-109; Charles King to Rufus King, April 5, 1824, King, *Correspondence*, VI,
563; Goldstein, "Albany Regency," p. 84.

Wright in the senate, where it promptly passed. The plan backfired, for according to King, "public feeling everywhere condemn[ed] the removal" and public meetings were called to protest. Van Buren admitted later that the removal gave Clinton "what he had never before possessed—the sympathies of the people."[57]

Governor Yates now struck back at the Regency by threatening to call a special session of the legislature to revise the electoral law before the presidential election took place. The Regency first refused to take the threat seriously because they did not believe that Yates had enough courage to act. But as the summer approached, Van Buren received disturbing reports that Yates was losing his temper and behaving so unreasonably that there was no telling what he might do. When Thurlow Weed taunted Yates, saying that the Regency was making fun of him, the governor sprang to his feet and shouted that he would "show" them. On June 2, 1824, he did by calling a special session.[58]

By the time the legislature convened on August 2, Van Buren had returned to Albany to take charge of the situation. He first wrote an article for the *Argus* explaining why the session should never have been called. Then he had Azariah Flagg ask for immediate adjournment of the assembly on the grounds that nothing new had happened since the regular session. In the senate Van Buren relied upon Silas Wright, who succeeded in getting Yates' proposals laid on the table. When both houses adjourned within a week, Van Buren had once again fought off electoral reform. Michael Hoffman of the Regency observed accurately a few days later, that Van Buren would be "censured and abused for a too busy interference in our state affairs," but Hoffman maintained that he himself still had "the greatest confidence" in Van Buren's ability.[59]

[57] Edwin Croswell had worried about Clinton in December 1823. Croswell to Flagg, Dec. 9, 1823, Flagg Papers. Van Buren blamed the removal on Skinner, but the Magician had been warned as early as January that Skinner wanted Clinton off the board. Marcy to MVB, Jan. 11, 1824, VBP. For two views of this affair, see Weed, *Autobiography*, pp. 109-111, and *Autobiography*, pp. 143-145. See also Rufus King to Charles King, April 21, 1824, King, *Correspondence*, VI, 567-568; *Argus*, Jan. 2, Jan. 6, April 20, 1824; *Albany Daily Advertiser Extra*, April 22, 1824; *Albany Gazette*, April 23, 1824.

[58] James A. Hamilton tried vainly to talk Yates out of calling the session. Hamilton to MVB, May 19, 1824 (two letters), VBP. Rufus King was certain that Yates would act. Adams, *Memoirs*, VI, 350-351. For Weed's role in the story, see Weed, *Autobiography*, pp. 115-116. See also Campbell to MVB, May 19, 1824, MVB to Thomas Jefferson, July 13, 1824, VBP.

[59] Weed, *Autobiography*, pp. 116-117; *Autobiography*, pp. 147-148; Adams, *Memoirs*, VI, 407; *Argus*, Aug. 10, 1824; Michael Hoffman to——, Aug. 14, 1824, Marcy Papers, LC.

To carry New York and Virginia for Crawford Van Buren continued his efforts to bring the Crawford and Clay camps together. The Regency never faltered in backing Young for governor even though Young preferred Clay to Crawford. When Senator Benjamin Ruggles of Ohio, wrote saying that Crawford could not possibly win without Clay, Van Buren, who agreed, sent back a seven-page reply. The union of Clay and Crawford, said Van Buren, would make a "great & powerful party." Convinced by Walter Lowrie of Pennsylvania, and Claiborne W. Gooch of Virginia, that Albert Gallatin was a weak candidate for Vice President, Van Buren plotted with them to get Gallatin to withdraw. He handled the vice presidential matter with characteristic political skill. Lowrie, not Van Buren, talked Gallatin into resigning. The resignation was announced, not in the *Albany Argus*, the mouthpiece of the Regency, but in the Washington *National Intelligencer*, which supported Crawford. Van Buren then arranged for Andrew Stevenson of Virginia, to leak to the press the idea that Clay would make a good Vice President. Under the deft guidance of Van Buren the Crawford campaign continued in high gear all fall.[60]

In New York Crawford benefited from divisions within the ranks of the opposition. Adams backers were divided between Clintonians and those who hated Clinton, who was himself supporting Andrew Jackson. Learning that a group of Clintonians had nominated Jackson in the spring, former House speaker John W. Taylor warned Adams that the state would probably go to Crawford. Thurlow Weed found his own position "somewhat embarrassing" because he was firmly committed both to Adams and Clinton. The situation became even more difficult with the Adams camp divided over whom to support for governor, Clinton or James Tallmadge. Weed embarked on a whirlwind tour of the state to determine whether he could rally all opponents of Crawford behind Tallmadge. Finding that it was impossible, Weed then arranged for the People's party to nominate Clinton for governor and Tallmadge for lieutenant governor. The stage was thus set for a showdown between the Weed-Adams-Clinton forces on one side and the Van Buren-Crawford-Young organization on the other.[61]

[60] Ruggles to MVB, July 31, 1824, MVB to Ruggles, Aug. 26, 1824, Gooch to MVB, Sept. 14, 1824, Lowrie to MVB, Sept. 14, Sept. 24, 1824, Gallatin to Lowrie, Oct. 2, 1824, Gallatin to MVB, Oct. 2, 1824, Gales and Seaton to MVB, Oct. 14, Oct. 17, Oct. 19, 1824, VBP; Lowrie to Gooch, Oct. 4, 1824, MVB to Andrew Stevenson, Oct. 13, 1824, Gales and Seaton to Thomas Ritchie, Oct. 17, 1824, Gooch Family Papers, UVL; Henry Storrs to Clay, Sept. 23, 1824, Clay, *Papers*, III, 847.

[61] Adams, *Memoirs*, VI, 371; Weed, *Autobiography*, pp. 117-120; *Argus*, July 9, Sept. 28, 1824; Rammelkamp, "Campaign of 1824 in New York," pp. 194-196; Fox, *Decline of Aristocracy*, p. 293.

The campaign that fall was vicious. Even before it began Clinton predicted that the Regency would buy whatever votes were needed to win. When the *Albany Argus* called Clinton a "factious and intriguing" trimmer, the *Daily Advertiser*, the newspaper of former Federalists, attacked "Martin the Pope" for his "arrogance." As Van Buren arrived at the polls to vote on election day, a hostile crowd shouted "Regency! Regency!" and a dozen opponents challenged his right to vote on the flimsy charge that he was not a resident of Albany. The Regency was routed. Not only did Clinton defeat Young by 103,452 votes to 87,093, but in the senate only two of the eight elected were Regency men, and three-quarters of the new assembly would be opponents of the Regency. Rudolph Bunner summed it up when he said, "We have been most shamefully beaten."[62]

It was fortunate for Van Buren that the lame duck legislature, not the new one, would select the presidential electors, but even so he could not guarantee the outcome. The system for choosing electors was the same one that Van Buren had exploited in 1812. Each branch of the legislature was to select a slate of electors by majority vote. If the slates were identical, the matter was settled. If not, then the thirty-two senators and one hundred and twenty-five assemblymen had to meet in joint session to choose the electors. Since the Regency controlled the senate but could no longer count on the assembly, it was assumed that a joint session would be necessary, with seventy-nine votes needed to elect a slate. The outcome would be close: Crawford and Adams each counted on about sixty votes, and Clay expected to secure forty.[63]

The outcome would also be important because New York's thirty-six electoral votes could determine the election. As the legislature assembled, it was estimated that in the nation Jackson had sixty-six sure votes from New Jersey, Pennsylvania, and the South and West, Adams had fifty-one, all from New England, Crawford thirty-three from Virginia and Georgia, and Clay thirty-three from Kentucky, Missouri and Ohio; that left seventy-eight undecided, including New York's thirty-six. Since it seemed likely that no one candidate would get an electoral majority, the top three candidates would vie for the presidency in the House of Representatives, where each state would have one vote. Even though Jackson had no chance in New York, he was

---

[62] Adams, *Memoirs*, VI, 408; *Argus*, Oct. 5, Oct. 29, Nov. 5, 1824; *Albany Daily Advertiser*, Oct. 18, 1824; Rudolph Bunner to Gulian Verplanck, Nov. 18, 1824, Gulian C. Verplanck Papers, NYHS; Rammelkamp, "Campaign of 1824 in New York," p. 68; Alexander, *Political History*, I, 332-333; *Autobiography*, p. 144.

[63] Alexander, *Political History*, I, 338-339.

certain to be one of the three national candidates. The Empire State could decide which one of the other three would be forced out.[64]

Anticipating a close election in the state legislature, Van Buren had taken steps to win a few additional votes. In mid-August, Thurlow Weed became suspicious when he spied William Kibbe, a Regency go-between, boarding the canal boat at Palmyra, near Rochester. When Weed saw Kibbe mailing a letter in Syracuse to an Adams man in the legislature, he became even more suspicious. He followed Kibbe back to Albany, then down the Hudson to New York City, where Kibbe conferred with Henry Eckford, a wealthy Crawford man. Weed trailed Kibbe and another Crawford man back to Albany and on to Montgomery County. There Weed discovered that Eckford's money was being used to secure the votes of three Clay legislators for Crawford. Weed kept the information to himself until the eve of the vote; then he called on the three hapless men and threatened to tell all unless they promised to vote for Clay. When the three agreed, Weed insisted that they use initialed ballots so that they could not change their minds. Weed won that round, but Van Buren was busy influencing other wavering votes.[65]

Since he despaired of winning all thirty-six electoral votes, Van Buren called a party caucus to bring Clay and Crawford men together on a mixed slate. Van Buren assumed that if he gave Clay about one-fourth of the electoral votes, the rest could be held for Crawford. The caucus, which met on November 5, decided to support a slate of twenty-nine electors for Crawford and seven for Clay. When voting began in each House on November 10, the list drawn up by the caucus was soon selected in the senate, but in the assembly, the Crawford, Clay and Adams groups all voted for separate lists, none of which received the necessary majority. The impasse continued for three days while the Regency held evening meetings to decide what to do. Since a joint session of the legislature seemed inevitable, the Regency decided to bring it on at once by voting for either a Clay or an Adams slate in the assembly. Benjamin Butler advocated a Clay ticket because then the joint session would divide its votes between Crawford and Clay and shut Adams out. But Azariah Flagg and Van Buren persuaded the Regency to swing the assembly to Adams on the assumption that the joint session would prefer the Crawford-Clay ticket to the Adams slate.

[64] Asbury Dickins to MVB, Oct. 2, 1824, VBP; Benjamin Butler to Jesse Hoyt, Nov. 13, 1824, Benjamin F. Butler Miscellaneous Papers, NYPL.

[65] Weed, *Autobiography*, pp. 124-128.

On November 13, the assembly selected an Adams slate, and a joint session was called for two days later.[66]

Unfortunately for Van Buren the Clay legislators were shocked and angry at the turn of events because they had not been consulted and thought that the Regency was deserting Clay for Adams. Seeing the opportunity, Thurlow Weed called a secret meeting of Adams and Clay legislators, who agreed to vote for a combined slate made up of thirty Adams electors and six Clay electors. To make certain that word did not leak out Weed printed the ballots himself.[67]

Unaware of what was going on, Van Buren and the Regency were confident when the joint session began. They assumed that there would be only two slates offered, and that the Crawford-Clay group would win. After the ballots were cast, Lieutenant Governor Erastus Root reached into the box to begin counting the ballots. When he drew out the first Adams-Clay ballot, he was so stunned that he could only exclaim, "A printed split ticket!" According to Weed, Regency stalwart Perley Keyes "sprang to his feet, and in a loud, angry voice, said 'Treason, by G__!' " At that, "the greatest confusion instantly ensued," until James Tallmadge rose and "in a stentorian voice called for order" and insisted that the balloting go on. The tabulation of votes produced a confusing result:

Crawford-Clay electoral ticket	76
Adams ticket	59
Adams-Clay ticket	19
Blank ballots	3
Total ballots	157 (necessary majority, 79)
Total votes cast	154 (necessary majority, 78)

It was agreed at once that the seven Clay electors who were on two tickets and had ninety-five votes were elected. The Regency was less willing to agree that the twenty-five Adams electors who received seventy-eight votes from two tickets should be declared elected. For two hours the Regency tried to argue that seventy-nine votes were needed for a majority because, including the three blank ballots, the total was one hundred and fifty-seven. When the twenty-five were

[66] Butler to Hoyt, Nov. 6, Nov. 9, Nov. 13, 1824, Butler Papers, NYPL; MVB to Crawford, Nov. 17, 1824, VBP; Oran Follett to the editor of the New York *Tribune*, Feb. 10, 1881, included in Weed, *Autobiography*, pp. 123, 130-135; L. Belle Hamlin, ed., "Selections from the Follett Papers," *Quarterly Publications of the Historical Philosophical Society of Ohio*, 5 (1910), 35-36; Ralph Lockwood to Francis Brooke, Nov. 17, 1824, Henry Clay Papers, LC.

[67] Weed, *Autobiography*, p. 123.

declared elected, Root was so disgusted that he led a group of Regency men out of the chamber. After four Crawford electors were chosen on a second ballot, the final result was Adams twenty-five electors, Clay seven, Crawford four.[68]

"Van Buren and his invincibles are beaten," crowed one of the Adams men; Van Buren, said another, "looks like a wilted cabbage, and poor Judge Skinner has quite lost his voice." Knowing they had failed, the members of the Regency for once lost their poise and snapped at each other as they sought scapegoats. The very next morning at breakfast Van Buren accused Judge Skinner of starting it all with his scheme for pushing Clinton off the canal commission. "There is such a thing in politics," said Van Buren, "as *killing a man too dead!*" Van Buren also blamed Yates and Young—"two very honest men but impracticable politicians"—for their part "in breaking down the party," and he informed Crawford that the friends of Clay had "deceived" the Regency. Though admitting that the Regency had contributed to its own defeat by opposing electoral reform, Van Buren still held the Clay men responsible for the outcome.[69]

Van Buren and the Regency hated to admit that they had blundered and let Thurlow Weed and his Adams allies outwit them. Adams defeated Crawford by exactly two votes, 78-76, and Weed provided that margin. If he had not uncovered the Kibbe-Eckford attempt to buy three electors, the margin would have evaporated. There would have been no Adams electors at all if Weed had not set up the Adams-Clay ballot and kept it secret. Van Buren and Flagg erred in letting the Adams ticket win in the assembly. Van Buren's refusal to consult the Clay organization was another bad miscalculation, as was his assumption that he could offer Clay a handful of electors and keep all the rest for Crawford. The Regency had been so successful that they had become overconfident and prone to make mistakes. Encouraged by their success to try to emulate their tactics, Weed beat an overconfident Van Buren at his own game.

But Van Buren still had a chance to get Crawford into the final election in the House of Representatives, as one of the three top national candidates of the Electoral College, and to keep Clay out. Henry

[68] Weed, *Autobiography*, pp. 126-127; *Niles' Register*, 27 (1824), 193-194, 225; T. S. Smith to Gouverneur, Nov. 15, 1824, Gouverneur Papers, NYPL; *Autobiography*, p. 145.

[69] T. S. Smith to Gouverneur, Nov. 15, 1824, H. Wheaton to Gouverneur, Nov. 21, 1824, Gouverneur Papers, NYPL; Joseph Gales to MVB, Nov. 11, 1824, MVB to Crawford, Nov. 17, 1824, VBP; *Autobiography*, pp. 144-146; MVB to John Lansing, Jr., Nov. 28, 1824, John Lansing, Jr., Miscellaneous Papers, NYHS.

Wheaton, who had shifted over to Adams after Calhoun had left the race, warned perceptively, that Van Buren would not stop scheming as long as there was any hope, and as the results trickled in from other states, it became apparent that a shift of one or two electoral votes in New York would be decisive. When the New York electors cast their ballots on December 1, one Clay man, under great pressure, voted for Andrew Jackson, and two others who failed to appear were replaced by Adams men. The Regency convinced one Adams elector to vote for Crawford. As a result the final tally showed that Adams' vote had risen from the expected twenty-five to twenty-six; Crawford's had gone from four to five, Jackson had picked up one solitary vote, and Clay had dropped from seven to four. If the November results in the New York legislature had stood, the national outcome would have been Jackson 98, Adams 83, Crawford 40, Clay 40, but the late changes in New York produced the final result: Jackson 99, Adams 84, Crawford 41, Clay 37. Van Buren had failed to carry New York for Crawford, but he had managed to nudge Crawford into the election in the House.[70]

"I left Albany for Washington," wrote Van Buren in his autobiography, "as completely broken down a politician as my bitterest enemies could desire." During the trip he encountered one embarrassment after another. On the Hudson River steamboat he had the bad luck to run into Governor Clinton's wife, and in New York City he had to pay off his election bets. Irritated at Rufus King for his role in the election, Van Buren decided to forgo his usual practice of traveling from New York to Washington with the senior senator. But King overtook Van Buren in Philadelphia and asked obtusely why Van Buren had "passed on without calling."[71]

On his arrival in Washington he found the Capital alive with rumors and bustling with dinner parties, most of them connected with the coming election. At the start of the session friends of Jackson were anxious about whispers of "good will" between Adams and Crawford, but the whispers were soon replaced by talk of a rapprochement between Adams and Clay. Not to be outdone, Andrew Jackson made overtures to Crawford and even sent his wife Rachel to visit Mrs. Crawford (she returned the call promptly). Jackson also tried wooing Henry Clay by giving him a ride home after a party, and then the two

[70] Wheaton to Gouverneur, Nov. 21, 1824, Gouverneur Papers, NYPL; Weed, *Autobiography*, pp. 128-130; *Autobiography*, p. 145; Roger Skinner to MVB, Dec. 1, 1824, VBP; A. Conkling to John W. Taylor, Dec. 24, 1824, Taylor Papers; MVB to John Lansing, Jr., Nov. 28, 1824, John Lansing, Jr., Miscellaneous Papers, NYHS.

[71] *Autobiography*, p. 149.

men exchanged dinner parties. The rivalry became so intense that Margaret Bayard Smith, wife of the president of the Washington branch of the Bank of the United States, described Washington society as "divided into separate batallions." After Mrs. Adams and Mrs. Calhoun had taken large parties to the theater, Mrs. Smith, who was for Crawford, urged Mrs. Crawford to do the same, "to show our strength." With the help of Louis McLane and Van Buren, they made up a party of ten women and twice as many men and spent a pleasant evening at the theater. Mrs. Crawford sat in the front box, flanked by senators Thomas W. Cobb of Georgia, and Walter Lowrie of Pennsylvania, on one side, and Van Buren on the other, "with a phalanx behind."[72]

Even though Crawford was an underdog, his followers had not given up, and Van Buren was as committed to Crawford as ever. The day after Christmas Van Buren reassured Benjamin Butler that Crawford's chances were "far, very far, from desparate [sic], and are believed to be every day improving." When friends Roger Skinner and Thomas Ritchie wavered, Van Buren admitted misgivings as to the outcome, but on January 26, he predicted that Adams would fail on the first ballot, and then Crawford's chances would be good. The Crawford side also clung to the belief that "when Jackson's friends lost hope of success, they would prefer C. to A." On the eve of voting, Louis McLane, Van Buren and the other Crawfordites predicted that the balloting would go on indefinitely until finally Adams and Jackson would compromise on Crawford.[73]

Van Buren, who had stuck with Crawford in order to create a national party, could do little but continue his support. He hardly wanted to see Adams in the White House since that would give Thurlow Weed power in New York. Andrew Jackson would be no better because he had not followed Old Republican principles and if elected would make DeWitt Clinton "premier" in New York. Roger Skinner

---

[72] Rufus King to John King, Jan. 12, 1825, Rufus King, memoranda, Jan. 29, 1825, King, *Correspondence*, V, 581-583; Bassett, *Jackson*, p. 352; Smith, *First Forty Years of Washington Society*, pp. 170-173.

[73] Skinner to MVB, Dec. 24, 1824, MVB to Butler, Dec. 27, 1824, VBP; Thomas Ritchie to Archibald Ritchie, Jan. 11, 1825, Ambler, "Ritchie Letters," *Branch Papers*, 3 (1911), 203; MVB to William C. Hoopham, Jan. 15, 1825, Gilbert H. Montague Collection, NYPL; MVB to Hamilton, Jan. 26, 1825, Hamilton, *Reminiscences*, pp. 62-63; Smith, *First Forty Years of Washington Society*, pp. 181-182, Rufus King, memoranda, Jan. 29, Jan. 31, 1825, King, *Correspondence*, VI, 583, 585-586; Adams, *Memoirs*, VI, 474, 493. James Buchanan believed that the Crawford people held the balance of power between Adams and Jackson. James Buchanan to Thomas Elder, Jan. 2, 1825, John B. Moore, ed., *The Works of James Buchanan* (Philadelphia, 1908), I, 119-121.

warned Van Buren that if Crawford lost, Clinton might even be elected President in 1828. Van Buren could only hope that Crawford would somehow win and thereby give the senator political power both nationally and in New York.[74]

Washington was busy doing arithmetic. When the House finally voted, thirteen votes—a majority of the state delegations—would be necessary to be elected. Crawford had Delaware, Virginia, North Carolina, and Georgia. Jackson seemed certain of seven states: New Jersey, Pennsylvania, South Carolina, Tennessee, Alabama, Mississippi, and Indiana. Adams could count on the six New England states, and expected also to win Maryland, Louisiana and Illinois. To get thirteen votes Adams needed in addition the three states that Henry Clay could deliver—Kentucky, Ohio, and Missouri—and New York.[75]

Attention naturally centered on Clay, who could bring Adams close to election. On January 9, Adams coyly wrote in his diary that Clay had arrived at six and "spent the evening with me in a long conversation . . . prospective of the future." Two weeks later Clay announced that he was supporting Adams, and Clay's aides began to urge others to back Adams too. When Congressman Francis Johnson of Kentucky found Van Buren "unyielding," Johnson warned that Clay might carry the House for Adams without the New Yorker's assistance. Van Buren admitted that it was "very possible," but added, "if you do so you sing Mr. Clay's political death warrant. He will never become President." Both predictions proved accurate.[76]

At the same time Adams was making overtures toward the men who could help bring him New York. Just before Clay paid his crucial visit, Adams used the time between two church services to visit congressmen John W. Taylor and Albert H. Tracy of New York, and that evening Adams received a letter from Lieutenant Governor James Tallmadge of New York. Adams also paid a call on Van Buren and promised to help a Van Buren protégé obtain an appointment as consul in South America. Intent on winning New York, Adams exchanged many other visits with New Yorkers right up to the election.[77]

On February 9, the day of the House election, Adams had won

[74] Adams, *Memoirs*, VI, 474; Williams to MVB, Nov. 25, 1824, Skinner to MVB, Dec. 24, 1824, VBP; Hammond, *Political Parties*, II, 189.

[75] King, memoranda, Jan. 29, 1825, King, *Correspondence*, VI, 583-584; MVB to James A. Hamilton, Jan. 26, 1825, Hamilton, *Reminiscences*, pp. 62-63.

[76] Adams, *Memoirs*, VI, 464-465; *Autobiography*, p. 150, Glyndon Van Deusen, *The Life of Henry Clay* (Boston, 1937), pp. 186-190.

[77] On January 12, Van Buren called on Adams, and later that day Adams had dinner with Van Buren. Adams, *Memoirs*, VI, 458, 462, 464-466, 469.

twelve states and needed only New York to become President. To keep Adams from carrying New York on the first ballot, Van Buren counted on the vote of Stephen Van Rensselaer. Although the Patroon had fluctuated from one candidate to another, Van Buren finally got Van Rensselaer to promise that he would "not vote for Adams." But just before the vote Clay and Daniel Webster took the Patroon into the speaker's room, where the three held "an animated conversation." When Louis McLane and William S. Archer of the Crawford group noticed how "staggered" Van Rensselaer was by the pressure, they asked Van Buren to hurry over to keep his messmate in line. Van Buren, who arrived just as the voting began, was "pained" to see Van Rensselaer's "obvious agitation and distress." Van Buren later told a wonderful but hardly credible story of how the Patroon had made up his mind to vote for Adams. According to Van Buren, the Patroon "dropped his head" to pray and "saw on the floor directly below him a ticket bearing the name of John Quincy Adams." Deciding that the Lord had spoken, Van Rensselaer voted for Adams, who carried New York and the House.[78]

It was charged many years later that Van Buren never expected Crawford to win, but plotted to keep New York divided so that on some later ballot he could bring the state over to Adams and receive the rewards due a kingmaker. There is not enough evidence to prove that Van Buren schemed to have the election come out exactly that way; it is more likely that he wanted to force the election to several ballots with the faint hope that the House would eventually compromise on Crawford. Van Buren had opposed Adams so persistently that he could hardly expect favors, even for delivering the New York vote.[79]

[78] The New York vote was Adams 18, Crawford 14, Jackson 2. Van Buren to James A. Hamilton, Jan. 26, 1825, Hamilton, *Reminiscences*, pp. 62-63; *Autobiography*, pp. 149-153; Stephen Van Rensselaer to Solomon Van Rensselaer, Jan. 22, 1825, Bonney, *Historical Gleanings*, I, 415; Adams, *Memoirs*, VI, 493; Weed, *Autobiography*, I, 176, 462; Smith, *First Forty Years of Washington Society*, pp. 175-176, 184-186, 190-193; Rufus King, memoranda, Jan. 31, 1825, King, *Correspondence*, VI, 585. William B. Fink does not take the Van Rensselaer story seriously. Fink denies that Van Rensselaer had ever promised to vote for Crawford, and points out that Van Buren is the only source for the prayer incident. William B. Fink, "Stephen Van Rensselaer and the House Election of 1825," *New York History*, 32 (1951), 323-330.

[79] The charge that he plotted to make Adams President came from Nathan Sargent, *Public Men and Events from the Commencement of Mr. Monroe's Administration in 1817, to the Close of Mr. Fillmore's Administration in 1853* (Philadelphia, 1874), I, 75-77. Jabez Hammond in his *History of Political Parties* accepted the thesis, but changed it in a later edition after Van Buren sent him a letter of protest. Van Buren to Hammond, Aug. 21, 1842, VBP. See also Wheaton to Gouverneur, Feb. 15, 1825, Gouverneur Papers, NYPL. Robert V. Remini denies that Van Buren had any intention

The question of why Van Buren behaved exactly as he did during the vote in the House is less important than the question of why he blundered so badly during the entire election of 1824-1825. It is difficult to explain how the man whose rise to power in New York had earned him the nickname of the "Magician" came to make so many disastrous mistakes during the campaign. He chose Crawford as his candidate and then stuck with him even after Crawford suffered a stroke and failed to rally the usual Republican support in the congressional caucus. He obstinately opposed the popular choice of electors in New York in the vain hope of improving Crawford's presidential chances. During the voting in New York he refused to compromise with the forces of Adams, Clay, or Jackson, and when the scene shifted to Washington he refused to go over to Adams or Jackson, even when it was evident that one of the two would win. As a result Van Buren suffered personal humiliation, the Regency received a serious setback, and Van Buren's national party organization was temporarily damaged.

The answer to the question lies in Van Buren's determination to place national goals ahead of state goals, and to create a political party based upon Old Republican principles and an alliance of New York and Virginia, North and South. Since Van Buren's Old Republican credentials were not impeccable and since he represented the New York or northern part of the alliance, he had to support a candidate in 1824, who was an acceptable Old Republican and who represented the South. Adams, Jackson, Clay, Calhoun—none of them would do. Once having decided on Crawford for these political-ideological reasons, Van Buren was forced into error after error, leading to eventual defeat. He lost because he had set nation over state. In trying to revive the old contest throughout the United States he had weakened his hold on New York.

---

of ever supporting Adams. Remini, *Van Buren and the Democratic Party*, pp. 85-90, 221-224.

·5·

PLANTERS AND PLAIN REPUBLICANS

Badly stung by his humiliating setback in 1824 and 1825, Van Buren set about strengthening his political base in New York before resuming his quest for a national party. He had learned through experience that it was a mistake to sacrifice his interests in New York to his national goals. Although he was still determined to restore the old Jeffersonian alliance of New York and Virginia, he first had to regain control of New York.

Van Buren's Bucktails were on the defensive in New York in January 1825, when their nemesis DeWitt Clinton delivered his inaugural address calling for popular choice of presidential electors and for a new program of internal improvements. The Bucktails were forced to accept the former, which was voted into law in March, but they managed to resist many of the roads and canals that Clinton proposed. When it came to choosing a senator to replace Rufus King, who had decided not to serve again, the Regency had to adopt delaying tactics to postpone the election and keep Clinton's old ally Ambrose Spencer from being chosen.[1]

The Regency was in transition as defeat, death and age respectively removed Samuel Young, Roger Skinner and Erastus Root from the top of the organization. Since young Azariah Flagg and Silas Wright had taken the lead in every crisis during the election of 1824 and in the session of the legislature that followed, they now joined William L. Marcy as the Regency leaders in Albany; despite his setback, Van Buren remained the unquestioned boss.[2]

In their weakened condition, Van Buren and the Regency found it expedient to deal with DeWitt Clinton, whose prospects in 1825 had never been better. Clinton's Erie Canal was just going into operation and the man he had supported for President, Andrew Jackson, was already the leading contender with John Quincy Adams for the presidency. Van Buren was even afraid that Clinton himself might win in 1828. As Van Buren saw it, Adams was not popular enough to be reelected, Henry Clay had damaged his chances by accepting the position of Secretary of State—in what many called a "corrupt bar-

---

[1] Fox, *Decline of Aristocracy*, pp. 285, 300, 305-308; Remini, *Van Buren and the Democratic Party*, pp. 93-94, 97-99.
[2] Remini, *Van Buren and the Democratic Party*, p. 95.

gain"—John C. Calhoun had failed to gather any strength, and Jackson could not "stand the test of a four year's exposure to the public scrutiny." When Clinton turned down an offer to become minister to England, many believed that he was looking ahead to the presidency. Although Van Buren did not want Clinton to succeed, he needed Clinton's help in 1825 and 1826, and Clinton needed Regency support in any serious bid for the presidency. Since both men shared an antipathy for Adams, they were ready to reach an understanding.[3]

Clinton had made the first move directly after the election of 1824, but Van Buren replied that his "fortunes were at too low an ebb" at that time for him to come to any understanding. When the Bucktails had gained control of the legislature in the fall election of 1825, Van Buren felt that the time had come to deal with Clinton. After meeting with Van Buren at the home of a friend, Clinton made an offer by way of former New York mayor Edward Livingston, who was now congressman from Louisiana. If Van Buren would remain uncommitted and not oppose Clinton in the next presidential campaign, Clinton would back Van Buren for governor or any federal job he wanted. Although Van Buren replied primly that he would not make any agreement just out of "personal interest," a rapprochement was under way.[4] In Richmond, for example, the *Enquirer*, which often reflected Regency opinion, began to print comments praising Clinton.[5]

The cooperation between the Regency and Clinton became apparent in Albany during the winter of 1826. In return for the election of Bucktail Nathan Sanford as senator, the Regency allowed Clinton's brother-in-law, James Jones, to replace Sanford as chancellor. After Flagg, Marcy and Samuel A. Talcott were safely installed as secretary of state, comptroller and attorney general, the Bucktails voted to confirm a Clintonian as recorder of Albany. And when it came to appointing a circuit judge, Clinton selected a man he knew would be "the least obnoxious" to the Regency. He even passed the word that he no longer considered Van Buren simply "a noisy . . . politician."[6] The reconciliation did not go unnoticed. Clay's friend Peter Porter

[3] *Autobiography*, pp. 157-159; Alfred Conkling to Jabez Hammond, Mar. 13, 1825, Alfred Conkling Miscellaneous Papers, NYHS.

[4] *Autobiography*, pp. 149, 158-159; Marcy to MVB, Dec. 17, 1825; Edward Livingston to MVB, Nov. 30, 1825, MVB to Livingston, Dec. 7, 1825, VBP; William B. Hatcher, *Edward Livingston: Jeffersonian Republican and Jacksonian Democrat* (University, 1940), p. 313.

[5] *Richmond Enquirer*, April 5, June 17, 1825.

[6] *Autobiography*, p. 158; Alexander, *Political History*, I, 346-348; Hammond, *Political Parties*, II, 211-215; Jesse Hoyt to MVB, June 11, 1826, VBP.

warned that Van Buren was leading Clinton on; Rufus King's son Charles called it "coquetry" and "open prostitution"; the lawyer Jabez Hammond labeled it "backstairs intercourse," and Erastus Root complained that the Bucktails were in a "d   l of a pickle."[7]

The Bucktails' problems grew in the spring of 1826 when Clinton decided to run for reelection. As part of their understanding with the governor, the Regency first considered letting him run unopposed, but Erastus Root and Silas Wright could not bring themselves to let their old enemy be reelected without a challenge. They convinced Van Buren that the Regency should put up a candidate, but could not talk him into accepting a supporter of Andrew Jackson. Van Buren reasoned that if they ran a Jackson man, backers of Adams and Clay would then unite behind Clinton. If they nominated a Clay-Adams man instead, then they stood a chance of splitting the opposition because New Yorkers who liked Clinton as well as Clay and Adams would have to choose. He proposed William B. Rochester, a supporter of Clay who had served briefly in the foreign service, and though Wright disapproved of Rochester, the party nominated him for governor.[8]

As usual Van Buren's motivation was complex. Since Rochester was likely to be a weak candidate, Van Buren did not endanger his reconciliation with Clinton, and by nominating a Clay-Adams man, he hoped to split the opposition and attract a few Adams followers over to the Bucktails. As long as the election was close, Van Buren expected to benefit no matter who won. In the unlikely event of a win for Rochester, the Adams men would abandon Clinton, leaving the Regency in command of the state. If, as expected, Clinton won, he and Van Buren would remain on good terms and could unite against Adams in 1828. The major risk lay in a sweeping Clinton victory that might encourage the governor to abandon his entente with Van Buren.[9]

The campaign was confusing because the Regency was so badly divided. While Edwin Croswell worked diligently for Rochester, Congressman Michael Hoffman and Mordecai Noah of the New York *National Advocate* did not. Many New Yorkers including Rochester

[7] Porter to Clay, Feb. 17, Mar. 4, 1826, Charles King to Clay, Mar. 21, 1826, Hammond to Clay, Mar. 16, 1826, Henry Clay Papers, LC; Root to MVB, April 2, 1826, VBP.

[8] Hammond, *Political Parties*, II, 212-213, 232; Alexander, *Political History*, I, 350; *Autobiography*, pp. 159-163; Root to MVB, April 2, 1826, VBP; *Argus*, Sept. 26, 1826.

[9] For various interpretations of Van Buren's motives in the election, see Hammond, *Political Parties*, II, 203, 232-234; Alexander, *Political History*, I, 350-352; Fox, *Decline of Aristocracy*, pp. 312-313; Remini, *Van Buren and the Democratic Party*, pp. 229-230; *Autobiography*, pp. 160-164.

suspected that Van Buren wanted Clinton to win, but the senator insisted that he gave his candidate "faithful support." And so he did, even wagering large amounts on a Rochester victory. Van Buren had to campaign hard because he wanted the Regency to keep control of the legislature, where his reelection to the Senate would be decided in February. When Rochester claimed that he had the administration's support, many Adams followers voted for him instead of Clinton. Van Buren had split the opposition exactly as he had anticipated.[10]

For several days after the election it appeared that Clinton had lost. The governor became resigned to defeat, and, just as Van Buren had expected, blamed the result on the People's party, not the Regency. On the Sunday morning following the election, Van Buren "heard the sound of the steam being blown off, signaling the arrival of the Southern boat." Soon a messenger carrying the final returns ran by on his way to the governor's mansion. On the way to church Van Buren told Marcy that "the mystery would be solved" as soon as Governor and Mrs. Clinton arrived at the service. When they did arrive, Mrs. Clinton gave Van Buren such a triumphant look that he knew at once that her husband had been reelected.[11]

Van Buren's commitment to a new national party now had to await his reelection to the Senate, and in the month following Clinton's victory Van Buren looked ahead nervously to the reconvening of the legislature when his reelection would be decided. On December 12, 1826, Marcy warned that the unreliable Noah was attacking Van Buren in the *National Advocate*. Two days later an anxious Van Buren wrote to the inner circle of the Regency to ask whether he needed to make a speech in the Senate against Clay and Adams. As the legislature gathered, friends of Adams put pressure on Clinton to oppose Van Buren. Jabez Hammond urged Henry Clay to support Peter Porter, Stephen Van Rensselaer, or John W. Taylor for senator in place of Van Buren. After talking with him, Congressman Romulus M. Saunders of North Carolina, reported that "Van B. [had] a delicate and difficult part to play."[12]

---

[10] Philip Nicholas to MVB, Oct. 13, 1826, MVB to Cambreleng, Nov. 7, 1826, W. C. Bouck to MVB, Nov. 17, 1826, VBP. For Rochester's suspicions, see Alexander, *Political History*, I, 352. For a contrary view see Peter Porter to Henry Clay, Oct. 8, 1826, Henry Clay Papers, LC. See also *Autobiography*, pp. 163-164; Hoffman to Azariah Flagg, Oct. 7, 1826, Flagg Papers; *Argus*, Oct. 17, 1826.

[11] Van Buren lost a large sum of money and a suit of clothes on the election. *Autobiography*, pp. 164-165; *Argus*, Nov. 18, Nov. 25, 1826; Alexander, *Political History*, I, 352.

[12] *Autobiography*, p. 165; Marcy to MVB, Dec. 10, Dec. 27, 1826, MVB to Butler, Dec. 12, 1826, VBP; A. Conkling to John W. Taylor, Jan. 7, 1827, J. Hammond to

Despite his fears, Van Buren was easily reelected on February 6. Since many Clintonians voted for Van Buren, the story spread that Clinton and Van Buren had made a deal, that Van Buren had helped make Clinton governor in return for Clinton's support. It is unlikely that there was any formal arrangement because Van Buren would never have committed himself to such a dangerous rival as Clinton, who could have destroyed him by revealing the plot. But Van Buren's behavior between 1825 and 1827 does suggest his overall strategy. After his defeat in the presidential election, he was determined to avoid national commitments and concentrate on rebuilding his power in New York. He achieved a reconciliation with Clinton, strengthened the Regency, gained control of the legislature, and won reelection to the Senate.[13]

WHILE they strengthened their home base by cooperating with Clinton, the Bucktails at first avoided making any open commitment to a presidential candidate for 1828. In April 1826, Edwin Croswell published an editorial in the *Albany Argus* advising Republicans to avoid any "collisions of opinion" because they were not yet "ready to take sides for 1828." In Washington Van Buren admitted that he and the other Crawford men "lay upon our oares" and would not "lightly commit ourselves." When Van Buren's opponents later accused him of "non-committalism" in 1826, he denied any responsibility. It is difficult to accept the denial because Croswell informed Van Buren of the editorial before it was published, and the *Argus* rarely printed anything that Van Buren had not approved. Although opposition to Adams was growing in New York, the Regency decided not to attack the President for fear of driving him into Clinton's arms. Van Buren and the Regency preferred to remain uncommitted and let the latent hostility between Clinton and Adams come to the surface. For the time being state interests were being placed ahead of national interests.[14]

Taylor, Feb. 5, 1827, Taylor Papers; J. Hammond to Henry Clay, Jan. 28, 1827, Henry Clay Papers, LC; Saunders to Bartlett Yancey, Jan. 20, 1827, "Letters to Bartlett Yancey," *The James Sprunt Historical Publications*, X, No. 2 (1911), 60-62.

[13] *Argus*, Dec. 28, 1826, Jan. 4, Jan. 15, Feb. 6, 1827; John C. Hamilton to MVB, Dec. 21, 1826, VBP; A. Conkling to John W. Taylor, Jan. 27, 1827, Taylor Papers; Hammond, *Political Parties*, II, 246-252.

[14] James Tallmadge to John W. Taylor, Feb. 22, 1826, Taylor Papers; MVB to Benjamin Butler, Dec. 25, 1825, Croswell to MVB, April 3, 1826, VBP; *Argus*, April 4, 1826; Hammond, *Political Parties*, II, 206. Van Buren urged Bartlett Yancey of North Carolina, to remain uncommitted. Romulus Saunders to Bartlett Yancey, Jan. 10, 1826, "Letters of Romulus M. Saunders," p. 454; William S. Hoffman, *Andrew Jackson and North Carolina Politics* (Chapel Hill, 1958; reprint, 1971), p. 12. In 1842, Van Buren

Although Van Buren did not commit himself in favor of any presidential candidate in 1826, everyone knew that he was opposed to President Adams. Eager as ever to restore the old two-party system, Van Buren could hardly support an administration that he believed was intent on continuing the amalgamation policies of James Monroe and did not seem to care whether its backing came "from Jew or Gentile." With his hard-earned reputation as a Jeffersonian Republican Van Buren could not approve of Adams' first annual message, which embraced many of the national economic principles of Henry Clay's American System. Van Buren took the opportunity to attack what he later called the "latitudinarian doctrines" of the message and to propose his resolution calling for a constitutional amendment limiting federal internal improvements. As a New Yorker, Van Buren had other good reasons for opposing Adams. He was angry at the administration for arranging to have New York Clintonian John W. Taylor returned as speaker of the House of Representatives. Van Buren also warned New Yorkers to oppose Adams' economic program because their state already had its roads and canals and would be responsible for "like works in other states."[15]

Even though the administration held a majority in the Congress, a large number of congressmen and senators were opposed to Adams. In addition to Van Buren, old Crawford men such as Nathaniel Macon and Louis McLane were quick to attack Adams. So were the South Carolinians Robert Y. Hayne and James Hamilton, Jr., who were followers of Vice President John C. Calhoun. And Andrew Jackson's western supporters, Thomas Hart Benton and John H. Eaton, were openly critical.

The first opportunity for these groups to join forces came when Adams proposed sending ministers to an assembly of American nations to be held in Panama. Even though the Panama Congress was popular with the American people, the President's opponents decided to take a stand against it. Van Buren paid a special call on Calhoun and found the South Carolinian just as opposed to the mission as he was. The two men agreed to oppose the nomination of the ministers in the Senate and then go on to overthrow the administration.[16]

On February 15, 1826, Van Buren fired the first shot by introducing

---

wrote a note on the 1826 letter from Croswell: "Origin of the non-committal charge." In his *Autobiography* Van Buren interrupted his account of politics in 1826 with a four-page refutation of the charge. *Autobiography*, pp. 196-199.

[15] *Autobiography*, pp. 194-195; *Register of Debates*, 19th Congress, 1st session (1825-1826), 20; MVB to Butler, Dec. 25, 1825, VBP.

[16] *Autobiography*, pp. 199-201.

a resolution asking the President whether he objected to opening the debate over the nominations to the public, and to publishing the documents. Those voting yea on the resolution, which passed, included Jacksonians Benton and Eaton, Calhoun supporter Hayne, and former Crawford men such as Macon, John Randolph and Van Buren. Adams, who opposed the resolution, responded sarcastically that he would leave such decisions up to the Senate because he could not understand the "motives" behind the questions. Since many newspapers were calling the mission "patriotic," Van Buren stalled and for several weeks the Senate discussed the Panama affair in secret session. Finally on March 14, he moved that it was unwise to send delegates to Panama because the power of joining political associations belonged to the people rather than to the Congress. When the motion failed, Adams was able to have his ministers to Panama confirmed.[17]

Despite the setback, the opposition continued to attack the mission. Senator Hayne, who concentrated on the issue of race, warned that the American delegates would have to discuss the question of suppressing the slave trade and would have to deal with black representatives from Haiti. Van Buren, who defended the policies of the early republic, relied upon the isolationist tradition of Washington, Jefferson and Monroe when he opposed joining a confederacy such as the Panama Congress. Such a "political connexion," he argued, would be "at war with the established policy of our government." The arguments of Hayne and Van Buren gave a glimpse of the North-South alliance that lay behind the opposition to Adams.[18]

Although Adams managed to save the Panama mission, the long debate accelerated the formation of a new political party. The eccentric John Randolph did his part too with a vicious, rambling oration in which he accused Adams and Clay of having made a corrupt bargain. Assuming that his listeners had read *Tom Jones*, Randolph compared the coalition of Adams and Clay to that of "Blifil and Black George ... of the puritan with the blackleg." When Clay challenged Randolph to a duel, the confrontation turned into a farce, but the excitement

[17] *Ibid.*, pp. 200-201; *Register of Debates*, 19th Congress, 1st session (1825-1826), 111-131, 142, 149, 150.

[18] Several other speakers, including John Randolph, referred to race and slavery in their speeches. *Register of Debates*, 19th Congress, 1st session (1825-1826), 111-131, 150, 154-174. For Van Buren's speech, see *Speeech of Mr. Van Buren of New York, Delivered in the Senate of the United States, on the Mission to Panama, March, 1826* (Washington, D.C., 1826); and *Register of Debates*, 19th Congress, 1st session (1825-1826), 243-263. For a letter to Van Buren praising him for the speech, see Kent to MVB, April 15, 1826, VBP. See also *Argus*, June 5, 1826.

dramatized the new political movement. Adams, who knew what was going on, called it an attempt "to combine the discordant elements of the Crawford and Jackson and Calhoun men into a united opposition against the administration." Several administration newspapers put the blame on Jackson and Calhoun; others recognized the hand of Van Buren. When Adams first heard of the resolutions against the mission, he blamed them on Van Buren, while Clay spoke of the "zeal" with which Van Buren went "along with the faction." Clay believed that Van Buren and Calhoun had not "yet agreed upon the terms" but had agreed to "settle other matters" soon.[19]

As a first step toward such an agreement, Van Buren approached Calhoun about establishing a partisan newspaper in Washington. In May 1826, Van Buren suggested that they bring in Thomas Ritchie of the Richmond Junto to set up a newspaper, but Calhoun preferred to use the *United States Telegraph*, which had been started by Missouri editor Duff Green the year before. After returning to Albany in the summer, Van Buren sent Calhoun a letter from Churchill C. Cambreleng recommending Ritchie, to which Calhoun replied that two papers "on the same side [would] distract and excite jealousy." He praised Green and reported that the circulation of the *Telegraph* was increasing rapidly. Calhoun, who could count on Green, did not want to get involved with Van Buren's friend Ritchie. Finding it easier to agree on political principles than on editors, Calhoun assured Van Buren that the "liberty and happiness [of the nation] depend[ed] on maintaining . . . republican grounds and republican principles."[20]

Back in New York during the summer of 1826, Van Buren continued to work on the new political party while he was preparing for the state election and even while he was vacationing at Saratoga Springs. As John Quincy Adams' nineteen-year-old son Charles Francis described it, Saratoga that August was in its "glory, [with] riding, singing, drinking, dancing . . . the constant order of the day and night." Young Adams, who was almost as serious as his father, was ashamed of spending five weeks in such an ugly, dusty place, where nothing was "pursued but pleasure," and where very few were content to drink the spring waters. Furthermore, it was crowded with politicians who were opposed to his father. Van Buren, on the other hand, enjoyed Saratoga that summer because it gave him the opportunity to cement the alliance of Crawford, Calhoun and Jackson. He invited Senator

[19] *Register of Debates*, 19th Congress, 1st session (1825-1826), 401; Adams, *Memoirs*, VII, 112, 117; Henry Clay to Peter Porter, Feb. 22, 1826, Clay, *Papers*, V, 126; *Richmond Enquirer*, April 28, 1826.

[20] Calhoun to MVB, July 7, 1826, quoted in *Autobiography*, pp. 514-515.

Levi Woodbury of New Hampshire, who was leaning toward Jackson, to visit him there. Calhounite Robert Y. Hayne spent the early summer visiting other parts of New York before settling down in Saratoga in August. Churchill C. Cambreleng and Louis McLane were there to represent the old Crawford movement, and Jackson's leading supporter in New York, DeWitt Clinton, arrived to speak for the general.[21]

While Van Buren was concentrating on state politics that summer and fall, the movement against Adams was rapidly becoming a campaign for Andrew Jackson. Ever since Jackson's defeat in 1825, John Overton's Tennessee clique had been making a sustained effort to put the Old Hero in the White House. By the summer of 1826, the South Carolinians Calhoun, Hayne and Hamilton had announced for Jackson, and Southerners John Randolph, Thomas Ritchie and Duff Green were tending in that direction. In New York Jackson could count on Clinton and former Federalists Gulian Verplanck and Rudolph Bunner, who promised in May that he and his friends at Oswego were ready to back Old Hickory.[22]

Van Buren had long been interested in Jackson, but only if the general would support sound republican principles. In 1825, Van Buren had reassured Judge William Smith of South Carolina that Jackson had been "well grounded" in these principles but had let them gather "rust" during his long military career. Van Buren was confident that they could defeat Adams if they added "the General's personal popularity to the strength of the old Republican party" and if Jackson would "put his election on old party grounds." As Van Buren waited uncertainly in December 1826 to find out if he would be reelected to the Senate, he still could not decide whether to join the swelling movement for Jackson or insist on someone with proven Republican credentials. He instructed the Regency to do everything to destroy the Adams administration but not to support anyone who did not stand on Jeffersonian principles.[23]

During a visit at the Virginia home of William H. Fitzhugh at Christmas, Van Buren and Calhoun finally "united heart and hand to pro-

[21] Aida DiPace Donald and David Donald, eds., *Diary of Charles Francis Adams* (Cambridge, Mass., 1964-1968), II, 73-74; MVB to Benjamin Butler, June 26, 1826, Levi Woodbury Papers, LC.

[22] Ambler, *Thomas Ritchie*, p. 106; John Eaton to Duff Green, Aug. 16, 1826, Duff Green Papers, LC; Duff Green to Thomas Ritchie, Sept. 10, 1826, Gooch Family Papers, UVL; *Richmond Enquirer*, Nov. 24, 1826, Jan. 4, 1827, Bunner to Verplanck, Mar. 5, May 8, Oct. 8, 1826, Verplanck Papers, NYHS.

[23] *Autobiography*, p. 198; MVB to Philip N. Nicholas, Nov. 1826, MVB to Benjamin Butler, Dec. 12, 1826, VBP. Van Buren's instructions to the Regency are in MVB to Azariah Flagg, Dec. 22, 1826, Flagg Papers, CUL.

mote the election of General Jackson." Van Buren agreed to prepare a letter to Ritchie outlining campaign plans and show it to Calhoun and Congressman Samuel D. Ingham of Pennsylvania, for approval. This Christmas agreement uniting men from South Carolina, Virginia, Pennsylvania, and New York in support of the Tennessee hero shaped the Jackson movement for the next few years. Although Van Buren felt obliged to keep his decision hidden until after his reelection in February, he was now committed to Jackson.[24]

In his letter to Ritchie, dated January 13, 1827, Van Buren returned to his theme of restoring the old two-party system. His strategy was first to call a national nominating convention because Adams would refuse to participate, and they would then be able to "draw anew the old Party lines." By thus "substituting *party principles* for *personal preferences*," they would help Republicans in the Northeast and Northwest. Van Buren used phrases that make this letter a political classic. By combining, he wrote "the planters of the South and the plain Republicans of the north," they would prevent conflict between the slave and free states. For the next three decades and more, the Democratic party tried desperately to keep this unwieldy alliance alive. "Political combinations," Van Buren concluded, were "unavoidable," and the old system was best.

Van Buren wanted Jackson as the party nominee, but only if he ran on a Republican platform. To "get rid of the present, & restore a

[24] *Autobiography*, p. 514. There has been some disagreement over when Van Buren committed himself to Jackson. To say that Van Buren had decided by November 1826, after the state election is to ignore his obvious indecision in early December. But George Dangerfield is incorrect in stating that Van Buren waited until the following summer. Dangerfield bases his position on a letter from Marcy referring to rumors that Van Buren was for Adams, and a letter from John W. Taylor citing Regency denials that Van Buren had any "political connection with the Jackson party." Marcy and other Regency men were simply tring to protect Van Buren until he was reelected. George Dangerfield, *The Awakening of American Nationalism 1815-1828* (New York, 1965), p. 274; Marcy to MVB, Dec. 27, 1826, VBP; Taylor to Charles Miner, April 16, 1827, Taylor Papers. Duff Green, who knew what was going on, predicted on December 29, 1826, that Van Buren would support Jackson. Green later wrote that Calhoun and Van Buren had been for Jackson from the start. James Hamilton, Jr., reported to Jackson in February 1827, that Van Buren was "*entirely* with us." Duff Green to Ninian Edwards, Dec. 29, 1826, E. B. Washburne, ed., *The Edwards Papers: Being a Portion of the Collection of the Letters, Papers, and Manuscripts of Ninian Edwards*, Chicago Historical Society's Collection, III (Chicago, 1884), 266; Duff Green to William B. Lewis, Sept. 2, 1827, Duff Green Letterbook, Duff Green Papers, LC; James Hamilton, Jr., to Jackson, Feb. 16, 1827, Jackson, *Correspondence*, III, 344. I concur with the view of Robert V. Remini that Van Buren had gone over to Jackson by January 1827. Remini, *Van Buren and the Democratic Party*, pp. 125-130.

better state of things," he said, they must combine "Genl. Jackson's personal popularity with the portion of the old party feeling yet remaining." Jackson should not be elected because of "his military services without reference to party. ... his election as the result of a combined and concerted effort of a political party, holding in the main, to certain tenets" would be much different. Van Buren's letter is an important contribution to American political theory because in it he combines his nostalgic desire to return to old political principles with his new concept of political parties as a positive good. He permits himself a backward glance at the old struggle between Federalists and Republicans, and looks ahead to the debate over slavery.[25]

During the winter and spring Van Buren attracted increasing political attention. Ritchie ran a series of articles in the *Enquirer* defending the "Great Magician" from charges that he was ambitious and was seeking the vice presidency. The editors of the *National Intelligencer*, Joseph Gales and William W. Seaton, who had deserted Crawford for Adams, blamed Van Buren when the Senate removed its printing from their newspaper and gave it to Green's *Telegraph*. They called Van Buren the "life and soul" of the movement against the administration and claimed that he held weekly meetings all winter. The hopes of the new party, they said, rested on Van Buren's ability to deliver New York's votes at next winter's Republican caucus. They taunted Ritchie and the other "Virginia Dons" for playing "second fiddle to the little Dutchman."[26]

To keep his southern allies in line the Dutchman took off on another of his tours of the South as soon as Congress ended. Accompanied by Cambreleng and congressmen James Hamilton, Jr., and William Drayton of South Carolina, Van Buren stopped first at Charleston. Here, at a political dinner, he offered a traditional Republican toast calling for the end of "sectional and State jealousies," and asking for the "appropriate sacrifice ... upon the altar of State Rights." He was so well received that he reported to the Regency that his trip was proceeding favorably.[27]

After waiting three days for the seas to calm, Van Buren left by ship

[25] MVB to Ritchie, Jan. 13, 1827, VBP.

[26] *Richmond Enquirer*, Mar. 20, Mar. 23, April 13, April 24, 1827; *Argus*, Mar. 29, April 4, April 5, May 19, 1827; *Niles' Register*, 32 (1827), 21-22.

[27] James Hamilton, Jr., to Andrew Jackson, Feb. 16, 1827, Jackson, *Correspondence*, III, 344; *Autobiography*, p. 169; clipping from a southern newspaper, reprinted in the Charleston *Southern Patriot*, Mar. 30, 1827, VBP; MVB to Azariah Flagg, April 2, 1827, Flagg Papers, CUL; MVB to Jesse Hoyt, April 23, 1827, Mackenzie, *Van Buren*, p. 200; Remini, *Van Buren and the Democratic Party*, pp. 138-146.

for Savannah, Georgia, and then journeyed inland to visit William Harris Crawford at Woodlawn. Although many of the Crawford men of 1824 had already gone over to Jackson, Van Buren wanted to make certain of Crawford himself. Van Buren knew that relations between the two old Southerners had never been good—especially after misunderstandings that stemmed from Jackson's Florida adventure of 1818—and he also knew that Crawford hated Calhoun, the likely vice presidential candidate.[28] Having agreed to join the coalition, Crawford urged Van Buren to drop Calhoun in favor of Nathaniel Macon, but Van Buren resisted the suggestion.[29]

On his way home through the Carolinas, Van Buren received more advice about the coming campaign, and heard arguments for and against Calhoun. An article in the *Western Carolinian* on May 1, praised both Van Buren and Calhoun. At Raleigh Van Buren and Cambreleng received an elaborate dinner invitation that accused Adams of violating state rights. Van Buren refused the invitation reluctantly, but agreed that "the spirit of encroachment [had] assumed a new and far more seductive aspect" under Adams than ever before.[30]

When Van Buren reached Virginia, he stopped to attend the horse races at Petersburg, and found a lot of backing for Jackson. While Van Buren had been in the deep South both Randolph and Ritchie had formally endorsed the Old Hero. Ritchie conceded that Jackson's votes in favor of tariff protection and internal improvements had been unwise, but insisted that since then Jackson had been converted to republicanism. In Richmond the columns of the *Enquirer* reflected the growing enthusiasm for Jackson in the Old Dominion.

By the time Van Buren crossed the Potomac into Washington, it was apparent that the Magician had become, as John Quincy Adams put it, "the great electioneering manager for General Jackson." Adams observed that Van Buren was playing the part of Aaron Burr in the election of 1800, but, Adams went on, Van Buren had "improved as much in the art of electioneering upon Burr as the State of New York [had] grown in relative strength and importance in the Union." Adams

---

[28] When Jackson had gone beyond James Monroe's orders and invaded Spanish Florida, Crawford, who was Secretary of the Treasury, and other members of Monroe's cabinet had secretly recommended that Jackson be disciplined. Robert V. Remini, *Andrew Jackson and the Course of American Empire, 1767-1821* (New York, 1977), pp. 366-367.

[29] *Autobiography*, pp. 367-368; Crawford to MVB, Dec. 21, 1827, VBP.

[30] Crawford to MVB, Dec. 21, 1827, VBP; *Autobiography*, p. 360; Cooper to Gulian Verplanck, April 13, 1827, Verplanck Papers, NYHS; *Niles' Register*, 32 (1827), 198.

correctly understood that while Burr had played second fiddle to the Virginia Dynasty, Van Buren was likely to outrank the Virginians.[31]

When Van Buren returned to New York in June, he found considerable disagreement about his party and his candidate. J. S. Schermerhorn of Utica, for example, was enthusiastic about Jackson, but Rudolph Bunner was beginning to have doubts. Bunner feared that if elected, Jackson would be controlled by Clinton and Calhoun, and "what a monster of a President" he would be![32] Jabez Hammond was against both Jackson and Van Buren's concept of a party. Hammond told Van Buren that Calhoun was a "high toned Hamiltonian Federalist" and that Adams was a better Republican than Jackson. Hammond denied that the two old parties had ever divided over internal improvements or the Bank of the United States. As Hammond saw it, the only issue that counted was the protective tariff, which northern interests needed and southern did not. He used history to show that the South would "never support a northern candidate for the Presidency." He believed that a New Yorker such as Van Buren or Clinton would make a better President than Jackson and asked why New York and Pennsylvania had to give the presidency to the South. Anticipating the Republican party of the 1850s, Hammond urged the two states to unite with the West instead of the South. "I can not be charmed [by] party names," he concluded. If Republicanism meant "agreement of the Executive authority to the Slave holding States," he could not be a Republican.[33]

To win over such doubters and to prepare for the state election in November, Van Buren set out on a tour of western New York, where he visited his property in Oswego, and then stopped at Auburn and Geneva. He found to his dismay that Anti-Masonic sentiment had swept through the western counties. The strange disappearance and supposed murder of William Morgan, who had threatened to expose the secrets of the Masonic order, had enraged the farmers of western New York, who were already suspicious of the Masons. Since the Anti-Masons threatened to blackball any candidate who supported Masonry, the delicate political balance of the Empire State was in danger. Even though his allies assured him that the Bucktails could carry the state in November, Van Buren knew that the Anti-Masonic movement would have to be kept under control.[34]

---

[31] Adams, *Memoirs*, VII, 272; *Richmond Enquirer*, Mar. 10, April 27, June 15, 1827.

[32] MVB to Charles Butler, July 27, 1827, Charles Butler Papers, LC; J. S. Schermerhorn to MVB, July 11, 1827, VBP; Bunner to Gulian Verplanck, Mar. 6, 1827, Verplanck Papers, NYHS.

[33] Hammond to MVB, May 23, 1827, VBP.

[34] MVP to Charles Butler, Aug. 23, 1827, Charles Butler Papers, LC.

During the fall campaign Van Buren worked hard to neutralize Anti-Masonry. In New York City Mordecai Noah, now editor of the *New York Enquirer* and a Mason, had been stirring up feelings by attacking the Anti-Masons. Van Buren, who was "heart sick" at such "reckless indiscretion," wrote urging Cambreleng to "beseech [Noah to] let the Morgan affair alone." Above all, Noah should not "run in face of" public opinion in the western counties. Typically, Van Buren ended: "Burn this letter." The problem was eased when Noah moderated his stance.[35]

In this affair and in others during the fall Van Buren and the Bucktails showed that they had recovered from their setback in 1824. They worked so effectively that one opponent was moved to comment on "the perfection of Mr. Van Buren's party discipline." "The wires [of his] political machinery [were] attached to strings in every county," and the Magician "pull[ed] all at his pleasure." Duff Green predicted that the Regency would win that fall because they took advantage of their regular caucuses and controlled some fifty newspaper presses. With the Bucktails, said Green, "*party* is everything." Van Buren, who now felt sure of his home support, told Jackson in September that he could count on New York.[36]

As the election neared, the Jackson movement began to gain momentum. On September 26, the Republican committee of New York City at Tammany Hall resolved that it had "full confidence [in the] worth, integrity and patriotism" of General Jackson. The committee urged Republicans to elect only those candidates who were "favorable to the man whom the American people delight to honor; and who, in the language of the immortal Jefferson, has filled the measure of his country's glory." The election resulted in a complete victory for the Jackson party, which won firm control of the legislature and carried New York City by four thousand votes. The *Albany Argus* boasted that the results expressed not only the "popular feeling now" but foreshadowed what it would be in 1828.[37]

As New York was falling into line, Van Buren was also reaping the rewards of his efforts in the South, particularly in Virginia. In July,

---

[35] MVB to Cambreleng, Oct. 23, 1827, VBP.

[36] William L. Stone to John Bailey, Jan. 1, 1828, John Bailey Papers, NYHS; Duff Green to William B. Lewis, Sept. 2, 1827, Duff Green Papers, LC; MVB to Jackson, Sept. 14, 1827, VBP.

[37] Hammond, *Political Parties*, II, 258-259; MVB to Cambreleng, Oct. 22, 1827, VBP; Bunner to Verplanck, Oct. 27, 1827, Verplanck Papers, NYHS. *Argus*, Nov. 9, Nov. 16, Nov. 23, 1827.

Van Buren's congressional friend William C. Rives said that he had no "squeamishness" in supporting Jackson and was "thoroughly satisfied" that Jackson was a Republican who opposed a protective tariff, a standing army and foreign alliances. In December, newly elected senator John Tyler ended six months of hesitation by announcing for Jackson. Tyler hoped that Jackson's administration would be characterized by "Republican simplicity" and that he would choose his cabinet from Virginians such as Littleton Tazewell and Philip P. Barbour, and Republicans such as Van Buren who agreed with Virginians in principle. That same month Van Buren was confiding in Claiborne W. Gooch of Richmond, about problems in New York, and on Christmas Day Van Buren wrote that it was "gratifying to meet the Republicans of the South upon the old platform which was laid by Jefferson & supported by Madison."[38]

In Kentucky Van Buren found another important man to campaign for Jackson. Amos Kendall grew up on a New Hampshire farm, taught school to pay his way through Dartmouth, and in 1814 at the age of twenty-five, migrated westward to Kentucky; there he served as a tutor in the home of Henry Clay, and soon became editor of the *Argus of Western America*. For some years Kendall was in league with Clay, but in 1827, when Clay began to press Kendall to repay a loan, the latter was ready to switch. While in New York City awaiting a steamboat for Providence, Rhode Island, Kendall wrote to Van Buren asking for a loan. As Van Buren had already received a letter from Richard Mentor Johnson of Kentucky, introducing Kendall and pledging security for the loan, he complied, and from then on Kendall was in the Jackson camp.[39]

At the same time Van Buren was making friends in the Nashville Junto. In 1827, John Overton, who had seconded Jackson in several duels, still headed the Junto, but younger men had risen in the or-

---

[38] Even in December the *Richmond Enquirer* was lukewarm about Jackson, and considered him the lesser of several evils. *Richmond Enquirer*, Nov. 27, 1827; William C. Rives to Thomas W. Gilmer, July 20, July 22, 1827, "Letters of William C. Rives, 1823-1829," *Tyler's Quarterly Historical and Genealogical Magazine*, 5 (1924), 230-237; Dingledine, "Political Career of William C. Rives," pp. 97-98; Tyler to Henry Curtis, Dec. 16, 1827, Lyon G. Tyler, *The Letters and Times of the Tylers*, 3 vols. (Richmond, 1884-1886), I, 379; MVB to Gooch, Dec. 5, 1827, Gooch Papers, UVL; MVB to Croswell, Dec. 25, 1827, VBP.

[39] Amos Kendall, *Autobiography of Amos Kendall*, William Stickney, ed. (Boston, 1872; reprint, 1949), pp. 269-274; Johnson to MVB, Sept. 22, 1827, Kendall to MVB, Nov. 10, 1827, VBP; Robert V. Remini, *The Election of Andrew Jackson* (Philadelphia, 1963), p. 82.

ganization. Jackson's wealthy neighbor John H. Eaton, aged thirty-seven, had served since 1818 in the United States Senate, where he had made important contacts for the Old Hero and helped establish Duff Green as editor of the *Telegraph*. Jackson's chief-of-staff in the New Orleans campaign, Major William B. Lewis, aged forty-three, was closer to the general than anyone else. Another popular member of the Junto was Sam Houston, who was elected governor in 1827. Many members of the rival clique of Andrew Erwin, including former governor William Carroll and Davy Crockett, were also supporting Jackson for President.[40]

Van Buren had known Jackson and Eaton in the Senate and had been corresponding with Lewis, but his closest friend in Tennessee was Alfred Balch, who as a law student and Crawford man became acquainted with Van Buren in Washington in 1824. The friendship had developed to the point that Balch swore he would "go to [his] death for V Buren." In 1827, Balch won a number of Tennesseans over to Van Buren's side, including Sam Houston, who saw the New Yorker as an alternative to Calhoun for Vice President.[41]

Van Buren was also establishing himself with Jackson. In the letter predicting that New York would go for Jackson in 1828, Van Buren boasted that his state could "settle the question." Trying to impress Jackson with the importance of party, Van Buren remarked that the politics of most of the northern states were "governed by old Party feelings." In blunt language he insisted that all they needed to carry New York was to be left alone and he warned Jackson not to get involved in the vice presidential debate. In a somewhat patronizing way Van Buren advised Jackson not to reply to attacks, but simply to publish a few speeches. He wrote again two months later, telling Jackson to ignore Duff Green's suggestion that the general come to Washington. Over the years Van Buren had written and would write hundreds of verbose, obscurely worded letters, but these two important letters to Jackson in 1827 were terse and direct. After receiving the

[40] Anyone who studies Tennessee politics in the 1820s is indebted to Charles Sellers. I have drawn from his "Banking and Politics in Jackson's Tennessee, 1817-1827," *Mississippi Valley Historical Review*, 41 (June 1954), 61-84, and his *James K. Polk Jacksonian 1795-1843* (Princeton, 1957), pp. 68-70, 135-137.

[41] Sellers, *James K. Polk Jacksonian*, pp. 137-138; Balch to MVB, Nov. 27, 1828, VBP; Marquis James, *The Raven: a Biography of Sam Houston* (Indianapolis, 1929; reprint, 1949), pp. 44-45, 50-52, 58-60; Balch to James K. Polk, Jan. 6, 1831, Herbert Weaver, ed., *Correspondence of James K. Polk* (Nashville, 1969), I, 376; Balch to Jackson, Jan. 8, 1830; Jackson *Correspondence*, II, 116.

first letter, Jackson took pains to pass it on to Lewis and declared himself impressed by New York politics and by Van Buren's political skill; he was not a politician, he remarked, but if he were one, he would like to be one in New York.[42]

In order to strengthen his ties with Jackson, Van Buren dispatched the Bucktail and former Federalist James A. Hamilton to accompany the general to New Orleans in December for a celebration of the battle that ended the War of 1812. When Hamilton arrived at the Hermitage, Jackson went out of his way to be gracious to Van Buren's envoy. Since the house was crowded with visitors, the two found it necessary to go on horseback rides in order to talk freely. To his dismay Hamilton found that Jackson "thought very highly" of DeWitt Clinton, and was worried about Van Buren's "reputed cunning." Hamilton countered by pointing to Van Buren's patriotism during the War of 1812 and by insisting that he was "cautious" rather than "cunning." Aboard the *Pocahontas* on the way down the Mississippi Hamilton had ample time to win over Jackson, William B. Lewis and Sam Houston, and he gained further approval by purchasing bonnets for Rachel Jackson and the other ladies in the party from "the most fashionable milliner" in the city. But when Hamilton left for New York, Jackson was still trying to decide between Clinton and Van Buren.[43]

Hamilton was not entirely surprised by this turn of events because a struggle for power in the Jackson ranks had been looming for some time between these two protagonists. Jackson had always liked Clinton, and owed a great deal to him for his support in the election of 1824. Clinton was ambitious and, as Duff Green pointed out, wanted at least to be Vice President. Green, who was backing Calhoun, warned that the party could not afford to nominate either Clinton or Van Buren because then the loser would go over to Adams. Cornelius Van Ness of Vermont, told Van Buren that Clinton would help the party in New England if he ran for Vice President, but Van Ness admitted that many New Yorkers would not like it. Green and Daniel Webster began to think that Clinton had dreams of becoming President, and a drive to make him President actually started in Virginia in the late summer of 1827, when the *Virginia Advocate* announced for him and

---

[42] MVB to Jackson, Sept. 14, Nov. 4, 1827, VBP; Parton, *Jackson*, III, 136; Jackson to Lewis, Nov. 25, 1827, Jackson-Lewis Letters, NYPL, photostats of letters at the J. Pierpont Morgan Library, New York City; Remini, *Van Buren and the Democratic Party*, p. 161.

[43] *Autobiography*, p. 368; Hamilton, *Reminiscences*, pp. 67-72; Jackson to Lewis, Dec. 25, 1827, Jackson-Lewis Letters, NYPL; Parton, *Jackson*, III, 137-140; Bassett, *Jackson*, p. 506.

Thomas Ritchie visited him in New York; but these efforts had collapsed by the fall.[44]

When the Regency gathered in Albany to stage its own celebration of the Battle of New Orleans, the specter of DeWitt Clinton hung over the gathering. Some members wanted to nominate Jackson at once in order to attract southern allies and gain an advantage over Clinton, but Van Buren and Wright feared that moving so quickly would weaken the Regency. Wright warned that a surprise nomination would upset the entente with Clinton and would give him the chance to form another People's party and accuse the Regency of being under "southern influence."[45] Van Buren again put state ahead of national interests; according to Wright he preferred to "jeopardize the Presidential election [rather than] risk . . . breaking up . . . our ranks at home."[46] Van Buren was particularly anxious to postpone choosing between John C. Calhoun and Clinton for Vice President. The Regency finally arranged to have Jackson nominated by the legislature on January 31, but avoided a rift with Clinton by naming no one for Vice President.[47]

Less than two weeks later, on February 11, DeWitt Clinton dropped dead. His demise brought great "gloom and shock" to Albany, for he had been a dominant figure in the Empire State ever since he became mayor of New York in 1803. Charismatic and aristocratic, the Magnus Apollo represented the old generation of factional politicians who ruled through deference but were ill-at-ease in the new world of party politics. For Van Buren his death brought an end to a struggle that had been going on since 1812. If Clinton had lived, he instead of Van Buren might have represented Jackson in New York, thereby gaining control of federal patronage and even advancing to the presidency.

Van Buren's eulogy for Clinton revealed as much about the former as the latter. With his sense of history and occasion, Van Buren gave Clinton credit for "the greatest public improvement of the age." It

---

[44] Duff Green to Ninian Edwards, Dec. 29, 1826, May 6, 1827, Washburne, *Edwards Papers*, p. 266; Van Ness to MVB, Feb. 22, 1827, VBP; Webster to George Mason, April 10, 1827, Fletcher Webster, ed., *The Private Correspondence of Daniel Webster* (Boston, 1857), I, 418; Green to Calhoun, Sept. 5, 1827, Duff Green Papers, LC; *Richmond Enquirer*, Nov. 9, 1827.

[45] Adams, *Memoirs*, VII, 427-428; *Argus*, Jan. 11, 1828; MVB to Thomas Olcott, Jan. 8, 1828, Thomas Olcott Papers, CUL; Michael Hoffman to Azariah Flagg, Dec. 21, 1827, Flagg-Hoffman Letters; Wright to Flagg, Dec. 20, 1827, Flagg-Wright Correspondence; MVB to Flagg, Feb. 5, 1828, Flagg Papers, CUL.

[46] Wright to Flagg, Dec. 20, 1827, Flagg-Wright Correspondence.

[47] MVB to Crawford, Feb. 15, 1828, William Harris Crawford Papers, LC; Hammond, *Political Parties*, II, 280-281; T. Rudd to Taylor, Feb. 26, 1828, R. M. Livingston to Taylor, Jan. 31, 1828, Taylor Papers.

gave him, he said, "deep-felt, though melancholy, satisfaction, to know [that their] political differences" had been free from "personal hatred." He had "never envied Clinton anything while alive" but now was "tempted to envy him his grave with its honours." The graceful words though no doubt sincerely meant by the agreeable, ambitious speaker, gave no hint of the rivalry that prompted New York merchant John Pintard to say that Van Buren had been one of Clinton's "two most virulent enemies."[48]

Politicians on all sides sensed that Clinton's death would have important consequences. The leaders of the Adams party rejoiced privately because they believed that Clinton had been the only one who could stop them from carrying New York. Some Jacksonians in the state thought that his death would help Adams because it left Jackson's fortunes in the hands of Van Buren, whom they considered less of a statesman than Clinton. Silas Wright, on the other hand, thought that the death would help Jackson because many New Yorkers had shied away from supporting him for fear of elevating Clinton in the process. Wright reported that since the death, a number of southern and western politicians in Washington had begun to speak favorably of Van Buren. In Tennessee Archibald Yell, who had served with Jackson in Florida, told Congressman James K. Polk that the loss of Clinton was "melancholy news," but that they still had Van Buren. Clintonians who had been flirting with Jackson began to go over to Adams, while Regency men who had held back from the Old Hero because of his loyalty to Clinton now had fewer pangs about joining him. As for Van Buren, the death left him—as Jackson's biographer James Parton put it—with a hand "full of cards," all of them "trumps."[49]

Van Buren began to play these cards in Congress that winter in the debate over the tariff. Ever since the tariff of 1824 manufacturers and producers of raw materials had both been demanding increased tariff protection. When a woolens bill with high rates for woolens and low rates for raw wool reached the Senate early in 1827, Van Buren was just as undecided as he had been in 1824, because woolen manufac-

[48] Hammond, *Political Parties*, II, 266-267; Francis Granger to M. P. Granger, Feb. 12, 1828, Gideon and Francis Granger Papers, LC; *Autobiography*, pp. 166-167; John Pintard to Eliza Davidson, Feb. 23, 1828, "Letters from John Pintard to His Daughter Eliza Noel Pintard Davidson," III, *Collections of the New-York Historical Society*, 72 (1939), 9-11.

[49] Wright to Flagg, Feb. 18, 1828, Flagg-Wright Correspondence; John Van Fossen to John C. McLemore, June 29, 1828, Andrew J. Donelson Papers, LC; Archibald Yell to Polk, Mar. 2, 1828, Polk, *Correspondence*, I, 160; Russell Jarvis to A. Ware, Feb. 23, 1828, Duff Green to——, Feb. 23, 1828, Duff Green Papers, LC; Hammond, *Political Parties*, II, 268; Parton, *Jackson*, III, 131.

turers in New York favored the bill, while wool growers and shippers opposed it. During the debates in 1827 Van Buren first tried unsuccessfully to raise the duties on raw wool, and then did what he could to avoid taking a stand. When the bill came up for a vote, Senator Robert Y. Hayne, who led Southerners in opposing protection, moved to defeat the bill by asking that it be laid on the table. Since the vote was 20-20, Van Buren had a chance to strengthen his alliance with the South by voting for tabling, but he left the room to avoid voting, thereby allowing Vice President Calhoun to cast the vote that tabled the bill.[50]

Even before Van Buren arrived home in May, complaints about his evasion began to reach him. Stopping to visit his son Abraham at West Point, he was notified that the "Farmers, Wool Growers, and Friends of the American system in the city of Albany" had called a tariff convention, at which the protectionists planned to denounce him for not voting in favor of the tariff. The protective tariff was so popular in New York that Van Buren was subjected to great "vituperation" in the press for not taking a stand. Some even said that he would not have been elected in February if the selection had been made after his failure to vote. The *Argus* was filled with reports of tariff meetings, and William L. Marcy reported that western New Yorkers were demanding protection.[51]

When Van Buren faced the convention in Albany in July, he pointed out that he had voted for high tariffs in 1824 and denied that he had missed the vote in 1827 "with the miserable design of evading responsibility." Although he admitted that woolens needed some protection from English competition, he insisted that manufacturers already had protection enough. Wool growers, he said, were the ones who needed help. Van Buren conceded that he had a personal interest in the subject because he had $20,000 invested in sheep farms, but he

---

[50] For a letter supporting tariff protection, see Ebenezer Sage to John W. Taylor, Dec. 14, 1826, Taylor Papers. For one opposing the woolens bill, see Gabriel Mead to MVB, Feb. 13, 1827, VBP. Edward Stanwood, *American Tariff Controversies in the Nineteenth Century* (Boston, 1903), I, 258; F. W. Taussig, *The Tariff History of the United States*, 6th ed. (New York, 1914), pp. 80-82; *Argus*, Mar. 9, 1827; *Autobiography*, pp. 169, 171; *Register of Debates*, 19th Congress, 2nd session (1826-1827), 337, 387-390, 496. The proadministration *Albany Sentinel* accused Van Buren of being purposely absent. *Argus*, Aug. 15, 1827.

[51] The Albany meeting was called to select delegates for the state tariff convention, which was held on July 16, 1827. *Autobiography*, p. 169; George C. McClure to Clay, April 11, 1827, Henry Clay Papers, LC; *Argus*, June 11, June 14, June 23, 1827; Marcy to MVB, July 4, 1827, VBP; William E. Richmond to John Bailey, April 16, 1827, John Bailey Miscellaneous Papers, NYHS.

also claimed a deep "admiration and respect" for all the "farmers of America." Since farmers and those who wore clothing far outnumbered those who made it, they should not let the manufacturers have their own way. Van Buren maintained that commerce not manufacturing was responsible for prosperity in New York, and that shipping would suffer if the tariff were raised. Above all, said Van Buren, they should not let the tariff become a political issue because it had already split Pennsylvania and Kentucky.[52]

According to legend, Van Buren managed to avoid committing himself in the speech. In one popular tale a wool buyer told Benjamin Knower that it was a "very able speech," but neither Knower nor the buyer could decide on which side of the tariff question it came down. Van Buren himself recalled that "directness on all points had not been [the] most prominent feature" of the address. But tradition and Van Buren's memory were both at fault. In this speech Van Buren stood clearly for wool farmers first, shippers second and manufacturers last. With its admiration for farmers and suspicion of manufacturers, the speech was worthy of the old Jeffersonian Republicans.[53]

Without evading the issue, Van Buren had disarmed his critics. Since he had not directly opposed protection and since the *Argus* maintained that he was for the American system, which was based on high tariffs, manufacturers did not turn against him. Daniel Webster observed wryly that Van Buren had been "too wise to place himself in opposition to the woolens bill," but wondered how Van Buren's southern friends would like the speech. Webster guessed correctly that in quieting his critics in New York, Van Buren would alarm many Southerners. Thomas Cooper of South Carolina, for example, wrote that Van Buren was "treading on the crest of a Lava not yet solid." If the American System became reality, Cooper threatened that South Carolina would declare Charleston a free port. Thomas Ritchie said that tariff protection endangered the Union.[54]

By the opening of Congress in December 1827, the pressure in favor of tariff protection had grown. In New York and Pennsylvania, for

---

[52] *Speech of the Hon. Martin Van Buren, Delivered at the Capitol, in the City of Albany, Before the Albany County Meeting, Held on the 10th July, 1827* (Albany, 1827).

[53] *Autobiography*, p. 171; *Argus*, July 11, 1827.

[54] *Argus*, July 17, July 24, 1827; "Biography of Van Buren," *Argus Extra*; T. Rudd to Taylor, July 20, 1827, Webster to Taylor, July 15, 1827, Taylor Papers; Cooper to MVB, July 5, July 31, 1827, James Wolcott to MVB, Nov. 10, 1827, VBP; *Richmond Enquirer*, Aug. 7, 1827.

example, woolen and iron manufacturers wanted higher tariffs because cheap English goods were flooding the market, while sheep farmers in those states and the Northwest demanded protection for raw wool. The delegates at the Harrisburg Convention in 1827 spoke for those interests by asking for increases in tariffs. Van Buren recognized—as Benton put it later—that the tariff had become an important "appendage" of presidential elections. The Jacksonians, or Democrats as they were beginning to be called, were expected to carry the eighty-three votes of the South in 1828, leaving them only forty-nine votes short of a majority. Since Adams and his National Republicans were likely to sweep New England, Van Buren had to look for the needed votes in New York, Pennsylvania and the Northwest, where tariff protection was popular. The previous summer farmer-assemblyman Jesse Buel of New York, had predicted that New York politicians would "ride the wollens [sic] bill with hemp and iron," and that Pennsylvania and Kentucky would "help hold on the *rider.*" Van Buren was destined to be the rider.[55]

In New York the greatest support for high tariffs came from manufacturers near Albany and wool growers in the west; shippers in New York City opposed any increase in rates. Of the fourteen memorials sent to Congress that spring from New York, nine favored protection and five opposed. Particularly striking was the plea from Ontario County in the west where sheep raisers complained that they would have to "sacrifice their fine Merino and Saxon flocks to the knife of the butcher" unless duties were increased. In Albany interest in tariffs was so great that a committee of correspondence was established to spread the word. Regency men responded by supporting high tariffs, especially hat maker and woolen manufacturer Benjamin Knower, whose politics, it was said, were "tied up in a sack of wool." Jesse Buel and banker Thomas Olcott shared Knower's concern for protecting manufactures, while William L. Marcy, Azariah Flagg and

---

[55] Benton, *Thirty Years' View*, I, 101; Frederick Jackson Turner, *Rise of the New West 1819-1829* (New York, 1907), pp. 314-316; Arthur H. Cole, *The American Wool Manufacture* (1926; reprint, New York, 1969), I, 250; Victor S. Clark, *History of Manufactures in the United States* (Washington, D.C., 1929; reprint, 1949), I, 500-501, 567; George Rogers Taylor, *The Transportation Revolution 1815-1860* (New York, 1951), p. 245; Paul W. Gates, *The Farmer's Age: Agriculture 1815-1860* (New York, 1960), pp. 116-117, 326; Taussig, *Tariff History*, pp. 82-84; Buel to Azariah Flagg, Aug. 3, 1827, Flagg Papers. In this paragraph and in those that follow I have followed in part the interpretations of Robert V. Remini and John Garraty. Remini, "Martin Van Buren and the Tariff of Abominations," *American Historical Review*, 63 (July 1958), 903-917; Remini, *Van Buren and the Democratic Party*, ch. 12; Remini, *Election of Jackson*, pp. 171-180; Garraty, *Wright*, pp. 53-67.

Edwin Croswell cared more about protecting wool. Only Churchill C. Cambreleng and Gulian Verplanck, who represented the shipping interest in New York City, dissented. Since supporters of Adams also favored a high tariff, Knower was able to say that all congressmen from the state except those from New York City were in favor of a "just and liberal tariff."[56]

To secure such a tariff Van Buren relied upon the majority that the Jackson coalition had finally achieved in both Houses of Congress. The Jacksonians took command of Congress in December 1827, electing Duff Green printer for the Senate and Andrew Stevenson of the Richmond Junto speaker of the House by a close vote over Clintonian John W. Taylor of New York. In a post-mortem after his defeat, Taylor complained that Regency votes from New York had beaten him, and that if all thirty-four members of the New York delegation had voted for him, he would have won; but eighteen, including Regency men Churchill C. Cambreleng, Silas Wright, Gulian Verplanck, Michael Hoffman, and Rudolph Bunner, voted for Stevenson. Wright, who was in his first session in Congress, reported that "the triumph was glorious," and that they had selected "a very sound democrat." On the other side, Henry R. Storrs of New York, complained that the eighteen had sold their state to Jackson's supporters in the House.[57]

---

[56] Between 1820 and 1840 the percentage engaged in manufacture in New York rose from 19 percent of those employed to 26 percent. Tucker, *Progress of the United States*, pp. 135-137, 195. For capital invested in manufactures in New York in 1822, see United States Census Office, *Fourth Census. Digest of the Accounts of Manufacturing Establishments in the United States and of Their Manufactures . . . 30th March, 1822* (Washington, D.C., 1823), pp. 8-13; for capital invested in woolen and iron manufactures in 1831, see Louis McLane, *Documents Relative to the Manufactures in the United States*, 2 vols. (Washington, D.C., 1833; reprint, 1969), II, 89-90, 115-122; for the number of woolen mills in 1840, see J. Disturnell, *A Gazetteer of the State of New-York* (Albany, 1843), p. 446; for the number of sheep in New York in 1855, see French, *Gazetteer of New York*, p. 107. For memorials, see *American State Papers: Documents, Legislative and Executive* (Washington, D.C., 1832-1861), *Finance*, V, 613-614, 680, 697-701, 723 (Ontario County Memorial), 745, 750, 847-848, 862, 864-869, 895-897, 899-900, 992-994, 1023-1024. See also Flagg to Wright, Jan. 22, Mar. 13, Mar. 16, 1828, Flagg-Wright Correspondence; Buel and Others to MVB, Mar. 1828, Marcy to MVB, Jan. 29, 1828, Knower to MVB, Jan. 27, 1828, VBP; Michael Hoffman to Flagg, Feb. 3, 1828, Flagg-Hoffman Letters; *Argus*, Feb. 12, 1828; Ambrose Spencer to John W. Taylor, April 5, 1828, Taylor Papers.

[57] Jacksonians outnumbered supporters of the administration 28-20 in the Senate and 119-94 in the House. *Register of Debates*, 20th Congress, 1st session (1827-1828), 1-2, 8-11; John W. Taylor, "memorandum," Dec. 27, 1827, Taylor Papers; Henry R. Storrs to———, Dec. 11, 1827, Henry R. Storrs Miscellaneous Papers, NYHS; Wright to Flagg, Dec. 13, 1827, Flagg-Wright Correspondence; Hammond, *Political Parties*, II, 260; Parton, *Jackson*, III, 135; *Argus*, Dec. 18, 1827.

Speaker Stevenson immediately repaid the Regency by appointing Van Buren's lieutenant Silas Wright to the House Committee on Manufactures, which was to deal with the tariff. No one better represented New York Jacksonians on the tariff than Wright, who spoke for the sheep raisers and iron manufacturers of northern New York. Like Van Buren, Wright wanted to protect both farmers and manufacturers, and like Van Buren he put farmers first. On being appointed to the Committee on Manufactures, Wright reassured Flagg that the committee was "perfectly safe" because there was only one "anti-tariff" man on it. But Wright indicated that he would not give manufacturers all they wanted when he tried in vain to keep archprotectionist Rollin C. Mallary of Vermont, off the committee. In opposing Mallary, Wright declared that he intended to "put the screws into the Tariff men" and "drive them to the wall." He later argued that the United States should protect competent manufacturers but not those who were inefficient. Wright and Van Buren sought a tariff bill that would help New York farmers first and manufacturers second, and would at the same time please voters in Pennsylvania and points west.[58]

When the Committee on Manufactures held hearings, New York businessmen lobbied hard for additional protection. Manufacturers of woolens and cottons along the Hudson and an iron producer near the Canadian border all testified in favor of higher tariffs. Benjamin Knower exerted so much pressure that Van Buren accused the hat maker of "mischief making," and Flagg complained that Knower put his economic interests ahead of his "political feelings and considerations." The legislature responded by passing a resolution in favor of protection for both manufacturers of iron and woolens, and for the farmers who produced wool, hemp and flax.[59]

The bill reported by the committee on Janaury 31 benefited farmers more than manufacturers by increasing rates on wool while reducing those on certain woolens. Since the duty on wool was set at seven cents a pound plus fifty percent of the value, the rate for standard wool worth about fifteen cents a pound would be in the vicinity of one hundred percent. At the same time the rate for some manufactured woolens dropped as low as forty percent. When the debate began,

[58] Wright to Flagg, Dec. 13, Dec. 20, 1827, Jan. 16, 1828, Flagg-Wright Correspondence. Calhoun later claimed that Van Buren controlled the choice of members of the Committee on Manufactures. *Register of Debates*, 24th Congress, 2nd session (1836-1837), 905.

[59] *American State Papers, Finance*, V, 680, 780-844, 862; Wright to Flagg, Dec. 13, 1827, Jan. 16, 1828, Flagg to Wright, Jan. 10, Jan. 22, April 13, 1828, Flagg-Wright Correspondence; Knower to Van Buren, Jan. 27, 1828, VBP.

Mallary, who represented New England, explained the plight of the manufacturers and urged the House to support amendments increasing the rates on manufacturers. Wright spoke in defense of the original bill as one that helped the farming interest. Although conceding the importance of manufacturing and commerce, he insisted that they were "subservient to the great interests of agriculture." Wright had his way when all of Mallary's amendments except one were rejected.[60]

While the debate was going on, Wright had to resist pressure from Knower in favor of manufacturing. The hat maker sent letters to Washington, held meetings, drew up resolutions, and even sent a special lobbyist to confront Wright directly. But Wright would not budge. He warned Knower that if rates on manufactures were raised, the "Southorns" would be so "exasperate[d]" that they would "cut out" raw materials such as hemp, flax and wool, forcing Jacksonians in the western states to "kill the bill." Wright reminded Knower that they had put duties on "woolen cloths as high as *our own friends* in Pennsylvania, Kentucky & Ohio" would vote for them. The lobbyist blundered when he accused Wright and the rest of the delegation of being under Van Buren's control. Stung by such impertinence, Wright called the man a "fool" and lectured him for half an hour in front of several New Yorkers. When Knower learned about the incident, he gave up all efforts to change the bill.[61]

Wright's bill, which passed the House on April 22 by a vote of 105 to 94, was a triumph for the northern farming interest, the new Jacksonian alliance, and New York. Votes for the bill came largely from northern and western farming states stretching from New York west to Illinois and Missouri, states that would later vote for Jackson. Since a shift of only six votes would have changed the outcome, the strong support from New York, whose delegation voted 27-6 for the bill, was particularly important. In the weeks before the vote the Regency had rallied behind the bill so strenuously that they were accused of "gull[ing] many of the ignorant, by their hollow & hypocritical cant about the interests of the wool grower." Wright and other New Yorkers had helped put the bill over.[62]

[60] *Register of Debates*, 20th Congress, 1st session (Mar. 4, Mar. 10, April 9, 1828), 1727-1737, 1835-1870, 2347; *Niles' Register*, 35 (1828), 57; Taussig, *Tariff History*, pp. 89-97; Wright to Flagg, April 7, 1828, Flagg-Wright Correspondence.

[61] Wright to Flagg and James Porter, April 13, 1828, Wright to Flagg, Mar. 21, Mar. 30, April 7, 1828, Flagg-Wright Correspondence; Knower to MVB, April 23, 1828, VBP.

[62] All the New York congressmen voted for the bill except six from the region in and around New York City. Five of these six nay votes were from Jacksonians. *Register of*

Van Buren also had played an important role in getting the bill through the House. After helping Speaker Stevenson construct the Committee on Manufactures, Van Buren had hovered over the members as they worked on the bill. One opposition newspaper accused Van Buren "of calling out the Jackson members of the committee daily, to hold talks with them," and complained that "nothing important was done [without his] knowledge and consent." Another critic claimed that everything had been planned by Van Buren, who had "taken upon himself the management of congress, so far as relates to the tariff." Van Buren had also kept the Regency informed and had seen to it that the Jacksonian newspapers in New York carried articles supporting the bill.[63]

Van Buren's role became even more important when an amended House bill calling for higher rates on manufactures was presented in the Senate. Caught between his agrarian supporters, who opposed the changes, and his manufacturing friends such as Knower, who favored them, Van Buren was in a difficult position. Characteristically, he temporized, voting against most of the amendments, but supporting one that increased rates on woolen manufactures. In almost every case he was among the majority. The crucial woolens amendment, which squeaked through by only two votes, passed largely because he and Levi Woodbury, who had also been opposing the amendments, voted for it. As in the House, the final bill passed in the Senate because of support from New York, Pennsylvania and western states.[64]

There were historians and some of his contemporaries who believed that Van Buren had engineered a "Tariff of Abominations" that raised rates on manufactures in order to please the middle and western states, but had also made the rates on raw materials so high that manufacturers in New England would find them intolerable. If so, congressional supporters of Adams from New England, according to historians, would then have been forced to defeat the bill; or Adams himself would have had to veto it. In any case the Jacksonians would have

---

Debates, 20th Congress, 1st session (April 22, 1828), 2471-2472; *Niles' Register*, 35 (1828), 52-55; Taussing, *Tariff History*, p. 98; Peter Porter to Henry Clay, Mar. 15, 1828, Henry Clay Papers, LC.

[63] *National Journal*, Feb. 19, Feb. 23, 1828, quoted in Remini, *Van Buren and the Democratic Party*, p. 174; MVB to Flagg, Mar. 31, 1828, Flagg Papers, CUL; *Argus*, April 4, April 8, April 11, April 22, 1828.

[64] MVB to Wright, May 1828, Wright to MVB, May 1828, MVB, "Notes," May 7, 1828, VBP; *Register of Debates*, 20th Congress, 1st session (1827-1828), 750-770, 786, 2576, 2700, 2708; *Niles' Register*, 35 (1828), 178-179; Remini, *Van Buren and the Democratic Party*, pp. 180-183.

won support in the East and West by favoring protection, but would not have lost the South because the bill would never have passed.

John C. Calhoun and Van Buren himself were largely responsible for the spread of the story. While debating another tariff in 1837, Calhoun angrily referred to a plot in 1828. Southerners, he said, had let Van Buren's friends dominate the House committee with the assurance that rates on raw materials would be so high that the bill would be defeated by New Englanders. Calhoun accused Van Buren of reneging on the deal by voting to amend the bill in the Senate. In 1840, Van Buren contributed to the idea of a plot by denying that he had really favored tariff protection in 1828. He had voted for the tariff, he maintained, simply because the state legislature had insisted on it. Others added to the story. During the debate in 1828, Henry Clay wrote Kentucky lawyer John J. Crittenden that the Jacksonians were framing a tariff that was designed not to pass. In February Hezekiah Niles, the publisher of *Niles' Weekly Register*, predicted that the bill would be defeated unless it was "materially altered." And in 1844, George McDuffie of South Carolina, who was an antitariff congressman in 1828, declared that the bill was drawn up with the idea of having it defeated later.[65]

The story of a plot is not convincing. After the tariff passed in 1828, the *Albany Argus* stated several times that Van Buren favored tariff protection and had not simply bowed to pressure from the legislature. Churchill C. Cambreleng referred to Van Buren's tariff policy as one of "equal protection to all branches of industry." Silas Wright flatly denied that there was any plot, and if there had been one it is surprising that Calhoun did not expose it in 1831 or 1832, when he quarreled with Van Buren and Jackson. There may have been some sort of casual arrangement among northern and southern Jacksonians, but it could not have been much of a plot if Clay and Niles knew about it. Van Buren had worked too hard at developing a close relationship with the South to mastermind a plot with Southerners and then back out of it. When Van Buren recalled in 1840 that he had really been against

---

[65] *Register of Debates*, 24th Congress, 2nd session (Feb. 23, 1837), 904-906, 926-927; MVB to John B. Cary and others, July 31, 1840, MVB, "Comment on his speech delivered at Albany, July 1827, on the woolen bill," printed in the *Richmond Enquirer*, Aug. 4, 1840, and reprinted in *The Crisis*, Aug. 12, 1840, Wright to Joseph S. Watkins, Feb. 9, 1835, VBP; Holland, *Van Buren*, p. 275; MVB, *Abolition of Slavery*, p. 15; Bancroft, *Van Buren*, pp. 151-152; Clay to John J. Crittenden, Feb. 14, 1828, Ann Mary B. Coleman, ed., *The Life of John J. Crittenden with Selections from His Correspondence and Speeches*, 2 vols. (1871; reprint, New York, 1970), I, 67; Niles to John W. Taylor, Feb. 14, 1828, Taylor Papers; *Congressional Globe*, 28th Congress, 1st session (1843-1844), appendix, 747.

the tariff in 1828 and had voted for it only because ordered to do so by the legislature, he was not telling the truth. The legislature had indeed instructed him to vote for the tariff, but Van Buren would have voted as he did anyway. In 1840, he wanted to pose as an opponent of the tariff in order to win southern votes in his quest for reelection. The evidence suggests that Van Buren and Wright really wanted higher tariffs in 1828 in order to help their agrarian constituents in New York and to strengthen Jackson's chances in New York, Pennsylvania and the West. The tariff of 1828 was a successful maneuver by northern Jacksonians to attract the "plain Republicans of the north" without losing the "planters of the South."[66]

WITH the tariff out of the way Van Buren turned his full attention to the election and to his national political organization. At the head of the organization was a central Democratic committee in Washington, chaired by John P. Van Ness, president of the Bank of Metropolis, the man who had loaned Van Buren money when Van Ness was a congressman from New York. A short letter from Cornelius Van Ness to Isaac Hill, the Jackson leader in New Hampshire, gives some idea of the extent and nature of the party structure. Cornelius, former governor of Vermont and brother of John P. Van Ness, was visiting in Washington. His letter lists prominent party members who sent their best wishes to Hill, including brother John, Senator James Hamilton, Jr., of South Carolina, and Van Buren. Cornelius Van Ness names four Jacksonians representing political constituencies from northern New England to the deep South, and his letter can be taken as evidence that Van Buren had succeeded in recreating the old alliance of North and South.[67]

In the North Van Buren relied on a number of local political groups including his own in New York. The Concord Regency in New Hampshire led by Hill and Levi Woodbury failed to carry the state in March, but had hopes of giving the state to Jackson in November. Banker David Henshaw and Justice Marcus Morton of the state supreme court led the Jacksonians in Massachusetts, editors Gideon Welles and John M. Niles of the *Hartford Times* in Connecticut. In Maryland and Delaware Van Buren counted on Louis McLane, who put so much

[66] Unlike Garraty and Remini, I believe that Van Buren and Wright followed a consistent policy aimed at pleasing northern farmers. *Argus*, May 20, Oct. 31, 1828, Mar. 3, 1829; Cambreleng to MVB, Mar. 1, 1829, VBP; *Register of Debates*, 24th Congress, 2nd session (Feb. 23, 1828), 921.

[67] Cornelius P. Van Ness to Hill, April 6, 1828, Isaac Hill Papers, New Hampshire Historical Society.

"heart and soul" into his state campaign that he was called the "Delaware Martin Van Buren *in miniature*."

Van Buren's closest friend in Virginia continued to be Thomas Ritchie, head of the Richmond Junto, a man who knew so much about New York politics that he could write to Van Buren on topics so diverse as Anti-Masonry and speeches by Benjamin Butler. Van Buren also kept in touch with another member of the Junto, the erratic John Randolph, who urged the New Yorker to visit him in August, promising horses, servants, and a "well-stocked cellar and a library not indifferently furnished." Farther south Van Buren continued to get on well with Old Republicans such as Nathaniel Macon and with followers of Calhoun such as Robert Y. Hayne.[68]

Despite his commitment to the national organization, Van Buren refused to repeat his 1824 mistake of putting national interests ahead of state, and devoted most of his attention to the campaign in New York. He was determined to have his state play "a respectable role" in the national election, and he wanted to make certain that the Regency won the governor's seat. With the death of Clinton, Lieutenant Governor Nathaniel Pitcher, a Bucktail, had become governor, but no one was sure that he could be reelected because of the Anti-Masonic movement, which had worried Van Buren the previous fall. Pioneers traveling west found themselves in Anti-Masonic country as soon as they crossed the famous mile-long bridge over the northern end of Lake Cayuga. In towns like Auburn, Rochester and Buffalo, young Anti-Masons such as Thurlow Weed, Francis Granger and William Henry Seward were beginning to challenge the Regency.[69]

[68] Gulian Verplanck to Woodbury, Woodbury Papers, LC; Woodbury to Verplanck, Aug. 29, 1828, Verplanck Papers, NYHS; Arthur B. Darling, *Political Changes in Massachusetts 1824-1848: a Study of Liberal Movements in Politics* (New Haven, 1925), pp. 56-65; John Niven, *Gideon Welles: Lincoln's Secretary of the Navy* (New York, 1973), pp. 24-51; Mark Haller, "The Rise of the Jackson Party in Maryland 1820-1829," *Journal of Southern History*, 28 (Aug. 1962), 307-326; Munroe, *Louis McLane*, pp. 234-239; Ambler, *Thomas Ritchie*, p. 113; Ritchie to MVB, Mar. 11, 1828, Randolph to MVB, Aug. 4, 1828, VBP.

[69] Hammond to John W. Taylor, April 14, 1828, Taylor Papers; MVB to David E. Evans, Mar. 31, 1828, Charles Hamilton Auction, Cat. No. 12, p. 58 (typed copy), VBP. Van Buren's preoccupation with state politics can be seen in his letters at the Library of Congress. Of 87 letters between January 1827 and Dec. 3, 1828, 48 were either to or from New Yorkers. No other state came close. Virginia was second with only 6 letters. For Anti-Masonry, see Alexander, *Political History*, I, 318, 361, 377; *Argus*, Nov. 23, 1827; Weed, *Autobiography*, pp. 299-309; Charles McCarthy, "The Antimasonic Party, a Study of Political Antimasonry in the United States, 1828-1840," American Historical Association, *Annual Report 1902* (Washington, D.C., 1903), I, 375.

The Regency began to deal with the Anti-Masonic threat early in March, when Azariah Flagg complained that the opposition was using Anti-Masonry to save the state for Adams, who was not a member of the secret order. Since the Jacksonians were in trouble west of the Genesee River, Flagg urged the Regency to do everything possible to control the choice of clerks and sheriffs in the west, because they were so important to the organization as legmen and patronage dealers. He hoped that the Anti-Masons would nominate their own candidate for governor, who would then draw from Adams' candidate and thus assure a victory for the Regency. To conciliate the Anti-Masons the Regency forced a bill through the legislature calling for a special investigation of the abduction of William Morgan. Daniel Moseley, who handled the inquiry, went out of his way to be impartial in order to demonstrate that Democrats were not protecting Masonry.[70]

Fearful that their opponents might combine and carry the state in November, the Regency sought the strongest possible candidate for governor. On March 7, Flagg told Wright that Van Buren could win the election, and although Van Buren was comfortably established in the Senate, members of the Regency urged him to run. At the end of March he confided that the Regency was "persecut[ing]" him to run, and he was afraid that he might not be able to "avoid a nomination without a rupture" of the party. Since Van Buren did not wish to hurt his state party during the national campaign, he believed that a crisis in his political life was approaching.[71]

Van Buren's sense of crisis intensified in April when he received a perceptive letter from Regency lawyer Lot Clark, who was head of the bar in Chenango County. Clark told Van Buren bluntly that he should run for governor, not just to help the party but also to help himself. No one, said Clark, could get ahead in politics unless he had a military record or had run for office in a major campaign. Even though Van Buren had campaigned for the state senate, he had never really been "before the people," but if he ran for governor, "justices, constables & all the minor active men in the towns [would become] familliar" [sic] with his name. People, Clark said, were used to "man-worshipping," and would not join a party unless some "distinguished individual" was at its head. He insisted that if Van Buren stayed in the Senate, he would be a target of both North and South; if he joined

---

[70] Flagg to Wright, Mar. 7, 1828, Flagg-Wright Correspondence; McCarthy, *Anti-masonic Party*, p. 376; Weed, *Autobiography*, pp. 258-259.

[71] Flagg to Wright, Mar. 7, 1828, Flagg-Wright Correspondence; MVB to David E. Evans, Mar. 31, 1828, Charles Hamilton Auction, Cat. No. 12, p. 58 (typed copy), VBP.

Jackson's cabinet, hostility to the President would be aimed at Van Buren and there would be little patronage. As governor he could avoid trouble in Washington, strengthen his position by handing out patronage in Albany, and prepare to campaign later for the presidency.[72]

The letter showed that Clark understood the new political system and Van Buren's place in it in 1828. Van Buren, who had failed in 1824 because he had put national ahead of state politics, should return to New York in 1828 and strengthen his base before trying for the presidency. Clark recognized, furthermore, the importance of heroes in national campaigns. At the local level, especially in New York where parties were well-established, patronage and organization were more important than personality; but at the national level, where parties were just emerging, heroes were indispensable. If Van Buren could gain a popular following in New York, he and his party would have a better chance in future campaigns. Clark believed that even in the throes of a national election, the state party was more important than the national organization.

Before deciding to follow Clark's advice, Van Buren came home and started on a tour of western New York, making his first stop near Auburn on the shores of Lake Owasco to visit Judge Enos T. Throop. If Van Buren was to run for governor, practical politics demanded that someone from the west such as Throop be given the second spot. The year before when Throop presided over the first trial of the Morgan kidnappers, he pleased Anti-Masons by "flaying" the defendants and handing out stiff sentences. When Van Buren left Throop's country estate, rumors spread that the two had agreed to head the Democratic ticket.[73]

Continuing west, Van Buren reached Rochester, where he dazzled worshipers at the First Presbyterian Church one August Sunday with his "exquisite . . . personal appearance." According to Henry B. Stanton (only twenty-three and not yet married to Elizabeth Cady):

> His complexion was a bright blond and he dressed accordingly. On this occasion he wore an elegant snuff-colored broadcloth coat, with velvet collar to match; his cravat was orange tinted silk with modest lace tips; his vest was of pearl hue; his trousers were white duck; his silk hose corresponded to his vest, his shoes

[72] Clark to MVB, April 10, 1828, VBP; MVB to Charles Dudley, Aug. 24, 1828, Van Buren Miscellaneous Papers, NYHS.

[73] Hammond, *Political Parties*, II, 288; Alexander, *Political History*, I, 365-366; Weed, *Autobiography*, pp. 236-237; MVB to Charles Butler, Sept. 9, 1828, Charles Butler Papers, LC.

were Morocco; his nicely fitting gloves were yellow kid; his hat, a long-furred beaver, with broad brim, was of Quaker color.

Here was Van Buren on a long, difficult political tour still managing to look like a dandy. Although he did complain at the end of the trip that he had "been upon the go" all summer, he insisted diplomatically that the "western excursion" had been "very pleasant."[74]

By the time he returned to Albany in late August, Van Buren had made up his mind to run for governor and had outlined plans for the campaign. He anticipated an "oppressive struggle," but was confident of winning if the Regency could only neutralize the Anti-Masons. He therefore asked James A. Hamilton to "beg" editors Mordecai Noah and William Coleman of the *Enquirer* and the New York *Evening Post* in New York City, to treat Anti-Masonry "cautiously." Van Buren was optimistic because the Anti-Masons had stubbornly insisted on running their own candidate for governor instead of combining with the Adams party. In a three-way race with the eccentric former editor Solomon Southwick, the Anti-Masonic candidate, and Supreme Court Justice Smith Thompson, who had been nominated by the supporters of Adams, Van Buren had a good chance to win. Some cynics suggested that Van Buren had bribed Southwick to run, but there is no evidence to support the charge, and the ambitious Southwick needed no encouragement anyway. There is no doubt, however, that Van Buren arranged to have the Democrats nominate Throop for lieutenant governor, rather than acting governor Nathaniel Pitcher. To keep Pitcher from rebelling at the convention, Van Buren asked Benjamin Butler to take the governor aside and explain "frankly and kindly" why the lieutenant governor had to be a westerner. When the delegates voted, they selected Van Buren and Throop.[75]

The New York campaign had national as well as local importance because in 1826 the electoral law had finally been changed to give the choice of presidential electors to the people instead of the legislature. To clinch New York, which Jackson needed to win the election, William B. Lewis tried to get Van Buren to have the state's electoral law

---

[74] Henry B. Stanton, *Random Recollections* (Johnstown, 1886), pp. 20-21; Flagg to Wright, Aug. 24, 1828, Flagg-Wright Correspondence; MVB to William C. Rives, Sept. 10, 1828, James Madison Papers, LC; MVB to James A. Hamilton, Aug. 25, 1828, Hamilton, *Reminiscences*, pp. 78-79.

[75] MVB to Hamilton, Aug. 25, 1828, Hamilton, *Reminiscences*, pp. 78-79; Weed, *Autobiography*, pp. 43-44; McCarthy, *Antimasonic Party*, pp. 375-383; Hammond, *Political Parties*, II, 283-287; Alexander, *Political History*, I, 360-364; Alexander, *American Talleyrand*, p. 240; MVB to Charles Butler, Sept. 9, 1828, Charles Butler Papers, LC; *Autobiography*, p. 220.

changed back so that the legislature would continue to choose the electors. He refused, but when the *National Intelligencer* picked up the story, Van Buren had to issue a series of denials in the *Argus*. John Quincy Adams, meanwhile, was reported to be giving "almost undivided attention" to New York, where he too thought the outcome would be decided.[76]

During the campaign politicians on both sides cultivated images of Van Buren and Jackson that shaped their careers and determined their places in history. Gales and Seaton, who edited the *National Intelligencer*, summed up the public view when they called Van Buren "the most adroit but also the most powerful politician of the present day," who could "accomplish more than any other man would dream of." The editors respected Van Buren's "powers of persuasion" and his "imperturbable temper," but worried that he had substituted "combination, management and party discipline" for "open and fearless appeals to public sentiment."[77]

Jackson, on the other hand, was portrayed as a pious, open and fearless hero. When asked about Jackson's "moral character," Van Buren instructed James A. Hamilton to "mention . . . modestly [that] the old gentleman [had] prayers in his own house." The *Argus* called on New Yorkers to vote for "THE SOLDIER BOY / OF THE FIRST WAR OF INDEPENDENCE / THE VETERAN HERO / OF THE SECOND; / NOW THE HONEST, UNASSUMING FARMER OF TENNESSEE." Jackson was said to combine the "Military" qualities of Washington, the "Democrat[ic]" qualities of Jefferson, and the "unostentatious" demeanor of Franklin. Long before historians wrote about symbol, restoration and nostalgia, Van Buren and Ned Croswell played upon similar themes in 1828. By the end of the campaign, images of Van Buren the politician and Jackson the hero were imbedded in people's minds.[78]

Van Buren cultivated another theme—that the election marked a renewal of the old party battles of the Jeffersonian era. In the columns of the *Argus* he hammered away at the idea that the Jacksonians were simple old-time Jeffersonians opposing aristocracy, waste and a powerful executive. The election, he insisted, was a crisis similar to those

[76] Lewis to MVB, Aug. 8, Sept. 27, 1828, Richard Mentor Johnson to MVB, Sept. 25, 1828, MVB to the Albany *Daily Advertiser*, Oct. 1828, VBP; *Argus*, Sept. 2, Sept. 19, Sept. 24, 1828; *National Intelligencer*, Sept. 11, Sept. 13, Sept. 23, Sept. 25, Oct. 4, 1828; Gales and Seaton to Taylor, Oct. 25, 1828, Taylor Papers.

[77] *Argus*, Sept. 2, 1828.

[78] Matthew Warner to MVB, Sept. 4, 1828, Matthew Warner Miscellaneous Papers, NYHS; MVB to Hamilton, Sept. 16, 1828, Hamilton, *Reminiscences*, p. 79; *Argus*, Oct. 31, Nov. 4, Nov. 7, 1828.

in 1776, 1798 and 1812. To attract Clintonians, the *Argus* pointed out that Clinton and Van Buren had both firmly supported state rights. The obvious connection with another Jeffersonian, Aaron Burr, posed several problems. Just a few months earlier Burr and Van Buren had stood side by side as lawyers in the case of Varick *v*. Johnson, and it was all too easy for the public to connect Van Buren with the corrupt Burr. Some people were also reminded that Burr had almost succeeded in dragging Andrew Jackson into the conspiracy to seize New Orleans and conquer the Southwest in 1806.[79]

During the campaign Van Buren lived up to his reputation as a political manipulator. To keep Mordecai Noah in line, he agreed to let the editor run for sheriff of New York County. When William Harris Crawford renewed his earlier efforts to have Nathaniel Macon replace Calhoun as the vice presidential candidate, Van Buren again fended off the proposal. Despite the demands of his own campaign in New York, he kept in close contact with his allies in other states. Little wonder that one opponent remarked shrilly that there had never been "such a wicked combination [as the one] headed by little Van Buren."[80]

As the election approached, Adams' backers became more and more pessimistic. John W. Taylor heard reports of apathy in September, Thurlow Weed was ready to concede the election in October, and Charles Francis Adams warned his mother in early November that defeat lay ahead. In New York the result was closer than they had anticipated, for Jackson carried the state by only 5,000 popular votes, and 20 electoral votes to 16 for Adams. Van Buren was elected governor with 136,794 votes to 106,444 for Thompson, and 33,345 for Southwick. The Jacksonians carried New York City, the lower Hudson, the southern tier, and the center of the state, but lost the upper Hudson around Albany, the northern region, and the Anti-Masonic counties in the west. Van Buren compared the results with the elections at the start of the century when Republicans had carried New York City, but had lost the counties near Albany to the Federalists. He blamed the closeness of the election on a revival of "old 98 Federalism"

[79] In 1805, Burr visited Jackson in Nashville and interested him in vague plans to conquer the Spanish Southwest. Jackson backed out when he learned that Burr was considering attacking New Orleans. Remini, *Jackson and the Course of Empire*, pp. 144-153. *Argus*, May 2, Oct. 31, Nov. 4, Nov. 7, 1828; *Richmond Enquirer*, Aug. 22, Aug. 29, 1828.

[80] MVB to Cambreleng, Oct. 18, Oct. 29, 1828, MVB to Jackson, Nov. 16, 1828, Noah to MVB, Oct. 2, 1828, Crawford to MVB, Oct. 21, 1828, MVB to Crawford, Nov. 14, 1828, VBP; William M. Oliver to Charles Butler, Nov. 10, 1828 (typed copy), Charles Butler Papers, LC.

and the "manor influence" on the upper Hudson. He ignored the obvious point that the election would have been even closer had not the Anti-Masons insisted on running Southwick. In the overall presidential election the outcome in New York was not decisive because Jackson won a sweeping victory and would have had more than enough electoral votes without those of the Empire State.[81]

But even so Van Buren deserved much credit for his accomplishments. Three years earlier in 1825, the Regency had lost the presidential election, Clinton was governor, Van Buren was not certain that he would be sent back to the Senate, and no Democratic party existed. In the intervening years Van Buren had made friends with Clinton, had restored the power of the Regency, had been reelected senator, had organized a national political party, had maneuvered his way around the pitfalls of tariff-making, had made the bold decision to run for governor, and had won the election. His persistent efforts to unite North and South were rewarded when Jackson carried five northern states, eight southern states, and two on the border as well. Victory in New York, Pennsylvania, Kentucky, Ohio, Illinois, and Indiana was in part due to Van Buren's tariff policy. In doing all this he helped create a new national political system better suited to the American society that was emerging than the old state-dominated system that held sway after the War of 1812, while at the same time he preserved the strength of his own state party.

IN spite of Van Buren's accomplishments the members of the Regency looked ahead uncertainly after the election. Although Van Buren was about to become governor, there was already talk that he would return to Washington to join the cabinet. The Regency was shaken when Attorney General Samuel A. Talcott, destroyed by drink, stepped down, and Comptroller William L. Marcy, passed over for governor, moved up to the state supreme court. There was internal debate over who should replace Van Buren in the Senate, and with election returns incomplete, Silas Wright was not certain for weeks whether he had

---

[81] New York was divided into electoral districts. In the nation Jackson received 178 electoral votes, Adams 83. R. M. Livingston to Taylor, Sept. 12, 1828, Taylor Papers; Weed to Francis Granger, Oct. 26, 1828, Granger Papers, LC; Charles Francis Adams to Louisa C. Adams, Nov. 8, 1828, John Quincy Adams Papers, Massachusetts Historical Society, quoted in Jerome Mushkat, *Tammany: the Evolution of a Political Machine 1789-1865* (Syracuse, 1971), p. 114; *Argus*, Dec. 5, Dec. 16, 1828; MVB to Cambreleng, Nov. 7, 1828, VBP. Dixon Ryan Fox agreed with Van Buren that the election followed the pattern of earlier elections. Fox, *Decline of Aristocracy*, p. 249. See also Goldstein, "Albany Regency," pp. 169-170; *Autobiography*, pp. 220-221; McCarthy, *Antimasonic Party*, p. 383; Hammond, *Political Parties*, II, 289-290.

been reelected to the House of Representatives. He was finally declared reelected, but the Regency decided to strengthen the party at home by bringing him back to fill the important patronage post of state comptroller. In January, the party decided on Mayor Charles Dudley of Albany, for Van Buren's Senate seat.[82]

In the midst of the politicking, on January 6, 1829, Van Buren delivered his inaugural address as governor. Some historians have argued that Jacksonians had little concern for the economic and social issues of the day, but in this message Van Buren addressed important new problems. Somewhat hypocritically perhaps, he proposed a bill to restrict campaign expenditures to printing only. Conscious of the growing slums in New York City, he asked for a system of houses for juvenile delinquents, and for a Republican he showed unusual concern for banking by promising to present a plan to help the state banks protect one another.[83]

His address drew an immediate response. Within three months laws were passed forbidding the entertainment of voters and requiring the commissioner of health in New York City to pay $8,000 a year to the Society for the Reformation of Juvenile Delinquents. The banking plan, drawn up by the lawyer Joshua Forman, who was a leading advocate of the Erie Canal, proposed the establishment of an association in which member banks would protect the credit and solvency of one another. Bankers in Albany and along the Erie Canal were enthusiastic about the plan, which Thomas Olcott called almost "too perfect," but New York City bankers, suspicious of Van Buren, Olcott, the Regency, and Albany banks, did not want to be drawn into a scheme in which they would be guaranteeing country banks. Despite their opposition, the Safety Fund plan passed the legislature, and provided a model for similar laws in other states. Van Buren's modest program showed once again his ability to respond to some of the social issues of his day. In New York and elsewhere Jacksonian Democrats at the state level were trying to find solutions to new problems.[84]

[82] MVB to Benjamin Butler, Nov. 17, 1828, Wright to MVB, Dec. 7, 1828, VBP; Wright to Flagg, Dec. 19, Dec. 28, 1828, Wright-Flagg Correspondence; *Argus*, Dec. 16, 1828; Hammond, *Political Parties*, II, 302-304.

[83] Hammond, *Political Parties*, II, 297-302; MVB, "Annual Message," 1829, Lincoln, *Messages*, III, 230-259.

[84] Hammond, *Political Parties*, II, 297-320. For another example of Jacksonian state reform, see Cole, *Jacksonian Democracy in New Hampshire*, pp. 170-184. I cannot accept the point of view that Jacksonians ignored those in need and opposed social and humanitarian reforms. For such an interpretation, see Edward Pessen, *Jacksonian America: Society, Personality and Politics*, rev. ed. (Homewood, 1978), pp. 296-303; Benson, *Concept of Jacksonian Democracy*, pp. 39, 44-46.

As Van Buren adjusted to the emergent society and the new national politics, he ran the risk of damaging his reputation as an Old Republican. In December, Democratic congressman John DeGraff of New York, had urged Van Buren to appeal to national interests in his inaugural by supporting tariff protection and by avoiding state rights. Although Van Buren ignored the advice about the tariff, he did steer clear of state rights, but he managed to sound enough like a Republican to please state-righters John Randolph and Thomas Ritchie. Randolph declared that Van Buren "came nearer to our old doctrines than any other prominent *publick* man." The inaugural, according to Randolph, was "so praised by friends & foes" that it did not "need [his] commendation."[85]

Ritchie and other Southerners had such confidence in Van Buren that they began to urge him to join Jackson's cabinet in order to protect republican principles. One Virginian thought that Van Buren deserved to be in the cabinet because of his "talents," not because of "intrigue"; another preferred Van Buren over fellow Virginian Littleton Tazewell. James Hamilton, Jr., William B. Lewis and Duff Green all agreed that Van Buren would become Secretary of State. Support for Van Buren was so widespread that members of the Regency reported that he could become the "premier" of the new cabinet, but at the same time rumors abounded that Van Buren would prefer to remain in New York.[86]

Rumors and doubt about the cabinet continued into the new year because Jackson made no appointments until he arrived in Washington in February. In addition to Van Buren, attention centered on Levi Woodbury, Louis McLane, Littleton Tazewell, John H. Eaton of Tennessee (with whom Van Buren kept in touch), William T. Barry of Kentucky, John McLean of Ohio, and Samuel D. Ingham of Pennsylvania. Van Buren depended on his New York colleagues in Washington to represent him and to pass along the news. Although James A. Hamilton was the most influential of these representatives, the

[85] John DeGraff to Azariah Flagg, Dec. 2, 1828, Flagg Papers; Randolph to MVB, Feb. 1, 1829, John Randolph Collection (# 6489), MSS Dept., UVL; Ritchie to MVB, Jan. 31, 1829, VBP.

[86] John Randolph to MVB, Dec. 16, 1828, William B. Lewis to James A. Hamilton, Dec. 12, 1828, Silas Wright to MVB, Dec. 9, 1828, James Hamilton, Jr., to MVB, Jan. 23, 1829, VBP; *Richmond Enquirer*, Nov. 21, Dec. 11, Dec. 23, 1828; James Campbell to Gulian Verplanck, Dec. 23, 1828, Verplanck Papers, NYHS; Duff Green to General T. Lyman, Dec. 7, 1828, Duff Green to Isaac Hill, Dec. 17, 1828, Duff Green Papers, LC; John DeGraff to Azariah Flagg, Dec. 2, 1828, Flagg Papers; Rudolph Bunner to James A. Hamilton, Jan. 14, 1829, Hamilton, *Reminiscences*, p. 88; Nehemiah Knight to J. F. Simmons, Dec. 29, 1828, James Fowler Simmons Papers, LC.

gregarious Churchill C. Cambreleng sent the most interesting letters. Soon after the election Van Buren wrote encouraging Cambreleng to report, even if it was only to describe intrigue. As he said, "You might as well turn the current of the Niagara with a ladies fan as to prevent scheming & intrigue at Washington." Quick to oblige, Cambreleng dispatched a humorous letter on New Year's Day filled with such salacious gossip about the notorious Peggy O'Neale Timberlake Eaton that he chose not to sign it.[87]

The question of whether Van Buren would join the cabinet came to a head in February when Jackson arrived in Washington. As soon as Hamilton came to call, Jackson made it clear that he wanted Van Buren as Secretary of State. In the letter tendering the office, the inexperienced Jackson said that he needed Van Buren's "intelligence & sound judgment," and asked him to come as soon as possible. When the news spread, many of Van Buren's friends told him to reject the offer. Joshua Forman, Jabez Hammond and Lot Clark thought that Van Buren should stay in New York and build a new northern party instead of playing second fiddle to a southern President in the Democratic party. Others such as Louis McLane and Senator Elias Kent Kane of Illinois, argued that Van Buren would be making too great a sacrifice in joining an administration that was doomed to fail. As one Southerner put it, Van Buren would "cut his throat" if he went. Realizing that Van Buren might refuse, the anxious Jackson asked Hamilton "repeatedly" during the next few days whether the governor would accept.

In deciding whether or not to accept Jackson's offer, Van Buren once again had to confront the question of whether state or national politics came first. Ever since 1825 he had been determined to put state over nation, and there had been ample reason to stick to that position. But the situation had changed. Clinton was dead, the Regency was in control of the state, and Van Buren could continue to help the state organization from Washington. Furthermore, he had never abandoned the goal of creating a national political party based upon Old Republican principles and an alliance of North and South. Even while running for governor he had always had in mind the possibility of giving up the office if the expected offer came from Washington. And finally the ambitious Van Buren was aware that the job of Secretary of State could lead to the White House. On February 20, he accepted

[87] Verplanck to MVB, Dec. 6, 1828, Wright to MVB, Dec. 9, 1828, MVB to Cambreleng, Dec. 17, 1828, Cambreleng to MVB, Jan. 1, 1829, Bunner to MVB, Feb. 21, 1829, VBP; Hamilton to MVB, Dec. 20, 1828, MVB to Hamilton, Dec. 28, 1828, Feb. 2, 1829, Hamilton, *Reminiscences*, pp. 81-82, 92.

Jackson's offer. Since Van Buren needed time to wind up his affairs as governor, he arranged to have James A. Hamilton serve as Secretary of State during the first few weeks of the new administration.[88]

Van Buren had hardly any influence on the make-up of the cabinet he was joining because, as Duff Green predicted, Jackson shaped the cabinet himself, paying little attention to the advice of anyone except Eaton and Lewis. In his letter accepting appointment to the cabinet, Van Buren recommended McLane as Secretary of the Treasury, but Jackson appointed Ingham instead. When Ritchie and Andrew Stevenson of Virginia, tried to influence Jackson, they were ignored. Jackson believed that there was no need to appoint a Virginian because politicians from the Old Dominion had had more than their share of cabinet positions in the past. Robert Y. Hayne and James Hamilton, Jr., of South Carolina, conferred with Jackson, but found that the cabinet had already been filled, and even though James A. Hamilton saw a great deal of Jackson in February, the New Yorker had no more influence than anyone else.[89]

Jackson's cabinet, announced on February 26, consisted of Van Buren in State, Ingham in Treasury, Eaton, Secretary of War, John Branch of North Carolina, Secretary of the Navy, John M. Berrien of Georgia, Attorney General, and John McLean, Postmaster General, all but McLean taken from the Twentieth Congress. The list included many less than distinguished figures, prompting British minister Sir Charles R. Vaughan to remark that Jackson's announcement was met by a "general expression of disappointment." Louis McLane, Elias Kent Kane and James Hamilton, Jr., all told Van Buren that he was not going to be working with powerful associates. Margaret Bayard Smith wrote that the new President's enemies were "delighted," his friends "grieved." "Even Van Buren," she added, "altho' a profound

---

[88] James A. Hamilton to MVB, Feb. 12, 1829, Hamilton, *Reminiscences*, pp. 89-90; Jackson to MVB, Feb. 15, 1829, James A. Hamilton to MVB, Feb. 19, 1829, MVB to Jackson, Feb. 20, 1829, Forman to MVB, Feb. 12, 1829, Clark to MVB, April 10, 1828, McLane to MVB, Feb. 19, 1829, Kane to MVB, Feb. 19, 1829, Rudolph Bunner to MVB, Feb. 21, 1829, Cambreleng to MVB, Mar. 1, 1829, VBP; *Autobiography*, pp. 224, 231.

[89] Green to John Pope, Dec. 11, 1828, Duff Green Papers, LC; MVB to James A. Hamilton, Feb. 2, Feb. 15, Feb. 21, 1829, Hamilton, *Reminiscences*, pp. 92-94; *Autobiography*, p. 231; James A. Hamilton to MVB, Feb. 12, Feb. 13, 1829, Hayne to MVB, Feb. 14, 1829, Louis McLane to MVB, Feb. 19, 1829, VBP; Hamilton, *Reminiscences*, pp. 90, 101; James C. Curtis, *Andrew Jackson and the Search for Vindication* (Boston, 1976), p. 96; Richard B. Latner, *The Presidency of Andrew Jackson: White House Politics 1829-1837* (Athens, 1979), pp. 31-46.

politician is not supposed to be an able statesman. . . . Yet on him, all rests."[90]

The gossip over the selection of the cabinet focused attention on the growing struggle between Van Buren and Calhoun for power within the new party. "Disguise it as we may," observed James Buchanan of Pennsylvania, "the friends of Van Buren and those of Calhoun are becoming very jealous of each other." Van Buren apparently gained an advantage by becoming Secretary of State, the post that usually went to the heir apparent; but Calhoun scored when his man Ingham beat out Van Buren's friend McLane for Secretary of the Treasury. In addition Branch and Berrien soon became allies of Calhoun. William B. Lewis tried to convince James A. Hamilton that the cabinet leaned toward Van Buren, but the latter was not convinced; Van Buren later recalled that no critic of the new cabinet was "more disappointed than myself by the composition of the administration." Since Jackson kept insisting that he would serve but one term, the alliance between Van Buren and the South Carolinian that had helped make Jackson President, was likely to continue to deteriorate. The alliance of planters and plain Republicans was already in danger.[91]

[90] William T. Barry of Kentucky, replaced McLean on March 9, 1829. British Foreign Office, Correspondence, 5: United States, 248 (1829) (photostats, LC), pp. 128-129; McLane to MVB, Feb. 19, 1829, Kane to MVB, Feb. 19, 1829, James Hamilton, Jr., to MVB, Feb. 19, 1829, Cambreleng to MVB, Mar. 1, 1829, James A. Hamilton to MVB, Feb. 21, Feb. 23, 1829, VBP; Smith, First Forty Years of Washington Society, p. 287.

[91] Argus, Dec. 16, 1828; Gulian Verplanck to MVB, Dec. 6, 1828, VBP; Duff Green to John Pope, Dec. 11, 1828, Duff Green Papers, LC; Rudolph Bunner to James A. Hamilton, Jan. 14, 1829, Hamilton, Reminiscences, p. 88; Buchanan to George B. Porter, Jan. 22, 1829, James Buchanan Papers, NYHS; Charles Dillingham to Azariah Flagg, Feb. 16, 1829, Flagg Papers; Charleston Courier, Feb. 16, 1829; Autobiography, p. 231.

· III ·

JACKSONIAN DEMOCRAT
1829-1837

3. Martin Van Buren c. 1837, from an original painting by Henry Inman

· 6 ·

THE MAGICIAN AND OLD HICKORY

Early in March 1829, Van Buren visited his old political opponent, former lieutenant governor John Tayler, who lay dying in Albany. After reminiscing about past party struggles, Van Buren described his "new duties" in the Jackson administration, which he was about to join. He was saying farewell not only to Tayler but also to New York, for a few days later Van Buren resigned as governor and left to go to work with Old Hickory. Though he had left once before to serve as senator, he had kept close ties to New York, realizing that he needed a strong local base to succeed in national politics; and every spring had found him heading home to his law office and the Regency. But this time was different. He would spend only five months at home in the next forty as he carried out his duties as Secretary of State and minister to England. He would never practice law again, and others would take control of the Regency.[1]

The trip down the Hudson to New York, across New Jersey to Philadelphia, and on by boat and carriage to New Castle, Delaware, Baltimore, and finally to Washington was far from a triumphal journey. At each stop along the way Van Buren was greeted by political friends, who urged him to turn back and not get involved with the weak, inexperienced Jackson administration. In New York Van Buren felt so ill that he went to bed, but Levi Woodbury burst into the room to enumerate those "who were dissatisfied" with the Cabinet. In Philadelphia the Secretary had "a long and gloomy interview" with Edward Livingston, now senator from Louisiana, who feared that foreigners would hold the new White House in "contempt." As Van Buren's boat approached the wharf in New Castle, he observed "disappointment and deep mortification stamped upon every line [of Louis McLane's] intelligent countenance." While waiting for the stage to leave, McLane took Van Buren by the arm and led him along the road, delivering an "excited harangue [on the] degraded condition" of affairs in Washington, which he blamed on the "evil counsellors" surrounding Jackson. Van Buren, who was still sick and found the walk tiring, was relieved when the stage overtook them and he was able to bid McLane goodbye. In Baltimore Senator Samuel Smith

[1] *Autobiography*, pp. 224-228.

renewed the tale of woe, but despite all advice, Van Buren pressed on to Washington to embark on his national career.[2]

It was after dark on March 22 when a tired Van Buren reached his hotel. It was surrounded by a crowd of office seekers and for the next hour he lay on a sofa listening to their requests before departing for the White House to pay his respects to Andrew Jackson. Many years later in writing his autobiography, Van Buren vividly recalled the dramatic moment:

> A solitary lamp in the vestibule and a single candle . . . gave no promise of the cordiality with which I was . . . greeted by General Jackson. . . . His health was poor, and his spirits depressed. . . . This was our first meeting as political friends and it was certainly a peculiar feature in that interview and no insignificant illustration of his nature that he received with most affectionate eagerness, . . . the individual destined to occupy the first place in his confidence, of whose character his only opportunities to learn anything by personal observation had been presented during periods of active political hostility.

Noticing Van Buren's exhaustion, Jackson "considerately [postponed] all business" until the next day, and sent his new colleague off to bed.[3]

The friendly meeting that evening was the beginning of a close personal relationship that lasted until Jackson's death sixteen years later. During the first eight years, while Jackson was President, the two leaders worked together most of the time in Washington, and when they were separated, they exchanged dozens of letters. They were particularly close the first two years, spending all but two months together in the Capital. Although the western clique of John H. Eaton, William B. Lewis and Andrew J. Donelson, who was Jackson's private secretary, had the most influence over the President during the first year of his administration, by 1830 Van Buren had used the Peggy Eaton affair and the Maysville veto to assert his supremacy. Van Buren's absence in much of 1831 and 1832 weakened his influence, but the President still relied on him for advice and support. When Van Buren became President, Jackson persisted in sending his successor letters filled with advice—advice that was often ignored. Van Buren had more influence over Jackson's administration than Jackson had over Van Buren's. Since the Magician and the Hero approached politics differently, they occasionally disagreed and tension sometimes arose,

[2] *Ibid.*, pp. 228-231.
[3] *Ibid.*, p. 232.

but the warmth and respect that developed that first evening never dissipated. Van Buren may have exaggerated when he claimed that the "cordial and confidential" relationship between the two had "never ... been surpassed among public men," but no study of Jacksonian Democracy is complete without a consideration of their partnership.[4]

Contemporary observers and historians have portrayed Jackson and Van Buren in terms of a classic contrast: Jackson, who was sixty-two years old in 1829, was the Hero—tall, lean, rugged, strong, virile, a fighter with a temper and emotions that were sometimes unleashed, straightforward, a man of iron will; Van Buren, who was forty-six, was the Magician—short, fat, soft, weak, a dandy who loved fancy clothes, a shrewd politician who suppressed his emotions and used his intellect to get his way. No one could imagine Van Buren losing his temper or fighting a duel. Whigs cleverly played upon these stereotypes in 1840 when they contrasted Van Buren, who drank wine out of silver goblets, with the frontier hero William Henry Harrison, who was made to seem remarkably like Jackson. As Davy Crockett put it, Jackson was "all *openness* and *feeling*," Van Buren "all *slyness* and *cold calculation*."[5]

In reality Jackson and Van Buren were far more similar than different, both exhibiting many of the qualities that marked Jacksonian Democracy. Born poor, they made their way upward until they captured the presidency and then retired to handsome country estates. Leaving home at an early age with little education, they were admitted to the bar at twenty and became powerful leaders in their communities. Married at twenty-four, widowers later in life, they were devoted family men. Reared in the tradition of the Revolution, Jeffersonians by the turn of the century, associates for a while of Aaron Burr, they became prominent during the War of 1812, and served as senators in the 1820s before joining forces against Clay and Adams. Both were

---

[4] *Ibid.* Between June 1831 and October 1833 they were apart most of the time, but exchanged over 100 letters. During the next 40 months (until March 1837), they spent 28 months together. Between 1837 and 1845 they exchanged another 100 letters. Richard B. Latner presents the thesis that Westerners had more influence over Jackson than did Van Buren. Latner, *Presidency of Jackson*, pp. 4-6, 54. But Latner concedes that Van Buren also had considerable influence.

[5] Crockett, *Van Buren*, pp. 167-168. Jessie Frémont referred to Van Buren's "effeminate life." Jessie Benton Frémont, *Souvenirs of My Time* (Boston, 1887), p. 30. John William Ward has captured many of the themes of Jackson's presidency in *Andrew Jackson—Symbol for an Age* (New York, 1953). Two works that depart from the stereotypes are Marvin Meyers' *Jacksonian Persuasion*, pp. 142-162, and Albert Somit's "Andrew Jackson: Legend and Reality," *Tennessee Historical Quarterly*, 7 (Dec. 1948), 291-313.

shrewd politicians who planned their moves with care; both loved the outdoors, rode horseback well, and gambled on horse races and elections. Both worked long hours, punishing themselves to achieve victory. During the War of 1812, Jackson went without sleep at New Orleans; Van Buren worked through the night on wartime problems in Albany. As vain as Van Buren, Andrew Jackson kept an artist in the White House to paint his portrait; like Jackson, Van Buren was manly enough to resort to bluff (he forced John Suydam to back down in a duel).

Of course, there were differences between the two men. Van Buren was never a military man and in temperament, was not capable of Jackson's towering rages. Jackson was never a new-style politician, nor was he conciliatory like Van Buren. Jackson was more of a nationalist than the republican-minded Van Buren, but the two had much in common.[6]

Both men resisted the false stereotype of a conniving Van Buren, shrewd, yes, but no more an intriguer than many other politicians. At the end of their first year together, Jackson wrote that his Secretary of State was not "selfish and intriguing," but was really "frank, open, candid, and manly." Impatient with those who singled Van Buren out as a plotter, Jackson insisted that Van Buren was "one of the most frank men" he had ever known—"*a true man* with no guile." Nothing bothered Van Buren more than the charge of being a sly plotter. On leaving New York he felt the need to say that he entered his new post "uncontaminated by court intrigue." And later he wrote wryly that if he had "possessed a tithe of the skill in subtle management and the spirit of intrigue" imputed to him by his enemies, he "could have turned aside the opposition . . . without much difficulty."[7]

Comfortable with each other because of their similarities, Van Buren said that he was "enamored" of the "affectionate, confidential" general, while Jackson described Van Buren as "one of the most pleasant men" he had ever known. The two spent so much time together that Van Buren was called the President's "constant riding, walking and visiting companion." Though Van Buren had his own quarters, he dined at the White House so often that he was considered one of the President's family. There he gave fatherly advice to Andrew J. Donelson's

---

[6] Robert E. Moody has noted a few of the similarities in "The Influence of Martin Van Buren on the Career and Acts of Andrew Jackson," *Papers of the Michigan Academy of Science Arts and Letters*, 7 (1926), 225-240.

[7] Jackson to John Overton, Dec. 31, 1829, Jackson to Hugh L. White, April 9, 1831, Jackson, *Correspondence*, IV, 108-109, 259-260; *Niles' Register*, 36 (1829), 89; *Autobiography*, p. 226n.

wife, Emily, who served as hostess at the White House because of the death of Jackson's wife, Rachel. On occasion Van Buren romped with the Donelson family after supper, playing games such as blindman's buff. Emily Donelson's niece, Mary Eastin, who also lived at the White House, told a friend that Van Buren had "fine manners," and was "pleasing in conversation." Even when Van Buren retreated to Decatur House, his home across Lafayette Square, he sent notes and signaled to the White House from his skylight.[8]

The relationship between the elderly Jackson and the middle-aged Van Buren was something akin to that of mentor and protégé. Having neither child nor wife, Jackson enjoyed protecting and guiding Van Buren. Accustomed to deferring to older men such as Rufus King, the widowed Van Buren, whose children were now largely independent or cared for by others, was content to play the role of the obedient junior. Once when Van Buren rode too close to the action at a horse race, Jackson bellowed, "Get behind me, sir! They will run over you," and Van Buren quickly fell back. As is common in such relationships, Jackson called Van Buren by his first name and teased him; the latter addressed the President formally and treated him seriously. When Jackson complained about his failing health, Van Buren responded solicitously. When Van Buren's son, Smith, complained that he had been unfairly disciplined by the principal of his school, Jackson reacted as though Smith were his own child. Smith's letter, said Jackson, was a "gem!" Unless the principal "*atone*[d] for the punishment of innocence," Van Buren should remove the boy from the school; "I would not take a *million*," roared the Old Hero, "for such a *son*, and I protest against permitting his *high sense* of honor [to be] subdued into abject servility."[9]

Van Buren was as much at home in Washington society as he was in the White House. On his morning rides with Jackson, Van Buren often rode the gentle bay gelding sent him by John Randolph. On more formal occasions he used a carriage made in Russia and drawn by a "pair of superb trotters." In the evenings he attended or presided

[8] MVB to Hoyt, April 13, 1829, Duff Green Papers, LC; MVB to James A. Hamilton, July 13, 1829, Hamilton, *Reminiscences*, p. 142; Jackson to John Overton, Dec. 31, 1829, Jackson, *Correspondence*, IV, 108; Smith, *First Forty Years of Washington Society*, p. 310; Pauline Wilcox Burke, *Emily Donelson of Tennessee* (Richmond, 1941), I, 188, 209-217, II, 95; Mary Eastin to Phila Ann Donelson, April 9, 1829, *Ibid.*, I, 188; Marie Beale, "Decatur House," p. 10, typescript, Decatur House Papers, LC.

[9] Ben: Perley Poor, *Perley's Reminiscences of Sixty Years in the National Metropolis* (Philadelphia, 1886), I, 190-191; Irelan, *Van Buren*, p. 225; MVB to Jackson, July 29, 1831, VBP; Burke, *Emily Donelson*, II, 92; Jackson to MVB, Nov. 15, 1830, Jackson, *Correspondence*, IV, 205.

over many elaborate dinners. His parties were so "frequent [and so] aristocratic," one critic complained, that "although a Republican, [Van Buren had no] taste for republican habits." He was still vain and "foppish" enough to have his portrait painted at least twice while he was Secretary of State. When John Barton Derby of Boston, sought a job in the State Department, he found himself "before a bald-headed, but whiskered little gentleman, dressed in the extreme of fashion, full of smirks and smiles, soft as the 'sweet South, breathing o'er violets,'— but penetrating as a mercurial bath, or the poison of Upas."[10]

The parties and fashionable dress attested to Van Buren's avid interest in women. When he returned to the Capital in 1829, it was accurately predicted that the Secretary would split his time between "international law [and] the ladies." Some women, the wives of Louis McLane and William C. Rives for example, were close to Van Buren's age, but Emily Donelson, Mary Eastin, and McLane's daughter Rebecca were much younger. He squired Emily to balls, took Emily and Mary on a visit to Delaware, gave all of them advice, and sent them letters. In one letter to Rebecca in 1830 he wrote in jest: "I mean to try to get married this summer if I can find time, & if not, I will give it up altogether." He did neither. Two months later he was off to Saratoga, "taking the waters," and paying "attention to some agreeable ladies." Despite his protestations and flirtations, Van Buren never remarried. According to one interpretation, which seems exaggerated, he was so ambitious that he could not bring himself to love or marry for fear that either would interfere with his political career. It is more likely that he was comfortable in middle age, and preferred to flirt rather than to marry.[11]

[10] Smith, *First Forty Years of Washington Society*, p. 310; Burke, *Emily Donelson*, I, 210, 217, 277; *Autobiography*, pp. 347-349, 402-403; Jackson to MVB, Oct. 23, 1830, William Leigh to MVB, Mar. 7, 1831, VBP; Adams, *Memoirs*, VIII, 154; *Niles' Register*, 40 (1831), 63; Esther Singleton, *The Story of the White House* (New York, 1907), I, 209; Colonel McKenney to Andrew J. Donelson, Aug. 14, 1829, Andrew J. Donelson Papers, LC; Henry Van der Lyn, "Journal," pp. 175, 177, NYHS; John Barton Derby, *Political Reminiscences* (Boston, 1835), p. 59.

[11] For the Delaware trip, see Burke, *Emily Donelson*, I, 203; Van Buren to Andrew J. Donelson, July 27, 1829, Andrew J. Donelson Papers, LC; *Richmond Enquirer*, July 31, 1829. For the interpretation of Van Buren's failure to remarry, see Joseph Hergesheimer, "Washington," *The Saturday Evening Post*, 199 (June 4, 1927), 16-17, 127, 129-130, 135. See also Singleton, *Story of the White House*, I, 205; MVB to Mrs. Catherine McLane, July 5, 1829, MVB to Rebecca McLane, May 4, 1830, Hamilton-McLane Series, Alexander Hamilton Papers, LC; MVB to Mrs. William C. Rives, Feb. 21, 1829, MVB to Rives, April 6, 1830, Rives Papers, LC; MVB to Mary Eastin, July 4, 1830, George Washington Campbell Papers, LC; Munroe, *Louis McLane*, pp. 257-261, 267-268.

Van Buren did not, however, allow his political and social life to interfere with his family responsibilities. After graduating from West Point, Abraham became his father's private secretary and in 1829 was courting Mary Eastin and Rebecca McLane. John, who graduated from Yale in 1828, began to enjoy such a full life in New York that his father asked James A. Hamilton to "keep a good look-out" to see that the young man did not "spend too much money." After a few weeks with John in 1830, Van Buren returned to Washington reflecting on "the course of life [that his son had] marked out for" himself, in which "eating, and drinking, & dressing appear[ed] to be the most important" activities. John, who respected his father, neither heeded nor resented his occasionally hypocritical advice. When John appeared in Washington to help with letter writing, Emily Donelson noted that the dashing young man cut a "very fine figure, with the aid," she imagined, of "pads & London taylors." Van Buren's third son, Martin, lived with his father at Decatur House, while the youngest, Smith, was battling the Yankee schoolmaster in Massachusetts. It took a great deal of managerial skill for Van Buren to keep track of his family.[12]

But Van Buren did not spend much time during the spring and summer of 1829 going to parties or caring for his family because he was overwhelmed by a multitude of political problems. On March 28, after a few days of rest, he took over the operation of the State Department from the interim secretary, James A. Hamilton. Van Buren quickly found that he had joined an inexperienced President and a disorganized administration, which was having difficulty coping with patronage, party squabbles, foreign affairs, and economic policy. Some observers even shared the opinion of Margaret Bayard Smith and the celebrated constitutional lawyer David B. Ogden, that Jackson was an "utterly incompetent [man of] violence and imbecilities," who was in his "dotage." As Ogden put it, "fears were entertained that the Government would run down unless Van Buren could sustain it." These fears proved to be groundless, but Van Buren himself began to believe that the future of the country depended on him, and was soon complaining that he was "occupied from early in the morning until

[12] For Abraham, see Irelan, *Van Buren*, p. 550; Burke, *Emily Donelson*, II, 19, 42. For John, see MVB to John Van Buren, April 19, May 15, 1828, Sept. 3, 1830, VBP; MVB to James A. Hamilton, Sept. 11, 1829, Hamilton, *Reminiscences*, pp. 144, 216; John Van Buren to Azariah Flagg, July 7, 1840, Flagg Papers, CUL; Burke, *Emily Donelson*, II, 19. For Martin, see MVB to John and Martin Van Buren, May 24, 1831, VBP. For Smith, see Jackson to MVB, Nov. 15, 1830, Jackson, *Correspondence*, IV, 205.

late at night." By the middle of the summer, according to John Quincy Adams, Van Buren's "pale and haggard looks" showed the strain.[13]

One reason for his exhaustion was the pressure for a party patronage—especially from Virginia and New York. As soon as he arrived in Washington, Van Buren received a letter from Thomas Ritchie saying that Jackson's appointments had "thrown a cloud over [their] friends." Ritchie was "sorry to see the personal friends of the President appointed" and "so many of the Editorial Corps favored." He and Andrew Stevenson were also afraid that Virginians would not play much of a role in the new administration. Ritchie told Mordecai Noah that Van Buren's "admirable talents" would "be of little avail unless he [had] the courage to tell Gen. J. the truth." Van Buren was content to pass the letter along to Jackson and to send Ritchie a bland reply defending the good intentions of the President. But Ritchie had made his point. Within ten days Jackson was asking Van Buren to consult Ritchie about naming John Campbell of Virginia, as Treasurer of the United States. He got the job, and Van Buren was soon corresponding with Judge Richard E. Parker of Virginia, about another appointment in May.[14]

Appointments in New York caused Van Buren even more anxiety because the members of the Regency expected to reap what William L. Marcy later called "the spoils of the enemy." Mordecai Noah and Jonathan I. Coddington, both friends of the Regency, expected posts in the customs office in New York City. In mid-April, Van Buren received a nasty letter from Regency henchman Jesse Hoyt, warning that Van Buren's friends were "falling off" because they doubted that he had much influence in the new government; Hoyt asked to be appointed United States attorney for southern New York. Since Van Buren had doubts of his own, he replied irritably, saying that he would do what he could in spite of Hoyt's "harsh" letter. Van Buren was worried because he knew that Jackson intended to appoint a member of the opposition, Samuel Swartwout, to an even more important post, that of collector of the Port of New York. The President preferred the

---

[13] Ogden's statement is in William Coleman to James A. Hamilton, Mar. 18, 1829, Hamilton, *Reminiscences*, p. 127. Smith, *First Forty Years of Washington Society*, pp. 320, 329; MVB to Jackson, Mar. 31, 1829, VBP; MVB to Jesse Hoyt, April 13, 1829, Duff Green Papers, LC; Adams, *Memoirs*, VIII, 154.

[14] Ritchie to Noah, Mar. 14, 1829, Ritchie to MVB, Mar. 27, April 13, April 19, 1829, Stevenson to MVB, April 19, 1829, Jackson to MVB, April 9, 1829, MVB to Ritchie, April 9, 1829, Campbell to MVB, April 21, 1829, MVB to Parker, May 11, 1829, VBP; MVB to Jackson, Mar. 31, 1829, Jackson to MVB, Mar. 31, 1829, MVB to Ritchie, April 1, 1829, *Autobiography*, pp. 245-250.

rough old scoundrel Swartwout because he had supported Jackson in the Aaron Burr trial in 1807 and in the election of 1824. Jackson placed old loyalties above new political debts.[15]

In his first crisis as Secretary of State, Van Buren turned to his political friends as he had so often in New York. He asked Churchill C. Cambreleng to tell the President that Swartwout's appointment would be intolerable because Swartwout had a dubious reputation as a land speculator. At the same time Van Buren called on both New York senators—Charles Dudley and Nathan Sanford—for help, and consulted Secretary of the Treasury Ingham about the collectorship. When Van Buren heard on April 20 that Swartwout was still likely to be appointed, the Secretary directed Cambreleng and Mayor Walter Bowne of New York City to organize a letter-writing campaign. To keep the Regency working Van Buren insisted that the President had not irrevocably made up his mind. Then Van Buren himself wrote to Jackson saying that Swartwout was not the man for the job because he was backed by enemies of the Regency. As a last resort, Van Buren suggested that since the incumbent collector—Jonathan Thompson—was a man of "Republican character," he need not be replaced. Van Buren also recommended Coddington for surveyor of customs, but ignored Noah and Hoyt. To cover himself in case all this failed, Van Buren told Cambreleng that their friends back home would have to bear some of the blame because they had not fought hard enough against Swartwout.[16]

Van Buren's efforts did fail. Not only was Jackson determined to appoint Swartwout—that "warm hearted, zealous, and generous man, strictly honest and correct"—but the President also rebuffed Van Buren by appointing Noah surveyor instead of Coddington. The President tried to protect Van Buren from blame by writing a letter to be sent on to New York, saying that the President had appointed Swartwout against Van Buren's advice. In addition Jackson appointed James A. Hamilton United States attorney for southern New York. Showing that he knew something about political horse-trading, Jackson offered to let Van Buren name his friend Alfred Balch of Tennessee, or someone

[15] *Register of Debates*, 22nd Congress, 1st session (Jan. 24, 1832), 1325; Parton, *Jackson*, I, 318, 335-336, III, 30, 75, 211-212; Coddington to Hoyt, Feb. 13, Feb. 20, Mar. 29, 1829, MVB to Hoyt, April 13, 1829, Duff Green Papers, LC; Hoyt to Samuel D. Ingham, Mar. 8, 1829, The Ferdinand Julius Dreer Collection, HSP; Hoyt to MVB, April 11, 1829, VBP.

[16] Cambreleng to Jackson, April 15, 1829, MVB to Cambreleng and Walter Bowne, April 20, 1829, VBP; Jackson to MVB, April 20, 1829, *Autobiography*, p. 263; MVB to Jackson, April 23, 1829, Jackson, *Correspondence*, IV, 25-27.

else attorney for Nashville. As Jackson put it, "Fair reciprocity is always right, and as I have given you in your State, a collector, I shall leave you, in mine, to give us an Attorney."

But Jackson's attempts at compromise failed. Van Buren had no interest in appointing an attorney for Nashville, and the appointment of former Federalist Hamilton hurt more than it helped in certain quarters in New York even though Hamilton was Van Buren's friend. The appointment caused further embarrassment because news of it arrived while Hamilton was with Van Buren, who was forced to admit that he could not support the major because the Regency wanted someone else.[17]

Van Buren's patronage setbacks hit him at a moment, he later recalled, when his "health was feeble and [his] spirits depressed." After "resist[ing]" for months the gloomy predictions of his friends about the administration, he was forced by the appointments to reconsider his position in Washington. "Deeply disturbed [that others had] acquired an influence over the President's mind," Van Buren "walked the streets . . . until a late hour of the night deliberating whether" he ought to resign. The next morning, however, he rationalized that Jackson had erred not because of any "defect in his character," but because he lacked "experience." Van Buren decided to stay on and see to it that Jackson did not make the same errors again.[18]

Van Buren's inability to make appointments for his own state revealed that he did not at first have as much power in the administration as he and others had thought he would. In the Swartwout affair he had not dealt directly with Jackson, but had been forced to use Cambreleng and write letters. Instead of becoming "king de facto" or the President's "right hand man" at once, as many had been predicting, Van Buren had to compete for power with two warring factions: the Calhounites, consisting of the Vice President and John Branch, Samuel D. Ingham and John M. Berrien in the cabinet; and the western group of Andrew J. Donelson and William B. Lewis, who worked and lived in the White House, John H. Eaton in the War Department, and Amos Kendall in the Treasury. Since Calhoun was not in Washington between March and December 1829, the Calhoun clique was in no position to exercise much influence; it was the Westerners and Jackson himself who had the upper hand during the first year of the admin-

[17] MVB to Jackson, April 24, 1829, Jackson to MVB, April 24, 1829, VBP; *Autobiography*, pp. 264-265; James A. Hamilton to friend, April 25, 1829, Hamilton, *Reminiscences*, p. 123.
[18] *Autobiography*, pp. 266-267.

istration. Van Buren could only bide his time and build his strength by developing his relationship with Jackson.[19]

Van Buren's role in the Swartwout episode and in other patronage decisions further suggests that he was not quite the ruthless spoilsman that the opposition and historians have made him out to be. His biographers have used such expressions as "chief patronage dispenser" to describe his role, and two of the most striking sections in James Parton's life of Jackson focus on Van Buren the spoilsman. But these assessments exaggerate. Van Buren used patronage to build the Regency and to strengthen the Democratic party, but he instituted no purge of existing officeholders in Washington. Jackson and Lewis had already begun to dispense patronage before Van Buren joined the cabinet. When he did arrive, he was dismayed by the crowds of office seekers awaiting him and immediately suggested a plan for getting them out of the city. Later on Van Buren resisted efforts to remove Superintendent Thomas P. Jones of the Patent Office, even though he was a National Republican.

But back in New York as the year went on Van Buren was able to strengthen the Regency through wholesale removals of local postmasters. By March 22, 1830, there had been 131 removals in New York out of a total of 491 removals in the entire postal department. It is apparent that Van Buren had much more influence in the administration than either Thomas Ritchie or John C. Calhoun because there were only eight removals in Virginia and none in South Carolina. The most successful spoilsman, however, was Isaac Hill of New Hampshire, who arranged for the removal of fifty-five postmasters in a state that was one-seventh the size of New York. Van Buren demonstrated that he was not greedy; he left Samuel L. Gouverneur as postmaster in New York City even though Gouverneur had been a long-time confidant of John C. Calhoun.[20]

---

[19] Francis Brooke to Henry Clay, Feb. 23, 1829, Clay, *Private Correspondence*, p. 223; Samuel F. Vinton to Duncan McArthur, Dec. 24, 1829, Duncan McArthur Papers, LC; "Letters of John Pintard," III, 204-205; Smith, *First Forty Years of Washington Society*, p. 310; Hamilton, *Reminiscences*, pp. 124, 126; Rudolph Bunner to Gulian Verplanck, July 25, 1829, Verplanck Papers, NYHS; Duff Green to————, June 16, 1829, Duff Green Papers, LC; Latner, *Presidency of Jackson*, pp. 4-6, 54.

[20] Calhoun, of course, may not have wanted many removals because as Vice President in the previous administration he had already had a chance to influence the choice of postmasters. Lynch, *Epoch and a Man*, p. 326; Alexander, *American Talleyrand*, p. 251; Shepard, *Van Buren*, pp. 173, 178; Parton, *Jackson*, III, 122-124, 227-255; Hamilton, *Reminiscences*, p. 129; *Autobiography*, pp. 231-232; Bassett, *Jackson*, p. 440; Moody, "Influence of Van Buren on Jackson," p. 230; MVB to Andrew J. Donelson, May 14, 1829, Andrew J. Donelson Papers, LC; John C. Calhoun to Gouverneur, Mar.

In making appointments in the State Department Van Buren followed the same pattern as in domestic appointments: he ran into trouble early but soon began to exert great influence. On arriving in Washington he found that the President had already plunged ahead and named ministers to England and France. Not only had Jackson failed to consult Van Buren but the President had also appointed two men who had little in common with the new Secretary, men whom he would have difficulty controlling. Senator Littleton Tazewell of Virginia, who had been appointed minister to England, was older than and almost as famous as Van Buren. As former chairman of the Senate Committee on Foreign Relations Tazewell had more experience in diplomacy than his new chief. In addition he was closer politically to Calhoun than to Van Buren. Edward Livingston, who had been named minister to France, had become a close friend of Jackson after leaving New York to settle in New Orleans. Van Buren, who had just seen Livingston in Philadelphia, believed that the senator was part of the Tennessee-western clique that had the President's ear, and feared that it would be hard to control diplomacy with France under the circumstances.

Fortunately for Van Buren the two men hesitated long enough for the Secretary to take steps to ease them out. Instead of confronting Jackson directly, Van Buren suggested tactfully that at fifty-four and sixty-four Tazewell and Livingston were too old for such demanding posts. Less stubborn on foreign appointments than domestic, Jackson promptly agreed. To get the two old-timers out of the way, Van Buren pressed them to make up their minds at once and agree to sail by August. Tazewell and Livingston refused to leave on such short notice, giving Van Buren what he wanted—the chance to appoint some of his own friends, younger men, to office.

Van Buren's scheme for replacing Tazewell was a little too elaborate. To make room for his friend Louis McLane in the cabinet, Van Buren convinced Jackson to send a letter to the new Attorney General Berrien, who had not yet assumed office, appointing him minister to England instead. Assuming that Berrien would prefer London to Washington, Van Buren dispatched James A. Hamilton to Delaware to offer McLane the attorney generalship without waiting for Berrien to answer. To make the offer as tempting as possible Hamilton promised McLane that if he agreed to be Attorney General, he would be appointed to

12, 1829, Gouverneur Papers, NYPL; Carl Russell Fish, *The Civil Service and the Patronage* (New York, 1904), p. 118; Leonard D. White, *The Jacksonians: a Study in Administrative History 1829-1861* (New York, 1954), p. 321; *Niles' Register*, 38 (April 3, 1830), 105; Paul E. Johnson, paper on local activists in New York in 1828.

the Supreme Court as soon as an opening occurred. McLane made Hamilton wait until he returned to Washington before sending a letter accepting the position. Then Berrien turned down the post in London and Van Buren had to offer it to McLane. Although McLane accepted on April 15, he did so in such an overbearing manner that Van Buren must have smarted, agreeing to go to London only to keep Van Buren and Jackson from being embarrassed by "too many rejected offers," and in return he expected to be rewarded later with an appointment to the Supreme Court. Van Buren had got the friend that he wanted in the diplomatic service, but McLane was hardly as grateful as Van Buren would have liked.

The task of replacing Livingston went more smoothly. After Livingston had expressed doubt that he could be ready to leave by August, Van Buren immediately appointed William C. Rives, before Livingston could change his mind. When Rives accepted in early May, Van Buren had not only secured a place for a loyal associate in the foreign service but he had found a place in the government for a Virginian other than Tazewell. Furthermore, the appointments of Rives and McLane strengthened Van Buren's standing in Washington at a time when he was frustrated by his inability to control patronage in his home state, and demonstrated his ability to attract talented subordinates. In addition, Van Buren was able to name other competent men, including Cornelius Van Ness to Spain, William Pitt Preble to the Netherlands, John Randolph to Russia, and Thomas Patrick Moore to Colombia. There were political benefits as well, for Van Ness was a deserving New Yorker, and Preble's appointment pleased mercantile interests in Maine. Van Buren also tried to reward loyal Jacksonians in New Hampshire, but his friend Levi Woodbury turned down the President's offer to become minister to Spain.[21]

Van Buren's next task was to establish a sound Jacksonian foreign policy. He was particularly anxious to reassure many of the foreign diplomats in Washington, who mistrusted Jackson's inexperience and belligerent nationalism. Accustomed to dealing with the experienced John Quincy Adams and Henry Clay, the diplomats doubted whether

---

[21] *Autobiography*, pp. 251-254, 256-260; Hamilton, *Reminiscences*, pp. 130-131; McLane to MVB, April 14, April 15, 1829, MVB to Livingston, April 6, April 19, 1829, Jackson to MVB, April 20, 1829, Livingston to Jackson, May 3, 1829, Livingston to MVB, May 3, 1829, MVB to Rives, May 5, 1829, VBP; Munroe, *Louis McLane*, pp. 253-256; John S. Bassett, "Martin Van Buren," Samuel F. Bemis, ed., *The American Secretaries of State and Their Diplomacy*, IV (New York, 1928), 161-168; MVB to Christopher Hughes, May 29, 1829, Samuel Smith Papers, LC; *Autobiography*, pp. 16-17.

the new party could summon much expertise in foreign affairs. The new President had tried to reduce their fears by saying in his inaugural that the United States would use "the forbearance becoming a powerful nation rather than the sensibility belonging to a gallant people," but the foreign corps was still uneasy. Fortunately the new Secretary had several good friends among the diplomats including his "brother Dutchman," Chevalier Huygens, and Van Buren's British crony, Sir Charles R. Vaughan. Van Buren met with the two men in order to "remove the unjust impressions," and to describe a reception that he was planning for Jackson and the diplomatic corps. Huygens suggested that the President would soothe the diplomats more effectively by making a short statement repeating the peaceful sentiments of his inaugural than by giving an elaborate address. Van Buren passed the advice on to Jackson, helped him compose a short, informal speech that was even more peaceful-sounding than his inaugural, and arranged a reception that went a long way toward dispelling suspicions on both sides. The President followed up his success with a formal dinner at which, according to Van Buren, "the simple yet kindly, old-school manners of the host" impressed the diplomats. Vaughan reported to his superiors that Adams could not have reassured the foreign ministers as well as Jackson did.[22]

Vaughan's remark was significant because Van Buren was anxious to improve relations with Great Britain in order to open ports in the British West Indies to American ships. As an Anglophile and a good friend of Vaughan, Van Buren was better equipped to win over the British than either Andrew Jackson, who was a well-known nationalist and Anglophobe, or John Quincy Adams, who as Secretary of State and President had presided over twelve years of controversy with the British. After the American Revolution the British refused to admit American shipping to the British West Indies. When negotiations failed, James Monroe retaliated in 1818 by closing American ports to British ships from the West Indies. In 1825, the British agreed to open the West Indies if the United States would reciprocate, but the rise of protectionist sentiment prevented Congress from taking any action. Since the Jacksonians had criticized Adams for failing to win trade with the West Indies, Jackson and Van Buren felt obliged to take action.

Jackson left the negotiations up to Van Buren, who delegated much

---

[22] *Autobiography*, pp. 260-262; Bassett, "Martin Van Buren," p. 169; Vaughan to Lord Aberdeen, April 12, 1829, British Foreign Office, Correspondence, 5: United States, 248 (1829), 273-276.

of the responsibility to McLane; he in turn sought advice from James A. Hamilton and Churchill C. Cambreleng. The latter, who had had years of experience in foreign affairs, recommended lowering tariffs and making other concessions in order to stimulate trade with Great Britain. Instead of waiting for instructions from the Secretary of State, McLane composed a long letter on the West Indies trade and sent it to Van Buren. Despite Cambreleng's advice, McLane said nothing about lowering tariffs. At the heart of his letter was a proposal that outraged the political opposition later when it became known, and caused Van Buren a great deal of trouble. McLane suggested that he be allowed to tell the British that the Jackson administration wished to "disconnect" itself from the "errors" of the Adams administration, errors that had been repudiated by the people in the election of 1828. McLane also recommended that instead of seeking a treaty the United States should simply offer to pass an act opening American ports if the British would do the same (as they had in 1825). Van Buren received McLane's letter in mid-June, consulted Jackson, waited a bit, and then on July 20 wrote instructions that read much like McLane's letter. He instructed McLane to say that in order to redress errors of the past, the President would accept reasonable terms and would like to be able to report progress in his annual message in December.[23]

Van Buren made plans to deliver the instructions himself to McLane in Delaware (the new minister was preparing to sail in early August from Cape May). When Cambreleng, "the anti-tariff champion," arranged to join McLane, Hamilton, and Van Buren in Wilmington, rumors spread that the administration had decided to lower tariffs in order to open the Indies. Unwilling to play into the hands of the opposition and determined to make McLane's mission a success, Van Buren prevailed on Cambreleng to stay in New York. Cambreleng would still have a chance to see McLane because the point of embarkation had been shifted to New York, but Van Buren would not be present at that meeting. Van Buren then made up a party that included himself, his sons Abraham and John, Mary Eastin, and Emily Donelson even though she was eight months pregnant, to visit the McLanes at

[23] Frank L. Benns, *The American Struggle for the British West India Carrying Trade, 1815-1830* (Bloomington, 1923); George Dangerfield, *The Era of Good Feelings* (New York, 1952), pp. 254-263; *Autobiography*, pp. 520-531; Bassett, *Jackson*, pp. 656-659; Bassett, "Martin Van Buren," pp. 183-184; Munroe, *Louis McLane*, pp. 262-263; McLane to MVB, July 11, 1829, Hamilton to Van Buren, June 6, 1829, Notes and Memoranda in reference to the British West India Trade, July 20, 1829, VBP; MVB to McLane, July 20, 1829, State Department, Diplomatic Instructions, Great Britain, XIV, National Archives; *Niles' Register*, 39 (1831), 363-368.

Wilmington and Charles Carroll, the sole surviving signer of the Declaration of Independence, at Carrolton, Maryland. Van Buren spent about a week in Delaware, his only vacation during his first year in Washington. He returned to the Capital and the rest of the party went on to New York City, where they saw McLane off for England on August 11. The care with which Van Buren arranged for McLane's instructions and departure showed the high priority that he gave to the West Indies trade.[24]

In October, a month after he arrived in London, McLane brought the subject of the West Indies to the attention of British Foreign Secretary Lord Aberdeen, after which discussions were suspended by the British for the duration of the hunting season. With no news from England Jackson was unable to report any progress in his December message, but what he said about the British made McLane's job easier. Unlike the year before when Adams had chastised them, Jackson said that he looked forward "to years of peaceful, honorable, and elevated competition" with Great Britain, based on "sentiments of mutual respect." The London *Times* called it the best annual message since the days of George Washington. Jackson, who on this occasion was unusually patient, authorized Van Buren to tell McLane to take his time. The negotiations dragged on throughout the winter.

As spring warmed the Capital, Jackson's patience waned. "In case of a failure," he wrote Van Buren on April 10, "we ought to be prepared to act . . . with that promptness and energy due to our national character." If McLane's terms were rejected, said Jackson, Van Buren should ask Congress to cut off trade with Canada and back the decision with a "sufficient number of cutters commanded by our naval officers." Van Buren did not have to act because a few days later a despatch arrived from McLane asking Van Buren to have Congress pass legislation authorizing the President to open American ports to the British as soon as they reciprocated in the West Indies. McLane also sent a message directly to Cambreleng, who was chairman of the House Committee on Commerce, recommending the same program. Andrew Jackson waited until May 26 before officially asking Congress to pass the legislation. The speed with which Congress complied suggests that Cambreleng and Van Buren had already prepared the way. The bill passed on May 29, 1830, and after McLane received assur-

[24] *Niles' Register*, 36 (1829), 330-331, 345, 387-388, 418-419; MVB to Hamilton, July 18, 1829, Hamilton, *Reminiscences*, p. 143; MVB to Cambreleng, July 19, 1829; Cambreleng to McLane, July 25, 1829, VBP; MVB to Andrew J. Donelson, July 27, 1829, Andrew J. Donelson Papers, LC; *Richmond Enquirer*, July 31, 1829; Burke, *Emily Donelson*, I, 203-204; Munroe, *Louis McLane*, pp. 263-269.

ances from Lord Aberdeen, Jackson issued a proclamation opening American ports to British ships from the West Indies on October 5. The British opened the ports in the Indies a month later.

By their efforts McLane and Van Buren had succeeded in reversing half a century of British and American policy. It was such a stunning diplomatic triumph that the administration rushed through the last stages of the negotiations in order to use the results in the fall congressional election. McLane carried despatches himself to Liverpool and handed them over to a ship's captain bound for the United States; Jackson hurried back from Tennessee in order to get the good news as soon as it arrived; and Van Buren spread the word where it would have the best effect. The news arrived in time to help the party in Maine, where shipping interests were pleased that they could now compete on even terms with the Canadians for the West Indies trade.[25]

Van Buren deserved credit for the West Indies victory. By giving McLane a free hand, by holding back the impetuous Jackson, and by first restraining and then using Cambreleng, Van Buren had succeeded where the trained diplomacy of Adams had failed. Moreover, Van Buren had succeeded in putting his own imprint on foreign policy and the State Department. Although Jackson controlled foreign affairs, the success of McLane's mission strengthened Van Buren's role in setting policy and demonstrated that Van Buren could use his political skills to good effect in diplomacy. It was not by chance that two of Van Buren's political allies, McLane and Cambreleng, played leading roles in the affair.

Van Buren's other diplomat, William C. Rives, faced a task more difficult than McLane's. Van Buren sent Rives off with McLane on the same ship to collect a sum of money from the French government. This was intended to settle the claims of American citizens against France dating from the days of Napoleon. Previous negotiations had accomplished nothing, and continued delays in the fall of 1829 aroused the fighting spirit in Jackson, who was far less conciliatory toward France than he was toward Great Britain in his first annual message. "The claims of our citizens," warned Jackson, could lead to "possible collisions between the two Governments." After soothing French feelings, Rives asked Van Buren for permission to offer a reduction in the

---

[25] James D. Richardson, *A Compilation of the Messages and Papers of the Presidents, 1789-1897*, 10 vols. (Washington, D.C., 1897-1899), II, 408-409, 443, 480-481; McLane to MVB, Mar. 22, 1830, State Department, Diplomatic Despatches, Great Britain, XXXVII, National Archives; McLane to Cambreleng, Mar. 30, 1829, VBP; Jackson to MVB, April 10, 1830, Jackson, *Correspondence*, IV, 133; Munroe, *Louis McLane*, pp. 271-279.

duty on imported French wines. Preoccupied with domestic problems and the West Indies, Jackson was more willing to make concessions in April than in December, and agreed to accept a modest sum. Rives renewed his efforts in the fall and asked Van Buren to have Jackson make a friendly statement about the new French government in his December message. Heartened by the West Indies victory, Jackson found it easy to accommodate. After boasting about the agreement with Great Britain, the President praised the "enlarged views and pure integrity" of the new French monarch, Louis Philippe. Rives pressed on, keeping Van Buren informed in frequent letters, and finally achieved a settlement which was signed July 4, 1831. The French agreed to pay 25,000,000 francs and to forget their own claims in return for reduced tariffs on wine. Even though the affair dragged on for another five years, Van Buren and his minister had made a good start.[26]

Van Buren and his subordinates were less influential in setting foreign policy in the Southwest than they had been in Europe. As a nationalist, an old filibustering Indian fighter, and a western empire builder, Jackson was deeply interested in acquiring Texas and rounding out the western frontier. "The god of the universe," he told Van Buren, "had intended this great valley to belong to one nation." On taking office Jackson suspended action on a commercial treaty which John Quincy Adams had arranged with Mexico and which declared the Sabine River the boundary between Mexico and the United States. Instead, Jackson authorized Van Buren to spend up to $5,000,000 to purchase Texas from the Mexican government. It is some indication of Jackson's dominant role in the Texan negotiations that the President insisted on preparing personally the instructions to Minister Joel Poinsett in Mexico. With the arrogance of an old frontiersman, Jackson told the Mexicans that they would benefit from selling Texas because they would thereby reduce the chances of war with the United States and save themselves the bother of governing the region. He claimed also that the United States needed Texas in order to protect New Orleans and to provide a home for Indians being moved westward. The instructions reflected the western influence on the administration in 1829.

Although Van Buren did not share Jackson's devotion to nationalism and western expansion, he did recognize the political advantages that

[26] *Autobiography*, p. 272; Bassett, *Jackson*, pp. 663-673; Rives to MVB, Oct. 17, 1829, Sept. 18, Sept. 29, Dec. 30, 1830, Feb. 14, May 30, Sept. 29, Oct. 22, Oct. 25, 1831, Rives to Edward Livingston, Oct. 8, 1831, VBP; Jackson to MVB, April 10, 1830, Sept. 5, 1831, MVB to Jackson, Oct. 11, 1831, Jackson, *Correspondence*, IV, 133, 347, 355; Richardson, *Messages and Papers*, II, 502.

would result from purchasing Texas. At the start of Jackson's administration southern Democrats such as Thomas Ritchie were almost as interested in Texas as they were in tariff reduction. If Texas could be acquired, both the party and the Secretary of State would gain support in the South. Jackson would have none of this political argument. When President David G. Burnet of Texas, wrote Jackson a letter outlining the political benefits of annexation, he rejected Burnet's argument, and insisted on national reasons for expansion. Van Buren dutifully followed Jackson's instructions but without much vigor. Since the Mexican government was not inclined to sell Texas and since the Texan independence movement had barely gotten underway, little was accomplished.[27]

Van Buren's performance as Secretary of State benefited both the nation and Van Buren himself. He opened the Indies, made a start toward settling the French claims, and directed Poinsett toward the acquisition of Texas. He restrained the President and convinced Europeans that the Democrats could carry on an effective foreign policy. These accomplishments helped Van Buren rise to the top of the administration and gave him valuable experience in working with Jackson. Jackson let Van Buren lead in the European negotiations; Van Buren did the President's bidding over Texas. As might be expected, Van Buren used political tactics and let political considerations govern his diplomacy so that by the time Van Buren left the State Department, Jackson had learned to consider the political implications of foreign affairs. In September 1831, the President wrote an enthusiastic letter to Van Buren in England describing the political reactions in New York to the settlement of the French claims. Jacksonian foreign policy was less spectacular but also less destructive than Jacksonian policies on the Bank and the tariff, and one reason was that Van Buren played a larger role in foreign than he did in domestic affairs.[28]

But Van Buren's standing in the administration depended as much on his reaction to the Peggy Eaton affair as on his handling of foreign policy. Pert, pretty Peggy O'Neale grew up fast waiting on tables at her father's boardinghouse midway between the White House and Georgetown. After several scandalous affairs, she married navy purser

---

[27] Jackson to MVB, Aug. 12, Aug. 14, Aug. c. 15, 1829, Jackson, Notes on instructions to be given Poinsett, Aug. 13, 1829, MVB to Poinsett, Instructions for negotiations for the purchase of a part of Texas, Aug. 25, 1829, Ritchie to MVB, Sept. 1829, VBP; *Richmond Enquirer*, Sept. 9, Sept. 11, 1829; Wayland, *Stevenson*, p. 220; Bassett, *Jackson*, pp. 673-675; E. C. Barker, "President Jackson and the Texas Revolution," *American Historical Review*, 12 (1906-1907), 789-791.

[28] Jackson to MVB, Sept. 5, 1831, Jackson, *Correspondence*, IV, 347.

John Timberlake when she was only sixteen, but while Timberlake was at sea, she maintained her reputation as a loose woman. During his ten years as senator, John H. Eaton boarded at O'Neale's and carried on a lively and well-known affair with Peggy. Andrew Jackson, who had also boarded there when he was senator, was apparently the only man in the city who considered Peggy a woman of virtue, and informed his wife Rachel that Peggy "play[ed] the piano delightfully, and every Sunday evening entertain[ed] her pious mother with sacred music." Timberlake having conveniently died abroad, Eaton married Peggy on New Year's Day 1829 and tongues wagged faster than ever. Churchill C. Cambreleng summed it up when he wrote Van Buren: "Poor Eaton is to be married tonight to Mrs. T——! There is a vulgar saying of some vulgar man, I believe Swift, on such unions—about using a certain household . . . , [Cambreleng's ellipsis] and then putting it on one's head." But Jackson was not amused, for he had urged Eaton to marry the widow Timberlake and had every expectation that Washington society would welcome the wife of his new Secretary of War.[29]

Soon after his inauguration Jackson found that contrary to his expectations, the wives of many members of his administration refused to pay courtesy calls on Peggy Eaton. Emily Donelson, the wives of Calhoun, Ingham and Berrien, and the daughters of widower John Branch all snubbed Mrs. Eaton. Jackson overreacted. Already convinced that enemies were plotting to destroy him, he believed that opponents inside and outside the party were using the affair as a means of attacking his administration. At first he blamed Henry Clay, but then settled on Calhoun because Ingham, Berrien, and Branch were all Calhounites. Always loyal to his friends, Jackson felt obliged to defend John H. Eaton's wife and William O'Neale's daughter to the very end. Because the attacks on Peggy reminded the grieving Jackson of the slanders against his own beloved Rachel during the campaign, Jackson spent the next twelve months defending Peggy and trying to force his official family to accept her. He became so preoccupied with his mission that the "Eaton malaria," as Van Buren dubbed it, dominated the political scene.[30]

[29] Margaret L. Eaton, *The Autobiography of Peggy Eaton* (New York, 1932); Marquis James, *Andrew Jackson: Portrait of a President* (Indianapolis, 1937), pp. 68-71, 204-213, 226-232; Parton, *Jackson*, III, 184-205, 287-309; Jackson, *Correspondence*, IV, passim; *Autobiography*, pp. 339-355; Charles M. Wiltse, *John C. Calhoun, Nullifier, 1829-1839* (Indianapolis, 1949), pp. 26-38; *Niles' Register*, 41 (1831), 49-62.

[30] For an old and new assessment of the Peggy Eaton affair, see Parton, *Jackson*, III, 184-205; and Curtis, *Andrew Jackson*, pp. 94-101.

The Eaton affair gave Van Buren an opportunity to gain ground on his rivals because Calhoun and his wife had taken a stand against Peggy, and the Tennessee clique was divided. Even though Jackson and Eaton both implored Emily Donelson to change her mind, she stubbornly refused, and eventually returned to Tennessee. In this situation, Van Buren won immediate credit with Jackson by calling on Peggy Eaton as soon as he arrived in Washington. And when Van Buren's friends the Riveses and the McLanes also called on the Eatons, Van Buren piled up more credit. Even young Rebecca McLane ignored the hostility of Emily Donelson and Mary Eastin to pay a call on Mrs. Eaton. With no wife or daughters to stir up a fuss, Van Buren was under no pressure to snub the notorious Peggy and since the President, whom Van Buren wished to please, was defending her, it was not surprising that Van Buren should follow suit.[31]

Van Buren kept out of the way as much as possible during the summer while Jackson was investigating the charges against the Eatons. The President put Lewis to work collecting affidavits praising Peggy's character and sent Reverend E. S. Ely to New York to disprove stories about Peggy's behavior there with Eaton while Timberlake was at sea. Finally, in September, Jackson held a curious cabinet meeting at which Lewis and Ely presented their evidence and Jackson tried to bully his administration into accepting the Eatons. But no one changed his mind. On the way home that evening Samuel D. Ingham was still hostile to the Eatons and Van Buren was still defending them.[32]

As the time drew near for the traditional dinner parties at the opening of Congress in December 1829, Van Buren began to assert himself in the Eaton affair. He tried so hard to prevail over Mary Eastin that he brought her to tears, but she did not change her mind. He escorted

[31] Parton, *Jackson*, III, 287-288; John Eaton to Emily Donelson, April 8, April 9, 1829, Andrew J. Donelson to John Eaton, April 10, 1829, Richard K. Call to Jackson, April 28, 1829, Jackson to John C. McLemore, May 3, 1829, Jackson, *Correspondence*, IV, 28-31; Emily Donelson to John Eaton, April 10, 1829, quoted in James, *Andrew Jackson President*, p. 208; *Autobiography*, pp. 339-343; Munroe, *Louis McLane*, pp. 259-261. Charles M. Wiltse has claimed without much evidence that Van Buren acted as he did to undermine Calhoun. Wiltse bases his position on statements by John Branch and Virgil Maxcy, both opponents of Van Buren. Wiltse, *John C. Calhoun, Nullifier*, pp. 32-33.

[32] Jackson to Ely, Sept. 3, 1829, Memorandum by Donelson, Sept. 3, 1829, Jackson to Lewis, Sept. 10, 1829, Jackson, *Correspondence*, IV, 67-73; Jackson, Narrative concerning Peggy Eaton, c. Sept. 3, 1829, Jackson to Reverend J. N. Campbell, Sept. 10, 1829, Lewis, Account of the September 10 Cabinet Meeting, Parton, *Jackson*, III, 197-205; MVB to James A. Hamilton, Sept. 24, 1829, Hamilton, *Reminiscences*, p. 146; Samuel D. Ingham to———, Jan. 18, 1832, Personal Papers, Miscellaneous, LC.

Emily Donelson to the President's official party, but Emily and her friends distressed Jackson by continuing to snub Peggy. Van Buren then tried to help by inviting the Eatons to two elaborate dinner parties of his own. Even though Van Buren escorted Thomas Jefferson's widowed daughter Martha Randolph to the first dinner, the effort was in vain because no cabinet wife except Peggy attended. Peggy herself ruined the second dinner by bumping into the wife of an army officer and starting a quarrel. In desperation, Van Buren turned to his bachelor friends, the diplomats Sir Charles R. Vaughan and Baron Krudener, who cheerfully agreed to give parties. Vaughan's went reasonably well, but at Krudener's Chevalier Huygens' wife left in a huff when she found herself seated next to Peggy. Van Buren had failed.[33]

By this time Van Buren had concluded that little more could be done, and so when Jackson tried to force a showdown in January 1830, he discovered that his Secretary of State would not cooperate. Van Buren took one look at the ultimatum that Jackson had prepared for Ingham, Branch and Berrien, and insisted on softening the language. Jackson finally did confront the three cabinet members, but allowed them to remain in the administration even though they refused to order their women to accept Peggy socially. The Eaton affair began to fade, but not before Van Buren had proved his loyalty and shown his ability to restrain the impulsive President.[34]

The "Eaton malaria" greatly strengthened Van Buren's position in the administration by weakening both the Tennesseans and John C. Calhoun. The affair put Eaton on the defensive, kept Lewis busy writing reports, and forced Donelson and his wife into temporary retirement. Of the Westerners only Kendall remained unscathed. Calhoun was badly hurt because Jackson continued to believe that the South Carolinian was responsible for the whole sorry business. Before long, as Adams noted, the administration was split into two factions with Calhoun at the head of the "moral party" and Van Buren leading the "frail sisterhood." In the fall and winter of 1829-1830, observers began to sense that Van Buren was coming up and Calhoun "going down." Congressman Robert Letcher of Kentucky, reported that Van Buren had become so popular with Jackson that Calhoun would have to support the Secretary in 1832. Jackson had been ill all summer with dropsy, which caused his legs to swell, and deciding once again that

[33] *Autobiography*, pp. 343-352; Burke, *Emily Donelson*, I, 209; Parton, *Jackson*, III, 291; Smith, *First Forty Years of Washington Society*, pp. 309-311.

[34] *Autobiography*, pp. 353-356; Jackson to MVB, Jan. 24, 1830, Jackson, Memorandum, c. Jan. 29, 1830, Jackson, *Correspondence*, IV, 122-124; Adams, *Memoirs*, VIII, 184; Ingham to——, Jan. 18, 1832, Personal Papers, Miscellaneous, LC.

he was about to die, began looking for a replacement. He confided in December that Van Buren was his choice and sent a letter to John Overton attacking Calhoun and praising Van Buren. The President gave a copy to Lewis to be used in an emergency. Van Buren, said Jackson, had won his "confidence."[35]

But the cautious Van Buren was not ready to attack Calhoun or to seek the presidency. When the *New York Courier and Enquirer* put his name forward as the next President, he made no response. Again in March he refused to speculate. Then in April he announced that he would have nothing to do with "intrigues" about succeeding Jackson because the people wanted to reelect "the old chief." At Van Buren's bidding, the *Albany Argus* called on Jackson to run again. Duff Green was probably correct when he suggested cynically that Van Buren and the party needed Jackson's popularity. By the spring of 1830, Van Buren had moved ahead of Calhoun, but had not defeated him. Van Buren was content to remain in Old Hickory's shadow.[36]

With Congress in session during the first half of 1830, political and economic issues overshadowed—and influenced—the battle between Van Buren and Calhoun. These issues gave Van Buren another opportunity to assert leadership in the administration by representing the old Jeffersonian position. From the moment Jackson took office, Jeffersonian Republicans—mostly from the South—had kept after the administration to remain faithful to republican orthodoxy. Reminding Jackson that he had been brought up in the "School of '76 and '98," the *Richmond Enquirer* praised him for emphasizing state rights and economy in his inaugural, but attacked him for supporting internal improvements. When the Virginia constitutional convention met in October 1829, every self-respecting Republican politician, including Van Buren, was there to hear Southerners discuss the old principles.[37]

Van Buren was deluged with letters from Southerners with Old Republican views. Thomas Cooper and James Hamilton, Jr., insisted on lower tariffs; William Harris Crawford opposed federal roads;

[35] Jackson to Richard K. Call, July 5, 1829, Jackson to John Overton, Dec. 31, 1829, Jackson, *Correspondence*, IV, 51-52, 109; Adams, *Memoirs*, VIII, 185; Caleb Atwater, *Remarks Made on a Tour to Prairie du Chien; Thence to Washington City in 1829* (Columbus, 1831); Letcher to Clay, Dec. 21, Dec. 26, 1829, Henry Clay Papers, LC; Hamilton, *Reminiscences*, p. 151; Jackson to John Overton, Dec. 31, 1829, with note by William B. Lewis, Jackson, *Correspondence*, IV, 108-110.

[36] James Webb to MVB, Dec. 19, 1829, MVB to William Jack, Mar. 8, 1830, MVB to James Gordon Bennett, May 2, 1830, VBP; MVB to Rives, April 6, 1830, Rives Papers, LC; *Argus*, April 3, 1830; Duff Green to Ninian Edwards, April 27, 1830, Washburne, *Edwards Papers*, p. 488.

[37] *Richmond Enquirer*, Mar. 6, Aug. 28, Oct. 6, 1829, Mar. 9, 1830.

James Madison reached into the past to advise Van Buren on internal improvements; Andrew Stevenson assured Van Buren that Virginians were still loyal to the beliefs of the Old Republicans. Most striking of all was a letter from the famous Old Republican Nathaniel Macon, now seventy-one, who had recently retired from the Senate. Macon was pleased with the administration, but warned Van Buren that Jackson had not gone far enough, that a "half revolution never produce[d] lasting benefits." Paying off the public debt, said Macon, would "place the administration on very high ground"; reducing the tariff so that it bore "equal[ly] in every state, would immortalize it." Like many Southerners Macon complained that the money raised from the tariff was spent in "the middle the Eastern & western states," not in the South.[38]

Given this sort of pressure Van Buren sought domestic policies that would satisfy the nationalism of Andrew Jackson and the Old Republicanism of the South. The first test came early in 1830 in the Webster-Hayne debate, which began when Senator Robert Y. Hayne of South Carolina, accused Easterners of wanting to restrict the sale of western land. Daniel Webster denied the charge, and Hayne replied with a speech defending state rights and the right of individual states to nullify acts of Congress. In his famous second reply to Hayne, Webster dismissed the doctrine of state rights and maintained that only the federal government exercised sovereign power over the people. During the debate Andrew Jackson, who believed in strict construction of the Constitution but not in the theory of nullification, sided with Webster. When one of the President's friends reported that Webster was "demolishing" Hayne, Jackson is supposed to have replied, "I expected it."

The debate posed more of a problem for Van Buren. Since he wanted to maintain his good relationship with Hayne and other Southerners, Van Buren had reason to take the state-rights side, but could not do so because it would have meant opposing Jackson and supporting Calhoun along with Hayne and nullification. While the debate was in progress, the *Albany Argus* and Regency senator Charles Dudley defended Hayne, but Van Buren took no position.[39]

Van Buren and Jackson got the chance to make their positions on

---

[38] Cooper to MVB, Mar. 29, 1829, Hamilton to MVB, April 28, 1829, Crawford to MVB, May 31, 1830, Madison to MVB, July 5, 1830, Stevenson to MVB, April 4, 1831, Macon to MVB, Oct. 1, 1830, VBP. See also Joseph Harrison, Jr., "Martin Van Buren and His Southern Supporters," *Journal of Southern History*, 22 (Nov. 1956), 438-458.

[39] *Argus*, Jan. 20, Jan. 22, 1830; Dudley to Azariah Flagg, Feb. 1, 1830, Flagg Papers.

state rights more explicit at the Jefferson Day dinner held on April 13 at Brown's Indian Queen Hotel in Washington. The idea for the dinner began with Hayne and Thomas Hart Benton; they hoped that it would bring together southern and western Democrats, who could not agree on nullification. But Van Buren became immediately suspicious that the dinner was a plot designed by Calhoun to link nullification with the old Jeffersonian tradition of '98 and to win Southerners away from Jackson. The Secretary had no trouble convincing Jackson, who believed that Calhoun was using the "Virginia model"—Jefferson's state-rights arguments of 1798—as a "stalking horse" to attack the administration. The two men prepared a toast that would present the President as the "guardian and Champion" of the Union, rebuking Calhoun and rejecting nullification.[40]

At the dinner the main courses were followed by dozens of prepared toasts praising such Jeffersonian principles as the rights of the states and the need to restrict federal power by limiting taxes. There was no outright defense of nullification, but Hayne did compare South Carolina's opposition to the tariff with Virginia's rejection of the Alien and Sedition Acts in 1798. Finally, at ten in the evening "all hilarity ceased," the audience grew still, and the little Van Buren stood on his chair so that he could see as Jackson rose to give the first of the volunteer toasts. Looking squarely at Calhoun, the Old Hero declared sternly: "Our Union: It must be preserved." Calhoun was so upset by the rebuke that the glass "trembled in his hand, [and] a little of the amber fluid trickled down the side." Recovering quickly he replied with his own toast: "The Union—next to our liberty most dear."[41]

The dramatic confrontation gave Van Buren, who spoke next, the perfect opportunity to be the harmonizer. His toast placed him in

---

[40] *Niles' Register*, 38 (April 24, 1830), 153-154; *Richmond Enquirer*, April 23, 1830; Richard R. Stenberg, "The Jefferson Birthday Dinner, 1830," *Journal of Southern History*, 4 (Aug. 1938), 334-345; *Autobiography*, pp. 412-414; Jackson to John Coffee, April 10, 1830, Jackson, *Correspondence*, IV, 134.

[41] *Autobiography*, pp. 414-415. The description of Calhoun's glass trembling is from Isaac Hill, quoted in Augustus C. Buell, *History of Andrew Jackson* (New York, 1904), II, 240-242. Jackson had planned to say "Federal Union," and added the word "Federal" in the published version of his toast. *Niles' Register*, 38 (1830), 153-154. James C. Curtis uses the story of Van Buren climbing on a chair to argue that Van Buren had little influence over Jackson's behavior at the dinner. According to Curtis, Van Buren was so far away from the center of the action that he had to climb on a chair to see. Perhaps so, but no matter where he sat Van Buren was influential. He did, after all, discuss the toasts with Jackson before the dinner. James C. Curtis, "In the Shadow of Old Hickory: the Political Travail of Martin Van Buren," *Journal of the Early Republic*, 1 (Fall 1981), 252.

principle close to Jefferson and Jackson, and midway between Webster and Calhoun. "Mutual forbearance and reciprocal concessions," he began, "thro' their agency the Union was established—the patriotic spirit from which they emanated will forever sustain it." Van Buren set the tone for a decade by asking his generation to support the Union but also to make concessions to the South. With their toasts he and Jackson anticipated the position taken by the administration in the nullification crisis in 1832 and 1833. More important for Van Buren at the time, he emerged from the dinner united with Jackson against Calhoun.[42]

Van Buren and Jackson were not the only ones to suspect a plot. Even before the dinner began, the Pennsylvania delegation smelled nullification and walked out. One of the original planners, Thomas Hart Benton, later concluded that he too had been taken in by a plot designed to "dissolve the Union." And on the opposition side Daniel Webster and John Quincy Adams agreed that Calhoun had planned the dinner in order to reorganize the party on state-rights principles against Van Buren.[43]

The conspiracy thesis, however, does not hold together, although it attracted historians for the next hundred years. The dinner was organized by too many northern friends of Van Buren including Cambreleng, Henry Hubbard and Levi Woodbury of New Hampshire, and Daniel Miller of Pennsylvania, to have been a southern plot. None of the toasts came out openly for nullification, and even if the nullifiers were laying plans, they would not have carried them out at such an affair because it could have been predicted that Jackson would side with Van Buren. What happened was that a wide range of party members planned a dinner to please Southerners, who were upset over the tariff, and after five hours of eating, drinking and toasting, a flare-up occurred.[44]

But even though there was no nullifier plot, Van Buren acted as though there were one and succeeded in embarrassing Calhoun. After convincing Jackson of the need to rebuke Calhoun and discredit his

[42] *Autobiography*, p. 416. Paul C. Nagel calls Van Buren's toast the most important of the three. Nagel, *One Nation Indivisible: the Union in American Thought 1776-1861* (New York, 1964), pp. 115-128.

[43] Webster to Clay, April 18, 1830, Clay, *Private Correspondence*, pp. 259-260; Webster to Jeremiah Mason, April 14, 1830, C. H. Van Tyne, ed., *The Letters of Daniel Webster* (New York, 1902), p. 152; Adams, *Memoirs*, VIII, 222; *National Intelligencer*, April 19, 1830; Benton, *Thirty Years' View*, I, 148.

[44] Richard Stenberg was the first to attack the plot thesis. Stenberg, "Jefferson Birthday Dinner."

theory of nullification, Van Buren prepared a toast of his own that was a model of Jacksonian moderation. More than Jackson and certainly more than Calhoun, he spoke for Democrats at the Jefferson Day dinner.[45]

Soon after the dinner, Jackson and Van Buren had another chance to define their republicanism when the Maysville Road bill authorizing the government to buy stock in a road from Lexington to Maysville in Kentucky, passed Congress on May 20. In the past, the two had differed on internal improvements: Jackson had favored roads and canals, especially national projects that would strengthen the Union; Van Buren had voted funds for the Cumberland Road, but had otherwise opposed bills for internal improvements. The Democratic party was also split. Democrats from Pennsylvania and the West wanted feeder roads like the one to Maysville to link their communities with the Ohio River or the National Road. William T. Barry and Richard Mentor Johnson of Kentucky, urged the Old Hero to sign the bill because the road ran through a Democratic stronghold in Kentucky, where two newspapers had already come out in favor of it. Pulling the other way were strict Jeffersonians such as Thomas Ritchie and Alfred Balch. The administration, wanting to please both the state-rights South and the nationalistic West, was in a tight spot.[46]

While the bill was working its way through Congress, Van Buren was encouraging the President to take a stand against the road. On one of their horseback rides, Van Buren handed Jackson a brief he had written opposing internal improvements, which the President later declared "furnish[ed] clear views upon the constitutional powers of Congress." Van Buren warned that the opposition would try to trap Jackson into approving a bill that was "most emphatically *local*," so the President was ready when Johnson called to lobby for the road. "General!" shouted the strong-minded Johnson, "If this hand were an anvil on which the sledge hammer of the smith was descending and a fly were to light upon it in time to receive the blow he would not

[45] Charles M. Wiltse has argued that at the dinner Van Buren was engaged in a plot to "eliminate Calhoun," but this interpretation is a bit extreme. Van Buren was not ready to "eliminate Calhoun" in April 1830. Wiltse, *John C. Calhoun, Nullifier,* pp. 68, 73, 425.

[46] *Autobiography,* pp. 297-321; Leland W. Meyer, *The Life and Times of Colonel Richard M. Johnson of Kentucky* (New York, 1932), pp. 274-275; Thomas Ritchie to Colonel A. Ritchie, June 8, 1830, Ambler, "Ritchie Letters," *Branch Papers,* 3 (1911), 204; Clay to Webster, June 7, 1830, Webster, *Private Correspondence,* I, 504; *Richmond Enquirer,* Mar. 30, April 6, May 11, May 25, June 4, June 11, 1830; Balch to Jackson, Jan 8, 1830, Jackson, *Correspondence,* IV, 114-116; Crawford to MVB, May 31, 1830, VBP.

crush it more effectually than you will crush your friends in Kentucky if you veto that Bill!" But Jackson silenced Johnson by replying in good republican style that the administration was "committed [to] pay off the National Debt" and could not "borrow a cent" for such a road. To keep Johnson guessing Van Buren convinced the senator before he left that Jackson was uncertain whether or not to veto the bill. During the month-long debate on the road Van Buren had prepared the way for a veto without tipping the President's hand.[47]

Van Buren also wrote the veto message that Jackson issued on May 27. In his message Jackson said that national internal improvements were valuable and might be constitutional, but pointed out that this one was a local project. He insisted, furthermore, that to preserve the "republican principle" it was necessary to save money and do away with the national debt. "What a salutary influence" it would have, he added loftily, if the United States could show "the world the sublime spectacle of a Republic . . . free from debt." Referring to the plan that Van Buren had suggested earlier in the Senate, Jackson said that if the people wanted internal improvements in the future, they should support a constitutional amendment. With this message Van Buren showed his ability to retain old ideals and yet take steps to allow for change. He pleased those Jeffersonians who looked to the past, but he did it without ultimately rejecting the roads and canals that an expanding society demanded. By convincing Jackson that he should defend state rights and veto the bill, Van Buren had turned Jacksonian Democracy imperceptibly away from the uncompromising nationalism of the President.[48]

Van Buren had also strengthened himself and his party politically, for the veto was sustained in Congress and well-received in the nation. Ritchie would have liked it couched in more sweeping terms and there was some "growling" in New York and opposition in Pennsylvania, but Jackson was able to conclude that the veto *work[ed] well*." After a survey of the east coast, Van Buren reported that Republicans were "vociferous in their approbation and the Opposition silent." In the South James Hamilton, Jr., praised "the noble and heroic stand," while another Republican said that the veto sounded "like the music of other days." When Democrats made gains that fall in the congressional elections, Van Buren knew the veto was a success.[49]

[47] *Autobiography*, pp. 321-326, Jackson to MVB, May 4, May 15, 1830, MVB to Jackson, May 4, 1830, *Autobiography*, pp. 321-322; Meyer, *Life of Johnson*, p. 274.

[48] Van Buren implies that he wrote the message, and John S. Bassett concurs. *Autobiography*, pp. 326-329; Jackson, *Correspondence*, IV, 137n. For the two drafts, see Jackson, *Correspondence*, IV, 137-139.

[49] *Richmond Enquirer*, June 1, 1830; Ritchie to Col. A. Ritchie, June 8, 1830, Ambler,

Although Van Buren and Jackson did not go as far as some southern Republicans would have liked, the two did take a stand against federal internal improvements. In addition to the Maysville veto, Jackson vetoed bills for the Washington Turnpike Road, the Louisville and Portland Canal, and for several rivers and harbors. He accepted a number of other bills—notably $300,000 for the Cumberland Road only three days after the Maysville veto—and the sum spent on internal improvements in his administration exceeded that spent under John Quincy Adams. But Jackson supported only national projects, he spent the money over eight years rather than four, and he spent far less than western nationalists wanted. With Van Buren's help, Jackson broke the trend toward increasing national expenditures for roads and canals.[50]

Jackson found it easier to please Old Republicans on Indian removal than on internal improvements because on this issue the Southerners were as nationalistic as he was. The President, who shared the frontiersman's hatred of the Indian, announced in his inaugural address that he planned to move the Cherokee and Creek Indians west of the Mississippi. When he sent a bill to Congress calling for Indian removal, the *Richmond Enquirer* approved because it did not want Indians setting up independent governments in Georgia. The Indian removal bill passed on May 28, 1830, one day after the Maysville veto and one day before the passing of Cambreleng's bill to open American ports to ships from the British West Indies.[51]

Van Buren took no part in the debates, but he agreed with Jackson's Indian policy. During the debates, Van Buren's friend Senator Charles Dudley of New York, voiced his support for the removal bill; a few months later the *Albany Argus* praised "the liberal and humane provisions" of the law, and in his autobiography, Van Buren called the harsh removal bill "most generous." Van Buren, who had grown up

---

"Ritchie Letters," *Branch Papers*, 3 (1911), 204; Jackson to MVB, June 26, 1830, James Hamilton, Jr., to MVB, June 8, 1830, VBP; MVB to Jackson, July 25, 1830, Jackson, *Correspondence*, IV, 166-167.

[50] For the case that the veto made a difference, see Bassett, *Jackson*, pp. 490-496. For the view that Jackson did little to check such expenditures, see Pessen, *Jacksonian America*, pp. 95, 124-125, and Carlton Jackson, "The Internal Improvement Vetoes of Andrew Jackson," *Tennessee Historical Quarterly*, 25 (Fall 1966), 261-279. David J. Russo argues that Jackson was consistent. Russo, "The Major Political Issues of the Jacksonian Period and the Development of Party Loyalty in Congress, 1830-1840," *Transactions of the American Philosophical Society*, New Series, LXII, Part 2 (May 1972), 9-13.

[51] *Autobiography*, pp. 276-289; *Richmond Enquirer*, June 9, 1829, May 25, 1830.

in a slaveowning community and had owned a slave himself, shared the American belief in white supremacy. While on the one hand condemning the Indians for using "savage cruelties" to stop the advance of white civilization, he also feared that the Indians were becoming "hopeless[ly] dependen[t] upon the clemency and justice of the United States." He hoped that white Americans would become the "guardians" and "benefactors" of the Indians.[52]

During this session of Congress, the Jacksonians disappointed some Old Republicans by not reversing the protective tariff and by not preparing to oppose the recharter of the Bank of the United States. Southern Democrats, who had voted for Jackson despite the "Tariff of Abominations," had expected the administration to reward them with lower duties. While waiting for Jackson to take office, the legislatures of South Carolina, Georgia, Mississippi, and Virginia had all passed resolutions against the tariff, and during his first year in office Van Buren received a number of letters from James Hamilton, Jr., summing up southern discontent with the "robbery" and "larceny" of tariff protection. In his first annual message Jackson annoyed Southerners by calling for tariffs that would help American manufacturers compete with the rest of the world.[53]

The administration did not move at once against the recharter of the Bank of the United States because influential Democrats were divided on the issue. Jackson himself took office with a bias against the Bank, and advisers such as Benton, Isaac Hill, and Senator Felix Grundy of Tennessee, recommended an attack on the institution. Other voices including those of William B. Lewis and James A. Hamilton, were raised in defense of the Bank. Van Buren was something of an enigma. Before leaving New York he had criticized the "constitutional encroachments" of the Bank on state rights, but he had also tried to have branches established at Albany and Oswego. In the late fall of 1829, Van Buren joined those who were trying to keep the President from attacking the Bank in his annual message. Despite their efforts, Jackson uttered threats, saying that its "constitutionality [had to be] questioned" and wondering whether Congress would care to set up a new "national" bank. Since the charter of the Bank was not due to

---

[52] Charles Dudley to Azariah Flagg, May 20, 1830, Flagg Papers; *Argus*, Jan. 13, 1831, *Autobiography*, pp. 276-296. Regency men Van Buren, Wright, Flagg, and John A. Dix all believed that the election of 1832 showed that the American public supported Jackson's Indian policy. *Argus*, July 19, 1833; *Autobiography*, pp. 294-295.

[53] Hamilton to MVB, Mar. 4, April 28, July 16, Nov. 16, 1829, Mar. 21, 1830, Robert Y. Hayne to MVB, Oct. 23, 1830, VBP; Richardson, *Messages and Papers*, II, 442-462; *Argus*, Jan. 20, 1831.

expire until 1836, there was no pressure on the Congress to take immediate action.[54]

During his first year and a half as Secretary of State, Van Buren had accomplished much. He had run the State Department well, he had survived the "Eaton malaria," and he had overtaken the Tennessee clique and outmaneuvered Calhoun to become Jackson's chief adviser. In addition, he and Jackson had taken important steps in defining Jacksonian Democracy. In foreign policy Van Buren had muted Jackson's nationalistic impulses in order to win important concessions. In domestic affairs the Secretary found a middle ground between nationalism and Old Republicanism. By appealing to the Old Republican tradition while at the same time responding to the nation's economic growth, Jackson and Van Buren were able to develop a moderate program that was acceptable to a majority of Americans. Van Buren had been able to do all this because he had quickly learned how to work with Jackson. In some cases the Secretary followed the President—in defending Peggy Eaton, in removing Indians; in others Van Buren advised Jackson—in limiting the spoils system, in opening trade with the West Indies, in rebuking Calhoun for his lack of Unionism, and in vetoing local internal improvements. After a hesitant start the Magician had been able to practice his arts and succeed with Old Hickory almost as well as he had in the New York Regency. When he returned to New York in the summer of 1830, he was far stronger politically than he had been the year before at the start of his tiring journey to Jackson's Washington.

[54] Robert V. Remini, *Andrew Jackson and the Bank War* (New York, 1967), pp. 49-66; Bassett, *Life of Jackson*, pp. 589-600; *Autobiography*, p. 619; Holland, *Van Buren*, p. 303; Jean A. Wilburn, *Biddle's Bank: the Crucial Years* (New York, 1964), p. 94; Rudolph Bunner to MVB, June 1, 1829, VBP; Hamilton, *Reminiscences*, pp. 149-150.

TRANQUILLITY IN ENGLAND

In the middle of May 1830, part way between the Jefferson Day dinner and the Maysville veto, President Jackson wrote a letter that in time forced Van Buren into a new phase of his career—a tranquil interlude in England. In the letter the President asked John C. Calhoun to explain his behavior during Jackson's Florida campaign of 1818. When Jackson had exceeded his instructions that year and had invaded Florida, most of James Monroe's cabinet, including Secretary of War Calhoun and Secretary of the Treasury William Harris Crawford, had argued secretly that the general should be disciplined. Jackson heard rumors of Calhoun's hostile attitude in 1819, in 1827, and again in 1828, when Crawford sent word by way of John Forsyth of Georgia, that Calhoun had wanted Jackson arrested and tried, but Jackson took no action. Finally, on May 12, 1830, he received a letter from Crawford directly, accusing Calhoun. Already at odds with his Vice President, Jackson decided to act, and the next day sent off a letter calling Calhoun to account.[1]

The letter opened a new phase in the struggle for power within the administration. Instead of backing down, Calhoun first tried to prove that Jackson had exceeded his authority in 1818, and then criticized Jackson for accepting Crawford's story. Angered by the defiance, the President wrote that he now had "full evidence [of Calhoun's] duplicity and insincerity." During the summer and fall the administration intensified its policy of taking patronage away from Calhoun. As part of this policy Amos Kendall and William T. Barry brought their old Kentucky associate Francis P. Blair to Washington to establish a new administration newspaper, the *Globe*, in place of Duff Green's *Telegraph*, because Green had increasingly annoyed Jackson by supporting Calhoun and the Bank of the United States. Blair, who had been writing editorials for the *Argus of Western America* in Frankfort, was an outspoken writer much like Isaac Hill, and his impulsive style appealed to Jackson. The President liked Blair (whom he called "Blaar") and

[1] Narrative of William B. Lewis, in Parton, *Jackson*, III, 310-325; *Autobiography*, pp. 372-374; Jackson to Calhoun, May 13, 1830, Jackson to James A. Hamilton, May 18, 1830, Jackson, *Correspondence*, IV, 136-137; Wiltse, *John C. Calhoun, Nullifier*, pp. 76-80.

soon began to turn to him for advice. Since Blair was an ally of Kendall and since Van Buren had nothing to do with his appointment, the establishment of the *Globe* strengthened the position of the Westerners in the administration.

As the attacks on Calhoun mounted, Van Buren, who had the most to gain, remained quietly on the sidelines. When Jackson and William B. Lewis asked Van Buren to read the Florida correspondence, he refused because he wanted to be able to say that he was unaware of the contents. Later in the fall, Jackson proposed a plan whereby Van Buren would run for Vice President in 1832 and then succeed Jackson, who would resign shortly after his inauguration. But Van Buren rejected the plan.[2]

Calhoun saw no need to give in when Congress reassembled in December 1830, and since the Jacksonian coalition lacked complete control of Congress, its leaders proceeded with caution. Efforts were made by Samuel Swartwout and others to bring Jackson and Calhoun together; the *Globe* was not immediately designated as the official party newspaper, and in February Calhoun's friend Duff Green was reelected printer by both the House and Senate. As a result Calhoun, who had been collecting documents all summer, decided that the time was ripe to declare war on Van Buren. On February 17, 1831, Calhoun published his documents in Green's *Telegraph* and accused Van Buren of starting the controversy in order to make himself Jackson's successor.[3]

Calhoun tried to conciliate Jackson by showing the documents to Lewis ahead of time, but their publication infuriated the President. It also triggered open war between the *Telegraph* and the *Globe*, which began to speak for the administration and defend Van Buren. Thomas Ritchie tried to remain neutral at first, insisting that the party should reelect the President before worrying about his successor, but before long the *Enquirer* was condemning the "reckless conduct" of Calhoun.

---

[2] Calhoun to Jackson, May 29, 1830, Richard K. Crallé, ed., *Works of John C. Calhoun*, 6 vols. (New York, 1854-1857), VI, 360-381; Jackson to Calhoun, May 30, 1830, Jackson to Lewis, June 26, 1830, Jackson, *Correspondence*, IV, 140-141; Calhoun to Jackson, Aug. 25, 1830, with endorsement by Jackson, Jackson Papers, LC; *Autobiography*, pp. 374-376, 506-507; Parton, *Jackson*, III, 325-329; Wiltse, *John C. Calhoun, Nullifier*, pp. 84-85; Bassett, *Jackson*, pp. 509-513. For Van Buren's refusal to read the correspondence, see Lewis' narrative in Parton, *Jackson*, III, 327. For the appointment of Blair, see Latner, *Presidency of Jackson*, pp. 74-79; Remini, *Jackson and the Course of American Freedom*, pp. 291-297.

[3] Meyer, *Life of Richard M. Johnson*, p. 270; *Autobiography*, pp. 376-377; *Niles' Register*, 40 (1831), 447-448; 41 (1831), 11-24, 37-45.

With both the *Globe* and the *Enquirer* attacking Calhoun, Jackson was reading the South Carolinian out of the party.[4]

Democrats were divided: for every one who regarded Calhoun as the aggressor another blamed Van Buren. Since some of the evidence against Calhoun had been dug up by Van Buren's friend James A. Hamilton, the Secretary seemed to be involved. In Virginia, Ritchie warned that many believed Van Buren at fault, and Governor John Floyd reported that the whole state was "disgusted" at Van Buren. In the North, Congressman Henry R. Storrs of New York, declared that Van Buren's career was over, John Quincy Adams thought that Calhoun would have another term as Vice President, and James Buchanan predicted that Van Buren's friends would be forced out of the government. Even among those who assumed that Van Buren would come out on top some were cynical. According to Anti-Masonic assemblyman Francis Granger of New York, "Matty" would "use the claws of others to take his own chestnuts from the fire." Many would not believe Van Buren when he published a notice in the *Telegraph* denying any involvement in the dispute.[5]

The fierce battle between Calhoun, Green and the *Telegraph* on one side, and Van Buren, Blair and the *Globe* on the other prompted harsh attacks on the Magician for his supposed influence on the President. Although the term "Kitchen Cabinet" did not appear until Nicholas Biddle used it in December 1831, the concept of an unofficial group of advisers exercising great power over Jackson was introduced in the *Telegraph* and other antiadministration newspapers as early as the spring of 1831. Recent research reveals that formally there was no such thing as a Kitchen Cabinet, but that the President used a wide variety of informal advisers in order to make certain that he kept control of the administration. During Jackson's first year in office Lewis, Eaton and Donelson dominated the "Kitchen Cabinet," but before the second year was out Blair, Kendall and Van Buren had the inside track.

Despite Van Buren's strong position, the intense struggle with Cal-

---

[4] *Autobiography*, pp. 377-380; *Richmond Enquirer*, Feb. 19, Feb. 24, 1831; D. J. Fisher to James H. Hammond, April, 1831, James H. Hammond Papers, LC; Wiltse, *John C. Calhoun, Nullifier*, pp. 94-97; Washington *Globe*, Feb. 19, Feb. 23, Feb. 26, Mar. 2, 1831.

[5] *Autobiography*, pp. 383-389; Ritchie to MVB, Feb. 21, 1831, *Autobiography*, pp. 385-386; Floyd, "Diary," Mar. 11, 1831, Charles H. Ambler, *The Life and Diary of John Floyd* (Richmond, 1918), p. 126; Adams, *Memoirs*, VIII, 327-328; Storrs to Abraham Van Vechten, Feb. 22, 1831, Storrs Papers, NYHS; Francis Granger to Thurlow Weed, Feb. 15, 1831, Granger Papers, LC; S. Pleasanton to Buchanan, Mar. 22, 1831, James Buchanan Papers, LC.

houn raised doubts in the Secretary's mind about his standing in the administration. As he always did, he totaled up the credits and debits. After two years in the cabinet he had won the confidence of Andrew Jackson, he had established a sound Jeffersonian record, he had been a successful Secretary of State, and he had Calhoun on the defensive. On the other hand, Jackson might become reconciled with Calhoun, three Calhoun supporters—Samuel D. Ingham, John Branch, and John M. Berrien—were still in the cabinet, and enough Virginians had believed Calhoun's story to suggest that Van Buren's southern base was unstable. Van Buren, moreover, was not as important to Jackson in 1831 as he had been the year before. The Eaton affair and the Maysville veto were history, Van Buren had accomplished all he could as Secretary of State, the President did not need Van Buren's help to be reelected. Difficult issues such as the Bank and the tariff loomed ahead, in which Van Buren might have to oppose the President. The two months following Calhoun's "Appeal" were, Van Buren recalled, "clouded by doubt and anxiety." Perhaps it was time to move on.[6]

One April morning as Van Buren and Jackson were riding along the Potomac, Van Buren decided to break the news that he wanted to resign. Jackson at first argued heatedly that he would never let his Secretary go, but listened carefully for the next four hours as Van Buren described in detail his plan. Jackson apparently worried about it into the small hours, for the next morning Van Buren observed "the usual signs of a sleepless night" when he encountered the President. That afternoon as they rode again Jackson did most of the talking. Within days he and Van Buren had perfected a plan that would help both men. Jackson would use Van Buren's resignation as an excuse to break up the cabinet and get rid of Calhoun's three backers. The President would then appoint supporters of Van Buren in their places, send Van Buren and John Eaton, who would also resign, to posts overseas, and thus ensure a harmonious cabinet. On April 11, Van Buren wrote a long, rambling letter of resignation, and the rest of the cabinet, except for William T. Barry, followed suit. Levi Woodbury, Lewis Cass, and Louis McLane—all Van Buren men—took over Navy, War, and Treasury. Van Buren was also on good terms with the new Attorney General Roger B. Taney and the new Secretary of State Edward Livingston. The Magician himself replaced McLane as a minister to England.[7]

[6] Latner, *Presidency of Jackson*, pp. 52-57; Remini, *Jackson and the Course of American Freedom*, pp. 326-330; *Autobiography*, p. 398.

[7] Eaton to Jackson, April 7, 1831, MVB to Jackson, April 11, 1831, Ingham to Jackson, April 18, 1831, Branch to Jackson, April 19, 1831, Jackson, *Correspondence*,

As always Van Buren took great pains to protect his political flanks. Since he had not followed his usual practice of consulting the Regency, he sent a careful letter to Albany saying that he had resigned because he had become a presidential candidate, not because he had lost favor with Jackson. To protect his position in Virginia Van Buren wrote to inform Thomas Ritchie that no one else had been told except a few friends in Albany. And to maintain his relationship with the British, Van Buren sought out British minister Sir Charles R. Vaughan several times to explain the cabinet shuffle. Vaughan privately attributed it all to Peggy Eaton, even though Van Buren persisted in saying that it had happened because he had become the leading candidate for President. Van Buren wanted everyone to believe that the reconstitution of the cabinet was a victory for him.[8]

A number of observers agreed. Though they were astounded, Silas Wright and Benjamin Butler thought that Van Buren was sure to become Vice President. The idealistic Ritchie insisted that Van Buren would have to show his purity by refusing any further appointment, while the more practical James A. Hamilton said that Van Buren was lucky to get away and escape impending problems. Even some of Van Buren's enemies thought he had won. Calhoun protested, with justification, that Van Buren had increased his power while reducing his responsibility, and the *United States Gazette* predicted that he would rise from minister to Vice President, and finally, to President.[9]

But others considered the resignation a defeat for Van Buren. Ambrose Spencer claimed that Van Buren had been ousted by the complaints of Virginia and Pennsylvania; another critic maintained that Van Buren's "duplicity" had caused him to lose "the President's confidence." Several New Yorkers, including Stephen Van Rensselaer, thought Van Buren was making a mistake in going to England, where "out of sight [was] out of mind." Rudolph Bunner suggested that Jackson would also be hurt because he needed someone like the former Secretary to take care of difficult situations. Unsure of the future, Van Buren shared some of these fears. One observer noted that he looked

---

IV, 257-266; Parton, *Jackson*, III, 344-360; *Autobiography*, pp. 403-408; William H. Sparks, *Memories of Fifty Years*, 3rd ed. (Philadelphia, 1872), p. 55; *Niles' Register*, 40 (1831), 143-144.

[8] MVB to Benjamin Butler, April 16, 1831, MVB to Edward Livingston, April 9, 1831, MVB to Ritchie, April 17, 1831, VBP; Vaughan to British Foreign Office, April 20, April 27, 1831, British Foreign Office, Correspondence, 5: United States, 265 (1831), 320-325, 334-335.

[9] Butler to MVB, April 22-23, 1831, Ritchie to MVB, April 20-21, 1831, Hamilton to MVB, May 1, 1831, VBP; Calhoun to Virgil Maxcy, May 16, 1831, Galloway-Maxcy-Marboe Papers, LC; *Niles' Register*, 40 (1831), 180.

"pale and spiritless," had been "much secluded," and had "not appeared at the *fetes* as heretofore."[10]

Before leaving for England, Van Buren made a short tour of New York, where he deeply impressed editor James Gordon Bennett of the *New York Courier and Enquirer* when the two shared a carriage between Schenectady and Utica. According to the editor Van Buren was a rather "formal" person—"nothing grand or imposing"—who had "no appreciation of wit or satire—or learning—or fancy." Although he "talked frankly and freely," and made "acute and sensible remarks about men," he said "nothing very imaginative or striking." When other passengers argued over the state usury law, Van Buren took a position based on "expediency" and gave no firm opinion. Bennett was particularly impressed that Van Buren remembered people so readily, including one woman with whom he had traveled the Mohawk Valley twenty years before, and concluded that he had great "natural popularity [and] more of Jefferson's qualities" than Calhoun, Clay, or anyone else. The Van Buren who rode that stagecoach was still an unspectacular, moderate, personable Jeffersonian.[11]

And he still basked in the warm friendship of Andrew Jackson, who sought his advice on appointments and asked for ideas for the next annual message. While vacationing on Rip Raps Island in Chesapeake Bay, Jackson made a point of denying that he had lost confidence in Van Buren. On his return he referred to Van Buren's "likeness hung up" in his room, where it seemed "to look, and smile upon" the President and he later declared sadly that he "regret[ted]" Van Buren's absence. When Van Buren finally departed on August 16, he expressed his gratitude for Jackson's friendship.[12]

For the next eleven months, Van Buren found himself in a situation far different from anything he had known before. After thirty years of party battles, he was suddenly transported from the old "turmoils and contentions [to] the quietude of a midsummer Ocean" and then to the pleasures of England and the Continent. The first morning at

[10] Spencer to John W. Taylor, April 25, 1831, Taylor Papers; John Pintard to Eliza Davidson, April 22, 1831, "Letters of John Pintard," III, 245; Bennett, Diary, June 21, 1831; Bunner to Gulian Verplanck, April 26, 1831, Verplanck Papers, NYHS; General Van Rensselaer to Henry Clay, Henry Clay Papers, LC; Richard McCall to Thomas Cadwalader, April 20, 1831, Cadwalader Collection, HSP.

[11] Bennett, Diary, June 21, June 22, June 26, July 6, Aug. 12, 1831.

[12] Jackson to John Coffee, April 24, 1831, Jackson to Andrew J. Donelson, May 5, 1831, Jackson to MVB, April 12, May 20, June 23, July 11, July 23, Aug. 8, Aug. 10, 1831, MVB to Jackson, Aug. 14, 1831, Jackson *Correspondence*, IV, 263, 269, 275, 284, 301-302, 312-314, 316-317, 328-330, 332-335; Jackson to MVB, July 25, Aug. 1, 1831, MVB to Jackson, July 16, July 29, Aug. 15, 1831, VBP.

sea he was delighted to realize that there was no trouble to attend to, and "one tranquil day" after another carried him "further from the sight and the sound of the political strife and labour" to which he was accustomed. With him on the three-week passage were his son John, who was to be an attaché, and Aaron Vail, secretary of the legation.[13]

On arriving Van Buren settled down to the sort of comforts he had always liked. Since he was receiving a salary of $9,000 a year and had another $9,000 for expenses, he could afford to live graciously. For $2,500 a year he rented a house on fashionable Stratford Place; for a comparable sum he hired a steward, a valet, a coachman, a footman, a cook, and two maids; another $1,550 bought him a carriage in which to travel in style about London and the countryside. To stock his larder he imported from America fourteen hams, a barrel of rice and two large boxes filled with meats, buffalo tongues, jellies, and preserves. From Cádiz, Calais, Bordeaux, and elsewhere came three cases, sixteen hampers and several hogsheads of wine. Thanks to new regulations, Van Buren was allowed to depart from the severe dress that Jackson had originally prescribed for his ministers. No wonder the new Envoy Extraordinary and Minister Plenipotentiary boasted a month after arriving that the situation was the most agreeable he had ever known. "Money—money—" he wrote, "is the thing."[14]

Van Buren's social life was equally pleasant. Washington Irving had spent several years in Spain writing his *History of Columbus* and collecting material for *The Alhambra* before becoming secretary of the American legation in London. Growing up at the same time in the Hudson Valley, loving the same old Dutch culture, Irving and Van Buren had much in common. Now approaching fifty, loving society, and growing fat, the two men became fast friends. "The more I see of Mr. V.B.," said Irving, "the more I feel . . . a strong personal regard for him. He is one of the gentlest and most amiable men . . . with an affectionate disposition." Though Irving soon left the office, he stayed in London and moved in with Van Buren.[15]

[13] *Autobiography*, pp. 445-446.

[14] MVB to Edward Livingston, Sept. 14, 1831, State Department, Diplomatic Despatches, Great Britain, XXXVIII; State Department, Diplomatic Instructions, Great Britain, XIV, 97-100; MVB to James A. Hamilton, Oct. 14, 1831, Hamilton, *Reminiscences*, pp. 229-230; Foreign Service Posts of the Department of State: Great Britain, Notes to the British Government, 1 (1831-1836), 1-22, National Archives; Cooper to William C. Rives, Nov. 14, 1831, James F. Beard, ed., *The Letters and Journals of James Fenimore Cooper* (Cambridge, Mass., 1960-1968), II, 154.

[15] Pierre Munroe Irving, *The Life and Letters of Washington Irving, by His Nephew, Pierre M. Irving*, rev. ed. (New York, 1892-1895), II, 167-168, 170, 210-212, 234-

Irving introduced the new envoy to English society, but Van Buren needed little help. Sir Charles R. Vaughan had already spread the word that as minister Van Buren would show the "same spirit of harmony" that he had displayed as Secretary of State. And Van Buren on his part assumed that the British and American people were "Brethren in principle," sharing a common faith in "liberty of speech and of the press." Hearty King William IV entertained Van Buren on a number of occasions, once inviting him to Windsor Castle, where Van Buren was treated as though he were a member of the family. The King even confided that he had never shared the alarm of many Englishmen at the election of Jackson. Van Buren was so popular with the Queen that she sent him a gift of four engravings of the castle.[16]

Van Buren's instructions called for him to negotiate with Foreign Secretary Lord Palmerston about impressments, the northeast boundary, and several minor matters. Since the King of the Netherlands had made a decision on the boundary, there was not much more to do on that subject, and Van Buren could accomplish little on impressment. He did make some progress in the case of the American brig *Comet*, which had run aground in the Bahamas with one hundred and sixty-four slaves aboard. When British officials refused to return the slaves, Van Buren—sympathetic as ever to the South—defended the rights of the owners and secured compensation. Otherwise he spent little time on diplomacy.[17]

With such light duties Van Buren had plenty of time to follow the progress of the British voting reform bill, which was debated all winter amid violent demonstrations. As an American democratic leader, he might have been expected to side with the reformers, but instead he displayed remarkable understanding and sympathy for those in the House of Lords who were opposing reform. Change had been so rapid, wrote Van Buren, that some aristocrats feared an end to stability and the "ultimate prostration of the privileged orders." Van Buren considered it natural for Tories to "look with some unkind feeling, upon the great source of liberal principles." He even explained without

235; Lynch, *Epoch and a Man*, p. 347; Shepard, *Van Buren*, pp. 224-226.

[16] British Foreign Office, Correspondence, 5: United States, 265 (1831), 335-336; 266 (1831), 28; *Autobiography*, pp. 448-457; MVB, Speech on presentation to King William IV, Sept. 21, 1831, MVB to Edward Livingston, Sept. 21, 1831, MVB to Jackson, Sept. 21, Oct. 21, 1831, VBP.

[17] State Department, Diplomatic Instructions, Great Britain, XIV, 100-120; *Autobiography*, pp. 452-453, 465; Bassett, "Martin Van Buren," pp. 225-232; MVB to Lord Palmerston, Feb. 25, 1832, MVB to Edward Livingston, Feb. 28, 1832, VBP; Montgomery Blair, "Martin Van Buren, Diplomatist, Minister of the United States to England," *Harper's Monthly Magazine*, 119 (1909), 274-281.

criticism the British system of rotten boroughs. When the Lords vetoed the bill, Van Buren worried more about the violence that followed than about the setback to reform. He praised the King not for supporting the bill but for keeping the people in check. Instead of criticizing the Duke of Wellington for opposing the bill, Van Buren called the Duke a hero for not giving in when a crowd broke his window and pelted his carriage with mud. Van Buren showed more interest in the political process than in the outcome. Disappointed in the quality of the debates, in which speakers focused on a specific point instead of covering the entire ground, he concluded that it was not an "age of great men" in England. Van Buren favored reform but not at the expense of public order.[18]

Van Buren was no more radical in his attitude toward society. When an epidemic of cholera began to reach London, he remarked calmly that the public was quiet because only "the poorest and of course most destitute classes" were threatened. When meetings were held to protest the Lords' rejection of the reform bill, Van Buren was quick to point out that those attending were from the "working classes." Observing that aristocrats could do as they pleased in England, Van Buren commented that rank and station deserved such privilege. "The higher one rises in the atmosphere," he remarked complacently, "the purer the tone of society is." After reading an enthusiastic letter from Van Buren, James A. Hamilton, no democrat himself, had to remind his friend that after all he was a "republican *Minister*." In writing his autobiography two decades later Van Buren was still the small-town boy who had been attracted to American aristocrats Elisha Williams and Rufus King, and was later fascinated by the British peerage. The Duke of Richmond, Lord Grey and many more are described in devoted detail. Van Buren was particularly interested in the aging Prince Talleyrand, the French minister in London. On presenting the old diplomat with a saddle of venison, Van Buren was rewarded when Talleyrand, who hated to speak any language but French, launched into a conversation in English.[19]

---

[18] *Autobiography*, pp. 460-463, 478; MVB to Livingston, Sept. 21, Oct. 14, Oct. 21, Nov. 22, Dec. 14, 1831, Feb. 14, 1832, MVB to Cambreleng, Oct. 14, Nov. 25, 1831, VBP; MVB to Jackson, Oct. 11, 1831, Jackson, *Correspondence*, IV, 358; *Argus*, Dec. 16, 1831; MVB to Hamilton, Oct. 14, Dec. 14, 1831, Hamilton, *Reminiscences*, pp. 229-230, 235; MVB to Enos T. Throop, Feb. 15, 1832, Martin Van Buren–Enos Throop Letters, NYSL. Robert L. Kelley argues that Van Buren shared the liberal views of the British reformers and watched the debates "in excited approval." Van Buren did approve, but he was far from excited. Robert L. Kelley, *The Transatlantic Persuasion: the Liberal Democratic Mind in the Age of Gladstone* (New York, 1969), pp. 246-247.

[19] MVB to Edward Livingston, Nov. 5, Nov. 22, 1831, extracts from Thomas Moore's

Van Buren enjoyed the company of these men and their women at parties in the fall, and he further indulged his taste for English high life when he, his son John, and Irving took a tour of the countryside during the Christmas season. Driving northwest from London in an open carriage in the mild English winter, the three bons vivants stopped at Oxford and Blenheim Castle before going on to Shakespeare's Stratford and Scott's Kenilworth. They arrived at Barlborough Hall just in time for Christmas and a fortnight of "old English hospitality." On Christmas Eve glee singers came by, servants brought in a boar's head crowned with holly, a wassail bowl offered cheer, and a yule log burned in the fireplace. After a fancy dress ball on Twelfth-night, they made their way back to London.[20]

That February, Van Buren was invited to the Queen's first drawing room of the season, but not feeling well decided to spend the day in bed. When the mail was brought up, he was greeted by the unpleasant announcement that the Senate had failed to confirm his appointment. Shaken by the news, he dressed hastily in order to make an appearance at the Queen's party, where he knew that his rejection would have set tongues wagging. In the receiving line the King honored Van Buren by stopping the flow of guests in order to "express in very kind terms his regret at what had happened." Even though Palmerston assured Van Buren that he should not feel ill-at-ease remaining in England, he knew that his carefree respite from American politics was over.[21]

Van Buren's rejection came as no surprise. Since the Democratic coalition had only shaky control of the Senate, Jackson had always had a hard time getting his controversial nominations confirmed. During the Twenty-first Congress the Senate had turned down editors Isaac Hill and Henry Lee; Mordecai Noah and Amos Kendall had barely squeezed through. With President of the Senate Calhoun no longer in the party as the Twenty-second Congress opened in December 1831, the administration faced rough going. As soon as Van Buren's name came before the Senate, Calhoun joined Clay and Webster in making plans to turn the nomination down. When debate began in late January, Webster attacked Van Buren for putting "party over country" in his instructions to McLane during the West Indies negotiations. According to Webster, Van Buren had invited the British

---

diary, Mar. 30, 1832, James A. Hamilton to MVB, Dec. 7, 1831, VBP; *Autobiography*, pp. 451-479.

[20] Irving, *Life and Letters of Washington Irving*, II, 213, 220-223; Aaron Vail to Colonel Aspinwall, Dec. 19, 1831, State Department, Diplomatic Despatches, Great Britain, XXXVIII.

[21] *Autobiography*, pp. 453-456.

to intervene in American politics by announcing that the Democrats were repudiating the policies of the National Republican administration. By making a settlement the British had helped the Democrats. Clay followed with a speech denouncing Van Buren for bringing the spoils system from New York to Washington. The best defense came from John Forsyth, who said that Van Buren had risen in politics because of his "extraordinary talent," not because of "the artifices of intrigue." William L. Marcy did less well. He boasted that New York politicians had always fought to win, and made his famous pronouncement that "to the victor belong the spoils of the enemy." In the end partisanship ruled and Van Buren lost, 24-23, with Vice President Calhoun casting the deciding vote.[22]

Calhoun was so elated that he exclaimed to Thomas Hart Benton: "It will kill him, sir, kill him dead. He will never kick, sir, never kick." Benton disagreed, declaring that Calhoun had "broken a minister, [but had] elected a Vice-President." Cambreleng had already told Van Buren that many of his friends hoped he would be rejected so that he could come home and run for Vice President. Some of Van Buren's enemies also suspected that the vote might make him Vice President. Duff Green could only hope that if Van Buren ran for Vice President, he would antagonize the other Democrats who had hoped to run with Jackson.[23]

The rejection started a storm of protest. In New York the columns of the *Argus* were filled with letters, and as many as fifty town and county meetings were held. One speaker reached into ancient history to compare Van Buren with Aristides and Cimon, who were opposed because they had done too much for the people. In the *Richmond Enquirer* Thomas Ritchie feared prophetically that the rejection would encourage Henry Clay in his efforts to raise the tariff and recharter the Bank of the United States. Dozens of other newspapers defended Van Buren, including the *Georgia Journal*, the *Ohio Monitor*, and the

[22] Bowers, *Party Battles*, pp. 82-87; Adams, *Memoirs*, VIII, 184; Sidney H. Aronson, *Status and Kinship in the Higher Civil Service: Standards of Selection in the Administrations of John Adams, Thomas Jefferson, and Andrew Jackson* (Cambridge, Mass., 1964), pp. 161-163; MVB to Rives, Jan. 25, 1832, Rives Papers, LC; *Register of Debates*, 22nd Congress, 1st session (1831-1832), 1309-1386; Washington *Globe*, Jan. 17, Feb. 2, 1832; *Niles' Register*, 41 (1832), 416-434, 453-466; *Autobiography*, pp. 523-533; Benton, *Thirty Years' View*, I, 214-217; Parton, *Jackson*, III, 378-379; Emmons, *Van Buren*, pp. 127-128.

[23] Benton recalls Calhoun's statement in *Thirty Years' View*, I, 219. For Benton's remark, see Parton, *Jackson*, III, 379. See also Cambreleng to MVB, Jan. 27, 1832, *Autobiography*, p. 454; Cambreleng to MVB, Jan. 4, 1832, VBP; Green to R. K. Crallé, Jan. 3, 1832, Duff Green Papers, LC.

Columbian Centinel. The Washington *Globe* carried articles from North Carolina, Maryland, Pennsylvania, and Rhode Island. As Rudolph Bunner told Gulian Verplanck, the action of the Senate had brought the Democratic party together.[24]

In New York the opposition was united too. A meeting in Van Buren's own Oswego approved of the rejection, and John Pintard, who had long disliked Van Buren, said he hoped that the minister would never come home because he was so dangerous. Another critic called Van Buren a spoilsman who had driven Jackson's "friends below decks" while "manning the good old ship United States with his own crew." National Republicans began to hope that the efforts of the Regency to "create an excitement" over Van Buren had failed. It was typical of the man that even in defeat he stimulated partisan feelings.[25]

The fate of Van Buren focused attention on the Democratic nomination for Vice President, which would take place at a convention—the first ever for the party—to be held in Baltimore in May. As the cabinet was breaking up the year before, William B. Lewis and Amos Kendall had thought of a convention as a means of uniting the party and naming a candidate for Vice President. In May 1831, while Kendall was in New Hampshire shortly after the cabinet breakup, he received a letter from Lewis commenting on the vice presidency and suggesting that the New Hampshrie Democrats call for a national party convention. The Granite State Democrats responded promptly, and after publicity in the Washington *Globe*, the idea caught on.[26]

In his letter Lewis comments on Van Buren's rivals for the vice presidency, dismissing former speaker Philip P. Barbour on the grounds that he would not be "acceptable to Pennsylvania and New York"; Senator Mahlon Dickerson of New Jersey, would not be "willingly supported by Southern anti-tariff States," and there would be "insurmountable objections" to Louis McLane. In the months that followed senators William Wilkins of Pennsylvania, and John Forsyth of Geor-

[24] *Argus*, Feb. 3, Feb. 7, Feb. 10, Feb. 14, Feb. 17, Feb. 24, Feb. 28, Mar. 2, Mar. 6, 1832; *Richmond Enquirer*, Jan. 31, Feb. 2, Feb. 4, Feb 7, Feb. 9, Feb. 11, Feb. 14, Feb. 18, Feb. 21, Feb. 24, Feb. 28, Mar. 8, 1832; Washington *Globe*, Feb. 9, 1832.

[25] John Pintard to Eliza Davidson, Jan. 30, 1832, "Letters of John Pintard," IV, 9; *Resolution of a Meeting of the Citizens of the Village of Oswego held on the 18th February, 1832*, A. Spencer to John W. Taylor, Feb. 29, 1832, Walter Case to Taylor, Mar. 4, 1832, T. J. Sutherland to Taylor, April 9, 1832, Taylor Papers; William Stone to Henry Clay, Feb. 5, 1832, Hiram Ketchum to Clay, Feb. 12, 1832, R. W. Stoddard to Clay, Feb. 21, 1832, Henry Clay Papers, LC.

[26] Lewis to Kendall, May 25, 1831, Parton, *Jackson*, III, 382-383; Lewis to MVB, April 22, 1859, *Autobiography*, p. 584; Cole, *Jacksonian Democracy in New Hampshire*, p. 97.

gia, joined the list, but as Lewis remarked, it would be difficult to find any one person who would be "satisfactory to the different local interests." Lewis preferred Van Buren and Jackson agreed.[27]

In September, after arriving in England, Van Buren received a letter from Jackson saying that he hoped soon to retire to "open the door" for others, and concluding significantly, "You will understand me." In December, the President wrote that he wanted to arrange "the *selection of a vice president*" as previously suggested, so that he could retire "to the peaceful shades of the Hermitage." In asking the Senate to confirm Van Buren as minister to England, Jackson boasted that the opposition did not dare defeat the nomination because they knew that the people would then elect Van Buren Vice President "without a nomination." When Van Buren was rejected, Jackson denounced the Senate for its "blackguardism," and roared that the people would welcome Van Buren home "with open arms" and elect him Vice President by "acclamation." Marcy wrote happily that Jackson was "rapped [sic] up in Van Buren."[28]

Up to the time of his rejection Van Buren had played coy. At first he denied any interest in the vice presidency, and his letters about England were so enthusiastic that Jackson must have wondered whether Van Buren would even consent to come home. But when William C. Rives, who was still minister to France, began to consider running for Vice President himself, Van Buren quickly poured cold water on the scheme, and after Christmas he began to drop hints. He had asked, he said, to state that he was not available for the vice presidency. "Let me know," he wrote the President, "how it strikes you."[29]

The Regency gave Van Buren conflicting advice. Marcy and Cambreleng, who put national ahead of state politics, urged Van Buren to run for Vice President in 1832 and President in 1836, and unite the Democratic party. Otherwise they feared that the party would split into factions, and the election of 1836 would end in the House of Representatives. Rejection, wrote Cambreleng, had doubled Van Buren's strength, creating a "party" for him "in the nation," and giving him

[27] Lewis to Kendall, May 25, 1831, Parton, *Jackson*, III, 382-383; Lewis to MVB, April 22, 1859, *Autobiography*, p. 584.

[28] Jackson to MVB, Sept. 5, Dec. 16, Dec. 17, 1831, Jackson to James A. Hamilton, Jan. 27, 1832, Jackson, *Correspondence*, IV, 348, 379, 385, 402-405; *Autobiography*, pp. 506, 584-585; Jackson to MVB, Feb. 12, 1832, Jackson to John Campbell, c. Feb. 9, 1832, VBP; Marcy to Flagg, Feb. 6, 1832, Flagg Papers.

[29] Rives to MVB, Oct. 25, Nov. 12, 1831, MVB to Rives, Nov. 1, 1831, MVB to Jackson, Oct. 29, 1831, VBP; *Autobiography*, p. 385; MVB to Jackson, Sept. 21, Oct. 11, 1831, Jan. 11, 1832, Jackson, *Correspondence*, IV, 352, 354-355, 396-397.

the opportunity to replace Clay as national mediator. The pragmatic Marcy pointed out bluntly that Jackson was in such "feeble health" that he would probably not last five more years. But Azariah Flagg, Silas Wright and Edwin Croswell, who put state politics first, preferred to have Van Buren run for governor. As in the election of 1824 and in February 1829, when Van Buren agreed to be Secretary of State, national interests won over state interests, and Marcy and Cambreleng were able to convince the others. "Don't be fastidious," Marcy counseled Flagg. "When party feeling is strong almost anything that is done is right."[30]

Outsiders also wanted Van Buren to run. Francis P. Blair told Van Buren that the rejection was to his advantage; Isaac Hill wrote that Van Buren was certain to be nominated, and Andrew J. Donelson thought that Van Buren's friends would help him get revenge. When Thomas Ritchie held back, fellow Virginian Andrew Stevenson told the editor that his "scruples" about Van Buren's nomination "must give way." The *Globe* spread the word that Jacksonians everywhere were responding to public opinion by supporting Van Buren. According to Elijah Haywood of Ohio, Van Buren had become "the property of the old republican party."[31]

As Van Buren moved closer to the nomination, his old friend Louis McLane began to loom as an obstacle. After returning from England, the new Secretary of the Treasury had rapidly become the strongest member of the cabinet. McLane, who was a former Federalist and sympathized with the Bank of the United States, was able to convince Jackson of the need to make a soft statement about the Bank in his annual message on December 6, 1831. The following day McLane showed his confidence by issuing a strong Treasury report. In a balanced document he pleased former Republicans by recommending the sale of public lands to the states and the elimination of the national debt, while at the same time appealing to former Federalists by sug-

[30] Marcy to Flagg, Feb. 6, 1832, James A. Hamilton to Flagg, Feb. 17, 1832, Flagg Papers; Cambreleng to MVB, Jan. 4, Feb. 4, Feb. 5, 1832, Marcy to MVB, Jan. 26, 1832, Butler to MVB, Jan. 31, 1832, William A. Duer to MVB, Feb. 1, 1832, James A. Hamilton to MVB, Feb. 1, 1832, James W. Webb to MVB, Dec. 31, 1831-Jan. 7, 1832, Feb. 5, 1832, Jesse Hoyt to MVB, Feb. 7, 1832, Flagg to———, Feb. 7, 1832, VBP.

[31] Hill to MVB, Jan. 29-Feb. 12, 1832, Blair to MVB, Jan. 28, 1832, Webb to MVB, Dec. 31, 1831-Jan. 7, 1832, Stevenson to Ritchie, Feb. 4, 1832, copy by Webb, Elijah Hayward to MVB, Jan. 30, 1832, VBP; Donelson to John Coffee, Jan. 26, 1832, Andrew J. Donelson Papers, LC; Stevenson to———, Feb. 28, 1832, Miscellaneous Papers, UVL; Washington *Globe*, Feb. 2, 1832.

gesting higher tariffs and the recharter of the Bank. It began to appear that McLane had the most power in the administration.[32]

Van Buren became alarmed at the news that began to filter across the Atlantic. First there was a letter from the President saying that he was "pleased" with the "honorable" McLane and his "lucid" report. Then James A. Hamilton reported that the entire cabinet sided with McLane. Hamilton was incorrect, but Van Buren did not know that. When a letter from McLane defending the report failed to ease Van Buren's mind, he asked Cambreleng to show the President the errors and faults in the document. Van Buren felt worse when he learned that three days after the rejection of his nomination McLane had suggested that Van Buren take a seat in the Senate instead of running for Vice President. McLane not only made the suggestion to Cambreleng and Flagg, but went so far as to tell Jackson that Van Buren would endanger the "success and safety of the whole party." Van Buren recalled later that the reports caused him much "pain and mortification."[33]

At this crucial point on February 20, Van Buren wrote a clever letter to Jackson. The New Yorker brushed off the idea of returning at once to join the Senate because people would say that he just wanted to be on hand for the vice presidential nomination in May. He would remain abroad until after the convention, leaving his political future up to his "friends," with the understanding that he had a "strong repugnance" for returning to the Senate. At the same time Van Buren reminded Jackson that Federalists had ruined good Republicans Aaron Burr, DeWitt Clinton, Henry Clay, and John C. Calhoun. The unwritten corollary was that the Federalist McLane could hurt good Republicans Jackson and Van Buren. Without saying so Van Buren was asking for Jackson's help and was warning him about McLane.[34]

To make sure there was no misunderstanding Van Buren told the Regency that he would accept the nomination for Vice President. To renew his ties with New York he sent long letters to various groups that had protested his rejection, and to strengthen his ties with the

[32] Munroe, *Louis McLane*, pp. 302-316.

[33] Jackson replied to McLane that Van Buren had such "common sense and good judgment" that he should decide his own future. Cambreleng to MVB, Jan. 28, 1832, Lewis, "Notes," *Autobiography*, pp. 502-503, 589; Jackson to MVB, Dec. 6, 1831, Jackson, *Correspondence*, IV, 379; McLane to MVB, Dec. 14, 1831, James A. Hamilton to MVB, Dec. 23, 1831, MVB to Cambreleng, Jan. 19, Feb. 4, 1832, VBP; *Autobiography*, pp. 531, 581; Charles Dayan to Flagg, Jan. 29, 1832, Flagg Papers; Poinsett to Dr. Joseph Johnson, Feb. 4, 1832, Joel R. Poinsett Papers, in the Henry D. Gilpin Papers, HSP.

[34] MVB to Jackson, Feb. 20-21, 1832, VBP.

White House Van Buren told Jackson that the opposition had really meant to attack the President when it accused Van Buren of partisanship in the instructions to McLane. Van Buren, producing a typically convoluted argument, assured Jackson that he did not think that the President's popularity had declined, but offered to run for Vice President in order to give the people a chance to record a vote of confidence for Jackson. This was a bold move and only a highly skilled politician would have made it.[35]

With business out of the way, Van Buren decided to make the most of his last months abroad by taking a tour of the Continent. After a short stay in Paris, he left for Cologne and Holland, where he investigated his family background. As usual John caused his father anxiety. Since John was enjoying himself in Naples when news of the rejection arrived in London, his father had to send out a series of letters and despatches to bring the two together. They sailed for New York in early June.[36]

By extending his stay abroad Van Buren avoided the Democratic convention. In the weeks before the convention the carefully laid plans to make Van Buren Vice President showed signs of going awry. First a state convention in Pennsylvania nominated William Wilkins for Vice President, then Duff Green spread the rumor that Jackson's informal advisers in the Kitchen Cabinet were preparing to shift from Van Buren to Richard Mentor Johnson. At first Lewis, who was masterminding Van Buren's nomination, did not believe the talk, but two days before the convention he was shocked to learn that John Overton, William T. Barry and John H. Eaton might not stick with Van Buren. When Overton suggested Senator Samuel Smith for Vice President, Lewis smelled a plot because Smith was a friend of McLane. But McLane in May was not as influential as McLane in February. As the campaign against the Bank of the United States heated up in the spring, McLane's stock with Jackson had begun to fall. Lewis took care of Eaton by sending him a stiff letter warning that he had better back

[35] MVB to Jackson, Mar. 6, Mar. 9, Mar. 13, 1832, MVB to Marcy, Mar. 14, 1832, MVB to Abraham Bloodgood and others, Feb. 24, 1832, VBP.

[36] MVB to John Van Buren, Feb. 23, 1832, April 8-9, April 10, 1832, MVB to Jackson, Mar. 13, 1832, VBP; Irving, *Life and Letters of Washington Irving*, II, 233-234; MVB to Livingston, Feb. 14, April 1, 1832, State Department, Diplomatic Despatches, Great Britain, XXXVIII; Palmerston to MVB, Feb. 13, 1832, Robert Chester to MVB, Mar. 21, 1832, Foreign Service Posts of the Department of State: Great Britain, Notes Received from the British Government, 1 (1829-1832), 219-220, 237, National Archives; Cooper to William C. Rives, April 9, 1832, Cooper, *Letters and Journals*, II, 242-243.

Van Buren or be *"prepared to quarrel with the General."* Eaton promptly gave in, sending back word that Van Buren would be selected.[37]

The Democratic convention served to pull the party together after the purge of Calhoun and the divisive congressional debates over the tariff and the Bank. To force the party to unite behind Jackson and Van Buren, the delegates adopted the rule that both the presidential and the vice presidential candidate of the party be nominated by a two-thirds vote. The rule remained in effect for a century. Despite a flurry of support for Johnson, Wilkins and Philip P. Barbour, Van Buren was nominated with 260 of 326 votes. With so much disagreement over the issues, party managers were wise enough not to adopt a platform, and the convention broke up after only two days.[38]

Van Buren's career as minister to England, which began so tranquilly in the "quietude of a midsummer Ocean," ended on a far more strident note.

[37] Lewis, "Notes," Major Eaton to Lewis, May 21, 1832, *Autobiography*, pp. 587-591; Green to R. K. Crallé, April 30, 1832, Frederick W. Moore, ed., "Calhoun as Seen by His Political Friends: Letters of Duff Green, Dixon H. Lewis, Richard K. Crallé during the Period from 1831 to 1848," Southern History Association, *Publications*, 7 (1903), 273; Parton, *Jackson*, III, 421; Munroe, *Louis McLane*, pp. 317-339.

[38] Samuel R. Gammon, Jr., *The Presidential Campaign of 1832* (Baltimore, 1922), pp. 100-101; Munroe, *Louis McLane*, p. 330; *Richmond Enquirer*, May 29, 1832; Washington *Globe*, June 7, 1832.

· 8 ·

THE BANK AND THE TARIFF

Shortly after midnight on July 5, 1832, the packet ship *New York* docked at Staten Island, bringing Martin Van Buren back from England. Awaiting him was a warm letter from Jackson discussing the Bank of the United States and other issues, and urging Van Buren to come as quickly as possible to Washington. Hearing that the cholera epidemic had spread from London to New York and not being one to tempt fate, Van Buren refused the offer of a public reception and left promptly for Washington.[1]

As soon as he arrived on the evening of July 7, Van Buren went to the White House, just as he had three years before, when he had first reported for duty at night. Van Buren recalled that Jackson looked like a "spectre," but was still the "hero in spirit." Holding Van Buren's hand and speaking without "passion or bluster," the President said, "the bank, Mr. Van Buren is trying to kill me, *but I will kill it!*" The New Yorker's arrival came at a dramatic political moment: the bill to recharter the Bank of the United States had passed Congress on July 3 and would be vetoed on July 10; the new tariff bill would pass on July 14, and Congress would adjourn two days later to await the election in the fall. Thanks to his interlude in England Van Buren had escaped the battles over the Bank and tariff, but now that he was back he would have to take a position.[2]

Even though Van Buren was out of the country during the debate over the Bank, contemporaries and historians have frequently blamed him and other members of the Regency for the Bank War. Congressman Erastus Root, who had turned against Van Buren and was no longer in the Regency, charged that that organization had attacked the Bank in order to protect Thomas Olcott's Mechanics' and Farmers' Bank in Albany against competition from branches of the Bank of the United States. On the basis of this and other flimsy evidence the historian Bray Hammond accused Van Buren of starting a war between Wall Street and Chestnut Street in order to "end Philadelphia's rivalry

[1] Allan Nevins, ed., *The Diary of Philip Hone 1828-1851* (New York, 1936), pp. 69-70; Jackson to MVB, June 14, 1832, Eldad Holmes to MVB, c. July 6, 1832, VBP; *Argus*, July 7, July 30, 1832; *Autobiography*, p. 510; Jackson, *Correspondence*, IV, 448.

[2] *Autobiography*, p. 625; W. Creighton to Nicholas Biddle, July 10, 1832, Biddle, *Correspondence*, p. 193.

of New York as a financial center."[3] Hammond's interpretation is hardly convincing. Some members of the Regency, particularly bankers such as Olcott and Benjamin Knower, were opposed to the Bank of the United States, and the Regency arranged to have resolutions against the Bank passed in the legislature in 1831 and 1832; the *Albany Argus* attacked the Bank, and almost every New York Jacksonian in the Congress voted against recharter. But in attacking the Bank, the Regency was trying to help banking in Albany not on Wall Street. Friends of the Regency in New York City such as Walter Bowne, Charles Livingston and Saul Alley opposed the resolutions against the Bank. Another New York City friend of the Regency, Congressman Gulian Verplanck, voted for the recharter. President Nicholas Biddle of the the Bank had no difficulty getting memorials in favor of the Bank from New York, and there is no evidence to link Van Buren directly with the attack on the Bank, or with Jackson's veto.[4]

Soon after the veto, Van Buren returned to a New York that had changed greatly since he had left as a freshman senator in 1821. Washington Irving had noted the change when he arrived back from England a month or so before Van Buren; as he sailed into New York Bay after seventeen years abroad, Irving was "astonished to see . . . a teeming city extending itself over heights [that he] had left covered with groves and forests." He found it hard to describe his emotion when the "city itself rose to sight," with the sun "brightening up the spires and domes." Albany, thirteen hours away up the Hudson, had doubled its population in the past decade and was no longer isolated. By steamboat and stagecoach a traveler could leave Albany and be in North Carolina within four days. He could already board a railroad train for Schenectady and Saratoga. Almost 15,000 canal boats bearing wheat, flour, firewood, and lumber passed through Albany's water-

---

[3] *Register of Debates*, 22nd Congress, 1st session (1831-1832), 2040-2041, 2074-2075; *Argus*, Mar. 24, 1832; S. DeWitt Bloodgood to Nicholas Biddle, April 18, 1831, Nicholas Biddle Papers, LC, quoted in Wilburn, *Biddle's Bank*, p. 94; Hammond, *Banks and Politics*, pp. 351-356. Hammond also used a letter from Judge Francis Brooke to Henry Clay, claiming that Van Buren and Felix Grundy were engaged in a "plot" against the Bank when they happened to meet in Richmond in the fall of 1829. Both James Robertson, who was cashier of the Richmond branch, and Frank Otto Gatell have successfully refuted Brooke. J. Robertson to Biddle, Nov. 27, 1830, Biddle Papers, LC; Gatell, "Sober Second Thoughts."

[4] Wilburn, *Biddle's Bank*, pp. 20-30, 93-117; Gatell, "Sober Second Thoughts"; Bloodgood to Biddle, April 18, 1830, quoted in Wilburn, *Biddle's Bank*, pp. 100-102; *Argus*, June 25, 1830, April 15, 1831, Jan. 16, June 26, 1832; Rudolph Bunner to Gulian Verplanck, Dec. 20, 1830, Verplanck Papers, NYHS; James Webb to Van Buren, April 12, 1831, VBP.

ways every year. The number of buildings had multiplied: 1,500 structures had been added between 1825 and 1830, and passengers on the top deck of the steamboat knew they had reached Albany when they saw the sunlight reflected off the tin roofs of these new buildings.[5]

Van Buren entered this new world quietly at the end of July, settling down at Lebanon Springs to enjoy the waters and wait for the cholera to abate. He was so unusually inconspicuous that John A. Dix of the Regency, asked anxiously whether anyone had seen "the Magician," and Francis Granger of the opposition remarked hopefully that Van Buren was "passing from the public mind." In September he emerged for his western tour, stopping first at the party convention at Herkimer, then at Oswego to inspect his real estate, and finally at Lake Owasco to visit outgoing governor Enos T. Throop.[6]

At Herkimer that September the Democrats prepared for the November election by nominating William L. Marcy to run for governor against Granger, who was named by both the National Republicans and the Anti-Masons. When a local election in Albany went against the party in September, the editor of the *Globe*, Francis P. Blair, wrote Van Buren a panicky letter asking whether they had any chance to carry the state in November. Sniffing victory, Peter Porter told Henry Clay scornfully that Van Buren's opponents were glad that he was on the Democratic ticket. But the Democrats won Anti-Masonic votes by rallying behind Jackson's Bank veto. Van Buren helped by luring influential state senator Albert H. Tracy away from Anti-Masonry, and the Old Hero was hard to beat in the presidential column. As Thurlow Weed complained, the "huzza-strength" of the Jacksonians was too much to overcome. Marcy, Jackson, and Van Buren carried New York by comfortable margins, and nationally, Jackson was reelected President with fifty-five percent of the popular vote.[7]

[5] Tucker, *Progress of the United States*, p. 128; *Argus*, April 7, Aug. 25, 1829, July 5, 1830, July 11, July 26, 1832, June 21, July 12, 1833; John Fowler, *Journal of a Tour through the State of New York in the Year 1830 with Remarks on Agriculture in Those Parts Most Eligible for Settlers* (1831; reprint, New York, 1970), pp. 37-58; Andrew Bell, *Men and Things in America; Being the Experience of a Year's Residence in the United States, in a Series of Letters to a Friend* (London, 1838), pp. 58-64.

[6] Nathaniel P. Tallmadge to MVB, July 31, 1832, MVB to Samuel Phillips and others, c. Aug. 1, 1832, MVB to Cambreleng, Sept. 15, 1832, VBP; Dix to Azariah Flagg, Aug. 16, 1832, Flagg Papers; Granger to Thurlow Weed, Aug. 10, 1832, Granger Papers, LC; Weed, *Autobiography*, pp. 417-419.

[7] Hammond, *Political Parties*, II, 397-399, 417-424; McCarthy, *Antimasonic Party*, pp. 406-420; Blair to MVB, Sept. 30, 1832, Jackson to MVB, Oct. 23, 1832, MVB to Jackson, Aug. 29, 1832, VBP; Porter to Clay, Aug. 30, 1832, Henry Clay Papers, LC; Weed to Granger, Aug. 2, 1832, Thurlow Weed Papers, NYHS; Weed to Granger, Nov.

During and after the campaign Van Buren began to resist Louis McLane and his efforts to turn the administration away from Republicanism toward Federalism, amalgamation, and the Bank of the United States. In a letter to a committee in North Carolina, later published as a campaign document, Van Buren spelled out Jeffersonian-Jacksonian doctrines designed for a party based on an alliance of North and South. As usual he straddled the tariff issue, but came down hard against a national debt, federal internal improvements and the Bank. When Edward Livingston asked to be relieved as Secretary of State, McLane began to maneuver for the position, and to keep party unity Jackson sent McLane to New York in November to discuss the cabinet with Van Buren. McLane became angry when Van Buren agreed that McLane could be Secretary of State but only if Attorney General Roger B. Taney moved up to the Treasury Department and Benjamin Butler of the Regency replaced Taney as Attorney General. Van Buren finally had to accept a compromise whereby William J. Duane of Pennsylvania, would become Secretary of the Treasury and McLane would take over the State Department. The transfer did not actually take place until the following May. McLane lost ground when the administration decided to attack the Bank, but he regained some of it by advancing to the State Department.[8]

Another threat to Van Buren's concept of party came from Amos Kendall, who suggested in November that Van Buren form a northern party based on principles of national Union to oppose Calhoun and the doctrine of nullification. The proposal was similar to the plans advanced by Jabez Hammond and Lot Clark just before Van Buren decided to join Jackson's cabinet. John Overton of Tennessee, also told Van Buren that he should lead the nation to *"permanent Republicanism and Union."* Van Buren turned Kendall down with the argument that it would be dangerous to join "Nationals" Webster and Clay, but Kendall, who was unconvinced, replied that there were many "good republicans" among the opposition.[9]

Southern Democrats, however, were counting on Van Buren to stick by the old alliance with the South and go on working for a lower

11, 1832, Thurlow Weed Barnes, *Memoir of Thurlow Weed* (Boston, 1884), pp. 45-46; John A. Dix to Azariah Flagg, July 13, 1832, Flagg Papers; *Argus*, July 14, 1832, June 13, 1833; Duff Green to R. K. Crallé, Sept. 11, 1832, Moore, "Calhoun as Seen by His Political Friends," p. 281.

[8] *Niles' Register*, 43 (1832), 124-125; MVB to Joseph H. Bryan and others, Oct. 4, 1832, VBP; *Autobiography*, pp. 592-600; Munroe, *Louis McLane*, pp. 356-363. I cannot agree with Munroe that Van Buren did not consider McLane a threat.

[9] Kendall to MVB, Nov. 2, Nov. 10, 1832, Overton to MVB, Dec. 12, 1832; VBP.

tariff. They had been encouraged during the tariff debates the previous spring when the *Albany Argus* had recommended lower tariffs in order to gain southern support for Van Buren. Ned Croswell had warned Marcy at the time that Van Buren would lose the votes of several southern states if John C. Calhoun could identify him with the high tariff. According to Daniel Webster, New York was "willing to sell the tariff" in order to make Van Buren Vice President. The South was disappointed, therefore, when most New Yorkers voted for tariff protection, and Van Buren was besieged by Ritchie and other Southerners with requests that the tariff be settled on "just principles." Anxious to conciliate the South, Churchill C. Cambreleng announced in the fall that the New Yorkers were tempering their tariff views.[10]

The fight over the tariff dated back to 1828, when South Carolinians issued their *Exposition and Protest*, written secretly by Calhoun, attacking tariff protection and outlining the theory of nullification. In 1831, Calhoun published a defense of nullification in a letter from his estate at Fort Hill, South Carolina. By July 1832, General William Henry Harrison was so worried that he offered to leave his farm in Ohio and lead troops against the nullifiers, and in September Andrew Jackson ordered a squadron held ready at Norfolk. On November 24, the stage was set for a confrontation when a special convention in South Carolina nullified the tariff act and threatened to secede if the President resorted to force.[11]

At the opening of Congress in December, Jackson first held out the olive branch by suggesting in his annual message that protective tariffs be reduced. On the same day the *Globe*, underlining the point, also recommended lower tariffs. Within a week the President swung in the opposite direction. In his powerful proclamation calling nullification *"incompatible with the existence of the Union,"* in words that sounded more Federalist than Republican, Jackson demolished state rights by declaring that the federal Constitution was "not a league," but a

---

[10] *Argus*, May 3, July 2, July 19, 1832; Croswell to Marcy, April 9, 1832, Marcy Papers, LC; Webster to Jeremiah Mason, June 23, 1832, G. J. Clark, ed., *Memoir, Autobiography and Correspondence of Jeremiah Mason*, rev. ed. (Kansas City, 1917), p. 331; Ritchie to MVB, June 25, 1832, Peter V. Daniel to MVB, July 12, 1832, Richard E. Parker to MVB, Sept. 5, 1832, VBP; Cambreleng to Claiborne W. Gooch, Oct. 24, 1832, Gooch Family Papers, UVL.

[11] *Exposition and Protest Reported by the Special Committee of the House of Representatives* (Columbia, 1829); Calhoun, "Fort Hill Letter," July 31, 1831, Calhoun, *Works*, VI, 59ff.; W. Harrison to James Findlay, July 4, 1832, Isaac J. Cox, ed., "Selections from the Torrence Papers," *The Quarterly Publication of the Historical and Philosophical Society of Ohio*, 3 (1908), 76-77; Jackson to Woodbury, Sept. 11, 1832, Jackson, *Correspondence*, IV, 474-475, 483.

government operating "directly on the people individually." In strong language, the President called "a State veto" an "absurdity," and said that he would have to "use the influence [of a] father [over] his children" in order to "admonish" the citizens of South Carolina. Jackson had pinned Calhoun between an annual message based on the Old Republicanism of Thomas Ritchie and a proclamation based on the nationalism of Daniel Webster.[12]

But the President found that he could not end the crisis so easily because his party was divided over the proclamation. Some Democrats such as Congressman William F. Gordon of Virginia, disapproved of its Federalist tone, while Thomas Hart Benton and others applauded its vigor. In Massachusetts Charles Francis Adams remarked that the proclamation reminded him of his "father's style and turn of thought." Lacking firm control of Congress, it seemed that the administration might be forced to turn to former Federalists such as Adams' father and Daniel Webster for help. As Christmas approached, Congress drifted, waiting for leaders including Webster and Clay to arrive. Cambreleng reported to Van Buren that since Congress was likely to "do nothing" to ease the situation, "somebody [might] get hanged and some killed."[13]

The nullification crisis put Van Buren in a difficult position. For years he had cultivated southern friends in order to revive the old North-South Republican party. He was on such good terms with South Carolinians Robert Y. Hayne and James Hamilton, Jr., that it was difficult for him to think of them as nullifiers. After the Jefferson Day dinner in 1830, Van Buren had assured Jackson that he had seen the "valedictory" of nullification because the "honest and good men" of the South were about to "return to better feelings and sounder principles." When the crisis came, Van Buren was less willing than Jackson to take a strong nationalist position. Van Buren preferred to go easy on South Carolina to prevent the nullifiers from becoming martyrs and to keep Virginia from coming to Calhoun's rescue.[14]

Since Van Buren was far away in Albany awaiting his inauguration as Vice President, he was able to duck the crisis in Washington, but he could not avoid a series of letters from Jackson, who eagerly sought Van Buren's opinion. When Jackson issued his proclamation, he had

---

[12] Richardson, *Messages and Papers*, II, 591-606; Washington *Globe*, Dec. 4, Dec. 7, 1832.

[13] Benton, *Thirty Years' View*, I, 308; Benton to MVB, Dec. 16, 1832, Cambreleng to MVB, Dec. 10-18, Dec. 18, 1832, VBP; Gordon to Thomas W. Gilmer, Dec. 11, 1832, *William and Mary College Quarterly Historical Magazine*, 21 (1912-1913), 1; Adams, *Diary*, IV, 419-420; Claude M. Fuess, *Daniel Webster* (Boston, 1930), I, 390.

[14] MVB to Jackson, July 25, 1830, Jackson, *Correspondence*, IV, 166.

sent a copy to Van Buren, asking for his views. Privately Van Buren disliked the proclamation because it asserted doctrines that were "heresies [to the] republican faith," and because he was afraid it might scare Republicans into supporting nullification. He blamed the proclamation on members of the cabinet such as McLane, who had been "brought up in the federal school." But Van Buren was not so outspoken in his reply. He merely called Jackson's attention to an issue of the *Albany Argus* in which Edwin Croswell supported both the proclamation and the doctrine of state rights. Worried about the reaction of Old Republicans in Virginia and Georgia, Croswell called for tariff reductions to prove that the administration was not trying to burden the South. The times, Van Buren concluded suavely, needed "great discretion & good temper."[15]

Before receiving this answer, Jackson sent a second letter saying that he planned to lay "the *acts of treason*" before Congress and "ask for the power to call upon volunteers" to crush "this wicked faction in its bud." "It will not do *now*, he said, "to temporise, or falter." Although Van Buren agreed that there must be no "faltering," he gently pointed out that just passing bills might not constitute treason or justify violent measures, and that perhaps the President should have "omitted . . . some of the doctrinal points of the proclamation" because they might bring him into conflict with Virginia. To keep the Old Dominion on the side of the Union the President should allow the Virginians "*honest* differences of opinion." "You will say," Van Buren wrote in a friendly tone, that "I am on my old track—caution—caution," but considering their "respective temperaments," there was no better way for him to serve Jackson.[16]

Too excited over the issue to wait for Van Buren's replies, Jackson dashed off two more letters to Albany, complaining that the Virginians were showing sympathy for South Carolina. The ideas of the nullifiers in Virginia reminded Jackson of "a bag of sand with both ends opened." "The moment the least pressure" was exerted, "the sand flow[ed] out at each end." Sounding more and more like John Marshall, Jackson denounced the "absurdity of the virginia [sic] doctrine" and said that "the preservation of the union [was] the supreme law." Once again Van Buren replied that the President should do as little as possible.[17]

Finally, after receiving the three letters from Van Buren, Jackson

[15] *Autobiography*, pp. 543-548; Jackson to MVB, Dec. 10, 1832, MVB to Jackson, Dec. 22, 1832, VBP; *Argus*, Dec. 15, Dec. 20, Dec. 21, Dec. 22, Dec. 27, 1832.

[16] Jackson to MVB, Dec. 15, 1832, MVB to Jackson, Dec. 27, 1832, Jackson, *Correspondence*, IV, 500-501, 506-508.

[17] Jackson to MVB, Dec. 23, Dec. 25, 1832, *ibid.*, 504-506; MVB to Jackson, Jan. 9, 1833, VBP.

wrote that he could not "sit by" with "arms folded" and let loyal Americans be "imprisoned, fined, and perhaps hung." He was prepared to arrest those committing treason even though they might be protected by "12,000 bayonets." "The union," he wrote, *shall* be preserved." Jackson did, however, promise to act with "forbearance."[18]

Meanwhile Van Buren's friends were trying to lower the tariff. Aided by Churchill C. Cambreleng and Virginian William S. Archer, Gulian Verplanck, chairman of the House Ways and Means Committee, reported a bill on December 27 that cut rates in half. The bill encountered rough sledding partly because Van Buren's enemies did not care to have him get the credit for ending the crisis. Samuel Swartwout, for example, said maliciously that he was glad Verplanck had presented the bill instead of a "certain little gentleman politician." Webster and Clay hoped to scuttle Verplanck's bill in order to make their own "peace offering" to the South in the Senate. Divided as usual over the tariff, the New York delegation could not be counted on. Silas Wright, Marcy's replacement in the Senate, tried to help by spreading the word that Van Buren wanted the tariff lowered in order to save the Union, but as amendment after amendment slowed the bill, Michael Hoffman of the Regency reported that "nothing but a Miracle" could save it.[19]

Disturbed by the ambivalence of the New Yorkers, Jackson asked Van Buren on January 25, 1833, why his legislature was "silent at this eventful crisis." The President warned that Van Buren's enemies were spreading "dark innuendoes" that he was holding New York back to await developments in Virginia, and for once in their generally warm relationship, Jackson vented his wrath on Van Buren; the President was so angry that he repeated the word "innuendoes" and three times made the point that the New Yorkers had not taken a stand. Van Buren had the good sense not to reply to the outburst, and put off writing to Jackson about the crisis for almost a month.[20]

Van Buren showed his usual caution during the crisis because he wanted to protect himself while helping to save the Union. He was afraid that the opposition would use the proclamation to divide Jackson and himself; he was also aware that his own supporters were

[18] Jackson to MVB, Jan. 13, 1833, Jackson, *Correspondence*, V, 2-4.

[19] Cambreleng to MVB, Dec. 18, Dec. 29, 1832, Mahlon Dickerson to MVB, Jan. 11, 1833, Wright to MVB, Jan. 13, 1833, Wright to Flagg, Jan. 14, 1833, McLane to MVB, Jan. 23, 1833, VBP; Thomas Cooper to Verplanck, Jan. 15, 1833, Rudolph Bunner to Verplanck, Jan. 3, 1833, Swartwout to Verplanck, Jan. 4, 1833, Verplanck Papers, NYHS; Benton, *Thirty Years' View*, I, 308-309; July, *Verplanck*, pp. 156-157.

[20] Jackson to MVB, Jan. 25, 1833, Jackson, *Correspondence*, V, 12-13.

divided. A Southerner—William H. Haywood of North Carolina—worried about the "despotism" of the proclamation, while a nationalist—James A. Hamilton—was urging Van Buren to back the President. When Van Buren returned one strong letter from Hamilton unopened, the latter understood that Van Buren feared "offending the dominant party in Virginia."[21]

Many New Yorkers were not willing to lower the tariff in order to satisfy the South. In his inaugural address, Governor Marcy insisted that a measure of tariff protection be retained. At a meeting to discuss the crisis on January 24, a committee dominated by protectionists, including Benjamin Knower, brought in a report instructing New York congressmen to oppose any change in rates. John A. Dix, who spoke for Van Buren, immediately proposed a substitute stating that tariffs should not operate at the expense of any section. At that point, according to Benjamin Butler, "bullies" in the audience drowned out efforts by Dix and Butler to speak in favor of the substitute. Butler also reported that even though two-thirds of the crowd voted for Dix's motion, the chair ruled otherwise. Butler, Dix, Croswell, and Azariah Flagg then led over half of those present to another room where Butler gave a patriotic address and resolutions were passed in favor of a compromise over the tariff. After the meetings the *Argus* praised Butler for working to save the Union, while the opposition *American* accused him of trying to help Van Buren with the South. Both were correct.[22]

The split within the Regency over an economic issue was not new. Knower and his group had wanted high tariffs for manufactures in 1828 and had backed their Albany banks against the Bank of the United States. Marcy and Croswell leaned toward Knower, with Flagg, Wright and Butler on the other side, and Van Buren trying to balance all interests. The fight over the tariff opened a rift between Van Buren and Marcy that gradually widened. When told that the party would have to choose between the tariff and Van Buren, Marcy supposedly put the tariff first. During the next few months he annoyed Wright and Van Buren by sending letters to New York congressmen urging

[21] *Autobiography*, pp. 547-549; Elias Kane to MVB, Jan. 2, 1833, Michael Hoffman to MVB, Jan. 4, 1833, William H. Haywood to MVB, Jan. 10, 1833, VBP; Hoffman to Azariah Flagg, Jan. 14, Jan. 15, 1833, Flagg-Hoffman Letters; Hamilton, *Reminiscences*, pp. 250-251.

[22] Peter Porter to Henry Clay, Jan. 21, 1833, Henry Clay Papers, LC. For the inaugural, see Lincoln, *Messages*, III, 420-429. Van Buren told Wright to support tariff reduction. MVB to Wright, Feb. 4, 1833, VBP. See also Flagg to Wright, Jan. 24, 1833, Flagg-Wright Correspondence; *Argus*, Jan. 26, Jan. 27, Jan. 28, Jan. 29, Jan. 31, 1833; New York *American*, Jan. 5, Jan. 26, Jan. 28, Feb. 1, 1833.

them to vote for protection. Flagg became so angry that he accused the "wool speculators [and] sordid manufacturers" of selling "the country for a bag of wool." The split became even more evident in early February when the party selected protectionist Nathaniel P. Tallmadge over Butler to replace Charles Dudley in the Senate.[23]

Two days before the caucus selected Tallmadge and shortly after Van Buren received the irate letter from Jackson, a report and a set of resolutions, both written by Van Buren, were brought in to the legislature. Though seeking a compromise that would satisfy both state-righters and the President, Van Buren sided with the former. The United States, he said, was not "one consolidated body," but a group of states. Although he was against nullification and would make "sacrifices" for the Union, he felt it his "duty" to reflect the principles of the states and suggest a reduction in the tariff. The report called Jackson a "good republican" for "believing in the people" and trying to stop "the increase in monopolies." The resolves made the same general points, repudiating nullification but calling for a lower tariff.[24]

Since the report and the resolutions ignored the proclamation, they were hardly the sort of defense that Jackson wanted. Congressman Mark Alexander of Virginia, observed that Van Buren had taken "his cue from Ritchie, by denouncing nullification, while . . . profess[ing] great devotion to the principles of —98," and the New York *American* correctly noted that the documents were aimed at improving Van Buren's "future prospects in the South." Van Buren had put himself and his party ahead of Jackson. As soon as the legislature had acted, Van Buren sent a letter to the President, boasting about the strength of the vote rather than the contents of the documents.[25]

In Washington Van Buren's efforts to see that New York got credit for lowering the tariff collapsed when Clay brought his own tariff reduction bill to the Senate on February 12. Calhoun, who had been elected United States Senator and had resigned as Vice President in December, decided to cooperate with Clay as a means of opposing

[23] Spencer, *Victor and the Spoils*, pp. 76-77; Marcy to MVB, Feb. 13, 1833, Wright to MVB, Jan. 29, 1833, VBP; Wright to Flagg, Jan. 20, 1833, Flagg to Wright, Jan. 21, Feb. 13, 1833, Flagg-Wright Correspondence; Hammond, *Political Parties*, II, 432-433.

[24] *Autobiography*, pp. 550-553; *State Papers on Nullification . . . Collected and Published by Order of the General Court of Massachusetts* (Boston, 1834), pp. 158-159; *Argus*, Jan. 29, Feb. 1, 1833.

[25] Alexander to Nathaniel Beverley Tucker, Feb. 6, 1833, "Correspondence of Judge N. B. Tucker," *William and Mary College Quarterly Historical Magazine*, 12 (1903-1904), 85; *Argus*, Feb. 18, Feb. 26, 1833; New York *American*, Feb. 4, 1833; MVB to Jackson, Feb. 25, 1833, Jackson, *Correspondence*, V, 19-21.

Jackson and ending the crisis. As a result Calhoun quickly supported the measure even though the rates were higher than those in Verplanck's bill, and since the new bill appealed to many New York congressmen who did not want drastic cuts in the tariff, the Regency made little effort to oppose it. Eight of eleven New York Jacksonian congressmen voted to replace Verplanck's bill with Clay's. Even the *Argus* came out in favor of Clay's bill. The historic compromise passed both Houses and was signed by the President before Congress adjourned on March 3. Since South Carolina had long before suspended nullification, the crisis was over.[26]

Van Buren had chosen to risk his relationship with Jackson over this issue partly because he wanted to maintain a party based on republican principles and an alliance of North and South, and partly because he needed southern support for 1836. Now that he had been elected Vice President, he had enough confidence in his position and his relationship with the President to be willing to arouse Jackson's wrath, with the result that he helped to restrain the headstrong President and made Jacksonian Democracy a little less nationalistic than Jackson would have liked.

But the Democratic party was never the same. As party discipline broke down during the crisis, the administration turned more and more to Daniel Webster, who approved of the President's proclamation. When someone was needed to speak in support of the Force bill, which gave the President the authority to use the military against South Carolina, the administration sent a carriage to bring Webster to the Senate floor. Jackson wrote delightedly of the New Englander's speech, that Webster had handled Calhoun, who opposed the bill, like "a child." Talk spread about a Union party uniting Jackson and Webster. Joel Poinsett, who led the Unionists in South Carolina, called for such a party in March; and in April Louis McLane noted that Roger B. Taney had developed a "recent affection for Webster." But Van Buren did not join the chorus, for he realized that a Union party would destroy not only the Democratic party as he knew it, but also his chances of becoming President. Instead of praising Webster for saving the Force bill, Van Buren criticized him for not backing a tariff compromise. Then newspapers that favored Van Buren began to attack Webster; Hill's *New-Hampshire Patriot* denied that Jackson wanted

[26] Rudolph Bunner to Flagg, Feb. 3, 1833, Wright to Flagg, Feb. 19, 1833, Flagg Papers; Benton, *Thirty Years' View*, I, 309-319; *Argus*, Mar. 4, 1833; New York *American*, Mar. 6, 1833.

Webster's support, and the *Globe* tried to smear Webster for cooperating with the nullifiers.[27]

On his arrival in Washington to be sworn in as Vice President, Van Buren ran into still another problem—the question of the removal of the deposits from the Bank of the United States. When Jackson had asked what he should say about the Bank in his 1832 annual message, Van Buren had suggested saying nothing. Ignoring the advice, the President asked Congress to determine whether the deposits were safe in the Bank. The question was referred to the House Ways and Means Committee, which decided after a short investigation that the deposits were in good hands. Despite this decision, the President sent the cabinet a memorandum in March outlining his views on the Bank and requesting theirs. Jackson stated that he had decided to do without a national bank after the charter expired. Meanwhile he favored putting future federal money into state banks and letting the amount in the Bank of the United States gradually dwindle. The policy came to be known imprecisely as removal of the deposits. Although Jackson got little support for deposit removal from the cabinet, Kendall and Blair of the Kitchen Cabinet favored going ahead.[28]

The two Westerners were disappointed to learn that Van Buren was opposed to removing the deposits. Kendall in particular became so indignant that his conference with Van Buren ended abruptly. But as usual Van Buren was willing to compromise when he realized that the President meant business. In a brief, ambiguous note to Jackson, the Vice President left the impression that he favored experimenting with deposit removal to see if it worked. In a second conversation with Kendall, Van Buren conceded that he had never "thought seriously" about the subject before, and was now ready to admit that he was

[27] Norman D. Brown, *Daniel Webster and the Politics of Availability* (Athens, 1969), especially pp. 33-37. Arthur B. Darling is less convinced than Brown that a rapprochement was likely. Darling, *Political Changes in Massachusetts*, pp. 148n-149n. Charles W. March, *Reminiscences of Congress* (New York, 1850), pp. 199, 224-243; Benton, *Thirty Years' View*, I, 333; Jackson to Joel Poinsett, Feb. 17, 1833, Poinsett to Jackson, Mar. 2, 1833, Jackson, *Correspondence*, V, 18; Tyler to John Floyd, Jan. 22, 1833, *William and Mary College Quarterly Historical Magazine*, 21 (1912-1913), 11; McLane to MVB, April 25, 1833, VBP; *Autobiography*, pp. 554-561, 672; *Cincinnati Gazette*, Mar. 8, 1833. *New-Hampshire Patriot*, Feb. 18, 1833; *Argus*, Mar. 8, 1833; Washington *Globe*, April 23, 1833.

[28] Parton, *Jackson*, III, 500-508; Richardson, *Messages and Papers*, II, 600; Munroe, *Louis McLane*, pp. 375-380, 384-388; Kendall, *Autobiography*, p. 375; Jackson to members of the cabinet, Mar. 19, 1833, Taney to Jackson, April 29, 1833, McLane to Jackson, May 20, 1833, Jackson, *Correspondence*, V, 32-41, 67-71, 75-101.

wrong and Kendall right. But he still seemed to be opposed to deposit removal as he left the Capital in late April.[29]

Van Buren could not escape the Bank question by leaving Washington. On reaching Philadelphia he received a letter from one of the New York Safety Fund commissioners recommending three banks in New York City to receive federal deposits if they were removed. Van Buren sent the letter on to the White House with a note of his own saying that he had already proposed an association of banks in New York City, and Jackson replied promptly that the note contained "much good sense." When Van Buren reached New York City, he was greeted by wild talk that the administration was about to establish a federal bank there with a capital of $50,000,000.[30]

Early in June 1833, the question of the deposits became associated with Andrew Jackson's trip to the Northeast. As he waited in New York City for Jackson's arrival, Van Buren made careful plans. He had a carriage built for the President, warned the committee in New York City not to ask too much of the Old Hero, and reminded Marcy to be on hand. Van Buren was prepared to discuss banking because Jackson had written ahead to say that he wanted to talk about the deposits when he reached New York. Secretary of State Louis McLane had also written a note on the same subject, which he planned to deliver in person to Van Buren. McLane wanted help from Van Buren in postponing the removal of the deposits until Congress had confirmed the appointment of new Secretary of the Treasury William J. Duane. At the same time Amos Kendall asked Van Buren to use his "great influence" with the President to get removal under way as soon as possible.[31]

Several incidents marred Jackson's arrival at Castle Garden island, New York City. On board a cutter in the harbor a gun exploded, tearing the hands off a gunner. As the presidential party rode across from the island to the Battery, the bridge gave way, throwing Secretary of War Lewis Cass, Andrew J. Donelson and others into the shallow water. Fortunately Jackson and Van Buren had already reached the

[29] Parton, *Jackson*, III, 504-506; Kendall, *Autobiography*, p. 376; MVB, Views on Removal of the Deposits, Mar. 1833, Jackson, *Correspondence*, V, 24-25; John G. Watmough to Nicholas Biddle, Mar. 23, 1833, Biddle, *Correspondence*, p. 202.

[30] C. Stebbins to MVB, April 17, 1833, MVB to Jackson, April 21, 1833, Jackson to MVB, April 25, 1833, VBP; *United States Telegraph*, Aug. 13, 1833; *Richmond Enquirer*, May 17, 1833.

[31] MVB to Jackson, May 2, May 16, 1833, Jackson to MVB, June 6, 1833, Kendall to MVB, June 9, 1833; VBP; MVB to Marcy, May 3, 1833, Van Buren Miscellaneous Papers, NYHS; New York *American*, May 1, 1833; McLane to MVB, June 4, 1833, *Autobiography*, p. 602; Munroe, *Louis McLane*, pp. 389-393.

shore, and no one was hurt. Then, on the way up Broadway, Jackson's horse reared, almost throwing its rider. On June 15 as Jackson and Van Buren boarded a steamboat for Connecticut, there was another scare when the burning wad from a cannon flew past the President's head.[32]

Although there were no more disasters, the rest of the trip became an ordeal for the aging President, who was already tired and ill. After countless receptions across Connecticut and Rhode Island, the party reached Massachusetts, where President Josiah Quincy of Harvard became the official guide. Quincy had rounded up several handsome horses so that Jackson and Van Buren could review the Boston Brigade in style, but unfortunately, Van Buren's horse behaved badly, backing the Vice President up against a wall. Jackson accepted an honorary degree from Harvard and visited the mill town of Lowell before moving north to Isaac Hill's Concord, New Hampshire. Hill outdid himself, putting Jackson through two parades, three receptions, two dinners, and three church services in forty-eight hours. The busy weekend proved too much for the old President, who decided suddenly to start back without completing his tour. By the Fourth of July, Jackson and Van Buren were back in Washington.[33]

Jackson's tour revived the old talk of a Union party. Even before he started north, newspapers like the *New-Hampshire Patriot* worried that the President's trip would lead to political amalgamation as Monroe's visit to New England in 1817 had done. Seba Smith, the author of the humorous letters of the imaginary Yankee Major Jack Downing, which poked fun at the administration, had a fictional Louis McLane and Edward Livingston tell Downing to treat Webster and other New England Federalists well. The real McLane predicted that an alliance between Jackson and Webster was "altogether probable," and Webster strengthened the rumors by taking a tour of his own to the West, where Democrats helped organize a dinner in Cincinnati and where Democrat Benjamin Tappan served as an escort. When the *Patriot* and the *Argus* stepped up their attacks on a Union party, the *Cincinnati*

---

[32] *Argus*, June 15, 1833; New York *American*, June 13, June 15, June 18, 1833; William L. Marcy, Diary, June 15, 1833, Marcy Papers, LC; Parton, *Jackson*, III, 489-491.

[33] Fletcher M. Green, "On Tour with President Andrew Jackson," *New England Quarterly*, 36 (1963), 209-228; John S. Bassett, "Notes on Jackson's Visit to New England, June, 1833," Massachusetts Historical Society, *Proceedings*, 56 (1922-1923), 243-260; Josiah Quincy, *Figures of the Past*, rev. ed. (Boston, 1911), pp. 298-313; Benjamin Brown French, Journal, 1 (July 20, 1833), Benjamin Brown French Papers, LC; *Argus*, June 22, July 6, July 10, 1833.

Gazette replied that as soon as Webster was mentioned for the presidency, he encountered the "blighting enmities" of Van Buren.[34]

The threat of a Union party made it easy for Jackson to get Van Buren to accept deposit removal when they talked about it in New York. Within a few days the *Argus* was supporting removal, and Van Buren later conceded that he "found the President so determined" that it was impossible to "oppose him." But there were still obstacles to be overcome. Duane threatened to resign if the deposits were removed, and the President and Vice President left for vacations at the Rip Raps and Saratoga at the end of July with the matter unsettled.[35]

The Bank War followed Van Buren to Saratoga. Before settling down, he received several letters from Jackson asking for "frank advice" about whether to remove the deposits at once or wait until January 1 as McLane and the cabinet preferred. Van Buren stalled, saying that he wanted to check with Silas Wright; then on August 11, he was called down to New York City to meet McLane, who persuaded him to recommend delay. The two men cornered Amos Kendall, who happened to be in the city lining up banks to receive the deposits, and brought him round temporarily to their point of view. On returning to Saratoga, Van Buren found a letter from Jackson with the rough draft of a statement on removing the deposits that he planned to present to the cabinet in September. A more ominous letter arrived a few days later, written because Jackson had heard hints that Van Buren was now opposed to removal, and, even worse, was "a friend to the Bank." "*This must be removed,*" warned Jackson, "*or it will do us both much harm.*"[36]

To buy time before answering the letters, Van Buren decided to

[34] *New-Hampshire Patriot*, May 5, July 15, July 20, 1833; Seba Smith, *My Thirty Years out of the Senate by Major Jack Downing* (New York, 1859), pp. 200-201; McLane to James Buchanan, June 20, 1833, George Ticknor Curtis, *Life of James Buchanan Fifteenth President of the United States* (New York, 1883), I, 191-192; William B. Lewis to James A. Hamilton, June 22, 1833, Hamilton, *Reminiscences*, pp. 258-259; *Cincinnati Gazette*, June 19, June 21, July 12, July 23, July 25, July 27, July 30, 1833; Barry to MVB, July 7, 1833, MVB to Jackson, July 22, 1833, VBP; *Argus*, July 9, July 12, 1833; Brown, *Webster and the Politics of Availability*, pp. 39-44; Washington *Globe*, Oct. 9, 1834; *Autobiography*, pp. 680-711.

[35] *Argus*, June 22, 1833; Jackson to Duane, June 26, July 17, July 22, July 23, 1833, Duane to Jackson, July 22, 1833, Jackson, *Correspondence*, V, 111-128, 131-146; Remini, *Jackson and the Bank War*, pp. 116-117; Kendall, *Autobiography*, pp. 601-603.

[36] Jackson to MVB; July 24, July 25, July 30, Aug. 12, Aug. 16, 1833, Kendall to Jackson, Aug. 11, Aug. 14, Jackson, *Correspondence*, V, 142-145, 150-159; MVB to Cambreleng, July 22, 1833, MVB to Jackson, July 29, 1833, VBP; Kendall, *Autobiography*, p. 383; Munroe, *Louis McLane*, pp. 398-400.

consult members of the Regency, who were scattered for the summer, Wright in Canton, New York, Flagg and Dix in Albany. On receiving a "summons from the Magician" to come to Saratoga, Wright confessed that he was "afraid [of] speculators," including Jesse Hoyt of the Regency, who hoped to profit from "instantaneous removal." When Wright came to Saratoga on August 18, he and Van Buren decided to postpone a decision until Wright had consulted others and Van Buren had made his customary western swing. On the canal boat between Oswego and Utica, Van Buren wrote a letter to Jackson explaining the delay. Wright finally reported on August 28 that the Regency was divided between those who wanted immediate removal and others, like himself, who preferred delay. Even then, almost forty days after Jackson had asked for an opinion, Van Buren could not give a decisive answer. After outlining three possible courses of action, he finally recommended waiting until January 1, but—noncommittal to the last—added that he was "not strenuous about it."[37]

Van Buren's evasive report failed to satisfy the President, who wrote back accusing him and Wright of siding with McLane. Convinced that their "republican Government" was at stake, Jackson sent word that he planned to act at once with Van Buren's support, and wanted his Vice President in Washington by October 1. Van Buren received the blunt letter in Kinderhook just as he and Washington Irving were setting forth on a tour of the old Dutch settlements along the Hudson. In his first reply Van Buren promised that he and Wright would "cheerfully acquiesce" if Jackson insisted on acting immediately, but said nothing about coming to Washington. Three days later he sent a second letter apologizing for "not notic[ing]" the order to report, but questioning whether he should comply. If he reported at once, he said, he would be playing "into the enemies' hands" because they would blame him and the "monied junto in N York" for removal. But if Jackson insisted, Van Buren agreed to come promptly and "share any portion [of Jackson's] responsibility." Van Buren, who had tarried in England and Albany to avoid battles over his nomination, the tariff and nullification, now wanted to hide along the Hudson until the Bank War was over.[38]

He succeeded. Jackson wrote that he was "well pleased" with Van

[37] Wright to Flagg, Aug. 8, Sept. 6, 1833, Flagg-Wright Correspondence; Wright to Erastus Corning, July 27, 1833, Silas Wright Papers, NYHS; MVB to Jackson, Aug. 19, Aug. 30, Sept. 4, 1833, Jackson, *Correspondence*, V, 159-160, 173, 179-182; Wright to MVB, Aug. 28, 1833, Jackson Papers, LC; Flagg to R. White, Aug. 11, 1833, Flagg Papers.
[38] MVB to Jackson, Sept. 11, Sept. 14, 1833, Jackson, *Correspondence*, V, 185-186.

Buren's "spirit," and then proceeded to act without waiting for his Vice President. When a cabinet meeting revealed that Attorney General Taney was the only member to support removal, the President went ahead on his own. On September 20, he announced that he planned to stop depositing funds in the Bank of the United States; three days later he replaced Secretary of the Treasury Duane with Taney, and on October 1, the day Van Buren was supposed to arrive, the government began to deposit its funds in state banks.[39]

Jackson acted independently, but he cared enough about Van Buren's opinion to send him eight letters describing the events between September 19 and October 5, letters in which Jackson portrayed himself as a courageous hero protecting the people against a host of enemies. In his version, he had presented an "ultimatum [to Duane in] a proper, calm, and dignified note," and dealt with McLane "kindly and firmly." After fighting off efforts to "alarm and deter" him, Jackson, though "indisposed" and a prey to "night-fevers," had done what his "God told [him was] right" and what "the Morals of the People" demanded. More than anything the letters reveal an insecure old man eager to win approval and sympathy from his subordinate.[40]

In his replies Van Buren promised all the support that was needed, reassuring Jackson that he would stay within "striking distance" in New York City, from which he could "communicate by letter every 24 hours." "All the Democrats," wrote the loyal Van Buren, were "enthusiastic in their support" of the President, and "public sentiment [was] strong" in his favor. Responding sympathetically to Jackson's illness, he wondered whether it stemmed from the "infernal hot coal fires" in his bedroom. Occasionally the Vice President slipped in political comments. He insisted that he and McLane differed fundamentally over the Bank, and suggested that McLane be allowed to resign. Still a staunch New Yorker, Van Buren hinted that Benjamin Butler would make a good Attorney General. In this series of letters Van Buren continued to play the role of the loyal subordinate.[41]

As the deposits were being removed, Van Buren did little to influence

[39] Jackson to MVB, Sept. 15, 1833, Jackson, *Correspondence*, V, 187. The story of deposit removal is told in Remini, *Jackson and the Bank War*, pp. 117-125; William J. Duane, *Narrative and Correspondence Concerning the Removal of the Deposits and Occurrences Connected Therewith* (Philadelphia, 1838); Jackson, *Correspondence*, V, 187-207; Bassett, *Jackson*, pp. 643-645.

[40] Jackson to MVB, Sept. 19, Sept. 22, Sept. 23, Sept. 26, Sept. 29, Oct. 15, 1833, VBP; Jackson to MVB, Sept. 24, Sept. 25, 1833, *Autobiography*, pp. 603-604.

[41] MVB to Jackson, Sept. 14, 1833, Jackson, *Correspondence*, V, 185-186; MVB to Jackson, Sept. 26, Sept. 28, Oct. 2, 1833, VBP; MVB to Jackson, Sept. 27, 1833, *Autobiography*, pp. 606-607.

the choice of the deposit banks. He did suggest that Jackson consult Thomas Olcott, but no deposits went to Albany during the first two years. The Mechanics' and Farmers' Bank in Albany finally became a deposit bank in 1835, but it never received funds on the scale of the banks in New York City. Recommendations from Van Buren certainly helped in the case of the Bank of America, the Mechanics' Bank, and the Manhattan Bank, but they were obvious choices to receive the deposits because of their size and because two of them were run by Jacksonians; Kendall had visited them when he came to New York in the summer to select deposit banks. But when Jackson asked Van Buren about a fourth bank for the city, the New Yorker made no recommendation.[42]

Van Buren played a larger role in rearranging the cabinet in 1833 and 1834 than he did in picking pet banks. His persistence was rewarded when he finally received permission to offer the post of Attorney General to Benjamin Butler. Since Butler preferred the world of law and scholarship to the political arena, Van Buren had to produce a convincing argument to lure his friend to Washington. As Attorney General, wrote Van Buren, Butler would gain the "national" standing that would enable him to make a large income—not as much as Webster, who made "tens of thousands," but an ample sum. To win over Butler's wife, who hated to leave home, Van Buren pointed out that Washington was but fifteen hours from New York City and a day and a night from Albany. He urged her to bring the family, since Louis McLane, Roger B. Taney, Levi Woodbury, and Lewis Cass each had "a household of little girls of the finest character." The Butlers succumbed. At about the same time, John Forsyth of Georgia, replaced McLane at the State Department, and when the Senate refused to confirm Taney's appointment Van Buren's friend Levi Woodbury moved from the Navy to the Treasury, opening the way for still another friend, Mahlon Dickerson, at Navy. Because of McLane's removal and the new appointments it was now Van Buren's cabinet.[43]

[42] Newbold and Others to MVB, Feb. 20, 1833, Jackson Papers, LC; C. Stebbins to MVB, April 17, 1833, MVB to Jackson, April 21, Sept. 28, 1833, Jackson to MVB, Sept. 26, 1833, VBP; MVB to Jackson, Sept. 4, Sept. 14, 1833, Jackson, *Correspondence*, V, 181-182, 187; Frank Otto Gatell, "Spoils of the Bank War: Political Bias in the Selection of Pet Banks," *American Historical Review*, 70 (Oct. 1964), 43-50; Kendall, *Autobiography*, pp. 380-381; Remini, *Jackson and the Bank War*, p. 117; *Argus*, Sept. 23, Oct. 3, 1833.

[43] MVB to Butler, Nov. 8, 1833, Butler, *Retrospect of Forty Years*, pp. 39-42; Munroe, *Louis McLane*, pp. 364, 422; Jackson to MVB, Nov. 16, 1833, Forsyth to MVB, Nov. 29, 1833, VBP; Irving to MVB, Oct. 5, 1833, *Autobiography*, pp. 610-611; Cole, *Jacksonian Democracy in New Hampshire*, p. 130.

While the cabinet was being reshuffled, Van Buren still had to contend with Daniel Webster. Although Hill, McLane and others had predicted that Webster and Jackson would split over the Bank, hope for a Union party persisted even after the removal of the deposits. Webster was still praising the President and still cooperating with the administration. At the opening of Congress in December 1833, Webster cooperated by voting to postpone selection of committees until Van Buren, who had not yet arrived, took his seat as President of the Senate. Within the administration Senator Felix Grundy of Tennessee, was trying to convince Jackson that he should unite with Webster in order to get his support on the issue of the deposits. If the Union party were to become a reality, Webster, not Van Buren, would be likely to succeed Jackson in 1837.[44]

When Van Buren arrived in the Capital, he had an immediate confrontation with Grundy and Jackson. First Grundy outlined his arguments for uniting with Webster, and then Van Buren replied with an emotional appeal to old party ties. He argued that if they followed Grundy's plan the public would desert them because people would assume that the party had made a deal with Webster. If Jackson, the "fearless opponent" of the Bank joined Webster, who had been one of the Bank's "most unscrupulous supporters," then there would be "confusion [and] alarm" among the President's friends. Van Buren said that he was prepared for a difficult struggle, but would "enter upon it in the full conviction that the people . . . would carry [the party] triumphantly thro' the crisis." Jackson was moved—he was never really committed to the idea of a Union party—and advised Grundy to drop the matter. The possibility of a Union party vanished.[45]

Van Buren faced a difficult task in presiding over the Senate because of the financial panic that swept the country in the fall and early winter. Henry Clay introduced resolutions censuring Jackson for removing the deposits and was particularly abusive on March 7, when he let loose a savage attack on the administration, demanding that Van Buren carry the message to the President. Comparing Jackson with "the worst of the Roman emperors," Clay insisted that Van Buren tell the President "of the tears of helpless widows . . . and of unclad and unfed orphans." Throughout the harangue Van Buren looked on "respect-

[44] Fuess, *Webster*, II, 4; *Argus*, Oct. 4, 1833; Curtis, *James Buchanan*, I, 191-192; John W. Forney, *Anecdotes of Public Men* (New York, 1873), p. 134; *Autobiography*, pp. 673-677, 703; Brown, *Webster and the Politics of Availability*, pp. 35, 66; Duff Green to Nicholas Biddle, Biddle Papers, LC.

[45] Jackson to MVB, Oct. 5, 1833, VBP; *Autobiography*, pp. 672, 676-679, 688-689, 699, 711.

251

fully, and even innocently . . . as if treasuring up every word." Then suddenly when it was over he rose from his seat and walked menacingly toward Clay. Anticipating a fight, the spectators gasped, but Van Buren simply stopped in front of Clay and asked for a "pinch of his fine maccoboy snuff." Clay was deflated and Van Buren returned calmly to his seat. Episodes like this prompted Webster's friend Charles March to concede that Van Buren was a "model presiding officer," who balanced "proper firmness" with a "quiet indifference [to] personal assault." "Master of his own passions," March reported, Van Buren was able to listen attentively, concealing his own thoughts, "unruffled in the midst of excitement."[46]

Deflating Clay was easier than coping with the panic and the conflicting advice that was coming from New York. Part of the Regency, including Olcott, Marcy, and now Butler, wanted the government to help New York bankers either by establishing a national bank in New York City, or by lending money to banks in the state. These Regency men were alarmed at the failure of Marcy's father-in-law, Benjamin Knower, who had been forced to suspend payment on his many debts. But other New York Democrats were hostile to banking in any form. Silas Wright opposed a national bank, rejected the idea of lending money to state banks, and said that Knower was nothing but a "gambler," who deserved what had happened to him. Both John A. Dix and Theodore Sedgwick, the editor of the New York *Evening Post*, wrote strong letters denouncing banking.[47]

[46] James A. Hamilton to MVB, Dec. 30, 1833, Jan. 18, 1834, VBP; Remini, *Jackson and the Bank War*, pp. 126-129, 135-139; Benton, *Thirty Years' View*, I, 402-406, 415-423; *Autobiography*, pp. 721-723, 771; Parton, *Jackson*, III, 545-546; March, *Reminiscences of Congress*, pp. 275-276.

[47] For the probanking side: Thomas Suffern to MVB, Jan. 12, 1834, Myndert Van Schaick to MVB, Jan. 28, Jan. 31, Mar. 12, Mar. 13, 1834, James King to MVB, Mar. 14, 1834, James A. Hamilton to MVB, Dec. 30, 1833, Jan. 18, 1834, James W. Webb to MVB, Jan. 22, 1834, Hoyt to MVB, Jan. 29, 1834, Charles Stebbins to MVB, Mar. 1, 1834, MVB to Marcy, Mar. 31, 1834, MVB to Gorham Worth, Feb. 28, 1834, VBP; Butler to Olcott, Jan. 27, Feb. 1, Mar. 20, 1834, Thomas Olcott Papers, CUL; Charles Butler to Wright, Feb. 10, 1834, Charles Butler to———, Charles Butler Papers, LC; Remini, *Jackson and the Bank War*, pp. 131-134; Spencer, *Victor and the Spoils*, pp. 79-80; *Argus*, Feb. 4, 1834; Wright to Flagg, Feb. 7, 1834, Flagg-Wright Correspondence.

For the antibanking side: *Argus*, Feb. 5, Mar. 31, 1834; Kendall, *Autobiography*, pp. 406-407; Wright to Flagg, Feb. 7, Feb. 21, Mar. 25, 1834, Dix to Wright, Feb. 11, 1834, Flagg-Wright Correspondence; Garraty, *Wright*, pp. 109-120; Sedgwick to MVB, Mar. 11, Dec. 20, 1834, George Strong to MVB, Dec. 23, 1834, VBP; Walter Hugins, *Jacksonian Democracy and the Working Class: a Study of the New York Workingmen's Movement* (Stanford, 1960), pp. 31-39.

Faced with this sort of pressure Van Buren stuck to his usual middle-of-the-road position. Too republican to side with the bankers' lobby, he dismissed the plan for a national bank, and under his guidance the *Albany Argus* published regular attacks on the Bank of the United States during the crisis. Van Buren reacted coldly to Knower, especially when an attempt was made to have Van Buren underwrite the hat maker's debts, but he was pragmatic enough to support the plan to lend money to the banks and conservative enough to resist the radical ideas of Dix and Sedgwick.[48]

The congressional battle over the causes of the panic and the removal of the deposits continued throughout the winter. As the opposition bore down on the administration, Van Buren turned to Silas Wright for help. Although the modest Wright was reluctant to seek the limelight, he finally agreed to speak, and gave two solid speeches attacking the Bank and defending the President on January 30 and March 20. But despite these efforts Clay's resolutions of censure passed the Senate on March 28, 1834. When Jackson responded with a strongly worded statement of "Protest," Van Buren prevailed on him to follow it with a softer message in order not to drive people out of the party. By the time Congress adjourned on June 30, any hopes of rechartering the Bank of the United States had vanished, and the Bank War was over.[49]

In trying to understand Jacksonian Democracy and the party battles of Jackson's first five years in office, historians have focused their attention on heroes and issues, such as Jackson and the spoils system, Calhoun and nullification, and Jackson, Nicholas Biddle and the Bank War.[50] But by examining the life of Van Buren and attempting to capture the outlook of a politician who was a better representative of the new class than most of his contemporaries, the historian can learn more than he could learn from heroes or issues. Van Buren, after all, had done much to create the new political system that Americans had embraced, and the new-style politician with whom most Americans could identify. Furthermore, in the first half of the nineteenth century Van Buren represented an important and pervasive American type—

[48] MVB to Thomas Suffern, Mar. 15, 1834, MVB to Gorham Worth, Feb. 20, 1834, MVB to Marcy, Mar. 31, 1834, VBP; MVB to Enos T. Throop, Feb. 16, 1834, Van Buren-Throop Letters, NYSL; *Argus*, Feb. 1834, Mar. 14, 1834.

[49] *Autobiography*, pp. 728-730; Kendall, *Autobiography*, pp. 406-407; Remini, *Jackson and the Bank War*, pp. 141-143, 165-166; Benton, *Thirty Years' View*, I, 423; Richardson, *Messages and Papers*, III, 69-94; R. H. Wilde to Gulian Verplanck, May 1, 1834, Verplanck Papers, NYHS.

[50] A historian with a novel look at these years has emphasized great men and issues: Major L. Wilson, " 'Liberty and Union': an Analysis of Three Concepts Involved in the Nullification Controversy," *Journal of Southern History*, 33 (Aug. 1967), 331-355.

the white, upwardly mobile Northerner, who began life on the farm but then turned to the new world of business. Southern slaveowners Calhoun, Clay and Jackson never quite understood the rise of business, while Northerners Adams and Webster were uncomfortable with the rising democratic movement that was changing politics. Van Buren was far more willing to temper his views and compromise than were any of his peers. If Jackson was the "Symbol for an Age," then Van Buren was the representative man of the age.[51]

The key to understanding the years after the War of 1812 and Jacksonian Democracy in particular, can be found in the lives of Americans like Van Buren who attempted to reconcile Old Republican traditions to the shifting demands of an urbanizing and modernizing society. As issues arose Van Buren compromised in ways that millions of Americans could understand, temporizing and compromising being part of the American way of life. In shaping Jacksonian democracy Van Buren succeeded in compromising by reconciling Jackson's nationalism with the state-rights tradition, the Old Republican ideology with the new partisanship of the Albany Regency, old ideals with new necessities emerging from new issues and a new generation. On economic and constitutional issues he remained as republican as he could, but he often gave ground and sacrificed ideology in order to preserve social and political gains.

In his career as a senator Van Buren was better able than Jackson to find a middle path between old and new, between nationalism and Old Republicanism. Van Buren's conciliatory toast at the Jefferson Day dinner was more in tune with the times than Jackson's nationalistic challenge and Calhoun's state-rights retort. Having annoyed some Old Republicans by his moderation that evening, Van Buren quickly balanced the books by favoring the Maysville Road veto, but even then he propitiated the Northwest by conceding that roads and canals were essential to the nation's future. By 1830, he had demonstrated that he was a Jeffersonian who understood the needs not only of northern and southern farmers but of businessmen in the North as well.

In the battles over the Bank and the tariff during the next few years Van Buren made his greatest concessions to economic and political necessity. Like most Americans he had trouble adjusting to the sudden increase in banks and paper money. Carefully weighing his banking allies in New York against his antibanking friends, he opposed the Bank of the United States, but whenever possible sought to modify

---

[51] For Jackson as symbol, see Ward, *Andrew Jackson*.

Jackson's attacks on the Bank. When the crisis arose over nullification, Van Buren tried to walk a tightrope between Jackson's belligerent Unionist stand and the equally bellicose state-rights position of many Virginians and South Carolinians. Like most Americans Van Buren was a trimmer. In a rapidly changing society he sprinted from point to point as modern politicians do, and in so doing he shaped Jacksonian Democracy and pulled divergent factions into a successful Democratic Party.

JACKSONIAN DEMOCRACY IN THE
ELECTION OF 1836

The end of the Bank War in 1834 saw the main outlines of Jacksonian Democracy firmly established. The administration would provide funds for internal improvements that benefited the nation, but not for local projects such as the Maysville Road. After some initial disagreement Jacksonians had united to destroy the Bank of the United States. Although Jacksonians would limit the power of the central government, they would not brook the nullification advocated by John C. Calhoun. Despite Andrew Jackson's desire for Texas, the Democratic party had restrained its expansionism in order to avoid an internal fight over slavery. Jacksonian Democracy was a nice blend of Old Republican state rights and old-fashioned American nationalism, a compromise between reverence for the past and adjustment to the present, a program well designed to unite the planters of the South and the plain Republicans of the North.

But the nation that the Jacksonians controlled in the 1830s was dramatically different from the one Andrew Jackson and Martin Van Buren had known in the early 1820s when they first began to develop Jacksonian Democracy. Changes were taking place, to be sure, in the 1820s, but change had become revolution by the mid-1830s as westward migration reshaped the patterns of American population. Between 1820 and 1840 the population of the eastern states rose slowly from 7.2 million to 10.7 million, while the population of the West increased rapidly from 2.2 million to 6.4 million. Michigan's population which was barely 55,000 in 1820, reached 476,000 twenty years later; Mississippi advanced from 75,000 to 376,000. By 1840, the western cities of New Orleans and Cincinnati had grown so large that they ranked third and sixth respectively in the United States.

These demographic changes were accompanied by equally significant changes in transportation. As New Orleans grew, the number of steamboats arriving there rose from 202 in 1820, to 1,958 in 1840. The age of the canal boat reached its high point in the 1830s as the miles of canals expanded from 1,277 in 1830, to 3,326 in 1840. Nowhere was the increase greater than in Ohio, where canals linking the Great Lakes and the Ohio River increased canal mileage in the state from 245 miles in 1830, to 744 miles in 1840. The completion of the first railroad in 1827 was the harbinger of another revolution: by 1840 railroad mileage equaled canal mileage in the United States. As a result of the changes, shipping time from New York City to Cincinnati dropped from seven weeks in 1820 to one week in 1850.

As America expanded, the products from her farms multiplied. The growth of the Southwest brought an increase in the number of bales of cotton produced from 335,000 in 1820, to 1,348,000 in 1840. The opening of new farms in the Northwest boosted corn and wheat production to 463,000,000 bushels by 1839. Large-scale agricultural exports—especially of cotton—helped limit the surplus of imports over exports, but even so the unfavorable balance of trade amounted to $140,000,000 between 1830 and 1837. Instead of demanding payment for this surplus, foreigners left most of it invested in American roads, canals and manufacturing establishments.

Encouraged by these liberal European investments, America enjoyed an unprecedented economic boom between 1830 and 1837. In the West federal land sales rose from 1,930,000 acres in 1830, to 12,565,000 acres in 1835. In the East the number of spindles in cotton manufacturing jumped from 220,000 in 1820, to 1,750,000 in 1835, and the value of all manufactured products reached almost half a billion dollars by 1840. To man the factories immigrants came from Europe, their numbers rising from 8,000 in 1820, to 84,000 in 1840. To finance the boom in land sales and the expansion of manufacturing, the number of banks in the United States rose from 307 in 1820, to 901 in 1840, while banking capital increased from $102,000,000 to $358,000,000. A good deal of this expansion took place in the West, and banking capital in Mississippi alone went from $3,000,000 in 1830, to $63,000,000 in 1839.[1]

The question facing Van Buren and his party in the 1830s was whether Jacksonian Democracy could cope with this large-scale economic transformation and the social shifts that followed. The Jacksonian program with its careful mixture of old and new had suited Americans well in the early stages of the great changes that were transforming America. Whether it could adjust to the social and economic revolution of the 1830s would depend upon Van Buren and those around him.

Before the congressional session of 1833-1834 ground to a close,

---

[1] *Statistical History of the United States*, pp. 13, 57, 239, 297, 302, 538, 623-625; Taylor, *Transportation Revolution*, pp. 79, 337, 443; Douglass C. North and Robert Paul Thomas, eds., *The Growth of the American Economy to 1860* (New York, 1968), p. 200; Reginald C. McGrane, *The Panic of 1837: Some Financial Problems of the Jacksonian Era* (Chicago, 1924; reprint, 1965), p. 25.

the presidential campaign of 1836 had already begun. At the start of the session Willie Mangum of North Carolina, warned that a drive to make Van Buren President would be underway that winter, and that every state legislature would become the "theatre of active intrigues." In February he complained that "the discipline of the Albany school" already held Maine, New Hampshire, New York, Ohio, and Pennsylvania "in chains." Henry Clay was just as concerned. When Van Buren offered to bet a suit of clothes on the election in New York City in the spring, Clay retorted angrily that if the people backed the administration in that election, they were likely to choose Van Buren and his "system of intrigue and corruption" in 1836. When the Democrats lost the New York City election, Clay directed a sarcastic speech at Van Buren, calling him responsible for the loss.[2]

The Van Buren who was preparing to run for the White House had changed in ways that made him look more dignified than before—more like a President. As his hair thinned and he grew bald, his forehead broadened, giving him a statesmanlike appearance. As the blond hair turned to white, he looked less romantic and more distinguished. He began to dress more formally—less like a dandy and more like a President. Years of good living had added inches to his waistline, and since he still carried himself erectly, the added girth gave him a solid, stately appearance.

But he was still as friendly and gregarious as ever on the campaign trail and in his personal life; he was surrounded by so many friends and relatives that John Quincy Adams compared him with "the Sosie of Molière's Amphitryon," who was "l'ami de tout le monde." Women were still attracted to him. He still entertained lavishly and Daniel Webster remarked—wistfully perhaps—that as Vice President, Van Buren lived as well as he had when he was Secretary of State. Still unfailingly cautious, he never cashed in on the land boom that was pushing up the value of house lots in upstate New York, though by selling the family property in Oswego he could have done so. It was this sort of caution that, while it may have kept him from making bad political mistakes, also tended to prevent him from making bold decisions.[3]

---

[2] Willie Mangum to David L. Swain, Dec. 22, 1833, Mangum to Duncan Cameron, Feb. 7, 1834, Henry T. Shanks, ed., *The Papers of Willie Person Mangum*, 5 vols. (Raleigh, 1950-1956), II, 51-52, 74; James Love to John J. Crittenden, May 27, 1834, John J. Crittenden Papers, LC; *Niles' Register*, 46 (1834), 126; Clay, *Private Correspondence*, p. 383.

[3] Adams, *Memoirs*, IX, 276; Mrs. Cambreleng to Mrs. Rives, June 27, 1836, Rives Papers, LC; Webster to Mrs. Daniel Webster, Feb. 9, 1836, Daniel Webster, *The Writ-*

Van Buren was too busy with politics in 1834 to spend much time worrying about land values. The bitter battles over the removal of the deposits in the winter of 1834 had marked the end of the Bank War and had also ushered in a new political era. The intensity of the party battles under Jackson had meant that National Republicans, Anti-Masons, former Federalists, and Democrats who opposed Jackson over nullification and the Bank were all drawn into the Whig party. Henry Clay helped to pull these groups together in April with his resolutions of censure against the President. Clay hoped to unite the new party behind his own nationalist program, but the Whig party was more of a negative, anti-Jacksonian federation than a unified party. In the Northeast the name "Whig" was bestowed on an uneasy alliance of old National Republicans such as Adams and Webster, and young Anti-Masons such as William Henry Seward of New York, and Thaddeus Stevens of Pennsylvania. In the South it meant dissident state-rights Democrats led by Calhoun and John Tyler, and nationalists led by Clay. But divided or not, the Whigs posed a serious obstacle to Van Buren in the election of 1836.

In 1834 Van Buren was faced with plenty of obstacles in his own party. Although Francis P. Blair claimed that the Democrats could count on a united majority of 147 votes out of a total of 260 in the House of Representatives, Blair's editorial rival Hezekiah Niles of *Niles' Register* was more accurate in his analysis. He listed no less than six political groups in the House. Three of these groups—the anti-Jackson party, the nullifying party and the Anti-Masonic party—held about 113 seats in the House, and constituted the basis of the Whig party. Niles insisted correctly that the 147 Jacksonian seats were divided among three groups: "The Jackson party, proper; the Jackson-Van Buren party; the Jackson-anti-Van Buren party." It was this division within the Democratic party that complicated voting in the House and stood in the way of Van Buren's nomination for President in 1836.[4]

The Democratic setback in the New York City election in the spring

---

ings and Speeches of Daniel Webster (Boston, 1903), XVI, 268; John Fairfield to Mrs. John Fairfield, Jan. 24, 1836, Arthur G. Staples, ed., *The Letters of John Fairfield* (Lewiston, 1922), pp. 81-83; Hone, *Diary*, p. 523; Adolphe Fourier de Bacourt, *Souvenirs of a Diplomat: Private Letters from America during the Administrations of Presidents Van Buren, Harrison, and Tyler* (New York, 1885), p. 66. Van Buren had earlier sold some property in New York City only to see the land go up forty percent in value shortly after the sale. MVB to Smith Van Buren, Jan. 5, 1835, MVB to Cambreleng, May 10, 1835, George McWhorter to MVB, Nov. 1, 1835, Joel Turrill to MVB, Nov. 6, 1835, VBP; Adams, *Memoirs*, IX, 236-237.

[4] *Niles' Register*, 45 (1833), 228.

of 1834 encouraged Whigs to hope that Seward could unseat Governor William L. Marcy in the fall. Young Whig Millard Fillmore reported that the majority of his constituents in Buffalo were opposed to Van Buren, and Thurlow Weed scoffed that the "jaded" Regency had gone to Washington "to get away from troubles at home." As a result of the Bank War dozens of "apostates" including Gulian Verplanck, Ogden Hoffman, Erastus Root, and Jesse Buel had deserted the Democratic party. But after traveling through western New York late in the summer of 1834, Van Buren was able to reassure Andrew Jackson that the state was safe. When Marcy squeezed by Seward in November, Van Buren told Jackson happily that the Democrats had even carried the "old Federal & Manor County" of Albany.[5]

With New York temporarily secure Van Buren was able to concentrate on Pennsylvania and Virginia. Van Buren had never been a favorite in Pennsylvania, and in 1832 had not been able to win the state's electoral votes for Vice President. To strengthen his position in the Keystone State Van Buren depended on United States Attorney Henry D. Gilpin, Speaker of the House James Thompson, and philanthropist Roberts Vaux. Van Buren also sought the backing of the shoemakers of Pennsylvania by sending them a flattering letter praising resolutions they had just published as having "true spirit." After reading a newspaper statement that Van Buren had stopped in Pennsylvania for his health on his way home in 1834, William B. Lewis, who knew what the Magician was up to, wrote tongue-in-cheek that he thought Van Buren had been in good health when he left Washington.[6]

Van Buren faced an even more difficult situation in Virginia, where the Bank War and the proclamation to South Carolina had cost the Democratic party the support of Tyler, Littleton Tazewell and Benjamin Leigh. When Tazewell was elected governor and Leigh senator early in 1834, the power of the Richmond Junto, which had long

[5] Mushkat, *Tammany*, pp. 154-157; Hugins, *Jacksonian Democracy and the Working Class*, pp. 30-35; Hammond, *Political Parties*, II, 441-442; Hutchins, *Civil List*, p. 151; Fillmore to John McLean, Dec. 9, 1833, Frank H. Severance, ed., "Millard Fillmore Papers," II, *Publications of the Buffalo Historical Society*, 11 (1907), 152; Weed to Granger, June 9, 1834, Weed Papers, NYHS; *Argus*, Sept. 30, Nov. 20, 1834, Feb. 11, 1835, Thomas Cooper to Gulian Verplanck, July 1834, Verplanck Papers, NYHS; MVB to Jackson, Oct. 2, Oct. 13, Oct. 18, Nov. 5, 1834, VBP.

[6] Charles M. Snyder, *The Jacksonian Heritage: Pennsylvania Politics 1833-1848* (Harrisburg, 1958), pp. 17, 24-30, 32-34, 50-57; McCarthy, *Antimasonic Party*, pp. 431-432, 444-450; MVB to the Cordwainers of Pennsylvania, Feb. 15, 1834, Thompson to MVB, Mar. 6, 1834, Gilpin to MVB, July 4, Aug. 31, 1834, April 5, 1835, Vaux to MVB, Sept. 29, Oct. 9, Dec. 6, 1834, Jan. 24, April 27, 1835, Lewis to MVB, July 19, 1834, VBP.

backed Van Buren, was seriously challenged. The leading Van Buren men in the state were Thomas Ritchie, Claiborne W. Gooch and William C. Rives. The administration considered Rives particularly important because he had supported deposit removal, finally resigning from the Senate over the issue in 1834. Rives's failure to win reelection later in the year convinced one observer that the Old Dominion was two-to-one against Van Buren.[7]

As Van Buren courted Virginia, he came under intensive scrutiny and was subjected to a series of charges. It was said that he had not supported the War of 1812, that he had opposed slavery in Missouri, and that he had favored federal internal improvements. After years of trying to please the South Van Buren was so infuriated by these accusations that in a letter to Judith Rives he burst out in frustration: "God knows I have suffered enough for my Southern partialities. Since I was a boy I have been stigmatized as the apologist of Southern institutions, & now forsooth you good people will have it . . . that I am an abolitionist." He added that he hoped a letter from Benjamin Butler to the *Richmond Enquirer* would end the attacks. Within a few days, however, William C. Rives replied that Van Buren would have to put up with the "cross-examination" because it was essential "to keep Virginia as the *Fulcrum* of the South in harmonious relations" with the administration. Van Buren decided to stay out of Virginia in 1834 and early 1835 because he was afraid that a visit would only weaken his chances.[8]

South of Virginia, Willie Mangum in North Carolina and Hugh L. White in Tennessee led such a persistent movement against Van Buren that Daniel Webster began to believe that Van Buren could not carry the South, and his vulnerability was confirmed in the spring of 1834 when Congressman John Bell of Tennessee, who also opposed Van Buren, defeated fellow Tennessean James K. Polk for speaker of the United States House of Representatives. The Nashville Junto was badly divided. Later that summer Jackson and Polk barely blocked a move at the Tennessee Democratic convention to nominate White for Pres-

[7] Gooch to MVB, Mar. 24, 1834, Rives to MVB, May 16, Oct. 14, Nov. 18, 1834, Richard E. Parker to MVB, Nov. 29, 1834, VBP; MVB to Rives, July 14, Oct. 23, MVB to Mrs. Rives, May 23, Dec. 12, 1834, Rives Papers, LC; G. Cooke to Edward Curtis, Oct. 5, 1834, G. Cooke Miscellaneous Papers, NYHS.

[8] Wright also wrote a letter defending Van Buren. Wright to Ritchie, Mar. 10, 1835, VBP. Butler's letter, which was sent to Hugh Garland, Mar. 1835, was published in MVB, *Abolition of Slavery*. See also Joseph Watkins to Wright, Jan. 29, 1835, Ritchie to Wright, Mar. 2, 1835, Peter V. Daniel to MVB, Mar. 9, 1835, Rives to MVB, April 10, 1835, VBP; MVB to Mrs. Rives, April 1, April 25, 1835, Rives Papers, LC.

ident. On his way back to Washington in the fall Jackson felt obliged to defend Van Buren against claims that two-thirds of the state assembly were against him.[9]

But armed with the support of Andrew Jackson, Van Buren was not to be denied. On learning that the Tennessee delegation in Congress had come out for White, the President angrily accused their "unprincipled leaders" of trying to "destroy" the administration. To make certain of the nomination for Van Buren Jackson started a campaign in the Washington *Globe*. Other Democrats joined in and after a swing through the West, Silas Wright reported that Van Buren's prospects looked good, especially in Ohio. In December Thomas Hart Benton declared for Van Buren and out in Illinois twenty-one-year-old Stephen A. Douglas had become one of his most enthusiastic supporters. As the convention approached, it became clear that Van Buren would win the nomination for President.[10]

There was far less certainty over the vice presidency. In order to balance the ticket, Jackson and others thought it important to run a Westerner, perhaps Congressman Richard Mentor Johnson of Kentucky, for the second spot. Johnson, a popular hero, who had supposedly killed Tecumseh in the War of 1812, had made no enemies in the Bank War and had made friends among eastern workers by opposing imprisonment for debt. But the Kentuckian was hated by slaveholders because he kept a mulatto mistress, who bore him two mulatto daughters. Chief Justice John Catron of the Tennessee supreme court complained that Johnson was "not only positively unpopular [but] affirmatively odious in Tennessee." Catron was shocked that Johnson's consort had "claimed equality" and that Johnson had tried to "force his daughter into society." No one believed, Catron declared,

[9] Arthur Charles Cole, *The Whig Party in the South* (Washington, D.C., 1914; reprint, 1962), p. 42; Mangum, *Papers*, II, 217-294, passim, especially p. 294; Webster to Jeremiah Mason, Feb. 1, 1835, Clark, *Memoir of Mason*, pp. 345-347; Sellers, *James K. Polk Jacksonian*, pp. 234-303; Polk to White, Sept. 2, 1834, Orville Bradley to White, Aug. 23, 1836, Nancy N. Scott, ed., *A Memoir of Hugh Lawson White* (Philadelphia, 1856), pp. 254, 302-303; Jackson to MVB, Sept. 14, 1834, VBP.

[10] Sellers, *James K. Polk Jacksonian*, pp. 256-262; Jackson to Alfred Balch, Feb. 16, 1835, Jackson to Joseph C. Guild, April 24, 1835, Jackson, *Correspondence*, V, 327-328, 338-341; Washington *Globe*, Jan. 5, Jan. 16, Jan. 24, Mar. 9, April 1, 1835; Wright to Azariah Flagg, Sept. 8, 1834, Flagg-Wright Correspondence; Benton to ———Davis, Dec. 16, 1834, William Conclin, Charles Cist and William L. Hatch to MVB, Nov. 3, 1834, John M. Goodenow to MVB, Nov. 26, 1834, VBP; E. Malcolm Carroll, *Origins of the Whig Party* (Durham, 1925; reprint, 1964), p. 133; Douglas to Julius N. Granger, April 25, 1835, Robert W. Johannsen, ed., *The Letters of Stephen A. Douglas* (Urbana, 1961), p. 14.

"that a lucky random shot, even if it did hit Tecumseh, qualifie[d] a man for Vice President." Virginians, who wanted a New York-Virginia ticket, started a drive to nominate William C. Rives in place of Johnson.[11]

The Democratic convention, which met in the Fourth Presbyterian Church in Baltimore on May 20, 1835, was ridiculed by the opposition as the "Van Buren Convention" or the "convention of officeholders." Over two-thirds of the six hundred and twenty-six delegates came from Maryland and the neighboring states of Virginia, New Jersey and Pennsylvania, while South Carolina, Alabama and Illinois were completely unrepresented. The convention was almost as unrepresentative as the caucus that had nominated Crawford in 1824. Since Tennessee also had no representatives, an unknown Tennessean named Edmund Rucker was dragooned into casting that state's votes (a process henceforth known as "to Ruckerize"). In short order the convention decided that two-thirds of the votes were needed for nomination and named Van Buren, who was unopposed, for President. But the convention split over the vice presidency when the Virginians insisted on Rives instead of Johnson. In order to secure two-thirds of the votes for Johnson the administration in desperation had to use the fifteen Tennessee votes, which were cast by Rucker.[12]

For many Virginians Johnson's nomination was the latest in a series of snubs by the Jackson administration. When the Virginians had helped establish the Democratic party in 1827, they thought they had revived the old New York-Virginia alliance, but Jackson shut them out of key positions. Now the alliance of the North and the West at the convention seemed to them to have scuttled the interests of the Old Dominion. Rives was especially angry because after risking his future by defending the administration, he had been bypassed for Vice President. Richard E. Parker warned Van Buren that he could never carry Virginia with Johnson as his running mate, and alarmed by the danger, Van Buren decided it was time for another of his southern trips. Driving his own carriage along difficult roads at night he paid a social-political call on Rives and his wife at Castle Hill. By the end of the year, emotions had cooled enough to reassure Van Buren that

[11] Catron to Jackson, Mar. 21, 1835, Blair to Jackson, May 19, 1835, Jackson, *Correspondence*, V, 330-332, 348-349; Wright to MVB, May 22, 1835, VBP.

[12] Edward Stanwood, *A History of the Presidency* (Boston, 1898), pp. 178-183; Joel H. Silbey, "Election of 1836," Arthur M. Schlesinger, Jr., Fred L. Israel and William P. Hansen, eds., *History of American Presidental Elections*, 4 vols. (New York, 1971), I, 584-585; Bowers, *Party Battles*, pp. 429-431; Sellers, *James K. Polk Jacksonian*, pp. 269-273.

the vice presidency was no longer seriously dividing the party in Virginia.[13]

As the presidential campaign unfolded, the character of the Democratic candidate became increasingly important. Starting in 1833 the opposition had sought to discredit Van Buren by portraying him as a sly fox. The humorists Seba Smith and Charles A. Davis contributed a great deal to this characterization through their letters of the fictional Major Jack Downing in which the quaint down-Mainer poked fun at Van Buren. In one of Davis' more amusing sequences "Gineral" Jackson asked Downing why Van Buren's slice of bread always landed butter side up when knocked out of his hand. Downing said it was because the Magician "butter[ed] both sides at once." According to the Major, Van Buren was a "plaguy cunnin . . . master hand at trippin folks who stand in his way." Others emphasized the metaphor of the sly fox. In the scurrilous biography of Van Buren supposedly written by frontier hero Davy Crockett before he died at the Alamo in 1836, Van Buren was described as "all slyness." During a Senate debate in 1836 Calhoun compared Jackson to a "lion or tiger," but found Van Buren more like "the fox and the weasel."[14]

Van Buren's critics contributed to the formation of an American stereotype when they condemned him as "only a politician." Crockett even claimed that Van Buren was not content merely to become a politician, but had "pushed it as a *trade*." According to the critics Van Buren was a "third rate man," a "master hand at managin things, and gittin all his folks into office," while his friends in the Regency were "a knot of cat-paced, sly-faced, cringing, artful, busy fellows." One cartoon entitled "Going the Whole Hog," showed officeholders under Van Buren as a litter of pigs.[15]

[13] Rives to MVB, June 2, 1835, Parker to MVB, June 18, Aug. 21, 1835, Hudson Garland to MVB, June 25, July 16, 1835, Richard Baptist to MVB, Sept. 2, 1835, VBP; MVB to Rives, Nov. 3, 1835, Rives Papers, LC; *Niles' Register*, 49 (1835), 228-229.

[14] Charles A. Davis, *Letters of J. Downing, Major, Downingville . . . to Mr. Dwight* (New York, 1834), pp. 60, 230; Jack Downing, *The Life of Andrew Jackson, President of the United States* (Philadelphia, 1834), p. 201; Crockett, *Van Buren*, pp. 43, 167; *Congressional Globe*, 24th Congress, 1st session (Feb. 17, 1836), 113.

[15] Davis, *Letters of J. Downing, Major*, p. 230; Crockett, *Van Buren*, p. 30; Francis Baylies to General Wool, Nov. 16, 1837, Rezneck, "Letters from a Mass. Federalist," pp. 269-270; "Report and Resolutions of Orange County, N. C. Whig Meeting," Feb. 24, 1836, J. G. de Roulhac Hamilton, ed., *The Papers of William Alexander Graham, 1825-1856* (Raleigh, 1957-1961), I, 411-412; *United States Telegraph*, Feb. 3, 1835, quoted in Erik M. Eriksson, "Official Newspaper Organs and the Presidential Election of 1836," *Tennessee Historical Magazine*, 9 (1925-1926), 122; *Argus*, Jan. 26, 1835; Frank Weitenkampf, "New York State in National Politics: Notes for a Cartoon Record," *The New-York Historical Society Quarterly*, 30 (1946), 78-79.

He was also pictured as an effeminate fop. In a devastating caricature Crockett described how Van Buren looked in the Senate "laced up in corsets, such as women in a town wear, and, if possible, tighter than the best of them. It would be difficult to say, from his personal appearance, whether he was man or woman, but for his large *red* and *gray* whiskers." "Aunt Matty," who rode in a fancy coach, was "the *perlitest* cretur amongst the wimmen" Davy had ever seen. In his novel *The Partisan Leader*, published in 1836, Nathaniel Beverley Tucker of Virginia, portrayed Van Buren as "tastily and even daintily dressed." On each foot he wore a "delicate slipper," while his hands were "fair, delicate, small, and richly jewelled." In nineteenth-century America, which gloried in masculinity and assigned women to the home as a separate sphere, the image of femininity hurt.[16]

As part of their attack Whigs kept insisting that Van Buren had accomplished nothing on his own, that he was entirely dependent on Andrew Jackson, who had hand-picked the New Yorker as his successor and was trying to force his dynasty on the nation. Even though Van Buren had not actually fallen into the water when the bridge from Castle Garden collapsed on Jackson's arrival in New York in 1833, Charles A. Davis in one of his Jack Downing stories painted a humorous and damaging picture of the Magician being pulled to safety holding on to the tail of Jackson's horse. On the basis of this scene countless cartoons appeared depicting the Vice President holding on to the horse's tail or on to Jackson's coattails. In another of Jack Downing's memorable scenes Van Buren was observed late at night trying on Jackson's coat and hat; they turned out to be much too big for the Magician.[17]

Once in office, warned the Whigs, Van Buren would be just as much of a dictator as Jackson; or, as Duff Green put it, Van Buren following Jackson would be like the Emperor Augustus succeeding Julius Caesar.

---

[16] Crockett, *Van Buren*, pp. 80-81; cartoon entitled "*Uncle Sam Sick with La Grippe*," William Murrell, *A History of American Graphic Humor* (New York, 1933), I, 133; *United States Telegraph*, Sept. 7, 1836, Eriksson, "Newspaper Organs and the Election of 1836," p. 123; Jack Downing, *Letters Written during the President's Tour "Down East," by Myself, Major Jack Downing of Downingville* (1833; reprint, Freeport, 1969), p. 23; Tucker, *Partisan Leader*, pp. 133-134.

[17] Downing, *Letters Written during the President's Tour*, pp. 35, 44-47; Murrell, *American Graphic Humor*, pp. 106-108, 120; cartoon entitled "Race over Uncle Sam's Course," Mar. 4, 1833, HSP; John Taylor to Whig Electors of Schenectady, Oct. 19, 1836, Taylor Papers; Henry Clay to————, June 22, 1835, Henry Clay Miscellaneous Papers, NYHS; Hugh Walker to Thomas Walker, Oct. 1, 1835, Walker Family Papers, UVL; *Resolutions and Address Adopted by the Antimasonic Members of the Legislature of Massachusetts* (Boston, 1836), p. 8, UVL.

In 1836, Green secretly published Tucker's *Partisan Leader* and distributed it in the South. Tucker, who followed the doctrines of John C. Calhoun, used the novel to warn readers that the election of Van Buren would so threaten the rights of the southern states that they would eventually secede. The novel was set in 1849, thirteen years later, with Van Buren in his fourth term as President and Virginia trying to decide whether to join the rest of the South, which had seceded from the Union. In one scene Tucker described Van Buren "in his palace," plotting to send troops to Virginia to force the "superfluous State Legislature, this absurd relic of imperium in imperio [to] abolish itself." After that, said Tucker, the people would "acquiesce in the union of all power in the hands of the Central Government."[18]

Democrats used an old theme—republicanism—and new ones—democracy and Unionism—to present a different Van Buren, a democratic republican who could unite the nation. Old Republican Claiborne W. Gooch attempted to convince his fellow Virginians that Van Buren came close to representing the high Jeffersonian principles that they believed in. Gooch was certain that Van Buren had the "cool judgement" and "practical wisdom" needed to "soothe the feelings of his countrymen." Congressman Charles J. Ingersoll of Pennsylvania, argued that Van Buren had the "democratic principles" necessary to lead the party; Jabez Hammond called Van Buren "the most *National Candidate* ever presented to the American people." In his campaign biography of Van Buren, Professor William M. Holland tried to develop the democratic theme while playing down Van Buren's reputation as a crafty politician. Holland described Van Buren as the "champion [of] democratic doctrines," who had risen from being the "son of a humble farmer . . . to the second office in the government." But these favorable descriptions often ended on a defensive note. Holland insisted, for example, that Van Buren had risen to power through "ability and virtue," not through "intrigue and accident," and Stephen A. Douglas attacked the Whigs for being "so extravagant in their abuse."[19]

[18] *United States Telegraph*, June 11, 1834, quoted in Eriksson, "Newspaper Organs and the Election of 1836," p. 122; Tucker, *Partisan Leader*, pp. 132, 151-156.

[19] Claiborne W. Gooch to William C. Rives, May 5, 1835, Rives Papers, LC; Charles J. Ingersoll, Speech at Bush Hill to Democrats of the third Congressional District, Pennsylvania, quoted in the Washington *Globe*, Aug. 10, 1835; Jabez Hammond to N. R. Packard or Edwin Croswell, July 19, 1835, VBP; Holland, *Van Buren*, pp. 355-356; Stephen A. Douglas to the Democratic Republicans of Illinois, Dec. 31, 1835, Douglas, *Letters*, p. 28.

Unable to compete with the colorful attacks on Van Buren, the Democrats stressed their party and their old leaders more than their new candidate during the campaign. The party statement, which was published in the summer of 1835 in place of an official platform, gave a preview of the Democratic campaign. Instead of praising the candidate, the statement mentioned Van Buren only once, while naming Jackson fifteen times, Jefferson ten, and Madison seven. Attention was lavished on the political organization and the term "party" appeared thirty-four times. Since Van Buren had been trying for years to recreate the old two-party system, it was entirely fitting that he should be the first presidential candidate to run in a campaign that downplayed the nominee and stressed the party.

In their party statement the Democrats ignored specific issues and relied upon the same combination of old and new themes that had served to defend Van Buren. Looking to the past, they used the word "Republican" twice as often as they used "Democratic," and claimed that, like the Republican party of 1800, their party in 1835 was based upon the old themes of state rights and strict construction of the Constitution. But the statement was not simply a nostalgic review of the past, for the Democrats addressed the new theme of democracy by using the word "people" no less than forty-eight times. They also called attention to several themes associated with Van Buren: the role of the party nominating convention, the use of the new party spirit as a means of protecting the Union, and the cooperation of North and South.

But like Van Buren the authors of the statement, including Silas Wright, refused to commit the party to specific positions on specific issues. Even though their declaration ran to over twenty pages, there was no reference to any of the issues facing the United States in the 1830s, no recognition that the United States was undergoing substantial economic change, no awareness of the financial boom. In addition the authors made no reference to internal improvements, no reference to the tariff, no acknowledgment of the new urbanization. Nor did they refer to the state banking system that had expanded so rapidly as a result of the boom and the removal of deposits from the Bank of the United States. They gave no sign that the Democratic party had any intention of modifying Jacksonian Democracy to meet the needs of the 1830s.[20]

Instead, the statement played upon the fears of the public by warning

[20] "Statement by the Democratic Republicans of the United States, Washington, July 31, 1835," Silbey, "Election of 1836," pp. 616-638.

267

of the dangers that would result from a Whig victory. According to the Democrats, their opponents, "whatever . . . their motives or professions"—whether they were "federal or National Republican, Whig or Tory, Abolitionist or Nullifyer"—were all "anti-republican in principle." They had endorsed the Alien and Sedition acts, nullification and the Bank of the United States. In a series of powerful paragraphs the statement attacked the Bank for its "bitter and vindictive war upon the President" and praised Andrew Jackson for "the manly and fearless manner" in which he had fought back. Now, the Bank War over, the opposition was planning to *"Divide and conquer"* by creating sectional animosities and sending the election to the Congress. Instead of supporting such dangerous men, the people should return to "the Republican fold of their fathers" and vote Democratic. It was a negative, aggressive message, not a response to the changing times.[21]

But by stressing their ability to unite a wide range of political points of view under the aegis of only a few fixed principles the Democrats were calling attention to the obvious divisions within the Whig organization. Unlike the Democrats the Whigs had not yet been able to unite disparate groups into a unified party. Old northern National Republicans such as Daniel Webster and John Quincy Adams could not cooperate with former southern Democrats John C. Calhoun, John Bell and Hugh L. White. Unable to hold a national convention, the Whig party was so dependent on state conventions that it entered the election with several candidates for President. After Whigs in Tennessee had nominated White, those in Ohio named John McLean, and others in Massachusetts put up Webster.[22]

Whigs were more willing than Democrats to seek Anti-Masonic support. As Webster traveled about the North campaigning for the presidency, he courted Anti-Masons both in Pennsylvania and in Massachusetts. But when Anti-Masons in New York and Boston sounded out Van Buren to see whether he was interested in the Anti-Masonic presidential nomination, Van Buren ignored the offers; he suspected that such support would hurt more than help. In New York the Anti-Masons had established ties with Whigs—in fact, many Whigs had once been Anti-Masons. Webster used the votes of Anti-Masons to win the nomination in Massachusetts and sought the support of the

[21] *Ibid.*, pp. 624, 638.

[22] Carroll, *Origins of Whig Party*, pp. 127-137; Darling, *Political Changes in Massachusetts*, pp. 119-127, 186; Sydney Nathans, *Daniel Webster and Jacksonian Democracy* (Baltimore, 1972), pp. 74-98; Hammond, *Political Parties*, II, 399, 442; Snyder, *Jacksonian Heritage*, pp. 65-67; McCarthy, *Antimasonic Party*, pp. 465-471; Sellers, *James K. Polk Jacksonian*, pp. 289-290; Silbey, "Election of 1836," pp. 584-585.

Anti-Masonic convention in Pennsylvania in the fall of 1835. The convention disappointed Webster and complicated the election by nominating William Henry Harrison for President.[23]

Van Buren found it more difficult to skirt the emerging issue of Roman Catholicism. In the 1830s, a steady increase in the immigration of Irish Catholic laborers to the Northeast led many native Americans to worry about the threat of Catholicism to Protestant America. The Irish drew attention to themselves in 1831 by attacking a parade of Orangemen from Northern Ireland in Philadelphia, and again in 1834 by staging a riot on the Chesapeake and Ohio Canal. Native Americans reacted against Catholicism in 1834 by burning down the Ursuline Convent in Charlestown, Massachusetts. Van Buren was drawn into the nativist controversy because of a letter he had sent to the Vatican in 1829 when he was Secretary of State, saying that Roman Catholics were always free to worship in the United States. Although the letter was not particularly liberal and could even have been considered patronizing, Whigs used it as evidence of Van Buren's involvement in a *"popish plot,"* and the next year the Native American Protective Association of New York demanded Van Buren's views on naturalization and foreign officeholders. When Cambreleng warned Van Buren that he was being accused of supporting Catholicism, Van Buren backed off and reminded people that he was not a Roman Catholic.[24]

A more important issue in the election campaign was the abolition of slavery. Since New York had over two hundred abolitionist societies and since Van Buren was on friendly terms with abolitionists such as Roberts Vaux of Pennsylvania, and Arthur and Lewis Tappan of New York, Southerners suspected Van Buren of opposing slavery himself. In 1834, he learned that he was being accused in Mississippi of planning to free the slaves by act of Congress, and a year later he was complaining to Judith Rives of being cross-examined on slavery by the Virginians. Davy Crockett exploited the issue by linking Van Buren

[23] Nathans, *Webster and Jacksonian Democracy*, pp. 83-98; Ward to Elam Tilden, Jan. 9, 1835, Tilden to MVB, Jan. 16, 1835, William Wright to Amos Kendall, Jan. 7, 1836, William Foster to Silas Wright, Feb. 12, 1836, VBP.

[24] David Grimsted, "Rioting in Its Jacksonian Setting," *American Historical Review*, 77 (April 1972), 390-392; Leonard L. Richards, *"Gentlemen of Property and Standing": Anti-Abolition Mobs in Jacksonian America* (New York, 1970), pp. 14, 18; Felix Cicognani to MVB, May 8, 1829, MVB to Cicognani, July 20, 1829, MVB to John A. Parker, Mar. 24, 1835, Parker to MVB, Mar. 24, 1835, Noah Wilson to MVB, June 8, 1835, MVB to Wilson, June 20, 1835, Cambreleng to MVB, June 24, 1835, Hiram Hunt to MVB, Feb. 22, 1836, Stafford Parker to MVB, Mar. 28, 1836, MVB to Parker, Mar. 4, 1836, J. M. Gemmill to MVB, May 6, 1836, VBP; *Niles' Register*, 46 (1834), 389.

to that antislavery "fanatic" Rufus King, while a circular in North Carolina accused Van Buren of having opposed slavery in Missouri. Willie Mangum received a letter calling Van Buren a "radical abolitionist."[25]

These charges were unfounded; as in earlier campaigns, Van Buren was too intent on keeping the support of the southern planters to say anything against slavery. To reassure his critics he denied that the federal government had the authority to interfere with slavery anywhere except in the District of Columbia, and added that the government should take no action there. He called slaveowners "sincere friends to the happiness of mankind," and accused abolitionists of being former Federalists trying to cause trouble. To make his position clear, he published a pamphlet opposing abolition and in so doing he reflected the views of his northern colleagues. New Hampshire Democrats Isaac Hill, Henry Hubbard, Franklin Pierce, and John Parker Hale all agreed that abolitionism was the work of "misguided fanatics." Farther south in New England, Orestes Brownson declared that the abolition movement endangered the Union, while John M. Niles labeled such efforts foolish, as foolish as agitation on "behalf of the poor Indians." Nowhere in the North were Jacksonians more outspoken than in New York, where Silas Wright called abolitionists "fanatics," and Van Buren's friend James K. Paulding denounced them as "enemies of the law of the land."[26]

Throughout the North the public was opposed to abolitionism. The presidential campaign of 1836 coincided with the worst period of antiabolitionist, racial riots during the entire ante-bellum era. Conditions were particularly serious in New York City, where there were three riots against the abolitionists between October 1833 and August 1834. The climax was reached during three days in July when rioters ran at will through the city destroying six churches and sixty other buildings. Whig merchant Philip Hone filled several pages of his diary

[25] Samuel Gwin to MVB, Mar. 20, 1834, VBP; Crockett, *Van Buren*, pp. 71, 94; "Circular to the Freemen of Orange County, North Carolina," Graham, *Papers*, I, 442-447; John Chavis to Mangum, April 4, 1836, *Papers*, II, 420.

[26] MVB to William Schley, Sept. 10, 1835, MVB to Junius Amis, Mar. 4, 1836, MVB to J. J. Lockhart, Sept. 18, 1836, VBP; *Argus*, July 31, Aug. 12, Aug. 13, Aug. 21, Aug. 24, Sept. 22, Sept. 25, Dec. 28, 1835, Jan. 6, 1836; MVB, *Abolition of Slavery*; Cole, *Jacksonian Democracy in New Hampshire*, pp. 176-177; Gerald S. Henig, "The Jacksonian Attitude Toward Abolitionism," *Tennessee Historical Quarterly*, 28 (Spring 1969), 42-49; *Niles' Register*, 52 (1837), 239; James K. Paulding, *Slavery in the United States* (New York, 1836), quoted in Henig, "Jacksonian Attitude Toward Abolitionism," p. 45; Paulding to Van Buren, Dec. 16, 1835, Ralph M. Aderman, ed., *Letters of James K. Paulding* (Madison, 1962), p. 172.

with descriptions of the terrifying events, which he blamed on "a set of fanatics who [were] determined to emancipate all the slaves." Hone correctly predicted that "the diabolical spirit [was not yet] quenched."[27]

But Southerners still distrusted Van Buren, especially when the *Oneida [N.Y.] Standard and Democrat* supported both Van Buren and abolition, and when the American Anti-Slavery Society centered in New York, began to distribute antislavery pamphlets in the South. The issue came to a head in August 1835, after citizens in Charleston, South Carolina, had seized the offending literature and burnt it in the streets. Van Buren's southern backers were so alarmed that they implored him to take some action against the abolitionists. Secretary of State John Forsyth complained that the authorities showed far too much "tolerance [toward] the wretches [who were] scattering fire-brands." He exhorted Van Buren to use his "magician's skill," and added, "the sooner you set the imps to work the better." Peter V. Daniel reported that Virginians were upset at abolitionist efforts "to bring down the whites to a level with the blacks," and asked Van Buren to stop the "bombs and torpedoes" that were being sent south from New York.[28]

Responding to the pressure, Van Buren and the Regency went to work at once. The postmaster of New York City announced that he would no longer forward any of the objectionable material and received the support of Postmaster General Kendall. Antiabolitionist meetings were held in New York and in Albany, where Governor Marcy presided and John A. Dix drew up resolutions denouncing abolitionists for "meddling." When abolitionists in Utica planned a statewide convention, local Democrats opposed the meeting because they believed it would hurt Van Buren's presidential chances. As the convention got under way on October 21, Jacksonian congressman Samuel Beardsley led a mob that broke up the meeting and destroyed the office of the *Oneida Standard and Democrat*. Silas Wright used the episode to show that New Yorkers were opposed to abolitionism, pointing out that after the riot, the legislature had overwhelmingly approved the appointment of Beardsley as attorney general. After consulting the Regency, Van Buren directed Marcy in December to include a strong statement against abolitionism in his annual message. Marcy responded in January by denouncing the "vi-

---

[27] Richards, *Gentlemen of Property and Standing*, pp. 113-122, 156-157; Hone, *Diary*, p. 134.

[28] Forsyth to MVB, Aug. 5, 1835, Butler, *Retrospect of Forty Years*, pp. 78-79; William Schley to MVB, Aug. 22, 1835, Daniel to MVB, Sept. 25, 1835, VBP.

sionary and pernicious . . . schemes" of the abolitionists because they could lead only to "violence."[29]

The battle over abolition continued in Washington, where Jackson asked Congress to "prohibit . . . the circulation . . . of incendiary publications." Anxious to stop the literature without increasing federal power, Calhoun proposed a bill in the Senate allowing postmasters to intercept any literature that state laws prohibited. When the bill came up for engrossment in the Senate, Calhoun tried to embarrass Van Buren by arranging for a tie vote, but the Vice President promptly voted yea, thus preventing Southerners from blaming him when the bill was finally defeated. Van Buren also supported a policy of referring antislavery petitions in the House to committee, on the grounds that such a policy would give "the abolition question . . . its quietus [and protect] the harmony of our happy Union." Later in the session Van Buren was asked to *"rally the Northern clans"* in favor of Congressman Henry L. Pinckney's resolution laying all antislavery petitions on the table. This so-called "gag rule" passed the House on May 18, 1836. To keep his southern support Van Buren was willing to restrict freedom of speech.[30]

During the abolitionist controversy Van Buren was also plagued by debates on banking. Within the ranks of Jacksonian Democrats, both in New York and in Washington, there had long been division between those who retained the Old Republican hostility to banking in general and other Democrats who were interested in local banking as a means of financing business growth. The war against the Bank of the United States had given these two groups the chance to unite against Biddle's "Monster." But when the Bank War was over, many hard-money Democrats were embarrassed to find that by defeating the Bank of the United States and transferring federal deposits to state banks they had inadvertently built up a new system of pet banks and paper bank

[29] *Argus*, Aug. 31, Sept. 3-5, Sept. 7, 1835, Jan. 5-6, 1836; Dix, *Memoirs*, I, 330-331; Richards, *Gentlemen of Property and Standing*, pp. 85-92; *Congressional Globe*, 24th Congress, 1st session (Jan. 19, 1836), 121; Henig, "Jacksonian Attitude Toward Abolitionism," pp. 48-49; Garraty, *Wright*, pp. 165-166; Marcy to MVB, Nov. 22, Dec. 3, 1835, MVB and Benjamin Butler to Marcy, Nov. 1835, Wright to Marcy, Dec. 18, 1835, VBP; Lincoln, *Messages*, III, 570-584; Spencer, *Victor and the Spoils*, pp. 103-104. Grimsted goes too far in suggesting that Van Buren ordered the Utica riot. Grimsted, "Rioting in Its Jacksonian Setting," p. 376n.

[30] Richardson, *Messages and Papers*, III, 175-176; Wiltse, *John C. Calhoun, Nullifier*, pp. 273-277; *Charleston Courier*, June 9, 1836; MVB to Nathaniel Macon, Feb. 13, 1836, William E. Dodd, "Nathaniel Macon Correspondence," *The John P. Branch Historical Papers of Randolph-Macon College*, 3 (June 1909), 93; George W. Owens to MVB, May 16, 1836, VBP.

notes. These so-called "radicals," including Thomas Hart Benton, Silas Wright and Francis P. Blair, yearned for an economy based on gold and silver coins rather than one supported by paper bank notes. "Conservatives," on the other hand, including William C. Rives and Nathaniel P. Tallmadge of New York, believed in paper money and state banks. In their campaign statement of 1835 the Democrats had tried to cover up the differences within their party by renewing the old attack on the Bank of the United States and avoiding any discussion of paper money and state banks, but the differences would not go away.

In New York City the struggle over banking was tied in with the Workingmen's movement, which had sprung up in the Northeast in the late 1820s to promote the interests of the new laboring class. The Workingmen's party of New York City supported free public education, the ten-hour day, and free land in the West as a means of benefiting this class. The Workies and their radical newspaper editors George Henry Evans and William Leggett also attacked paper money and the banking system because banks in New York and elsewhere had been granted special monopoly privileges and went virtually unchecked. The radicals demanded a "free banking" system, with strict state regulation of banks and a general incorporation law making any group eligible to receive a banking charter—not just a privileged few. In order to win the support of the Workingmen in the fall election of 1834, William L. Marcy and Tammany Hall Democrats had taken a stand against the extension of the old privileged banking monopolies, but soon after winning the election they went back on their campaign promises and supported a number of additional monopolistic bank charters. Evans and Leggett of the New York *Evening Post* were quick to protest that they had been "damnably deceived."

Within the Regency, Cambreleng, Wright, Dix, and Azariah Flagg backed the radicals; Marcy, Thomas Olcott and Benjamin Knower favored the bankers, and both sides tried to win over Van Buren. Leggett's assistant Theodore Sedgwick urged Van Buren to endorse free banking because farmers would approve, while bankers warned him against the "Jacobinical Creed" of the *Post*. Dix summed up Van Buren's dilemma by declaring that the Regency had its "hands full with the inroads of aristocracy on the one side and agrarianism on the other." Van Buren held the middle by opposing free banking but supporting the use of hard money in place of paper bank notes in minor dealings.[31]

---

[31] Hugins, *Jacksonian Democracy and the Working Class*, pp. 35-37; Mushkat, *Tam-*

The radical, agrarian, antimonopoly, or Equal Rights Democrats, as they came to be called, broke openly with conservative Tammany Hall in March 1835. The split widened late in the summer when some of the radicals, including Leggett in the *Evening Post*, began to defend the abolitionists. Alarmed at such radicalism, the Jackson administration sided with the conservatives and withdrew federal printing contracts from the *Post*, and the Washington *Globe* denounced the *Post* for its "spirit of agrarianism" and for "running into extremes." In October the Equal Rights Democrats held a dinner to honor—not Van Buren, but Richard Mentor Johnson, who had endeared himself to the radicals earlier by his radical stand in favor of delivering the mail on Sunday and against imprisonment for debt. At the dinner there was a toast denouncing "Banks, Banking and paper money," and a radical speech by Cambreleng. A few weeks later Cambreleng wrote to Van Buren recommending that New York adopt a system of free banking and exclude all bank notes from circulation.[32]

The showdown occurred on the evening of October 29, when the Democratic party met at Tammany Hall to nominate candidates for Congress and the state assembly. Before the doors opened, party regulars sneaked up the back stairs, called a rump meeting to order, and nominated one of their men for moderator. When the Equal Rights Democrats gained control of the meeting shortly after and nominated their own man for moderator, the regulars left, turning off the gaslights on the way out. Prepared for just such an event, the radicals brought out friction matches, which were known as loco-focos, lit candles, and nominated their slate of candidates. The next day representatives of the Whig and regular Democratic press vied with one another to see who could cast the strongest epithets at the Equal Righters: "*Agrarians*," "*Rowdies*," "*Noisy Brawlers*," "*Fire flies of faction*," were bandied about, and finally, the term that stuck—the "*Loco Foco party*." The Loco Focos ran poorly in both the November and spring elections,

---

many, pp. 158-160; *Argus*, Oct. 18, Dec. 22, 1834, Jan. 5, Jan. 9, Jan. 17, Feb. 3, 1835; John M. McFaul, *The Politics of Jacksonian Finance* (Ithaca, 1972), pp. 102-106, 144-146; "Character of Mr. Van Buren," *Evening Post*, Jan. 19, 1835, quoted in Theodore Sedgwick, ed., *A Collection of the Political Writings of William Leggett*, 2 vols. (New York, 1839), I, 178-185; Sedgwick to MVB, Dec. 29, 1834, Jan. 2, 1835, John Van Buren to MVB, Jan. 14, 1835, Gideon Lee to John T. Morgan, Dec. 25, 1834, George Strong to MVB, Dec. 23, 1834, Van Buren to——, Aug. 11, 1835, VBP; Dix to George C. Shattuck, Jan. 5, 1835, "Letters from Dix to Shattuck," p. 163.

[32] Fox, *Decline of Aristocracy*, p. 383; Fitzwilliam Byrdsall, *The History of the Loco-Foco or Equal Rights Party* (New York, 1842), pp. 13-20; Cambreleng to MVB, Nov. 2, 1835; VBP.

but they made their presence felt in the legislature, where they co-operated with Whigs to block new bank charters.[33]

Many of Van Buren's radical friends urged him to support the Loco Focos when the latter sent copies of their political principles to Van Buren and Johnson in the summer of 1836. Calling themselves "the original Democratic party," they demanded *"equal rights* [for] every citizen" and every enterprise, and denounced special privileges such as monopoly charters and the special right granted certain banks to issue bank notes. While Johnson endorsed the platform, saying that he opposed "monopolies and vested rights," Van Buren was much more circumspect. He agreed that republican government was based on "equal rights," but said that efforts to protect those rights should be "temperate." On the subject of banks and paper money, he answered by referring to his earlier statements. Declaring Van Buren's answer "evasive" and "unsatisfactory," the Locos decided to endorse no one in the election. Though surrounded by radicals—Cambreleng, Flagg, Wright, Dix, Beardsley, Vaux, Sedgwick, Leggett, and Evans—Van Buren went into the final months of the campaign without Loco Foco support.[34]

In Washington, meanwhile, Democrats who were uneasy about promoting pet banks and paper money, sought ways to regulate the state banks that received federal deposits. During both sessions of the Twenty-third Congress administration Democrats introduced a bill in the House to regulate the pet banks, but neither bill passed. William F. Gordon of Virginia, a supporter of John C. Calhoun and an ardent hard-money Democrat, went even further and proposed that all federal funds be removed from state banks and deposited in Treasury vaults. This was the first attempt at what later came to be called the independent treasury, but the proposal made no headway in either 1834 or 1835. In March 1835, Secretary of the Treasury Levi Woodbury succeeded where Democratic congressmen had failed by ordering pet banks to refuse bank notes under $5 in receipt for government dues. The ban was to extend to notes under $10 after March 1836.[35]

[33] Byrdsall, *History of the Loco-Foco Party*, pp. 23-29, 43-49, 51-52; Mushkat, *Tammany*, pp. 165-170; Hammond, *Political Parties*, II, 490-495; Hugins, *Jacksonian Democracy and the Working Class*, pp. 41-42.

[34] *Argus*, April 25, April 29, Aug. 10, Aug. 13, 1836; Byrdsall, *History of the Loco-Foco Party*, pp. 54-61; Beardsley to MVB, April 17, 1836, Cambreleng to MVB, April 24, 1836, Edgar W. Davies to MVB, May 28, 1836, Dix to MVB, June 7, 1836, VBP.

[35] McFaul, *Politics of Jacksonian Finance*, pp. 107-127; Harry N. Scheiber, "The Pet Banks in Jacksonian Politics and Finance, 1833-1841," *Journal of Economic History*, 23 (June 1963), 202-203.

Efforts at regulation were complicated by the question of how to dispose of the surplus in the federal Treasury. Since the end of the War of 1812 a federal debt of $127,000,000 had been gradually reduced until it was completely paid off in 1834. Because of the boom in federal land sales a substantial surplus was anticipated for the next few years. Whigs and conservative Democrats wanted to distribute the surplus funds to the states, while radical Democrats feared that such a distribution would only add fuel to the financial fire and cause a conflagration. Since Democrats had talked for years about extinguishing the federal debt, something had to be done.

In the debate over money and banking in 1836 conservative pro-banking Democrats opposed the regulation of state banks but supported distribution of the surplus and an increase in the number of banks receiving federal deposits. The radicals sought to restrain the banks by limiting their power to issue notes based on their deposits. The compromise deposit-distribution bill that passed on June 23, 1836, provided that all money in the Treasury in excess of $5,000,000 on January 1, 1837, be loaned to the states in four equal installments. In all, some $28,000,000 was eventually distributed to the states with no expectation that it be repaid. In another provision that pleased the conservatives, the act called for an increase in the number of deposit banks so that there would be at least one in each state and territory. To satisfy the radicals deposit banks were forbidden to issue notes of small denominations in place of coinage, and the amount of federal money to be held by any deposit bank was strictly limited. The act was a classic Jacksonian compromise with something to please each group, but it was an inadequate response to the new economic needs of the nation. The new banking regulations took a necessary first step in regulating the banking system, but the distribution of the surplus and the increase in pet banks only added to the speculative boom under way. Van Buren, who was sliding toward the radicals, favored regulation and opposed distribution, but he supported both because he dared not lose the backing of Rives and other conservatives in the midst of the presidential campaign.[36]

The hard-money men were displeased by the act. Alarmed by the land boom and other forms of speculation sweeping the country, they encouraged William M. Gouge in the Treasury to draw up detailed plans for Gordon's proposal to stop all depositing of federal funds in state banks. According to these plans excess federal money would be

[36] McFaul, *Politics of Jacksonian Finance*, pp. 130-138; Davis R. Dewey, *Financial History of the United States*, 10th ed. (New York, 1928), pp. 219-222.

placed in subtreasuries where it could not be used to increase the supply of bank notes in circulation. Less than three weeks after passage of the Deposit-Distribution Act, Andrew Jackson, who was a committed hard-money radical, ordered Secretary Woodbury to issue a Treasury circular requiring gold or silver coin to be used for the purchase of public lands. According to the specie circular of July 11, 1836, the principal goal of the President was to discourage "the monopoly of the public lands in the hands of speculators and capitalists." Jackson, worried that his pet banks were encouraging the land boom, was committing his administration to the hard-money cause. On his way home from Congress that summer, Van Buren, who bore no responsibility for the decision, found that the circular was unpopular in the eastern cities because there was a shortage of hard money. To protect its candidate, the *Albany Argus* remained silent on the specie circular instead of defending the administration. In both New York and Washington Van Buren had shown an awareness of the new economic situation, but he was too cautious to take a decisive stand.[37]

In August, however, Van Buren took two steps that brought him closer to the hard-money position. Afraid to desert the President on the eve of the election, Van Buren sent Jackson a letter supporting the specie circular; at the same time he took a radical position in a campaign letter to Congressman Sherrod Williams of Kentucky. Van Buren began by agreeing with Jefferson that state governments were "the surest bulwarks against anti-republican tendencies," and went on to align himself with Jackson by defending the Maysville Road veto and the veto of the recharter of the Bank of the United States. In past statements Van Buren had stopped there, but this time he was prepared to make more radical assertions. The best he could say for the deposit banks was that they should be given a "fair trial," but should be strictly regulated and not allowed to issue bank notes in small denominations. He joined the hard-money wing by asserting that the federal government should "confine itself to the creation of coin" and by arguing that "gold and silver should constitute a much greater proportion of the circulating medium of the country" than at present. Although Van Buren would not support the Loco Focos and the other radicals, he attempted to win their votes by endorsing several of their policies. Van Buren's motives were political. He was willing to exploit

[37] McFaul, *Politics of Jacksonian Finance*, pp. 126-127, 172-174; Henry Toland to MVB, Nov. 9, 1836, VBP; Elisha Whittlesey to Samuel Burch, Sept. 19, 1836, Samuel Burch Papers, LC; *Argus*, July-Nov. 1836.

the emotional issues of hard money and the Bank of the United States as a means of tying himself to Jackson.[38]

Reaction to Van Buren's letter reflected its moderately radical tone. Radicals Silas Wright, Charles J. Ingersoll of Pennsylvania, Charles G. Atherton of New Hampshire, and L. F. Linn of Missouri, praised the letter. Moderates Richard E. Parker and Peter V. Daniel of Virginia, approved but with less enthusiasm. Conservative William C. Rives, moving away from Van Buren, said he liked the statement, but disapproved of Van Buren's criticism of the Deposit-Distribution Act. For the time being Van Buren had succeeded in pleasing the radicals without losing conservatives such as Rives. With the presidency at stake, Van Buren followed his old pattern of compromising and avoiding ideological commitments. He had outlined a vague program that would help win the election but which did not directly attack the root economic problem.[39]

Van Buren kept up his careful political maneuvering as he moved toward the election. As soon as Congress adjourned he traveled north, renewing as many friendships as possible. From August until November he divided his time as usual between work at his Albany office and excursions to Lebanon Springs, Saratoga Springs, and Oswego; but his attention was on the campaign as the reports rolled in. Rives, still friendly, wrote that Ritchie was "buoyant and *betting*." Jackson, who was out campaigning, predicted victory in Ohio, but remained ominously quiet about Tennessee. Blair stood ready to obey the candidate's commands. Van Buren was still on the defensive. He was still being accused of sympathy for Catholics, slaves, or slaveowners. His statements on banking continued to receive close scrutiny. He still had to prove that he could be trusted. In a frank letter to Rives Van Buren confided that one reason he had decided not to sell his land at Oswego was because he was afraid of being criticized for speculating. It was not the first time, he lamented, that he had sacrificed "money to politics."[40]

[38] MVB to Jackson, Aug. 5, 1836, MVB to Sherrod Williams, Aug. 8, 1836, VBP; Williams to MVB, April 7, June 9, 1836, MVB to Williams, April 20, Aug. 8, 1836, *Niles' Register*, 51 (1836), 25-30.

[39] Ingersoll to MVB, Aug. 21, 1836, Wright to MVB, Sept. 4, 1836, Daniel to MVB, Sept. 7, 1836, Rives to MVB, Sept. 20, 1836, Parker to MVB, Sept. 20, 1836, Linn to MVB, Oct. 9, 1836, Atherton to MVB, Oct. 11, 1836, VBP.

[40] *Argus*, Aug. 3, 1836; MVB to Rives, Oct. 11, 1836, Rives to MVB, Oct. 13, 1836, Rives Papers, LC; MVB to Benjamin Butler, Oct. 19, 1836, Rives to MVB, Aug. 29, Oct. 13, 1836, Jackson to MVB, Aug. 22, Sept. 19, 1836, Blair to MVB, Aug. 28, Oct. 8, 1836, William Christy to MVB, Sept. 24, 1836, MVB to J. J. Lockhart, Sept. 18, 1836, A. Logan to MVB, Oct. 12, 1836, Richard E. Parker to MVB, Sept. 20, 1836, VBP; MVB to Blair, Aug. 25, Oct. 15, 1836, Blair Family Papers, LC.

The sacrifice was worth it. A warning that the election would be close came in October when Ohio and New Jersey, which had been Democratic in 1832, went Whig in state elections. The presidential election was held between November 4 and November 23, and Van Buren was in suspense until the end of the month. The final result showed that he had won with 170 electoral votes, compared to 73 for Harrison, 26 for White, 14 for Webster, and 11 for Willie Mangum. Van Buren narrowly defeated his combined Whig opponents in the popular vote, 762,987–736,250. In New York he won by a substantial margin and Marcy was reelected governor.[41]

The election of 1836 marked an important turning point in American political history because of the part it played in establishing the second American party system. In the early 1830s the political party structure was still changing rapidly; the Democratic party had been organized, but factional and personal leaders still played a major role in politics. By the end of the campaign of 1836 the new party system was almost complete, as nearly every faction had been absorbed by either the Democrats or the Whigs. Within a year Rives and Tallmadge would lead the last group from the Democratic party to the Whig, and Calhoun would lead the last group the other way. Aside from desertions over slavery, the two parties would remain relatively stable until the mid-1850s.[42]

As the new political system emerged, close elections became the order of the day. In the presidential election of 1832 the contest was close in only ten of twenty-three states, but by 1836 there were close elections in nineteen of twenty-five, and in 1840, in twenty-two of twenty-five. The average difference in the percentage of votes cast for the winner and the loser in each state dropped from thirty-six percent in 1832 to eleven percent in 1836 and 1840. Old Hickory swept to victory in eleven states in 1832 and was swamped in two; Van Buren, on the other hand, could sweep in only one and was swamped in none in 1836.[43]

There were other fundamental changes as well. The state line-up was drastically altered as Ohio, Indiana, Tennessee, and Georgia joined the Whigs, while Rhode Island and Connecticut supported the De-

---

[41] Stanwood, *History of the Presidency*, p. 184; Silbey, "Election of 1836," p. 595; MVB to Butler, Oct. 19, 1836, MVB to John Van Buren, Nov. 25, 1836, VBP.

[42] Joel Silbey discusses the "shakedown" of the two parties in his "Election of 1836"; and also in his "The Election of 1836," American Philosophical Society, *Crucial American Elections* (Philadelphia, 1973), pp. 14-29. See also William G. Carleton, "Political Aspects of the Van Buren Era," *South Atlantic Quarterly*, 50 (April 1951), 167-185.

[43] McCormick, "New Perspectives on Democratic Politics," pp. 299-301.

mocracy. Sectional assumptions were shattered as Democrats gained in New England, but lost in the South and the Northwest. Southern suspicion of Van Buren's position on slavery was the first crack in the alliance of North and South that Van Buren had built. Nowhere was the shift more dramatic than in Tennessee where, despite Jackson's active campaign, a Democratic plurality of 27,000 votes in 1832 was turned into a deficit of 10,000 votes in 1836. The new patterns showed little variation until the second party system fell apart in the 1850s.[44]

The election of 1836 has particular significance because of the many changes taking place in the 1830s. The expansion of the economy, the land boom, the outburst of urban riots, and the emergence of the new party system are but four examples of the enormous economic, social and political changes that were sweeping the United States. A technological and transportation revolution, great urban growth, economic expansion, the westward movement, a new awareness of class, racial and ethnic distinctions, and a new surge of reform—especially abolitionism—all forced Americans to face new problems and new issues during the election of 1836. A crucial question that year was the ability of the new parties and the new politicians to respond to the changes.

Neither Van Buren nor the Democratic party responded as effectively as they might have. The Democratic party statement in 1835 ignored the issues, played upon fears, and relied upon the Old Hero, the old issue of the Bank of the United States, and emotional themes to appeal to the voters. Faced with a runaway financial boom in the midst of the campaign, the Democrats responded with the contradictory Deposit-Distribution Act and specie circular. Since his party was divided, Van Buren refused to commit himself deeply on any issue, but despite his doubts he finally backed slavery and the specie circular. There is little evidence that either Van Buren or his party made a conscious effort to reshape Jacksonian Democracy to meet the new challenge.

But as students of American history are well aware, politicians and parties rarely respond as well as they might, and in the election of 1836 Van Buren's record was better than his opponents'. It was Van Buren, first of all, who had done more than anyone else to create the new political system that was so firmly established and accepted by Americans in 1836. Although it was not apparent at the time of the election, two parties had emerged, each substantially different from

[44] Silbey, "Election of 1836," pp. 596-599.

the other on the issues—something that had not been true since the 1790s. Though Van Buren was equivocal toward the Loco Focos, he did move with his party toward a radical, hard-money position in the midst of a banking boom. By siding with Wright and Dix in New York instead of with Knower and Olcott, Van Buren made his party more responsive to the "plain Republicans of the north" than before. As anti-Catholic nativism spread, Van Buren leaned toward the Catholics and the immigrants.

Even in his slavery policy Van Buren showed some inclination to adapt. His letter to Judith Rives complaining that he had "suffered" because of his "Southern partialities" revealed an awareness of antislavery sentiment in the North. He did, to be sure, work hard to keep the support of the southern planters. Too hard, for there was nothing attractive about the Utica riot. But Van Buren's policy had changed. He was now opposing abolition instead of defending slavery. In this way he was faithfully representing most northern Republicans, who liked neither blacks nor the reformers who sought to free them. In the years ahead this change would lead to the Free-Soil movement and drive a number of Democrats, including Van Buren, out of the party— some permanently. Van Buren had not changed Jacksonian Democracy in the 1836 campaign, but he did give indications that changes might be forthcoming in his administration.[45]

[45] William G. Carleton makes the point that the issues dividing the parties after 1836 were economic and social in "Political Aspects of the Van Buren Era." John M. McFaul argues persuasively that northern Jacksonians opposed abolition only because it threatened the Union, not because they had a proslavery policy. John M. McFaul, "Expediency vs. Morality: Jacksonian Politics and Slavery," *Journal of American History*, 42 (June 1975), 24-39.

4. Martin Van Buren c. 1840, from an original painting by Daniel Huntington

· 10 ·

RESPONDING TO THE PANIC

After the election Van Buren basked for a few serene weeks in the approval of his admirers. Writing in his journal, Benjamin Brown French, later clerk of the House, commented that Van Buren's behavior illustrated the adage that men become less haughty as they near the top. French considered Van Buren "ever so agreeable, . . . one of the most perfect gentlemen" he had ever met. James Buchanan was equally generous, praising Van Buren's "prudence, sagacity & judgment." Henry S. Foote of Mississippi, added to the friendly assessment calling Van Buren "as polished and captivating a person in the social circle as America has ever known." Surrounded by his friends, Van Buren confidently awaited his inauguration in March.[1]

But there were indications that the serenity would not last. Thomas Ritchie predicted that the "cares of office" would soon teach Van Buren "a melancholy lesson." A complaining letter from Enos T. Throop reminded Van Buren that he would still have to deal with Regency quarrels, even when he was President. A mob rioting against high flour prices in New York City in February gave warning that there was economic danger ahead. Privately, Thurlow Weed was predicting that Van Buren would last only one term, and Nicholas Biddle was trying to decide whether the Bank of the United States, which had been chartered in Pennsylvania as a state bank when its federal charter expired in 1836, was "to have war or peace" with the new administration. There were problems ahead that would give the new President a chance to change Jacksonian Democracy—if he were so inclined.[2]

Andrew Jackson best summarized the problems awaiting Van Buren when the retiring President delivered his annual message to Congress on December 5, 1836. Early in the message Jackson described the diplomatic conflict with Mexico that had arisen as a result of the

[1] French, *Journal*, 3 (Dec. 2, 1836), Benjamin Brown French Papers, LC; Buchanan to Benjamin E. Carter and others, Dec. 17, 1836, Buchanan, *Works*, III, 130; Gilman Lee to James M. Miller, Dec. 20, 1836, VBP; Henry S. Foote, *Casket of Reminiscences* (Washington, D.C., 1874; reprint, 1968), p. 59.

[2] Ritchie to———Green, Jan. 16, 1837, Ambler, "Ritchie Letters," *Branch Papers*, 4 (1916), 380; Throop to MVB, Jan. 28, 1837, VBP; Hone, *Diary*, pp. 241-242; Biddle to Roswell Colt, Jan. 28, 1837, Roswell L. Colt Papers, HSP; Weed to Francis Granger, Dec. 5, 1836, Granger Papers, LC.

successful Texan revolution the previous June, and toward the end he reviewed the bloody Seminole War going on in Florida; but the main body of the message was taken up with an analysis of the economic problems then facing the United States. The President reported with alarm that at the end of the year there would be a surplus of at least $16,000,000 in the Treasury, the result of the wild boom in the sale of federal lands between 1834 and 1836. Jackson, who had never liked the idea of distribution, was sorry that the surplus would have to be distributed to the states because the money would be used by state banks to "make loans" and would increase the "spirit of wild speculation." By distributing the surplus, he reasoned, Congress would be encouraged to increase the tariff in order to create an additional surplus. To avoid distribution in the future, Jackson recommended that the next administration "collect revenue enough only to meet the wants of the Government." Jackson concluded by defending his specie circular and by attacking the Bank of the United States.[3]

The wave of speculation to which Jackson was reacting was threatening to engulf the economy. Since 1830, prices had risen fifty percent, interest rates had climbed to twenty-four percent, the supply of money had more than doubled, and in New York City the value of real property had risen from $250,000,000 to more than $400,000,000. If this boom continued, Van Buren would have to decide whether to follow the hard-money, radical advice of Andrew Jackson or the expansionist arguments of Whigs and conservative Democrats.[4]

In selecting his cabinet Van Buren gave some indication of the direction his policies would take. Instead of making a clean break with the past, he decided to retain Jackson's cabinet almost intact. In many ways this was the obvious decision to make and there was ample precedent for it. Previous Republican Presidents—James Madison, James Monroe and John Quincy Adams—had kept at least half of their predecessors' cabinets, and because Van Buren had played a major role in shaping the cabinet since 1831, almost all of the incumbent secretaries were his friends. He had every reason to trust Secretary of State John Forsyth, Treasury Secretary Levi Woodbury, Attorney General Benjamin Butler, Postmaster General Amos Kendall, and Secretary of the Navy Mahlon Dickerson. He needed only to find a Secretary of War to replace Lewis Cass, who had left to become minister to France.

[3] Richardson, *Messages and Papers*, III, 236-260.
[4] McGrane, *Panic of 1837*, pp. 44-45; Peter Temin, *The Jacksonian Economy* (New York, 1969), pp. 68-71.

After the bitter tumult of the Jackson years, Van Buren sought the calm and order that keeping the old cabinet would ensure; but because he showed considerable anxiety about making any changes, his stand-pat policy takes on more than ordinary significance. When Benjamin Butler, who did not like Washington, began to talk about leaving, Van Buren frantically asked his son John to have the Regency put pressure on Butler to stay. "You have no idea," Van Buren told his son, what "conflicting interests" would arise if the office of Attorney General became vacant. Democrats from Virginia and Pennsylvania, states that had contributed 53 of Van Buren's 170 electoral votes, were already clamoring for a seat in the cabinet, and in the old days the Magician would have welcomed the opportunity to hand out such rich patronage plums as cabinet positions. But now, after years of struggling to reach the White House, Van Buren showed signs of losing his combative edge—of becoming more cautious than ever—and so he was greatly relieved to learn that Butler would stay on. During the campaign Whigs had ridiculed Van Buren for being Jackson's hand-picked successor and that fact alone might have provoked him to make changes in order to prove the criticism unfounded, but evidently he felt a deep need for continuity and calm.

In replacing Cass in the War Department Van Buren showed his caution and his desire to maintain party harmony. William C. Rives, a Virginian and a friend of Van Buren, was the obvious choice. His appointment would bring a conservative voice and a second Southerner into the administration, and would heal some of the wounds incurred when the Virginian had been denied the vice presidential nomination. When Rives turned down the offer on the grounds that he preferred the State Department, Van Buren was served warning that Rives would soon make a clean break with the administration and he promptly appointed Joel Poinsett of South Carolina, Secretary of War. In so doing Van Buren kept an important link with the Jackson years because Poinsett had demonstrated his loyalty to the Democratic party and the Union during the nullification crisis.[5]

In the months just before Van Buren's inauguration there were other

---

[5] In this and other questions involving Van Buren's presidency I have been guided by James C. Curtis, *The Fox at Bay: Martin Van Buren and the Presidency 1837-1841* (Lexington, 1970). Curtis discusses the selection of the cabinet on pp. 53-57. I emphasize Van Buren's desire to keep the old cabinet more than Curtis does. See also Rives to Judge R. S. Parker, Nov. 9, 1836, William Cabell Rives Papers, UVL; MVB to John Van Buren, Dec. 30, 1836, Richard E. Parker to MVB, Feb. 7, 1837, MVB to George M. Dallas, Feb. 16, 1837, Buchanan to MVB, Feb. 19, 1837, VBP; Buchanan to MVB, Feb. 28, 1837, James Buchanan Papers, NYHS.

indications that the new President would not cut his ties with the past and with the states. Instead of focusing on national issues he continued to show unflagging interest in state problems and state politicians, particularly those of the three key states of New York, Pennsylvania and Virginia. Some incoming Presidents might have dismissed problems in the organization of the party back home as not worthy of their attention, but not Van Buren. When Enos T. Throop wrote petulantly in January that other members of the Regency were not treating him properly, Van Buren asked Silas Wright to do all he could to smooth the matter over. Azariah Flagg was also writing to Van Buren, urging him to help restore the *Albany Argus* to its old "democratic tone." According to Flagg, Edwin Croswell had far too much sympathy for banks. Correspondence between Van Buren and Virginians flourished, and there was a striking increase in letters to and from Pennsylvanians. If Van Buren could not appoint a Virginian or a Pennsylvanian to the cabinet, he could at least maintain close ties by mail.[6]

During Jackson's last months, Congress returned to the old battles over money and banking. When Silas Wright and Thomas Hart Benton led a move in the Senate to expunge Henry Clay's resolution censuring Jackson for removing the deposits, Whigs retaliated with long speeches designed to filibuster the expunging resolution to death. To forestall such tactics as the time to vote approached, the Democratic leaders made plans for an all-night meeting, laying in, according to Benton, supplies of "cold hams, turkeys, rounds of beef, pickles, wines and cups of hot coffee" to keep the faithful comfortable and awake. It was a classic battle between the great Jacksonians Benton, Wright and Felix Grundy, and the Whig triumvirate of Clay, Calhoun and Webster. Just before midnight the votes were counted and the Jacksonians had won, 24-19. On January 16, 1837, the secretary of the Senate wrote across the offending page of the Journal in broad black strokes the words: "Expunged by order of the Senate." The Old Hero's record had been cleared.[7]

Another of Jackson's controversial policies, the specie circular, was also debated in this session. Both Whigs and conservative Democrats introduced bills in the Senate to repeal the circular, partly to get rid

---

[6] Throop to MVB, Jan. 28, 1837, MVB to Throop; Feb. 6, 1837, Flagg to MVB, Jan. 11, 1837, VBP; Wright to Flagg, Jan. 9, 1837, Flagg to General S. Maison, Nov. 15, 1837, Flagg to Jesse Hoyt, Sept. 18, 1836, Flagg Papers. Van Buren's correspondence between the election and the inauguration included an exchange of seventeen letters with Pennsylvanians and six with Virginians. West, *Calendar of Van Buren Papers*, pp. 271-280.

[7] Benton, *Thirty Years' View*, I, pp. 727-730.

of a restraint on the economy and partly to smoke out the attitude of the new administration toward paper money. In order to compromise with hard-money Democrats Rives proposed a bill that coupled repeal of the circular with a reform clause that prohibited the government from accepting after 1840, bank notes from banks issuing paper notes under $20. The bill passed the Senate by a vote of 41 to 5, and the House by a vote of 143 to 59. The second vote revealed that the House was divided into three groups: 54 Democrats and 89 Whigs combined to pass the bill, while 59 Democrats and no Whigs voted against it. Most of the 59 Democratic votes in support of the specie circular came from committed hard-money radicals, but some came from loyal Democrats voting to support Jackson. Even though the circular had been criticized for diverting specie from the East to the West, most of the votes for the circular were from the East, and most Westerners voted against it. Since Silas Wright in the Senate and twenty-two New York congressmen voted to keep the circular, the impression was left that Van Buren was for it. Ideology and party loyalty played a more important role in the voting than did sectional interest. Andrew Jackson protected his pet measure by giving the bill a pocket veto at 11:45 P.M. on March 3, the day before he left office, thereby putting Van Buren in a position where he would have to choose between remaining loyal to Jackson and responding to the opinion of Congress and the public.[8]

When Inauguration Day arrived with its "clear sky [and] balmy vernal sun," reverence for the old took precedence over concern for the new. Though ill and in pain, Jackson insisted on taking part in the ceremony. He and Van Buren arrived at the Capitol in a phaeton made of wood from the *U.S.S. Constitution* and drawn by four gray horses. As the writer N. P. Willis described the scene: "A murmur of feeling rose up from the moving mass below, and the infirm old man . . . bowed to the people, and, still uncovered in the cold air, took his seat beneath the portico." Van Buren then read his address "with great dignity" and "with a voice [so] remarkably distinct" that 20,000 persons easily heard him. Thomas Hart Benton recalled that the audience was "profoundly silent [out of] reverence and affection" for the Old Hero. Not until the inauguration was over and Jackson walked down the steps did "the deep repressed feeling" of the crowd finally burst

[8] McFaul, *Politics of Jacksonian Finance*, pp. 178-184; Tallmadge to MVB, Feb. 14, Mar. 15, 1837, MVB to John Van Buren, Dec. 22, 1836, MVB to Tallmadge, Feb. 14, 1837, Butler to MVB, Feb. 15, 1837, VBP; Richardson, *Messages and Papers*, III, 282-283.

forth and cheers fill the air. For once, said Benton, "the rising was eclipsed by the setting sun."[9]

In his inaugural Van Buren had a chance to outline his views on the economy and to indicate whether he intended to diverge substantially from Jacksonian Democracy, but he said nothing specific and nothing new. Instead he was content to generalize and present views with which most Jacksonians could agree. It was an address remarkably similar to the farewell address that Jackson and Roger B. Taney had prepared the previous fall. Conscious of the passage of time, Jackson had then reminded his compatriots that they had lived "almost fifty years under the Constitution"; Van Buren in March marveled that they had seen "half a century, teeming with extraordinary events." Both men expressed faith in the Jacksonian balance of old and new. The Old Hero summed up the Old Republican tradition by defending state rights and attacking the public debt; the Magician, by pledging loyalty to the "sovereign power" of the states and by opposing an "ever ready military organization." Both tempered their nostalgia with concessions to the realities of the 1830s. Jackson, for example, recognized that the old American homogeneity was gone by referring several times to the new social "classes" and by warning the people against the "moneyed interest." Van Buren called attention to new forms of business, new political parties and new means of transportation.

Of the two, Andrew Jackson was much more forthright than Van Buren on economic policy. Repeating some of the hard-money arguments that he had made in his final annual message, Jackson bragged that his administration had extinguished the national debt, but warned his listeners that his opponents had not "yet abandoned [their] design to collect an extravagant revenue and to burden you with taxes." In a strongly worded declaration reminiscent of his Bank veto Jackson blamed "the wild spirit of speculation" on those who advocated paper money, and accused them of an "eager desire to amass wealth without labor." Such people, he said, held "the power to inflict injury upon the agricultural, mechanical, and laboring classes of society." To the last Jackson was unsparing in his portrayal of bankers and businessmen as enemies of the American people and the Democratic party.

Van Buren gave no hint at all of the direction his administration would take. Instead of offering something new, he sought to keep the political peace. Instead of trying to rally the troops and destroy the

---

[9] Benton, *Thirty Years' View*, I, 735; N. P. Willis, quoted in Parton, *Jackson*, III, 628.

enemy, he sought to satisfy his followers and placate the opposition. It took two of his political opponents to sense what he was doing. William Henry Seward found it "refreshing" to read an address "imbued once more with the sense of responsibility [and the] dignity" that had characterized presidential messages before Andrew Jackson. Hezekiah Niles on the other hand, thought that Van Buren's address was so bland that it disappointed both friend and foe, but harmony, said Niles was coming.[10]

After taking office Van Buren refused to exploit his opportunities for patronage. Even though Democrats in Albany were supposedly "calculating the amount of 'spoils' " due them and despite demands for "rotation in office" coming from Boston, Philadelphia and Baltimore, Van Buren replaced relatively few officeholders. In his first two years he removed only three of the postmasters who were appointed directly by the President, while Postmaster General Kendall removed but 364 out of 12,000 of the other postmasters. Nor did the President choose between Democratic factions—between conservative David Henshaw and radical Benjamin F. Hallett in Massachusetts, between William L. Marcy and Azariah Flagg in New York, or between George M. Dallas and Henry A. P. Muhlenberg in Pennsylvania.[11] Van Buren postponed a problem in New York by ignoring Enos T. Throop's maneuvers to replace Samuel Swartwout as collector of the Port of New York. Since Swartwout's term did not expire until 1838, Van Buren decided to wait. To soothe Democrats in Pennsylvania, who had been thwarted in efforts to win a cabinet position, he offered the diplomatic post in Moscow to Muhlenberg. After he turned it down, Muhlenberg was sent to Austria and the position in Moscow went to Dallas.

Van Buren's attention was soon drawn from patronage to finance

[10] Richardson, *Messages and Papers*, III, 298-308, 313-320; Frederick W. Seward, ed., *Autobiography of William H. Seward from 1801 to 1834, with a Memoir of His Life, and Selections from His Letters from 1831 to 1846* (New York, 1877), p. 328; *Niles' Register*, 52 (1837), 17. Because of its review of a half-century of American progress, Van Buren's was one of the most interesting inaugural addresses since Jefferson's famous first inaugural. But Van Buren's address broke no new economic ground.

[11] Weed to Francis Granger, Dec. 5, 1836, Granger Papers, LC; John B. Turner, Junius Tilden, and Jonathan Nayson to MVB, Mar. 31, 1837, Democratic Convention Committee of Baltimore to MVB, April 2, April 15, 1837, John M. Read to MVB, April 5, 1837, James N. Barker to MVB, April 5, 1837, Philadelphia General Ward Delegation Committee to MVB, April 26, 1837, VBP; Darling, *Political Changes in Massachusetts*, pp. 204-209; Prosper Wetmore to Marcy, Mar. 19, 1837, Gratz Collection, HSP; White, *Jacksonians*, p. 309; Samuel Champlain to Joel Poinsett, Mar. 2, 1837, Joel R. Poinsett Papers, HSP.

as the economy began a downward spiral. After the dizzy expansion of 1835 and 1836 the bottom suddenly fell out. On the very day of Van Buren's inauguration, the prominent trading firm of Philip Hone's son Isaac stopped payment, and three days later failures began among the cotton houses in New Orleans. By the middle of March several banking firms in New York City had suspended payments, including the great banking house of I. and L. Joseph. Financiers Philip Hone, Gorham Worth and Prosper Wetmore were dismayed by the "fearful crisis" and the latter declared that he had never seen "such gloom and despondency."[12]

The Panic of 1837 resulted from the interaction of events on both sides of the Atlantic Ocean. As the economy in the United States boomed, American imports from England exceeded exports. Part of the unfavorable balance of trade was covered by exports of cotton to England, while a large percentage of the English profits was invested in American transportation and manufacturing. Concern about the outflow of gold and silver led the Bank of England to demand specie from American banks and to raise its rediscount rate in order to force British merchant bankers to curtail their investments in America. At the same time a decrease in the price of cotton made the situation worse by increasing the unfavorable balance of trade. The panic began when Herman, Briggs, and Co. of New Orleans, failed because it could not honor its notes to British banks. Since I. and L. Joseph in turn could not collect payment on money loaned to Herman, Briggs, the Josephs suspended payment, setting in motion a series of bank suspensions.

The monetary policies of the Jackson administration also played an important part in the panic. By removing the deposits from the Bank of the United States and depositing them in state banks the administration had contributed to the boom. It did so again by distributing the surplus to the states. Then, conscious of his part in the expansion, Jackson issued the specie circular in order to put a brake on the speculation. Contemporary observers blamed the panic on the specie circular, which they believed had caused a sudden shift of gold and silver reserves from East to West to pay for the sale of lands. As a result, they argued, there was a decline in specie reserves in eastern cities, which led to suspension of payments and the ensuing panic. Evidence now suggests that there was no great flow of specie from East to West, but that does not eliminate the specie circular as a cause

[12] Benton, *Thirty Years' View*, II, 10-11, Hone, *Diary*, pp. 245, 248-249; Worth to MVB, Mar. 12, 1837, VBP; Wetmore to Marcy, Mar. 19, 1837, Gratz Collection, HSP.

of the panic. When Jackson issued the circular and followed it with his annual message and farewell address denouncing the great wave of speculation, the public both in America and in England assumed that Jackson and his successor would do all they could to contract the currency. As a result banks became cautious, began to call in loans and helped bring on the panic.[13]

Bankers and politicians were quick to add their voices to those who blamed the panic on the specie circular, and Henry Toland, Gorham Worth and other bankers wrote to Van Buren urging him to rescind it. Whigs sponsored a giant meeting in New York City, at which Daniel Webster predicted that the repeal of the Treasury order would bring about a much "better state of things." Among Democrats, Rives and Nathaniel P. Tallmadge warned that the circular would saddle Van Buren with such a heavy burden of unpopularity that it could cause him to lose both the South and the West. Even supporters of the circular began to favor modification; Andrew J. Donelson, for example, suggested that land buyers be allowed to use paper money, but only in large bills. Soon after the inauguration the *Albany Argus* and the *Richmond Enquirer* hinted that the administration would at least change the terms of the circular.[14]

But there was counterpressure from Andrew Jackson and other Democrats who were committed to a hard-money policy. Even before reaching Tennessee the Old Hero began sending a series of letters to Washington demanding that the specie circular be retained. From Kentucky he assured his successor that "nineteen twentieths, of the whole people approve[d]" of the circular, and from the Hermitage he declared that the circular was still "popular with the people." To rally support he told Francis P. Blair that the circular was "popular with all but the speculators, and gamblers." Blair, Taney, Henry D. Gilpin of Pennsylvania, and other Jacksonians agreed with the former President.[15]

---

[13] McGrane, *Panic of 1837*, pp. 41-42, 91-99; Temin, *Jacksonian Economy*, pp. 113-117; Dewey, *Financial History*, pp. 229-231.

[14] Democratic congressmen John F. Claiborne and Robert I. Ward asked for repeal, and Whig William Henry Seward predicted that Van Buren would soon comply. Claiborne to MVB, April 10, 1837, Ward to MVB, Mar. 22, 1837, VBP; Seward, *Autobiography*, p. 328. Toland to MVB, Mar. 9, April 3, 1837, Worth to MVB, Mar. 12, 1837, Tallmadge to MVB, March 15, 1837, Rives to MVB, April 7, April 10, 1837, Abijah Mann to MVB, Mar. 23, 1837, Campbell P. White to MVB, Mar. 14, 1837, Donelson to MVB, May 17, 1837, VBP; Donelson to MVB, April 3, 1837, Andrew J. Donelson Papers, LC; Benton, *Thirty Years' View*, II, 13; *Argus*, Mar. 11, Mar. 16, 1837; *Richmond Enquirer*, April 27, 1837.

[15] Jackson to MVB, Mar. 22, Mar. 30, 1837, Jackson to Blair, April 2, April 18,

For a President who hoped to establish calm during his administration Van Buren was faced with a potentially devastating emergency,
probably the worst facing any new President on taking office until
James Buchanan had to cope with slavery and the Dred Scott decision
in 1857. Among Van Buren's predecessors John Adams was confronted
with the expulsion of Charles C. Pinckney from France in 1797, and
James Madison had to put the Non-Intercourse Act into effect in 1809,
but neither of these problems had the same far-reaching impact on
the American people as did the Panic of 1837. Instead of presiding
calmly over a unified Democratic party and restoring harmony to the
political scene, Van Buren had to try to pull together several Democratic factions in his efforts to react coherently to the panic. Instead
of being able to ignore a divided Whig party, he had to respond to
powerful attacks from a suddenly united opposition.

Thomas Hart Benton argued years later that Daniel Webster's speech
in New York in March against the specie circular was the first gun in
an organized conspiracy to destroy Van Buren. Believing that Van
Buren lacked "firmness," said Benton, the Whigs decided to start "an
experiment upon his nerves"—"a pressure of public opinion . . . under
which his gentle temperament was expected to yield." John C. Calhoun
believed that Van Buren had entered office "very weak" and could be
"easily crushed with anything like a vigorous effort." A contemporary
cartoon summed up Van Buren's position; it showed him riding on a
fox, his gown flying off, saving himself as Jackson on a pig and Benton
on a donkey are about to ride off a cliff in pursuit of the "gold
humbug." The caption read, "Although I follow in the footsteps of
Jackson, it is expedient at this time that I deviate a little."[16]

With his party split, with the Whigs applying pressure and with the
panic worsening daily, Van Buren was tempted to abandon Jackson's
specie circular. In trying to decide what to do, he followed his old
practice of moving cautiously, treating everyone tactfully, and asking
for advice. He was also firmer than critics expected. The draft of Van
Buren's first letter to Rives after the inauguration gives a good indication of the new President's caution and indecision because the letter
is filled with crossed-out sentences. Van Buren concluded tactfully by

---

1837, Blair to Jackson, April 5, 1837, Jackson, *Correspondence*, V, 465, 467, 472,
474, 476; Taney to MVB, April 1, 1837, Thomas Fletcher to MVB, Mar. 28, 1837,
Henry D. Gilpin to MVB, April 7, 1837, VBP.

[16] Benton, *Thirty Years' View*, II, 15-16; Calhoun to James Edward Calhoun, Mar.
22, 1837, J. Franklin Jameson, ed., "Correspondence of John C. Calhoun," American
Historical Association, *Annual Report for the Year 1899* (Washington, D.C., 1900),
II, 370; cartoon, "Fifty Cent Note," HSP.

assuring Rives that despite their differences they were still friends and Rives's advice was always welcome. In writing to William L. Marcy, who was not in sympathy with the circular, Van Buren said that he respected the integrity of Marcy's views and regretted that Marcy could not visit him. After some differences with Thomas Ritchie, Van Buren wrote that he still regarded Ritchie highly.[17]

Van Buren was surprisingly firm as well as tactful in dealing with Andrew Jackson. Only a few weeks after taking office Van Buren felt obliged to send Jackson a careful letter to warn him that his specie circular might be abandoned. It was a difficult task because Jackson was so committed to the circular, but Van Buren accomplished it with considerable skill. He wrote sadly that he had been receiving "bundles of letters [from their] friends in favor of rescinding the Treasury order." Even though the letters were filled with "a kind & liberal spirit toward" Jackson, the authors were insisting that the specie circular must go. Van Buren added tactfully that the critics were only "relieving themselves from self reproaches by laying [their] misfortunes at the door of the Treasury order," but in effect he had warned Jackson that a change in policy was being considered.[18]

Since Van Buren believed in using his cabinet and intended to hold regular cabinet meetings, he might have been expected to consult the cabinet about the specie circular. But knowing that the cabinet would be divided and not wishing to provoke a fight within his administration, he resorted as usual to compromise. On March 24, he sent a memorandum to the members of the cabinet asking them for their views in writing, but he did not insist on receiving answers. The general sentiment among the cabinet members, including Secretary of the Treasury Levi Woodbury, was in favor of modification or outright repeal of the specie circular. But Woodbury's clerk William M. Gouge, who had drawn up a plan to deposit federal money in subtreasuries, disagreed, insisting that the circular did not go far enough in divorcing the government from the economy of the nation.[19]

Van Buren showed that he still prized his state ties by asking the Regency for advice and by sending Silas Wright to look into the sit-

[17] MVB to Rives, April 8, 1837, MVB to Marcy, June 18, 1837, MVB to Ritchie, Aug. 11, 1837, VBP.

[18] MVB to Jackson, Mar. 1837, VBP. John M. McFaul suggests that Van Buren may not have sent this particular letter to Jackson, but I agree with James C. Curtis that Jackson did receive the letter. It was entirely in keeping with Van Buren's character that he would try to get Jackson's support in this crisis. McFaul, *Politics of Jacksonian Finance*, p. 185; Curtis, *Fox at Bay*, p. 69.

[19] Gouge to MVB, Mar. 19, 1837, MVB, Memorandum, Mar. 24, 1837, VBP.

uation in New York City. Wright, who arrived on the heels of the collapse of the banking house of Joseph, expected to find businessmen blaming the federal government, but found instead that most of them thought that the Josephs had only themselves to blame. Just as cautious as Van Buren, Wright recommended keeping but perhaps modifying the circular. More radical and less circumspect than Wright, Azariah Flagg and Churchill C. Cambreleng told the President bluntly that he should retain Jackson's circular. According to Flagg, "Laxness and Corruption [had] made fearful strides" in the country, and the speculators were like "drowning men [who] catch at straws." Cambreleng said that it would be better if the speculators failed.[20]

After hearing all views, Van Buren decided to retain the specie circular. He issued no formal announcement, but by mid-April the *Globe* made the President's position clear by publishing strong statements supporting the circular. It was not an easy decision, coming less than two months after a majority in Congress had declared against the specie circular, and with the preponderance of advice from those in Washington and outside favoring rescission. Van Buren kept the circular because Andrew Jackson and the Regency wanted it, because Van Buren himself had become increasingly sympathetic to the hard-money point of view, and because he hated to go against the wishes of old associates. With his party divided Van Buren considered it important to retain a tie with the Old Hero, and it could be inferred in April at least, that Van Buren had no intention of making any dramatic change in Jacksonian Democracy. But it did not mean that he had gone over to the radicals or that he had given up compromising. The tone of his letters to those advocating repeal showed that he was trying to keep communications open in order to prevent his party from splitting further apart. The decision did mean, however, that the Democratic party, which had been maneuvered into a noncompromising attack on the Bank of the United States while Jackson was President, was now moving closer to a noncompromising attack on paper money and banks.[21]

As spring advanced, the panic increased. On April 25, a group of merchants held a meeting in New York City presided over by Philip Hone. The merchants resolved that the "widespread disaster [could

[20] Wright to MVB, Mar. 21, 1837, Cambreleng to MVB, April 8, 1837, Flagg to MVB, April 10, 1837, VBP; Garraty, *Wright*, pp. 137-140. Enos T. Throop favored repeal as a means of restoring confidence. Throop to MVB, April 29, 1837, VBP.

[21] Washington *Globe*, April 14, April 15, April 17, April 19, 1837. For other views on why Van Buren stayed with the specie circular, see Curtis, *Fox at Bay*, p. 70; McFaul, *Politics of Jacksonian Finance*, p. 186; Dewey, *Financial History*, p. 232.

be] ascribed to the interference of the general government with the commercial and business operations of the country; its intermeddling with the currency; its destruction of the national bank; its attempt to substitute a metallic for a credit currency; and finally, to the issuing ... of ... the 'specie circular.' " They voted to send a committee to Washington to ask the President to rescind the specie circular and to call a special session of Congress. In the week that followed Van Buren received letters preparing him for the visit of the committee. Jesse Hoyt, who knew the merchants, reassured the President that there was no cause for alarm even though the committee would "talk very big," but Peter V. Daniel warned Van Buren of the "eager cupidity" of the delegation. He took the view that the New Yorkers had caused their own trouble by their speculation and urged Van Buren to meet the delegation in private and to ask for questions ahead of time in writing. Watch out, said the suspicious Daniel, for "this new diplomacy."[22]

Van Buren took Daniel's advice and asked the merchants to present their demands in writing before the meeting on May 3. In their address the merchants said that they spoke for "a community which trembles upon the brink of ruin." Within the last six months, they claimed, the value of real estate in New York City had depreciated by $40,000,000 and the value of merchandise in New York City warehouses had dropped by thirty percent; furthermore, there were 20,000 out of work. In their view, "the error of our rulers [had] produced a wider desolation than the pestilence" that attacked New York in 1832. The merchants asked Van Buren to repeal the specie circular, call a special session of Congress, and grant a moratorium on duty bonds owed for United States customs. Benton reported that Van Buren listened with his usual "composure," treated his visitors with "exquisite politeness," but gave no immediate reply. The next day, May 4, he issued—as Benton put it—"a calm, quiet, decent, peremptory refusal."[23]

Van Buren's firmness did not end the matter, for as soon as the delegation returned home, a run began on the banks in New York City. A million dollars in specie was withdrawn on May 8 and May 9, and the next day soldiers guarded the streets as all but three banks suspended specie payments. When suspensions followed all over the United States, Van Buren's network relayed the news to the White

---

[22] *Argus*, April 18, May 2, 1837; Hone, *Diary*, p. 254; Benton, *Thirty Years' View*, II, 16-19; John McClure to MVB, April 26, 1837, Morgan Lewis to MVB, April 27, 1837, Hoyt to MVB, April 30, 1837, "Real Friend" to MVB, c. May 1, 1837, Daniel to MVB, April 29, 1837, VBP; *Richmond Enquirer*, May 12, 1837.

[23] Benton, *Thirty Years' View*, II, 18.

House. Although some insisted that Nicholas Biddle and other bankers had manufactured the panic to put pressure on the President, almost all agreed that the situation was serious. Jesse Hoyt and conservative banker Myndert Van Schaick both called the situation a crisis. Silas Wright wrote that the panic had created bad feeling in Albany. British minister Henry S. Fox reported to the Foreign Office that the "terror [and] indignation" was so great that Van Buren was likely to be overthrown. To cope with the situation Van Buren held daily cabinet meetings, but did little other than allow delays in the payment of duty bonds that merchants owed the custom houses. Finally, in desperation, the beleaguered President gave way and on May 15, called a special session of Congress for September. According to Benton it was "a mortifying concession to imperative circumstances."[24]

As the Democratic party continued to split under the pressure of the panic, Van Buren received increasing and conflicting advice from conservatives defending the state banks and from radicals who wanted to separate the federal government from any banking institution. Though conceding that the system of depositing funds in state banks was temporarily "out of gear," Rives insisted that it could continue to care for the financial needs of the nation. He warned Van Buren against following the "new-fangled Jacobinism" of isolating the federal Treasury from local communities. Conservatism was gaining ground in Albany, where Nathaniel P. Tallmadge told a group of listeners not to "submit to have Loco Focoism poked down their throats," and letters appeared in the *Argus* supporting Tallmadge. Governor Marcy, who was rapidly becoming more conservative, favored the use of paper money and opposed the separation of government and banking. In Washington Rives and Tallmadge founded a newspaper called the *Madisonian* to advance the interests of the state banks.[25]

[24] Hone, *Diary*, pp. 257, 260; Benton, *Thirty Years' View*, II, 20-21, 28; Hoyt to Flagg, May 10, 1837, Flagg Papers; George F. Lehman to MVB, May 11, 1837, Van Schaick to MVB, May 12, 1837, James N. Barker to MVB, May 13, 1837, V. M. Saresche to MVB, May 14, 1837, Silas Wright to MVB, May 13, 1837, Henry D. Gilpin to MVB, May 14, 1837, VBP; Curtis, *Fox at Bay*, p. 73; Woodbury, Circular to Banks, May 16, 1837, Letters from the Secretary of the Treasury to Banks, Treasury Department Records, National Archives; Richardson, *Messages and Papers*, III, 321-322; Fox to Lord Palmerston, May 21, 1837, British Foreign Office, Correspondence 5: United States, 314 (1837), 208-213.

[25] Van Buren also received letters supporting a revival of the Bank of the United States. Myndert Van Schaick to MVB, Aug. 28, 1837, Henry D. Gilpin to MVB, May 21, 1837, John Kane to MVB, May 20, May 24, 1837, MVB to Jackson, July 28, 1837, VBP. See also *Argus*, June 2, June 28, July 4, July 11, July 25, Aug. 4, Aug. 22, 1837; Marcy to MVB, May 25, 1837, MVB to Rives, May 25, 1837, Rives to MVB, June 3,

Radicals were just as busy. Democrats in the New Hampshire legislature and laboring men in Philadelphia passed resolutions attacking banks, while from Virginia Richard E. Parker asked Van Buren to stop the "gambling" of state banks. In strongly worded letters Nathaniel Macon and Churchill C. Cambreleng tried to stiffen Van Buren's radicalism. Macon professed "great confidence" in Van Buren's "republican character," and Cambreleng reported that public sentiment in New York was "decidedly anti-bank."[26]

Seeking a program to present to Congress in September, Van Buren turned to Gouge's plan for holding federal funds in an independent treasury instead of depositing them in state banks. When Dr. John Brockenbrough, the Democratic president of the Bank of Virginia, who was not a radical, offered his support for the independent treasury, Van Buren saw the possibility of rallying a united party behind the plan. Brockenbrough and other moderate Democrats liked the proposal because it left state banks free from the federal regulations that Woodbury and other Jacksonians—even Rives—had been trying to attach to the system of pet banks. The independent treasury was, furthermore, a practical plan because Woodbury had already been placing surplus funds in federal vaults instead of depositing them in pet banks that had suspended specie payments. He was complying with the Deposit-Distribution Act of 1836, which prohibited federal deposits in banks that had suspended payments. Deciding to support the independent treasury plan was typical of Van Buren's essential flexibility. Although he rarely came up with new ideas himself, he had always been willing to accept someone else's idea and turn it to his own political advantage. He had taken the same approach to the War of 1812, to the Erie Canal, to democratic changes at the New York constitutional convention, to Andrew Jackson's presidential candidacy, and to the war against the Bank of the United States.[27]

1837, Taney to MVB, July 20, 1837, Ritchie to MVB, Aug. 20, 1837, Welles to MVB, Aug. 26, 1837, VBP; Rives to David Campbell, June 18, 1837, Tallmadge to Rives, June 30, 1837, David Campbell Papers, Duke University Library; *Richmond Enquirer*, June 2, 1837; [Washington, D.C.] *Madisonian*, Aug. 16, Aug. 19, Aug. 23, 1837.

[26] New Hampshire Legislature, Instructions to senators and representatives in Congress to oppose a Bank of the United States, July 7, 1837, Parker to MVB, May 29, 1837, Benton to MVB, May 31, 1837, Welles to MVB, July 24, 1837, Macon to MVB, June 18, 1837, Cambreleng to MVB, Aug. 2, 1837, VBP.

[27] McFaul, *Politics of Jacksonian Finance*, pp. 123-127; James Roger Sharp, *The Jacksonians versus the Banks: Politics in the States after the Panic of 1837* (New York, 1970), pp. 10-11; Brockenbrough to Rives, May 20, 1837, Rives Papers, LC; Brockenbrough to MVB, May 22, 1837, Gouge to MVB, July 17, 1840, Gouge, Draft of a Request for Advice on Questions to Come before Congress in Special Session on the

With the independent treasury as the cornerstone of his program, Van Buren spent the rest of the summer working with Gouge, Woodbury and Benjamin Butler, fashioning a balanced set of proposals that would satisfy as many Democrats as possible. To attract radicals and Old Republicans he offered the independent treasury and postponement of the final installment of the distribution of surplus revenue to the states. To satisfy state bankers he suggested delaying federal lawsuits against banks that had suspended payments. To please conservatives he proposed issuing paper money in the form of federal Treasury notes. A sense of drama filled the inner circle of administrators as they mobilized the press and sent letters to win over prominent Democrats. A few years later Gouge recalled that "in that crisis" Butler was the President's "confidential counsellor," while Gouge himself advised Butler. Van Buren, who gave up his usual vacation that summer, was as tense and distraught as he had been at the height of his struggle with DeWitt Clinton. When Silas Wright wrote that he was reluctant to support the program and warned that it would have difficulty getting through Congress, Van Buren revealed his tension and insecurity by scribbling across the face of the letter: the "discouraging" contents, he wrote, showed that his friend Wright was "in a moody frame of mind."[28]

As the special session approached, Van Buren's careful work seemed to be succeeding. To keep Jackson's support Woodbury had explained carefully just why they had been so lenient with defaulting banks. Jackson was delighted that Van Buren wanted to separate the government from the banks. In hopes of holding the conservatives, Van Buren tactfully asked Rives again for his views on banking and government agencies, and assured Marcy that they could all appreciate why he was sympathetic to state banks. Although Cambreleng disapproved of the Treasury notes, both he and Azariah Flagg applauded the independent treasury. So did Isaac Hill and James Buchanan, who wrote that he liked "Dr. B's plan." Wright soon fell in line after discovering that the farmers in St. Lawrence County approved of the program. Announcing that he would fight for the independent treasury until the "labouring classes" were safe from the "caprice and cupidity" of the banks, Wright wrote a series of articles for the *St. Lawrence*

National Revenues and the Banks, with Corrections by Woodbury and Van Buren, June 21, 1837, VBP.

[28] Woodbury to Jackson, June 28, 1837, Jackson, *Correspondence*, V, 490-491; MVB to Rives, May 25, 1837, Gouge to MVB, July 17, 1840, Wright to MVB, June 4, 1837, VBP; Garraty, *Wright*, pp. 144-146, MVB to Marcy, June 18, 1837, Gratz Collection, HSP.

Republican supporting Van Buren's proposals. A note of caution was sounded by Thomas Ritchie, who feared that the establishment of a number of subtreasuries would strengthen the power of the executive by increasing federal patronage. To keep peace in Virginia Ritchie preferred not to have the controversial plan brought up. But Van Buren appeared to have most of his party behind him as the special session convened.[29]

On September 5, Abraham Van Buren delivered his father's message to the clerks of both Houses of Congress. The message inaugurated a new Van Buren, one who was clear, direct and to the point—far different from the Van Buren who had managed to reach the White House by avoiding commitment on specific issues and whose inaugural address was singularly noncommittal. This time, dispensing with a wordy, rhetorical introduction, Van Buren moved right to the heart of the matter. The Deposit-Distribution Act of 1836, he pointed out in his first sentence, required the Secretary of the Treasury to stop using banks that "refuse[d] to redeem their notes in specie." Since most deposit banks had suspended specie payments in May, Woodbury had discontinued deposits and thereby made congressional regulations for the "safe-keeping of the public moneys . . . inoperative." In addition, because of a shortage of federal funds, it would be difficult to make the final distribution to the states due in October. Realistic politician that he was, Van Buren warned the Congress that the panic had become "connected with the passions and conflicts of party," but he told them confidently that "a community [as] intelligent" as theirs would "ultimately [reach] correct conclusions." He had called the special session to enable Congress to reach just such conclusions. The quintessential new-style politician, Van Buren was confident that the new politics that he had created would be able to solve the economic ills of the nation.[30]

After this straightforward start, Van Buren launched into a clear and sophisticated analysis of the causes of the panic. Attributing the present situation primarily to "overaction in all the departments of business," and to "excessive issues of bank paper," he documented fact by fact the great "expansion of credit": an increase in bank notes in 1834 and 1835 from $95,000,000 to $140,000,000; a jump in the

[29] Cambreleng to Abraham Van Buren, May 30, 1837, Cambreleng to MVB, June 13, 1837, Flagg to Butler, July 12, 1837, Wright to MVB, June 22, 1837, Hill to MVB, July 4, 1837, Buchanan to MVB, July 5, 1837, Ritchie to MVB, Aug. 20, 1837, VBP; Jackson to MVB, Aug. 7, 1837, Jackson Papers, LC; Garraty, *Wright*, pp. 144-146; *St. Lawrence* [N.Y.] *Republican*, June 20-Aug. 15, 1837.

[30] Richardson, *Messages and Papers*, III, 324-346; Adams, *Memoirs*, IX, 366.

sale of public lands from $4,500,000 in 1834 to $39,500,000 during the next two years. He made the critical point that the money invested in lands had been particularly inflationary because it was temporarily an "unproductive" investment that had not increased the supply of real goods in the country. He called attention to the costly fire in New York City in 1835, and to the bad grain crops that had forced Americans to spend money on grain from Europe. He blamed the panic directly on "the measures adopted by the foreign creditors . . . to reduce their debts and to withdraw from the United States a large portion of our specie." Suddenly, said Van Buren, England and the United States—the two "most commercial [nations] in the world"— had been "plunged into a state of embarrassment and distress." The message was a classic statement of the international interpretation of the Panic of 1837.

By elimination Van Buren made his way toward the independent treasury. "For the deposit, transfer, and disbursement of the revenue," he went on, first the Bank of the United States and then state banks had been tried, but reviving the former would be improper because it would violate the will of the people. The pet bank system must be rejected because it had "stimulate[d] a general rashness of enterprise and aggravate[d] the fluctuations of commerce and the currency." Therefore, he concluded, federal funds should be controlled by the government rather than by banks. The latter were not any "more able than the Government to secure the money in their possession against accident, violence, or fraud." It was foolish to argue that "a vault in a bank [was] stronger than a vault in the Treasury." The government had been keeping funds in federal vaults since the suspension of specie payments in May.

In order to rally Old Republican and radical support, and to keep the backing of Andrew Jackson, Van Buren couched his analysis in language reminiscent of Nathaniel Macon and the Old Hero himself. In a series of paragraphs Van Buren denounced not just "speculation," but also "reckless speculation" and "adventurous speculation"—not only in land sales but in "the whole range of human enterprise." The excessive use of credit especially endangered the "laboring classes" when it "inflame[d] the public mind with the temptations of sudden and unsubstantial wealth." He blamed the panic on "luxurious habits founded too often on merely fancied wealth, and detrimental to . . . the morals of our people." Government, he said, should not contribute to such "excesses in speculation." He showed that he was still a Jeffersonian by remarking that "all communities are apt to look to government for too much," and in words that William Jennings Bryan would echo a half-century later, he concluded that conditions were not as serious as they might be because "the great agricultural interest [had] suffered comparatively little," and "the proceeds of our great staples [would] soon furnish the means of liquidating debts at home and abroad." Conscious of Thomas Ritchie's warning, Van Buren denied that his plan would increase executive patronage. He promised to keep the specie circular and cancel the fourth distribution to the states.

Van Buren sought to attract broad support by outlining other proposals that would appeal to conservatives. The President insisted that he had no desire to "undervalue the benefits of a salutary credit to any branch of enterprise," for credit was the "just reward of merit and an honorable incentive to further acquisition." He reported that he had postponed the due date of duty bonds owed by merchants until October 1, and asked Congress to consider further postponement. In spite of radical proposals that the Treasury accept only hard money for all debts owed the government, Van Buren did not recommend such a requirement. And he annoyed radicals by proposing that the government issue Treasury notes to make more money available. With this combination of radical and conservative planks Van Buren had fashioned a program that he believed would unite his party. He had finally shown himself willing to make some changes in Jacksonian Democracy. Whether these changes would be voted into law, whether they would be enough to pull the nation out of the panic, and whether Van Buren's program was well-suited to the expanding America of the 1830s remained to be seen.

Politicians reacted, and in many cases overreacted, to the message in accordance with their political and economic views. Party stalwarts Richard E. Parker, Ritchie and Buchanan agreed that the message demonstrated Van Buren's great "moral courage" and "dissipated the charges against him of timidity." The *Globe* called the message "the boldest and highest stand ever taken by a chief magistrate, . . . a second declaration of independence." John K. Kane of Pennsylvania, predicted that it would become one of the great statements of principle of the American people. Loco Focos were particularly flattering because they considered the independent treasury their brainchild. Old Republicans liked the "beauty and force" of Van Buren's argument for limited government.

But there were many critics of the speech. Conservatives and Whigs, who received the message as an "electric shock," denounced it as "ultra," and "locofoco to the very core." The Democratic Republicans of New York City were fearful that an increase in "corrupt political patronage [would] endanger the liberties of the Republic." Even loyal newspapers were cautious. The *Albany Argus* praised the message, but was not enthusiastic about the independent treasury, while the *Richmond Enquirer* feared that executive authority might be increased by the plan.[31]

Ever since 1837 historians have tried to fit Van Buren's message and the independent treasury into their own interpretations of Jacksonian Democracy. Van Buren's biographer Edward M. Shepard, a laissez-faire Democrat writing in the late nineteenth century, considered the message "one of the greatest of American state papers" because it argued that "the government had not caused [and] could not cure" the panic. Arthur M. Schlesinger, Jr., viewing history from the perspective of the New Deal, praised Van Buren for trying to block the rise of "a moneyed aristocracy" and for warning the business class that it did not have "a proprietary right to government favor." Reacting to Schlesinger, Bray Hammond called the independent treasury an "ingenious" scheme that seemed to attack state banks while all the while freeing them from federal control. According to Hammond, the plan "breathed the sound and fury of Loco Foco distrust of banks," but did nothing more than call them "hard names."[32]

Such evaluations missed the point of Van Buren's message. The message was neither as bold and courageous as supporters claimed, nor as "loco-foco" and "corrupt" as detractors insisted. An independent treasury plan that called for additional federal patronage was hardly a laissez-faire program. The new system, after all, offered the possibility of federal regulation of banking because the receivers at the subtreasuries could put pressure on state banks by accumulating their bank notes and then presenting them for specie. Nor is it reasonable to suggest as Schlesinger does that a cautious politician such

---

[31] For statements of praise, see VBP; also Buchanan to Jackson, Oct. 26, 1837, Buchanan, *Works*, III, 324; Washington *Globe*, Sept. 5, 1837; *Richmond Enquirer*, Sept. 8, 1837. For criticism, see Democratic Republicans of New York City, Resolutions, Sept. 27, 1837, Thomas Olcott to MVB, Sept. 19, 1837, Myndert Van Schaick to MVB, Sept. 23, 1837, Azariah Flagg to MVB, Nov. 5, 1837, VBP; *Argus*, Sept. 8, Sept. 15, 1837; *Richmond Enquirer*, Sept. 8, 1837; Claiborne W. Gooch to Thomas Ritchie, Sept. 7, 1837, Gooch Family Papers, UVL; *Madisonian*, Sept. 6, 1837; Charles A. Davis to Nicholas Biddle, Sept. 27, 1837, Biddle, *Correspondence*, pp. 292-293; Hone, *Diary*, p. 282.

[32] Glyndon Van Deusen revived Shepard's interpretation in *The Jacksonian Era 1828-1848* (New York, 1959), pp. 121-122. Dixon Ryan Fox and John M. McFaul interpreted the message as Schlesinger did. Fox, *Decline of Aristocracy*, p. 398; McFaul, *Politics of Jacksonian Finance*, pp. 194-199; Shepard, *Van Buren*, pp. 325-327; Schlesinger, *Age of Jackson*, pp. 239-240; Hammond, *Banks and Politics*, pp. 496-499.

as Van Buren, with his great respect for wealth, would lead a crusade against the business class. And if Van Buren had been trying to protect the state banks as Hammond maintains, he would have come right out and said so in order to win the support of Rives, Tallmadge and the other conservatives. Each interpretation is too theoretical and far too much influenced by the economic and political view of the writer.

Furthermore, none of the interpretations considers the message from the vantage point of Van Buren himself, with his particular personal and political goals. In determining his course of action in the past Van Buren had always behaved cautiously, had tried to avoid unnecessary action, and when forced to act had sought to balance republican principles with practical adjustment to economic change. In a showdown he invariably put his personal career and his political party ahead of the issues. It was not likely that at the age of fifty-four Van Buren was going to change. He did not. Cautious as always, he had tried to move slowly and to do as little as possible. He refused to repeal the specie circular and he refused at first to call a special session of Congress. But facing economic disaster and a divided political party, Van Buren adopted a carefully balanced program designed to save his presidency, his party, and the nation—in that order. He compromised over the issues. By divorcing the government from the banks he joined the radicals and showed his loyalty to Jackson and the Old Republicans. By calling for Treasury notes and postponing lawsuits against the banks he signaled his acceptance of an economy based on paper money and state banks. Van Buren did what he thought most of his party and most Americans could agree on.[33]

But there was no certainty that this program would save either Van Buren or his party. From a personal standpoint he had done well. He had behaved much more firmly and resolutely than most observers had expected and was clearly in control of the party. He had also managed to free himself from dependence on Andrew Jackson without losing his ties with the Old Hero. By warning Jackson tactfully that the administration was not tied permanently to the specie circular, by dealing more gently with the banks than Jackson would have liked, by ignoring some of Jackson's letters, and by presenting his own program—the independent treasury was not Jackson's idea—Van Buren had won his freedom. By retaining the specie circular—for the time being at least—he had salvaged the symbolic tie with Jackson. But

[33] In this interpretation I have been influenced by James C. Curtis in *The Fox at Bay*, ch. 4, ch. 5, but I go further than Curtis in tying Van Buren's program to his previous career.

this was not enough to counteract the public's fundamental suspicion of Van Buren.

As far as the Democratic party was concerned, Van Buren had offered what appeared to be the best possibility for unification. The program was radical enough to hold Benton, conservative enough to keep Marcy, Jacksonian enough to satisfy Blair, and sufficiently anti-bank to attract Calhoun. But by conjuring up the Loco Foco image of the independent treasury Van Buren ran the risk of starting a crusade that might alienate enough conservatives and potential Whigs to create a powerful opposition to the Democratic party, especially in the two states on which he had always relied—New York and Virginia. Tall-madge and Rives might yet defeat the Democratic party.

Nor was there any assurance that Van Buren's program would meet the needs of the nation. With its combination of nostalgic symbols and grudging acceptance of change, Jacksonian Democracy had satis-fied enough Americans to carry the nation through the Bank War and the nullification crisis while largely ignoring the economic boom. But with thousands unemployed in cities that had been only towns a decade earlier, with thousands surging to the Northwest and the Southwest, with the insistent demand for factories, railroads and farms, it was unreasonable to base a program on Jeffersonian principles and on the thesis that the government should remain separated from the economy. And there were other national problems that Van Buren chose not to address in his message, notably the growing antislavery movement and the territorial expansion that created diplomatic problems on the fron-tiers. Many Americans may have been committed to Jefferson's theory of republicanism, but just as many were committed to the acquisition of wealth, and to the pursuit of progress and personal freedom. Van Buren would have to modify his program to satisfy these changing class and sectional needs. A party based upon the planters of the South and the plain republicans of the North would have to be flexible enough to satisfy Americans who considered themselves neither.

The success of Van Buren's plans depended on the Twenty-fifth Congress, which had gathered for its first session to hear his message. The task would be easier in the Senate, where one tabulation counted 30 Democrats out of 52 members, than in the House, where the same count showed 108 Democrats, 107 Whigs and 24 others. With nul-lifiers, Anti-Masons, hard-money Democrats, Loco Focos, Bank of the United States supporters, conservative Democrats, administration Democrats, National Republicans, and the American System Whigs in the Congress, as well as complicated sectional and economic align-ments, the terms "Democrat" and "Whig" did not mean a great deal.

Simply put, in 1837 Whigs and conservative Democrats could outvote administration Democrats; so political maneuvering and effective party leadership would be essential. The administration made a good start in the House by electing as speaker Jackson's friend James K. Polk of Tennessee, who in turn chose Van Buren's friend Churchill C. Cambreleng as chairman of the Ways and Means Committee. But it was a measure of the administration's weakness that the House printing went to the conservative *Madisonian* rather than to the administration *Globe*. Van Buren had fewer worries in the Senate because the reliable Silas Wright was made chairman of the Finance Committee. Perhaps Polk, Cambreleng and Wright could translate Van Buren's program into law.[34]

The administration moved rapidly in the Senate, where Wright introduced five bills embracing Van Buren's entire program between September 11 and September 15. Since all of the bills except the independent treasury were practical measures designed to help the banks and the Treasury weather the panic, these four passed the Senate by September 19 and the House by October 16. With the surplus in the Treasury dwindling, Congress quickly approved a bill to postpone the fourth installment of the distribution bill. Congress also passed a bill requiring the Secretary of the Treasury to withdraw federal funds from deposit banks that had suspended specie payments, but giving the banks eight months of grace in which to make the necessary payments to the Treasury. In another measure to help bankers and merchants, Van Buren secured passage of a bill allowing merchants to delay payment of custom house bonds. He had difficulty with his bill authorizing the issuance of $10,000,000 of Treasury notes because Cambreleng and Jackson disapproved of such expansion of paper money, but the drastic need for funds to pay immediate government expenses made the bill mandatory. By mid-October Van Buren could boast that he had put four-fifths of his program into operation.[35]

Hoping to avoid controversy over the remaining fifth—the independent treasury—he presented it as a practical measure to help the country through the crisis, not as a dramatic governmental reform; and to forestall criticism that the independent treasury would increase the number of public officials, he decided to create no new federal

[34] The tabulation listed 30 Democrats, 18 Whigs, and 4 others in the Senate. *Statistical History of the United States*, p. 691; *Congressional Globe*, 25th Congress, 1st session (1837), 3, 11, 13, 15, 16; Sellers, *James K. Polk Jacksonian*, pp. 326-327; Blair to Jackson, Sept. 9, 1837, Jackson, *Correspondence*, V, 509-510.

[35] *Congressional Globe*, 25th Congress, 1st session (1837), 17, 22, 26-27, 32, 38, 41, 91, 120, 123, 145.

agencies such as subtreasuries. Instead, on Thursday, September 14, Silas Wright brought to the Senate a bill that merely sought to impose "additional duties as depositories, in certain cases, on public officers." The bill authorized officers of the Treasury, the Mint, the land offices, the customs offices, and the Post Office to collect and disburse public funds without the use of banks.[36]

Prospects for early passage of the independent treasury bill brightened when rumors spread that Senator John C. Calhoun and other Southerners who had left the Democratic party over nullification, were planning to return to the fold and support the bill. On the day the independent treasury bill was introduced, Calhoun gave an indication that the rumors were correct by joining the administration in blocking an attempt by Rives to postpone consideration of one of the other bills. Two days later, on Saturday, September 16, Calhoun asked postponement until Monday of the Treasury notes bill so that he could have time to prepare an amendment. It was obvious that Calhoun's speech on Monday would go well beyond Treasury notes to the broad question of the divorce of banking from the government. Since the administration had no desire to put Calhoun in the spotlight, Benton and Wright tried to block postponement, but they were unable to do so.

The galleries were thronged on Monday to hear the great nullifier speak. Buttressing his opinions with historical data, Calhoun pleased Van Buren by supporting the independent treasury, but he embarrassed the President by offering an amendment requiring the Treasury to accept nothing but specie from state banks after 1840. In his message Van Buren had avoided committing himself to such an arbitrary hard-money position because he did not want to alienate conservative Democrats. Calhoun's cool arrogance also annoyed the administration. The self-centered South Carolinian gave every impression of being in complete command, calling the independent treasury bill his own measure and asking for administration help. After the speech he bragged that he stood "in the breach in this great conflict," bore "the brunt of the action," and controlled "the fate of the country." Although he boasted that the administration had been forced to "play directly" into his hand, others assumed that Calhoun had returned to the Democratic party in order to strengthen his chances for the presidency. The caustic John Quincy Adams referred to the move as "Calhoun's bargain and sale of himself to Van Buren."[37]

[36] *Ibid.*, 27-28.
[37] Charles Wiltse went much too far in accepting Calhoun's own assessment of his

Calhoun's hard-money amendment to the independent treasury bill turned the discussion in the Senate into a full-fledged debate over the relationship between the government and banking in the United States. On the radical side of the debate was Calhoun supporting hard money; more toward the middle but still on the radical side was Van Buren supporting the independent treasury; far over on the conservative side were Daniel Webster and Henry Clay, who were urging the reestablishment of the Bank of the United States. Between them and Van Buren stood the conservative Democrats William C. Rives and Nathaniel P. Tallmadge, who supported the system of pet banks. On the day after Calhoun proposed his amendment Rives offered his own bill, which would allow the government to continue depositing funds in state banks provided they agreed gradually to eliminate small notes under $20. Attacking the Bank of the United States on the one hand and the independent treasury on the other, Rives argued that the state banks were "able . . . to perform all the duties required of them," and blamed the woes of the country on the specie circular rather than on the banks. In supporting Rives on September 22, Senator Tallmadge expressed the fear that the independent treasury bill marked an attack on the entire system of credit in the United States, a system that the French traveler Michel Chevalier had called "the primary element of life in the United States." With Rives's amendment the whole spectrum of political attitudes toward banking was represented.[38]

Confident that there were enough votes to dispose of the Bank of the United States, the administration decided to settle that matter first before going on to the independent treasury. Therefore on September 21, Silas Wright brought in a resolution from the Finance Committee against the establishment of a national bank. Despite Henry Clay's objections, Wright's resolution passed the Senate, 31-15, on September 26, with the voting along straight party lines. When the same resolution passed the House on October 5, the specter of Nicholas Biddle was laid to rest. Since Rives and Tallmadge voted with the Democratic

---

role in the debate. In describing Calhoun's speech Wiltse wrote: "Everyone knew that the occasion was momentous, for it meant that the most powerful single individual in public life was going to take a position on the great issue of the day." Wiltse, *John C. Calhoun, Nullifier*, pp. 342-356. For a less charitable view, see Gerald M. Capers, *John C. Calhoun—Opportunist: a Reappraisal* (Gainesville, 1960), p. 189. Calhoun to James Edward Calhoun, Sept. 7, 1837, Calhoun to Anna Maria Calhoun, Sept. 8, Sept. 30, 1837, Calhoun, *Correspondence*, pp. 377-380; Adams, *Memoirs*, IX, 398; *Congressional Globe*, 25th Congress, 1st session (1837), 28, 35-37.

[38] *Congressional Globe*, 25th Congress, 1st session (1837), appendix, 156-164, 229-236; *Argus*, Oct. 17, Oct. 24, 1837.

party against the Bank of the United States, there was still a chance that Van Buren could maintain party unity.[39]

With the Bank out of the way, the Senate returned to the independent treasury. First Clay and Webster spoke wistfully of the Bank of the United States, but said they would accept the state bank system in preference to the independent treasury. On September 28, Webster leveled a particularly powerful attack against Van Buren for abandoning "the duty of government [in refusing] to recommend any measure for the relief of commerce, for the restoration of currency." The following day James Buchanan stoutly opposed Webster's broad construction of the Constitution and insisted that the founding fathers had conferred on the general government only "certain enumerated powers." In conclusion Buchanan praised Van Buren, declaring that he had "put to flight the charge of non-committalism" and had "shown himself worthy to succeed General Jackson." This was welcome support, but even as President, and even when being defended by a supporter, Van Buren could not escape qualified praise and could not avoid being compared with Andrew Jackson.[40]

The climax of the Senate debate came on October 2, when Silas Wright, who obviously spoke for Van Buren, presented the major administration defense of the independent treasury. Unlike Webster, Wright made no personal references, unlike Calhoun, no historical analogies, unlike Buchanan, no constitutional analysis. Instead the speech was vintage Silas Wright—even vintage Martin Van Buren— sober, reasoned, well-organized, placing the independent treasury in the context of the administration's well-balanced economic package. He finished by denying the two charges the administration most feared— that the bill would increase executive patronage, and that it would destroy the credit of the United States. It might have been Van Buren speaking, urging his colleagues to "take a calm dispassionate view."[41]

After Wright's speech the administration was ready to vote on amendments. Calhoun spoke in defense of hard money on October 3, and his amendment was brought to a vote. Convinced by this time that they could not hold the votes of the conservative Democrats, the administration decided to support the amendment in order to keep Calhoun and his southern supporters in line. Silas Wright led the way by voting in favor of the amendment, which passed by a vote of 24 to 23, with Rives and Tallmadge voting nay. Next, Rives' bill in favor

[39] *Congressional Globe*, 25th Congress, 1st session (1837), 49, 73-76, 103-105.
[40] *Ibid.*, appendix, 94-103, quotation, 103, 167-174, 179-184; *Argus*, Oct. 27, 1837.
[41] *Congressional Globe*, 25th Congress, 1st session (1837), 94; appendix, 113-121.

of the pet bank system was defeated, 26-22. By adding Calhoun's amendment to the independent treasury and by defeating Rives' bill, Van Buren allowed the administration to slide further toward the radical end of the spectrum and forced conservative Democrats out of the party.[42]

With the fate of the amendments decided, the administration brought the independent treasury bill to a final vote on the floor of the Senate. When it passed, 26-20, it was again by a party vote. The victory in the Senate reflected well on the administration, showing that Van Buren could provide executive leadership in that body. Within a month they had pushed five financial bills and an anti-Bank of the United States resolution through the upper chamber, and in the process had adjusted well to the return of Calhoun to the party. Although their margin of success slipped from 31-15 on the Bank of the United States resolution, to a bare 24-23 on the specie amendment, Wright had managed to hold Democratic ranks firm when it counted. He cracked the whip so effectively that on the average only one administration senator missed any given vote and administration Democrats voted with Wright ninety-one percent of the time.[43]

When the independent treasury bill was sent to the House, it encountered more difficulty than in the Senate because the administration lacked a clear majority of the votes. In hopes of saving time and winning a few nullifier votes, Cambreleng passed up the opportunity to speak first on the bill and gave the honor to Francis W. Pickens of South Carolina. It was a mistake, because on October 10, Pickens antagonized both friends and foes of the bill by making a slashing attack on banking in general and by concluding with an irrelevant defense of slavery. John Quincy Adams best summed up the reaction:

> Pickens is a fixture in the house of Calhoun, and Van Buren bought him with Calhoun. Cambreleng tickles his vanity by pushing him forward as the champion of this bill. . . . Pickens is . . . pompous, flashy, and shallow. . . . Pickens' speech was a jumble . . . of abuse upon Jackson . . . of abuse, repeated from Calhoun, upon banks, . . . of South Carolina nullification, of slave-driving autocracy, and of ranting radicalism.[44]

Cambreleng, who spoke three days later, made matters worse with a tactless speech accusing the opposition of rejoicing "at the embar-

[42] *Ibid.*, 96; appendix, 121-126.

[43] *Ibid.*, 100; Curtis, *Fox at Bay*, pp. 104-105.

[44] *Congressional Globe*, 25th Congress, 1st session (1837), appendix, 174-179; Adams, *Memoirs*, IX, 398-399.

rassment of our treasury." Instead of placating the state bankers, he denounced them. Instead of avoiding the question of increased federal power, he boasted that the independent treasury would allow the government to regulate notes issued by state banks. When he attacked Ogden Hoffman of New York, for deserting Tammany Hall after receiving spoils for years, Hoffman retorted with "tremendous invective." According to Adams' description, congressmen "formed a perfect ring" around the two, listening so intently that "a pin might have been heard to drop" as Cambreleng "cowered under the castigation, and implored Hoffman's mercy."[45]

It was a bad moment for the Regency and Van Buren, and a bad omen for the independent treasury. Most of the speeches before and after Cambreleng's speech were against the bill. On October 14, only four days after Pickens' speech, John C. Clark, a Whig from New York, rose to observe that since the public had not had time to make up its mind on the bill, he believed it wise to postpone consideration until the next session. Clark argued that there was a "difference of opinion [among] the friends of the administration," and he drew attention to the embarrassing fact that even the *Albany Argus* had not yet taken a position. By a vote of 120-107 Clark's motion passed, and the independent treasury was postponed until the next session.[46]

The bill might have failed anyway, but the administration had not managed as well in the House as it had in the Senate. Cambreleng's choice of Pickens and the New Yorker's own crude speech were disastrous. On the bill to postpone, sixteen Democrats voted against the administration and seven more did not vote at all. Despite the concessions to the South, five Virginians and all South Carolinians except Pickens voted to postpone. Since a shift of seven votes might have saved the bill, the southern defections were decisive. If a President can be judged on the performance of his aides, Van Buren was a failure in the House.[47]

Van Buren had difficulty winning votes in the state elections that fall, and his independent treasury failed to receive a vote of confidence. In New York the Albany Regency entered the fall election badly divided by the panic and the independent treasury. Edwin Croswell, the editor of the *Albany Argus*, was so involved in speculation that he was not interested in an independent treasury plan that threatened state banks and bank notes. Thomas Olcott considered Van Buren's

---

[45] *Congressional Globe*, 25th Congress, 1st session (1837), appendix, 146-151; Adams, *Memoirs*, IX, 406.

[46] *Congressional Globe*, 25th Congress, 1st session (1837), 140-141.

[47] Curtis, *Fox at Bay*, p. 109.

message "ultra" and regretted the "harsh and offensive course of the *Globe*." Governor Marcy told Van Buren that the President's message showed "great ability," but warned him to be ready for "some diversity of opinion." Despite his "great admiration [for Van Buren's] talents, wisdom and discretion," Marcy still would not "submit." He was tired of the "scolding" he had received from Washington and believed that someone should do some "scolding back" because he could not "see the wisdom of the sub-treasury suggestion." When a group of bankers in Albany published an attack on Van Buren, Azariah Flagg felt obliged to deny that members of the Regency were involved.

Democratic prospects in New York were bleak that fall because of the shakeup in the political parties. As a result of the independent treasury conservative Democrats went over to the Whigs, while Loco Focos in New York City were accepted back by Tammany Hall. Whigs took advantage of the changes to accuse all Democrats of being Loco Focos and campaigned against hard money, Locofocoism, agrarianism, and the panic. When Benjamin Butler visited Albany in October to drum up support for the independent treasury, Marcy asked sarcastically who would shield the party in New York from the work of "the loco-focos" in Washington. Shaken by the attack, Butler changed the subject and sent word back to Van Buren that the Democrats could not expect to carry ten of the state's fifty-eight counties in November if they ran on the administration's program. John Van Buren also warned his father in October that the party's chances were poor. The Regency organized the traditional mass meeting in Albany late in the month, but to no avail. In the election in November the Whigs turned a deficit of 28,000 votes in 1836 into a majority of 17,000, winning 121 of 148 seats in the assembly, and ten out of twelve elections for the senate. Worse still for the Regency, the Democrats lost many of the elections for sheriffs and clerks. Marcy and Cambreleng, who disagreed on the independent treasury, agreed that they had lost because of the Loco Focos, while Croswell and Flagg, who also disagreed, shared the view that it was Van Buren's worst defeat since the election of 1824.[48]

[48] Marcy to Wetmore, Sept. 9, Nov. 9, 1837, Marcy to Albert Gallup, Sept. 23, 1837, Marcy Papers, LC; Olcott to MVB, Sept. 19, 1837, Marcy to MVB, Sept. 18, 1837, John Van Buren to MVB, Oct. 15, 1837, Flagg to MVB, Nov. 5, Nov. 9, 1837, Cambreleng to MVB, Nov. 15, 1837, "A Chart Showing the Progress of the Great Political Trends Which Swept over the Empire State during the 6th, 7th, & 8th, November, 1837," VBP; *Argus*, Sept. 8, Sept. 12, Sept. 22, Sept. 29, Oct. 24, Oct. 27, Nov. 14, Nov. 17, Nov. 24, 1837; Hammond, *Political Parties*, II, 478-479; McGrane, *Panic of 1837*, pp. 152-156.

Elsewhere the results were just as discouraging. In addition to New York, the states of Rhode Island, Ohio, Illinois, and North Carolina moved from the Democratic to the Whig column, and nowhere did the Democrats win back a state. Whigs swept the Northwest because Van Buren's program seemed to threaten future expansion in lands, transportation and banking. For the same reason Democrats were weakened in the South, where the defection of Tennessee continued; but the party was too well-entrenched to lose the cotton states of Alabama and Mississippi. The Whigs scored a decisive victory in Massachusetts by exploiting the unemployment and the bankruptcies caused by the panic. Only in Pennsylvania, where suspicion of Biddle and the Bank of the United States hurt the Whigs, did the Democrats win an important victory.[49]

Although there was no election in Virginia that fall, there was ample evidence that Van Buren could no longer count on his banner southern state. In a cordial letter Thomas Ritchie said that he liked and respected the "generous . . . honest and able" Van Buren, but could not support his program because it would increase the power of the executive and hurt the banks of Virginia. Governor David Campbell predicted that the South and West would desert Van Buren in the next election and said that only "silly pride" kept many Virginians from doing so at once. One of the most loyal Virginians, Richard E. Parker, warned Van Buren not to push the conservatives into joining the Whigs, and John Brockenbrough complained that Secretary of the Treasury Levi Woodbury had been too severe in withdrawing federal funds from deposit banks. By December, the *Richmond Enquirer* was adamantly opposed to the independent treasury.[50]

The Democratic losses not only cast doubt on the political wisdom of Van Buren's response to the panic; they also suggested that his program had economic limitations. Democratic and Whig critics exaggerated when they accused him of being a Loco Foco and when they asserted that the independent treasury would destroy the economy by denying it the credit needed for expansion. Since the federal government held only two percent of the money supply of the country, no banking plan, however radical, was likely to have a decisive long-term impact on the economy; in fact the nation's economy expanded rapidly

---

[49] McGrane, *Panic of 1837*, pp. 156-163.

[50] Ritchie to Thomas Green, Sept. 20, 1837, Ambler, "Ritchie Letters," *Branch Papers*, 4 (June 1916), 282; David Campbell to——, Sept. 18, 1837, Campbell to William C. Rives, Nov. 4, 1837, Campbell to——, Nov. 25, 1837, David Campbell Papers, Duke University Library; Richard E. Parker to MVB, Nov. 14, 1837, Brockenbrough to MVB, Nov. 12, 1837, VBP; *Richmond Enquirer*, Dec. 8, 1837.

between 1846 and 1913 while the independent treasury was in operation. Two percent of the money supply could, however, have a short-term effect, and exaggerated fears of the administration's policies could seriously endanger the economy. Jacksonian policies had aroused such fears, and they had contributed to the coming of the panic. Sober and cautious as he was, Van Buren understood the need to build up the confidence of the banking and merchant community; he designed his special session message and his financial program to meet this need.

But Van Buren was too cautious, he tried too hard to balance all interests, bowing to Jackson and the specie circular, Ritchie and Old Republicanism, Calhoun and hard money. If only Van Buren and Cambreleng had been able to hold the southern votes in the House and pass the independent treasury bill, then perhaps the President could have weathered the fall defeats and gone on to cope with the country's real needs during the remainder of his presidency. After all, the expanding nation needed roads, railroads, banks, credit, factories, and jobs. Many of Van Buren's constituents believed that the borders should be pushed south and west toward Mexico and the Pacific; others believed that the institution of slavery should be examined. But Van Buren was stuck with a crusade to win the independent treasury— a crusade that would make him and his party appear more radical than was the case and would interfere with the pursuit of more worthwhile goals.[51]

Van Buren reacted to his setbacks in Congress and in the states with his usual poise and optimism. When Adams called at the White House in the uncertain days after the special session message, he expected to find the President looking "wretched," but instead found him displaying "every appearance of composure and tranquillity." A few weeks later Van Buren was optimistically declaring that "the Democracy [was] everywhere rallying [with] fervor" behind the "principles" of his message. Within a month he was insisting that the defeat in New York was only temporary. Perhaps he was simply whistling in the dark, perhaps he was resorting to the self-control that had always been his strongest characteristic. In one reflective moment Van Buren told Adams that it was a "delusion" for a President to expect to be happy, and spoke admiringly of the "calm, philosophical spirit" of James Madison. Adams generously conceded that Van Buren resembled Madison in his "calmness [and] gentleness."[52]

[51] Temin, *Jacksonian Economy*, pp. 166-167.

[52] Adams, *Memoirs*, IX, 368-369; MVB to Andrew J. Donelson, Oct. 4, 1837, Andrew J. Donelson Papers, LC; MVB to Andrew Jackson, Nov. 18, 1837, MVB to Richard E. Parker, Nov. 16, 1837, VBP.

In his first eight months as President Van Buren showed many of the qualities that had brought him to the White House. Despite the party split over banking policy, he was still the same cautious, tactful harmonizer who sought to bring politicians of divergent views together. He still prized his philosophical ties with Jefferson and his political and personal ties with Jackson. And yet he was showing signs of becoming a new man, upsetting expectations. Instead of bowing to Jackson whenever the general "roar[ed] like a lion," as one observer put it, Van Buren exhibited independence by cooperating with the conservatives and the nullifiers. James Buchanan acknowledged that Van Buren displayed far more "firmness" than Buchanan had anticipated. Whigs who had portrayed him as a "sly fox" and Democrats who had hoped that he would continue to be the "Little Magician" found that he was neither. His handling of patronage and his management of the independent treasury bill produced no evidence either of chicanery or political magic. In short there were signs that Van Buren had lost some of the sharpness that had shaped his reputation.[53]

But in the Indian summer of late October after Congress had adjourned, Van Buren's thoughts turned to less weighty matters. He relaxed at his retreat in Georgetown before departing for a short vacation at Berkeley Springs, Virginia, where members of the cabinet joined him to prepare for the next session of Congress.[54]

[53] N. Knight to J. T. Fowler, Dec. 22, 1839, J. F. Simmons Papers, LC; Buchanan to Jackson, July 28, 1837, Jackson, *Correspondence*, V, 501.
[54] *Niles' Register*, 53 (1837), 129.

· 11 ·

THE INDEPENDENT TREASURY

Gunfire ended Van Buren's brief respite on the evening of November 21, when Whigs gathered near the White House, shooting off cannon to celebrate their victories in New York and Massachusetts. It was a rude reminder of his political and legislative defeats during the fall. With the opening of Congress only two weeks away, Van Buren focused on the goals that he had set for himself during the summer— passage of the independent treasury bill and political success for the Democratic party. He yearned to hear cannon sounding in the night celebrating his victories in these battles.[1]

But during the next two years Van Buren found that entirely different issues—slavery and manifest destiny—claimed his attention and interfered with his efforts to win the independent treasury. Hints of trouble ahead over slavery appeared during the fall of 1837, with the news of the murder of abolitionist Elijah Lovejoy in Alton, Illinois. The outbreak of a revolt against the crown in Canada that fall pointed up problems of neutrality and peace-keeping on the northern border. And as he awaited the opening of Congress, Van Buren was already deeply involved in negotiations with Mexico over monetary claims, and in similar negotiations with Texas over possible annexation.

Since the election of 1836, Van Buren and Jackson had followed a moderate policy toward Texas. Even though his old friend Sam Houston had won independence for Texas at San Jacinto in April 1836, the usually expansionist Jackson hesitated to recognize the new republic. Finally, on December 8, he asked Amos Kendall to draft a message on recognition that the President could send to Congress, and on December 21, Jackson informed Congress that he would recognize Texan independence only when both Houses told him to do so. The President argued that since recognition might lead to war with Mexico the decision should be left in the hands of the legislature. He said that he preferred to wait until Mexico or one of the European powers recognized the Lone Star Republic.[2]

In adopting a wait-and-see policy toward Texas Jackson was influenced by the cautious views of Van Buren, who was in Washington

[1] Adams, *Memoirs*, IX, 431-432.
[2] Jackson to Kendall, Dec. 8, 1836, Jackson, *Correspondence*, V, 441; Richardson, *Messages and Papers*, III, 265-269.

at the time and had every opportunity to counsel the President. As soon as the message was delivered, Van Buren told his son John that "the thinking and responsible portion of our people [would] sustain the views of the President." William H. Wharton, who had just arrived from Texas to seek recognition and annexation, quickly blamed Van Buren for Jackson's hesitation. According to Wharton, Van Buren wanted to postpone the Texas question because he knew that both his party and his nation were badly divided between Southerners who wanted a new slave state, and antislavery Northerners. The worst policy for the party would be immediate recognition and annexation by an outgoing southern President. If these steps had to be taken, it had better be done by the moderate, proslavery Northerner, Van Buren. It was Wharton's view that Van Buren wanted to delay as long as possible because he did not want to be forced to take a stand on Texas early in his administration and risk repudiation in the congressional elections. Wharton concluded that "the fear then of throwing Mr. Van Buren into a minority in the next Congress induces his friends to desire a postponement of recognition at present, thereby keeping down the exciting question of annexation at the next elections and giving Mr. Van Buren more time to manage his cards and consolidate his strength."

As Wharton had predicted, Van Buren's friends did their best to stall recognition during the last months of the Jackson administration. When Congressman Linn Boyd of Kentucky, moved in February to instruct the House Committee on Foreign Affairs to report a resolution in favor of recognition, Churchill C. Cambreleng moved to suspend the rules in order to take up an appropriation bill instead of Boyd's motion. Cambreleng's delaying tactics failed when he could not secure the necessary two-thirds vote to suspend the rules, but the House tabled the resolution of recognition. In the Senate Silas Wright succeeded in having a similar resolution postponed until March. Finally, however, in the last days of the Jackson administration, both House and Senate passed resolutions in favor of recognition, and on March 3, the President appointed Alcée La Branche chargé d'affaires to the Republic of Texas. Although Jackson and Wharton celebrated the appointment over a glass of wine, the incoming President had little cause to take cheer.[3]

[3] MVB to John Van Buren, Dec. 22, 1836, VBP; Wharton to Stephen Austin, Dec. 11, Dec. 22, Dec. 25, Dec. 31, 1836, Jan. 6, 1837, Wharton to Sam Houston, Feb. 2, Feb. 5, Feb. 12, 1837, Wharton to T. J. Rusk, Feb. 1837, Wharton and Memucan Hunt to J. P. Henderson, Mar. 5, 1837, George P. Garrison, ed., "Diplomatic Correspondence of the Republic of Texas," Part I, American Historical Association, *Annual Report 1907* (Washington, D.C., 1908), II, 151-154, 157-160, 166-172, 179-194, 201; George

During the early months of his administration Van Buren did his best to defuse the Texan situation. He did not officially receive the Texan minister Memucan Hunt until July 6, but as the summer wore on and the panic worsened, Hunt became unreasonably optimistic about the chances for the annexation of Texas. Hunt believed that the panic had so weakened Van Buren that he would have to annex Texas in order to appease the South and win reelection. "Nothing," wrote Hunt, "would so much strengthen" the Democratic party in the South as "hearty support of the annexation of Texas." In the cabinet Hunt counted on support from Southerners Joel Poinsett, Amos Kendall and Secretary of State John Forsyth, and buoyed by misplaced self-confidence, he sent an arrogant message to Forsyth on August 4, asking for immediate annexation. If the United States did not comply, said Hunt, Texas would make commercial treaties with European powers that would further undermine American prosperity.

But Hunt had overestimated the strength of his position and underestimated Van Buren's ability to delay. Properly preoccupied with the panic, Van Buren ignored Hunt's message, and Hunt was soon to discover that Forsyth cared more about party unity than he did about the desires of southern annexationists. On August 11, an angry Hunt wrote: "I have ascertained beyond a doubt, that Mr. Forsyth Secretary of State of the United States is violently opposed to annexation!!" After holding a cabinet meeting on the subject, Van Buren and Forsyth waited until August 25—a week before the special session began— and then rejected the Texan proposal. Basing their decision on the "just principles" of international peace, they declared that while Texas was at war with Mexico the United States could not agree to annexation because it would involve the country in the war.[4]

Van Buren was doing his best to stay out of the war despite the persistent issue of claims by American citizens against the Mexican government. Neither President Adams nor President Jackson had been able to get the ineffectual Mexican government to settle these claims. Jackson became so frustrated that on February 6, 1837, he sent Con-

L. Rives, *The United States and Mexico, 1821-1848* (New York, 1913), I, 393-401; Richardson, *Messages and Papers*, III, 281-282.

[4] Hunt to J. P. Henderson, April 15, 1837, Fairfax Catlett to Henderson, May 25, 1837, Hunt to R. A. Irion, July 11, Aug. 10, Aug. 11, Oct. 21, 1837, Jan. 31, 1838, Irion to Hunt, Dec. 31, 1837, Garrison, "Diplomatic Correspondence of Texas," I, 208-211, 218-221, 235-241, 252-256, 266-267, 277-281, 284-288; MVB, Notes on Annexation of Texas, Aug. 1837, VBP; James K. Paulding to MVB, Sept. 22, 1837, Paulding, *Letters*, pp. 201-202; Curtis, *Fox at Bay*, pp. 156-160; Rives, *United States and Mexico*, I, 406-411.

gress a message urging "reprisals, and the use of the naval forces of the United States" against Mexico. The Mexican "outrages," said Jackson, "would justify . . . war." In June, Van Buren decided to send Robert Greenhow of the State Department to Mexico City to make one last attempt at a diplomatic settlement. Hopes were raised when Francisco Martinez arrived from Mexico in October, but the official Mexican response on November 18 ignored all but eight of the fifty-seven American claims outstanding.[5]

The combination of Mexican arrogance and persistent Texan demands for annexation gave Van Buren ample justification for returning to Andrew Jackson's old policy of expansion in the Southwest; but in his annual message in December 1837, Van Buren chose instead to advocate keeping the peace. After reviewing the many "aggravated cases of personal wrongs," and reporting that the Mexicans had given almost no "satisfaction," Van Buren left it up to Congress to determine "the mode, and the measure of redress." He said nothing at all about the annexation of Texas.[6]

His efforts for peace satisfied neither Southerners, who demanded action, nor antislavery Northerners, who suspected the administration of secretly wanting Texas in order to expand slavery. John Quincy Adams called Van Buren's message nothing more than Jackson's message of December 1832, "covered with a new coat of varnish." The words, said Adams, were so full of "cunning and duplicity" that they gave him a "fit of melancholy for the future fortunes of the country." He accused Van Buren of planning to sacrifice "the rights of Northern freedom to slavery and the South" by annexing Texas and waging war on Mexico. A flood of petitions had poured in all summer and fall supporting Adams in opposing the annexation of Texas. On December 2, Adams proposed that all such petitions be sent to a select committee instead of the House Committee on Foreign Affairs, which was chaired by an administration Democrat. On December 18, he presented a petition in favor of settling Mexican claims by arbitration instead of war. The former President believed that he was fighting a battle against "the thirst of the slave-holders for Texas."[7]

Southerners and antiabolitionist Northerners began an immediate

[5] Rives, *United States and Mexico*, I, 417-430; Curtis, *Fox at Bay*, pp. 160-165.

[6] Richardson, *Messages and Papers*, III, 377-379; Curtis, *Fox at Bay*, pp. 165-166.

[7] *Congressional Globe*, 25th Congress, 2nd session (1837-1838), 19-20, 24, 31; Adams, *Memoirs*, IX, 440-446, 451, 457; *Niles' Register*, 53 (1837), 267; Curtis, *Fox at Bay*, p. 166; Hunt to R. A. Irion, Jan. 31, 1838, Garrison, "Diplomatic Correspondence of Texas," I, 284-288; Rives, *United States and Mexico*, I, 411.

counterattack. In the Senate John C. Calhoun and his colleague from South Carolina, William C. Preston, offered separate resolutions calling for the annexation of Texas. Later in the session Robert Walker of Mississippi, asked why the Senate Committee on Foreign Relations had done nothing to secure "redress" from the "insults" offered by Mexico.[8]

Caught in the crossfire of the debate Van Buren had to set priorities. He had been elected by the votes of expansionist Southerners and he acknowledged a debt to Andrew Jackson, who favored war and annexation; but he was also aware of the growing antislavery movement in the North. To keep the Democratic party united and to keep Congress headed toward the independent treasury, Van Buren decided to sweep the Mexican claims and Texan annexation under the House rug. In the Senate Calhoun's and Preston's resolutions were tabled. James Buchanan answered Walker's question by saying that any action against Mexico should start in the House of Representatives. And in the House nothing was done. With this sort of evasion the administration bought time until the next fall when the Texan government withdrew its request for annexation and the Mexican claims were turned over to arbitration. By blocking manifest destiny in the Southwest Van Buren had moved his administration away from the nationalistic expansionism of Jacksonian Democracy.[9]

Van Buren followed the same antiexpansionist policy in the Northeast when the insurrection against the British broke out in Canada. Late in the fall of 1837, William L. Mackenzie and Louis Jean Papineau led a revolt in the Province of Upper Canada across the border from New York. British soldiers dispersed the rebels, but Mackenzie escaped in disguise to New York, where he began to enlist volunteers. On December 15, he stirred a large crowd in Buffalo and had soon enrolled over one thousand Americans, led by Rensselaer Van Rensselaer, the son of Solomon Van Rensselaer. Many Americans were lured by Mackenzie's offer of three hundred acres of Ontario soil to every volunteer, while others sympathized with an independence movement like that of 1776, or wanted to retaliate against the British. Unemployed canal diggers were attracted by the chance to earn some money. Within a few days Van Rensselaer had seized Navy Island on the Canadian side

[8] Calhoun to James E. Calhoun, Dec. 20, 1837, Calhoun, *Correspondence*, p. 386; *Congressional Globe*, 25th Congress, 2nd session (1837-1838), 55, 76, 298-299; Hunt to Irion, Jan. 31, 1838, Garrison, "Diplomatic Correspondence of Texas," I, 286-287.

[9] Rives, *United States and Mexico*, I, 430-432; MVB to Forsyth, Sept. 18, 1838, VBP; *Congressional Globe*, 25th Congress, 2nd session (1837-1838), 299-301, 453.

of the Niagara River, just above the falls. Here he erected fortifications, and Mackenzie issued a declaration of Canadian independence.[10]

The spirit of the movement was personified by its leader Van Rensselaer, who, as one observer put it, "was a true hearted, noble man, ... possessing heroism, strong patriotic enthusiasm, and generosity; ever ready to unfurl the standard of liberty." He was also a heavy drinker and a reckless reprobate with an unsavory reputation who had been dismissed from the military academy; furthermore, he had a special incentive because his father had been wounded in the unsuccessful and inglorious invasion of Canada at Niagara in 1812. The fiery young man sent a letter home at Christmas saying that "as an American" he did not "fear ... the Red-coats, be they few or many." Many New Yorkers apparently shared his enthusiasm because his sister Adeline reported that "sympathy for the Patriots [had] the predominance" in Albany. They were supported by the *Albany Argus* and a few of the Troy papers, she said, and Thurlow Weed of the *Albany Evening Journal* "came out ... with a strong, good piece for them and now we are all democrats to the back bone." Adeline told her brother that he was the sort of hero Lafayette had been in the revolution.[11]

The British soon retaliated against the Americans on Navy Island. On the night of December 29, Canadian militia crossed over to Fort Schlosser on the American side of the Niagara River and boarded the American ship *Caroline*, which had been running supplies to Navy Island. After subduing the American crew the Canadians set the *Caroline* afire, and cut her loose to drift aground just above Niagara Falls. Only one American was killed and there was no one aboard when the *Caroline* went aground, but exaggerated accounts of the episode aroused such "indignation [that] the frontier from Buffalo to Lake Ontario ... bristle[d] with bayonets." Young George Templeton Strong of New York City recorded his excitement over the incident in his diary: "It's infamous—forty unarmed American citizens butchered in cold blood, while sleeping, by a party of British assassins, and living and dead sent together over Niagara." Strong hoped that the outrage would lead to war.[12]

[10] Hugh L. Keenleyside and Gerald S. Brown, *Canada and the United States*, rev. ed. (New York, 1952), pp. 82-92; Curtis, *Fox at Bay*, p. 173; Richardson, *Messages and Papers*, III, 399-400, 461-463; Bonney, *Historical Gleanings*, II, 61-64, 76-81.

[11] *Ibid.*, 62, 66-68; M. Sterling to Benjamin Butler, Feb. 23, 1838, VBP; Charles W. Elliott, *Winfield Scott: the Soldier and the Man* (New York, 1937), p. 337; *Memoirs of Lieut.-General Scott, LL.D.* (New York, 1864), pp. 305-306.

[12] Bonney, *Historical Gleanings*, II, 72; Richardson, *Messages and Papers*, III, 402;

News of the conflict reached Van Buren as he was trying to guide Congress toward the independent treasury. Before Congress convened, Benjamin Butler's barkeeper, who had just returned from Montreal, reported that there was a "state of actual war" in Canada. Since the American army, small to start with, was engaged in the bloody Seminole War in Florida, Van Buren turned first to the states to maintain American neutrality. On December 7, he asked the governors of New York, Vermont and Michigan to arrest anyone caught aiding the Canadian rebels. In New York Governor Marcy did little at first because he considered foreign policy the responsibility of the federal government, but after the *Caroline* affair he asked the legislature for funds in case he had to call out the militia. Van Buren learned about the *Caroline* on January 4, as he was entertaining a group of Whigs including Henry Clay and Major General Winfield Scott, at dinner. Keeping his guests waiting, Van Buren came into the dining room, took Scott aside and whispered, "Blood has been shed; you must go with all speed to the Niagara frontier." Marcy and Van Buren had decided that they could not afford to let the disturbance on the frontier continue.[13]

While waiting for Scott and Marcy to take charge in New York, Van Buren took immediate action in Washington to establish American neutrality. On January 5, 1838, the day after he had spoken to Scott, Van Buren issued a proclamation of neutrality in which he called on all to return home, and warned that any who "compromise[d] the neutrality of this government" would be "liable to arrest." Aware that he lacked power to enforce the proclamation, he asked Congress to review all neutrality laws and find ways to give him "adequate power [to] restrain all persons" from violating the laws. To avoid criticism for failing to defend the honor of the United States Van Buren made an official representation to the British minister protesting "the destruction of property and assassination of citizens of the United States on the soil of New York." Unlike Andrew Jackson, who had dallied while Americans were aiding rebels in Texas, Van Buren was doing his best to maintain neutrality on the northern border.[14]

As he moved north General Scott carried orders that testified to the difficulty of his task. Van Buren hoped that Scott would "be able to

---

Allan Nevins and Milton H. Thomas, eds., *The Diary of George Templeton Strong, 1835-1875*, 4 vols. (New York, 1952), I, 81.

[13] Butler to MVB, Nov. 28, 1837, VBP; Curtis, *Fox at Bay*, pp. 171-172; Marcy to Sir Francis Head, Dec. 21, 1837, in Spencer, *Victor and the Spoils*, pp. 105-106; Richardson, *Messages and Papers*, III, 399-403; Scott, *Memoirs*, I, 306-307.

[14] Richardson, *Messages and Papers*, III, 399-404, 481.

maintain the peace . . . without being called upon to use" the state militia. If he did use the militia, he could do so only with the permission of state authorities. Admitting that he had no "authority to employ [the army] to restrain persons . . . from . . . making incursions" into Canada, Van Buren relied upon Scott's "discretion, military skill, and intimate knowledge of the country."[15]

Less than a week after receiving his orders Scott arrived in Albany, where he picked up Governor Marcy and hurried on to Niagara Falls. When Scott and Marcy arrived at Navy Island on January 13, the general first tried, as Van Rensselaer put it, to "intimidate" the young rebel commander by describing the large Canadian army forming across the river. When intimidation failed, Marcy tried persuasion, and finally managed to convince Van Rensselaer of the need to evacuate the Island. Freezing weather and the heavy Canadian bombardment had as much to do with Van Rensselaer's decision as pressure from Scott and Marcy. Within a day the Americans had fallen back to Fort Schlosser, and on January 18, Van Rensselaer told his father that the volunteers were "all disarmed," and "like good quiet fellows" were on their way "West to get a job at canal digging." Van Rensselaer was arrested for his part in the affair but was released on bail.[16]

Despite the setback, the disorders continued and Scott and Marcy were kept busy stamping out brush fires wherever they sprang up. In order to move as quickly as possible, Scott often journeyed by stagecoach at night, bundled up in fur robes. When he left for Tennessee in March, he had been so successful that James Gordon Bennett praised him in the *New York Herald* for behaving with "prudence [and] circumspection," and winning "the admiration of all." During the summer Marcy carried the burden. When guerrillas burned the Canadian steamer *Sir Robert Peel*, Marcy rushed to the scene, took charge of the militia, and convinced the patriots that they should return home.[17]

While Scott and Marcy were busy in the North, Van Buren was trying to obtain congressional support for his neutrality efforts. Congress was slow to act because it was preoccupied with the independent treasury and a debate over slavery, but it finally passed a bill giving the President $625,000 for operations on the frontier. Then on March 10, Congress passed a two-year neutrality act giving civil authorities the power to confiscate arms and other equipment from any force trying to cross the border. The appropriations and the neutrality act

[15] *Ibid.*, 403.
[16] Elliott, *Winfield Scott*, pp. 338-340; Bonney, *Historical Gleanings*, II, 82-93.
[17] Elliott, *Winfield Scott*, pp. 340-346; Spencer, *Victor and the Spoils*, pp. 106-107.

strengthened Van Buren's hand, but he still lacked the power to stop the organization of an invading army.[18]

Van Buren's efforts to establish American neutrality on the northern border were challenged early in November 1838, when Americans and Canadians crossed the St. Lawrence to attack the Canadian town of Prescott. Even though the Canadian defenders captured the invaders within a few days, Van Buren felt obliged to respond. On November 21, he issued a second neutrality proclamation addressed to "those misguided or deluded persons" who were engaged in "projects dangerous to their own country, fatal to those whom they profess a desire to relieve, impracticable of execution." He asked Americans to "use every effort . . . to arrest . . . every offender," and warned that the government would not intervene to help anyone captured in Canada. To underline his concern Van Buren once again called upon Winfield Scott, who soon restored quiet along the border from Michigan to Maine.[19]

Van Buren's strong words frightened members of the Regency because Marcy's role in enforcing neutrality had reduced his popularity in New York. As Jabez Hammond put it, Van Buren's policy made it "easy for artful electioneers . . . to turn the sympathy felt by our border citizens, for the Canadian patriots, . . . into a hostile feeling towards Governor Marcy." Before the opening of Congress in December, both Azariah Flagg and Edwin Croswell wrote to Van Buren asking him not to make matters worse by defending neutrality in his annual message. Flagg told Van Buren to say nothing that might appear to "censure [the] cause of liberty," while Croswell warned the President not to repudiate the young men who had been lured into the revolt. Nonetheless, in his message on December 3, 1838, Van Buren bluntly denounced the "criminal assaults upon the peace and order of a neighboring country" carried out by "misguided or deluded persons," and reminded Congress that Americans had always opposed such attacks. Conceding that it was "natural" for Americans to "feel an interest in the spread of political institutions as free as they regard their own," he reminded his fellow citizens that only Congress could wage war to help the Canadian rebels acquire these institutions.[20]

Only a few weeks after Van Buren had delivered his message, his policy of peace with Great Britain over Canada was once again threat-

[18] Curtis, *Fox at Bay*, pp. 174-177.

[19] Richardson, *Messages and Papers*, III, 482-483; Elliott, *Winfield Scott*, pp. 356-357.

[20] Hammond, *Political Parties*, II, 487; Flagg to MVB, Nov. 23, 1838, Croswell to MVB, Nov. 25, 1838, VBP; Richardson, *Messages and Papers*, III, 486-487.

ened—this time on the northeast border between Maine and Canada. For years Maine and New Brunswick had engaged in a dispute over possession of parts of the valley of the St. John River. When the government of Maine sent an expedition under Rufus MacIntire into the Aroostook River valley to clear it of Canadian "trespassers," the Canadians promptly captured MacIntire and put him in jail. To make matters worse Lieutenant Governor John Harvey of New Brunswick, then announced that he would use force to keep Americans out of the disputed area. Van Buren's friend, former senator and old Jacksonian John Fairfield, now governor of Maine, was so angry at what he considered a British incursion into American territory, that he sent three hundred militiamen into the Aroostook and gathered an additional force of one thousand. Andrew Jackson would have approved.[21]

Once again Van Buren responded by using diplomacy in Washington and by sending Winfield Scott to the border. Following his established policy of consulting his cabinet, he called a cabinet meeting and then on February 26, sent a message to Congress reviewing events in the Aroostook Valley. Van Buren defended the United States claim to the disputed region and said that Fairfield had every right to expel "a numerous band of lawless and desperate men" from the valley. But, said the President, Fairfield had gone too far in carrying out "a military occupation . . . of the territory with a view to hold it by force while the settlement is a subject of negotiation." Van Buren asked both sides to withdraw their troops and to release all prisoners, and the next day British minister Henry S. Fox and Secretary of State John Forsyth signed a memorandum calling for withdrawal of all troops from the disputed area.

In January 1839, British-American cooperation was a growing force for peace, but Van Buren still had to worry about firebrands in Congress and in Maine. On February 22, the impetuous Fairfield sent a threatening letter to the President. "Should you go *against* us upon this occasion," he wrote, "God only knows what the result would be politically." Then on March 2, Congress passed a warlike bill granting the President $10,000,000 and the power to call out fifty thousand militiamen to defend the Aroostook Valley. But even before the bill passed Scott had convinced Fairfield that he should withdraw his troops if Lieutenant Governor Harvey would do the same. On March 23, both sides officially agreed to withdraw and the crisis was over.[22]

[21] Curtis, *Fox at Bay*, pp. 181-183; Richardson, *Messages and Papers*, III, 516-520.
[22] *Ibid.*, 516-527; Curtis, *Fox at Bay*, pp. 183-187; Fairfield to MVB, Feb. 22, 1839, VBP.

Although Van Buren was not able to settle his diplomatic disputes either with Mexico or Great Britain during his term of office, he achieved a good diplomatic record. By postponing the question of the Mexican claims and refusing to annex Texas, he had reversed almost a decade of Jacksonian aggression in the Southwest. By keeping the peace in the Northeast he had furthered the policy of Anglo-American cooperation that he had started as Secretary of State and minister to England. It was a solid record of accomplishment.

But no ceremonial gunfire celebrated these accomplishments. Nor did they satisfy the President, for his diplomatic goals were always secondary to his overriding desire to win passage of the independent treasury bill. Against the wishes of many members of his party and in the face of public opinion he opposed expansion in order to keep the nation's attention riveted on the problem of money and the panic, and on his solution to the problem—the independent treasury. In his first annual message, delivered December 5, 1837, he showed his order of priorities by devoting far more space to the financial crisis than he did to Texas and Mexico. After reiterating his support for the independent treasury, Van Buren tried to gloss over his political defeats in the fall, insisting that "questions of far deeper and more immediate local interest than the fiscal plans of the National Treasury were involved in those elections." "Above all," he argued, "we can not overlook the striking fact that there were at the time in those States more than one hundred and sixty millions of bank capital" which had a great effect on the outcome of the elections. Van Buren declared resolutely that the elections had given him no "reason to change" his mind about his banking program.

As the message continued, Van Buren showed that he had learned from the debates in Congress and in the press that fall. In order to win the support of conservative Democrats and state banking interests, he proposed a modification of the independent treasury bill whereby the federal government would be allowed to make special deposits in state banks. Van Buren also showed a new awareness of the importance of the West, where his party had lost ground during the fall. Noting that the population of the West now made up one-fifth of the total population of the United States, he appealed to these new voters by proposing a new land bill, which would allow the government to reduce the minimum price of land according to actual valuation. To this graduation concept, which he had taken from Thomas Hart Benton, Van Buren added a preemption provision allowing squatters on federal land to purchase land at the minimum price. As another gesture to the West Van Buren reviewed the "beneficial effects" of the Indian removal policy, which, he said, had started with Thomas Jefferson and was in 1837 "the settled policy of the country."

He was rewarded for his moderation by a favorable response from various ideological and regional segments of the party, and of course, Jackson himself was pleased. Convinced by the President's moderation that he was not really a Loco Foco, the *Albany Argus* and the *Richmond Enquirer* for the first time in a long while sang his praise.[23]

But before Van Buren could induce Congress to take up the independent treasury, his administration had to deal with a month-long congressional debate over the issue of slavery. The debate, which was sparked by the question of the annexation of Texas, began on December 12, when John Quincy Adams presented a series of petitions to the House "praying for the abolition of slavery and the slave trade in the District of Columbia." These and other petitions that day were laid on the table. Northern congressmen brought in similar petitions on December 18 and December 20, which were also laid on the table. On December 21, in an effort to discourage any further petitions, Congressman John M. Patton of Virginia, proposed a gag rule that was even tougher than Henry L. Pinckney's gag rule of 1836. "All petitions touching the abolition of slavery," said Patton, were to be laid on the table "without being debated," and there would be "no further action whatever." When the resolution passed by the substantial margin of 122 to 74, most of the Democratic votes were recorded in support of slavery.[24]

A similar debate began in the Senate on December 18, when Garret D. Wall presented a petition from 115 women in New Jersey asking for the abolition of slavery in the District of Columbia. When Henry Clay suggested innocently that the Senate should inquire into the broad question of abolitionism and the right of petition, John C. Calhoun protested that such an inquiry would "produce an excitement." "If a single step was yielded," said Calhoun, "the fanatical spirit would be reanimated." Calhoun "despaired" about the attitude of the North toward slavery because the spirit of abolition had "control over the political parties" of that section of the country. After further debate, Henry Hubbard of New Hampshire, who spoke for the administration, moved that Wall's petition be laid on the table. The vote carried, 25-20, with all but two of the yea votes coming from the Democratic

[23] Richardson, *Messages and Papers*, III, 373-395; Jackson to MVB, Dec. 18, 1837, Pierce to MVB, Dec. 25, 1837, Welles to MVB, Dec. 12, 1837, Enos T. Throop to MVB, Dec. 6, 1837, William L. Marcy to MVB, Dec. 8, 1837, VBP.

[24] *Congressional Globe*, 25th Congress, 2nd session (1837-1838), 19-21, 24, 30-33, 41, 45.

party and all but seven of the nay votes from Whigs or conservative Democrats.[25]

On December 27, not satisfied with the tabling motions, Calhoun offered a series of six resolutions designed to force the Senate to commit itself in defense of slavery. The first resolution, which summarized the compact theory of government, and the second, which forbade any interference in the affairs of the individual states, passed by wide margins on January 3, 1838. Calhoun's third resolution declared that it was the duty of the federal government to use its powers "to give ... increased stability and security to the domestic institutions of the states." That resolution passed easily too, but only after the Senate had watered it down to the negative stipulation that the federal authority was "not to interfere with the stability and security" of these institutions.

In his fourth and fifth resolutions Calhoun referred specifically to the institution of slavery. The fourth, which declared that any "attack" on slavery was a "violation of the most solemn obligations," passed after the Senate had weakened the language a bit. In his fifth resolution Calhoun tried to get the Senate to declare that any effort to abolish slavery in the District of Columbia constituted a "dangerous attack on the institutions of the slaveholding states"; but before it passed, Clay softened the wording so that such an effort on the part of abolitionists was simply labeled a "violation of the faith implied in the cessions by the states of Virginia and Maryland." Calhoun's final resolution, which condemned any refusal to expand American boundaries that was based on antislavery considerations, was tabled on January 12, because the same argument was included in William C. Preston's resolution on the annexation of Texas.

Since all five of Calhoun's motions passed the Senate by margins of 31 to 11, or better, and since almost all Democrats voted with the majority, the position of the administration on slavery was unmistakable. Although the administration would not support the most extreme of Calhoun's statements, it was willing to endorse the institution of slavery and oppose any attempts to "intermeddle" with it. Even when Democratic senator William Allen of Ohio, introduced a resolution stating that nothing in Calhoun's resolutions should be interpreted as an abridgment of the freedom of speech, the administration senators voted for slavery and against freedom of speech. On a motion by John M. Niles of Connecticut, Allen's resolution was laid on the table by a vote of 23 to 21. Fourteen Democrats joined Niles in voting for

[25] *Ibid.*, 33-39.

tabling. The tabulation of the vote showed that 20 out of 23 voting to table were from slaveholding states.[26]

With the slavery question temporarily in abeyance, Silas Wright was finally able to introduce the independent treasury bill in the Senate on January 16. To attract both conservatives and hard-money advocates Van Buren had added two new sections to the original bill: clause twelve, which allowed special federal deposits in state banks, and clause twenty-three, which required gold or silver for payments owed the United States after 1842. With these new clauses, prospects for passage were excellent, but Henry Clay led a combination of Whigs and conservative Democrats that succeeded in postponing the bill until the end of the month.[27]

While waiting for the bill to return to the floor of the Senate, administration leaders sought to bolster western support by pushing for renewal of the preemption policy, which had first been enacted into law in 1830. The new preemption bill, first taken up in the Senate on January 23, authorized settlers who had been squatting on government land on December 1, 1837, to purchase 160 acres at the minimum price before the land was put up for public sale. According to Democrat Robert Walker of Mississippi, the bill would give the "worthy and enterprising [settler] preference [over the] cold and heartless speculator," and would ensure that "the honest and hardy cultivator [was not] driven from his property that he had toiled so hard to secure." The bill passed on January 30 by a vote of 30 to 18, with the division more on partisan than on regional lines. Only three Democrats voted against the bill, and only two Whigs voted for it. Even though the bill benefited the West, four Westerners opposed it, while eleven Easterners—with less reason to support it—voted yea. Van Buren, who had tried to cement his alliance with the South by supporting Calhoun's proslavery stand, sought to strengthen his backing in the West by securing preemption.[28]

The day after the preemption bill was passed, Silas Wright presented Van Buren's case for the independent treasury. Although Wright's presentation was for the most part sober and straightforward, he resorted at times to emotional rhetoric. At the start he cited as one of the two basic principles of the bill, the necessity of separating the "public treasure, the money of the people [from] the business of individuals and incorporations." In the course of the speech he reminded

[26] *Ibid.*, 55-60, 73-74, 80-81, 88, 96-99; appendix, 21-32, 36-41, 53-65, 69-74; Wiltse, *John C. Calhoun, Nullifier*, pp. 369-373.

[27] *Congressional Globe*, 25th Congress, 2nd session (1837-1838), 109-112, 119-120.

[28] *Ibid.*, 130, 136-144, 147, 149.

the Senate that expansion of credit under the pet bank system had caused public lands to be sold too rapidly: "The whole splendid public domain, that rich inheritance from our fathers of the Republic," had been "exchanged [for] bank rags." He asked "in all sincerity" if anything "could show, more conclusively, the impropriety of this connection between the finances of the country" and the banks. Using language strongly reminiscent of Andrew Jackson's in the Bank veto, Wright was committing the administration to a crusade against the state banks.

In the rest of his speech Wright contented himself with an analytical defense of the bill. He pointed out that clause twenty-three, the specie clause, contained proposals first offered by Calhoun. He minimized the added expense of the independent treasury. He denied that executive patronage would be increased. He made the significant point that even with the independent treasury, the Treasury could control the state banks by deciding which state bank notes would be accepted for payment of government dues. As Wright put it, the system "would constantly circulate among the people a basis for the paper currency of the State banks." Like Van Buren in his special session message, Wright reviewed the alternatives—the Bank of the United States and the pet banks—and concluded that neither would do.[29]

Wright's speech triggered a strong reaction in both Whigs and conservative Democrats. On February 1, Daniel Webster attacked the independent treasury and accused Wright and Van Buren of leaving the people to "take care of themselves." A day later William C. Rives introduced an alternative bill, proposing a return to the old system of depositing federal funds in state banks. On February 5 and February 6, Rives delivered a long speech in which he destroyed any hopes Van Buren may have had of reaching an accommodation with the conservatives. Rives asked his colleagues not to be "led away, under the dominion of well-sounding phrases, of plausible or pompous commonplaces, to disregard the real interests of the country." If only "the honorable Senator from New York," said Rives scornfully, "had taken the trouble to look at" the independent treasury bill before making his speech, "he might have saved himself the labor of a great deal of superfluous ingenuity." Rives insisted that the bill would increase federal expense and executive patronage. Like Webster, Rives attacked the administration's proposal because it contained "no provision for the relief of the country." The Virginian ended sarcastically; he knew, he said, that he would "incur the anathemas of *party*," but he had a

---

[29] *Ibid.*, 151-152; appendix, 82-93.

"country to serve, as well as a party to obey." This was a direct attack on Wright and Van Buren, who had long believed that they could best serve their country by obeying their party.[30]

The Senate seemed headed for a vote on the independent treasury as speeches were delivered during the next few days both for and against the plan. Henry Hubbard put forward a staunch Jacksonian defense of the administration's proposal, and Nathaniel P. Tallmadge rebutted with arguments supporting Rives' state bank bill. Finally, on February 15, Calhoun delivered what he expected to be the decisive speech in favor of the independent treasury. Calhoun took what he called "higher and broader" grounds by offering a series of "constitutional objections" to Rives' proposal. If Rives had his way, said Calhoun, a league of twenty-five state banks would gain control of the financial resources of the country, and one of them—the Bank of the United States—would soon dominate the other twenty-four. Before long Biddle's bank would control the nation as it had during the days of Andrew Jackson. As he had in the fall, Calhoun had taken a commanding position in the debate over the independent treasury.[31]

Just as the Senate seemed ready to vote on the independent treasury, the administration was thwarted once again—this time by a savage duel involving two congressmen. The duel came about when Democrat Jonathan Cilley of Maine, criticized James Watson Webb, editor of the New York *Courier and Enquirer*, in the House of Representatives, and William Graves, a Whig from Kentucky, came to Webb's rescue. In the duel that followed, Cilley and Graves exchanged rifle fire at eighty yards, and on the third round Cilley was killed. Official Washington, though long accustomed to duels, was so shocked by the savagery of this one that little was accomplished until mid-March. To show their displeasure, the justices of the Supreme Court refused to attend the funeral and Congress responded by debating the merits of an antidueling bill for the next few weeks.[32]

Even if there had been no duel and no death, the Senate would not have been able to vote at once on the independent treasury because the bill became entangled in a debate over the character of John C. Calhoun. As Thomas Hart Benton recalled, the "storm had been gathering since September," when Calhoun left the Whigs to rejoin the Democrats, and "burst in February," when Calhoun spoke in defense of the independent treasury. Henry Clay fired the opening round on

[30] *Ibid.*, 153-154, 156-157, 161; appendix, 608-614.

[31] *Ibid.*, 169-172, 184; appendix, 188-195.

[32] *Niles' Register*, 54 (1838), 5-6; Wiltse, *John C. Calhoun, Nullifier*, pp. 379-380.

February 19, by adding a personal attack on Calhoun to a speech against the independent treasury. In response Calhoun complained that Clay had "perverted almost" everything that he had said, and asked permission to prepare a reply to this "personal attack."[33]

Calhoun spent the next three weeks preparing to answer Clay, even reading, said Benton, Demosthenes' "Oration on the Crown." When Calhoun finally decided to speak, he refuted Clay's charges one after another. Two days later Webster came to the defense of Clay, attacking Calhoun for nullification and prompting Calhoun to make still another rebuttal. The speeches and the impromptu exchanges of "the great Debate" marked a high point in the oratory of the three senators. According to one observer, "Calhoun beat them all out and out," but John Quincy Adams thought that Clay had had the better of it.[34]

As soon as debate on the independent treasury resumed Van Buren won one battle but lost another. First the Senate defeated Rives' substitute bill by a straight party vote, 29-20. The only Democrats who voted for the bill were the five conservatives, Rives, Tallmadge, John Tipton of Indiana, Robert C. Nicholas of Louisiana, and John Ruggles of Maine. But directly after the vote Democrat Alfred Cuthbert of Georgia, alarmed the administration by making a motion to strike Calhoun's specie clause from the independent treasury bill. Since James Buchanan and Felix Grundy had already indicated that their legislatures would not allow them to vote for the independent treasury, Cuthbert's defection put the administration in a difficult position. If Cuthbert's motion passed, Calhoun might desert the Democrats, and hard-money advocates such as Benton would have less reason to fight for the bill. But if the motion lost, Democrats leaning toward the conservatives would desert the bill. Unable to resolve the dilemma, the administration for the first time failed to take a decisive stand, and the party divided. When seven Democrats, including Grundy and Buchanan, voted in support of Cuthbert, the motion passed, and the specie clause was stripped from the bill.[35]

Two days later, on March 26, the independent treasury came to a final vote and passed by the narrow margin of 27 to 25. The twenty-five nay votes came from seventeen Whigs, five conservative Democrats, and Buchanan, Grundy and Calhoun. It was apparent that Van Buren's gamble to accept Calhoun's assistance had hardly been a suc-

---

[33] Benton, *Thirty Years' View*, II, 97-123; *Congressional Globe*, 25th Congress, 2nd session (1837-1838), 191; appendix, 614-619.

[34] *Congressional Globe*, 25th Congress, 2nd session (1837-1838), appendix, 176-181, 243-250, 632-641.

[35] *Ibid.*, 253, 259; Curtis, *Fox at Bay*, pp. 124-125.

cess. After stomaching Calhoun's posturing and gloating at the special session, the administration had rallied behind his slavery resolutions in January and had added his specie clause to the bill. By February, the administration bill seemed to many to be Calhoun's bill, and the three-cornered debate in February and March did nothing to dim the spotlight focused on the South Carolinian. Although the administration never lost control of the bill, Van Buren was less in command in March than he had been in October and in the end Calhoun deserted the party and voted against the independent treasury. A reconciliation between the South Carolinian and Van Buren, which had seemed likely during the winter, was no longer possible.[36]

Van Buren was further embarrassed by Daniel Webster and Henry Clay when they took steps to abolish the specie circular. Just before Calhoun's specie clause was voted down, Webster had offered in its place an amendment making it unlawful for the Secretary of the Treasury "to make, or continue in force, any general order which shall make any difference as to the money or medium of payment in which the debts or dues to the Government . . . may be paid or discharged." Since the amendment required Woodbury either to abolish the specie circular or to apply its terms to all debts owed the government, and since the latter requirement was unlikely to be enacted, the amendment in effect repealed the circular. Weary of defending Jackson's specie circular, Van Buren capitulated, and the amendment passed promptly with only fourteen Democrats voting against it.

On April 30, not content with Webster's amendment, which would not go into effect unless the independent treasury bill passed the House, Clay offered a joint resolution that "no discrimination [should be] made as to the currency or medium of payment in the several branches of the Public Revenues, or in debts or dues to the Government" and that "the notes of sound banks" should be received for such debts. Clay's resolution was more direct than Webster's and was not dependent on passage of the independent treasury bill. But Clay, who could not leave well enough alone, lost whatever chance he had of getting Democratic support for his resolution when he coupled it with a bold speech advocating the reestablishment of the Bank of the United States. On May 26, Democratic votes stripped Clay's resolution of everything except the prohibition of "discrimination" in the mode of the payment of debts owed the government. When the resolution passed the Senate on May 26 and the House on May 30, it was identical

[36] *Congressional Globe*, 25th Congress, 2nd session (1837-1838), 264; Niles to Gideon Welles, Mar. 26, 1838, Gideon Welles Papers, LC.

to Webster's amendment. But the resolution ended Andrew Jackson's specie circular and weakened Van Buren, who had tied his administration to it for over a year.[37]

In the House of Representatives, Churchill C. Cambreleng introduced his own independent treasury bill on March 6. Since Cambreleng's bill contained a specie clause, the bill differed from the Senate version that was sent to the House on March 27 and laid on the table. Alarmed by the close vote in the Senate and uncertain whether or not to fight for the specie clause in the House, Cambreleng and Speaker James K. Polk decided to move slowly. They hoped that by waiting they would pick up two Democratic votes from Mississippi after a special election to be held there later in the spring. There was also the prospect of enticing western congressmen by passing the preemption bill, which had come over from the Senate.

Finally, by mid-June 1838, Cambreleng and Polk could wait no longer, for the House stood ready to adjourn. The passage of the preemption bill on June 14 was a favorable omen for western votes, but the victory of two Whig congressmen in Mississippi augured less well for southern support. Hopeful of keeping the allegiance of Calhoun supporters in the South, the administration decided to offer Cambreleng's bill with the specie clause instead of the bill that had arrived from the Senate without such a clause. In moving his own bill on June 19, Cambreleng spoke more decorously than he had in October and urged passage of the independent treasury as a way to end "agitation." Francis W. Pickens, who spoke soon after Cambreleng, also tried to avoid his errors in the special session by omitting any reference to slavery. Instead, Pickens followed Van Buren's lead and appealed to western votes by telling his colleagues that "no part of the country [had] more interest than the interior West" in the passage of the independent treasury. As the time for the final vote approached, Van Buren and his agents applied a great deal of political pressure in order to keep wavering Democrats in line. Van Buren had much at stake, but if he was alarmed, he did not show it to John Quincy Adams the night before the vote when they held a leisurely conversation about the uses of the Smithsonian bequest.[38]

Over a year of political maneuvering by Van Buren went for nothing on June 25 when the House defeated his independent treasury bill by

[37] *Congressional Globe*, 25th Congress, 2nd session (1837-1838), 259, 344, 396-397, 412-413, 416-417.

[38] *Ibid.*, 216-222, 266-267, 452 (preemption bill), 457-459, 463, 465, 473-475; appendix, 428-433, 451-452; Curtis, *Fox at Bay*, pp. 126-132; Adams, *Memoirs*, X, 24-25.

a vote of 125 to 111. In a desperate effort to hold conservative votes, the administration allowed the specie clause to be stricken from Cambreleng's bill, but the change only alienated Calhoun's supporters, who voted against the bill. Democratic support for the preemption bill did not help, for congressmen from six key western states voted 19-14 against the independent treasury. Blame for the defeat, however, rested squarely with sixteen Democrats who voted against the bill. If seven of them had voted for the bill, it would have passed. As in the special session, Van Buren had succeeded in the Senate but failed in the House of Representatives. Andrew Jackson tried to comfort the President by pointing out that "the divorce between the Government and the Banks" had actually been in effect ever since the administration had stopped depositing federal funds in banks that had suspended payments. But both Jackson and Van Buren knew that they had suffered a crushing defeat—especially since Nicholas Biddle was shamelessly boasting that the repeal of the specie circular and the rejection of the independent treasury had resulted "exclusively" from "the course pursued by the Bank of the U.S."[39]

Van Buren was also losing ground in Virginia and New York. In the Old Dominion the conservative revolt had so weakened support for the administration that Van Buren could not even count on the backing of Thomas Ritchie. When Benjamin Butler resigned as Attorney General in April, Van Buren made an overture to Ritchie by offering the position to his son-in-law Richard E. Parker, but Parker declined. With only nominal support from the *Richmond Enquirer*, the Democrats were beaten in the spring election, losing thirty-four seats in the senate and house. In May, a distraught Ritchie wrote Van Buren a touching letter, apologizing for deserting him and imploring him to stop listening to the "Ultra Hotspurs." Anxious for the message to reach Van Buren as soon as possible, Ritchie considered taking the train to Washington to deliver the letter in person. He abandoned the idea only because he feared that Calhoun would misinterpret it if he saw Ritchie and Van Buren with their heads together.[40]

[39] *Congressional Globe*, 25th Congress, 2nd session (1837-1838), 475-480; Curtis, *Fox at Bay*, p. 133; Sellers, *James K. Polk Jacksonian*, 331-334. The six western states were Ohio, Indiana, Illinois, Michigan, Missouri, and Arkansas. Jackson to MVB, July 6, 1838, Jackson, *Correspondence*, V, 555; Biddle to Samuel Jaudon, June 29, 1838, Biddle to Thomas Cooper, July 13, 1838, Biddle, *Correspondence*, pp. 314-315, 316-317.

[40] Howard Braverman, "The Economic and Political Background of the Conservative Revolt in Virginia," *Virginia Magazine of History and Biography*, 60 (1952), 278-282; Parker to MVB, Jan. 18, May 2, 1838, Butler to MVB, April 11, 1838, Ritchie to MVB, May, July 2, 1838, VBP.

Late in the summer Van Buren decided to combine politics and pleasure. With Abraham and Smith Van Buren and the Poinsetts, he traveled south to White Sulphur Springs in the hills of what is now southern West Virginia. Here, according to Rives, Van Buren "courted . . . every opportunity of enlisting the feelings of those about him, in his favor." Ritchie later reported that the President's "*fascinating manners*" had worked "miracles," but Rives was skeptical—he had not heard of a single convert. Even Parker conceded that the trip had failed, and that Van Buren should have traveled home through the Valley of Virginia, where the conservatives were strongest.[41]

The conservative revolt was also taking its toll in New York, widening the gap between Marcy and Van Buren. In his governor's message of January 2, 1838, Marcy tried to compromise by proposing that the independent treasury plan be modified. Marcy meant to leave the impression that he had taken a stand against the independent treasury, but the public and Van Buren understood that he was supporting it. When the *Albany Argus* praised Wright's speech defending the independent treasury, Van Buren was all the more convinced that he could take Marcy and New York for granted. As a result the President did not bother to keep the governor informed, leading Marcy to complain that he knew more about what went on in Parliament than about affairs in Congress.[42]

Not quite the Magician he had once been, Van Buren failed to keep in touch with his home base; and when it came to replacing Samuel Swartwout as collector of customs in New York City, he allowed the gap between himself and Marcy to become wider. Since Swartwout had opposed both Van Buren and the independent treasury, it was apparent that the President would appoint a new collector when Swartwout's term expired in March 1838. The position was a political and financial plum. Enos T. Throop had already applied for the job; Azariah Flagg and Wright opposed Throop and backed William S. Coe instead; Tammany Hall was pushing Jesse Hoyt, and Marcy wanted almost anyone but Hoyt. In making the appointment Van Buren pleased

[41] MVB to Jackson, July 22, 1838, Daniel to MVB, Aug. 8, 1838, Parker to MVB, Oct. 6, 1838, VBP; MVB to Levi Woodbury, Woodbury Papers, LC; Rives to David Campbell, Aug. 26, 1838, David Campbell Papers, Duke University Library; MVB to Joel Poinsett, Sept. 13, 1838, Joel R. Poinsett Papers, in the Henry D. Gilpin Papers, HSP; MVB to Rives, Sept. 18, 1838, Rives Papers, LC.

[42] Marcy, "Governor's message," Jan. 2, 1838, Lincoln, *Messages*, III, 654-666; Marcy to Wetmore, Jan. 22, Mar. 27, 1838, Marcy Papers, LC; Wetmore to Marcy, Jan. 23, 1838, Gratz Collection HSP; *Argus*, Feb. 20, 1838; Elam Tilden to MVB, Feb. 22, 1838, MVB to Jackson, April 29, 1838, VBP.

most of the conflicting interests. He eliminated Coe, but he did not antagonize Wright and Flagg because he assured them that Throop would not get the job. Coe and Throop were satisfied when they received other positions, and when the President finally settled on Hoyt, the appointment greatly strengthened Tammany Hall. But the relationship between Marcy and Van Buren was damaged once again.[43]

Marcy continued to move toward the Whigs and conservative Democrats in his state by supporting New York's free banking bill. According to long-established state law, no one could engage in banking in New York without a special legislative charter, and since the charters required a two-thirds vote and granted monopoly privileges, the system restricted the right of banking to a privileged few. Inasmuch as Van Buren and the Regency had adjusted to the system with their Safety Fund Act in 1829, they were not interested in change. But Whigs and conservative Democrats wanted a free banking act that would allow any person or corporation to engage in banking without a special charter. They hoped that such an act would stimulate banking and help New Yorkers recover from the panic. Marcy called for free banking in January, and the legislature responded by passing the New York Free Banking Act on April 18.[44]

With such deep party divisions the Democrats had an uphill battle trying to reelect Marcy in the fall. Led by editors Horace Greeley and Thurlow Weed, the Whigs accused the Democrats of hostility toward

[43] Jackson to Francis P. Blair, April 2, 1837, Jackson to MVB, Jan. 23, 1838, Jackson, *Correspondence*, V, 472, 530; Mushkat, *Tammany*, pp. 182-184; Hartman, "The New York Custom House: Seat of Spoils Politics," pp. 149-163; Prosper Wetmore to William L. Marcy, Mar. 19, 1837, Gratz Collection, HSP; James Campbell to MVB, Dec. 1, 1837, J. Oakley, Henry Ulshoeffer, William Cullen Bryant et al. to MVB, Dec. 4, 1837, Bryant to MVB, Dec. 5, 1837, Jonathan Coddington to MVB, Dec. 7, 1837, Democratic-Republican General Committee of New York to MVB, Dec. 15, 1837, Jabez Hammond to MVB, Dec. 24, 1837, New York delegation to MVB, Dec. 30, 1837, Marcy to MVB, Feb. 12, 1838, Throop to MVB, Jan. 10, 1838, Jackson to MVB, May 1, 1838, VBP; MVB to Throop, Nov. 15, 1837, Jan. 18, Mar. 20, 1838, Van Buren-Throop Letters, NYSL; Jesse Hoyt to Edward Curtis, Oct. 20, Dec. 27, Dec. 29, 1837, Jan. 9, Feb. 2, 1838, Jesse Hoyt Letters to Edward Curtis, NYPL; Marcy to Prosper Wetmore, Nov. 13, 1838, Marcy Papers, LC.

[44] The subject of free banking is complicated because both Loco Focos and conservatives wanted it, but for different reasons. Loco Focos hoped to get rid of monopoly; conservatives sought to increase banking in the state. Arthur M. Schlesinger, Jr., has stressed the radical features of free banking, while Lee Benson has emphasized the conservative features. Schlesinger, *Age of Jackson*, p. 286; Benson, *Concept of Jacksonian Democracy*, pp. 97-104. See also Bray Hammond, "Free Banks and Corporations: the New York Free Banking Act of 1838," *Journal of Political Economy*, 44 (April 1936), 184-209; Spencer, *Victor and the Spoils*, pp. 93-95.

banks and of supporting radical reformers such as Fanny Wright, who was unpopular because of her assault on slavery, religion and marriage. The Whigs also attacked Marcy and Van Buren for their role in blocking efforts to help the Canadian revolt. In the election the Whigs swept the state, electing William Henry Seward governor by 10,000 votes and improving their position in the legislature. In the aftermath, Flagg, John A. Dix, and Van Buren blamed the defeat on the influence of the "money" power, but Marcy pointed bitterly to Van Buren's policies. It was a harsh verdict, for the depression played a large part in the loss, but Van Buren deserved his share of the blame. It was he, not the money power, who had insisted on a financial program that made the party appear opposed to the banks. It was he, not the money power, who had alienated Marcy and Edwin Croswell. It was he who had insisted on an unpopular neutrality policy on the border and he who had hurt Marcy by not letting him attack slavery. When antislavery groups circulated a questionnaire, Seward gained ground by responding, while Marcy had to remain silent in order to help Van Buren keep his southern allies. By insisting on financial and slavery policies designed to unite the party nationally, Van Buren had helped drag his state party down to defeat.[45]

But the news was not all bad in 1838. In New York and in other states, banks began to resume specie payments as the panic temporarily lessened. As a result Democrats carried Maine, Ohio, Illinois, New Jersey, and Maryland—states they had lost a year earlier—and held on to Pennsylvania and New Hamphire. Only in Connecticut and Mississippi did Whigs overturn the Democrats, though Whigs also maintained control of Massachusetts, Rhode Island, North Carolina, Georgia, Louisiana, and Indiana. Whigs still controlled more states than the Democrats, but the situation was an improvement over 1837.[46]

As the election results came in, Van Buren received disquieting news from New York. Early in November a letter of ill-concealed triumph arrived from Cambreleng hinting that his prophecy about "a certain officer" had been "super-abundantly fulfilled." Cambreleng was referring to Samuel Swartwout. At the time of Swartwout's appointment as New York collector of customs over the objections of the Regency,

<hr/>

[45] Glyndon Van Deusen, *Thurlow Weed: Wizard of the Lobby* (Boston, 1947; reprint, 1969), pp. 96-102; Hammond, *Political Parties*, II, 486-488; Spencer, *Victor and the Spoils*, pp. 95-98; Flagg to MVB, Nov. 9, 1838, Cambreleng to MVB, Nov. 9, 1838, Dix to MVB, Nov. 12, 1838, MVB to Jackson, Nov. 16, 1838, VBP; Marcy to Prosper Wetmore, Dec. 11, 1838, Marcy to Albert Gallup, Feb. 17, 1838, Marcy Papers, LC; Hone, *Diary*, pp. 346-354.

[46] McGrane, *Panic of 1837*, p. 171.

Cambreleng had predicted that the new collector would become corrupt. When he was replaced as a collector in 1838, Swartwout fled to Europe with $1,250,000 of public funds. In the weeks that followed stunned Jacksonians exchanged unhappy letters trying to explain what had happened.[47]

The news of Swartwout's defalcation was particularly embarrassing for Van Buren because it came just as he was preparing to renew his quest for the independent treasury. Since the Congress that gathered in December was the final session of the Twenty-fifth Congress, the prospects of the bill were not good anyway. Time would be limited because the session would end in March, and the bill would have to be passed by the same House of Representatives that had rejected it in June. Swartwout's misconduct made it worse because the House would surely use up a good deal of precious time discussing him and the New York custom house. In his annual message Van Buren tried to make the best of the situation. He called attention to the incident and promised a special report from the Secretary of the Treasury, arguing in addition that the Swartwout affair "furnish[ed] the strongest motive for the establishment of a more severe and secure system for the safe-keeping and disbursement of the public moneys than any that [had] heretofore existed."[48]

Following Van Buren's lead, Cambreleng brought a bill to the House on December 21, which was not called an independent treasury bill, but was called instead a bill "more effectually to prevent frauds in the collection, keeping, transfer, and disbursement of the public revenue, and to punish defaulters." Wright introduced a bill with a similar title to the Senate on January 30, 1839. Instead of proposing the establishment of subtreasuries, both bills required the Secretary of the Treasury to continue the same temporary system of holding government funds that had been in operation ever since the start of the panic.

Instead of helping passage of the administration bill, the Swartwout affair got in the way. With evidence of corruption involving the Treasury Department and Van Buren's own state organization in front of them, Whigs in the House of Representatives started a long debate in which they attacked the Democrats and demanded a thorough investigation of the Treasury Department. As a result Cambreleng's bill never emerged from committee. In the Senate Wright's bill went to committee and was brought back to the floor on February 8. On

---

[47] Cambreleng to MVB, Oct. 30, Nov. 12, 1838, Jackson to MVB, Dec. 4, 1838, Jacob Harvey to MVB, Dec. 7, 1838, Benjamin Butler to MVB, Dec. 12, 1838, VBP; Hone, *Diary*, p. 375; Blair to Jackson, Dec. 23, 1838, Blair Family Papers, LC.

[48] Cambreleng to MVB, Dec. 27, VBP; Richardson, *Messages and Papers*, III, 492.

February 14, William C. Rives offered an alternate plan calling for a return to the system of pet banks, but the bill was defeated four days later by a party vote of 27 to 15. On February 21, Wright's bill "more effectually to secure public moneys" passed the Senate by a vote of 28 to 15, with all Democrats present including Cuthbert of Georgia voting for it, and Calhoun abstaining. Congress adjourned on March 4 without further action in the House of Representatives.[49]

With the adjournment of the Twenty-fifth Congress, Van Buren had completed his first two years in office. He had established a sound record in foreign policy by bringing peace to the southwestern and northeastern borders. In the Southwest the Mexican government had agreed to arbitrate the claims of American citizens, and the Republic of Texas had withdrawn its request for annexation. In the Northeast Van Buren had worked effectively with Winfield Scott to stop the intervention of New Yorkers in the Canadian revolution, and soon after Congress adjourned Van Buren and Scott ended the conflict over the Maine border. By avoiding the annexation of Texas and by supporting Calhoun's slavery resolutions the President had done much to ease sectional tensions over slavery. But his program had done little to ease the economic depression and he had not succeeded in separating the government from the nation's banks. He had not changed the Jacksonian formula. The election of 1840 loomed ahead. Van Buren had yet to hear cannon sounding in the night for the independent treasury and it was far from certain that they would ever sound in the night for his reelection.

[49] *Congressional Globe*, 25th Congress, 3rd session (1838-1839), 57, 149, 169, 191, 197.

· 12 ·

THE END OF THE MAGIC

By the spring of 1839, Van Buren had reached a fork in the road. After two years of unsuccessful efforts to secure the independent treasury, he was beginning to look ahead to the presidential campaign of 1840. As he prepared for the campaign he had to take account of significant changes. The Regency, having dominated New York politics for two decades, had been overtaken by Thurlow Weed's Whig machine and would never have the same power again. William L. Marcy had been ousted as governor, John A. Dix as secretary of state, and Azariah Flagg as comptroller. In Washington, Churchill C. Cambreleng had been defeated as congressman and Benjamin Butler had resigned from the cabinet. Although all would move on to other high government positions, they would never again be united in a common cause. They were getting older, some were not well, and a new generation of leaders was emerging; Flagg, forty-eight, had had a stroke; Marcy, fifty-two, had been ill and talked of getting back to his books, and Cambreleng was well past fifty. It was a sign of the passing of the old guard that Van Buren's son John, now twenty-eight, was beginning to rise in New York politics.[1]

The organization in Washington was also changing. Butler and Mahlon Dickerson had already left the cabinet; Amos Kendall was complaining of his health and murmuring about a post in sunny Spain. One after another Jackson's old friends passed from the scene. Andrew J. Donelson was back in Tennessee negotiating with Van Buren for a personal loan; John H. Eaton had left his ministry in Spain; the painter Ralph Earl, who had spent so much time in Jackson's White House, had died, and there was talk of replacing Francis P. Blair as editor of the *Globe*. Since Cambreleng had lost his seat and Polk had decided to run for governor of Tennessee, there would soon be a new chairman of Ways and Means and a new speaker in the House.[2]

Adapting to these changes, Van Buren had settled in as President and had developed a style in running his administration that was

---

[1] Marcy to Prosper Wetmore, Nov. 13, 1838, Marcy Papers, LC.

[2] Cambreleng to MVB, Nov. 12, 1838, Dix to MVB, Dec. 12, 1838, Duff Green to MVB, Nov. 23, 1838, Jackson to MVB, Oct. 22, 1838, April 20, 1839, Kendall to MVB, July 30, Aug. 13, 1838, MVB to Kendall, Aug. 6, 1838, MVB to Donelson, Oct. 8, 1838, VBP; Sellers, *James K. Polk Jacksonian*, pp. 350-355. MVB to Donelson, May 11, 1838, Andrew J. Donelson Papers, LC.

marked by consultation, openness and personal attention to detail. During the first two years his closest advisers in Washington were the three New Yorkers Cambreleng, Butler and Silas Wright, but after the departure of the first two the President was forced to rely on Wright alone. Van Buren also prized the advice of his son Martin, who acted as private secretary and later held a job in the General Land Office; and after some hesitation about using his cabinet during the crisis over the panic in the spring of 1837, he fell into a pattern of holding regular cabinet meetings and of relying on his cabinet officers for advice. During the dispute with Canada in January 1838, for example, Van Buren told James A. Hamilton that he had not ever considered war because the cabinet was opposed to it.[3]

Accessible and a master of detail, Van Buren received advice from scores of obscure citizens and often dealt with matters that other Presidents might have left to subordinates. He dealt with army engineer Thomas Warner, for example, who went over Secretary of War Joel Poinsett's head to complain about being dismissed. Sometimes Van Buren let sentiment intrude on his decisions; when William Leggett was dying of tuberculosis, Van Buren appointed him agent to Guatemala so that he could enjoy his last months in a warm climate. And as before, his tact helped in handling delicate situations, especially in appeasing Eaton when he was withdrawn from Spain. The skills that were evident in Albany were still at work in the White House.[4]

A surprisingly large number of men of letters served his administration. His long-established friendship with Washington Irving continued during the White House years even though the conservative Irving disapproved of Van Buren's banking policies. Another New Yorker, James K. Paulding, who published the humorous magazine *Salmagundi*, became Secretary of the Navy in 1838 when Irving turned the job down. In 1837, after producing the first two volumes of his *History of the United States*, George Bancroft accepted the lucrative post of collector of customs in Boston. Two years later he in turn appointed Nathaniel Hawthorne as weigher and gager of the custom

[3] Adams, *Memoirs*, IX, 426; Francis P. Blair to MVB, Sept. 27, 1839, MVB to James A. Hamilton, Jan. 23, 1838, Notes from cabinet members, c. Sept. 4, 1837, VBP. On the basis of Mahlon Dickerson's diary for 1837 and 1838, James C. Curtis has concluded that Van Buren relied heavily on his cabinet. Curtis, *Fox at Bay*, p. 60.

[4] Warner to MVB, Nov. 1, 1837, V. P. Van Antwerp to MVB, Nov. 20, 1837, MVB to Joel Poinsett, Dec. 1838, Dabney S. Carr to MVB, Aug. 12, 1839, G. B. Wilson to MVB, Dec. 26, 1839, Joel R. Poinsett Papers, HSP; William Leggett to MVB, Mar. 7, 1838, Noel Lawhon to MVB, Aug. 26, 1837, VBP; Thomas Carlin to MVB, Sept. 25, 1838, Woodbury Papers, LC; John Davis to MVB, Feb. 20, 1839, Dreer Collection, HSP.

house. Hawthorne, who had just published *Twice-told Tales*, spent two years in the custom house before moving on to Brook Farm. Van Buren also considered James Fenimore Cooper for a position in 1839, but Cooper, who favored Jacksonians but mistrusted the rise of democracy, was not interested. As Van Buren moved closer to the Loco Focos, he won the support and friendship of William Cullen Bryant, Orestes Brownson and William Leggett. Even Henry Wadsworth Longfellow, who was no Democrat, felt impelled to spend fifteen minutes with Van Buren talking about the weather and the cost of wood and coal when the poet visited Washington in 1837.[5]

During his years as Secretary of State and Vice President Van Buren had established such a reputation for lavish entertaining that Washington society looked forward to a series of gracious levees as soon as he took office. But preoccupied by the panic, the new President disappointed such expectations during his first nine months in office. His first important effort was a reception on New Year's Day 1838—a traditional affair in Washington—and he held a formal open house two months later attended by five thousand people. Dinners presided over by Van Buren were nonpartisan affairs; he accepted many dinner invitations, and became the first President to dine with cabinet members in their homes. In his memoirs John Quincy Adams describes meeting Van Buren and his son Martin at a Washington dinner party and returning home with the two in a carriage at ten in the evening.[6]

As Van Buren stepped up the pace of his entertaining, critical reports began to emanate from Washington about elegance and luxury at the White House. According to one observer Van Buren had "fitted up the President's house in *princely stile*." The most elaborate attack came from Whig congressman Charles Ogle of Pennsylvania, who accused Van Buren of "*spending the money of the people with a lavish hand* [on] regal splendor." Ogle said that Van Buren lived in a "PALACE *as splendid as that of the Caesars, and as richly adorned as the proudest Asiatic mansion.*" With reports of French china, gold knives and forks, expensive artificial flowers, Brussels carpets, and stuffed and covered

[5] Irving, *Life and Letters of Washington Irving*, II, 336-341; Paulding to MVB, Sept. 22, 1837, Bancroft to MVB, Nov. 16, 1837, Irving to MVB, April 30, 1838, Benjamin Butler to MVB, April 30, 1838, MVB to Paulding, May 13, 1838, VBP; Henry W. Longfellow to his father, Feb. 9, 1839, Samuel Longfellow, ed., *Life of Henry Wadsworth Longfellow with Extracts from His Journals and Correspondence* (Boston, 1886), I, 313-314; George Combe, *Notes on the United States of North America during a Phrenological Visit in 1838-9-40* (Philadelphia, 1841), II, 216.

[6] Singleton, *Story of the White House*, I, 234, 261-263; Bryan, *History of the National Capital*, II, 447; Adams, *Memoirs*, IX, 425, X, 44; Lynch, *Epoch and a Man*, pp. 415-416, 444; Hone, *Diary*, p. 460.

mahogany chairs and sofas, Ogle left the impression that Andrew Jackson's successor was behaving in a most undemocratic way.[7]

Ogle's attack was politically motivated and grossly exaggerated. Van Buren did spend $20,000 on furnishings for the White House while he was President, but his expenditure compared favorably with the $65,000 spent by Andrew Jackson over eight years and the sums of $14,000 and $25,000 spent by James K. Polk and Franklin Pierce respectively during their single terms. The White House, furthermore, was in shabby condition when Van Buren took office. Levi Lincoln of Massachusetts, who was a member of the House committee on furnishing the White House at the time, disclosed that the receiving room did not even have a table or a mirror at which ladies might adjust their bonnets before being introduced to the President. And Thomas Hart Benton's daughter Jessie Benton Frémont reported that even after Van Buren placed a glass screen across the drafty entrance hall, "great wood fires [still had to] struggle against the chill of the house." The White House was so "badly underdrained," added Jessie, that "in all long rains the floors of kitchens and cellars were actually under water."[8]

An Englishman who visited Van Buren's White House failed to notice any luxury or ostentation. Member of Parliament James Silk Buckingham, who attended Van Buren's open house in March 1838, wrote that the White House was "greatly inferior in size and splendor to the country residences of most of [the British] nobility," and the furniture was "far from elegant or costly." "The whole air of the mansion," he said, was "unostentatious . . . without parade or displays, . . . well adapted to the simplicity and economy . . . of the republican institutions of the country." The servants wore no livery and Van Buren himself was dressed in a "plain suit of black." Buckingham was impressed that "every one present acted as though he felt himself to be on a footing of equality with every other person." As Buckingham noted, Van Buren in 1838 followed Andrew Jackson's policy of allowing anyone at all to attend a White House reception, and stationed no guards at the door. Van Buren himself walked to and from church alone and often rode horseback unaccompanied. A short time later, however, another British traveler, Captain Frederick Marryat, noted that Van Buren had taken a step that struck at "the

[7] James Graham to W. A. Graham, Sept. 17, 1837, Graham, *Papers*, I, 527; [Charles Ogle], *Speech by Mr. Ogle of Pennsylvania on the Regal Splendor of the President's Palace* (Boston, 1840), especially, I, 1-25, II, 1-19; Singleton, *Story of the White House*, I, 219-247.

[8] *Niles' Register*, 58 (1840), 387; Singleton, *Story of the White House*, I, 234, 248-252, 259-261, 267-268.

very roots of their boasted equality" by stationing police at the door to "prevent the intrusion of any improper person." It was Van Buren's concession to the changing times.[9]

In November 1838, Van Buren's eldest son Abraham married Angelica Singleton, daughter of South Carolina planter Richard Singleton, niece and protégée of Dolly Madison, and niece of the minister to England's wife, Sally Stevenson. Angelica had just the sort of aristocratic background that Martin Van Buren could appreciate. The marriage strengthened Van Buren's ties with the Richmond Junto, the Old Republican party and the old South. It also brought to the White House a beautiful woman, who had been educated at Madame Grelaud's seminary in Philadelphia and introduced to Washington society by Dolly Madison in 1837. As soon as they returned from their honeymoon in England with the Stevensons, Angelica and Abraham moved into the White House, where Angelica served as hostess for her father-in-law for the next two years. Angelica was "universally admired" in Washington, and even won the admiration of the critical French minister Adolphe Fourier de Bacourt. He scorned almost every other American belle, but admitted that "in any country" Angelica would "pass for an amiable woman of graceful and distinguished manners and appearance."[10]

While the young Van Burens were in England, they spent some time with John Van Buren, who had arrived just in time to see the coronation of Queen Victoria and to attend a dress ball at Buckingham Palace. Since John supposedly danced with the young queen and was listed on the guest list with a number of famous princes, the Whig press began sarcastically to call him Prince John—a nickname that stuck. It cost Martin Van Buren at least $1,000 that summer to maintain John in England, but for a President who had been born in a tavern and had always envied aristocrats, it must have been worth every penny.[11]

In the late spring of 1839 with the Twenty-fifth Congress behind him, Van Buren decided to make a trip home. He had not been to New York since the fall of 1836, and it was time to check on his home base before starting his campaign for reelection. Traveling part of the way by railroad, he reached New York City on July 2. Although Governor Seward found an excuse for not being on hand, the reception

[9] *Ibid.*, 261-264.

[10] *Ibid.*, 264-265; Lynch, *Epoch and a Man*, p. 416; Anne H. Wharton, *Social Life in the Early Republic* (Philadelphia, 1902), 269-272, 297-298.

[11] *Ibid.*, 269-270; MVB to Andrew Jackson, April 29, 1838, Lady Wellesley to MVB, Sept. 20, 1838, VBP; Hunt, *Biographical Sketch Book*, p. 53.

was even greater than the one given Jackson in 1833. Philip Hone was particularly distressed because the festivities replaced the normal Fourth of July celebration. Like Jackson Van Buren landed at Castle Garden, reviewed the troops, and led a parade up Broadway. During the week that followed he made a number of public appearances and spent most of his time in the company of radical Democrats John A. Riell and Alexander Ming, Jr., and others of what Hone called the "Loco-foco rabble."[12]

On July 9, Van Buren left for Kinderhook, arriving on July 20. Here a friendly crowd greeted him as Marcy, bearing no grudges, reviewed Van Buren's career and praised him for his speech supporting the Erie Canal and for his stand at the constitutional convention of 1821 in favor of extending the right to vote. Standing on the balcony of the village hotel, Van Buren responded with a rambling, sentimental account of his boyhood days. During their week in Kinderhook Van Buren and his son Smith spent a day or two at the old Van Ness family estate, which Van Buren had recently purchased. Celebrating with fricasseed ham and champagne, they decided on "The Locusts" as a name for their new home, remembering that Cooper had used it in *The Spy*; but when Van Buren retired to the estate later, he called it Lindenwald.[13]

Van Buren spent the first three weeks in August at the United States Hotel at Saratoga Springs, chatting, promenading, taking the waters, and politicking with other famous politicians. Claiming that "all the world" had come to the Springs, Philip Hone called that August the "meridian of the Saratoga season." At the end of the summer Van Buren took a tour of western New York, returned to spend a few more weeks at Albany and Kinderhook, then headed back to Washington and the start of his reelection campaign.[14]

During his summer in New York State Van Buren was much encouraged by the political news and by the warm reception he received. He was pleased to find Marcy still in the fold and the Democratic party far more united than it had been for several years. The *Albany Argus*, which had been lukewarm toward Van Buren during the panic,

[12] *Niles' Register*, 56 (1839), 275, 297-298, 310; Hone, *Diary*, pp. 402-405; *Argus*, July 9, 1839; William Henry Seward to Thomas G. Talmage, June 30, 1839, VBP.

[13] *Argus*, July 9, July 23, July 26, July 30, 1839; *Niles' Register*, 56 (1839), 365-367; Smith Van Buren to Martin Van Buren, Jr., July 31, 1839, VBP.

[14] Hone, *Diary*, pp. 405-411; Seward, *Autobiography*, pp. 435-436; MVB to Levi Woodbury, Sept. 1, 1839, Woodbury Papers, LC; MVB to Silas Wright, Sept. 21, 1839, James Fenimore Cooper to Mrs. Cooper, Oct. 5, Oct. 10, 1839, Cooper, *Letters and Journals*, III, 427, 430, 432.

was finally backing the independent treasury and was condemning the "apostasy" of William C. Rives and Nathaniel P. Tallmadge. Benjamin Butler, using one of Van Buren's favorite phrases, reported that the "sober second thought" of the New York voters was with the administration. Even though Weed's Whig machine retained control of the state, the Democrats managed to elect Isaac Varian mayor of New York City in the spring, and improved their representation in the state assembly in the fall.[15]

Back in Washington on October 18, Van Buren was cheered by the news of Democratic victories in other states as well. In New Hampshire the Democrats had widened their margin over the Whigs in March, and in Massachusetts Marcus Morton defeated Whig incumbent governor Edward Everett in the fall. Although Morton won by a majority of only one vote, his victory was significant because National Republicans or Whigs had held the governor's seat in the Bay State throughout the 1830s. Democrats had also gained ten seats in the Virginia house and senate, where the opposition was so deeply divided among Whigs, Rives-Whigs, and conservatives that the legislature was unable to elect anyone to fill Rives' seat in the United State Senate. In the late summer, news of Democratic successes had come from North Carolina and from Tennessee, where James K. Polk had campaigned so aggressively that he had increased the number of Democratic votes by 20,000 and had been elected governor. In the Northwest the Democrats carried Indiana, which had been Whig in both 1837 and 1838. Jabez Hammond later wrote that with the results so "favourable," Van Buren's reelection looked likely.[16]

The economic news was not nearly so good. The recovery that had begun the previous spring came to a halt when financial stringency once again forced English banks to call in specie from America. Van Buren was no sooner back in Washington than the Bank of the United States announced that it was once again suspending payments, and banks in the South and West followed suit. The effect of the new panic was devastating. Wholesale commodity prices, which had almost re-

[15] *Argus*, Jan. 4, Jan. 22, Jan. 25, Jan. 29, Feb. 1, Feb. 5, Mar. 19, Nov. 8, Dec. 13, 1839; Benjamin Butler to MVB, April 12, 1839, VBP; Hammond, *Political Parties*, II, 516-517; Fox, *Decline of Aristocracy*, p. 402.

[16] Cole, *Jacksonian Democracy in New Hampshire*, p. 196; Darling, *Political Changes in Massachusetts*, pp. 240-241; Braverman, "Conservative Revolt in Virginia," pp. 284-287; Ritchie to Andrew Russell, Thomas Ritchie Miscellaneous Papers, UVL; Wiltse, *John C. Calhoun, Nullifier*, p. 404; Sellers, *James K. Polk Jacksonian*, pp. 366-377; Levi Woodbury to MVB, Aug. 11, Aug. 16, 1839, John M. Niles to MVB, Oct. 27, 1839, VBP; Hammond, *Political Parties*, II, 516-517.

gained their pre-1837 highs in the late winter, started a long retreat that lasted well into the 1840s, while land sales by the federal government, which had risen in 1839, fell again in 1840.[17]

Any hopes Van Buren might have harbored of entering the campaign of 1840 with an improving economy vanished as the panic became a severe economic depression. The decline in business hit New York State hard by cutting into the tolls collected on the state's canal system. In the South, especially the deep South, planters went bankrupt, plantations lay uncultivated, and the price of slaves dropped precipitously. Farther west schemes for building roads, canals and railroads collapsed, forcing investors into bankruptcy and workers into unemployment. Conditions were worst of all in the eastern cities, where as many as one-third of all workers were thrown out of work. Shoe factories in Haverhill and textile mills in Lowell, Massachusetts, shut down, and it was estimated that over 50,000 were out of work in New York City. Even workers who could find jobs were hurt because wages dropped more rapidly than the price of food and rent. In the nation's Capital Van Buren could see relief centers ladling out soup to paupers and knew that there were similar lines in many other cities. The wealthy Philip Hone could not understand how a "poor man manage[d] to get a dinner for his family" when mutton was still selling at eighteen to twenty-five cents a pound. Another New Yorker, George Templeton Strong, noted that people everywhere were "out of kash, out of kredit, out of karacter and out of klothes." "The blossoms of hope," mourned Hone, "which had sprung up in the brief sunshine of confidence," had been "blighted by the frosts of suspicion."[18]

The deepening of the depression made the Whig presidential nomination all the more attractive. Two of the three Whig candidates in 1836 had removed themselves from consideration—Hugh L. White by backing Henry Clay, and Daniel Webster by spending the summer and fall of 1839 in England—but the third, William Henry Harrision, was very much in the running. After receiving the nomination of the Ohio Whigs in May 1838, and the nomination of the Democratic Anti-Masonic national convention that November, Harrison entered the year 1839 as the Whig front runner.

In order to defeat Harrison, Henry Clay needed votes from New York in addition to the support he could count on from southern states. Confident that he had the backing of the Whigs in New York

---

[17] Temin, *Jacksonian Economy*, pp. 69, 148-171.

[18] McGrane, *Panic of 1837*, pp. 103-132; Norman Ware, *The Industrial Worker, 1840-1860* (Boston, 1924), pp. 26-27; Hone, *Diary*, p. 385; Strong, *Diary*, I, 137.

City, Clay set forth on a tour of upstate and western New York in the summer of 1839, at the very moment that Van Buren was visiting his home state. Another candidate in New York that summer was Winfield Scott, who had won many supporters by his role in the border disputes with Canada, and who had the backing of Thurlow Weed. Clay, Scott and Van Buren all gathered at Saratoga in August, and Hone reported that the self-conscious candidates made "good-natured" jokes as they whiled away the hours with their "fair ladies." As Henry Clay tried to pass Van Buren in one of the narrow hallways on one occasion, the President remarked coyly, "I hope I do not obstruct your way." "Not here certainly," replied Clay.[19]

The festive gathering at Saratoga that summer had a bearing on the Whig national nominating convention scheduled to open in Harrisburg, Pennsylvania, on December 4. Weed traveled to Saratoga to try to convince Clay that he should drop out of the race and leave the way open for Scott, but Clay refused. Clay led on the first ballot at the convention with 103 votes, mostly from the South and West, but Thaddeus Stevens, the young Whig leader from Pennsylvania, was able to secure 91 votes for Harrison, half of them from Pennsylvania and Ohio; Weed mustered 57 votes for Scott, including 42 from New York. When Virginia deserted Clay on the second ballot and New York abandoned Scott on the third, the nomination went to General Harrison. John Tyler, who had left the Democratic party over nullification, was named for Vice President. At Brown's Hotel in Washington on December 11, Henry Clay assured the Whigs of unity in 1840 by announcing his full support for Harrison. Van Buren, who had faced a divided Whig party in 1836, would have no such advantage in 1840.[20]

Now united nationally, the Whigs were well-organized at the state level as well and thus doubly effective. In New York the Whig machine under Governor William Henry Seward and party boss Thurlow Weed ran the state just as Van Buren's Albany Regency had done. Weed controlled the New York Whigs by exploiting his position as state printer, by dispensing a variety of state jobs, and by spreading party propaganda through his own *Albany Journal* and James Gordon Bennett's *New York Journal*. Weed's Whig delegation in Washington included former Anti-Masons Francis Granger and Millard Fillmore in the House, and former conservative Democrat Nathaniel P. Tall-

---

[19] Robert G. Gunderson, *The Log-Cabin Campaign* (Lexington, 1957), pp. 41-47.
[20] *Ibid.*, pp. 47-69; William N. Chambers, "Election of 1840," Schlesinger, *American Presidential Elections*, I, 656-665.

madge in the Senate. Thaddeus Stevens, who had also started as an Anti-Mason, had developed an organization in Pennsylvania that rivaled Weed's. Despite their losses in 1839 the Whigs were also well-organized in important states such as Webster's Massachusetts and Harrison's Ohio. Since New York, Pennsylvania, Massachusetts, and Ohio had 101 of the 148 electoral votes needed to win the election in 1840, Van Buren's chances of success were much in doubt, and they were not helped by news of Democratic bickering in Tennessee, North Carolina and Virginia. Soon after his return from Europe in December Daniel Webster wrote optimistically that the Whigs felt "confident of the centre, the Northwest, and the North and East." In the South he was confident of Kentucky and Louisiana, "very probably Tennessee," and he even had "hopes of Virginia."[21]

At the crossroads of his presidency, faced by a deepening economic depression and by a united opposition, Van Buren had hard decisions to make about the campaign of 1840. He could return to old Jacksonian policies, he could continue with the moderate program that he had devised in 1837, or he could adopt new Loco Foco policies to cope with the depression and the Whigs. There was also the question of how he would react personally. In his first two and a half years in the White House Van Buren had tried to avoid trouble, had sought to calm troubled waters. He had retained Jackson's cabinet, kept the specie circular, avoided the excesses of political patronage, and had sought peace in foreign policy even when it threatened his political future. Would he now be forced to become more partisan, more political, in order to win reelection? And in an America that was changing both economically and politically, there was the question of whether Van Buren still had the ability to adapt. Although his enemies accused him of joining the Loco Focos, Van Buren had done little to win the support of the working classes. He was still using tactics that had succeeded in earlier years. In December 1839, just turning fifty-seven, Van Buren was being put to the test.

Since he had little hope in 1840 without winning his home state, he had already begun compensating for previous political errors and past political neglect by making key appointments of New Yorkers. In 1838, he had appointed Jesse Hoyt customs collector in New York City and James K. Paulding Secretary of the Navy; the next year he named his friend Harmanus Bleecker minister to the Netherlands and in 1840, Churchill C. Cambreleng was posted as minister to Russia.

[21] Van Deusen, *Thurlow Weed*, pp. 103-111; Weed, *Autobiography*, pp. 456-484; Webster to Samuel Jaudon, Mar. 29, 1840, Webster, *Private Correspondence*, II, 79.

Van Buren also succumbed to Regency pressure by finally replacing Solomon Van Rensselaer as postmaster in Albany with Azariah Flagg. To strengthen his ties with William L. Marcy and the conservatives, Van Buren appointed Marcy to the commission on American claims against Mexico, and offered him the prospect of becoming receiver-general in the independent treasury system, or of joining the cabinet. Van Buren was finally acting the way a Regency spoilsman was expected to act.[22]

He gave further evidence that he would be more partisan when he interjected himself directly into New York politics on November 25, by sending Flagg suggestions for the coming campaign. Pointing out that the Whigs were winning because they were well-organized at the grass roots, he asked for the names of Democratic leaders in each county so that he could send them election materials. Flagg and Wright seized the opportunity to undermine the occasionally disloyal Edwin Croswell and the *Argus* by suggesting that the party set up a new newspaper to "prepare the public mind against falsehoods." Van Buren was willing to go along with the plan and even supplied the name of *Rough Hewer*, but he showed that he was unwilling to be completely ruthless when he entertained an emissary sent by Croswell to Washington. In addition Van Buren arranged to have Thomas M. Burt, a former partner of Croswell, edit the new journal. The *Rough Hewer* boasted a circulation of 10,000 by March, but it did not replace the *Argus*.[23]

Early in 1840, Van Buren sent the Regency seventy-five pages of advice entitled "Thoughts on the Approaching Election in New York." It resembled other manuscripts of his in length, methodical organization, and in the many insertions and crossed-out sentences; and typically the contents looked to the past rather than to the future. Warning that the Whigs were plotting to "break down the spirit of the Democratic Party," he outlined plans for a caucus to call a state meeting. Instead of discussing campaign issues such as the depression

[22] William C. Bryant to MVB, April 27, 1839, Bleecker to MVB, Sept. 9, 1839, Marcy to MVB, April 26, May 9, 1840, VBP; Marcy to Prosper Wetmore, April 26, 1840, MVB to Marcy, April 29, 1840, Marcy Papers, LC; Lynch, *Epoch and a Man*, p. 426; Hammond, *Political Parties*, II, 514; Spencer, *Victor and the Spoils*, pp. 117-118; Fillmore, "Papers," II, 216n.

[23] MVB to Flagg, Nov. 25, Dec. 28, 1839, Flagg Papers, CUL; Flagg to MVB, Dec. 20, 1839, Wright to Flagg, Dec. 22, 1839; Flagg Papers; Garraty, *Wright*, pp. 180-181; Marcy and Croswell to MVB, Dec. 22, 1839, John A. Dix to MVB, Mar. 27, 1840, VBP.

or the independent treasury, he reviewed early party history and called for a vindication of "Republican principles."[24]

Most of the Democratic newspapers that Van Buren relied on that winter also looked backward. Old Jacksonian journals, especially the *New-Hampshire Patriot* and the *Richmond Enquirer*, could be counted on to remind voters of the Old Jeffersonian-Jacksonian tradition. So could Francis P. Blair of the Washington *Globe*, who reassured Old Hickory that "the Magician by his firmness, ability, and honesty justifie[d]" Jackson's "good opinion" and would "succeed in stamping [Jackson's] principles on the administration for years to come." When party leaders set up a new organ in Washington called the *Extra Globe* and needed an editor, they turned to Amos Kendall. Radical editor John L. O'Sullivan of the *United States Magazine and Democratic Review*, warned against this preoccupation with past issues, particularly the Bank of the United States.[25]

Instead of heeding such advice, Van Buren continued his efforts to maintain his links with the past—especially with Andrew Jackson. Since January 8, 1840, would be the twenty-fifth anniversary of the battle of New Orleans, Van Buren thought he would gain political advantage if the Old Hero were to attend the celebration in New Orleans. Jackson demurred, saying that he was "out of funds," but finally agreed to go. After four days of traveling by carriage along "rough roads" over ground "covered with snow," Jackson reached the mouth of the Cumberland River, where he boarded the first of three steamboats for New Orleans. Despite rough seas, "floating ice," and a severe hemorrhage he arrived on time and spent ten days at countless ceremonies "struggling against pain and sickness, . . . determined to go through or fail in the struggle."[26]

Van Buren had his first opportunity to outline his program when the Twenty-sixth Congress assembled on December 2, 1839. The congressional elections the previous year had left the new Congress with about the same party division as before. Although the Democratic

---

[24] "Thoughts on the Approaching Election in New York, Mar. 1840," VBP. Gunderson believes that the document was written by Kendall, but Curtis correctly points out that the handwriting is Van Buren's.

[25] Gunderson, *Log-Cabin Campaign*, pp. 86-87; Blair to Jackson, Mar. 17, 1840, Jackson, *Correspondence*, VI, 54; O'Sullivan to Levi Woodbury, Mar. 4, 1840, VBP.

[26] Jackson to William B. Lewis, Nov. 11, 1839, Jackson to Andrew J. Donelson, Dec. 10, 1839, Jackson to Andrew J. Hutchings, Dec. 19, 1839, Jackson to Andrew Jackson, Jr., Dec. 24, Dec. 27, Dec. 31, 1839, Jackson to Mrs. Sarah Jackson, Jan. 4, 1840, Jackson to Rev. Hardy M. Cryer, Feb. 5, 1840, Jackson to Amos Kendall, April 16, 1840, Jackson, *Correspondence*, VI, 40-49, 58; Kendall to Jackson, Mar 4, 1840, Jackson Papers, LC; James, *Andrew Jackson President*, pp. 446-448.

margin in both Houses was slightly reduced, the administration no longer had to contend with the conservative Democrats, who had been absorbed into the Whig ranks. When Congress opened, the Democrats had firm control of the Senate, but were immediately embroiled in a two-week dispute over organizing the House of Representatives. The Democrats arrived in Washington counting on a majority of 124 to 118 in the House, but most of their advantage was eliminated when the House temporarily refused to seat five Democrats from New Jersey whose seats were contested. In attempting to name a speaker, the Democratic caucus nominated John W. Jones of Virginia, but Jones was not elected because five nullifier Democrats from South Carolina, supporters of John C. Calhoun, threw away their votes to other candidates. When the Democrats turned to Dixon H. Lewis of Alabama, he too failed to be elected because he lacked the support of Thomas Hart Benton. Finally, on December 16, on the eleventh ballot, the Whigs succeeded in electing Robert M. T. Hunter of Virginia, by the slim majority of two votes and with the help of six Democratic votes from South Carolina.[27]

Because of the organizational battles, Van Buren was not able to deliver his message to Congress until the day before Christmas, and when he did, his emphasis indicated that he had no new program in mind. In an earlier letter to Silas Wright, he had written with good republican logic that the only way to prevent the abuse of power was to "confine legislation to as few subjects" as possible.[28] His message of December 24 rehearsed the by now familiar arguments. More realistic than usual, he began by admitting that "the past year [had] not been one of unalloyed prosperity" because "serious embarrassments yet derange[d] the trade of many of our cities." But he held fast to his Old Republican principles by offering no plan to end the depression and by bragging that he had reduced federal expenditures. Keeping taxes down and "expenditures within reasonable bounds," said Van Buren, was "a duty second only in importance to the preservation of our national character." Later in the message Van Buren returned to his Old Republican theme by attacking those who would "substitute

[27] One study of the 26th Congress lists 28 Democrats, 22 Whigs, and 2 uncertain in the Senate. *Statistical History*, p. 691; Wiltse, *John C. Calhoun, Nullifier*, pp. 405-407; *Congressional Globe*, 26th Congress, 1st session (1839-1840), 1, 40-41, 52-56; Benton, *Thirty Years' View*, II, 158-162.

[28] MVB to Wright, Sept. 21, 1839, VBP. Wright had suggested regulation of state banks in a speech in the Senate on January 31, 1838. *Congressional Globe*, 25th Congress, 2nd session (1837-1838), appendix, 91.

for republican simplicity . . . a sickly appetite for . . . reckless indulgence."

For the same republican reasons it was essential to end the connection between the federal government and the state banks, which had been responsible for "the extension [of a] system of extravagant credit." These banks, furthermore, were not a safe depository for federal funds because they were interrelated and the failure of one could lead to the failure of many others. "This chain of dependence," he went on, did "not stop here, [but] reach[ed] across the ocean and end[ed] in London, the center of the credit system." "The introduction of a new bank into the most distant of our villages," he declared, "places the business of that village within the influence of the money power of England." Lapsing into demagoguery, he said that if the government put its funds into state banks, American policies would be "entirely under the control of a foreign moneyed interest." He sounded like Jackson in his Bank veto when he insisted that such a policy would "impair [American] independence."

After these Jeffersonian and Jacksonian flourishes, Van Buren turned to his independent treasury plan. With no hope of holding conservative Democratic votes Van Buren came out flatly for a strong specie clause in the bill to be presented to Congress. Van Buren argued that the plan would enable the government to check state banks by "withholding the means of extravagance afforded by the public funds and restraining them from excessive issue of notes which they would be constantly called upon to redeem." Thus in one bill Van Buren proposed to avoid the evils of tying the federal government to the banks of the land, and to reap the benefits of having that government regulate those very banks. The President's proposals with their countervailing effect showed that he was still pursuing a moderate course.[29]

Van Buren's difficulties in organizing the House of Representatives underscored the importance of Calhoun and the southern nullifiers to the passage of the independent treasury. Calhoun's clique, wrote Benton, had assumed "control in the House [by] constituting themselves into a balance wheel between the two nearly balanced parties." Even though Calhoun had backed part of Van Buren's program during the Twenty-fifth Congress, the two men had had no personal contact for over eight years—since the dispute over the cabinet in 1831. Needing Calhoun's support both for the independent treasury and for reelection, Van Buren made the first overture, through Virginia senator William H. Roane. When Roane suggested at the opening of Congress

[29] Richardson, *Messages and Papers*, III, 529-555.

that Calhoun leave his card at the White House, the proud South Carolinian replied that he preferred to wait until he had heard Van Buren's message. Apparently satisfied—especially by Van Buren's insistence on a specie clause—Calhoun paid a private call on Van Buren and then made a public appearance at the White House at the New Year's day reception. Two days later when Calhoun introduced an administration land bill in the Senate, Henry Clay attacked his colleague for suddenly assuming "intimate, friendly, and confidential relations" with Van Buren. Angered by the implication, Calhoun replied that his action had been based on "principle," not on any personal political relationship. But he was not convincing. Calhoun had decided to help Van Buren, both in the Senate and in the presidential campaign, for pragmatic, political reasons.[30]

On January 6, 1840, a few days after the rapprochement between Van Buren and Calhoun, Silas Wright brought his fourth independent treasury bill to the Senate. As Van Buren had proposed, the bill included clauses empowering the Secretary of the Treasury to regulate state banks by "issu[ing] and publish[ing] regulations to enforce the speedy presentation of all Government drafts for payment." Calhoun promptly supported the bill. Henry Clay was so amused by the incongruity of state-righters Van Buren and Calhoun officially proposing government regulation of banking that he taunted them, claiming that he saw a "Government bank lurking in the bill." Sensitive to such comments, James Buchanan and Robert Walker devoted the better part of two major addresses to defending the bill against charges of excessive federal regulation. Wright's original bill allowed the use of paper bank notes in payment of federal debts, but Benton introduced an amendment that removed the paper money clauses and required payment of federal dues in specie. When the independent treasury bill came up for final vote on January 23, it still contained enough of Van Buren's strange mixture of hard money and federal regulation to make it the sort of balanced bill that appealed to Democrats of all persuasions. And Wright, Buchanan, Calhoun, Walker, and Benton promptly pushed it through by a vote of 24 to 18.[31]

[30] Benton, *Thirty Years' View*, II, 160; Wiltse, *John C. Calhoun, Nullifier*, pp. 407-408; Calhoun to Dr. Danall, Oct. 26, 1838, Calhoun to James E. Calhoun, Feb. 1, 1840, Calhoun to James H. Hammond, May 16, 1840, Calhoun, *Correspondence*, pp. 407-408, 444-445, 457; MVB to Jackson, Feb. 2, 1840, VBP; *Autobiography*, pp. 389-392; *Congressional Globe*, 26th Congress, 1st session (1839-1840), 96-98; Adams, *Memoirs*, X, 182; Francis Granger to————, Jan. 2, 1840, Granger Papers, LC; Benjamin Tappan's Journal, Dec. 31, 1839 (photostat of original), Benjamin Tappan Papers, LC; MVB to Jackson, Feb. 2, 1840, Jackson, *Correspondence*, VI, 48.

[31] *Congressional Globe*, 26th Congress, 1st session (1839-1840), 103, 120, 124, 127, 130, 139-141; appendix, 106-108, 123-125, 129-143.

Despite the impressive victory in the Senate, Van Buren was still far from certain that the independent treasury would become law. Three times before, the Senate had passed an independent treasury bill only to have it blocked in the House of Representatives, and Democrats had no assurance that they could prevail in the House in 1840. Hopes brightened on January 30 when Democrats succeeded in electing Blair and his partner John C. Rives printers for the House. Still the administration hesitated, waiting for a decision on the five contested New Jersey seats, and even when the House seated the five New Jersey Democrats on March 10, the administration moved slowly. John W. Jones introduced the Senate independent treasury bill in the House on March 11, but the bill was then buried in the Ways and Means Committee until the latter part of May.[32]

While the independent treasury was stalled in the House, Van Buren turned his attention to the Democratic convention, which was to meet in Baltimore on May 5. Although there was no question about Van Buren's renomination, there was strong opposition to the renomination of Vice President Richard Mentor Johnson, who was still unpopular in the South because of his mulatto mistress and mulatto children. In 1836, the electors in Virginia had refused to give their twenty-three votes to Johnson, and thus forced the vice presidential election into the Senate, where Johnson was finally chosen. In 1838, William H. Haywood of North Carolina, had remarked that southern hostility to Van Buren would vanish if only some Southerner other than Johnson were named for Vice President. After a trip south in 1839, Amos Kendall reported that Johnson was devoting "too much of his time to a young Delilah of about the complexion of Shakespears [sic] swarthy Othello"; and on returning from New Orleans in February 1840, Andrew Jackson, who had supported Johnson in 1836, had warned Van Buren that Johnson would be a "dead weight" on the ticket. Like many other Southerners Jackson preferred James K. Polk, and promised that if Polk ran with Van Buren, the party would carry the entire South.[33]

The vice presidency continued to divide the party at the convention in Baltimore on May 5 and May 6. Van Buren was unanimously

[32] *Ibid.*, 157, 256-257, 261-262.

[33] Haywood to Polk, Mar. 10, 1838, Elizabeth G. McPherson, ed., "Unpublished Letters from North Carolinians to Polk," *North Carolina Historical Review*, 16 (1939), 329; Anonymous to Kendall, Aug. 12, 1839, Jackson to MVB, Feb. 17, April 3, April 29, 1840, VBP; Sellers, *James K. Polk Jacksonian*, pp. 350-352, 399-403; Jackson to Blair, Feb. 15, 1840, Jackson to Kendall, April 1840, MVB to Jackson, April 1840, Jackson, *Correspondence*, VI, 50, 55, 58; MVB to Jackson, April 17, 1840, Jackson Papers, LC.

renominated for President, but the division over Johnson was so wide that the delegates voted to leave the nomination for Vice President up to the states. Since Van Buren wanted to keep Johnson on the ticket because of his popularity with workers and radicals in the North, the decision of the convention failed to bring harmony. Jackson told Van Buren angrily that enemies in disguise were backing Johnson because they knew that he would hurt the party in Kentucky, Tennessee and Pennsylvania. Jackson threatened to desert Van Buren if the states did not nominate Polk. Even when Van Buren had his way and Johnson's rivals withdrew, the party did not achieve the harmony that was needed. Secretary of State John Forsyth, who wanted the nomination, retired from the race with—as Philip Hone put it—"very bad grace, snarling and showing his teeth." Polk never officially withdrew, but his letter saying that he would not persist if he became an "obstacle" to party unity was taken as a resignation.[34]

Less divided on issues than men, Democrats agreed on a traditional, backward-looking party platform calling for strict construction of the Constitution. They denied that the Constitution gave the government the power to finance internal improvements, to assume state debts, to establish a national bank, or to "foster one branch of industry" through a protective tariff. The platform called for "the most rigid economy" in order to protect "republican institutions." Democrats continued to appeal to the South with statements that Congress could not "interfere with or control the domestic institutions of the several states, . . . that all efforts of abolitionists or others, made to induce congress to interfere with questions of slavery, . . . lead to the most alarming and dangerous consequences." Anticipating passage of the independent treasury bill, the platform also called for "the separation of the moneys of the government from banking institutions."[35]

In the campaign that followed Van Buren stuck to this platform, making every effort to present himself as an ideal Jeffersonian-Jacksonian. From the quiet shores of Derwentwater in England, Churchill C. Cambreleng reminded Van Buren that there was no other way to win an election. On the Fourth of July Van Buren wrote to a group of Democrats in Kentucky promising to "rebuke any attempt by the Whigs to mislead or intimidate the People . . . into a surrender of their Constitution and their liberties," and on July 31, he summed up his

[34] Jackson to MVB, May 21, 1840, MVB to Jackson, June 17, 1840, VBP; Hone, *Diary*, p. 479; Polk to Grundy, May 27, 1840, James K. Polk Papers, LC, quoted in Sellers, *James K. Polk Jacksonian*, p. 416.

[35] "Democratic Platform 1840," Schlesinger, *Presidential Elections*, I, 691-692.

views in a campaign letter that repeated the traditional Democratic opposition to the Bank, the tariff and internal improvements.[36]

As part of his campaign for reelection Van Buren returned to the task of securing the independent treasury. His administration brought the independent treasury bill back to the floor of the House on May 20, but even then Whig delaying tactics, Democratic absences, and long-winded speeches prevented action for over a month. Andrew Jackson became so angry at the delays that he told Francis P. Blair to "permit no leave of absence until this bill is passed." Recalling his old military days, Jackson compared the situation to that in which a general gives "his soldiers furlows until he becomes so weak, that the enemy sallies forth, defeats and destroys him." Absent Democrats, roared Jackson, "should be shot as deserters from their posts on the lines of the enemy." The administration ignored Jackson, but took advantage of the delay to secure passage of another preemption bill in the hope of encouraging western congressmen to vote for the independent treasury. Finally, on June 26, the administration nerved itself for a decision by passing a resolution calling for a vote on the independent treasury no later than June 30.

The Democratic delays and maneuvers were justified; the final vote showed 124 yeas and 107 nays. Having no conservative bloc to contend with, Van Buren was able to enforce party discipline. Only two Democrats failed to vote and only four who voted opposed the bill. Three years of catering to Calhoun paid off when five of the seven South Carolinians voted for the bill. And the preemption bill helped more than it did two years earlier, for members of the six western delegations, who voted 19-14 against the independent treasury in 1838, this time voted 18-10 for the bill.[37]

During the campaign of 1840 and in years to come Democrats praised the independent treasury bill as a magnificent achievement that, in Jackson's words, gave "light and strength [to the] republican cause." Benton called passage of the bill "the distinguishing glory of the Twenty-sixth Congress, and the 'crowning mercy' of Mr. Van

[36] Cambreleng to MVB, May 28, 1840, VBP; Poinsett, Notes for a speech in Virginia in 1840, Joel R. Poinsett Papers, in the Henry D. Gilpin Papers, HSP; MVB to a Committee in Lexington, Ky., July 4, 1840, Schlesinger, *Presidential Elections*, I, 733-736; Douglas, *Letters*, p. 90; MVB to Messrs. John B. Cary and others, of Elizabeth City County, Virginia, July 31, 1840, *Niles' Register*, 58 (1840), 393-396.

[37] For the independent treasury bill, *Congressional Globe*, 26th Congress, 1st session (1839-1840), 406, 488, 495. For the preemption bill, *ibid.*, 405, 421, 424-425. Jackson to Blair, June 27, 1840, Jackson, *Correspondence*, VI, 66-67; Curtis, *Fox at Bay*, pp. 148-151; Ray Allen Billington, *Westward Expansion: a History of the American Frontier*, 2nd ed. (New York, 1960), pp. 374-378.

Buren's administration." According to Calhoun it was "a great step," one that would bring about "a permanent and salutary change in the moral, social and political condition of the country." Radical Robert Rantoul of Massachusetts, asserted that the bill had "purifie[d] the political atmosphere" by ending the "corrupt alliance between Bank & State." Van Buren delayed signing the bill until the Fourth of July, when crowds gathered to celebrate both the Fourth and the independent treasury. From then on Democrats referred to the bill as the "Second Declaration of Independence."[38]

But despite the rhetoric the new law had little effect on the banking practices of the federal government. Ever since the bank suspensions of 1837 Levi Woodbury had followed the terms of the Deposit-Distribution Act by taking deposits from state banks and placing them in the vaults of various federal officials. The Independent Treasury Act simply made official Woodbury's de facto policy. For this dubious accomplishment Van Buren had split his party, lost the support of conservatives and damaged his ties with Virginia and New York. The *Albany Argus*, which had finally supported the bill with some reluctance, paid little attention to its passage.[39]

The question remains why a politician as astute as Van Buren devoted three years of his presidency to the pursuit of the independent treasury. To find the answer it is necessary first to examine his priorities on entering the White House. Instead of facing new issues such as slavery and manifest destiny that divided the party, he preferred dealing with the old Jacksonian issues of banking on which he thought the party could unite. Once he was in office the sudden economic panic by threatening to split the party increased the need for unity and raised anew the problem of banking. It was only natural that Van Buren should respond by shaping a compromise banking policy designed to hold the party together. Once having committed his administration to the independent treasury in the spotlight of a special session of Congress, Van Buren was trapped by the issue. From then on he felt obliged to secure passage of the bill in order to prove his administration a success; as a matter of prestige he must win at all costs. With the benefit of hindsight it can be seen that Van Buren was unwise to put such a premium on the independent treasury. He was no longer as astute as he had been.

[38] Jackson to MVB, July 13, 1840, Rantoul to Van Buren, July 10, 1840, VBP; Benton, *Thirty Years' View*, II, 167; Calhoun to James H. Hammond, July 5, 1840, Calhoun, *Correspondence*, p. 461; Washington *Globe*, July 6, 1840.

[39] *Argus*, July 7, 1840.

In his letter to the Kentucky Democrats on the day he signed the independent treasury bill, Van Buren showed that he also had a positive reason for being so persistent. He hoped the bill would demonstrate that he, like Andrew Jackson, was fighting for the common people. In describing the bill to the Kentucky Democrats, Van Buren boasted that it ended a half-century of "abuse" in which government funds had been used by banks to enable "privileged orders [to] profit at the expense of the many." He said that Jackson had defeated the Bank of the United States but had not ended the power of those who "derive[d] wealth from the use of the People's money." "In the triumph of the Independent Treasury," said Van Buren, "we witness the triumph of the popular intelligence . . . over the arts . . . of the interested few." Jackson had appealed to the common man in vetoing the recharter of the Bank of the United States in July 1832, and had gone on to a landslide victory in the election that followed. Eight years later Van Buren hoped that the independent treasury bill would win him the support of the common people and enable him to go on to a similar victory in the fall, but his hopes were ill-founded; in the campaign slavery proved to be more of an issue than the independent treasury.[40]

During the campaign of 1836 Van Buren had gained favor in the South by taking a stand against the rising tide of abolitionism in the North. He maintained his position by supporting Calhoun's resolutions defending slavery in 1838. But the emergence of political abolitionism in 1839 made Van Buren's stance more risky in 1840 than it had been in 1836. After a preliminary meeting in Warsaw, New York, in November 1839, political abolitionists held a convention in Albany on April 1, 1840, at which they nominated James G. Birney of Ohio, for President. Their organization, which soon became known as the Liberty party, won support in New England, the Old Northwest, and in the middle Atlantic states including Van Buren's own New York. Abolitionists from Madison, Wisconsin, wrote to Van Buren demanding that he express his views on human rights. Ned Croswell became so fearful of the abolitionist movement that he resisted Democratic suggestions that he use his *Albany Argus* to attack abolitionists. On the Fourth of July 1840, Benjamin Butler had to reassure Van Buren that abolitionism was not going to be discussed at a local party meeting in New York, and in Connecticut John M. Niles was worried that the state's Liberty party would nominate a separate ticket. An-

---

[40] MVB, "Letter to the Democratic Citizens Committee," July 4, 1840, Schlesinger, *Presidential Elections*, I, 733-736.

tislavery pressure began to rival the pressure that Van Buren had been subjected to all along from the defenders of the peculiar institution.[41]

Van Buren declared repeatedly that he was opposed to abolitionism, but many Southerners were not convinced. Some remembered his evasiveness over the Missouri Compromise and others worried because he would not defend slavery in the territories. Seeking help, Van Buren asked Senator Bedford Brown of North Carolina, to join in saving the state from "the fangs of the federalists and abolitionists." Van Buren's concern over the issue of slavery can be seen in the number of drafts he prepared of his letters to Southerners that summer and fall. John Van Buren reflected the same concern when he told his father that it was more important to carry "the Southern half of the Union" than to win "a few negro votes of white people" in New York.[42]

The case of naval lieutenant George Mason Hoe only added to the concern of the two Van Burens. Early in 1840, a naval court-martial in North Carolina convicted Hoe of flogging sailors on board ship. Hoe appealed on the grounds that black witnesses were used against him, but Secretary of the Navy James K. Paulding upheld the decision. When asked to review the case Van Buren backed Paulding but tried to straddle the issue of black witnesses. He first conceded that state law was ordinarily followed in such cases and admitted that the North Carolina code forbade the use of black testimony. But he also pointed out that blacks had always been allowed to act as witnesses in naval court-martials and concluded that until Congress passed a law forbidding the use of such testimony, it would be considered legitimate. By taking this position Van Buren aroused southern hostility. A broadside printed in North Carolina denounced him for supporting black witnesses, and the *Richmond Whig* called him "the advocate . . . of

[41] Louis Filler, *The Crusade against Slavery* (New York, 1960), p. 152; Gunderson, *Log-Cabin Campaign*, p. 93; John Van Buren to MVB, May 17, 1840, Convention of Friends of the Negro to MVB, June 12, June 13, 1840, H. P. Bennett to MVB, July 1, 1840, Butler to MVB, July 4, 1840, Niles to MVB, Aug. 29, 1840, VBP.

[42] W. F. Leak to MVB, Mar. 21, May 9, 1840, MVB to Leak, Mar. 27, 1840, Robert J. Steele to MVB, May 4, 1840, MVB to Steele, Aug. 6, Aug. 7, Aug. 18, 1840, MVB to Louisville Committee, April 21, 1840, MVB to Henderson Yoakum, June 29, 1840, MVB to Bedford Brown, Aug. 20, 1840, Thomas L. Smith to MVB, Sept. 11, 1840, John Van Buren to MVB, May 17, 1840, VBP; Elizabeth G. McPherson, ed., "Unpublished Letters from North Carolinians to Van Buren," *North Carolina Historical Review*, 15 (1938), 133-140; *Richmond Whig*, Oct. 7, 1840; Van Buren to W. Fithian et al., Aug. 20, 1840, *Niles' Register*, 59 (1840), 40-41; George W. Julian, *Political Recollections 1840 to 1872* (Chicago, 1883), p. 116.

Negro testimony." After the election Polk concluded that the Hoe case had hurt the party in Tennessee.[43]

In his handling of the *Amistad* case Van Buren went out of his way to win the favor of southern slaveholders. In June 1839, a group of about fifty slaves revolted and seized control of the Spanish schooner *Amistad* on its way from Havana to another port in Cuba. After killing the captain and three of the crew, the slaves tried to navigate the ship eastward to Africa, but instead sailed westward and landed on the coast of Long Island. Here, on August 26, the *Amistad* was boarded by Lieutenant Commander Thomas R. Gedney of the United States Navy, and taken into New London, Connecticut, where the slaves were accused of piracy and imprisoned to await trial in federal district court. When Spanish authorities in the United States demanded that the slaves be returned to their Spanish owners, Attorney General Felix Grundy, long a defender of slavery, ruled in favor of the owners. Secretary of State John Forsyth, a slaveholder himself, agreed, and assured the Spanish ambassador that the administration would take steps to return the slaves as soon as the district court had ruled. The administration, meanwhile, sued to obtain the persons of the slaves in order to return them to their owners. Anticipating a favorable decision, Van Buren issued an executive order on January 9, 1840, calling on the federal marshal to deliver the slaves to the United States schooner *Grampus*, which Secretary of the Navy James K. Paulding, another defender of slavery, had ordered to stand by off New Haven. The incident is memorable for the uniform position in support of slavery taken by Van Buren and his three proslavery cabinet officers.

Unfortunately for Van Buren, abolitionists led by Lewis Tappan and Theodore Sedgwick of New York, organized a committee to defend the slaves and publicize the case. When the district court and the court of appeals ruled against the administration, Grundy brought the case before the Supreme Court of the United States, where former President John Quincy Adams defended the slaves. The seventy-three-year-old Adams, who had not appeared before the Supreme Court since 1809, spoke on behalf of the blacks for four and a half hours on February 24, 1841, and then again the next day, presenting an argument that Justice Joseph Story called "extraordinary, for its power, for its bitter sarcasm." On March 9, the court decided in favor of the defense and

---

[43] MVB to Eugene Barras, Aug. 1840, Benjamin Howard to MVB, Aug. 26, 1840, VBP; *Niles' Register*, 58 (1840), 408; "Broadside," July 1840, Graham, *Papers*, II, 102; *Richmond Whig*, Oct. 7, 1840; Polk to Robert B. Reynolds, Nov. 18, 1840, James K. Polk Miscellaneous Papers, NHYS.

set the blacks free. While the *Amistad* case was being argued in the courts throughout the election year 1840 and early 1841, it was also debated in the press, where the President's proslavery position received great publicity. Van Buren won credit in the South for his stand in defense of slavery, but he incurred the wrath of abolitionists such as William Jay, who wrote indignantly that Van Buren's executive order should be "engraved on his tomb, to rot only with his memory."[44]

Van Buren's Indian policy, especially his management of the Seminole War, also won him support in the South and opposition in the North during the campaign. When Van Buren took over the presidency in 1837, most Indians had been moved west, but there were troublesome exceptions including the Cherokees in Georgia and the Seminoles in Florida. Early in his presidency Van Buren made it clear that he intended to continue Andrew Jackson's policy of moving the Indian tribes to land west of the Mississippi. In his first annual message he rationalized that the policy was "philanthropic and enlightened" because it protected the Indians from the "evil practices" that surrounded them in the East, then added honestly that he could not abandon the policy without "sacrificing important [white] interests." Under the leadership of Major General Winfield Scott in 1838, the army rounded up thousands of Cherokees so hastily that they were forced to leave their animals and other belongings behind. Driven relentlessly by Scott's soldiers, several thousand Cherokees died from disease, exposure and murder as they walked along the "Trail of Tears" on the way to present-day Oklahoma. The removal policy was carried out so vigorously that Van Buren was able to boast in December that almost all Indian titles had been extinguished. He added hypocritically that the government's dealings with the Indians had been "just and friendly . . . directed by the best feelings of humanity."[45]

[44] Hermann E. von Holst, *The Constitutional and Political History of the United States, 1828-1846* (Chicago, 1888), pp. 321-329; Filler, *Crusade against Slavery*, pp. 167-169; Forsyth to Van Buren, Sept. 23, 1839, Woodbury to Van Buren, Sept. 22, 1839, H. G. Ludlow to MVB, Nov. 28, 1839, MVB, "Order to the United States Marshal . . . to Deliver the *Amistad* Negroes to the United States Schooner *Grampus*," Jan. 9, 1840, Lewis Tappan to Benjamin Tappan, April 24, 1840, Ralph Ingersoll to MVB, Feb. 15, 1840, VBP; Benjamin Tappan, Journal, Jan. 26, April 25, 1840, Benjamin Tappan Papers, LC; William Jay, *A View of the Action of the Federal Government in Behalf of Slavery* (New York, 1839).

[45] Van Buren's policy was designed to "induce" Indians to "labor and acquire property," and thus to cultivate the Puritan ethic. Richardson, *Messages and Papers*, III, 391-392, 497-502; Grant Foreman, *Indian Removal: the Emigration of the Five Civilized Tribes of Indians*, rev. ed. (Norman, 1953), pp. 279-312; Ronald N. Satz, *American Indian Policy in the Jacksonian Era* (Lincoln, 1975), p. 101.

Van Buren could not afford to boast about the Seminoles, who in December 1838, had not been forced out of Florida. The Seminole Indians derived their name from the word "Simanoli," meaning "renegade," or "runaway," because in the eighteenth century they had seceded from the Creek confederacy and occupied the major part of Florida, including the swamp areas near Lake Okeechobee. When they attacked settlements in Georgia and Alabama in 1817 and 1818, Andrew Jackson invaded their territory and defeated them in the first Seminole War. Despite Jackson's victories, the Seminoles became an increasing source of annoyance to plantation owners in Georgia and northern Florida whose runaway slaves often found refuge with the Seminoles. As part of Jackson's Indian removal policy, treaties were made with Seminole chiefs in 1832 and 1833, according to which the Seminoles agreed to migrate to land west of the Mississippi within three years. But Seminole resistance stiffened in April 1835, when Osceola and other chieftains refused to acknowledge the removal treaties, and when Osceola followed resistance by murdering Indian agent Wiley Thompson in Florida in December, the second Seminole War began. During the next year and a half the war became more and more unpopular in the North as the Seminoles waged an effective guerrilla campaign, hiding their women and children in the swamps while catching the United States forces off guard with sudden hit-and-run tactics.[46]

Osceola and the Seminoles were so successful that heavy criticism of the war greeted Van Buren when he took office, criticism that was not quieted in October 1837, when Osceola was lured into a trap by a flag of truce and imprisoned. Van Buren responded by ordering Colonel Zachary Taylor to take command in Florida and step up the war. Taylor won a pyrrhic victory by leading 1,100 men deep into the Everglades and defeating the Seminoles on Christmas Day, in the battle of Lake Okeechobee. After that the conflict settled down into an inconclusive war of attrition as Taylor contented himself with arming the white settlers and avoiding pitched battles. Van Buren had to admit in his message in December 1838, that the Seminoles "constitute[d] at present the only exception to the successful efforts of the Government to remove the Indians to the homes assigned them west of the Mississippi." Casting rationalization but not hypocrisy aside, Van Buren declared angrily, "[The] treacherous conduct of these people; the savage and unprovoked murders they have lately committed,

[46] Foreman, *Indian Removal*, pp. 315-331; von Holst, *Constitutional and Political History 1828-1846*, pp. 295-298.

butchering whole families [gives] the Government no alternative but to continue the military operations against them until they are totally expelled from Florida."

By the spring of 1840, as Van Buren struggled for the independent treasury and prepared for the presidential campaign, the Seminole War had become a heavy burden. In February 1840, Secretary of War Poinsett had to respond to charges that Taylor's army was violating humanitarian standards of conduct by using thirty-three bloodhounds imported from Cuba against the Seminoles. Poinsett presented to the Congress correspondence between himself and Taylor that demonstrated that the dogs were muzzled, leashed, and used only to track down the Indians, not to bite them. Poinsett added that the "cold-blooded and inhuman murders lately perpetrated upon helpless women and children by these ruthless savages" justified the use of "every possible means." Two months later a discouraged Taylor left Florida with victory no closer than it had been when he first arrived. In the House of Representatives Democrats and Whigs bickered over proposals to increase the amount of money and the number of soldiers to be used against the Seminoles. While friends of the administration asked for more money and troops to protect southern plantation owners and to defend the "suffering people of Florida," opponents contended that such increases were designed merely to "increase the power and patronage of the Government." Faced by an unending war that appeared impossible to win, a war that put his administration clearly on the side of the plantation South, a war that had already cost over $30,000,000 and the lives of over a thousand of his fellow citizens, Van Buren was in trouble and could expect to face a good deal of hostility during the campaign.[47]

Joel Poinsett did not make Van Buren's position any easier by drawing up a plan to strengthen the American fighting force. It required all Americans between the ages of twenty and forty-five to serve in their state militia, and was in some ways reminiscent of Van Buren's classification bill of 1814. Whigs promptly attacked Poinsett's plan, insisting incorrectly that it would establish a standing army of 200,000 soldiers. Henry Clay warned that there would be a *"frightful union of purse and sword"* if the President controlled both a swollen treasury and an enlarged army. In the House of Representatives on June 27, 1840, Congressman William B. Campbell of Tennessee, who had once

[47] Foreman, *Indian Removal*, pp. 332-374; Satz, *American Indian Policy*, pp. 101-104; Richardson, *Messages and Papers*, III, 497-502; von Holst, *Constitutional and Political History 1828-1846*, pp. 298-310; *Congressional Globe*, 26th Congress, 1st session (1839-1840), 163, 203-205, 358, 431, 489.

served in Florida, denounced the plan as "more odious than the alien and sedition law of the elder Adams." Democrats protested lamely that Van Buren knew nothing about the proposed bill, but the evasion was unsuccessful. Though never implemented, the bill damaged Van Buren's claims that he was an economy-minded Jeffersonian.[48]

With the depression worsening on all sides, Van Buren was urged in 1840 to side with Loco Focos, workingmen and union leaders in backing the working class. Editor John L. O'Sullivan warned Levi Woodbury in March 1840 that the depression had become the major concern of the American people. When Democrats were beaten in Connecticut in April, John M. Niles agreed with O'Sullivan that unemployment was the issue of the day. Although hard times are never conducive to labor reform, advocates of the ten-hour day had also been bringing pressure to bear on the President. Some mechanics, including outdoor workers, had won the ten-hour day in a few states during the 1830s, but in New England textile operatives worked from twelve to fourteen hours a day. Before Van Buren took office, the ten-hour day had been established for federal workers in the Philadelphia navy yard, and Van Buren went further by setting the same limit for the New York navy yard. Elsewhere, however, workers on federal jobs reported at sunrise and left at sunset. Van Buren thus had the opportunity during the campaign to appeal broadly to urban workers by providing federal relief and by establishing the ten-hour day.

But the Jeffersonian President who had told the special session of Congress in 1837 that "all communities are apt to look to government for too much," was not likely to turn to radical measures in 1840. Van Buren proposed no measures for public relief, no measures to employ hungry workers. He did, however, take steps to reduce the hours of labor, steps that some historians have construed as evidence that Van Buren was a labor reformer. On March 31, 1840, Van Buren issued an executive order establishing a ten-hour day for laborers on all federal public works—not simply navy yards—with no reduction

[48] Thomas Ritchie to MVB, June 1, 1840, Poinsett to Ritchie, May 29–June 5, 1840, Rice Garland and others, *"Plan of the Standing Army of 200,000 Men,"* 1839-1840, G. C. Hurt to MVB, July 25, 1840, MVB to Garland and John C. Clark, Aug. 15, 1840, VBP; *Argus,* June 6, June 23, 1840; *Richmond Whig,* Sept. 8, 1840; Alfred Balch to Poinsett, May 4, 1840, Azariah Flagg to Poinsett, May 10, 1840, C. W. Hunton to MVB, June 13, 1840, W. W. Wallace to MVB, June 13, 1840, J. W. Stevenson to Poinsett, June 24, 1840, Joel R. Poinsett Papers, in the Henry D. Gilpin Papers, HSP; Anthony B. Norton, *The Great Revolution of 1840, Reminiscences of a Log Cabin and Hard Cider Campaign* (Mount Vernon, 1888), pp. 187-198; James Graham to William A. Graham, April 8, 1840, Graham, *Papers,* II, 83-84; *Congressional Globe,* 26th Congress, 1st session (1838-1840), 489.

in pay. Michael Shiner, a free black who worked in the Washington navy yard, wrote in his diary that "the Working Class of people . . . ought to never forget" Van Buren for the order; and Arthur M. Schlesinger, Jr. commented later that Van Buren "might have had a worse epitaph." But the ten-hour order was far from a landmark. Nine years later the Washington city council still found it necessary to pass a resolution asking the President to extend the ten-hour day to all government workers in the city. And Van Buren did not claim that he was trying to help the working class when he issued the order. Instead he wrote that he was issuing the order only as a means of ending the "inconvenience and dissatisfaction" that stemmed from having "different rules" for work at "different places." Van Buren, who was to brag about separating the government and the banks, refused to take credit for government intervention in setting working standards. The work order was a constructive step, but not enough to prove that he set a high priority on labor reform. Nor was it enough to win Van Buren many votes in the election.[49]

BUT Van Buren's failure to win votes by adopting new or popular policies was not decisive because in the election of 1840, techniques, symbols, personalities and—above all—the depression were what counted. After one hundred and forty years the election of 1840 is still familiar to Americans because of the slogans, the parades, the images, the nicknames, and the drama associated with it. "Little Van," "Tippecanoe and Tyler too," torchlights burning in the night, log cabins and cider jugs all left their mark. Three historical trends converged that year: the modernization of America with its national press and its revolutionized transportation; the severe economic depression that dominated the thinking of most Americans; and finally, the emergence of a new political party—the Whigs—and new political leaders—Thurlow Weed, Horace Greeley, William Henry Seward, and Thaddeus Stevens—who were able to use the new means of communication and take advantage of the depression to shape a new type of campaign.

The symbol of the log cabin emerged soon after the Whigs nominated William Henry Harrison. Harrison, an old man in his sixty-

[49] O'Sullivan to Levi Woodbury, Mar. 4, 1840, Niles to MVB, April 8, 1840, James K. Paulding, "Statement of Working Hours at the Different Navy Yards," Mar. 27, 1840, VBP; Ware, *Industrial Worker*, pp. 125-126; Richardson, *Messages and Papers*, III, 602; Michael Shiner, MS diary, p. 71, LC, quoted in Schlesinger, *Age of Jackson*, p. 266. See also Wilhelmus Bryan, *History of the National Capital* (New York, 1916), II, 231; MVB to Isaac Lippincott and others, Sept. 14, 1840, *Niles' Register*, 59 (1840), 59.

seventh year, had suffered financial reverses and in 1839 was barely eking out a living on a farm. Democrats were quick to ridicule him as "Old Granny" Harrison, who wanted nothing more than to spend the rest of his days in a log cabin with a barrel of cider. But the gibes soon backfired as Whig newspapers reminded their readers of Harrison's exploits at the battle of Tippecanoe, pointing out that he had been defending hardy pioneers who lived in log cabins. On January 20, two imaginative Whigs in Harrisburg, Pennsylvania, produced an enormous transparency of a log cabin with a cider barrel by the door and displayed the picture on the wall at a ratification meeting. The response was so rewarding that from that moment the log cabin became Harrison's identifying symbol.

Conscious that they had a winning formula, Whig party managers avoided the issues, published no party platform, and built their campaign instead around the log cabin. Before long log-cabin headquarters, log-cabin cider and log-cabin song books became standard fare. Tied to the symbol of the log cabin were nicknames such as "Old Tip," slogans such as "Tippecanoe and Tyler too," and songs promising that the "Log Cabin Candidate" would "march on Washington." In May Horace Greeley came out with the first issue of the *Log Cabin*, which soon became the leading Whig newspaper in the land, circulating 80,000 copies a week. The Whig campaign began officially on Washington's birthday with a gigantic rally at Columbus, Ohio, replete with log cabins, barrels of cider and cannon salutes. A series of great displays followed—at Tippecanoe, Nashville, Boston, and Cincinnati. Thanks to the new railroads and the new roads Whig speakers were able to move rapidly from one rally to another and large crowds of listeners were able to travel to hear them. John Quincy Adams, who disapproved of the new campaign style, complained about the "fearful extent [of this] itinerant speech-making." Alarmed by the "hostile collision between the parties," Adams wondered when this "revolution in the habits and manners of the people" would ever end.[50]

Part of the Whig technique was a brutal frontal attack on "Van, Van . . . a used up man." One Whig pamphet called Van Buren a "cunning magician," who bested his opponents through "intrigue"; in another he was described as a "cool, calculating, intriguing politician," who used his "low creeping arts" to get ahead. Since the accusations never ceased, the Democrats were on the defensive as they had been in 1836. One group of Democrats in Pennsylvania tried to

[50] Gunderson, *Log-Cabin Campaign*, pp. 74-77, 115-122; Chambers, "Election of 1840," p. 676; Adams, *Memoirs*, X, 351-353.

turn the table; "instead of pursuing that sly, scheming, intriguing . . . policy which we anticipated," they declared, Van Buren had shown "a bold and statesmanlike disposition to meet responsibility."[51]

The Whigs also put Van Buren on the defensive by pointing to inconsistencies in his record. They reminded voters that the same Van Buren who was attacking the Bank of the United States had once signed a petition calling for a branch of the Bank at Albany. They cited his votes for and against slavery, internal improvements, and the protective tariff. Van Buren's dedication to republicanism and state rights was also challenged. To refute the charge that he had actually been responsible for Jackson's proclamation against South Carolina, Van Buren had to prove that he was not in Washington during the nullification crisis. A report came in from Bloomfield, Illinois, saying that "the Prairies [were] all on fire" as the Whigs tried to show that Van Buren was a "rank Federalist," who had been opposed to the War of 1812. Hostile publications such as *The Claims of Martin Van Buren to the Presidency* dogged the Magician throughout the campaign.[52]

With Harrison established in the public mind as a rugged frontiersman living in rural simplicity in a log cabin, it was easy to portray Van Buren as an effete Easterner, living in urban elegance in a mansion. While Harrision drank hard cider from an earthenware mug, Van Buren supposedly drank French wine from a silver goblet. The lurid attacks of Charles Ogle accusing the President of living in "regal splendor" appeared in April 1840, just at the right time to influence the campaign. Even though the charges were unfair, they struck a responsive nerve in a public suffering from a severe economic depression, and made it difficult for Van Buren to maintain that he was following a policy of republican simplicity.[53]

Stable and calm as always, Van Buren responded without rancor to the barrage of attacks. Although he did not travel about the country, he kept in touch with the campaign as he always had by receiving and sending letters. All through the summer and fall reports came in from

---

[51] *A Brief Account of the Life and Political Opinions of Martin Van Buren* (n.p. 1840), pp. 6-21; Hildreth, *The Contrast*, pp. 30, 58, 63; Jonathan Stevens et al., "Address of Citizens of Bradford County Formerly Opposed to Martin Van Buren, Showing Why They Now Prefer Him to Gen. Harrison," Towanda, Pa., 1840; MVB to Governor Thomas Reynolds, Missouri, Mar. 6, 1841, *Niles' Register*, 60 (1841), 52.

[52] *The Claims of Martin Van Buren to the Presidency*, pp. 3-12; *Richmond Whig*, Sept. 1, 1840; Seaborn Jones to MVB, July 13, 1840, MVB to Seaborn Jones, July or Aug. 1840, Elisha Houtt to MVB, May 11, 1840, VBP.

[53] Ogle, *Speech by Mr. Ogle on the President's Palace.*

Democrats such as Mahlon Dickerson in New Jersey, James Buchanan in Pennsylvania, and Peter V. Daniel in Virginia, and replies went back with suggestions for local campaigns. There were also formal letters to political groups in different parts of the country explaining Van Buren's position on the issues. Observers differed in evaluating Van Buren during the campaign. John Quincy Adams, who did not believe that candidates should campaign for themselves, did not approve of Van Buren's efforts, especially his "controversial electioneering letters." On the other hand, Democrat Gideon Welles thought that Van Buren won the support of "reflecting men, acting from sober conviction of principle," even though he could not command "enthusiastic personal attachment." The European dancer Fanny Elssler, who caused a great commotion in America in 1840, was favorably impressed. After meeting the President, she remarked that his demeanor was "very easy, very frank, and very royal." He was, she thought, as distinguished as Prince Metternich of Austria.[54]

In New York the Democrats were on the lookout for a gubernatorial candidate because Whig governor Seward seemed vulnerable. Seward had alienated native Protestants by proposing to educate foreign-born Catholic children at public expense in their native language. When the *Oneida Democrat* suggested Senator Silas Wright for governor, he was alarmed. He dreaded the campaigning and entertaining that went with the governor's job, and thought that he could be more valuable in Washington. Nonetheless, John Van Buren told his father that most Democrats, especially those in Tammany Hall, were for the senator. But Wright could not be persuaded and the nomination went to William C. Bouck, an uneducated farmer from Schoharie County, who had served on the canal commission.[55]

Whigs in New York used the same tactics that were working in the other states. Daniel Webster was active in the city, and elsewhere. Horace Greeley's *Log Cabin*, which was set up to counter the Democratic *Rough Hewer*, soon far outstripped its rival in circulation. The *Log Cabin* and other Whig newspapers satirized the opposition, calling attention to William L. Marcy's sloppy dress, to Wright's heavy drink-

[54] Mahlon Dickerson to MVB, Sept. 11, 1840, Ten Eyck to MVB, Sept. 16, 1840, Andrew Jackson to MVB, Sept. 22, 1840, Peter V. Daniel to MVB, Sept. 28, 1840, James Buchanan to MVB, Sept. 25, 1840, VBP; Adams, *Memoirs*, X, 356-357; Gideon Welles, "Political History," Welles Papers, LC; Ivor Guest, *Fanny Elssler* (Middletown, 1970), pp. 128-137; Schlesinger, *Age of Jackson*, p. 48.

[55] John Van Buren to MVB, April 11, June 30, 1840, VBP; Wright to Flagg, Feb. 21, Mar. 10, 1840, Flagg Papers; Garraty, *Wright*, pp. 186-188; Alexander, *Political History*, II, 42-43; Hammond, *Political Parties*, II, 519-520.

ing, to Van Buren's lavish spending, and to the Regency's spoils system. On June 16, Whigs even went so far as to dedicate a log cabin on Broadway in New York City.[56]

Van Buren's Regency friends, like their leader, showed that they were still tied to the past by not taking the Whigs' new style of campaigning seriously. Ned Croswell, for example, made fun of the cabin that Whigs erected in Albany, and Marcy claimed that "the Whigs themselves [were] ashamed" of the "silly" log cabin in Buffalo. But members of the Regency fought hard to return Van Buren to office. On the Fourth of July, John A. Dix told his listeners that the election was as important as that of 1800, and Benjamin Butler put so much effort into the campaign that the Whigs accused him of deceitful plotting. Despite his own fears that he would be a failure, Wright proved particularly effective at answering Webster. Azariah Flagg reported in September that Wright "succeed[ed] admirably as a field preacher."[57]

But most of the reports coming in to Van Buren were less cheerful. By early October news of Whig victories in state elections in Maine, Ohio, Indiana, and Maryland alerted the President to what lay ahead. Jabez Hammond warned that "the power of money" might spell defeat because every bank in New York was against the Democrats. When Wright completed his campaign, the best he could offer was a cautious letter making no prediction. Long before the people voted for President the realistic Van Buren had given up all hope of victory and for one of the few times in his career was obviously discouraged.[58]

The results, which came in during the first three weeks in November, justified Van Buren's concern. After winning by some 26,000 popular votes and 46 electoral votes in 1836, Van Buren lost the presidency by about 150,000 popular votes and 174 electoral votes in 1840, and he carried only seven states. Van Buren could not even win in New York State, where Harrison was victorious by 13,000 votes and where Seward was reelected by 5,000 votes.

The election had great significance for the Whig party and for the new American political system. For the only time in the history of

[56] J. Hunter to MVB, Aug. 20, 1840, VBP; Garraty, *Wright*, pp. 192-197; Hone, *Diary*, p. 486; Fuess, *Daniel Webster*, II, 86-87; Hammond, *Political Parties*, II, 527.

[57] Marcy to G. W. Newell, April 10, 1840, Marcy Papers, LC; *Argus*, Aug. 4, 1840; Marcy to MVB, May 9, 1840, Wright to MVB, Aug. 20, 1840, Flagg to MVB, Sept. 24, 1840, Butler to MVB, Oct. 23, 1840, VBP; Garraty, *Wright*, pp. 196-202.

[58] Wright to MVB, Oct. 29, 1840, Hammond to MVB, Sept. 21, 1840, Benjamin Howard to MVB, Oct. 11, 1840, John D. Phelan to MVB, Oct. 13, 1840, VBP; Bacourt, *Souvenirs of a Diplomat*, p. 150; MVB to Gideon Welles, May 17, 1843, Welles Papers, LC; MVB to James Buchanan, Nov. 24, 1840, James Buchanan Papers, HSP; Hammond, *Political Parties*, II, 528; Weed, *Autobiography*, pp. 491, 494.

their party the Whigs were able to gain control of both Houses of Congress. They made the campaign so dramatic and exciting that they drew vast crowds of voters to the polls. The number of popular votes, which had inched up from 1.2 million in 1828 to 1.5 million in 1836, suddenly shot up to 2.4 million in 1840, and never fell back again. The percentage of adult white males voting, which had stabilized between fifty-five percent and fifty-eight percent in the three previous elections, rose to eighty percent in 1840. Despite the Whig sweep, the Democrats did well enough to show that the close margin between victory and defeat, so evident in 1836, had not disappeared. In carrying Alabama, Arkansas, South Carolina, Virginia, Missouri, Illinois, and New Hampshire, Van Buren showed strength in all sections of the United States. Although beaten he won almost 400,000 more popular votes than any previous Presidential candidate, and the winning margin was exceptionally close in every state but three.[59]

Although Democrats tried to blame the defeat on fraud, hallucination, excessive democracy, and the Mormon Church, none of these was responsible. There were more fundamental reasons for the defeat. It would have been a miracle if the Democrats had been able to survive the depression that had gripped the nation ever since Van Buren took office. Even though the Liberty party polled barely 7,000 votes, Van Buren's proslavery policies had alienated Northerners and contributed to the loss of six states that Van Buren had carried in 1836. The party, furthermore, had been in office long enough to develop factions. The Loco Foco movement, the conservative banking revolt, and the struggle over the vice presidency contributed to losses in New York, Pennsylvania, North Carolina, Georgia, and Tennessee. A decade of Democratic successes had goaded the opposition into unity and a hard-hitting campaign that brought out the votes. James K. Polk lamented that the Whigs were organized and his own party was not. The time was right for the Whigs.[60]

Van Buren himself bore much of the responsibility. In the election he was defeated by a political system and by political techniques that he more than anyone else had developed. Whig managers such as

---

[59] The statistics for the election are conveniently tabulated and analyzed in William N. Chambers, "Election of 1840," pp. 643-690. See also Hammond, *Political Parties*, II, 528.

[60] For some of the excuses, see Blair to MVB, Aug. 8, 1840, P. Kaufmann to MVB, Nov. 15, 1840, Thomas L. Hamer to MVB, Nov. 18, 1840, George McWhorter to MVB, Nov. 20, 1840, Abijah Mann to MVB, Dec. 28, 1840, VBP. See also MVB to James Buchanan, Nov. 28, 1840, James Buchanan Papers, HSP; Polk to Robert B. Reynolds, Nov. 18, 1840, James K. Polk Papers, NYHS.

Weed and Stevens used methods that Van Buren and the Regency had perfected in New York. In addition Van Buren lost because he ran a weak campaign. In 1836, he had won partly by adjusting to change better than his opponents had, but in 1840, the Whigs not the Democrats took advantage of what was new. With a national two-party system and nationwide means of communication, a national campaign with a national message was needed. With their log cabins, Tippecanoe slogans, and parades, the Whigs found the message that could produce votes. In Philip Hone's words, "the hurrah [was] heard and felt in every part of the United States." The Whigs allowed the common man to participate in their campaign, whereas the Democrats, who had based their previous campaigns on the common man, discouraged participation. Harrison, not Van Buren, broke with tradition and went out on the campaign trail for himself. Harrison, not Van Buren, replaced Andrew Jackson as the popular hero in the eyes of the people. Even though Van Buren had created a national political party, he did not run a national campaign in 1840, but devoted most of his attention to New York as he had done in 1828, but not in 1824. Instead of adjusting his republicanism as he had in the past, he remained in 1840 chained to the Jeffersonian tradition.[61]

Van Buren's personality played a part in his downfall. As Jabez Hammond observed, Van Buren lacked "those fascinating traits" and the "halo of military glory" that had made Jackson a successful President. The lack of charisma had not been a liability in state politics, but in a national election, popular appeal meant much. Hammond wrote that "the people of this country [were] fond of novelties," and Van Buren's bland personality gave them nothing to make them forget the depression. In addition, Hammond believed that Van Buren had lost his two genuinely exciting qualities—his "adroitness and skill"—during his years in the White House. This change had become apparent in the way Van Buren had run his presidency, especially in his preoccupation with the independent treasury and his failure to use patronage effectively. The skills and talents that opened the door to the White House did not last long enough to keep him there.[62]

[61] James C. Curtis points to the irony of Van Buren's situation. Throughout the Jackson years Van Buren carefully protected the state organizations that formed the Democratic party. Once he was in the White House, these very organizations revolted against him. In 1840, the nation focused its attention on national politics. Harrison, but not Van Buren, was able to respond to this interest. Curtis, *Fox at Bay*, p. 206; Hone, *Diary*, p. 472.

[62] Hammond, *Political Parties*, II, 529-531. For another opinion that Van Buren lost his "vitality" while President, see Samuel P. Orth, *Five American Politicians; a Study in the Evolution of American Politics* (Cleveland, 1906), p. 157.

Van Buren's self-control and his ability to rationalize enabled him to take the defeat with grace. Instead of admitting that he was at least partly responsible for the disaster, he blamed it on Whig fraud and a temporary popular delusion. From that moment until his death twenty-two years later he insisted that the outcome had been due to a "mistake in the public mind." He wrote that he had no regrets, and had much to look forward to—a "house to furnish, farm to stock, etc., etc." "Will you believe," he told Butler, "that I begin to hanker after the Hour of Separation between myself and my official honours." The defeat did not seem to change the social Van Buren. Still fascinated by men with the ability to lead, he kept one of the Tappans up until midnight one evening telling him stories about DeWitt Clinton. Still attracted to charming women, the President invited "some of the most beautiful" women in Washington to his holiday parties and "paid unusual attention" to Robert Walker's wife Mary, the belle of the city that winter. As good a family man as ever, he planned his parties around his son and daughter-in-law, Abraham and Angelica. When Harrison arrived in February, Van Buren showed his usual grace, receiving the general "with great politeness," and breaking with tradition the next day by returning his call. Philip Hone found the President so "calm and unruffled" that it was hard to tell that he had been defeated. Van Buren was far more distressed than he showed, but throughout his career he had learned to mask his emotions in order to succeed. He could behave no differently when he failed.[63]

Before leaving office Van Buren implemented two last-minute partisan decisions. The appointment of his friend Jesse Hoyt to the New York customs office in 1838 backfired when Hoyt was accused of overdrawing his account by some $30,000. Although Hoyt claimed that he had acted within the law and later won in court, his indiscretion placed his administration in a delicate position. The situation was particularly embarrassing for United States Attorney Benjamin Butler, who had urged Hoyt's appointment and was now responsible for prosecuting him. Silas Wright criticized Butler for recommending a man "immersed in stock gambling debts," and—much worse—one who put "his party, his friends, and his country . . . second to his passion for accumulation." The unhappy Wright had to suffer the

[63] Van Buren to James Buchanan, Nov. 24, 1840, James Buchanan Papers, HSP; MVB, *Political Parties*, p. 349; MVB to Jackson, Dec. 1840, James K. Polk Papers, transcripts by George Bancroft, NYPL; MVB to Butler, Dec. 21, 1840, copy of a letter held by Harriet A. Butler, VBP; Benjamin Tappan, Journal, Jan. 9, 1841, Benjamin Tappan Papers, LC; Gustave Koerner, *Memoirs of Gustave Koerner 1809-1896: Life-Sketches Written at the Suggestion of His Children* (Cedar Rapids, 1909), I, 453-454; Hone, *Diary*, pp. 520-523, 528.

taunts of Whigs who renewed the old charges of political dishonesty. Van Buren said that he still considered Hoyt a friend, but four days before leaving the White House removed him from the customs office. It was a final irony of the ill-fated administration that three of its most honest members, Van Buren, Butler, and Wright, should be linked at the end with the dishonest party hack Jesse Hoyt.[64]

Van Buren also drew fire for his hasty nomination of Peter V. Daniel of Virginia, to the Supreme Court. Justice Philip P. Barbour, also of Virginia, having died suddenly on February 25, Van Buren moved promptly to appoint a Democrat before Harrison took office. When the President sent Daniel's name to the Senate on February 27, the *Richmond Whig* accused the administration of "indecent haste," but Van Buren boasted that he had just appointed a man who would "stick to the principles of the constitution," a man who was in no "danger of falling off in the true spirit." He had replaced one Old Republican with another. He had now appointed three Southerners to the Supreme Court, two of whom would still be on the Court at the time of the Dred Scott decision in 1857.[65]

As President Van Buren was more experienced in politics than most—in a class with Buchanan and Nixon—since he came to the White House after a long career in state and national politics. Capable of adjusting to change, he had shown himself more in tune with his times than his opponents were in 1836. Van Buren analyzed the problems of the nation perceptively in his special session message; he showed himself to be a skillful politician, ranking with Polk and Truman, and he used political allies such as Wright, Benton and Calhoun to secure the independent treasury. A national unifier, he kept the nation at peace and avoided sectional confrontation over slavery and expansion. These were not mean achievements.

But Van Buren was neither a successful nor a great President, for he failed to grow in the White House and if anything showed signs of losing some of his native strength and ability. In a long career the Magician had succeeded up until 1837 largely because he was a shrewd,

[64] MVB to Butler, Oct. 29, 1839, copy of a letter held by Harriet A. Butler, Butler to MVB, Jan. 30, 1841, Butler to Henry D. Gilpin, Feb. 16, Feb. 17, 1841, VBP; Wright to Butler, Feb. 27, Feb. 28, Mar. 7, 1841, Silas Wright, Letters to Benjamin Butler, NYPL.

[65] *Richmond Whig*, Mar. 5, 1841; Henry A. Wise to MVB, Feb. 26, 1841, Miscellaneous Papers, UVL; John Brockenbrough to MVB, Feb. 27, 1841, Robert Ridley et al. to MVB, Feb. 27, 1841, MVB to Andrew Jackson, Mar. 12, 1841, VBP. Van Buren also appointed John Catron of Tennessee, and John McKinley of Alabama, both in 1837.

even ruthless, and above all adaptable politician. During the years in the White House some of the shrewdness and adaptability slipped away. The man who had built the Regency and the Democratic party failed to use patronage effectively as President. The man who had been quick to change his political tactics in the past could not abandon his reliance on fading, outdated state organizations such as the Regency and the Richmond Junto. The new-style politician who had always put party success ahead of ideology depended too much on one issue— the independent treasury—to hold his party together. As a result, in spite of isolated successes, the once great state politician was ineffective politically as President.

Furthermore, Van Buren and his party failed to adapt to the vast economic and social changes that were making the United States a new land. The man who had taken advantage of economic change in New York was unable to adjust to the new economy or to the Panic of 1837. At the head of a rapidly growing nation in the midst of a depression that needed more credit and more banks, Van Buren allowed himself to be maneuvered into committing himself and his party to hard-money policies that would restrict credit and discourage banks. The nation was expanding and looking forward, but Van Buren followed policies that restrained America in her money marts and on her frontiers, policies that looked backward to the Jacksonian and even Jeffersonian past. Financial restraint was needed in 1835 and 1836, but not in 1839 and 1840. Restraint on the frontiers may have been a wise policy that improved our relations with other nations, but it was not a policy that most Americans favored. And Jacksonian Democracy with its appeal to planters and plain Republicans was no longer appropriate or appealing to a nation of small capitalists and democrats. Where the nation was beginning to question the morality of slavery, Van Buren continued to back the slaveowners of the South. Brought up much like Lincoln with the same prejudices about white and black, Van Buren was not able to change as Lincoln did, at least not by 1840. The immediate economic problem during Van Buren's White House years was the Panic of 1837, and Van Buren as a matter of policy turned his back. He stuck with Jacksonian Democracy and lost.

And there was a matter of his personality. In the new democratic political system that Van Buren had created, Presidents and presidential candidates had to appeal to the nation by taking advantage of the new system of communications. As a result military heroes, popular figures, or candidates with charisma were needed to put over programs and win elections. Andrew Jackson, William Henry Harrison, Zachary

Taylor, and Abraham Lincoln succeeded, but not Van Buren, who lacked the necessary appeal. Instead of trying so hard to live down his reputation as a spoilsman, Van Buren could have accepted and exploited his old image. But he did not. It was only as the "Magician" that Van Buren had the appeal needed to win. By 1840 the magic was gone.[66]

[66] Hammond, *Political Parties*, II, 530; Thomas C. Thornton to MVB, Mar. 2, 1841, VBP; Orth, *Five American Politicians*, p. 157.

· V ·

COUNTRY GENTLEMAN
1841-1862

5. Lindenwald, after a rendering by Richard Upjohn

· 13 ·

NEW PRINCIPLES

"In the midst of a storm of wind and rain," Van Buren landed at the Battery and was greeted by a "tumultuous" crowd on March 23, 1841. Armed firemen and a corps of lancers headed a procession that escorted him up Broadway to Tammany Hall. New York Whig George Templeton Strong wrote sourly that he had never seen "a more rowdy, draggletailed, jailbird-resembling gang of truculent loafers," but Van Buren called it "the happiest day [in his] whole political life."[1]

In early May, after several weeks of receptions, rallies, and theatergoing, Van Buren took the steamboat up the Hudson to Stuyvesant Landing and Kinderhook. There he was warmly greeted before journeying two miles south to his country estate. Lindenwald stood amid elms, pines and fruit trees, looking out over broad meadows that led down to a creek winding its course to the Hudson five miles away. The view across the fields to the Catskills was so lovely that Henry D. Gilpin urged Van Buren not to block it with fences. Here in 1797, Peter Van Ness had built a brick farmhouse about four hundred feet back from the post road from Troy to New York. Washington Irving had once lived there after the death of his fiancée, while he completed *Knickerbocker's History*. Van Buren, who had dubious artistic taste, destroyed much of the estate's eighteenth-century character with elaborate renovations during the next ten years. When they were completed, he had transformed the house into a Venetian villa with a four-story loggia tower, a wide piazza, and an enormous main hall with ceilings twelve feet high and walls covered with cheerful Dutch wallpaper. Seven windows wide, four windows deep and three stories high, it was an imposing but garish building.[2]

---

[1] MVB to Gansevoort Melville and others, June 3, 1844, MVB to Andrew Jackson, Mar. 30, 1841, VBP; Hone, *Diary*, p. 533; Strong, *Diary*, I, 158.

[2] James K. Paulding to Andrew Jackson, Oct. 4, 1843, Paulding, *Letters*, p. 352; *Niles' Register*, 60 (1841), 179; MVB to Jackson, Mar. 30, 1841, Gilpin to MVB, April 21, 1843, VBP; William Cullen Bryant, "Journal," Sept. 18, 1841, Parke Godwin, *A Biography of William Cullen Bryant with Extracts from His Private Correspondence* (1883; reprint, New York, 1967), I, 389-390; Edward T. Booth, *Country Life in America as Lived by Ten Presidents of the United States* (New York, 1947), p. 140; Collier, *Kinderhook*, pp. 376-377; Gideon Welles, "Diary," Oct. 19, 1843, Welles Papers, LC; MVB to Levi Woodbury, July 24, 1841, Woodbury Papers, LC; MVB to Jackson, Mar. 15, 1841, Jackson, *Correspondence*, VI, 112; Alexander, *Political History*, II, 45-46.

On the two hundred acres surrounding Lindenwald, Van Buren developed a successful farm with a hired man to work the land. Not expecting much from a novice farmer, the neighbors agreed to sell him fruit and vegetables the first year, but a year later they were amazed to learn that he had his own surplus of hay, oats and potatoes. To increase his crops he reclaimed several acres of land from a bog; to provide fish he made a pond by damming up several brooks, and to make certain that he had fruit in season he cultivated orchards of pear, peach, plum, and apple. Van Buren was such a clever farmer that his crops often came earlier and his fruit and vegetables were often larger than those of his neighbors.[3]

The farmer's day began with a ride of up to fifteen miles about the estate and into town on Duroc, the horse given him by John Randolph. After a hearty breakfast—Van Buren now carried over 170 pounds on his small frame—he worked for a while in the fields before retiring to the library to read and to write letters. Van Buren owned a good many books, and spent $50-$75 a year to acquire others. In the evening he entertained so often that it seemed to Silas Wright always to be "open house." Van Buren still loved rich food and drink and his budget provided almost $400 a year for butter, wine and champagne, twice what he spent on taxes and church. Sundays, nevertheless, found him regularly in his family pew in the Dutch Reformed Church. It was a pleasant, comfortable life and with personal property and real estate worth as much as $200,000, Van Buren could well afford to live the life of a country gentleman.[4]

As a farmer Van Buren displayed "the same practical good sense," said James K. Paulding, that had "carried [the Magician] successfully through every stage of his political life." And Lindenwald brought out the Dutchman in him. After a year and a half on the farm he wrote to Harmanus Bleecker in Holland, asking him to bring back a "first rate Dutch cow." "How strange," commented Gouverneur Kemble, "that national tastes of this kind should descend from generation to

[3] MVB, Contract with Mr. Marquatte, 1841, MVB to Andrew Jackson, Sept. 8, 1843, VBP; MVB to Joel Poinsett, Oct. 1, 1842, Joel R. Poinsett Papers, in the Henry D. Gilpin Papers, HSP; MVB to Levi Woodbury, July 24, 1841, Woodbury Papers, LC; Booth, *Country Life*, pp. 141-143; MVB to James H. Hammond, Mar. 18, Mar. 20, 1843, James H. Hammond Papers, LC.

[4] Bryant, "Journal," Sept. 18, 1843, Godwin, *Life of William Cullen Bryant*, I, 389; Booth, *Country Living*, pp. 140, 146; Collier, *Kinderhook*, p. 422; Burt, "Personal Reminiscences," I, 83, 116; "Probable Expenses, May 1, 1842–Jan. 1, 1843," "Expenses, April 1, 1844–April 1, 1845," "Treatment by the assessors," 1855, Wright to MVB, Oct. 25, 1841, VBP; MVB to Bleecker, Jan. 27, 1841, Harmanus Bleecker Papers, NYSL.

generation." Friends who came to call found Van Buren as "vigorous and sprightly" as ever, full of "lively, idiomatic" talk, with an inexhaustible store of anecdotes, and protected by that "same calm philosophy which supported him in defeat." He still had a sense of humor. When Bleecker brought back a new wife from Holland, Van Buren wrote to say that he wished there had been another for him. Cheerful as ever, he vowed that he had "never spent as pleasant a summer" as his first one at Lindenwald.[5]

Van Buren was surrounded by his family. During that first summer a son was born to Abraham and Angelica, who had settled down in a cottage at nearby Stuyvesant. John also showed signs of settling down when he married a plain Dutch woman, Elizabeth Vanderpoel. Joel Poinsett remarked that John was better off with "a sensible person however homely than with the prettiest girl in the state that might aid and abet him in his extravaganzas." In typical fashion John brought his entire wedding party to Lindenwald to live at his father's expense for two weeks. A permanent resident of the farm was third son Martin, who was unmarried and chronically ill with tuberculosis. Though still in Washington, Smith kept in close touch with his father. By 1842, Smith had also married and had brought his wife to Lindenwald for a visit. Silas Wright told Van Buren that it was time his sons got married because they depended too much on the old man. But even when married, they never became completely independent of their father.[6]

[5] Paulding to Jackson, Oct. 4, 1843, Paulding, *Letters*, pp. 352-353; Gouverneur Kemble to Joel Poinsett, Nov. 28, 1841, Joel R. Poinsett Papers, in the Henry D. Gilpin Papers, HSP; MVB to Bleecker, Dec. 13, 1842, Harmanus Bleecker Papers, NYSL; MVB to Jackson, July 30, Oct. 12, 1841, VBP; Gideon Welles, "Diary," Oct. 19, 1843, Welles Papers, LC; William Cullen Bryant, "Journal," Sept. 18, 1841, Godwin, *Biography of William Cullen Bryant*, I, 390; MVB to Andrew Jackson, Mar. 15, 1841, Jackson, *Correspondence*, VI, 112; MVB to Levi Woodbury, July 24, 1841, Woodbury Papers, LC.

[6] For Abraham, see MVB to Joel Poinsett, Dec. 7, 1841, Joel R. Poinsett Papers, in the Henry D. Gilpin Papers, HSP; Jackson to MVB, Sept. 15, 1841, MVB to Jackson, July 30, 1841, MVB to Benjamin Butler, Oct. 23, 1843, copy of a letter held by Harriet A. Butler, VBP; Andrew J. Donelson to Elizabeth Donelson, Aug. 4, 1842, Andrew J. Donelson Papers, LC; MVB to Harmanus Bleecker, Dec. 13, 1842, Harmanus Bleecker Papers, NYSL. For John, see Wright to MVB, June 21, 1841, MVB to Jackson, July 30, 1841, VBP; Joel Poinsett to Henry D. Gilpin, 1840, Joel R. Poinsett Papers, in the Henry D. Gilpin Papers, HSP. For Martin, see MVB to Jackson, Mar. 12, 1841, VBP; Jackson to MVB, Mar. 31, 1841, Jackson, *Correspondence*, VI, 97. For Smith, see Smith Van Buren to MVB, Sept. 12, 1841, Wright to MVB, April 2, 1842, VBP; Gideon Welles, "Diary," Oct. 19, 1843, Welles Papers, LC. See also Wright to MVB, April 2, 1842, VBP.

Van Buren's contentment did not mean that he was done with politics. Life at Lindenwald was not a retirement but an interlude as he renewed his spirits and sharpened the edge that had been dulled in the White House. When he boasted about the size of his vegetables and the extent of his hay crop, it was a sign that the old competitive spirit was returning. The pictures of Jefferson and Jackson in the dining room showed that farmer Martin had not forgotten the past, and his elation at Democratic victories in the fall proved that he cared about the present. And letters began to arrive urging him to look to the future. Democrats writing from Maine, Pennsylvania, Ohio, and Indiana, all borrowed Van Buren's expression to tell him that the "sober second thought" of the people was beginning to turn in his direction. Thomas Hart Benton predicted that Missouri would nominate Van Buren for President, and George Bancroft assured William L. Marcy that the party would not rest until "justice [was] done to the cabbage-grower of Kinderhook." Van Buren said smugly that the "eyes of the people" were opening.[7]

With an eye toward renomination Van Buren set out on a journey to the South and West early in 1842. Accompanied by Paulding, he stopped in Philadelphia for a noisy reception, then took the steamboat from Baltimore to Charleston, South Carolina, arriving on March 1. After attending a dinner in their honor given by James H. Hammond, Van Buren and Paulding traveled up the coast to spend a week at the estate of Joel Poinsett on the Peedee River. They went on to visit Abraham and Angelica Van Buren at her father's plantation in Sumter County, before striking southwest through Georgia and Alabama to New Orleans.[8]

The high point of the tour came in late April, when after journeying

[7] Samuel Hart to MVB, June 28, 1841, Henry D. Gilpin to MVB, Oct. 19, 1841, John Hastings to MVB, Oct. 23, 1841, John Fairfield to MVB, Oct. 25, 1841, William Allen to MVB, Oct. 27, 1841, John Law to MVB, Nov. 23, 1841, Andrew Jackson to the 9th Ward, Sept. 11, 1841, quoted in the *Wayne Sentinel*, Henry Horn to MVB, Nov. 13, 1841, MVB to Henry Horn, Nov. 26, 1841, VBP; George Bancroft to Marcy, Nov. 5, 1841, William L. Marcy Papers, NYSL; Benjamin Tappan, "Journal," Dec. 9, 1840, Benjamin Tappan Papers, LC.

[8] Albert H. Tracy to MVB, Nov. 24, 1841, MVB to Andrew Jackson, Feb. 7, Mar. 26, 1842, VBP; Edmund Hubard to Robert T. Hubard, Feb. 22, 1842, Hubard Family Papers, UVL; Smith, *Blair Family in Politics*, p. 155; MVB to Paulding, Feb. 3, 1842, William I. Paulding, *Literary Life of James K. Paulding* (New York, 1867), p. 285; MVB to Poinsett, Feb. 6, Feb. 8, 1842, Joel R. Poinsett Papers, HSP; Silas Wright to Poinsett, Feb. 17, 1842, Poinsett to Gouverneur Kemble, Mar. 14, 1842, Joel R. Poinsett Papers, in the Henry D. Gilpin Papers, HSP; MVB to Henry Clay, Clay, *Private Correspondence*, p. 458; Paulding to Jackson, Sept. 22, 1842, Jackson, *Correspondence*, VI, 168-170.

up the Mississippi to Memphis and overland to Nashville, Van Buren arrived at the Hermitage. He had worked closely with Jackson for eight years, but had never entertained the Old Hero at Kinderhook or visited him at the Hermitage, and although Jackson came down with an "attack of chills and fever," both men considered the visit a social and political triumph. Jackson was delighted that Van Buren made a good enough impression to refute the stories that the Whigs had spread about him. "The people," said Jackson, saw that the New Yorker was "a plain man of middle size, plain and affable, [not] a dwarf dutchman," and not "a little dandy who you might lift in a bandbox." Jackson reported that Van Buren and his party "left in fine health and spirits, pleased with the reception" they had received.[9]

Van Buren was also happy about the way he was received in Columbia, Tennessee, where he visited James K. Polk, and in Henry Clay's Lexington, Kentucky, but the remainder of the swing through Kentucky went less well. At Louisville the crowd responded warmly— "fired their guns, threw up their Hats and Huzzaed with all their might,"—but unfortunately the cheers were received, not by Van Buren, but by Paulding, who had entered the city ahead of the main party.[10]

Before returning home Van Buren spent the month of June in the old Northwest following the advice of Thomas Hart Benton who stressed how important the Northwest would be for reelection.[11] On his way from St. Louis to Chicago Van Buren spent an evening in the little town of Rochester outside of Springfield, Illinois. Here he was entertained by a number of leading Democrats who brought along a young Whig named Abraham Lincoln, then aged thirty-three, to help amuse the former President. Lincoln, who had been going through a long period of indecision and melancholy, was full of fun that evening, swapping stories with Van Buren, Paulding, and the others until late into the night. Van Buren laughed so hard that he went to bed with

---

[9] In Tennessee Van Buren spent a day or two with James K. Polk, who tried in vain to sound out Van Buren on the vice presidency for 1844. Sellers, *James K. Polk Jacksonian*, pp. 466-477; Jackson to Francis P. Blair, April 23, May 23, 1842, Jackson, *Correspondence*, VI, 151-152.

[10] Clay to John Sargent, May 31, 1842, McGregor-Clay Papers, UVL; MVB to Jackson, May 27, 1842, Paulding to Jackson, Sept. 22, 1842, Jackson, *Correspondence*, VI, 154-155, 169; James C. N. Paul, *Rift in the Democracy* (Philadelphia, 1951), pp. 37-38; Letcher to John J. Crittenden, May 31, June 7, 1842, Crittenden Papers, LC.

[11] Mentor L. Williams, ed., "A Tour of Illinois in 1842," *Journal of the Illinois State Historical Society*, 42 (Sept. 1949), 292-294; Nathaniel West to MVB, Oct. 12, 1842, Benton to MVB, June 3, 1842, MVB to Benjamin Butler, May 24, 1842, VBP; Koerner, *Memoirs*, p. 475.

his sides aching, and said later that he had never "spent so agreeable a night in his life."[12]

The convivial evening in Rochester came at a turning point in Van Buren's career. He had left New York in February a defeated President, unsure of his position in the party, uncertain whether to try again for the White House. He returned in July determined to run, and with his campaign already under way. He returned more confident of himself than before and with a broader view of his country and his role. The tour, he reported enthusiastically, was all that anyone could imagine. Wherever he went he found the Whigs "respectful" and the Democrats "in high & sometimes uproarious spirits." Paulding best summed up the new spirit of national pride that he and Van Buren shared. "When I reflect that I have travelled nearly seven thousand miles on my own native soil without once 'crossing my track,' " he wrote, "I feel an impression of the vastness and grandeur of my country which swells my heart, and wakens a crowd of lofty anticipations. . . . I feel there is scarcely a limit to the power and prosperity of our country." Van Buren's travels took him to many parts of the nation, places such as New Orleans, St. Louis, and Chicago, that he had never seen before. His visit to the old Northwest further weakened his loyalty to the South and to the institution of slavery. A night with Lincoln did not make Van Buren a Free-Soiler, but his stay with the free farmers of Ohio, Indiana and Illinois helped push him in that direction.[13]

On his return to New York Van Buren was soon deeply involved in the fortunes of the New York Democracy, which was divided between conservatives, who favored extending the state canal system, and radicals, who opposed the extension. The conservatives were led by Edwin Croswell and William C. Bouck, the unsuccessful gubernatorial candidate in 1840. At the head of the radicals were old-timers Azariah Flagg and Silas Wright, and among their ranks were such newcomers as Van Buren's son John and Samuel J. Tilden, the eighteen-year-old son of Van Buren's henchman Elam Tilden. As a boy Tilden had become familiar with the Regency because its members had often gathered at his father's home. Something of a hypochondriac, young Tilden was unable to complete his studies at Yale, but nonetheless went on to become a lawyer in New York City. In later years his successful law practice and his shrewd investments during the Civil War made him one of the wealthiest men in America and eventually

[12] Williams, "Tour of Illinois," pp. 292-294.

[13] Paulding to Jackson, Sept. 22, 1842, Jackson, *Correspondence*, VI, 168-169; Van Buren to Jackson, July 30, 1842, VBP; MVB to C. J. Ingersoll, Aug. 9, 1842, Charles Jared Ingersoll Papers, HSP.

the unsuccessful Democratic candidate for President in 1876. In 1842 Tilden was a clever, outspoken, radical Democrat.

Aware of the deep rift in the party, Wright wrote Van Buren three anxious letters in early August asking for a conference at Kinderhook as soon as Congress adjourned. The result of the conference was a compromise at the state Democratic convention in September; Bouck was renominated for governor, but the party agreed to dig no more canals. Even though Bouck won in November, he was unable to achieve party harmony. As radicals and conservatives fought over patronage, both sides tried to secure the support of Van Buren.[14]

Van Buren's tour and the Democratic victory in New York encouraged many of his backers to start thinking about 1844. When Francis P. Blair asked Jackson whether he would return to Washington for the inauguration if Van Buren were reelected, the Hero replied that he would come "cheerfully" and would provide a carriage for the occasion. Wright was already at work enlisting John Law, whom Van Buren had appointed receiver of public money in Vincennes, Indiana, Senator Benjamin Tappan in Ohio, and former senator William H. Roane in Virginia, to start the bandwagon. Benton, Thomas Ritchie and Bancroft could all be counted on. After a swing through Pennsylvania, Virginia and Tennessee, old faithful Alfred Balch assured Van Buren that people everywhere wanted him restored to office. Early in 1843, the Washington *Globe* carried a long article supporting Van Buren, and the *United States Magazine and Democratic Review* published a sonnet in his honor. Van Buren had become the favorite for the Democratic nomination.[15]

But there were other candidates. Bancroft warned Van Buren that Lewis Cass, who had just returned from his post as minister to France, had a following in the Northwest, New Jersey and Tennessee, while Richard Mentor Johnson could depend upon Kentucky and Arkansas. There was also opposition in Pennsylvania, where James Buchanan was saying that Van Buren should not run a third time.[16]

[14] Wright to MVB, Aug. 2, Aug. 12, Aug. 17, 1842, Oct. 2, 1843, Croswell to MVB, Feb. 4, 1843, William L. Marcy to MVB, Jan. 27, 1843, draft for Bouck's inaugural address, Dec. 12, 1842, VBP; Alexander, *Political History*, II, 50-59; Garraty, *Wright*, pp. 228-231.

[15] Blair to Jackson, Nov. 13, 1842, Jackson to Blair, Nov. 25, 1842, Jackson, *Correspondence*, VI, 176, 178; Wright to John Law, Nov. 5, 1842, Silas Wright Miscellaneous Papers, LC; Wright to William H. Roane, Feb. 25, 1843, Wright Papers, NYHS; John Law to MVB, Nov. 3, 1842, Balch to MVB, Nov. 22, 1842, Abraham Van Buren to MVB, Jan. 29, 1843, VBP; *United States Magazine and Democratic Review*, 12 (1843), 78; Washington *Globe*, April 13, 1843.

[16] Bancroft to MVB, Dec. 9, 1842, July 18, 1843, Thomas N. Carr to MVB, July 15,

The most serious obstacle was John C. Calhoun, who had started looking for northern allies in 1841. Congressman Francis W. Pickens told Levi Woodbury in the fall that Calhoun would like to enter the campaign alongside someone from New Hampshire. Woodbury, who was interested in the vice presidency, sent his brother-in-law J. O. Barnes to Boston the next winter to work for Calhoun. Worried by Woodbury's behavior, Van Buren asked Blair what that "non committal" New Hampshireman was up to. Calhoun even tried to lure Silas Wright with hints about the vice presidency. During Van Buren's western tour he received two letters warning him about a ticket made up of Calhoun and Wright. Joel Poinsett reported that "the Devil" had taken Wright to "the summit of a lofty mountain" and offered him "dominion over . . . this fair land [if] he would fall down and worship" Calhoun. Wright reassured Van Buren that there was nothing to the rumors, but talk about Calhoun persisted in New York.[17]

Calhoun's campaign reached its peak in the spring and summer of 1843 when the South Carolinian resigned from the Senate to concentrate on the coming election. In addition to his contacts in New York, New Hampshire and the South, Calhoun was on good terms with David Henshaw of Massachusetts, and President John Tyler of Virginia. After Webster resigned as Secretary of State in May, Calhoun's influence on the administration became apparent. Not only did his friend Abel P. Upshur of Virginia, take over the State Department but in addition, Henshaw replaced Upshur as Secretary of the Navy. Observers interpreted Democratic talk of nominating Tyler as a disguised maneuver for Calhoun.[18]

1843, Jackson to MVB, Nov. 29, 1843, Polk to MVB, Nov. 30, 1843, VBP; S. H. Laughlin, "Diary," Oct. 18, 1843, St. George L. Sioussat, ed., "Diaries of S. H. Laughlin, of Tennessee, 1840, 1843," *Tennessee Historical Magazine*, 2 (Mar. 1916), 70; Buchanan to Jesse Miller, Dec. 28, 1842, James Buchanan Papers, LC; Buchanan to Campbell P. White, July 27, Dec. 19, 1843, James Buchanan Papers, NYHS.

[17] For Woodbury, see Charles M. Wiltse, *John C. Calhoun, Sectionalist, 1840-1850* (New York, 1951), pp. 89-90; Pickens to Woodbury, Oct. 17, 1841, Woodbury Papers, LC; William Allen to MVB, Jan. 18, 1843, Fernando Wood to MVB, Feb. 20, 1843, Gideon Welles to MVB, April 29, June 13, 1843, Wright to MVB, June 19, 1843, George Bancroft to MVB, June 22, 1843, William H. Roane to MVB, Sept. 11, 1843, Benjamin V. French to MVB, Sept. 12, 1843, VBP; MVB to Francis P. Blair, Mar. 18, 1843, Blair Family Papers, LC; Blair to Andrew Jackson, Jan. 29, 1843, Jackson, *Correspondence*, VI, 186; Robert M. T. Hunter to Calhoun, June 16, 1843, Calhoun, *Correspondence*, p. 865. For Wright, see Benton to MVB, April 17, Aug. 16, 1843, Joel Poinsett to MVB, June 5, 1842, Augustus Vanderpoel to MVB, Aug. 29, 1842, Marcy to MVB, July 30, 1843, VBP; Gouverneur Kemble to Joel Poinsett, Oct. 10, 1842, Joel R. Poinsett Papers, in the Henry D. Gilpin Papers, HSP; Wright to William Holdredge, Aug. 24, 1842, Wright Papers, NYHS.

[18] Wiltse, *John C. Calhoun, Sectionalist*, pp. 98-100, 103-104, 114-115, 134-139;

Calhoun's chances looked even better when the Democrats decided to postpone their nominating convention. Since Van Buren was in the lead, Wright and Van Buren's other managers wanted the convention held as soon as possible, perhaps in the fall of 1843. Calhoun preferred to delay it in hopes that something would come up to divide Van Buren's backing. Wright finally agreed to postpone the convention until the spring rather than run the risk of being blamed for party friction.[19]

The tariff of 1842, which had returned many duties to the protective rates of 1832, helped keep Calhoun's drive going by stirring up the South. As soon as the bill was passed, Calhoun put Van Buren on the defensive by attacking Wright and other northern Democrats for supporting the increased rates. Already losing patience with the South, Van Buren replied that Wright had tried to get southern senators to agree on a moderate tariff, but they had refused. Reviewing the past, Van Buren complained that northern Democrats had been "broken down entirely" by supporting the Southerner Crawford in 1824, and had been "brought to death's door" later by backing Jackson's pro-Southern Indian policy. In the 1830s the party had lost many Northerners by defending slavery, and if he helped the South again by supporting a low tariff, said Van Buren, he would risk losing more northern votes.[20]

The opportunity to discuss the tariff arose early in 1843 when Indiana Democrats asked the candidates to answer questions on economic issues. Van Buren drew up a fifty-four-page draft, which was cut and rewritten by Wright, Flagg, Marcy, and John Van Buren. In the final version Van Buren did his best to straddle the issue. Declaring that tariffs should be for revenue rather than for protection, he also argued that revenues should be high, and he called for protection for certain manufactured and agricultural products. The delegates at the Democratic convention in New York also tried to compromise by supporting a tariff that would bring in "revenue" but would encourage

Blair to Jackson, Sept. 26, 1843, Jackson to Blair, Oct. 9, 1843, Jackson, *Correspondence*, VI, 231, 233; Darling, *Political Changes in Massachusetts*, p. 272; Amos Kendall to MVB, Aug. 20, 1843, VBP.

[19] Garraty, *Wright*, pp. 239-242; Charles Sellers, "Election of 1844," Schlesinger, *Presidential Elections*, I, 760; Wright to John Law, Nov. 5, 1842, Silas Wright Miscellaneous Papers, LC; Gouverneur Kemble to MVB, Jan. 26, 1843, Robert McClellan to MVB, Feb. 3, 1843, VBP.

[20] Wright to MVB, Jan. 27, Feb. 27, 1843, R. B. Gooch to Auguste Davezac, Dec. 1842, William Hallet to MVB, Feb. 16, 1843, VBP; Calhoun to Robert M. T. Hunter, May 1843, Calhoun, *Correspondence*, pp. 533-534; Wiltse, *John C. Calhoun, Sectionalist*, pp. 86-88; Garraty, *Wright*, pp. 226-227; MVB to Francis P. Blair, Sept. 12, 1842, Blair Family Papers, LC.

"labor in agriculture, commerce, and manufactures" as well. Although some Southerners seemed mollified by the statement, others reported that there was still "bad feeling" over Van Buren and the tariff. Van Buren told Wright irritably that it was impossible to satisfy the South, and that Southerners were "given to complaining" about the tariff.[21]

Calhoun's presidential hopes were heightened in August 1843, when James K. Polk, who had become identified with Van Buren, was once again defeated for governor of Tennessee. On hearing the news Calhoun boasted that Polk had lost even though "the influence of V.B. Jackson and Polk was perfectly united." The *Knoxville Argus* reported that the Whigs had made "Van Burenism as odious among the people of Tennessee as Black Cockade Federalism had ever been." A few months later Van Buren told Polk that his defeat had been both "mortifying [and] incomprehensible."[22]

During the fall Calhoun's drive began to founder. In New Hampshire, New York and Massachusetts, Democratic conventions nominated Van Buren and endorsed planks on the tariff and slavery that were distasteful to the South. The Democratic convention in Georgia withdrew its nomination of Calhoun, and in other southern states his support ebbed away. By October Polk was confident that Van Buren would be the Democratic nominee. The Magician was in command in December when his wing of the party seized control of the House, elected Blair printer, and made John W. Jones of Virginia, speaker. Within a few weeks Calhoun gave up the race, and Buchanan and Cass followed suit. By January 1844, twelve party conventions had declared for Van Buren, five others remaining uncommitted. Van Buren was so confident that he made arrangements for George Bancroft to write a campaign biography and told Jackson that the convention would be "very harmonious."[23]

---

[21] Indiana State Democratic Convention, Resolutions providing for the questioning of Democratic candidates for the presidency and vice-presidency, Jan. 9, 1843, Wright to MVB, Jan. 27, Feb. 19, Feb. 27, 1843, Jan. 8, 1844, MVB to Democratic State Convention of Indiana, Feb. 15, 1843, "Opinions of Mr. Van Buren on the subject of a national bank, distribution of the proceeds of the public lands, an exchequer or government fiscal agent, a tariff, the veto power, and a national convention," Feb. 15, 1843, Peter V. Daniel to MVB, July 6, Nov. 15, 1843, Floyd Jones to MVB, May 8, 1843, Robert Walker to MVB, Aug. 4, 1843, William R. Hallet to MVB, Dec. 13, 1843, A. W. Smith to MVB, Dec. 5, 1843, Hugh A. Garland to MVB, Jan. 12, 1844, R. B. Rhett to MVB, Feb. 26, 1844, MVB to Wright, Jan. 9, 1844, MVB to William H. Roane, Jan. 24, 1844, VBP; Calhoun to Robert M. T. Hunter, May 1843, Calhoun to George McDuffie, Dec. 4, 1843, Calhoun, *Correspondence*, pp. 533-534, 552-553.

[22] Sellers, *James K. Polk Jacksonian*, pp. 489-492; Calhoun to Duff Green, Sept. 8, 1843, Calhoun, *Correspondence*, p. 547; James Buchanan to Lynch, Oct. 3, 1843, David Lynch Papers, LC.

[23] Wiltse, *John C. Calhoun, Sectionalist*, pp. 144-149; Sellers, "Election of 1844,"

But the question of Texas stood between Van Buren and the nomination. A year earlier, in January 1843, President Tyler's friend, Congressman Thomas W. Gilmer of Virginia, had sent a letter to the *Madisonian* calling for annexation. When Tennessee congressman Aaron Brown forwarded a copy to Jackson, the Old Hero wrote back saying that he wholeheartedly agreed. Brown held on to Jackson's letter, waiting for the right moment to publish it. The appointment of Upshur as Secretary of State brought one more annexationist into power, and by September the administration had opened secret talks with President Sam Houston of Texas. Supporters of Calhoun seized on the issue of Texas as a means of derailing Van Buren. According to Virgil Maxcy of Maryland, only "the immediate calling up of the Texas question" could prevent Van Buren's nomination. Upshur argued that on such a platform the South could nominate Calhoun as a third candidate and force the election into the House, where southern delegations would refuse to vote for Van Buren. With Texas, noted another writer, they could force the sly fox "out of his hole." Benton called these plans a "plot," but his term was exaggerated, for Southerners such as Gilmer and Jackson had been after Texas for years. And Van Buren knew what was going on, for John Bragg of Alabama, Andrew Stevenson and William H. Roane had all warned the New Yorker about the maneuvering.[24]

While Calhoun was exploiting the Texas issue, Tyler was making his own effort to get Van Buren out of the way. On New Year's Day

---

Schlesinger, *Presidential Elections*, I, 755-757; Jackson to Blair, Dec. 5, 1843, Blair to Jackson, Dec. 6, Dec. 16, 1843, Jackson, *Correspondence*, VI, 247-250; Polk to Andrew J. Donelson, Oct. 19, Dec. 20, 1843, St. George L. Sioussat, ed., "Letters of James K. Polk to Andrew J. Donelson, 1843-1848," *Tennessee Historical Magazine*, 3 (1917), 53, 56; MVB to Marcy, Feb. 12, 1844, Marcy Papers, LC; Wright to Marcy, Feb. 5, 1844, Marcy to MVB, Feb. 1844, MVB to Bancroft, Feb. 25, 1844, Worthington C. Ford, ed., "Van Buren–Bancroft Correspondence," Massachusetts Historical Society, *Proceedings*, 42 (1908-1909), 417-419, 425n; Garraty, *Wright*, p. 244; MVB to Jackson, Jan. 13, 1844, VBP; Jackson to MVB, Feb. 7, 1844, Jackson, *Correspondence*, VI, 258.

[24] Charles Sellers leans toward the "plot" interpretation; Charles M. Wiltse and Robert Seager do not. Charles Sellers, *James K. Polk Continentalist 1843-1846* (Princeton, 1966), pp. 49-53; Wiltse, *John C. Calhoun, Sectionalist*, pp. 150-156, 506; Robert Seager, *And Tyler Too: a Biography of John and Julia Gardiner Tyler* (New York, 1943), pp. 209-219. Gilmer's letter is in the *Madisonian*, Jan. 23, 1843. See also Brown to Jackson, Jan. 23, 1843, Andrew J. Donelson Papers, LC; Jackson to Brown, Feb. 9 [12], 1843, Jackson, *Correspondence*, VI, 201; Benton, *Thirty Years' View*, II, 582-583; John Letcher to Thomas Ritchie, Sept. 23, 1843, Stevenson to MVB, Oct. 8, 1843, Roane to MVB, Oct. 17, 1843, John Bragg to MVB, Oct. 28, 1843, VBP; Maxcy to Calhoun, Dec. 3, Dec. 10, 1843, Hunter to Calhoun, Dec. 19, 1843, Francis Wharton to Calhoun, Feb. 1, 1844, Calhoun, *Correspondence*, pp. 897, 903, 907-908, 920.

1844 the President sent an envoy to Silas Wright to suggest that Van Buren might be named to fill an empty seat on the Supreme Court. Wright first began to laugh, but sobered quickly when he realized that the offer was serious. The messenger argued that Van Buren could not be elected President and even suggested that Wright should become the Democratic candidate. When the interview was over, Wright sent word back that the nomination of Van Buren to the Court would give the country "a broader, deeper, heartier, laugh than it ever had." That ended the matter. Two months later Tyler offered the seat to Wright himself, but the New Yorker turned it down in order to go on helping Van Buren regain the presidency.[25]

On March 20, the Texas question burst into the open when Aaron Brown published in the *Globe* the letter he had been holding from Jackson. Ritchie reprinted it in the *Enquirer*, and warned Van Buren that he would lose the nomination if he opposed annexation. From all parts of the nation Democrats including Bancroft, Woodbury, Paulding, Jefferson Davis of Mississippi, and Cave Johnson of Tennessee, wrote to Van Buren supporting annexation. Pressure from the other side was just as great, especially from New York, where Wright, Benjamin Butler and Flagg stood opposed to slavery. Butler had never forgotten the awful day in Washington when he saw a slave woman kill herself after being sold away from her family. Wright feared that Texas would prove to be a "mill stone" that would "sink" Van Buren.[26]

Calhoun increased the pressure on Van Buren. After Abel P. Upshur had been killed by the explosion of a gun aboard the *U.S.S. Princeton* on February 28, Calhoun became Secretary of State. Within a few weeks the Tyler administration signed a treaty of annexation with Texas. Shortly afterward, on April 18, Calhoun decided it was time to answer British minister Richard Pakenham's letter in which he said that the British had been urging the Texans to abolish slavery. In his well-known reply Calhoun defended slavery as a positive good, and announced that the United States was annexing Texas in order to protect American slavery against British interference. The letter transformed a debate over Texas into one over slavery.[27]

[25] Wright to MVB, Jan. 2, Mar. 6, 1844, VBP; Garraty, *Wright*, pp. 234-238.

[26] Washington *Globe*, Mar. 20, 1844; *Richmond Enquirer*, Mar. 22, 1844; Ritchie to MVB, Mar. 20, 1844, Davis to MVB, Mar. 25, 1844, Bancroft to MVB, Mar. 28, 1844, Johnson to MVB, April 20, 1844, Smith Van Buren to MVB, April 23, 1844, Salmon Chase to MVB, Mar. 30, 1844, Jabez Hammond to MVB, April 7, 1844, Wright to MVB, April 3, April 6, 1844, Flagg to MVB, Mar. 24, 1844, VBP; Paulding to MVB, April 16, 1844, Paulding, *Letters*, p. 365; *New-York Evening Post*, Mar. 21, 1844; Butler, *Retrospect of Forty Years*, p. 55.

[27] Sellers, *James K. Polk Continentalist*, pp. 56-61; Wiltse, *John C. Calhoun, Sectionalist*, pp. 167-171.

Van Buren chose to take a stand by answering a letter dated March 27, from Congressman William H. Hammet of Mississippi. When Van Buren sent the draft of a reply to members of the Regency, he received conflicting advice. Paulding wrote that his "fingers itch[ed] a little to get hold of Texas"; Wright preferred to take the side of "truth and principle" by resisting annexation. He warned that Tyler would try to embarrass Van Buren by including a defense of slavery in the Texan treaty. Butler said that he would support annexation only if Mexico gave her consent and only if Texas were admitted as a territory rather than a state. With his usual caution Van Buren dispatched Butler to the Hermitage on April 6 to sound out Jackson.[28]

But Van Buren's reply to Hammet was far from cautious. Instead of waiting to hear from Tennessee, Van Buren wrote on April 20 that he was opposed to the annexation of Texas. Accusing Tyler of acting too secretly and too suddenly, Van Buren said that annexation would be an act of aggression against Mexico that would damage the United States' reputation for "reason and justice." Although he did say that he would annex Texas if the people were firmly in favor of it after he became President, the letter showed that he had abandoned his old proslavery position. After two decades of bending to the will of the South, he was willing to risk southern hostility by opposing the annexation of Texas. The Hammet letter was the culmination of a drift away from the South that had begun in 1835 with his letter of complaint to Judith Rives. The change was in part political because there were northern votes to be won in opposing annexation, but principle played a part. Van Buren had decided to follow what he called "the path of duty" and resist the extension of slavery.[29]

Van Buren's declaration of conscience immediately became the subject of political controversy because the letter arrived in Washington at the same time as a letter from Henry Clay also opposing annexation. Afraid that some of Van Buren's backers might commit themselves in favor of annexation, Wright decided to publish Van Buren's letter at once. As a result, Clay, who was about to become the Whig nominee, and Van Buren, who expected to run for the Democrats, came out against annexation on the very same day. The coincidence led to the assumption that during Van Buren's visit with Clay the two had agreed on this course of action in order to duck the issue of Texas. This interpretation is a dubious one because a politician as cautious as Van Buren was not likely to have made an agreement with an opponent

[28] Hammet to MVB, Mar. 27, 1844, Wright to MVB, April 1, April 3, April 6, April 8, April 11, 1844, Paulding to MVB, April 16, 1844, Butler to MVB, Mar. 29, April 6, April 29, 1844, VBP.

[29] MVB to Hammet, April 20, 1844, MVB to Wright, May 10, 1844, VBP.

two years before an election. It is more likely that Van Buren did on his own what he thought was best both morally and politically in 1844.[30]

For once in his life Van Buren evoked a strong moral response with a political decision. Those closest to him agreed with Wright that they had never "felt more proud" of their leader "than at that moment"; whatever the outcome, said Wright, he had "much less care" because their "principles [and their] character [were] safe." Azariah Flagg and Samuel J. Tilden believed that Van Buren's letter took "the true ground [of the] northern democracy." But the letter aroused "fever and fury" in Van Buren's rivals. Flagg reported that Cass and Woodbury were prepared to "fish for immortality in the Texas pool," and according to Wright, Buchanan declared that Van Buren was "a dead cock in the pit."[31]

Van Buren's letter had a pronounced effect in Tennessee. Nashville Democrats who were holding a meeting in favor of annexation were jubilant when Clay's letter appeared on the morning of May 4, but before the day was over the arrival of Van Buren's letter spread gloom in their ranks, and Alfred Balch reported that it had started "a political conflagration" against Van Buren. Acknowledging the possibility that Polk might emerge as a compromise choice for the nomination, Jackson brought up the question when Polk visited the Hermitage on May 13. With this prospect in mind Polk was all the more determined to send the Tennessee delegation to Baltimore united in favor of Van Buren. If the New Yorker won the nomination, he would owe Polk the vice presidency, and if Van Buren lost, he would not be able to blame it on Polk. With some difficulty Polk managed to keep Jackson from coming out openly against Van Buren.[32]

The letter also had an impact on Virginia, where Van Buren still had a great deal of support. When Ritchie, Roane, and others in the

[30] Garraty, *Wright*, pp. 251-252; "Letter from Henry Clay to the Washington *National Intelligencer*, April 17, 1844," Schlesinger, *Presidential Elections*, I, 814-817.

[31] Approval letters: Wright to Butler, May 15, 1844, Benjamin F. Butler Papers, NYSL; Wright to MVB, April 21, May 6, May 13, 1844, Tilden to MVB, April 1844, VBP; Flagg to O. Hungerford, May 9, 1844, Flagg Papers. Warning letters: Wright to Tilden, April 30, 1844, John Bigelow, ed., *Letters and Literary Memorials of Samuel J. Tilden* (New York, 1908), I, 23; Kendall to MVB, April 19-20, April 29-30, 1844, Wright to MVB, May 6, 1844, Flagg to MVB, May 23, 1844, VBP.

[32] Jackson to editor of the Nashville *Union*, May 13, 1844, Jackson to Butler, May 14, 1844, Kendall to MVB, May 16, 1844, Balch to MVB, May 22, 1844, VBP; Jackson to William B. Lewis, May 7, May 11, 1844, Jackson-Lewis Letters, NYHS; Jackson to Benton, May 14, 1844, Jackson to Blair, May 18, 1844, Jackson, *Correspondence*, VI, 291-294; Sellers, *James K. Polk Continentalist*, pp. 67-76.

Richmond Junto heard about the Texas "plot" in 1843, they disavowed it and passed word along to Van Buren. The Hammet letter changed everything, for the Virginians wanted Texas. On April 30, Roane told Van Buren that all was "lost" in Virginia; a day later he heard that the Junto was "all out against [him,] *positively, openly, and unequivocally.*" Ritchie gathered the angry letters repudiating Van Buren in a package and sent it to New York. Van Buren, suspecting that all was, indeed, lost in Virginia, sent the package back without a word.[33]

As the bad news arrived, Van Buren remained calm as ever, pleased that for once he could lay claim to being a man of principle. If the southern delegates distrusted his "fidelity, . . . self respect would forbid [him from] adding another word." After all he had "said and done in respect to the rights of the South . . . and all the opposition and persecution" he had received on that account, he had no intention of bowing any further. He still hoped to win, and he kept up a steady correspondence about the convention.[34]

Although the members of the New York delegation to the convention remained loyal to Van Buren, they began to prepare for the worst. Silas Wright's friend Judge John Fine suggested that Van Buren announce that he would withdraw if he did not have a "fair majority" on the first ballot. Since Van Buren was not going to the convention, he wrote a letter to Butler giving the delegates permission to shift to Wright whenever they thought that Van Buren could not win. Wright, who also planned to stay away from the convention, was distressed at the thought of being the nominee. Suspecting that annexationists were using him to divide the delegation, he gave Fine a strong letter refusing to be a candidate. The New York delegates knew about Van Buren's letter but not about Wright's.[35]

[33] Charles H. Ambler, "Virginia and the Presidental Succession, 1840-1844," Guy S. Ford, ed., *Essays in American History Dedicated to Frederick Jackson Turner* (New York, 1910), pp. 165-202; Charles H. Ambler, ed., "Virginia and Texas, 1844," *The John P. Branch Historical Papers of Randolph-Macon College*, 4 (June 1913), 116-137; Roane to MVB, April 30, 1844, ———to MVB, May 1, 1844, Ritchie to MVB, May 5, 1844, Ritchie, editorial, *Richmond Enquirer*, July 28, 1849, MVB to Ritchie, May 16, 1844, VBP.

[34] MVB to Wright, May 10, 1844, MVB to Butler, May 20, 1844, copy of letter owned by Harriet A. Butler, VBP.

[35] Flagg to MVB, May 17, 1844, Butler to MVB, May 20, 1844, Wright to MVB, May 20, 1844, MVB to Butler, May 20, 1844, VBP; Jabez Hammond, *Life and Times of Silas Wright, Late Governor of the State of New York* (Syracuse, 1848), pp. 444-459; Wright to Fine, May 23, 1844, quoted in Hammond, *Wright*, pp. 456-459; Wright to Flagg, May 22, 1844, Flagg-Wright Correspondence.

Since a majority but not two-thirds of the delegates preferred Van Buren, his opponents were intent on blocking him by retaining the rule established in 1832 requiring a two-thirds vote for nomination. It was ironic that a rule adopted in 1832 to help Van Buren was now being used to hurt him. Butler reported to Van Buren that "plots and counterplots" flourished as the annexationists fought for the two-thirds rule and compromise candidates maneuvered for support. The New Hampshire delegation was told that if they voted for the rule, Woodbury would have a good chance at the nomination. Pennsylvania was promised the same for Buchanan, Michigan for Cass. The badly divided Tennessee delegation was swinging away from Van Buren toward either Cass or Wright. Bancroft, who wanted Texas but was loyal to Van Buren, declared that the Southerners would accept "any Northern man that was a Texan, be it Cass! [or,] Heaven save the mark, Levi Woodbury!!!"[36]

During the first two days of the convention the two-thirds rule kept Van Buren from being nominated. Butler, who headed the delegation in the absence of Van Buren and Wright, did all he could to block the rule. "White" with anger, he "carried the body by storm" with a one-hour harangue, jumping up and down and receiving great applause. But he failed. Fifty-four delegates pledged to Van Buren bolted, allowing the rule to pass by a vote of 148 to 116. Some of the defectors then voted for Van Buren for a ballot or two, knowing full well that he could not win a two-thirds vote. On the first ballot Van Buren held most of the Northeast and Northwest, receiving 146 of the 177 votes needed, and Cass came in second with 83. In the next six ballots Van Buren lost first Vermont, Connecticut and Illinois, then Pennsylvania as he dropped behind Cass. The convention adjourned at the end of the second day with no one close to winning.[37]

During the evening Butler, George Bancroft, and Polk's former law partner Gideon Pillow agreed that the convention needed a new candidate, but could not agree on a name. Bancroft and Pillow turned to Polk, Butler to Wright. Though aware of Wright's letter to Fine, Butler thought he could prevail on the senator to run, and dashed off a letter to Wright in Washington asking him to accept the nomination. But

[36] Butler to MVB, May 27, 1844, Wright to Flagg, May 23, 1844, Wright to MVB, May 26, 1844, Bancroft to MVB, May 23, May 24, May 25, 1844, Auguste Davezac to MVB, May 27, May 28, 1844, VBP; Andrew J. Donelson to MVB, June 2, 1844, Van Schaack Papers, NYSL; Sellers, *James K. Polk Continentalist*, pp. 76-85.

[37] Garraty, *Wright*, pp. 268-272; John L. O'Sullivan to MVB, May 27, 1844, VBP; "Proceedings of the Democratic National Convention, Baltimore, May 27-30, 1844," Schlesinger, *Presidential Elections*, I, 829-839.

when Butler caucused the New York delegation a short time later, Fine refused to go along with the plan. As the convention got under way the next morning Polk's managers went into action and the New Yorkers were stalled.[38]

At the start of the eighth ballot Henry Hubbard of New Hampshire, and Bancroft of Massachusetts, announced thirteen votes for Polk. When Tennessee, Alabama and Louisiana also came out for Polk, his total stood at forty-four at the end of the voting. At this moment Samuel Young, who had supported Van Buren in New York for decades, delivered a bitter diatribe against Tyler, Calhoun and the annexationists for denying Van Buren the nomination. "Nero fiddled whilst Rome . . . was burning," shouted Young, "and no doubt the political Nero of this country . . . was looking on, and rejoicing." Young demanded that the two-thirds rule be given up so that the delegates would not "be kept here for all eternity." Fistfights threatened as Southerners responded angrily to Young's insults. While the shouting raged, the New Yorkers left the room to caucus beneath the stands.[39]

As the New York delegation huddled, Hubbard and Samuel Medary of Ohio, who had once been for Van Buren, calmed the convention with speeches supporting Polk. The ninth ballot began, with the states as usual voting geographically. After all of New England except Vermont had voted for Polk, and several delegations including New York had passed, William H. Roane drew a roar from the crowd when he cast Virginia's votes for Polk and then held out his hand to Hubbard, who had been the first to go over to Polk. Leading the New York delegation back on the floor, Butler, tears streaming down his cheeks, withdrew Van Buren's name and launched into a speech in support of party harmony. Recalling the old Jeffersonian alliance, Butler promised that the Empire State would be found beside the Old Dominion fighting for the Democratic party in the fall. Although Butler could not speak for the rest of his delegation, he gave his own vote to Polk. Delegation after delegation then switched to Polk until the vote was unanimous.[40]

[38] Garraty, *Wright*, pp. 272-273; Sellers, *James K. Polk Continentalist*, pp. 92-95.

[39] "Proceedings of the Democratic National Convention . . . 1844," Schlesinger, *Presidential Elections*, I, 841-842; O'Sullivan to MVB, May 29, 1844, VBP; Garraty, *Wright*, pp. 273-276.

[40] "Proccedings of the Democratic National Convention . . . 1844," Schlesinger, *Presidential Elections*, I, 842-849; Hammond, *Wright*, 461-464; Sellers, *James K. Polk Continentalist*, pp. 96-98; Bancroft to MVB, June 14, 1844, O'Sullivan to MVB, May 29, 1844, VBP.

After rejecting Van Buren, most delegates wanted to please the New Yorkers by nominating Wright for Vice President. To speed matters up word went out by way of the newly invented telegraph to Wright, who was standing by in Washington at the Capitol. The answer came back—not once but several times—that Wright would not run. When his telegraphed refusal was not accepted, Wright sent an emissary to Baltimore overnight by wagon with a handwritten letter turning down the nomination. The party settled for a ticket of Polk and lawyer George M. Dallas of Pennsylvania.[41]

Wright's explanation of his decision reflected the self-righteousness and self-pity that gripped Van Buren and his followers. He refused, he said, because acceptance would have detracted from Van Buren's courageous stand. Committed to the old partisanship and the new concern for principle, he assured Van Buren that their "honor [and] character, as individuals, as a party, and as a state [had been] preserved." Van Buren, in his new role, insisted that he would not modify his views on Texas because he did not want to trim his "sails to catch the passing breeze."[42]

Van Buren's rejection dealt a blow to the alliance of North and South on which the Democratic party had been based. James S. Wadsworth of New York, denounced the "dictation & selfishness of the south," while Andrew J. Donelson of Tennessee accused Southerners of dumping the very man who had fought alongside Andrew Jackson for years. Peter V. Daniel, a Southerner himself, blamed Van Buren's defeat on the "selfish ambition and avarice" of men like Calhoun. The only consolation for Van Buren's supporters was the thought that Calhoun had not won the nomination for himself. As John L. O'Sullivan put it, they were "weeping with one eye while [they] smile[d] with the other at the overthrow of the intriguers and traitors."[43]

Despite their disappointment at the convention, Van Buren and the New York Democrats did their part in the fall campaign. Learning that some of his friends were withholding their support from Polk, Van Buren persuaded them to back the national ticket. When Wright

[41] Wright to Butler, May 29, 1844, Silas Wright, Letters to Benjamin Butler, NYPL; Wright to Marcy, Sept. 13, 1844, Marcy Papers, LC; Garraty, *Wright*, pp. 279-286.

[42] Wright to MVB, June 2, 1844, MVB to Amos Kendall, June 12, 1844, VBP; Wright to Flagg, June 8, 1844, Flagg Papers; Wright to Marcy, Sept. 13, 1844, Marcy Papers, LC; MVB to Joel Poinsett, June 29, 1844, Joel R. Poinsett Papers, in the Henry D. Gilpin Papers, HSP.

[43] Tracy to MVB, June 2, 1844, Wadsworth to MVB, June 1, 1844, Daniel to MVB, June 11, 1844, O'Sullivan to MVB, May 29, 1844, VBP; Donelson to MVB, June 2, 1844, Van Schaack Papers, NYSL.

was nominated for governor, he tried to refuse to run, but gave way under pressure from Polk and Van Buren. The campaign was complex as issues such as abolitionism, nativism, and canal policy vied with annexation to decide votes. Since the outcome was in doubt as the election approached, each side intensified its efforts. Philip Hone described Whig and Democratic processions, both five miles long. On election eve, said Hone, there were "little knots of men at every corner," and Tammany Hall was a "perfect jam." Hone was disappointed by the outcome, for New York gave Polk a plurality of 5,000 over Clay, and Wright 10,000 over Millard Fillmore, the Whig candidate. Without New York Polk would have lost the election. On receiving the news, Andrew Jackson wrote that the "stern virtue of the democracy" had prevailed in New York. He was ready "to depart in peace."[44]

In the wake of the narrow victory radicals, who were loyal to Van Buren, and conservatives, who looked to William L. Marcy, fought for control of Democratic politics in New York. Wright set a radical tone for his administration when he asked that revenues be used to reduce the state debt. Radicals also managed to keep Azariah Flagg as comptroller and to elect John Van Buren attorney general. Control of the assembly, however, went to the conservatives when Horatio Seymour was chosen speaker. The party divided the two seats in the Senate between conservative Daniel Dickinson and radical John A. Dix.[45]

Van Buren and the radicals also vied with the conservatives to see which side could influence Polk in selecting his cabinet. After accepting Polk's nomination and helping him carry New York, Van Buren believed that Polk should let him control the choice of the ranking member of the cabinet. Polk understood this obligation, but he was under pressure from Southerners and Westerners who did not want any Van Buren man appointed. The conservatives in New York hoped that Polk would appoint Marcy. Communication between Polk and the New Yorkers was slow because the persons involved were so many miles apart. Van Buren, for example, was at Lindenwald, Butler in

[44] Hammond, *Wright*, p. 412; George W. Roach, "The Presidential Campaign of 1844 in New York State," *New York History*, 19 (1938), 155-167; Alexander, *Political History*, II, 59-64, 76-82, 86-89; Wright to Benjamin Tappan, Oct. 17, 1844, Wright Papers, NYHS; MVB to O'Sullivan, Oct. 30, 1844, MVB to Jackson, Nov. 2, 1844, Amos Kendall to MVB, Oct. 13, 1844, VBP; Hone, *Diary*, pp. 718-720; Hough, *New York Civil List*, p. 166; Schlesinger, *Presidential Elections*, I, 861; Jackson to Andrew J. Donelson, Nov. 18, 1844, Jackson, *Correspondence*, VI, 329-330.

[45] Garraty, *Wright*, pp. 333-339; Alexander, *Political History*, II, 90-94; Dix, *Memoirs*, I, 194. Flagg was reelected comptroller in 1842.

New York City, Wright in Canton or Albany, and Polk in Tennessee or Washington. Polk could get a letter from Washington to New York City in twenty-four hours, but it often took three more days to reach Kinderhook.[46]

Polk started correctly on December 7 by offering the post of Secretary of the Treasury to Wright. Although he did not want Wright and did not expect him to accept, party protocol demanded that the offer be made. No one was surprised or disappointed when Wright rejected it. But Polk's gesture was costly because four of the thirteen weeks between his election and inauguration were used up by the time Wright's refusal arrived in Tennessee.[47]

With Wright out of the way, Polk wrote friendly letters to him and Van Buren asking them to nominate another New Yorker for Secretary of State or Treasury. Regretting that he had not seen Van Buren since they had conferrred in 1842, Polk thanked him for "the disinterested and magnanimous ground" he had "so promptly assumed" after the convention. Encouraged by the warm letters, Van Buren and Wright conferred hurriedly and sent off replies nominating Butler for State or Flagg for Treasury. Van Buren admitted that the former would not want to return to Washington, but thought that a letter from Jackson would change Butler's mind. Wright praised Butler as a man "who could wear a window in his breast" and whose mind was as "clear as light." Van Buren made a special point of recommending that Polk rely on the radical Senator John A. Dix rather than the conservative Daniel Dickinson for advice about New York. The tone of these letters suggests that Van Buren and Wright sincerely believed that Polk wanted to cooperate.[48]

Before the letters arrived Polk had already made tentative plans for his cabinet. Anticipating a refusal from Butler, Polk leaned toward Flagg for Treasury, leaving State for James Buchanan of Pennsylvania. Robert Walker of Mississippi, was in the lead for Attorney General because Polk wanted to reward one of the annexationists. George Bancroft of Massachusetts, for the Navy Department, Andrew Ste-

[46] Welles to MVB, Nov. 13, 1844, Bancroft to MVB, Dec. 3, 1844, John Fairfield to MVB, Dec. 21, 1844, VBP. For a thorough study of Van Buren and the choice of Polk's cabinet, see Joseph G. Rayback, "Martin Van Buren's Break with James K. Polk," *New York History*, 36 (1955), 51-62.

[47] Polk to Wright, Dec. 7, 1844 (copy), Polk Papers, LC; Wright to Polk, Dec. 20, 1844, R. H. Gillet, *The Life and Times of Silas Wright* (Albany, 1874), II, 1632; Sellers, *James K. Polk Continentalist*, p. 178; Garraty, *Wright*, pp. 340-341.

[48] Polk to MVB, Jan. 4, 1845, MVB to Polk, Jan. 18, 1845, VBP; Wright to Polk, Jan. 21, 1845, James K. Polk Papers, NYPL.

venson of Virginia, for War, and Cave Johnson of Tennessee, for Postmaster General rounded out a cabinet representing important parts of the nation. When the letters from New York finally reached Polk on January 30, he was about to leave for Washington. Instead of revealing his plans, he replied that he had decided to put off cabinet choices until he reached the Capital.[49]

Arriving in Washington on February 13, Polk spent another week getting settled before replying to Van Buren. By the time he did write on February 22 he had begun to have second thoughts about appointing any New York radical. On the way to Washington Polk had heard a number of complaints from Southerners against Butler, and on Capitol Hill he began to listen to conservatives from New York, who preferred Marcy to Butler or Flagg. Polk said in his letter of February 22 that he could not appoint a New Yorker Secretary of State because the post had to go to Buchanan. Furthermore, Polk claimed that southern pressure made it impossible for him to name a New York Democrat Secretary of the Treasury. Though willing to appoint Butler or Flagg to the War Department, Polk pointed out that Marcy had been "strongly recommended." When Van Buren received the letter on February 26—only six days before the inauguration—he began to fear that Polk was about to appoint the conservative Marcy to the cabinet.[50]

Horrified, Van Buren spent a day consulting with Wright, and then wrote an angry reply to Polk, whose letter, said Van Buren, had caused him "embarrassment, and not a little pain." Polk's failure to give first or second place in the cabinet to New York had outraged those whose "state pride [was] stronger than the love of office." "The honest Democracy" of New York, who had supported Polk, would "feel their pride severely wounded [and their] recollection of past events painfully revived" if Polk gave in to those who "look[ed] upon our state with an evil eye." Without waiting to hear from Butler Van Buren took it upon himself to say that his former partner would accept the position of Secretary of War. Otherwise it should go to Churchill C. Cambreleng—not Marcy.[51]

Unfortunately Polk had decided by February 25 that since time was running out he had to make a decision. He therefore wrote to Butler

[49] Sellers, *James K. Polk Continentalist*, pp. 180-192; Polk to MVB, Jan. 30, 1845, MVB, memorandum on three letters to Polk after Jan. 18, 1845, VBP; MVB to Polk, Feb. 10, 1845, Polk Papers, LC.

[50] Polk to MVB, Feb. 22, 1845, VBP; Sellers, *James K. Polk Continentalist*, pp. 193-198.

[51] MVB to Polk, Feb. 27, 1845, MVB, memorandum appended to Polk to MVB, Feb. 22, 1845, VBP.

in New York City asking him to become Secretary of War. Butler received the offer twenty-four hours later, on February 26—the very day that Polk's letter reached Van Buren. The unhappy Butler, who wanted to help Van Buren but had no interest in returning to Washington, wrote back at once saying that he would have accepted State or Treasury, but would not take the War Department. At the same time Butler's wife Harriet, who hated Washington, wrote to Van Buren taking the blame for her husband's decision. "Do not scold at me if I have done wrong," she begged; "you cannot imagine how disagreeable to me Washington & its dull rounds are." In great anguish Butler wrote to Van Buren twice on February 28th, first a one-page note recommending Cambreleng for the War Department and then twelve pages worrying about whether he had acted correctly "as a loyal son of New York," and blaming what had happened on Marcy.[52]

When Samuel J. Tilden and John L. O'Sullivan delivered Butler's refusal on March 1, Polk had to make some difficult decisions. The New Yorkers told him that a letter was on the way from Kinderhook, but Polk decided to wait no longer. He announced Marcy's appointment as Secretary of War even though John A. Dix warned that it would break up the Democratic majority in the Senate. Polk then wrote to Van Buren explaining that Marcy had been selected rather than Cambreleng or Flagg because neither of the latter had sufficient "reputation."[53]

As fate would have it, Van Buren's bitter letter opposing Marcy arrived just a few hours after Polk had made up his mind. Van Buren had entrusted the letter to his son Smith, who boarded the steamboat at Albany on February 28th, changed to the train in New York City the next day, and might have reached Washington that evening had he not been delayed by a train accident. When he finally arrived on March 2nd, he had to wait because Polk was at church. Sleepless and frustrated, Smith was ready to do battle when he was received by Polk in the afternoon. On reading Van Buren's letter, Polk said with embarrassment that he wished he had received it the night before. When Smith replied hotly that the letter "*guaranteed* [Butler's] *acceptance*," Polk insisted that it was too late. Polk went on to explain why he had

[52] Polk to Butler, Feb. 25, 1845 (copy), Polk Papers, LC; Butler to Polk, Feb. 27, 1845 (two letters), Polk to MVB, Feb. 25, 1845, Harriet Butler to Van Buren, Feb. 27, 1845, Butler to MVB, Feb. 28, 1845 (two letters), MVB, memorandum appended to Polk to MVB, Feb. 22, 1845, VBP.

[53] Polk to MVB, Mar. 1, 1845, O'Sullivan to MVB, Mar. 1, 1845, Smith Van Buren to MVB, Mar. 2, 1845, VBP.

acted as he did, but Smith, who was unconvinced, told his father that the story must have taken barely a "half hour to concoct."[54]

The next day Smith received a much more conciliatory letter from his father to Polk. Having learned that Polk had actually offered the War Department to Butler, Van Buren apologized for putting "too much feeling" in his previous letter. Smith passed it along with great reluctance because he knew that it "would turn out a plaister for the other." The handwriting was so bad that Polk had to hold it up and let Smith read it aloud looking over Polk's shoulder. Much relieved, Polk protested lamely that he had not realized that Van Buren and Marcy were on opposite sides, and promised in the future to give control over patronage in New York to Van Buren and Wright. Unmoved, Smith reported to his father that Polk had sold out to Buchanan, Cass and Walker. Smith also tried to get Tilden and O'Sullivan to join him in an ultimatum to Polk demanding that Butler be named in place of Marcy, but the two refused to go along. That evening Polk sent out letters appointing Buchanan to the State Department, Walker to Treasury, Marcy to War, and Bancroft to Navy.[55]

The cold, rainy weather at Polk's inauguration reflected the chilly attitude of the radical New Yorkers toward the President. They had gone to the convention expecting to nominate Van Buren for President, but had backed off first in favor of Wright for President, then Wright for Vice President, and then for nothing at all. In the correspondence over the cabinet, they had assumed that they would be awarded the State Department, but had settled for the Treasury Department, finally in desperation for the War Department, and then saw that prize go to the enemy. Shortly after the inauguration Van Buren put in order the letters he had exchanged with Polk, numbered them from one to nine, and composed a memorandum reflecting his suspicions and anger. Polk had erred, wrote Van Buren, in not giving at least the Treasury position to New York, and the President had not told Van Buren about the decision until it was too late for him to send a reply, or to try to get Butler to accept. Van Buren implied that Polk had acted deviously. Polk interpreted the events differently. Several years later he wrote in his diary: "Mr. Van Buren became offended with me . . .

[54] Smith Van Buren to MVB, Mar. 2, 1845, VBP.

[55] MVB to Polk, Mar. 1, 1845, Polk to MVB, Feb. 25, Mar. 3, 1845, Smith Van Buren to MVB, Mar. 3, Mar. 4, 1845, Smith Van Buren, Tilden and O'Sullivan to Polk, Mar. 3, 1845 (never sent), VBP; Tilden to William H. Havemeyer, Mar. 4, 1845, Tilden, *Letters*, I, 26-28; Sellers, *James K. Polk Continentalist*, pp. 202-203.

because I chose to exercise my own judgment in the selection of my own Cabinet, and would not be controlled by him."[56]

Since the make-up of the cabinet contributed to a deep rift within the Democratic party, the events are worth evaluating. What happened was in part the accident of history, in part the result of careful politics. If Polk and Van Buren had not lived so far apart, if Polk had not squandered so much time, if Van Buren had been better represented in Washington, if Smith Van Buren had arrived the night before he did, history might have been different. But such variations might not have made any difference. Worried about the divided Democracy in New York, the cautious Polk did not want to commit himself to Van Buren's wing. Since Polk was in debt to Walker, Buchanan, Cass, and Bancroft, the new President had to consider their interests before those of Van Buren. Polk also wanted to build a pro-Southern, conservative, annexationist cabinet, one in which Butler, Cambreleng, or Flagg would be out of place. Polk played a careful, clever political game, but in the end his decision to ignore Van Buren split the party.[57]

To appease Van Buren and Wright Polk tried to dispense patronage to the radicals in New York. He appointed Benjamin Butler district attorney in New York City, Michael Hoffman naval officer for the Port of New York, Ely Moore federal marshal for New York City, and Silas Wright's friend Ransom H. Gillet solicitor of the Treasury. In addition, such jobs as surveyor of customs in New York, postmaster and collector of customs in Buffalo, and federal marshal for western New York went to Van Buren's wing. The harvest would have been even richer if Flagg, Tilden, O'Sullivan, and William Cullen Bryant had accepted posts that Van Buren and Wright convinced them that they should reject. But at least as many other appointments went to conservatives, including the most crucial and powerful position of collector for the Port of New York. And in Washington Polk reduced

[56] MVB, memorandum appended to Polk to MVB, Feb. 22, 1845, VBP; Milo M. Quaife, ed., *The Diary of James K. Polk during His Presidency, 1845 to 1849* (Chicago, 1910), III, 74.

[57] Joseph G. Rayback is correct in his opinion that Polk should have named Butler, Flagg, or Cambreleng to the cabinet. To satisfy Van Buren it should have been Butler or Flagg in either State or Treasury. Rayback, "Van Buren's Break with Polk." Charles Sellers is unfair when he says that Van Buren took too long responding to Polk's letter of Feb. 22. Van Buren received that letter on the evening of Feb. 26, and sent his reply on Feb. 28, a day and a half later. It was Polk who wasted two precious months, first offering a post to Wright and then asking Wright and Van Buren to name someone for the top position in the cabinet. Polk also encouraged the expectations of the New Yorkers and then took away the prize. Sellers, *James K. Polk Continentalist*, pp. 199-201.

Van Buren's influence by removing Francis P. Blair as official spokes-man of the administration.[58]

In another attempt to please the radicals, Polk asked George Ban-croft to offer Van Buren the post of minister to England after Calhoun and others had turned it down. Bancroft started tactfully, pointing out that Metternich, Guizot and Talleyrand had all served as foreign minister after stepping down as prime minister. Furthermore, the crit-ical state of affairs with Great Britain demanded that a truly important figure be sent. Appealing to Van Buren's love of comfort, Bancroft estimated that the salary and Van Buren's private income would give him $20,000 a year. Bancroft concluded kindly that he and his wife felt that Van Buren's "personal happiness" would improve in England. Van Buren asked the opinion of his closest friends. Wright, Flagg and John Van Buren all agreed that the British crisis was not big enough to involve him and that Polk was simply trying to "plaster over all the rascality from the Baltimore Convention." "Nestled snugly, quietly and contentedly in a retirement," Van Buren wrote, he could not accept a favor from Polk, especially after the way New York had been treated.[59]

And so the campaign to regain the presidency ended as it had begun back in 1841, with Van Buren in retirement and with political sus-picion and rivalry very much in evidence, only this time directed at Polk rather than Calhoun. Three years later, two generations of Van Burens would not forget what Polk had done.

[58] Sellers, *James K. Polk Continentalist*, pp. 284-292; Butler to MVB, Mar. 10, May 7, 1845, Wright and MVB to O'Sullivan, Mar. 15, 1845, O'Sullivan to MVB, Mar. 29, 1845, Bancroft to MVB, April 19, 1845, Blair to MVB, Mar. 29, April 11, 1845, VBP; Tilden to———, Mar. 17, 1845, Dix to Tilden, June 21, 1845, Tilden, *Letters*, I, 29-30; Garraty, *Wright*, pp. 348-354; Polk, *Diary*, I, 103-104.

[59] Polk to Butler, May 5, 1845, Bancroft to MVB, May 5, 1845, Flagg to MVB, May 16, 1845, MVB to Bancroft, May 12, 1845, John Van Buren to MVB, May 14, 1845, VBP.

6. Martin Van Buren c. 1848

· 14 ·

FREE SOIL

Soon after his defeat in 1844, Van Buren wrote that his second retirement had reduced neither the "happiness [nor the] cheerfulness at
Lindenwald." Busy with building "a beautiful cottage . . . on the brow
of the hill" and a large hay barn in the meadow, he looked forward
to the "life of quiet contentment" that had once again been forced on
him. In the years that followed, Van Buren became more and more
the Dutch farmer, who bragged about having a thousand pear trees
and seventeen acres of potatoes. Still vigorous, he brushed away disappointment by going fishing with his son Martin, James K. Paulding,
Churchill C. Cambreleng, and Gouverneur Kemble. The Magician still
managed the light touch that encouraged Samuel J. Tilden to write
that perhaps he might select a wife for Van Buren. His four sons, now
aged twenty-eight to thirty-seven, still participated in his daily life: John
the attorney general in Albany, Smith and Abraham married and living
nearby, Martin living at Lindenwald. The sons still caused their father
concern—Abraham when he served in the Mexican War, Martin because he was never well. When John went to Washington to appear
before the Supreme Court, the anxious father asked his friend Francis
P. Blair to keep the unsteady young lawyer "from getting into any
scrapes."[1]

A charming glimpse of Van Buren in retirement is to be found in a
description by the English traveler Sarah M. Maury, who visited Lindenwald in July 1846. When Mrs. Maury and her son arrived without
warning one evening, Van Buren answered the door himself and immediately invited the two to stay overnight. After offering iced water,
lemonade and wine, he took them to his garden to gather flowers for
their room. Then, with his arm around the boy's neck, Van Buren led
the way to his potato patch, of which he was especially proud. Mrs.
Maury was entranced by this amiable "magician," who told stories
well, and whose conversation flowed "like a strain of varied music."[2]

Van Buren maintained his interest in such state affairs as the Anti-

[1] MVB to James S. Wadsworth, June 8, 1844, James W. Wadsworth, Jr., Family
Papers, LC; MVB to Paulding, April 25, 1846, Paulding, *Letters*, p. 429; MVB to
Kemble, June 2, 1847, Tilden to MVB, Mar. 29, 1845, VBP; MVB to Henry D. Gilpin,
Sept. 4, 1845, Joel R. Poinsett Papers, in the Henry D. Gilpin Papers, HSP; MVB to
Blair, Mar. 13, 1846, Nov. 6, 1847, April 9, 1849, Blair Family Papers, LC.

[2] Sarah M. Maury, *The Statesmen of America in 1846* (London, 1847), pp. 114-139.

Rent War, which swept through New York from Rensselaer County to Delaware County. For centuries much of the land in these counties had been rented out by the Van Rensselaers and other landowners to tenant farmers. Since rents were rarely collected, the farmers began to believe that they would never have to pay, and when Stephen Van Rensselaer's heirs tried to collect $400,000 in back rents in 1839, tenants donned Indian disguises and drove off sheriffs and rent collectors. During the campaign of 1844, Wright, Van Buren and the Regency courted the hostility of the farmers by declaring that the state should not help tenants who used force. Late in December 1844, just before Wright was sworn in as governor, Van Buren sent a letter in which he revealed where his sympathies lay. "We are," wrote Van Buren, "on the eve of a bloody insurrection by the Tenants . . . although I have strong hopes that the matter will be suppressed without much bloodshed." The landlords, he continued, were calling on the "Democracy" for help "as the only true conservative party in the Country," and the Democrats would have to put the uprising down. After he took office, Wright secured a law forbidding Indian disguises and providing state aid to quell the disturbances. Although Van Buren, Wright, and other Jacksonians supported part of the radical Loco Foco program, they showed their fundamental conservatism when the Anti-Rent revolt threatened property interests.[3]

The rebellion came to a climax in 1845 in Delaware County when farmers killed a sheriff trying to confiscate cattle. Wright declared the county in a state of insurrection, sent in troops and arrested a number of Anti-Renters including Dr. Smith A. Boughton, known as "Big Thunder." At the trial John Van Buren got into a fist fight with the defense counsel, but managed to win the conviction of "Big Thunder." During the next session of the legislature Wright had a law passed abolishing the right of landlords to seize the property of defaulting tenants, but this tardy reform was not enough to bring the rebels over to Wright's side.[4]

Wright's unpopularity with the Anti-Renters was only one reason that he was at a disadvantage when he ran for reelection in 1846. His veto of a bill to extend the canal system disturbed many conservatives and cost him support in western New York. There was little help

[3] Christman, *Tin Horns and Calico*, pp. 1-33; Garraty, *Wright*, pp. 319-322, 356-357; Wright to MVB, Oct. 8, 1844, Flagg to MVB, Dec. 23, 1844, VBP; Wright to Flagg, Dec. 4, 1844, Flagg-Wright Correspondence; MVB to Joel Poinsett, Dec. 27, 1845, Joel R. Poinsett Papers, in the Henry D. Gilpin Papers, HSP.

[4] Christman, *Tin Horns and Calico*, pp. 179, 240-249; Garraty, *Wright*, pp. 357-365.

coming from Washington. New York radicals were pleased when the independent treasury system, which had been done away with by the Whigs in 1841, was restored by Congress in 1846, but they were unhappy when Polk appointed the conservative William C. Bouck as receiver of federal money in New York City. Last-minute efforts by Polk to swing his administration behind Wright came too late. The conservative *Albany Argus* carried Wright's name on its masthead, but otherwise ignored him. His position became desperate when his Whig opponent John Young promised to pardon those sent to jail during the Anti-Rent riots. Just before the election Wright and John Van Buren asked the elder Van Buren to line up Anti-Renters to help the governor, but Van Buren was not the man to win over Anti-Renters. The Whigs defeated Wright and carried the state.[5]

During Wright's two years as governor, he and other radicals had been drawn into the rising controversy over slavery in the Southwest. In January 1845, Wright, Senator John A. Dix, and fourteen Democratic congressmen from New York opposed the resolution to annex Texas with its slavery. At the same time the New York legislature came close to passing a resolution against the annexation. When Texas was finally annexed and war broke out with Mexico, the debate shifted from Texas to the issue of slavery in the territories. In August 1846, Democratic congressmen Preston King of New York, and David Wilmot of Pennsylvania, added to an appropriation bill a proviso forbidding slavery in any territory to be acquired from Mexico. Congress adjourned without taking any action; so King introduced a resolution in the next session forbidding slavery in any territory thereafter acquired. This proviso was defeated in the House, and Polk's appropriation bill passed with no limitation on slavery.[6]

The debate over slavery widened the split between radicals and conservatives in New York. While radicals including King, Wright, Dix, and the Van Burens opposed the spread of slavery, Marcy and other conservatives supported Polk's expansionist policies regardless of slavery. As the division deepened, conservatives became known as Hunkers (because they hungered after spoils) and radicals as Barnburners (because they were radical enough to burn down the barn to get rid of the rats). In choosing his cabinet and dispensing patronage Polk had tried to satisfy both sides, but had alienated the radicals.

[5] Alexander, *Political History*, II, 114-125; Garraty, *Wright*, pp. 362-388; Christman, *Tin Horns and Calico*, pp. 268-275; Wright to MVB, Oct. 14, Nov. 10, 1846, VBP.

[6] Dix to MVB, Jan. 30, Feb. 18, 1845, Gideon Welles to MVB, Feb. 20, 1845, VBP; MVB to Blair, Feb. 11, 1845, Blair Family Papers, LC; Frederick J. Blue, *The Free Soilers: Third Party Politics* (Urbana, 1973), pp. 20-23, 27-29.

Many of them looked forward to nominating Silas Wright in place of Polk in 1848.[7]

But Wright was not destined to run for President. In the summer of 1847, he was living in retirement on his farm in Canton. There one hot August day he worked for many hours in the blazing sun digging ditches and bringing in loads of hay. The exertion was too great, and the next morning he suddenly dropped dead. In the days that followed Americans stopped to mourn the passing of the man who more than anyone else had come to symbolize the plain Republican of the North. As the young editor Walt Whitman put it, they "confess[ed] that [they] loved Silas Wright as a true democratic friend of the people. . . . The late governor was a MAN." Van Buren, for whom the death meant a heavy personal loss, commented as he had in the past, that Wright was a completely disinterested person. The Barnburners had been deprived of one of their strongest antislavery voices.[8]

The death heightened tension as the Democrats gathered for their state convention in Syracuse two weeks later. "The great chiefs of both factions," wrote abolitionist Henry B. Stanton, "were on the ground, and never was there a fiercer, more bitter and relentless conflict between the Narragansetts and the Pequods than this memorable conflict between the Barnburners and the Hunkers." The Barnburners became angry and bitter when Hunkers managed to seat a majority of the delegates and then voted down a resolution in favor of the Wilmot Proviso. When a Hunker "sneeringly" remarked that it was too late to do justice to Wright because he was dead, James S. Wadsworth sprang upon a table and warned the Hunkers: "Though it may be too late to do justice to Silas Wright, it is not too late to do justice to his assassins." The convention broke up with the party badly divided.[9]

In the weeks that followed, leadership in the Barnburner ranks began to fall on John Van Buren and other young Democrats who cared more about opposing Hunkers and stopping the spread of slavery than they did about keeping the Democratic party united. When John proposed a mass meeting of Barnburners, his father wrote Azariah Flagg an anxious letter asking him to stop the plan before it further divided the party. Despite the efforts of the old party leaders 4,000 Barnburners gathered at the railroad station in Herkimer in late October 1847, to

[7] Alexander, *Political History*, II, 126-127; Herbert D. A. Donovan, *The Barnburners . . . 1830-1852* (New York, 1925), pp. 15-47; Joseph G. Rayback, *Free Soil: The Election of 1848* (Lexington, 1970), pp. 60-61.

[8] Garraty, *Wright*, pp. 404-409. See also MVB to John M. Niles, Oct. 14, 1847, VBP.

[9] Stanton, *Random Recollections*, p. 159; Alexander, *Political History*, II, 126-128; Rayback, *Free Soil*, pp. 75-76.

hear David Wilmot and "Prince John" denounce slavery in the territories. Unlike his father John Van Buren could sway crowds with his speaking. According to one observer "the father was grave, urbane, wary, a safe counsellor, and accustomed to an argumentative and deliberate method of address," while "the son was enthusiastic, frank, bold, and given to wit, repartee." Won over by John's oratory, the Barnburners pledged to oppose any Democratic nominee in 1848 who favored the extension of slavery. In the state election the elder Van Buren's fears were realized when the Whigs won a sweeping victory over the divided Democrats. Unabashed, John told his father: "Mr. W. [Wright] is dead and I assume that you are sincere in not wishing to return to public life. I can therefore, hurt no one but myself." He promised to square accounts with his father's enemies.[10]

Not everyone shared John's assumption. During the fall his father received many letters seeking his views on the Wilmot Proviso and wondering whether he intended to run again for President. Wilmot himself implored Van Buren to "speak out" on the issue of slavery in the territories. With Wright dead, said Wilmot, "you Sir, are the only man left for us in the North, to whom we can look for advice." Supreme Court Justice Peter V. Daniel, on the other hand, assumed that Van Buren's devotion to the Constitution would make it impossible for him to support the proviso. Although Van Buren answered these letters evasively, he left the impression that he favored keeping slavery out of the territories.[11]

After the Christmas holidays Van Buren moved into Julian's Hotel in Washington Square, New York City, for the rest of the winter of 1847-1848, and began to take political initiative. Toward the end of the winter he brought Samuel J. Tilden a manuscript, saying humorously that the young man might make himself "immortal" by rewriting it. After revising the document, Tilden and John Van Buren read it to Barnburners in the legislature and then published it in April, in the *New York Atlas*, as the "Barnburner Manifesto." In addition to defending the Wilmot Proviso, the manifesto demanded that the Democratic national convention seat only Barnburners from New York.[12]

[10] The comparison of the two Van Burens is from Stanton, *Random Recollections*, p. 175. See also MVB to Flagg, Oct. 12, 1837, Flagg to MVB, Oct. 13, 1847, John Van Buren to MVB, Nov. 13, 1847, VBP; Alexander, *Political History*, II, 127-130; *Niles' Register*, 73 (1847), 144; Blue, *Free Soilers*, pp. 31-32.

[11] Wilmot to MVB, Oct. 6, 1847, MVB to Wilmot, Oct. 22, 1847, Daniel to MVB, Nov. 1, 1847, MVB to Daniel, Nov. 13, 1847, Daniel to MVB, Nov. 19, 1847, MVB to Campbell P. White, Nov. 29, 1847, VBP.

[12] MVB to Gorham Worth, Jan. 2, 1848, "Address of the Democratic members of the Legislature of the State of New York," April 12, 1848, VBP.

The manifesto was so well-received that John Van Buren asked his father if he would let the Barnburners name Van Buren for President at the Democratic convention. Van Buren's reply was a lecture on party politics. The Barnburners, said Van Buren, had been successful because they had worked within the party and had not challenged party traditions. In addition they had stressed all along that their only concern was in opposing slavery in the territories. If they suddenly tried to nominate their own candidate, they would be accused of trying to gain control of the party for their selfish interests. Moreover, said Van Buren, he could not win the election without the support of the South. Even though Van Buren had apparently turned against slavery in the territories, the letter showed that he was still the same old canny politician, still a party man.[13]

Van Buren did not slam the door on the nomination, and in the rest of the letter proved that he was out of retirement by giving the Barnburners detailed political instructions for the convention. These showed that he was not unalterably committed to opposing slavery in the territories. Although he suggested men such as Thomas Hart Benton, Governor Francis R. Shunk of Pennsylvania, and Henry Dodge of Wisconsin, all of whom opposed slavery in the territories, Van Buren did not insist on one of these candidates. He told the Barnburners that they should be prepared to back such proslavery Democrats as Lewis Cass, James Buchanan, Vice President George M. Dallas, or Levi Woodbury. During the campaign, Cass, who was eventually nominated, began to support popular sovereignty, or letting territories decide for themselves on slavery, as an alternative to opposing slavery in the territories, and it is tempting to wonder whether Van Buren might have been content with popular sovereignty in 1848. But Cass was not speaking out for popular sovereignty before the convention, and none of those that Van Buren would accept—Buchanan, Dallas, or Woodbury—was noted for backing the idea. On the eve of the Democratic convention of 1848 Martin Van Buren was leaning toward opposing slavery in the territories.

But Van Buren was more concerned about party factions than ideology in preparing for the convention. In his letter he told the Barnburners that they must insist on being recognized by the party. If the convention refused to seat the Barnburners or admitted Hunkers, the Barnburners should walk out. Van Buren also revealed his bitterness

[13] John Van Buren to MVB, April 20, 1848, MVB to John Van Buren, May 3, 1848, VBP; Rayback, *Free Soil*, pp. 175-181; Blue, *Free Soilers*, pp. 44-47; Joseph G. Rayback, "Martin Van Buren's Desire for Revenge in the Campaign of 1848," *Mississippi Valley Historical Review*, 40 (Mar. 1954), 707-716.

toward Polk by claiming that the President had persisted in attacking New York intentionally ever since he was elected in 1844. If the convention renominated Polk, Van Buren told the Barnburners to march out in protest.[14]

The Barnburners followed these instructions closely at the Democratic convention, which was held in Baltimore in May. At the start they refused to agree ahead of time to support any candidate who might be selected by the convention. (Polk had decided not to run.) When the credentials committee tried to seat both Barnburners and Hunkers, neither side would accept the ruling. Finally, the Barnburners exceeded Van Buren's suggestions by marching out as a group to show their displeasure at the nomination of Lewis Cass.[15]

On returning home John Van Buren and other young Barnburners made plans for their own convention in Utica in June and began to seek a presidential candidate. When they asked Benton, he turned them down, saying that such a move would make the Hunkers the regular party in New York. Benton, Francis P. Blair, Dix, and Flagg all tried to keep the elder Van Buren from joining a third party, but Benjamin Butler convinced Van Buren that he should join the Barnburners and form the "nucleus [for a] northern *Democratic* party, [which would] bring the despots & ingrates of the South . . . to their senses." Van Buren told Blair bitterly that the New York Democrats had been so "grossly humiliated" by the party that they might never take part in a national convention again. He predicted that the Barnburners would nominate Butler for President and carry New York.[16]

Despite his prediction, it is apparent that Van Buren was interested in the nomination for himself. When the letter came asking whether he would let his name be put forward at Utica, he and his son Martin prepared two lengthy drafts before sending a nineteen-page reply. Van Buren said that he did not wish to run, but he outlined a party platform. Since the founding fathers had understood the inconsistency between slavery and the "principles of the Revolution," they had tried to curtail it with measures such as the Northwest Ordinance, but had otherwise

[14] MVB to John Van Buren, May 3, 1848, VBP; Rayback, *Free Soil*, pp. 177-181; Alto L. Whitehurst, "Martin Van Buren and the Free Soil Movement" (Doctoral dissertation, University of Chicago, 1935), pp. 134-137.

[15] Rayback, *Free Soil*, pp. 186-191; Whitehurst, "Van Buren and the Free Soil Movement," pp. 144-145.

[16] Benton to MVB, May 31, 1848, Butler to MVB, May 29, May 30, May 31, 1848, Flagg to MVB, June 19, 1848, MVB to Butler, June 20, 1848, MVB to Dix, June 20, 1848, VPB; Oliver C. Gardiner, *The Great Issue: or, the Three Presidential Candidates: Being a Brief Sketch of the Free Soil Question* (New York, 1848); Smith, *Blair Family*, pp. 230-233; MVB to Blair, June 22, 1848, Blair Family Papers, LC.

left decisions on slavery up to the states. Van Buren disagreed with the plank in the Democratic platform that said that Congress had no power to stop slavery in the territories; he would keep "the evils of slavery" out of the territories. Won over by Van Buren's rhetoric, the delegates disregarded his refusal, and nominated him unanimously for President.[17]

The Democratic opposition reacted in horror. Polk called the Barnburners a "dangerous attempt to organize Geographical parties upon the slave question, . . . more threatening to the Union than anything . . . since . . . the Hartford convention." Calhoun received a letter accusing Van Buren of seeking revenge, and calling his Utica letter "the fierce war-cry of a new and formidable party," led by "a bold, unscrupulous and vindictive demagogue."[18]

Northern antislavery leaders reacted sympathetically but suspiciously to Van Buren's conversion. Salmon Chase, who led the Liberty party in Ohio, preferred John Van Buren to his father, and "conscience" Whig Charles Francis Adams, the son of John Quincy Adams, was worried about Van Buren's assurance that he would veto any attempt to abolish slavery in the District of Columbia. When Adams raised the point with Van Buren, the New Yorker gave him what Adams called an "enigmatic" answer. But despite their hesitation the antislavery men began to fall in line. John Parker Hale of New Hampshire, was nominated for President by the Liberty party, but he was willing to stand aside. As Charles Sumner of Massachusetts said, "things tend to Van Buren as our candidate; I am willing to take him. With him we can break the slavepower; that is our first aim."[19]

On August 9, a throng of about 20,000 politicians gathered in Buffalo, the Queen City of the Lakes, to meet in an enormous tent in the city park. Henry B. Stanton noted some of those who were there: New York Democrats who wanted "to punish the assassins of Silas Wright"; proslavery Whigs who hoped "to strike down" Whig presidential candidate Zachary Taylor because he had "dethroned" Henry

[17] The Barnburners nominated Henry Dodge for Vice President, but he turned the offer down. MVB to Samuel Waterbury and others, June 20, 1848, VBP; Gardiner, *The Great Issue*, pp. 110-116; Rayback, *Free Soil*, pp. 209-210.

[18] Polk, *Diary*, III, 502; Joseph W. Lesnesne to Calhoun, July 5, 1848, Calhoun, *Correspondence*, pp. 450-451.

[19] Blue, *Free Soilers*, pp. 54-65; Rayback, *Free Soil*, pp. 212-218; Chase to John Van Buren, June 19, 1848, Tilden, *Letters*, I, 50-52; Adams to MVB, July 16, 1848, MVB to Adams, July 24, 1848, VBP; MVB to Francis P. Blair, July 26, 1848, Blair Family Papers, LC; Charles Sumner to John Greenleaf Whittier, July 12, 1848, Edward L. Pierce, *Memoir and Letters of Charles Sumner* (1893; reprint, New York, 1969), III, 168-170; Frank Otto Gatell, " 'Conscience and Judgment'; the Bolt of the Massachusetts Conscience Whigs," *The Historian*, 21 (1958-1959), passim, especially pp. 42-44.

Clay; antislavery Whigs who "breath[ed] the spirit" of John Quincy Adams. While the crowd sweltered under the tent listening to the oratory, a smaller meeting of delegates hammered out the platform and selected the candidates. By prior consultation delegates from the Liberty party agreed to support Van Buren if the Barnburners voted for a strong antislavery platform. The final wording contrived by Salmon Chase did not go as far as many wanted, but it directly opposed slavery in the territories and denounced the "reckless hostility of the Slave Power." The platform called for the Bentonian policy of free land for "ACTUAL SETTLERS," and supported the Jacksonian ideal of paying off the national debt. To attract Whigs there were also planks calling for a protective tariff and for "river and harbor improvements." The platform, which had something in it for everyone in the North, ended with the slogan: "Free Soil, Free Speech, Free Labor, and Free Men!" The new party, which was called the Free-Soil party, then nominated Van Buren for President with 244 votes—a strong majority over Hale, who received 183 votes. In an ironic aftermath, the delegates named Charles Francis Adams for Vice President, thereby linking the son of Andrew Jackson's old opponent with Jackson's former Vice President.[20]

Though disagreeing with a few of the planks in the platform, Van Buren promptly accepted it. With its mixture of old Jacksonianism and the newer Free-Soil, Bentonian and Whiggish planks, the platform was just right for Van Buren, who had been modifying Jacksonian Democracy ever since he helped create it and who had begun to swing away from the South after the nullification crisis. In his acceptance speech he showed how his views had matured. Clutching his Jacksonian credentials, he opposed tariff protection and said that Congress should give land to settlers only if revenue could be found elsewhere. But he went on to point out that he had opposed the annexation of Texas because it meant adding new slave territory; he believed that slaveowners did not have the right to take slaves to the territories, and he had even changed his mind and would not veto a bill to abolish slavery in the District of Columbia.[21]

Though other Free-Soilers were far more idealistic—Adams, for example, said that the United States must choose between slavery and the Declaration of Independence—they rallied behind Van Buren with good grace. The skeptical Salmon Chase admitted that Van Buren's nomination was well-received in the Western Reserve. Before a cheer-

---

[20] Blue, *Free Soilers*, pp. 70-80; Stanton, *Random Recollections*, pp. 162-163; "Free Soil Platform," Schlesinger, *Presidential Elections*, II, 902-905.

[21] MVB to Benjamin Butler and others, Aug. 22, 1848, VBP.

ing crowd at Faneuil Hall in Boston, Charles Sumner said that he was proud to support "the Van Buren of to-day,—the veteran statesman, sagacious, determined, experienced, who at an age when most men are rejoicing to put off their armor girds himself anew, and enters the lists as the champion of freedom." Politicians in New York even began to look beyond their state and dream of victory. Reminding his old law partner that he had been nominated by a national party, Benjamin Butler urged Van Buren to stress "broad grounds" and stop talking about "the injustice done to the democracy of *this state*." Jabez Hammond believed that Van Buren was leading a party that could force the election to the House in 1848 and then win in 1852. Other Democrats—John M. Niles and Gideon Welles of Connecticut, Walt Whitman and John A. Dix, to name a few—joined in the crusade.[22]

But the crusade failed to overcome the suspicion and scorn of Van Buren's opponents. Van Buren was, said Polk privately, "the most fallen man" he had ever known. Calhoun's correspondents called Van Buren an "unprincipled intriguer" and the "most unprincipled of politicians." Webster dismissed his old antagonist with a series of quips. To "express confidence in Mr. Van Buren," sneered Black Daniel, "would border on the ludicrous, if not on the contemptible"; "with his accustomed good humor," Van Buren must surely laugh to think that "the leader of the Free Spoil party should have so suddenly become the leader of the Free Soil party." Van Buren had to answer charges that he owned a southern plantation and that he was an infidel. One cartoon showed him milking a cow held by Cass and Taylor, with Cass saying: "Matty is at his old tricks again and going in for the spoils." Another showed Van Buren on the back of son John, fording "Salt River" with the White House on the other side. Taylor and Clay are seen drowning while John says: "Hold on Dad & I'll put you through."[23]

---

[22] Charles G. DeLavan of Baltimore, agreed with Hammond. In a letter to Calhoun DeLavan wrote that Van Buren had "set the ball in motion" that Webster would carry to victory in 1852. Calhoun himself predicted that the Free-Soil movement would lead to "two great sectional parties." DeLavan to Calhoun, Oct. 24, 1848, Chauncey S. Boucher and Robert P. Brooks, eds., "Correspondence Addressed to John C. Calhoun, 1837-1849," American Historical Association, *Annual Report for the Year 1929* (Washington, D.C., 1930), pp. 484-485; Calhoun to Thomas G. Clemson, Aug. 11, 1848, Calhoun, *Correspondence*, p. 761; Chase to MVB, Aug. 21, 1848, Hammond to MVB, Aug. 7, 1848, Butler to MVB, Aug. 16, 1848, Adams, letter of acceptance, Aug. 22, 1848, quoted from *Orleans Republican*, Sept. 6, 1848, VBP; Sumner, *Letters*, III, 170-171.

[23] Charles G. DeLavan to Calhoun, Oct. 24, 1848, J. T. Trasker to Calhoun, Jan. 2, 1849, Boucher and Brooks, *Correspondence Addressed to Calhoun*, pp. 485, 489;

John did carry his father in the campaign, for while the candidate stayed home tending his garden, his son was out on the hustings. Thirty-eight, taller and more handsome than his father, John Van Buren had great political promise. The passage of time had matured him, stripping away some of his deviltry without removing the wit, the humor, the sharpness of mind, and the enormous vitality. Here was a Van Buren who had not been forced to make his own way; one who had graduated from Yale and had visited the court of Queen Victoria; a Van Buren with charisma rather than caution. At ease with each other, father and son enjoyed being together, did not hesitate to show their love and respect, exchanging wit and laughter whenever they had the chance. Loyalty to his father stirred John Van Buren to a strenuous effort. When asked why he was campaigning so vigorously, he told a story about a boy who was seen furiously pitching hay. To a bystander who wanted to know why he was working so hard, the lad replied: "Stranger, Dad's under there."[24]

The Free-Soil movement did not sweep the North. Too many Democrats—even Van Buren's friends Benton, Blair, George Bancroft, Robert Rantoul, and Theodore Sedgwick—stuck with the party of Andrew Jackson. No great stampede of Whigs took place. Zachary Taylor won the presidential election with 1,360,967 popular and 163 electoral votes, over Lewis Cass, who polled 1,222,342 popular and 127 electoral votes. Van Buren won but 291,804 popular votes—ten percent of the total—and carried no states. Even so, the Free-Soilers did far better than the Liberty party in 1840, and in the states of Massachusetts, Ohio and New York, they won 193,922 votes—over twenty-one percent of the total.

And Van Buren's candidacy had an effect on the outcome of the election, especially in New York, where Taylor won the state with 218,603 votes, compared to 120,510 for Van Buren and 114,320 for Cass. Most of Van Buren's votes were at the expense of Cass, who received 123,000 fewer votes than Polk in 1844, rather than Taylor, who did almost as well as Clay in 1844. Van Buren ran best in the old Jacksonian counties from Delaware County north to St. Lawrence County, but he also did well in the old Anti-Masonic, Whiggish western part of the state. By running John A. Dix, the Free-Soilers also

---

Webster, speech, Sept. 1, 1848, Webster, *Writings and Speeches*, XVI, 123-129; MVB to Robert E. Remsen, Oct. 13, 1848, VBP; cartoons at the HSP.

[24] For a glimpse of father and son together, see L. E. Chittenden, *Personal Reminiscences, 1840-1890, Including Some Not Hitherto Published of Lincoln and the War* (New York, 1893), pp. 11-17; Alexander, *Political History*, II, 129; Schlesinger, *Age of Jackson*, p. 467; Shepard, *Van Buren*, pp. 1-2.

split the Democratic vote for governor, enabling the Whig candidate, Hamilton Fish, to be elected. But the Free-Soil movement did not determine the outcome of the presidential campaign. If there had been no Free-Soil candidate, New York would probably have gone Democratic, but Ohio would in all likelihood have remained Whig instead of going to Cass. Changes in New York and Ohio would have still left Taylor the winner.[25]

In New York the leaders of the Free-Soil movement ranged from men such as Preston King who were mainly concerned about slavery, to Dix and others who were swayed by more practical political considerations. Silas Wright's neighbor King, who had opposed slavery in the territories since 1846, was the only Free-Soiler in New York to win a seat in Congress. Even Dix at first resisted the idea of a third party, and only agreed reluctantly to run for governor. James S. Wadsworth and William Cullen Bryant were closer to King, Samuel J. Tilden, Benjamin Butler and John Van Buren were closer to Dix.[26]

As for Van Buren, his motives were mixed. In part, his decision to run was a further step in the evolution of his Jacksonianism, the logical culmination of his shift away from defending slavery and relying on the South. At the same time a desire to get back at his opponents in the party played an important part. Van Buren had convinced himself that Polk, Cass, the southern Democrats, and the Hunkers had willfully sought to destroy the Democratic party in New York, and in so doing had endangered both the national party and the nation. This is not to say that Van Buren's campaign was pure revenge. Van Buren was not the sort of man who harbored grudges or sought to destroy anything—especially a political organization. If anything, he believed that he was defending his organization in New York and was helping his Barnburner friends. In a letter four years later he said he had run because John Van Buren, "Sammy" Tilden and others needed help. The campaign, wrote Van Buren, had been "an exceedingly unpleasant but unavoidable sacrifice to the feelings and unsurpassed injuries of Friends who had stood by me throughout evil and through good report, & had, more than any others, helped to make me what I had been." In 1848, Van Buren acted neither as a moral idealist nor as a revengeful cynic, but rather as the loyal New York Democrat he had always been.[27]

[25] Rayback, *Free Soil*, pp. 279-287; Holman Hamilton, "Election of 1848," Schlesinger, *Presidential Elections*, II, pp. 892-896.

[26] Blue, *Free Soilers*, pp. 81-103; Schlesinger, *Age of Jackson*, pp. 450-468.

[27] MVB to Andrew Beaumont, Feb. 10, 1852, reproduced from a private collection, Andrew Beaumont Papers, LC. John Van Buren denied that his father acted out of

In the years that followed it would have been logical for Van Buren to stand with the thousands of northern Democrats who continued to oppose slavery in the territories. But he was sixty-five in 1848, and there were no more campaigns in him. As his younger and more committed antislavery friends moved on to new battles, Van Buren returned to Lindenwald and the old Democratic party. In 1850, he quickly fell in line behind his old rival Henry Clay and the rising young Democrat Stephen A. Douglas, in defending the compromise over slavery. Chatting with Clay at Kinderhook in 1849, Van Buren had predicted correctly that "old prejudices" would force the Kentuckian to defend slavery. In 1850, after Clay offered his compromise proposals putting no restriction on slavery in the territories acquired from Mexico, Van Buren wrote that Clay's speeches had "added a crowning grace to his public life."

In 1852, Van Buren refused to support the Free-Soil ticket. When the Democrats endorsed the compromise of 1850 and nominated the proslavery Franklin Pierce, Salmon Chase was disturbed that the Democratic convention had given "sanctions and guarantees to slavery," and asked Van Buren to "raise a warning." Van Buren refused. Instead, he sent a letter to Tammany Hall backing the entire Democratic ticket, and then suggested that Chase read the letter. Later Van Buren told the Young Men's Club of Chicago that slavery was no longer an issue because Americans had turned their attention to "bringing into successful operation the vast resources of our country." "Ours," he said complacently, "has become a land of unequalled prosperity and plenty." Ever in tune with his fellow Americans, Van Buren had again let loyalty to party and love of prosperity obscure his moral view.[28]

Not only was he becoming accustomed to the new prosperity, but he was adjusting to new political ideals as well. Writing to Gideon Welles in 1851, he commented that the republican principles of '98 were waning. It was the fate of Van Buren and other Northerners of his generation to support—in theory at least—the republican ideals of Jefferson as these were subjected to social and economic change; in the middle of the nineteenth century, Jeffersonians and their successors turned to broader principles that had national significance. Van Buren was recognizing this shift.[29]

---

pique. *New York Evening Post Extra*, Nov. 8, 1849.

[28] MVB to Francis P. Blair, Mar. 3, July 9, 1850, Blair Family Papers, LC; Chase to MVB, June 27, 1852, MVB to Tammany Society, July 1, 1852, MVB to Chase, July 7, 1852, MVB to Young Men's Club of Chicago, Sept. 14, 1852, printed in the *New-York Evening Post*, Oct. 18, 1852, VBP.

[29] For the ideals of republicanism, see Wood, *Creation of the American Republic.*

Van Buren had known for some time that an era had passed. The break began in June 1845, when word passed north that the Old Hero had died at the Hermitage. Van Buren was gratified to learn that he had been on Jackson's mind near the end. When asked to name the men in whom he had had the greatest confidence, Jackson had started with Van Buren, calling him "perfectly Honest—as A Statesman— quick and penetrating—possessing A powerful mind—Governed by strict Integrity." But still smarting from the blows delivered by Polk, Van Buren did not respond emotionally when news of the death came. Asked to contribute $250 to a monument for Jackson, he offered only $100. He also declined to give a eulogy in New York City, promising instead that some day he would write a memoir. The day never came, but Van Buren's autobiography was in part a tribute to Jackson, and son John did deliver a eulogy in Albany that June.[30]

From then on Van Buren was frequently reminded that time was slipping by. At the New York constitutional convention in 1846 James Tallmadge was the only important member from the 1821 convention to participate. Daniel D. Tompkins, Rufus King, William W. Van Ness were dead; Erastus Root and James Kent were dying. Soon after the convention Gorham Worth wrote to Van Buren to describe the passing of the "political veterans of 1810," and to ask whimsically how they would all feel when they met in the next world. As the debate over slavery began in 1850, Henry D. Gilpin sent Van Buren a list of those no longer in the Congress and described how Clay, Webster and Calhoun had aged. In the spring Jabez Hammond lamented: "*The* great Southern Statesman is no more. What a mind has gone out! *John C. Calhoun!*" Woodbury and Clay followed. The last time he saw Woodbury, wrote Van Buren, the New Hampshireman had "the stamp of death upon him." Early in 1852, Benton warned Van Buren that Clay was "calmly viewing the approaches of death." By the end of the year Van Buren had seen the passing of a generation: Jackson, Wright, Kent, Adams, Polk, Calhoun, Woodbury, Clay, and Webster were gone.[31]

For the concept of the Union, see Nagel, *One Nation Indivisible*. See also Wilson, "Liberty and Union"; MVB to Welles, July 31, 1851, Welles Papers, LC.

[30] George E. Purser to MVB, June 18, 1845, William Tyack to MVB, July 12, 1845, VBP; John Van Buren, "Eulogy to Andrew Jackson, June 30, 1845," Benjamin M. Dusenbery, *Monument to the Memory of General Andrew Jackson Containing Twenty- five Eulogies and Sermons Delivered on the Occasion of His Death* (Philadelphia, 1845), pp. 96-107; MVB to John L. O'Sullivan, July 29, 1845, Dreer Collection, HSP.

[31] Alexander, *Political History*, II, 104; Worth to MVB, Jan. 24, 1847, William Kent to MVB, Dec. 17, 1847, Gilpin to MVB, Jan. 27, 1850, Benton to MVB, Jan. 11, 1852, VBP; Hammond to Henry S. Randall, April 23, 1850, Jabez D. Hammond Miscellaneous

Aware that he might not have much time left, Van Buren was eager to preserve his record. He had been not at all pleased by the two scurrilous books published by the old Canadian revolutionary William L. Mackenzie, who bore a grudge because President Van Buren had not released Mackenzie soon enough from jail. When the Polk administration took over the New York custom house, a trunk was discovered containing hundreds of revealing letters to and from Van Buren, Jesse Hoyt, Benjamin Butler, and other members of the Regency. Mackenzie had published these in two lurid volumes. After retrieving some of his correspondence from Blair, Andrew J. Donelson and Amos Kendall, Van Buren started work both on his autobiography and his *Origin and Course of Political Parties*. Jabez Hammond encouraged Van Buren, assuring him that "no living man [could] write so accurate an account of political operations in this country." Hammond impressed on his friend the need to describe events "as they *were* not as they *ought* to have been."[32]

Van Buren's family kept him as interested in the present as he was in the past. In the fall of 1849, John abandoned the Free-Soil party to try to bring about a reconciliation between the Barnburners and the Hunkers. He drew some Democratic support for Vice President in 1852, but succumbed to the weakness of character that led some to call him "Alcibiades" and soon began to fade from national political power. After the death of his wife he invited gossip by his indiscreet behavior. On one particularly flagrant occasion a sharp-tongued observer described John's female companion as the "suspicious 'Mrs. Jones' generally concluded to be chattel held in joint tenancy by some gentlemen." Maunsell Field, a member of the New York City bar, rightly observed that no one had ever "wasted such opportunities and talents" as John Van Buren.[33]

Van Buren's life now revolved more and more about his two younger sons, Martin and Smith. In 1849, deciding to leave Lindenwald to Smith, Van Buren invited his youngest son and family to live on the estate. It was a tragic year, for Smith's wife Ellen was slowly dying

---

Papers, NYHS; MVB to Francis P. Blair, Sept. 14, 1851, Blair Family Papers, LC.

[32] Mackenzie, *Butler*; Mackenzie, *Van Buren*; Lynch, *Epoch and a Man*, pp. 501-503; Blair to MVB, July 20, 1849, April 30, May 14, 1851, Hammond to MVB, Mar. 29, 1852, MVB to Butler, Dec. 3, 1856, VBP; MVB to Blair, June 16, 1849, Blair Family Papers, LC.

[33] Blue, *Free Soilers*, pp. 159-160; MVB to Francis P. Blair, July 15, Sept. 14, 1851, Blair Family Papers, LC; Bradford R. Wood to MVB, Feb. 25, 1851, VBP; John Van Buren to Isaac Fowler, Mar. 21, 1853, Tilden, *Letters*, I, 99-101; Strong, *Diary*, I, 356; Maunsell B. Field, *Memories of Many Men and Some Women* (New York, 1873), p. 181.

of consumption. Perhaps as a diversion Smith hired the architect Richard Upjohn, and planned changes in the structure of the house that were to cost $10,000. At the end of the year Ellen died, leaving her husband with three young children. The death drew Smith even closer to his father.[34]

Van Buren's son Martin had not much longer to live. The small, sickly Martin had never married but stayed close to his father, writing letters and occasionally joining him on fishing trips. In 1853, Van Buren took his son abroad, hoping that the European climate would prove beneficial. Even though Van Buren insisted on being treated as a private citizen, he was received by—among others—the King of Belgium, Pope Pius IX and Count Camillo Benso di Cavour during the tour. In June 1854, he established himself in Italy, at Villa Falangola, overlooking the bay at Sorrento, where he began serious work on his autobiography. "At the age of seventy-one, and in a foreign land," he wrote, "I commence a sketch of the principal events of my life." Young Martin, meanwhile, enjoyed the waters at Aix-les-Bains before departing for London to consult doctors. During the winter Van Buren corresponded with his son, worrying that the London weather might be injurious to his health, and eventually Martin joined his father in Paris. On March 15, 1855, Van Buren turned down a dinner invitation from Emperor Louis Napoleon, saying that his son lay dying, and four days later Martin was gone. Van Buren, who had suffered through the early deaths of his wife and two daughters-in-law, once again faced loss and the pain of bereavement.[35]

Back home in the spring Van Buren resumed the life he so much enjoyed. Although he suffered occasionally from asthma, and gout made it difficult for him to put his boot on, his health remained good. Age did not diminish his pleasure in comfortable living. Since he had accumulated a small fortune, he could afford to buy expensive shirts, silk handkerchiefs and good sherry. He could visit his sons in New York City and his friends Kemble at Cold Harbor and Paulding at Hyde Park. In the summer there were trips to his favorite watering

[34] MVB to Gorham Worth, April 9, 1849, VBP; MVB to Enos T. Throop, June 1, 1849, Van Buren-Throop Letters, NYSL; MVB to Francis P. Blair, Nov. 2, Dec. 11, 1849, May 6, 1850, Blair Family Papers, LC.

[35] MVB to Henry D. Gilpin, Sept. 16, 1851, Joel R. Poinsett Papers, in the Henry D. Gilpin Papers, HSP; MVB to William L. Marcy, Mar. 25, 1853, Marcy Papers, LC; Jules Van Braet to MVB, Aug. 6, 1853, MVB to Lord Palmerston, June 21, 1853, Count Cavour to MVB, Oct. 1, 1853, MVB to Martin Van Buren, Jr., Sept. 19, Nov. 12, 1854, MVB to Mr. Corbin, Mar. 15, 1855, MVB to Lord Breadalbane, June 19, 1855, VBP; Field, *Memories*, pp. 131-132.

places. At home he tended his farm, entertained his guests, wrote letters to attractive women, and read his books. Benjamin Butler presented Van Buren with the histories of George Bancroft and William Prescott, and Nathaniel Hawthorne sent a manuscript from Liverpool for Van Buren to forward to a publisher. In 1858, Van Buren asked Samuel J. Tilden to purchase the eight-volume set of *Scott's Family Bible* for Lindenwald if he could get it for $15. Tilden managed Van Buren's finances and Smith Van Buren looked after Lindenwald.[36]

Part of Van Buren's contentment lay in his calm acceptance of approaching death. He had watched so many younger people die, especially in his own family, that death was no stranger to him. He admonished Nicholas Trist to "remember that I am old and may slip off at any moment, a thing you young people can't remember." In a letter to Smith, the Magician admitted that at seventy-six he could expect only two more years of life. And he could jest about death to Tilden: "When I am gone I trust you will, as my confidential representative, be more punctual in the performance of your engagements." Reminders of his mortality became more frequent as death further thinned the ranks of great Jacksonians, claiming Marcy, Benton and Butler. Van Buren grew more and more anxious to complete his two books, and enlisted the aid of Smith. When Smith lagged in his efforts, his father wrote in his usual friendly fashion that if the work had become "irksome," Smith could drop it with no hard feeling. The well-organized Van Buren informed his son that the project needed three hours a day six days a week for two years. Van Buren had been dead a number of years before either book was published.[37]

Only occasionally did politics intrude on Van Buren's preparations for death. In the election of 1856 he could not bring himself to join old Jacksonians, Blair and Wadsworth in supporting the new Republican party and its presidential candidate John C. Frémont. Congrat-

---

[36] MVB to Kemble, Nov. 19, 1855, Butler to MVB, Mar. 20, 1856, I. U. Silleck to MVB, Sept. 9, 1858, Tilden to MVB, Feb. 2, 1859, John H. Gardner and William Landon, Jr., to MVB, June 17, 1859, VBP; MVB to Mrs. Henry D. Gilpin, May 21, 1857, Joel R. Poinsett Papers, in the Henry D. Gilpin Papers, HSP; MVB to Charlotte Cushman, April 5, 1858, Charlotte Cushman Papers, LC; MVB to Tilden, June 29, Oct. 18, 1858, Jan. 19, Aug. 22, 1859, Samuel J. Tilden Papers, NYPL; MVB to Tilden, Jan. 19, 1859, Tilden, *Letters*, I, 125.

[37] MVB to Trist, April 25, 1857, Nicholas Trist Papers, LC; MVB to Tilden, June 16, 1858, Tilden, *Letters*, I, 124; [Albany] *Atlas and Argus*, July 11, 1857; Charlotte A. Brown to MVB, Nov. 11, 1858, Joel R. Poinsett Papers, in the Henry D. Gilpin Papers, HSP; MVB to Butler, Dec. 3, 1856, MVB to Smith Van Buren, Mar. 24, Oct. 7-8, 1858, Francis P. Blair to MVB, April 12, 1858, Gilpin to MVB, Mar. 8, 1859, VBP.

ulating Tilden for sticking with the Democracy, Van Buren lectured his young colleague on what was wrong with the Republican party. For the first time, he said, one section of the country was trying to gain control of the government without the cooperation of the other. If the Republicans succeeded, other efforts would follow because men had too much of "wild beasts in them to stop the pursuit" after they had once "tasted blood." Democrats who thought they could vote Republican once and then go back to the old party were participants in a dangerous experiment. Returning to an old theme, Van Buren reiterated that in order to save the Union the Democratic party was indispensable because it alone could "maintain party cohesions between men of the free and slave states." He also showed flashes of his old New York partisanship, predicting that if Frémont were elected, he would be controlled by the New York Whigs William Henry Seward, Horace Greeley and Thurlow Weed, who had become Republicans.

Van Buren had been very disturbed by the repeal of the Missouri Compromise that formed part of the Kansas-Nebraska Act of 1854, but since he was away in Europe he could do nothing about it. By 1856, however, he had become sufficiently reconciled to the act to defend it in a letter to Tammany Hall. He defended the right of Congress to transfer its power to legislate for the territories to the territories themselves and commented favorably on James Buchanan's support for the Kansas-Nebraska Act in his acceptance message. The aging former Free-Soiler did not favor renewal of the Missouri Compromise or direct legislation by Congress for the territories. Whereas in 1848 he had campaigned to end slavery in the territories, he now believed that the most important goal was to end the "slavery agitation." If only Congress could avoid any action for a while, he thought that the excitement in the North would soon subside.[38]

Three years later, after John Brown's raid, Van Buren showed that he was still in sympathy with the South. He called Brown a man of "lawless . . . disposition," waging war on a section of the country "distinguished for hospitality, personal manners, amiable disposition, love of country and respect for principle & public virtue." Reverting to his old state-rights philosophy, Van Buren referred to the original thirteen states as the "old Confederacy." Distorting history, he praised Virginians for a long history of trying to restrict slavery. Although he

[38] MVB to Blair, May 21, 1856, Blair Family Papers, LC; Wadsworth to MVB, Aug. 1, 1856, MVB to Tammany Society, July 1, 1856, VBP; MVB to Tilden, Sept. 1, 1856, Tilden Papers, NYPL; MVB, *Letter of Ex-President Van Buren*; MVB, *Political Parties*, pp. 355-357.

believed that slavery was wrong, he felt it was equally wrong to resort to political solutions, or to abolish it "by the sword." The North, he concluded, should show good will toward the South.[39]

As Southerners moved toward secession in 1860, Van Buren maintained his position of moderation and conciliation by supporting Stephen A. Douglas over John C. Breckinridge for the Democratic nomination. One reason Van Buren backed Douglas was that the New Yorker agreed with Douglas' policy of popular sovereignty in the territories. Breckinridge went beyond popular sovereignty and believed that the federal government should defend slavery in the territories. But even if Van Buren had wanted to support Breckinridge, he could not have done much because Breckinridge was not on the ballot in New York State. There were only two candidates in New York that fall—the Republican Abraham Lincoln and the Unionist Douglas. Van Buren naturally was for the Union.

After secession began he agreed with the compromise proposals advanced by Senator John J. Crittenden in December 1860, to prevent a civil war. Van Buren favored some sort of accommodation that would stop the "ultra abolitionists." In a resolution for the state Democratic convention in 1861 he denounced both the secessionists for their "monstrous heresies" and the extreme Republicans, whose speeches were "full of mischief." He called for a special national convention to discuss the institution of slavery and if the convention failed, he was prepared to let the South go in peace. On the eve of the war Van Buren in his old age had the same sympathy for the South that he had had in his prime. And he was still not as strong a nationalist as Andrew Jackson had been. The Old Hero would have fought to save the Union.[40]

After Fort Sumter, Van Buren was involved briefly in one last effort to bring peace. On April 16, Franklin Pierce wrote to former Presidents Van Buren, Tyler, Fillmore, and Buchanan, to see whether they could meet to discuss the desperate situation. Pierce asked Van Buren as the senior man to call the meeting. In his reply couched in typically flowery phrases, Van Buren expressed doubt that it would do any good, and insisted that as the most recent incumbent Buchanan should call it. Because of his nature and because of his age Van Buren was not the man to do something dramatic to end the Civil War.[41]

While Van Buren was concerned about saving the Union, a call for help came from John Van Buren. On January 31, John, who was now

[39] Van Buren to——, c. Jan. 1-26, 1860, VBP.

[40] MVB to Reverdy Johnson, July 11, 1860, Reverdy Johnson Papers, LC; MVB to John J. Crittenden, Dec. 24, 1860, MVB, "Resolutions," c. Feb. 1861, VBP.

[41] "Pierce and Van Buren in the Crisis of '61," *Autograph*, 1 (Nov. 1911), 5-7.

fifty and showing signs of disorder of the liver, sent an anguished letter to his father, requesting a family conference. John wrote that he was anxious not only about his health for he had a bad cold and was losing weight rapidly, but also about how to care for his sick, motherless child and prepare for two impending legal cases. Worried by his "incapacity for business," he found his income declining and did not know how he was going to renew the lease on his office. Above all, John admitted, his "disposition to dwell on, & magnify trifles [made him] disagreeable to everybody." "The dashing of all my hopes in life," said John, "keeps me . . . in a state of despondency." John was "grieve[d]" that he had to "disturb & worry" Van Buren at a time when the "relation should be reversed," and the son should be caring for the father.[42]

There is no evidence to indicate whether Van Buren heeded his son's call or not, but it is hard to imagine that he did nothing. The letter shows to what an extent the family still relied on Van Buren. The sons depended on the father in one sense, just as such politicians as Butler, Wright and Jackson had depended on him in another. It is ironic that men with reputations for strength of character—Jackson and Wright in particular—should have relied so much on one who had a reputation for weakness. Van Buren was not a weak character.

As the attacks of asthma became more frequent, Van Buren spent more and more time in his bedroom on the second floor of Lindenwald, a room decorated with a tribute to Jackson and a small picture of Wright. In May 1862, he was well enough to walk for two hours, to plan a trip to the country, and to visit New York City. While in the city, he performed one last duty—writing farewell to Azariah Flagg, who was the only remaining member of the old Regency, Churchill C. Cambreleng having died in April. In his usual long sentences Van Buren praised Flagg for performing his public duties with little concern for his own "advancement."[43]

Back at Lindenwald he grew progressively weaker until Smith felt obliged to summon John and Abraham to their father's bedside. They arrived in time for Van Buren, a family man from first to last, to say good-bye to his sons before lapsing into a final coma. On July 24, as Robert E. Lee defended Richmond and prepared to invade the North, the man who had fought so hard to hold North and South together died at Kinderhook, where his story had begun at the end of the Revolution almost eighty years earlier.

[42] John Van Buren to MVB, Jan. 31, 1861, VBP.

[43] MVB to Flagg, May 28, 1862, Ellen Van Buren to Mrs. Gilpin, May 8, 1862, VBP. Lynch, *Epoch and a Man*, pp. 543-545.

CONCLUSION

Even before Van Buren died, historians and others began to render a verdict. James Parton cast the first vote in 1860, in his biography of Andrew Jackson. Parton, who had been born in England, served on the staff of the *Home Journal* in New York before turning his hand to biographies of Horace Greeley and Aaron Burr in 1855 and 1857. To prepare for his life of Jackson, Parton interviewed a number of the Old Hero's associates, notably Sam Houston and William B. Lewis. The result was a magnificent two-thousand-page biography, which together with Parton's lives of Franklin and Jefferson, earned the writer great popularity in his time and the reputation of being the father of American biography.

Although Parton conceded that the criticisms of Van Buren were "less than half true," the biographer did much to perpetuate the Magician's reputation as a ruthless political dealer. He began by concocting an imaginary "Code of the New York Politician," which he attributed to Aaron Burr and Van Buren. According to the code, politics was a "game" in which "fidelity to party" was the only virtue, and keeping "great men down [and] little men up" was a major goal. Parton focused on the spoils system, which he considered the great weakness of Jacksonian Democracy. Nothing did more to establish the view of Jacksonians as spoilsmen than his chapter "Terror among the Office-Holders," and nothing did more to identify Van Buren as the principal spoilsman than the chapter "Successful Politician's Story." The latter, which was based on interviews in New York, purported to be a description of Van Buren by an office seeker who followed the Magician to Washington. The description of Van Buren brusquely dismissing an officeholder is a devastating caricature.[1]

In his account of the Peggy Eaton affair Parton portrayed Van Buren as a shrewd manipulator. In a memorable phrase Parton said that political power shifted from Calhoun to Van Buren "from the moment when the soft hand of Mr. Van Buren" knocked on Mrs. Eaton's door. Not only did Parton's story show Van Buren as a schemer, but the phrase "soft hand" reinforced the image of him as an effeminate fop.[2]

Perhaps because he anticipated this sort of treatment, Van Buren

[1] Parton, *Jackson*, III, 120, chs. 18, 19.
[2] *Ibid.*, p. 287.

had been unwilling to cooperate when Parton asked for information, even refusing to answer the biographer's letter. One reason was that Van Buren had been preparing his own story for years. When he had asked his political friends to help by returning his letters, many had complied including Jackson, who had sent back a large number. It has been suggested that Van Buren destroyed some of his correspondence in order to protect his reputation, and even though there is little evidence, he may have done so because the collection at the Library of Congress is curiously unbalanced. For the twenty-nine years between 1800 and 1829, the period when Van Buren was developing his reputation as a manipulator, there are only eight volumes of letters, compared to nineteen volumes for the shorter but safer period between 1841 and 1862.[3]

The autobiography that Van Buren was preparing and his history of the origin of political parties (published by his sons in 1867) were efforts to establish his place in history. The latter emphasized the struggle between the Republicans and the Federalists and was so slanted in favor of the Republicans that it could be called the forerunner of the Progressive interpretation of American history. Although Van Buren says little about himself in the book, two letters in the appendix make it clear that he wanted to be thought of as a Jeffersonian. When Van Buren visited Monticello in 1824, he brought Jefferson a pamphlet by the Federalist Timothy Pickering. In it Jefferson was attacked for supposedly criticizing George Washington in a letter to the Italian liberal Philip Mazzei. Shortly after the 1824 visit, Jefferson sent Van Buren a long letter answering Pickering's charges. By appending that letter and the letter to Mazzei to the study of political parties, Van Buren portrays himself as both Jefferson's defender and heir apparent.[4]

Van Buren presents the same image in his autobiography, which was published in 1920. Since the book is incomplete and ends in 1834, it tells more about Van Buren's relation to events during the Jeffersonian and Jacksonian eras than about the man himself. The focus is often on others rather than on the author. Among the most dramatic moments in the autobiography are Van Buren's visit to Jefferson, and his reception by Jackson on arrival in Washington in 1829 and 1832. Van Buren describes himself in 1824 listening deferentially to Jefferson's "liberal views," dwells on the "cordiality" with which Jackson welcomed him in 1829, and paints the famous picture of Jackson on his sickbed in 1832 promising that he will "kill" the Bank. In each

---

[3] Alexander, *American Talleyrand*, p. 422.
[4] MVB, *Political Parties*, pp. 425-436.

instance Van Buren portrays himself as the devoted follower soaking up wisdom from his Republican and Democratic heroes.[5]

A similar impression of Van Buren is conveyed by the biography that Edward M. Shepard wrote for the American Statesmen Series in 1888. Shepard, who was born in 1850, was a New York Democrat who supported Grover Cleveland, the gold standard and the theory of laissez faire. At the beginning of the biography Shepard points out that Van Buren drew "profound inspiration" from Thomas Jefferson. In describing the election of 1828 Shepard praises Van Buren for fighting a Jeffersonian battle against the nationalist policies of John Quincy Adams. He also applauds Van Buren's republican statement in 1837 that society expected too much of government. Shepard, who believed that Van Buren had high principles, was uncomfortable with his subject's support of slavery, but delighted with his repudiation of the institution in 1844 and 1848.[6]

A twentieth-century writer who considered Van Buren a Jeffersonian man of principle was the poet Ezra Pound. Convinced that international Jewish bankers had ruined American life, Pound made a number of anti-Semitic radio broadcasts in Italy during World War II. After being indicted for treason, he spent ten years in a mental hospital before writers' organizations managed to secure his release. Pound was impressed by Van Buren's supposed opposition to the banking interests and his support for the independent treasury, and Pound's epic poem *Cantos* includes tributes to both Van Buren and Jefferson. The canto on Van Buren begins: " 'Thou shalt not,' said Martin Van Buren, 'jail 'em for debt.' " Presenting Van Buren as a defender of the common man, Pound quotes from Van Buren's speech at the New York constitutional convention in favor of extending the suffrage, and praises him for defending sailors against whipping. Most of the rest of the canto applauds Van Buren for standing up to banks, especially the Bank of the United States. Since Van Buren was not a consistent opponent of banking, this is not good history, but it does reflect the sympathy for the Magician that arose during the depression. In a letter to the poet Harriet Monroe in 1933, Pound called Van Buren a "national hero," whose story was one of the "few clean and decent pages" in American history.[7]

---

[5] *Autobiography*, pp. 182-188, 232, 625.

[6] Shepard, *Van Buren*, pp. 4, 159-164, 332, 414, 419-420.

[7] Ezra Pound, *The Cantos of Ezra Pound* (New York, 1948), pp. 31-36; Pound to Monroe, Sept. 14, 1933, D. D. Paige, *The Letters of Ezra Pound, 1907-1941* (New York, 1950), p. 247. For other favorable accounts of Van Buren, see Schlesinger, *Age of Jackson*, and Lynch, *Epoch and a Man*.

But the sly manipulator of Parton's *Jackson*, the pure Jeffersonian of the *Autobiography*, Shepard and the *Cantos*—none of these is the real Van Buren. The Magician was not purely either a politician or a man of principle. Since he never intentionally revealed himself to others, anyone studying him must peel off several layers before reaching the inner man. The outer layer, which everyone saw, was the social man; beneath it lay the politican Van Buren, and deeper still a hidden and profoundly enigmatic person.

The social Van Buren was the one Henry B. Stanton described in 1828 as dressed in a "snuff-colored" coat, with an orange cravat, white duck trousers and yellow gloves. He was a man of great tact with impeccable manners, the friend—as Adams said—of all the world. This was the Van Buren who craved comfort and liked nothing better than flirting with married women, exchanging jokes with younger men, or gossiping with his cronies. His office was the most attractive in Albany, his dinners the talk of Washington. Although Van Buren had many opponents, he had few enemies.

The social man formed the outer layer of the political man, for Van Buren's social bearing contributed much to his political success. One reason the Regency worked so effectively was that Van Buren and his allies enjoyed being with one another. Van Buren took his social nature to Washington, where it enabled him to play games with the Donelson children, entertain Peggy Eaton and ride with Andrew Jackson, and in each case help himself politically.

Since sociability did not guarantee political success, Van Buren needed other qualities. First of all, he was well-organized, always anticipating, always planning, always gathering information. The young Van Buren defeated more impressive lawyers because he was better prepared; the same characteristic helped him to form the Albany Regency and the Democratic party. The consternation that seized the Regency when Thurlow Weed took it by surprise in 1824 only underscored how unusual that episode was. In addition he was able to draw upon reserves of deception and ruthlessness that enabled him to carry the day in countless political battles. And, finally, he was unusually poised— in the words of one observer, "master of himself."[8] Whether receiving the news that his candidate had been beaten by DeWitt Clinton, or presiding over a difficult session of the Senate, Van Buren never lost his composure. His show of serenity in defeat in 1840 was classic.

Still, Van Buren needed a philosophy, and needing a philosophy he spent his career establishing and protecting his reputation as a Re-

---

[8] Jenkins, *Lives of the Governors*, pp. 436-437.

publican. Since the economy and the society around him were changing rapidly, he had to adapt, and adapt he did. At times the demands of the new economy challenged his republican ideals, but he always managed to reconcile the two. In the process he built a new political system which recognized the value of political parties both locally and nationally.

But Van Buren's obvious social and political assets masked liabilities. Though certainly not dull, he was not exciting either, for in spite of his flamboyant appearance he was blessed with neither style, presence, nor charisma. As James Gordon Bennett noted, Van Buren had no "appreciation of wit or satire." Van Buren was always conscious of these deficiencies. Though he joked about his lack of education, he regretted it. Though he often got the best of those who had more popular appeal, he never really believed himself their equal. Though he often exploited aristocrats, he still felt inferior, a feeling that surfaced frequently in the *Autobiography*. Whether dealing with the Silvesters in Kinderhook, Rufus King in New York, or with John Randolph in Washington, Van Buren believed that he was at a disadvantage. Conscious of being inferior, he played the role of outsider. As he rose to power in Columbia County, he was a Republican outsider in a Federalist world. In Washington his messmates were by his own choosing more aristocratic than he and the Westerners were closer to Jackson. Van Buren, to be sure, did rise to the top of the administration, but he never stopped acting like an outsider.[9]

The sense of being an outsider helped create the social and the political Van Buren. His dress became his trademark, a way of creating a style and attracting attention. So were his parties and his trips to Saratoga Springs, western New York, and the South. As a political outsider he had to plan more, organize better, and be more adaptable. He had to be more ambitious than others. Van Buren never stopped trying to improve his position.

Some of these social and political strengths were also weaknesses. He almost always kept himself under control; he never risked letting himself go. The well-dressed, well-mannered statesman was also the Van Buren who did not dare to dress badly or behave crudely. The calm, poised man of the world was also the cold Van Buren who dared not show emotion. On the death of his wife all he could say was that he felt anxiety. He never mentioned her in his writing again. The Van Buren who loved to gossip and flirt, never dared to have an affair. The Van Buren who liked to make money, never dared gamble with

[9] Bennett, Diary, June 22, 1831.

431

his land investments in the hopes of making a fortune. The hard-working, well-organized political man was also fatally cautious. The caution that Van Buren joked about during the nullification crisis, prevented him later from being a great President. And the Van Buren who built a Republican reputation was trapped by it. Once having built the reputation he did not dare deviate from it.

The one characteristic for which Van Buren was famous was the one that suggested that perhaps he was not always under control. This was his political ruthlessness. He was ruthless enough to stick with William Harris Crawford long after the Georgian had suffered a disabling stroke. He kept plotting to keep John Quincy Adams from the presidency in 1825. He cleared out most of the Adams postmasters in New York in 1829. As the stories about him spread, he acquired the nicknames of "Little Magician" and "Sly Fox." His reputation and political skill gave him a place in history, but he hated the image and sought steadily to be something else. He might have been a more successful President if he had been more willing to exploit his reputation.

The cost of keeping himself under control was high. Throughout his career periods of pressure and anxiety recurred, notably between 1817 and 1820 when the death of his wife and a temporary setback in his political career left him exhausted and angry. Anger exploded again in 1824 when Van Buren shouted at Judge Skinner for removing Clinton from the canal commission. Over-anxious about his status with Jackson in 1829, Van Buren walked the streets late at night and even thought of resigning, and unduly disturbed by the attacks from the Calhoun wing of the party, he did resign in 1831. Flashes of bitterness appeared in 1845 during the conflict over appointments to Polk's cabinet.

But the unsettled periods became more and more infrequent as Van Buren settled into his role in American politics. By keeping himself under control and by fighting off his attacks of insecurity, he was able to rebuild the American political system and make an enduring place for himself as a shrewd and creative new-style politician, a model for future generations.

BIBLIOGRAPHY

PRIMARY MATERIALS

1. MANUSCRIPTS

A. *Library of Congress*

Andrew Beaumont Papers.
Nicholas Biddle Papers.
Blair Family Papers.
British Foreign Office Correspondence, 5: United States, 248 (1829), 265 (1831), 266 (1831), 314 (1837). Photostats.
James Buchanan Papers.
Samuel Burch Papers.
Charles Butler Papers.
Henry Clay Papers.
William Harris Crawford Papers.
John J. Crittenden Papers.
Decatur House Papers.
Asbury Dickins Papers.
Andrew J. Donelson Papers.
Margaret L. O'Neale Eaton Papers.
Benjamin Brown French Papers.
Galloway-Maxcy-Marboe Papers.
Edmond Charles Genêt Papers.
Gideon and Francis Granger Papers.
Duff Green Papers.
Alexander Hamilton Papers, Hamilton-McLane Series.
James H. Hammond Papers.
Hugh Hughes Papers.
Andrew Jackson Papers.
Reverdy Johnson Papers.
David Lynch Papers.
Duncan McArthur Papers.
John McLean Papers.
James Madison Papers.
William L. Marcy Papers.
Personal Papers, Miscellaneous.
James K. Polk Papers.
William C. Rives Papers.
James Fowler Simmons Papers.
Samuel Smith Papers.

Benjamin Tappan Papers.
Martin Van Buren Papers.
James W. Wadsworth, Jr., Family Papers.
Gideon Welles Papers.
Charles Wilkes Family Papers.
Levi Woodbury Papers.

B. New-York Historical Society

John Bailey Miscellaneous Papers.
James Buchanan Miscellaneous Papers.
Silas W. Burt Personal Reminiscences.
Henry Clay Miscellaneous Papers.
Alfred Conkling Miscellaneous Papers.
G. Cooke Miscellaneous Papers.
Jabez D. Hammond Miscellaneous Papers.
Rufus King Papers.
John Lansing, Jr., Miscellaneous Papers.
James K. Polk Miscellaneous Papers.
Henry R. Storrs Miscellaneous Papers.
John W. Taylor Papers.
Martin Van Buren Correspondence and Papers. Microfilm.
Henry Van der Lyn Diary.
Gulian C. Verplanck Papers.
Matthew Warner Miscellaneous Papers.
Thurlow Weed Papers.
Silas Wright Miscellaneous Papers.

C. New York Public Library

James Barbour Papers.
James Gordon Bennett, Diary of a Journey through New York [June 12–Aug.
    18, 1831].
Benjamin F. Butler Miscellaneous Papers.
Azariah Flagg Papers.
Azariah Flagg–Michael Hoffman Letters, Azariah Flagg Papers.
Azariah Flagg–Silas Wright Correspondence, Azariah Flagg Papers.
Samuel L. Gouverneur Papers.
Jesse Hoyt, Letters to Edward Curtis.
Jackson–Lewis Letters. Photostats of letters at the J. Pierpont Morgan Library,
    New York City.
Lee Kohns Memorial Collection.
James Monroe Papers.
Gilbert H. Montague Collection.
James K. Polk Papers. Transcripts.
Samuel J. Tilden Papers.
Silas Wright, Letters to Benjamin Butler.

D. New York State Library

Harmanus Bleecker Papers.
Benjamin F. Butler Papers.
Edmond C. Genêt Miscellaneous Papers.
Kinderhook Law Society, Minute Book.
William L. Marcy Papers.
Martin Van Buren–Enos Throop Letters.
Van Schaack Papers.

E. Columbia University Library

DeWitt Clinton Papers.
Azariah Flagg Papers.
Thomas W. Olcott Papers.
Charlemagne Tower Diary.

F. Historical Society of Pennsylvania

James Buchanan Papers.
Cadwalader Collection.
Roswell L. Colt Papers.
Ferdinand Julius Dreer Collection.
Simon Gratz Collection.
Charles Jared Ingersoll Papers.
Joel Roberts Poinsett Papers.
Joel Roberts Poinsett Papers, in the Henry D. Gilpin Papers.

G. University of Virginia Library

Gooch Family Papers.
Hubard Family Papers.
McGregor-Clay Papers.
Miscellaneous Papers.
Henry Post Papers.
John Randolph Collection.
Thomas Ritchie Miscellaneous Papers.
William Cabell Rives Papers.
Walker Family Papers.

H. Other

David Campbell Papers, Duke University Library. Microfilm.
Isaac Hill Papers, New Hampshire Historical Society.

2. NATIONAL ARCHIVES

Foreign Service Posts of the Department of State: Great Britain, Notes Received from the British Government, 1 (1829-1832).
Foreign Service Posts of the Department of State: Great Britain, Notes to the British Government, 1 (1831-1836).

Fourth Census of the United States, 1820, Population Schedules, II, Albany County, New York.

Secretary of the Treasury, Letters to Banks.

State Department, Diplomatic Despatches, Great Britain, XXXVII, XXXVIII.

State Department, Diplomatic Instructions, Great Britain, XIV.

3. Published Works of Van Buren

Davis, Greer W. *Votes and Speeches of Martin Van Buren . . . in the Convention of the State of New-York.* Albany: Thurlow Weed, 1840.

Fitzpatrick, John C., ed. "The Autobiography of Martin Van Buren." *Annual Report of the American Historical Association for the Year 1918.* II. Washington, D.C.: Government Printing Office, 1920.

Ford, Worthington C., ed. "Van Buren–Bancroft Correspondence," Massachusetts Historical Society, *Proceedings*, 42 (1908-1909), 381-442.

Friedenberg, Albert M. "The Correspondence of Jews with President Martin Van Buren," *American Jewish Historical Society Publications*, 22 (1914), 71-100.

McPherson, Elizabeth G., ed. "Unpublished Letters from North Carolinians to Van Buren," *North Carolina Historical Review*, 15 (1938), 53-81, 131-155.

"Pierce and Van Buren in the Crisis of '61," *Autograph*, 1 (Nov. 1911), 5-7.

Van Buren, Martin. *Considerations in Favour of the Appointment of Rufus King, to the Senate of the United States. Submitted to the Republican Members of the Legislature of the State of New-York.* Albany, 1819.

———. *Inquiry into the Origin and Course of Political Parties in the United States.* New York: Hurd & Houghton, 1867.

———. *Letter of Ex-President Van Buren. June 28, 1856.* Philadelphia: William Rice, Printer, 1856.

———. *Opinions . . . Mr. Van Buren's Reply to the Democratic State Convention of Indiana.* New York, 1843.

———. *Opinions of Martin Van Buren, Vice President of the United States, upon the Powers and Duties of Congress, in Reference to the Abolition of Slavery either in the Slave-Holding States or in the District of Columbia.* Washington, D.C., 1836.

———. *Speech of Mr. Van Buren of New York, Delivered in the Senate of the United States, on the Mission to Panama, March, 1826.* Washington, D.C.: Gales & Seaton, 1826.

———. *Speech of the Hon. M: Van Buren of the Senate, on the Act to Carry into Effect, the Act of the 13th April, 1819, for the Settlement of the Late Governor's Accounts.* Albany: J. Buel, 1820.

———. *Speech of the Hon. Martin Van Buren, Delivered at the Capitol, in the City of Albany, Before the Albany County Meeting, Held on the 10th July, 1827.* Albany: Croswell & Van Benthuysen, 1827.

———. *Substance of Mr. Van Buren's Observations on Mr. Foot's Amendment to the Rules of the Senate, by which it was proposed to Give the*

Vice-President the Right to Call to Order for Words Spoken in Debate.
Washington, D.C.: Green & Jarvis, 1828.

4. PUBLISHED WRITINGS

Adams, Charles Francis, ed. *Memoirs of John Quincy Adams, Comprising Portions of His Diary from 1795 to 1848.* 12 vols. Philadelphia: J. B. Lippincott & Co., 1875-1877.

Adams, Cindy, ed. *The West Point Thayer Papers 1808-1877.* 11 vols. West Point, N.Y.: Association of Graduates, 1965.

Aderman, Ralph M., ed. *Letters of James K. Paulding.* Madison, Wis.: University of Wisconsin Press, 1962.

Ambler, Charles H. *The Life and Diary of John Floyd.* Richmond, Va.: Richmond Press, 1918.

———, ed. "Ritchie Letters," *The John P. Branch Historical Papers of Randolph-Macon College,* 3 (1911), 199-252; 4 (1916), 372-418.

Atwater, Caleb. *Remarks Made on a Tour to Prairie du Chien; Thence to Washington City in 1829.* Columbus, Ohio: Isaac N. Whiting, 1831.

Bacourt, Adolphe Fourier de. *Souvenirs of a Diplomat: Private Letters from America during the Administrations of Presidents Van Buren, Harrison, and Tyler.* New York: Henry Holt and Company, 1885.

Bassett, John S., and J. Franklin Jameson, eds. *Correspondence of Andrew Jackson.* 7 vols. Washington, D.C.: Carnegie Institution of Washington, 1926-1935.

Beard, James F., ed. *The Letters and Journal of James Fenimore Cooper.* 6 vols. Cambridge, Mass.: Harvard University Press, 1960-1968.

Bell, Andrew. *Men and Things in America; Being the Experience of a Year's Residence in the United States, in a Series of Letters to a Friend.* London, 1838.

Benton, Thomas Hart. *Thirty Years' View, or a History of the Working of the American Government for Thirty Years from 1820 to 1850.* 2 vols. New York: Appleton, 1854-1856.

Bigelow, John. "DeWitt Clinton as a Politician," *Harper's New Monthly Magazine,* 50 (1874-1875), 409-417, 563-571.

———, ed. *Letters and Literary Memorials of Samuel J. Tilden.* 2 vols. New York: Harper & Brothers, 1908.

Bonney, Mrs. Catharina V. R. *A Legacy of Historical Gleanings.* 2 vols. Albany: J. Munsell, 1875.

Boucher, Chauncey S., and Robert P. Brooks, eds. "Correspondence Addressed to John C. Calhoun 1837-1848," American Historical Association, *Annual Report for the Year 1929.* Washington, D. C.: Government Printing Office, 1930.

Brockway, Beman. *Fifty Years in Journalism Embracing Recollections and Personal Experiences.* Watertown, N.Y.: Daily Times Printing & Publishing House, 1891.

Brown, Everett S., ed. *The Missouri Compromises and Presidential Politics*

1820-1825 from the Letters of William Plumer, Junior. St. Louis: Missouri Historical Society, 1926.

Butler, William A. *A Retrospect of Forty Years 1825-1865.* New York: Charles Scribner's Sons, 1911.

Chittenden, L. E. *Personal Reminiscences, 1840-1890, Including Some Not Hitherto Published of Lincoln and the War.* New York: Richmond, Croscup & Co., 1893.

Clark, G. J., ed. *Memoir, Autobiography and Correspondence of Jeremiah Mason.* Rev. ed. Kansas City, Mo.: Lawyers' International Publishing Co., 1917.

Coleman, Ann Mary B., ed. *The Life of John J. Crittenden with Selections from His Correspondence and Speeches.* 2 vols. 1871. Reprint. New York: Da Capo Press, 1970.

Colton, Calvin, ed. *The Private Correspondence of Henry Clay.* 2 vols. New York: R. S. Barnes & Co., 1855.

Combe, George. *Notes on the United States of North America during a Phrenological Visit in 1838-9-40.* 2 vols. Philadelphia: Cary & Hart, 1841.

"Correspondence of Judge N. B. Tucker," *William and Mary College Quarterly Historical Magazine,* 12 (1903-1904), 84-95, 142-155.

Cox, Isaac J., ed. "Selections from the Torrence Papers," *The Quarterly Publication of the Historical and Philosophical Society of Ohio,* 1-4, 6 (1906-1911).

Crallé, Richard K., ed. *Works of John C. Calhoun.* 6 vols. New York, 1854-1857.

Derby, John Barton. *Political Reminiscences.* Boston: Homer & Palmer, 1835.

Dodd, William E. "National Macon Correspondence," *The John P. Branch Historical Papers of Randolph-Macon College,* 3 (June 1909), 27-93.

Donald, Aida DiPace, and David Donald, eds. *Diary of Charles Francis Adams.* 4 vols. Cambridge, Mass.: Harvard University Press, 1964-1968.

Duane, William J. *Narrative and Correspondence Concerning the Removal of the Deposits and Occurrences Connected Therewith.* Philadelphia, 1838.

Eaton, Margaret L. *The Autobiography of Peggy Eaton.* New York: Charles Scribner's Sons, 1932.

Field, Maunsell B. *Memories of Many Men and of Some Women.* New York: Harper & Brothers, 1873.

Foote, Henry S. *Casket of Reminiscences.* Washington, D.C.: Chronicle Publishing Co., 1874. Reprint. 1968.

Forney, John W. *Anecdotes of Public Men.* New York: Harper & Brothers, 1873.

Fowler, John. *Journal of a Tour through the State of New York in the Year 1830 with Remarks on Agriculture in Those Parts Most Eligible for Settlers.* 1831. Reprint. New York: Augustus M. Kelley, 1970.

Frémont, Jessie Benton. *Souvenirs of My Time.* Boston: D. Lothrop Company, 1887.

Gallatin, Albert. *Considerations on the Currency and Banking System of the United States.* New York: Carey & Lea, 1831.

Garrison, George P., ed. "Diplomatic Correspondence of the Republic of Texas." Part I, American Historical Association, *Annual Report 1907.* II. Washington, D.C.: Government Printing Office, 1908.

Godwin, Parke. *A Biography of William Cullen Bryant with Extracts from His Private Correspondence.* 2 vols. 1883. Reprint. New York: Russell & Russell, 1967.

Gouge, William M. *A Short History of Paper Money and Banking in the United States.* Philadelphia, 1833.

Hamilton, J. G. de Roulhac, ed. *The Papers of William Alexander Graham, 1825-1856.* 4 vols. Raleigh, N.C.: State Department of Archives and History, 1957-1961.

Hamilton, James A. *Reminiscences of James A. Hamilton; or Men and Events, at Home and Abroad, During Three Quarters of a Century.* New York: Charles Scribner and Co., 1869.

Hamlin, L. Belle, ed. "Selections from the Follett Papers," *Quarterly Publications of the Historical and Philosophical Society of Ohio,* 5, 9-11 (1910-1916).

Hay, Thomas R., ed. "John C. Calhoun and the Presidential Campaign of 1824: Some Unpublished Calhoun Letters," *American Historical Review,* 40 (1934-1935), 82-96, 287-300.

Holmes, Oliver Wendell. *The Poet at the Breakfast-Table.* Boston: Houghton Mifflin, 1891.

Hopkins, James F., et al., eds. *The Papers of Henry Clay.* 7 vols. Lexington, Ky.: University of Kentucky Press, 1959—.

Hunt, Gaillard, ed. *The Writings of James Madison.* 9 vols. New York: G. P. Putnam's Sons, 1910.

Irving, Pierre Munroe. *The Life and Letters of Washington Irving, by His Nephew, Pierre M. Irving.* 3 vols. Rev. ed. New York: G. P. Putnam's Sons, 1892-1895.

Jameson, J. Franklin, ed. "Correspondence of John C. Calhoun," American Historical Association, *Annual Report for the Year 1899.* II. Washington, D.C.: Government Printing Office, 1900.

Johannsen, Robert W., ed. *The Letters of Stephen A. Douglas.* Urbana, Ill.: University of Illinois Press, 1961.

Johnston, Henry P., ed. *The Correspondence and Public Papers of John Jay.* 1890-1893. Reprint. 4 vols. in 1. New York: Da Capo Press, 1971.

Julian, George W. *Political Recollections 1840 to 1872.* Chicago: Jansen, McClurg & Co., 1883.

Kendall, Amos. *Autobiography of Amos Kendall.* William Stickney, ed. Boston: 1872. Reprint. 1949.

King, Charles R., ed. *The Life and Correspondence of Rufus King.* 6 vols. New York: G. P. Putnam's Sons, 1894-1900. Reprint. 1971.

Koerner, Gustave. *Memoirs of Gustave Koerner 1809-1896. Life-sketches*

Written at the Suggestion of His Children. 2 vols. Cedar Rapids, Iowa: Torch Press, 1909.

"Letters from John Adams Dix to Dr. George Cheyne Shattuck, 1818-1848," Massachusetts Historical Society, *Proceedings,* 50 (1916-1917), 135-168.

"Letters from John Pintard to His Daughter Eliza Noel Pintard Davidson," *Collections of the New-York Historical Society,* 70-73 (1937-1940).

"Letters of William C. Rives, 1823-1829," *Tyler's Quarterly Historical and Genealogical Magazine,* 5-6 (1924-1925).

"Letters to Bartlett Yancey," *The James Sprunt Historical Publications,* X, no. 2 (1911), 25-76.

McGrane, Reginald C., ed. *The Correspondence of Nicholas Biddle Dealing with National Affairs, 1807-1844.* New York: Houghton, 1919.

McPherson, Elizabeth G., ed. "Unpublished Letters from North Carolinians to Polk," *North Carolina Historical Review,* 16-17 (1939-1940).

March, Charles W. *Reminiscences of Congress.* 3rd ed. New York: Charles Scribner, 1850.

Maury, Sarah M. *The Statesmen of America in 1846.* London: Longman, Brown, Green and Longmans, 1847.

Moore, Frederick W., ed. "Calhoun as Seen by His Political Friends: Letters of Duff Green, Dixon H. Lewis, Richard K. Crallé during the Period from 1831 to 1848," Southern History Association, *Publications,* 7 (1903).

Moore, John B., ed. *The Works of James Buchanan.* Philadelphia: J. B. Lippincott Company, 1908.

Nevins, Allan, ed. *The Diary of Philip Hone 1828-1851.* New York: Dodd, Mead and Co., 1936.

Nevins, Allan, and Milton H. Thomas, eds. *The Diary of George Templeton Strong, 1835-1875.* 4 vols. New York: Macmillan Company, 1952.

Newsome, A. R., ed. "Correspondence of John C. Calhoun, George McDuffie, and Charles Fisher Relating to the Presidential Campaign of 1824," *North Carolina Historical Review,* 7 (1930), 477-504.

————. "Letters of Romulus M. Saunders to Bartlett Yancey, 1821-1828," *North Carolina Historical Review,* 8 (1931), 427-462.

Norton, Anthony B. *The Great Revolution of 1840. Reminiscences of a Log Cabin and Hard Cider Campaign.* Mount Vernon, Ohio: A. B. Norton & Co., 1888.

"Original Letters," *William and Mary College Quarterly Historical Magazine,* 21 (1912-1913), 1-11, 75-84.

Pierce, Edward L. *Memoir and Letters of Charles Sumner.* 4 vols. 1893. Reprint. New York: Arno Press, 1969.

Poore, Ben: Perley. *Perley's Reminiscences of Sixty Years in the National Metropolis.* 2 vols. Philadelphia: Hubbard Brothers, Publishers, 1886.

Quaife, Milo M., ed. *The Diary of James K. Polk during His Presidency, 1845 to 1849.* 4 vols. Chicago: A. D. McClurg & Co., 1910.

Quincy, Josiah. *Figures of the Past.* Rev. ed. Boston: Little, Brown, and Company, 1911.

Rezneck, Samuel. "Letters from a Massachusetts Federalist to a New York Democrat, 1823-1839," *New York History*, 48 (July 1967), 255-274.

Sargent, Nathan. *Public Men and Events from the Commencement of Mr. Monroe's Administration in 1817, to the Close of Mr. Fillmore's Administration in 1853.* 2 vols. Philadelphia: Lippincott, 1874.

Scott, Winfield. *Memoirs of Lieut.-General Scott, LL.D. Written by Himself.* New York: Sheldon and Company, 1864.

Sedgwick, Theodore, ed. *A Collection of the Political Writings of William Leggett.* 2 vols. New York, 1839.

Severance, Frank H., ed. "Millard Fillmore Papers," *Publications of the Buffalo Historical Society*, 10-11 (1906-1907). Buffalo, N.Y.: Buffalo Historical Society, 1907.

Seward, Frederick W., ed. *Autobiography of William H. Seward from 1801 to 1834, with a Memoir of His Life, and Selections from His Letters from 1831 to 1846.* New York: D. Appleton and Company, 1877.

Shanks, Henry T., ed. *The Papers of Willie Person Mangum.* 5 vols. Raleigh, N.C.: State Department of Archives and History, 1950-1956.

Sioussat, St. George L., ed. "Diaries of S. H. Laughlin, of Tennessee, 1840, 1843," *Tennessee Historical Magazine*, 2 (Mar. 1916), 43-85.

———. "Letters of James K. Polk to Andrew J. Donelson, 1843-1848," *Tennessee Historical Magazine*, 3 (1917), 51-73.

———. "Selected Letters, 1844-1845, from the Donelson Papers," *Tennessee Historical Magazine*, 3 (1917), 134-162, 257-291.

Smith, Mrs. Samuel Harrison. *The First Forty Years of Washington Society.* Ed. Gaillard Hunt. 1906. Reprint. New York: Frederick Ungar Publishing Co., 1965.

Sparks, William H. *The Memories of Fifty Years.* 3rd ed. Philadelphia: Claxton, Remsen & Haffelfinger, 1872.

Stanton, Henry B. *Random Recollections.* Johnstown, N.Y.: Blunck & Leaning, Printers, 1886.

Staples, Arthur G., ed. *The Letters of John Fairfield.* Lewiston, Maine: Lewiston Journal Company, 1922.

Tocqueville, Alexis de. *Democracy in America.* 2 vols. 1835. Bradley edition. New York: Vintage Books, 1945.

Van Laer, A.J.F., trans., ed. *Van Rensselaer Bowier Manuscripts, Being the Letters of Kiliaen Van Rensselaer, Rensselaerswyck.* Albany: University of the State of New York, 1908.

Van Tyne, C. H., ed. *The Letters of Daniel Webster.* New York: Haskell House, 1902.

Washburne, E. B., ed. *The Edwards Papers, Being a Portion of the Collection of the Letters, Papers, and Manuscripts of Ninian Edwards.* Chicago Historical Society's Collection, III. Chicago: Fergus Printing Company, 1884.

Weaver, Herbert, ed. *Correspondence of James K. Polk.* I. Nashville, Tenn.: Vanderbilt University Press, 1969.

Webster, Daniel. *The Writings and Speeches of Daniel Webster*. XVI. Boston: Little, Brown and Company, 1903.

Webster, Fletcher, ed. *The Private Correspondence of Daniel Webster*. 2 vols. Boston: Little, Brown and Company, 1857.

Weed, Harriet A., ed. *Autobiography of Thurlow Weed*. Boston: Houghton, Mifflin and Company, 1883.

Williams, Mentor L., ed. "A Tour of Illinois in 1842," *Journal of the Illinois State Historical Society*, 42 (Sept. 1949), 292-312.

Worth, Gorham A. *Random Recollections of Albany from 1800 to 1808*. 3rd ed. Albany: J. Munsell, 1866.

5. NEWSPAPERS

Albany Advertiser, 1815-1817, 1824.

Albany Argus, 1814-1841.

Albany Gazette, 1824.

Albany Morning Chronicle, 1828.

Albany Register, 1812, 1816.

[New York] *American*, 1833.

[Albany] *Atlas and Argus*, 1857.

[Albany] *Balance and New-York State Journal*, 1809.

Charleston [S.C.] *Courier*, 1828, 1836.

Cincinnati Gazette, 1833.

[New York] *Evening Post*, 1844, 1849, 1862.

[Washington] *Globe*, 1831-1837.

[Washington] *Madisonian*, 1837.

[New York] *National Advocate*, 1820.

[Washington] *National Intelligencer*, 1819, 1824, 1828, 1830, 1841-1842.

New-Hampshire Patriot, 1833.

[Albany] *New-York Statesman*, 1820-1821.

Niles' Weekly Register, 1811-1849.

Richmond Enquirer, 1823-1844.

Richmond Whig and Public Advertiser, 1840-1841.

St. Lawrence [N.Y.] *Republican*, 1837.

United States Magazine and Democratic Review, 1836-1844.

[Washington] *United States Telegraph*, 1826-1837.

6. PUBLIC DOCUMENTS, DIRECTORIES, GAZETTEERS

American State Papers: Documents, Legislative and Executive. Washington, D.C., 1832-1862. *Finance*, V.

Annals of Congress. 1821-1824.

Carter, Nathaniel H., and William L. Stone, reporters: and Marcus T. C. Gould, stenographer. *Reports of the Proceedings and Debates of the Convention of 1821, Assembled for the Purpose of Amending the Constitution of the State of New-York*. Albany: E. and E. Hosford, 1821.

Congressional Globe. 1833-1841.

DeBow, J.D.B. *Statistical View of the United States . . . a Compendium of the Seventh Census.* Washington, D.C.: A.O.P. Nicholson, Public Printer, 1854.

Delano Judah. *The Washington Directory.* Washington, D.C.: William Duncan, 1822.

Disturnell, J. *A Gazetteer of the State of New York.* Albany: C. Van Benthuysen & Co., 1843.

French, John H. *Gazetteer of the State of New York.* Syracuse, N.Y.: R. Pearsall Smith, 1860. Reprint. 1969.

Hough, Franklin B. *Census of the State of New-York for 1855.* Albany: Charles Van Benthuysen, 1857.

―――. *The New York Civil List from 1777 to 1863.* Albany: Weed, Parsons & Co., 1863.

Hutchins, Stephen C. *Civil List and Constitutional History of the Colony and State of New York.* Albany: Weed, Parsons & Company, 1880.

Johnson, William. *Reports of Cases Argued and Determined in the Supreme Court of Judicature, and in the Court for the Trial of Impeachments and the Correction of Errors in the State of New-York.* 3 (1808). 3rd ed. Philadelphia, 1832.

Journal of the Assembly of the State of New York. 36-38 (1812-1815).

Journal of the Senate of the State of New-York. 36-40 (1812-1817).

Lincoln, Charles Z., ed. *Messages from the Governors.* 11 vols. Albany: J. B. Lyon Co., 1909.

McLane, Louis. *Documents Relative to the Manufactures in the United States.* Washington, D.C., 1833. Reprint. 1969.

Pitkin, Timothy. *A Statistical View of the Commerce of the United States of America: Its Connection with Agriculture and Manufactures: and an Account of the Public Debt, Revenues, and Expenditures of the United States.* Hartford, Charles Hosmer, 1816.

Register of Debates in Congress. 1824-1837.

Report of the Trial of Brig. General William Hull. New-York: Eastburn, Kirk, and Co., 1814.

Richardson, James D. *A Compilation of the Messages and Papers of the Presidents, 1789-1897.* 10 vols. Washington, D.C., 1897-1899.

The Statistical History of the United States from Colonial Times to the Present. Stamford, Conn.: Fairfield Publishers, 1965.

Treasury Department. *A Series of Tables of the Several Branches of American Manufactures, 1810.* Part II, *Tabular Statement.* Philadelphia, 1813.

Tucker, George. *Progress of the United States in Population & Wealth in Fifty Years.* 1855. Reprint. New York: Augustus M. Kelley, 1964.

United States Bureau of the Census. *Fourteenth Census of the United States: 1920. Bulletin. Population: New York.* Washington, D.C.: Government Printing Office, 1921.

United States Bureau of the Census. *Heads of Families at the First Census of the United States Taken in the Year 1790. New York.* Washington, D.C.: Government Printing Office, 1908.

United States Census Office. *Fourth Census. Digest of the Accounts of Manufacturing Establishments in the United States and of Their Manufactures, 30th Mar. 1822.* Washington, D.C.: Gales and Seaton, 1823.

7. PAMPHLETS AND MISCELLANEOUS SOURCES

Appeal to the Democratic Electors of the County of Lewis, Who, with the Undersigned, Supported the Election of Gen. Jackson and Martin Van Buren. N.p. 1840.

Byrdsall, Fitzwilliam B. *The History of the Loco-Foco or Equal Rights Party.* New York: Clement & Packard, 1842.

The Claims of Martin Van Buren to the Presidency. N.p., n.d.

"Corrector." *Letters Addressed to Martin Van Buren, Esq. Secretary of State: Correcting Many Important Errors in a Late Biography of that Gentleman.* New York, 1830.

Davis, Charles A. *Letters of J. Downing, Major, Downingville . . . to Mr. Dwight.* New York: Harper and Bros., 1834.

Downing, Jack. *Letters Written during the President's Tour "Down East," by Myself, Major Jack Downing of Downingville.* Reprint. Freeport, N.Y.: Books for Libraries Press, 1969.

————. *The Life of Andrew Jackson, President of the United States.* Philadelphia: T. K. Greenbank, 1834.

Dusenbery, Benjamin M. *Monument to the Memory of General Andrew Jackson Containing Twenty-five Eulogies and Sermons Delivered on the Occasion of His Death.* Philadelphia: Walker & Gillis, 1845.

Gardiner, Oliver C. *The Great Issue: or, the Three Presidential Candidates; Being a Brief Sketch of the Free Soil Question.* New York: Wm. C. Bryant & Co., 1848.

The Grand Canal Defeated by a Democratic Senate. N.p., 1816.

Hergesheimer, Joseph. "Washington," *The Saturday Evening Post,* 199 (June 4, 1927), 16-17, 127, 129-130, 135.

Hildreth, Richard. *The Contrast: or William Henry Harrison versus Martin Van Buren.* Boston: Weeks, Jordan & Company, 1840.

Inconsistency and Hypocrisy of Martin Van Buren on the Question of Slavery. N.p., n.d.

"Mr. Van Buren and the War," *Albany Argus Extra,* 1832.

[Ogle, Charles]. *Speech of Mr. Ogle of Pennsylvania on the Regal Splendor of the President's Palace.* Boston: Weeks, Jordan, and Company, 1840.

Paige, D. D., ed. *The Letters of Ezra Pound, 1907-1941.* New York: Harcourt, Brace, 1950.

Pound, Ezra. *The Cantos of Ezra Pound.* New York: New Directions Books, 1948.

Proceedings and Addresses on the Occasion of the Death of Benjamin F. Butler of New York. New York, 1859.

Resolutions and Address Adopted by the Antimasonic Members of the Legislature of Massachusetts. Boston, 1836. University of Virginia Library.

Roney, Lila James. "Inscriptions of the Historic Stones, Kinderhook, New York." Typescript, n.p., 1925.

Smith, Seba. *The Life and Writings of Major Jack Downing of Downingville, away down East in the State of Maine, Written by Himself.* Boston: Lilly, Wait, and Co., 1833.

——. *My Thirty Years out of the Senate by Major Jack Downing.* New York: Oaksmith & Co., 1859.

State Papers on Nullification . . . Collected and Published by Order of the General Court of Massachusetts. Boston, 1834.

Tucker, Nathaniel Beverley. *The Partisan Leader.* 1836. Reprint. Chapel Hill, N.C.: University of North Carolina Press, 1971.

SECONDARY WORKS

1. Books and Articles on Van Buren

Alexander, Holmes. *The American Talleyrand: the Career and Contemporaries of Martin Van Buren, Eighth President.* 1935. Reprint. New York: Russell & Russell, 1968.

Bancroft, George. *Martin Van Buren to the End of His Public Career.* New York: Harper & Brothers, 1889.

Bassett, John S. "Martin Van Buren," Samuel F. Bemis, ed. *The American Secretaries of State and Their Diplomacy.* IV. New York: Alfred A. Knopf. 1928.

"Biography of Martin Van Buren," *Albany Argus Extra,* 1832.

Blair, Montgomery. "Martin Van Buren, Diplomatist, Minister of the United States to England," *Harper's Monthly Magazine,* 119 (1909), 274-281.

A Brief Account of the Life and Political Opinions of Martin Van Buren. N.p., 1840.

Brown, Richard H. " 'Southern Planters and Plain Republicans of the North': Martin Van Buren's Formula for National Politics." Doctoral dissertation, Yale University, 1955.

Butler, William A. *Martin Van Buren: Lawyer, Statesman and Man.* New York: D. Appleton and Company, 1862.

Cone, Leon W., Jr. "Martin Van Buren: the Architect of the Democratic Party, 1837-1840." Doctoral dissertation, University of Chicago, 1951.

Conkling, Frank J. "Martin Van Buren, with a Sketch of the Van Buren Family in America," *The New York Genealogical and Biographical Record,* 28 (1897), 121-125, 207-211.

Crockett, David. *The Life of Martin Van Buren, Heir-Apparent to the "Government," and the Appointed Successor of General Andrew Jackson.* Philadelphia: Robert Wright, 1835.

Curtis, James C. *The Fox at Bay: Martin Van Buren and the Presidency.* Lexington, Ky.: University of Kentucky Press, 1970.

————. "In the Shadow of Old Hickory: the Political Travail of Martin Van Buren," *Journal of the Early Republic*, 1 (Fall 1981), 249-267.

Dawson, Moses. *Sketches of the Life of Martin Van Buren*. Cincinnati, 1840.

Emmons, William. *Biography of Martin Van Buren, Vice President of the United States*. Washington, D.C.: Jacob Gideon, Jr., 1835.

Gatell, Frank O. "Sober Second Thoughts on Van Buren, the Albany Regency and the Wall Street Conspiracy," *Journal of American History*, 53 (June 1966), 19-40.

Harrison, Joseph H., Jr. "Martin Van Buren and His Southern Supporters," *Journal of Southern History*, 22 (Nov. 1956), 438-458.

Holland, William M. *The Life and Political Opinions of Martin Van Buren Vice President of the United States*. Hartford, Conn.: Belknap & Hammersley, 1835.

Irelan, John R. *History of the Life, Administration and Times of Martin Van Buren, Eighth President of the United States*. Chicago: Fairbank and Palmer, 1887.

Jenkins, John S. *Lives of the Governors of the State of New York*. Auburn, N.Y.: Derby and Miller, 1851.

Joline, Adrian H. "Martin Van Buren, the Lawyer," *The Autograph Hunter and Other Papers*. Chicago: Alderbrink Press, 1907.

Lynch, Denis Tilden. *An Epoch and a Man: Martin Van Buren and His Times*. New York: Horace Liveright, 1929.

Mackenzie, William L. *The Life and Times of Martin Van Buren*. Boston: Cooke & Co., 1846.

Mayo, Robert. *A Word in Season; or Review of the Political Life and Opinions of Martin Van Buren*. Washington, D.C.: W. M. Morrison, 1840.

M'Elhiney, Thomas. *Life of Martin Van Buren*. Pittsburgh: J. T. Shryock, 1853.

Meyers, Marvin. "Old Hero and Sly Fox: Variations on a Theme," *The Jacksonian Persuasion: Politics and Belief*. Stanford, Calif.: Stanford University Press, 1957.

Mintz, Max M. "The Political Ideas of Martin Van Buren," *New York History*, 30 (Oct. 1949), 422-448.

Moody, Robert D. "The Influence of Martin Van Buren on the Career and Acts of Andrew Jackson," *Papers of the Michigan Academy of Science, Arts and Letters*, 7 (1926), 225-240.

Niven, John. *Martin Van Buren: the Romantic Age of American Politics*. New York: Oxford University Press, 1983.

Orth, Samuel Peter. *Five American Politicians; a Study in the Evolution of American Politics*. Cleveland: The Burrows Brothers Company, 1906.

Rayback, Joseph G. "Martin Van Buren's Break with James K. Polk," *New York History*, 36 (1955), 51-62.

————. "Martin Van Buren's Desire for Revenge in the Campaign of 1848," *Mississippi Valley Historical Review*, 40 (Mar. 1954), 707-716.

————. "A Myth Reexamined: Martin Van Buren's Role in the Presidential

Election of 1816," *Proceedings of the American Philosophical Society*, 124 (1980), 106-118.

Raymond, William. *Biographical Sketches of the Distinguished Men of Columbia County*. Albany: Weed, Parsons & Co., 1851.

Remini, Robert V. "The Early Political Career of Martin Van Buren, 1782-1828." Doctoral dissertation, Columbia University, 1951.

———. *Martin Van Buren and the Making of the Democratic Party*. New York: Columbia University Press, 1951.

———. "Martin Van Buren and the Tariff of Abominations," *American Historical Review*, 63 (July 1958), 903-917.

Roper, Donald M. "Martin Van Buren as Tocqueville's Lawyer: the Jurisprudence of Politics," *Journal of the Early Republic*, 2 (Summer 1982), 169-189.

Shepard, Edward M. *Martin Van Buren*. Rev. ed. Boston: Houghton Mifflin and Co., 1899.

Sievers, Harry J., ed. *Six Presidents from the Empire State*. Tarrytown, N.Y.: Sleepy Hollow Restorations, 1974.

Sloan, Irving, ed. *Martin Van Buren 1782-1862: Chronology-Documents-Bibliographical Aids*. Dobbs Ferry, N.Y.: Oceana Press, 1969.

Smith, Richard W. "The Public Career of Martin Van Buren in Connection with the Slavery Controversy through the Election of 1840." Doctoral dissertation, Ohio State University, 1959.

West, Elizabeth H. *Calendar of the Papers of Martin Van Buren*. Washington, D.C.: Government Printing Office, 1910.

Whitehurst, Alto L. "Martin Van Buren and the Free Soil Movement." Doctoral dissertation, University of Chicago, 1935.

2. Biographies

Ambler, Charles H. *Thomas Ritchie: a Study in Virginia Politics*. Richmond, Va.: Bell Co., 1913.

Barnes, Thurlow Weed. *Memoir of Thurlow Weed*. Boston: Houghton, Mifflin and Company, 1884.

Bassett, John S. *The Life of Andrew Jackson*. Garden City, N.Y.: Doubleday, Page, 1911. 2 vols. in 1. Reprint. 1967.

Bigelow, John. *The Life of Samuel J. Tilden*. 2 vols. New York: Harper & Brothers, 1895.

Brown, Norman D. *Daniel Webster and the Politics of Availability*. Athens, Ga.: University of Georgia Press, 1969.

Buell, Augustus C. *History of Andrew Jackson*. 2 vols. New York: Charles Scribner's Sons, 1904.

Burke, Pauline Wilcox. *Emily Donelson of Tennessee*. 2 vols. Richmond, Va.: Garrett and Massie, Inc., 1941.

Capers, Gerald M. *John C. Calhoun—Opportunist: a Reappraisal*. Gainesville, Fla.: University of Florida Press, 1960.

Curtis, George Ticknor. *Life of James Buchanan Fifteenth President of the United States*. 2 vols. New York: Harper & Brothers, 1883.

Curtis, James C. *Andrew Jackson and the Search for Vindication*. Boston: Little, Brown, 1976.

Dingledine, Raymond C. "The Political Career of William Cabell Rives." Doctoral dissertation, University of Virginia, 1947.

Dix, John A. *Memoirs of John Adams Dix compiled by His Son Morgan Dix*. 2 vols. New York: Harper and Brothers, 1883.

Driscoll, William D. "Benjamin F. Butler: Lawyer and Regency Politician." Doctoral dissertation, Fordham University, 1965.

Elliott, Charles W. *Winfield Scott: the Soldier and the Man*. New York: Macmillan, 1937.

Ernst, Robert. *Rufus King: an American Federalist*. Chapel Hill, N.C.: North Carolina Press, 1968.

Fink, William B. "Stephen Van Rensselaer and the House Election of 1825," *New York History*, 32 (1951), 323-330.

Fuess, Claude M. *Daniel Webster*. 2 vols. Boston: Little, Brown, 1930.

Garraty, John A. *Silas Wright*. New York: Oxford University Press, 1949.

Gillet, Ransome H. *The Life and Times of Silas Wright*. 2 vols. Albany: The Argus Co., 1874.

Govan, Thomas P. *Nicholas Biddle: Nationalist and Public Banker 1786-1844*. Chicago: University of Chicago Press, 1959.

Guest, Ivor. *Fanny Elssler*. Middletown, Conn.: Wesleyan University Press, 1970.

Hammond, Jabez D. *Life and Times of Silas Wright, Late Governor of the State of New York*. Syracuse, N.Y.: Hull & Dickson, 1848.

Hatcher, William B. *Edward Livingston: Jeffersonian Republican and Jacksonian Democrat*. University, La.: Louisiana State University Press, 1940.

Hofstadter, Richard. "William Leggett, Spokesman of Jacksonian Democracy," *Political Science Quarterly*, 58 (Dec. 1943), 581-594.

Hosack, David. *Memoir of DeWitt Clinton*. New York: J. Seymour, 1829.

Howe, Mark A. de Wolf. *The Life and Letters of George Bancroft*. 2 vols. New York: Charles Scribner's Sons, 1908.

Hunt, William. *The American Biographical Sketch Book*. New York: Cornish, Lamport & Co., 1848.

Irwin, Ray W. *Daniel D. Tompkins: Governor of New York and Vice President of the United States*. New York: New-York Historical Society, 1968.

James, Marquis. *Andrew Jackson: Portrait of a President*. Indianapolis: Bobbs-Merrill, 1937.

———. *The Raven: a Biography of Sam Houston*. Indianapolis: Bobbs-Merrill, 1929. Reprint. 1949.

July, Robert W. *The Essential New Yorker: Gulian Crommelin Verplanck*. Durham, N.C.: Duke University Press, 1951.

The Leading Citizens of Columbia County New York. Boston: Biographical Review Publishing Company, 1894.

Lichterman, Martin. "John Adams Dix: 1798-1879." Doctoral dissertation, Columbia University, 1952.

Longfellow, Samuel, ed. *Life of Henry Wadsworth Longfellow with Extracts from His Journals and Correspondence.* 2 vols. Boston: Ticknor and Company, 1886.

Mackenzie, William L. *The Lives and Opinions of Benjamin Franklin Butler, . . . and Jesse Hoyt.* Boston: Cook & Co., 1845.

Meyer, Leland W. *The Life and Times of Colonel Richard M. Johnson of Kentucky.* New York: Columbia University Press, 1932.

Miller, Peyton F. *A Group of Great Lawyers of Columbia County, New York.* Hudson, N.Y.: The De Vinne Press, 1904.

Munroe, John A. *Louis McLane: Federalist and Jacksonian.* New Brunswick, N.J.: Rutgers University Press, 1973.

Nathans, Sydney. *Daniel Webster and Jacksonian Democracy.* Baltimore: Johns Hopkins University Press, 1972.

Niven, John. *Gideon Welles: Lincoln's Secretary of the Navy.* New York: Oxford University Press, 1973.

Parton, James. *Life of Andrew Jackson.* 3 vols. New York: Mason Brothers, 1860.

Paulding, William I. *Literary Life of James K. Paulding.* New York: Charles Scribner and Company, 1867.

Peckham, Harriet C. *History of Cornelis Maessen Van Buren . . . and His Descendants.* New York: Tobias A. Wright, 1913.

Pray, Isaac C. *Memories of James Gordon Bennett and His Times.* New York: Stringer & Townshend, 1855.

Remini, Robert V. *Andrew Jackson.* New York: Harper and Row, 1966.

———. *Andrew Jackson and the Course of American Empire, 1767-1821.* New York: Harper and Row, 1977.

———. *Andrew Jackson and the Course of American Freedom, 1822-1832.* New York: Harper and Row, 1981.

———. "Hannah Hoes Van Buren," *Notable American Women 1607-1950: a Biographical Dictionary.* Ed. Edward T. James. III. Cambridge, Mass.: Harvard University Press, 1971.

Scott, Nancy N., ed. *A Memoir of Hugh Lawson White.* Philadelphia: J. B. Lippincott & Co., 1856.

Sellers, Charles. *James K. Polk Continentalist 1843-1846.* Princeton, N.J.: Princeton University Press, 1966.

———. *James K. Polk Jacksonian 1795-1843.* Princeton, N.J.: Princeton University Press, 1957.

Somit, Albert. "Andrew Jackson: Legend and Reality," *Tennessee Historical Quarterly,* 7 (Dec. 1948), 291-313.

Spann, Edward K. "The Souring of Good Feelings: John W. Taylor and the Speakership Election of 1821," *New York History,* 41 (1960), 379-399.

Spencer, Ivor D. *The Victor and the Spoils: a Life of William L. Marcy.* Providence: Brown University Press, 1959.

449

Tyler, Lyon G. *The Letters and Times of the Tylers*. 3 vols. Richmond, Va., 1884, 1886.

Van Deusen, Glyndon G. *The Life of Henry Clay*. Boston: Little, Brown, 1937.

————. *Thurlow Weed: Wizard of the Lobby*. Boston: Little, Brown, 1947. Reprint. 1969.

Wayland, Francis F. *Andrew Stevenson Democrat and Diplomat 1785-1857*. Philadelphia: University of Pennsylvania Press, 1949.

Wiltse, Charles M. *John C. Calhoun, Nullifier, 1829-1839*. Indianapolis: Bobbs-Merrill Company, 1949.

————. *John C. Calhoun, Sectionalist, 1840-1850*. Indianapolis: Bobbs-Merrill, 1951.

Young, William T. *Sketch of the Life and Public Services of General Lewis Cass*. Philadelphia: E. H. Butler & Co., 1851.

3. Other Monographs and Secondary Works

Adams, Henry. *History of the United States of America during the Administrations of Thomas Jefferson and James Madison*. 1889. Reprint. 9 vols. in 4. New York: Albert and Charles Boni, 1930.

Alexander, De Alva S. *A Political History of the State of New York*. 2 vols. New York: Henry Holt and Co., 1906.

Aronson, Sidney. *Status and Kinship in the Higher Civil Service: Standards of Selection in the Administrations of John Adams, Thomas Jefferson, and Andrew Jackson*. Cambridge, Mass.: Harvard University Press, 1964.

Bailyn, Bernard. *The Origins of American Politics*. New York: Knopf, 1967.

Benns, Frank L. *The American Struggle for the British West India Carrying-Trade, 1815-1830*. Bloomington, Ind.: Indiana University Press, 1923.

Benson, Lee. *The Concept of Jacksonian Democracy: New York as a Test Case*. Princeton, N.J.: Princeton University Press, 1961.

Billington, Ray Allen. *Westward Expansion: a History of the American Frontier*. 2nd ed. New York: Macmillan Company, 1960.

Blue, Frederick J. *The Free Soilers: Third Party Politics*. Urbana, Ill.: University of Illinois Press, 1973.

Booth, Edward T. *Country Life in America as Lived by Ten Presidents of the United States*. New York: Alfred A. Knopf, 1947.

Bowers, Claude G. *The Party Battles of the Jackson Period*. Boston: Houghton Mifflin Company, 1922.

Bradbury, Anna R. *History of the City of Hudson New York*. Hudson, N.Y.: Record Printing and Publishing Co., 1908.

Bryan, Wilhelmus B. *A History of the National Capital*. 2 vols. New York: Macmillan, 1916.

Carroll, E. Malcolm. *Origins of the Whig Party*. Durham, N.C.: Duke University Press, 1925. Reprint. 1964.

Casais, John A. "The New York State Constitutional Convention of 1821 and Its Aftermath." Doctoral dissertation, Columbia University, 1967.

Chandler, Alfred D. *The Visible Hand: the Managerial Revolution in American Business*. Cambridge, Mass.: Harvard University Press, 1977.

Christman, Henry. *Tin Horns and Calico: a Decisive Episode in the Emergence of Democracy*. New York: Henry Holt and Company, 1945.

Clark, Victor S. *History of Manufactures in the United States*. I (1607-1860). Washington, D.C.: Carnegie Institution, 1929. Reprint. 1949.

Cole, Arthur Charles. *The Whig Party in the South*. Washington, D.C.: American Historical Association, 1914. Reprint. 1962.

Cole, Arthur H. *The American Wool Manufacture*. I. 1926. Reprint. New York: Harper and Row, 1969.

Cole, Donald B. *Jacksonian Democracy in New Hampshire, 1800-1851*. Cambridge, Mass.: Harvard University Press, 1970.

Collier, Edward A. *A History of Old Kinderhook*. New York: G. P. Putnam's Sons, 1914.

Dangerfield, George. *The Awakening of American Nationalism 1815-1828*. New York: Harper and Row, 1965.

————. *The Era of Good Feelings*. New York: Harcourt, Brace and Company, 1952.

Darling, Arthur B. *Political Changes in Massachusetts 1824-1848: a Study of Liberal Movements in Politics*. New Haven, Conn.: Yale University Press, 1925.

Dewey, Davis R. *Financial History of the United States*. 10th ed. New York: Longmans, Green, 1928.

Donovan, Herbert D. A. *The Barnburners . . . 1830-1852*. New York: New York University Press. 1925.

Ellis, David M. *Landlords and Farmers in the Hundson-Mohawk Region*. Ithaca, N.Y.: Cornell University Press, 1946.

Ellis, Franklin. *History of Columbia County, New York with Illustrations and Biographical Sketches of Some of Its Prominent Men and Pioneers*. Philadelphia: Everts and Ensign, 1878.

Filler, Louis. *The Crusade against Slavery 1830-1860*. New York: Harper & Brothers, 1960.

Fish, Carl Russell. *The Civil Service and the Patronage*. New York: Longmans, Green, and Co. 1904.

Foreman, Grant. *Indian Removal: the Emigration of the Five Civilized Tribes of Indians*. Rev. ed. Norman, Okla.: University of Oklahoma Press, 1953.

Fox, Dixon Ryan. *The Decline of Aristocracy in the Politics of New York 1801-1840*. New York: Columbia University Press, 1919.

————. *Yankees and Yorkers*. New York: New York University Press, 1940.

Freehling, W. W. *Prelude to Civil War: the Nullification Controversy in South Carolina, 1816-1836*. New York: Harper and Row, 1965.

Gammon, Samuel R., Jr. *The Presidential Campaign of 1832*. Baltimore: Johns Hopkins University Press, 1922.

Gates, Paul W. *The Farmer's Age: Agriculture 1815-1860*. New York: Holt, Rinehart, and Winston, 1960.

451

Goldstein, Kalman. "The Albany Regency: The Failure of Practical Politics." Doctoral dissertation, Columbia University, 1969.

Gunderson, Robert G. *The Log-Cabin Campaign*. Lexington, Ky.: University of Kentucky Press, 1957.

Hamilton, Milton W. *The Country Printer: New York State 1785-1830*. 2nd ed. New York: Ira J. Friedman, 1964.

Hamm, Margherita A. *Famous Families of New York*. 2 vols. New York: G. P. Putnam's, 1901.

Hammond, Bray. *Banks and Politics in America from the Revolution to the Civil War*. Princeton, N.J.: Princeton University Press, 1957.

Hammond, Jabez D. *The History of Political Parties in the State of New-York, from the Ratification of the Federal Constitution to December, 1840*. 2 vols. Cooperstown, N.Y.: H. & E. Phinney, 1842.

Hoffman, William S. *Andrew Jackson and North Carolina Politics*. Chapel Hill, N.C.: University of North Carolina Press, 1958. Reprint. 1971.

Hofstadter, Richard. *The Idea of a Party System: the Rise of Legitimate Opposition in the United States, 1780-1840*. Berkeley and Los Angeles, Calif.: University of California Press, 1969.

Holloway, Laura C. *The Ladies of the White House, or, in the Home of the Presidents*. Philadelphia: Bradley, Garretson & Co., 1881.

Hugins, Walter. *Jacksonian Democracy and the Working Class: a Study of the New York Workingmen's Movement*. Stanford, Calif.: Stanford University Press, 1960.

Jenkins, John S. *History of Political Parties, in the State of New York*. Auburn, N.Y.: Alden & Parsons, 1849.

Kass, Alvin. *Politics in New York State 1800-1830*. Syracuse, N.Y.: Syracuse University Press, 1965.

Keenleyside, Hugh L., and Gerald S. Brown. *Canada and the United States*. Rev. ed. New York: Knopf, 1952.

Kelley, Robert. *The Transatlantic Persuasion: the Liberal-Democratic Mind in the Age of Gladstone*. New York: Knopf, 1969.

Kinderhook, N.Y., the Village Beautiful. The Story of To-day. Kinderhook, N.Y.: The Fellowship Shop, 1910.

Klein, Philip S. *Pennsylvania Politics: 1817-1832, a Game without Rules*. Harrisburg, Pa.: The Historical Society of Pennsylvania, 1940.

Latner, Richard B. "Andrew Jackson and His Advisors: White House Politics, 1829-1837." Doctoral dissertation, University of Wisconsin, 1972.

———. *The Presidency of Andrew Jackson: White House Politics, 1829-1837*. Athens, Ga.: University of Georgia Press, 1979.

McCarthy, Charles. "The Antimasonic Party: a Study of Political Antimasonry in the United States, 1828-1840," American Historical Association, *Annual Report 1902*. I. 365-574. Washington, D.C.: Government Printing Office, 1903.

McCormick, Richard P. *The Second American Party System: Party Formation in the Jacksonian Era.* Chapel Hill, N.C.: University of North Carolina Press, 1966.

McFaul, John M. *The Politics of Jacksonian Finance.* Ithaca, N.Y.: Cornell University Press, 1972.

McGrane, Reginald C. *The Panic of 1837: Some Financial Problems of the Jacksonian Era.* Chicago: University of Chicago Press, 1924. Reprint. 1965.

McManus, Edgar J. *A History of Negro Slavery in New York.* Syracuse, N.Y.: Syracuse University Press, 1966.

May, Ernest R. *The Making of the Monroe Doctrine.* Cambridge, Mass.: Harvard University Press, 1975.

Meyers, Marvin. *The Jacksonian Persuasion: Politics and Belief.* Stanford, Calif.: Stanford University Press, 1957.

Miller, Douglas T. *The Birth of Modern America, 1820-1850.* New York: Pegasus, 1970.

Miller, Nathan. *The Enterprise of a Free People: Aspects of Economic Development in New York State during the Canal Period, 1792-1838.* Ithaca, N.Y.: Cornell University Press, 1962.

Moore, Glover. *The Missouri Controversy.* Lexington, Ky.: University of Kentucky Press, 1953.

Munsell, Joel. *The Annals of Albany.* 10 vols. Albany: Joel Munsell, 1853-1859.

Murrell, William. *A History of American Graphic Humor.* 2 vols. New York: Whitney Museum of American Art, 1933.

Mushkat, Jerome. *Tammany: the Evolution of a Political Machine 1789-1865.* Syracuse, N.Y.: Syracuse University Press, 1971.

Nagel, Paul D. *One Nation Indivisible: the Union in American Thought 1776-1861.* New York: Oxford University Press, 1964.

Paul, James C. N. *Rift in the Democracy.* Philadelphia: University of Pennsylvania Press, 1951.

Pessen, Edward. *Jacksonian America: Society, Personality and Politics.* Rev. ed. Homewood, Ill.: The Dorsey Press, 1978.

————. *Most Uncommon Jacksonians: the Radical Leaders of the Early Labor Movement.* Albany: State University of New York Press, 1967.

Rayback, Joseph G. *Free Soil: the Election of 1848.* Lexington, Ky.: University of Kentucky Press, 1970.

Remini, Robert V. *Andrew Jackson and the Bank War.* New York: W. W. Norton, 1967.

————. *The Election of Andrew Jackson.* New York: J. B. Lippincott Co., 1963.

Richards, Leonard L. *"Gentlemen of Property and Standing": Anti-Abolition Mobs in Jacksonian America.* New York: Oxford University Press, 1970.

Risjord, Norman K. *The Old Republicans: Southern Conservatism in the Age of Jefferson.* New York: Columbia University Press, 1965.

Rives, George L. *The United States and Mexico, 1821-1848*. New York: Charles Scribner's Sons, 1913.

Satz, Ronald N. *American Indian Policy in the Jacksonian Era*. Lincoln, Neb.: University of Nebraska Press, 1975.

Schlesinger, Arthur M., Jr. *The Age of Jackson*. Boston: Little, Brown, 1945.

Schlesinger, Arthur M., Jr., Fred L. Israel and William P. Hansen, eds. *History of American Presidential Elections*. I, II. New York: Chelsea House, 1971.

Seager, Robert. *And Tyler Too: a Biography of John and Julia Gardiner Tyler*. New York: McGraw-Hill, 1943.

Sharp, James Roger. *The Jacksonians Versus the Banks: Politics in the States after the Panic of 1837*. New York: Columbia University Press, 1970.

Shaw, Ronald E. *Erie Water West: a History of the Erie Canal 1792-1864*. Lexington, Ky.: University of Kentucky Press, 1966.

Singleton, Esther. *The Story of the White House*. 2 vols. New York: The McClure Company, 1907.

Snyder, Charles M. *The Jacksonian Heritage: Pennsylvania Politics 1833-1848*. Harrisburg, Pa.: The Pennsylvania Historical and Museum Commission, 1958.

Somkin, Fred. *Unquiet Eagle: Memory and Desire in the Idea of American Freedom, 1815-1860*. Ithaca, N.Y.: Cornell University Press, 1967.

Stanwood, Edward. *American Tariff Controversies in the Nineteenth Century*. Boston: Houghton Mifflin Co., 1903.

———. *A History of the Presidency*. Boston: Houghton Mifflin, 1898.

Taussig, F. W. *The Tariff History of the United States*. 6th ed. New York: G. P. Putnam's Sons, 1914.

Taylor, George Rogers. *The Transportation Revolution 1815-1860*. New York: Holt, Rinehart, and Winston, 1951.

Temin, Peter. *The Jacksonian Economy*. New York: W. W. Norton, 1969.

Van Deusen, Glyndon. *The Jacksonian Era 1828-1848*. New York: Harper & Brothers, 1959.

Von Holst, Hermann E. *The Constitutional and Political History of the United States, 1828-1846*. Chicago: Callaghan and Co., 1888.

Ward, John M. *Andrew Jackson: Symbol for an Age*. New York: Oxford University Press, 1955.

Ware, Norman. *The Industrial Worker 1840-1860*. Boston: Houghton Mifflin, 1924.

Warren, Charles. *The Supreme Court in United States History*. 2 vols. Rev. ed. Boston: Little, Brown, 1926.

Wharton, Anne H. *Social Life in the Early Republic*. Philadelphia: Lippincott, 1902.

White, Leonard D. *The Jacksonians: a Study in Administrative History 1829-1861*. New York: Macmillan Company, 1954.

Wilburn, Jean. *Biddle's Bank: the Crucial Years*. New York: Columbia University Press, 1967.

Wood, Gordon. *The Creation of the American Republic 1776-1787.* Chapel Hill, N.C.: University of North Carolina Press, 1969.

Wyman, Mary Alice. *Two American Pioneers Seba Smith and Elizabeth Oakes Smith.* New York: Columbia University Press, 1926.

Young, Alfred E. *The Democratic Republicans of New York: the Origins, 1763-1797.* Chapel Hill, N.C.: University of North Carolina Press, 1967.

4. ARTICLES

Ambler, Charles H. "Virginia and the Presidential Succession, 1840-1844," Guy S. Ford, ed., *Essays in American History Dedicated to Frederick Jackson Turner.* New York: Henry Holt, 1910.

————, ed. "Virginia and Texas, 1844," *The John P. Branch Historical Papers of Randolph-Macon College,* 4 (June 1913), 116-137.

Ammon, Harry. "The Richmond Junto, 1800-1824," *Virginia Magazine of History and Biography,* 63 (1955), 395-419.

Barker, E. C. "President Jackson and the Texas Revolution," *American Historical Review,* 12 (1906-1907), 788-801.

Bassett, John S. "Notes on Jackson's Visit to New England, June, 1833," Massachusetts Historical Society, *Proceedings,* 56 (1922-1923), 243-260.

Braverman, Howard. "The Economic and Political Background of the Conservative Revolt in Virginia," *Virginia Magazine of History and Biography,* 60 (1952), 266-287.

Brown, Richard H. "The Missouri Crisis, Slavery and the Politics of Jacksonianism," *South Atlantic Quarterly,* 65 (1966), 55-72.

Carleton, William G. "Political Aspects of the Van Buren Era," *South Atlantic Quarterly,* 50 (April 1951), 167-185.

Ellis, David M. "The Yankee Invasion of New York, 1783-1850," *New York History,* 32 (Jan. 1951), 1-17.

Eriksson, Erik M. "Official Newspaper Organs and the Presidential Election of 1836," *Tennessee Historical Magazine,* 9 (1925-1926), 115-130.

Gatell, Frank O. " 'Conscience and Judgment'; the Bolt of the Massachusetts Conscience Whigs," *The Historian,* 21 (1958-1959), 18-45.

————. "Spoils of the Bank War: Political Bias in the Selection of Pet Banks," *American Historical Review,* 70 (Oct. 1964), 43-50.

Gitterman, J. M. "The Council of Appointment in New York," *Political Science Quarterly,* 7 (1892), 80-115.

Green, Fletcher M. "On Tour with President Andrew Jackson," *New England Quarterly,* 26 (1963), 209-228.

Grimsted, David. "Rioting in Its Jacksonian Setting," *American Historical Review,* 77 (April 1972), 361-397.

Haller, Mark. "The Rise of the Jackson Party in Maryland 1820-1829," *Journal of Southern History,* 28 (Aug. 1962) 307-326.

Hammond, Bray. "Free Banks and Corporations: the New York Free Banking Act of 1838," *Journal of Political Economy,* 44 (April 1936), 184-209.

Harrison, Joseph H., Jr. "Oligarchs and Democrats: the Richmond Junto," *Virginia Magazine of History and Biography*, 78 (April 1970), 184-198.

Hartman, William. "The New York Custom House: Seat of Spoils Politics," *New York History*, 34 (1953), 149-163.

Henig, Gerald S. "The Jacksonian Attitude Toward Abolitionism in the 1830's," *Tennessee Historical Quarterly*, 28 (Spring 1969), 42-56.

Jackson, Carlton. "The Internal Improvement Vetoes of Andrew Jackson," *Tennessee Historical Quarterly*, 25 (Fall 1966), 261-279.

Kenney, Alice P. "The Albany Dutch: Loyalists and Patriots," *New York History*, 42 (1961), 331-350.

Latner, Richard B. "The Kitchen Cabinet and Andrew Jackson's Advisory System," *Journal of American History*, 65 (1978-1979), 367-388.

McCormick, Richard P. "New Perspectives on Jacksonian Politics," *American Historical Review*, 65 (Jan. 1960), 288-301.

――――. "Suffrage Classes and Party Alignments: a Study in Voter Behavior," *Mississippi Valley Historical Review*, 46 (1959), 399-410.

McFaul, John M. "Expediency vs. Morality: Jacksonian Politics and Slavery," *Journal of American History*, 62 (1975-1976), 24-39.

Morgan, William G. "The Origin and Development of the Congressional Nominating Caucus," *Proceedings of the American Philosophical Society*, 113 (1969), 184-196.

Rammelkamp, C. H. "The Campaign of 1824 in New York," American Historical Association, *Annual Report for the Year 1904*. Washington, D.C.: Government Printing Office, 1905.

Remini, Robert V. "The Albany Regency," *New York History*, 39 (Oct. 1958), 341-355.

――――. "New York and the Presidential Election of 1816," *New York History*, 31 (1950), 308-324.

Roach, George W. "The Presidential Campaign of 1844 in New York State," *New York History*, 19 (1938), 153-172.

Russo, David J. "The Major Political Issues of the Jacksonian Period and the Development of Party Loyalty in Congress, 1830-1840," *Transactions of the American Philosophical Society*, New Series, LXII, Part 2 (May 1972).

Scheiber, Harry N. "The Pet Banks in Jacksonian Politics and Finance," *Journal of Economic History*, 23 (June 1963), 196-214.

Sellers, Charles. "Banking and Politics in Jackson's Tennessee, 1817-1827," *Mississippi Valley Historical Review*, 41 (June 1954), 61-84.

――――. "Jackson Men with Feet of Clay," *American Historical Review*, 42 (April 1957), 537-551.

Silbey, Joel H. "The Election of 1836," *Crucial American Elections*. Philadelphia: American Philosophical Society, 1973.

Stenberg, Richard. "The Jefferson Birthday Dinner, 1830," *Journal of Southern History*, 4 (Aug. 1938), 334-345.

Sutton, Robert P. "Nostalgia, Pessimism and Malaise: the Doomed Aristocrat in Late-Jeffersonian Virginia," *Virginia Magazine of History and Biography*, 76 (Jan. 1968), 41-55.

Van Schaack, Henry C. *An Old Kinderhook Mansion*. Reprinted from the *Magazine of American History*. Sept. 1878.

Wallace, Michael. "Changing Concepts of Party in the United States: New York, 1815-1828," *American Historical Review*, 74 (Dec. 1968), 453-491.

Weitenkampf, Frank. "New York State in National Politics: Notes for a Cartoon Record," *The New-York Historical Society Quarterly*, 30 (1946), 77-91.

Wilson, Major L. " 'Liberty and Union': an Analysis of Three Concepts Involved in the Nullification Controversy," *Journal of Southern History*, 33 (Aug. 1967), 331-355.

INDEX

Aberdeen, George H. Gordon, Earl of, 200

Adams, Charles Francis, 149, 175, 238, 414-15

Adams, John, 102, 294

Adams, John Quincy, 84, 144, 238, 254, 259, 311, 344, 415, 429, 432; on Rufus King, 57; in 1824 election, 116-17, 119, 122-23, 125-28, 130-41; on MVB, 119, 153-54, 192, 258, 315, 320; opposition to, 145, 147-50; in 1828 election, 152, 153, 163, 171-75; and economic issues, 167, 213; on foreign policy, 197, 202, 319, 320; and Peggy Eaton affair, 206; and Jefferson Day dinner, 210; on Calhoun, 308; on slavery, 328, 363; on Clay, 333; converses with MVB, 335; on campaign tactics, 369, 371; death, 420

Adelaide, Queen, 223

Albany, 21, 26, 82-85, 109, 161-62, 234-35, 271, 361, 372, 420

Albany Advertiser, 50, 133

Albany Argus, 37, 52, 55, 56, 64, 102, 103, 288, 312, 322, 409; and Missouri Compromise, 59; and Regency, 84, 87, 96; backs Crawford, 120, 124; backs Jackson, 122, 146, 174-75, 207; attacks Clinton, 133; in state elections, 155, 352; on tariff, 161, 162, 168, 237, 241, 243; on national issues, 208, 213, 239; on rejection of MVB, 226; on Bank of the U.S., 234, 253; on Union party, 246; on specie circular, 277, 293; on independent treasury, 304, 328, 337, 347-48, 360

Albany Journal, 322, 350

Albany Regency, 4, 85-98, 102, 132, 260, 312, 377, 421, 430; use of term, 82, 82n34; in Albany postmastership affair, 83-85; techniques, 86-88, 91, 94; leaders, 88-95; opinions of observers, 94, 95, 97, 133, 155; theory of political parties, 95-96; similar organizations, 96-98, 120; prototype of party machines, 98; in 1824 election, 128-31, 134, 136; transition 1825, 142; in politics 1826-1828, 144-45, 159, 171, 176-77; on tariff, 163-67, 241; and MVB, 220, 228-30; on banking, 233-34, 252-53, 273, 295-96, 312-13; on deposit removal, 248; loses election of 1837, 313; changes in, 342; advice on Texas, 393

Albany Register, 47, 123

Alexander, Mark, 242

Allen, William, 329

Alley, Saul, 234

amalgamation policy, 147, 246-47

American Anti-Slavery Society, 271

American Society for the Encouragement of Domestic Manufactures, 111

American System, 147, 162

Amistad case, 363-64

antiabolitionist riots, 270-71

Anti-Rent War, 29, 407-409

antislavery movement, 59, 269-72, 320-21, 328-30, 361-62

Archer, William S., 117, 125, 140, 240

Argus of Western America, 156, 216

Aroostook Valley War, 326

Astor, John Jacob, 93

Atherton, Charles G., 278

Bacourt, Adolphe Fourier de, 346

Balch, Alfred, 157, 193-94, 211, 387, 394

Baltimore, 227, 263, 357, 395-98, 413

Bancroft, George, 343, 384, 387, 405, 417, 423; on MVB, 29; on N.Y. constitutional convention, 77, 80; agrees to write MVB's biography, 390; favors annexing Texas, 392; at Democratic convention, 396-97; Secretary of Navy, 400, 403, 404

Bank of America, 26-28, 30, 250

Bank of the United States, 26, 27, 272-

Library of Congress Cataloging in Publication Data

Cole, Donald B.
Martin Van Buren and the American political system.

Bibliography: p.
Includes index.
1. Van Buren, Martin, 1782-1862.   2. United States—
Politics and government—1815-1861.   3. New York (State)—
Politics and government—1775-1865.   4. Presidents—United
States—Biography. I. Title.
E387.C65 1984   973.5'7'0924 [B]   84-3402
ISBN 0-691-04715-4